School Readiness
and the Transition
to Kindergarten
in the Era of Accountability

School Readiness and the Transition to Kindergarten in the Era of Accountability

Edited by

Robert C. Pianta, Ph.D.
Center for the Advanced Study of Teaching and Learning
University of Virginia
Charlottesville

Martha J. Cox, Ph.D.
Center for Developmental Science
University of North Carolina at Chapel Hill

and

Kyle L. Snow, Ph.D.
Center for Research in Education
RTI International
Rockville, Maryland

PAUL·H·
BROOKES
PUBLISHING CO.®

Baltimore · London · Sydney

Paul H. Brookes Publishing Co.
Post Office Box 10624
Baltimore, Maryland 21285-0624

www.brookespublishing.com

Typeset by Graphic World, St. Louis, Missouri.
Manufactured in the United States of America by
Versa Press, Inc., East Peoria, Illinois

Library of Congress Cataloging-in-Publication Data

School readiness and the transition to kindergarten in the era of accountability / edited
by Robert C. Pianta, Martha J. Cox, Kyle L. Snow.
    p.   cm.
  Includes bibliographical references and index.
  ISBN-13: 978-1-55766-890-5
  ISBN-10: 1-55766-890-6
  1. Readiness for school—United States.   2. Kindergarten—United States.   I. Pianta,
Robert C.   II. Cox, Martha J.   III. Snow, Kyle LaBrie, 1969–   IV. Title.
  LB1132.S325 2007
  372.21'8—dc22   2006100698

British Library Cataloguing in Publication data are available from the British Library.

CONTENTS

ABOUT THE EDITORS

Robert C. Pianta, Ph.D., is the Novartis U.S. Foundation Professor in the Curry School of Education, and Professor of Psychology at the University of Virginia, where he also directs the University of Virginia Center for Advanced Study of Teaching and Learning. Dr. Pianta's research and policy interests are research on classroom settings, their contributions to child outcomes in preschool and the early school years, and how to improve teaching and learning in classrooms. Dr. Pianta has published more than 200 scholarly papers, the majority having a focus on schooling and development in early childhood. He is the lead author of several influential books related to early childhood and elementary education and is the senior author and developer of the Classroom Assessment Scoring System (CLASS), a method for assessing teacher/classroom quality being used in many large-scale applications. Dr. Pianta is Principal Investigator and Director of the Institute of Education Sciences National Center for Research on Early Childhood Education and is Principal Investigator of MyTeachingPartner, a National Institute of Child Health and Human Development (NICHD)–funded clinical trial evaluation of web-based support for teachers in prekindergarten classrooms. He is also Principal Investigator on the NICHD Study of Early Child Care and Youth Development, a 10-site study of the effects of child care on the development of more than 1,300 children across the United States, and on the National Center for Early Development and Learning's 11-state study of pre-kindergarten programs and their effects on children's competence. Dr. Pianta is also Program Director of the University of Virginia's interdisciplinary doctoral training program in education sciences and Editor of *The Journal of School Psychology.* He consults with numerous foundations and agencies regarding early childhood issues.

Martha J. Cox, Ph.D., is Director of the Center for Developmental Science and Professor of Psychology at the University of North Carolina at Chapel Hill. Dr. Cox is known for her studies of families and young children and for her methodological contributions to the observational analysis of family interactions. Since the 1980s, she has studied the early years of family development and the processes of reorganization of families over the transition to parenthood and the transition to school with a special emphasis on the role of family relationships, including parent–child and marital relationships in children's successful adaptation to new challenges in the early years. She is 1 of 10 principal investigators in the NICHD Study of Early Child Care, a study of children from birth through the elementary school years. She is Principal Investigator of the National Science Foundation–funded North Carolina Child Development Research Collaborative (CDRC). A centerpiece of the CDRC activities is a longitudinal, collaborative, multidisciplinary research study focusing on multiple levels of factors associated with successful development of a diverse group of young children. Dr. Cox is also the Co-principal Investigator of the program project Rural Children Living in Poverty, funded primarily by the National Institute of Child Health and Human Development but also by the National Institute on Drug Abuse. The purpose of this program project is to understand the early school readiness of an understudied but important group of children: impoverished children living in low-resource, rural areas of the country.

Kyle L. Snow, Ph.D., is Program Director for research in early childhood education at Research Triangle Institute (RTI) International. He is also Principal Investigator for the Early Childhood Longitudinal Study–Birth (ECLS-B) cohort, a prospective longitudinal study of a nationally representative cohort of children studied from 9 months to kindergarten. Before joining RTI in 2005, Dr. Snow was Director of the National Institute of Child Health and Human Development (NICHD) Program in Early Learning and School Readiness. In this position, Dr. Snow had responsibilities for developing initiatives to support research on the processes and contexts of early learning. This included coordination and/or collaboration with other federal and private sources of research funding to support rigorous research on the most effective practices in preparing children from diverse backgrounds and experiences for school entry and success. His research program was also active in supporting research and development of outcome measures for use in early childhood that are appropriate for diverse populations and usable at scale. Before joining NICHD, Dr. Snow was a research analyst in the education studies division at Westat, a contract research firm located in Rockville, Maryland. In this position, Dr. Snow performed a diverse range of evaluation and research projects related to education and education policy. Dr. Snow has also held a faculty appointment at Wilkes University in Wilkes-Barre, Pennsylvania, and taught courses at Cornell University, American University, and Seton Hall University. Dr. Snow holds a bachelor's degree in psychology from Castleton State College in Vermont and master's and doctoral degrees in human development from Cornell University. Dr. Snow's areas of specialization include infant and child development, the interface between early social and cognitive development, and children's transition to school.

About the Contributors

David P. Baker, Ph.D., Eberly Professor of Education and Sociology, Department of Education Policy Studies, The Pennsylvania State University, 300 Rackley Building, University Park, PA 16802

As a sociologist of education, Dr. Baker publishes widely on the relationship between formal education and modern society. *National Differences, Global Similarities: World Culture and the Future of Schooling* (2005, Stanford University Press) is his most recent co-authored book on this topic.

Clancy Blair, Ph.D., Associate Professor, Human Development and Family Studies, The Pennsylvania State University, 110 Henderson South, University Park, PA 16802

Dr. Blair received a doctoral degree in developmental psychology and a master's degree in public health from the University of Alabama at Birmingham in 1996. He is an associate professor in the Department of Human Development and Family Studies at The Pennsylvania State University. His primary research interest concerns the development of self-regulation in children facing early psychosocial adversity.

Jeanne Brooks-Gunn, Ph.D., M.Ed., Co-director, National Center for Children and Families, Teachers College, Columbia University, 525 West 120th Street, Box 39, New York, NY 10027

In addition to being Co-director of the National Center for Children and Families, Dr. Brooks-Gunn is the Virginia and Leonard Marx Professor of Child Development at Columbia University's Teachers College and the College for Physicians and Surgeons in New York. As the author of more than 350 published articles, three books, and many edited volumes, she has received numerous awards from scientific organizations, including the American Academy of Political and Social Science (Margaret Mead Award), the American Psychological Society (James McKeen Cattell Award), the American Psychological Association (Distinguished Contributions to Public Policy Award), the Society for Research in Child Development (Public Policy Award), the Society for Research on Adolescence (John B. Hill Award), and the American Sociological Association (the William Goode Book Award), as well as from two divisions of the American Psychological Association (the Urie Bronfenbrenner Award and the Nicholas Hobbs Award).

Richard M. Clifford, Ph.D., Senior Scientist, FPG Child Development Institute, University of North Carolina, CB #8180, Chapel Hill, NC 27599

Dr. Clifford studies programs for young children and their impact on children's development. He has special interests in public policy, financing services for young children, and assessment of early learning environments. He is a past president of the National Association for the Education of Young Children.

Eric Cummings, Ph.D., Research Associate, Education Policy Studies, The Pennsylvania State University, 302D Rackley Building, University Park, PA 16802

Dr. Cummings's areas of interest include the history of educational policy and the implementation of policy, specifically on the role that personal beliefs play in the local interpretation and implementation of external reform mandates.

Nancy A. Denton, Ph.D., Professor of Sociology and Associate Director, Center for Social and Demographic Analysis, University at Albany, State University of New York, 1400 Washington Avenue, Albany, NY 12222

Dr. Denton received her master's and doctoral degrees in demography from the University of Pennsylvania and a master's degree in sociology from Fordham University. Her major research interests are race and residential segregation, and with Douglas S. Massey she is author of *American Apartheid: Segregation and the Making of the Underclass,* winner of the 1995 American Sociological Association Distinguished Publication Award and the 1994 Otis Dudley Duncan award from the Sociology of Population section of the American Sociological Association.

Fabienne Doucet, Ph.D., Assistant Professor, Steinhardt School of Education, Department of Teaching and Learning, New York University, 239 Greene Street, East Building, Suite 200, New York, NY 10003

Dr. Doucet received her doctoral degree in human development and family studies from the University of North Carolina at Greensboro. Her research interests include the schooling experiences of immigrant and U.S. ethnic minority children; parenting values and beliefs about education; and family, school, and community partnerships.

Jason Downer, Ph.D., Senior Research Scientist, Center for Advanced Study of Teaching and Learning, University of Virginia, 350 Old Ivy Way, Suite 100, Charlottesville, VA 22903

Dr. Downer's research focuses on the identification and understanding of contextual supports available to children during early childhood. In particular, his research emphasizes father–child and teacher–child relationships, as well as home–school connections for children at risk for school adjustment problems.

Paul Eslinger, Ph.D., Professor of Neurology, Neural & Behavioral Sciences, Pediatrics, and Radiology, College of Medicine, Penn State Milton S. Hershey Medical Center, Department of Neurology H037, Post Office Box 850, Hershey, PA 17033

Dr. Eslinger is a licensed clinical neuropsychologist and Director of the Clinical Neuropsychology and Cognitive Neuroscience Program in Neurology as well as a member of the Center for Nuclear Magnetic Resonance Research at The Pennsylvania State University College of Medicine and Milton S. Hershey Medical Center. His clinical and research interests center around diseases of the brain that affect executive functions, learning and memory, and the neuromaturation of cognitive functions.

Linda M. Espinosa, Ph.D., Professor of Early Childhood Education, College of Education, University of Missouri–Columbia, 211C Townsend Hall, Columbia, MO 65211

Dr. Espinosa served as Co-director of the National Institute for Early Education Research at Rutgers University from 2002 to 2004. Her practical experience and research interests focus on the design and evaluation of optimal learning environments for young children at risk for school failure. Her recent research and policy work has focused on effective curriculum and assessment practices for young children from low-income families who are dual language learners. Dr. Espinosa is currently on the board of examiners for the National Council for Accreditation of Teacher Education and a Commissioner for the National Association for the Education of Young Children Accreditation Standards and Criteria Commission. Dr. Espinosa has worked extensively with low-income Hispanic/Latino children and families throughout the state of California and has published many research articles and training manuals on how to establish effective educational services for low-income, minority families who are acquiring English as a second language. Dr. Espinosa completed her bachelor's degree at the University of Washington, her master's degree at Harvard University, and her doctoral degree in educational psychology at the University of Chicago.

Ruth A. Etzel, M.D., Ph.D., Adjunct Professor, George Washington University School of Public Health and Health Services, 4501 Diplomacy Drive, Suite 200, Anchorage, AK 99508

Dr. Etzel is a pediatrician and epidemiologist, Editor of *Pediatric Environmental Health*, published by the American Academy of Pediatrics, and Adjunct Professor at George Washington University School of Public Health and Health Services. Her research has focused on the effects of indoor air pollution on children. Dr. Etzel has received numerous research awards, including the Arthur Flemming Award from the Washington, D.C., Jaycees and the 1998 Clinical Society Award for discovering the association between infant pulmonary hemorrhage and exposure to indoor molds.

Shalini G. Forbis, M.D., M.P.H., Assistant Professor of Pediatrics, Wright State University School of Medicine, One Children's Plaza, Dayton, OH 45404

Dr. Forbis's main responsibilities include research, clinical patient care duties, and medical student and pediatric resident education. Her research interests encompass the topic of health disparities in underserved pediatric populations, and one of her main areas of study is in pediatric asthma along with an interest in parental health literacy. Dr. Forbis completed a fellowship in general academic pediatrics and a master's degree in public health at University of Rochester, New York, where she was named the 2001 Bradford Fellow. She completed medical school and pediatric residency training at the Medical College of Ohio at Toledo.

David Gamson, Ph.D., Assistant Professor of Education, Department of Education Policy Studies, The Pennsylvania State University, 310E Rackley Building, University Park, PA 16802

Dr. Gamson is a National Academy of Education/Spencer postdoctoral fellow. His research centers on educational policy and the history of educational reform and recently has focused on the evolution of the U.S. mathematics curriculum and the role played by school districts in education reform movements. He has been a fellow in the Advanced Studies Fellowship

Program (2002–2005) at Brown University and a fellow with the Pennsylvania Education Policy Fellowship Program, administered through the Institute for Educational Leadership. Before attending graduate school at Stanford University, he was a social studies and history teacher for grades 6–12 at the International School of Minnesota. His recent publications have appeared in *Paedagogica Historica, Journal of Educational Administration,* and *Intelligence.*

Pamela W. Garner, Ph.D., Associate Professor of Interdisciplinary Studies, New Century College, George Mason University, Enterprise Hall, 4400 University Drive, Fairfax, VA 22030

Dr. Garner received her doctoral degree from Texas A&M University. She is continuing her research on the social and emotional development of economically disadvantaged preschoolers, with particular emphasis on emotion socialization and emotion knowledge. She has begun to examine links among these emotion constructs and young children's school-related competence.

Bridget K. Hamre, Ph.D., Senior Research Scientist, Center for Advanced Study of Teaching and Learning, 350 Old Ivy Way, Suite 100, Charlottesville, VA 22903

Dr. Hamre is a clinical and school psychologist working as Senior Research Scientist at the Center for Advanced Study of Teaching and Learning at the University of Virginia in Charlottesville. Her research interests include identifying classroom-level processes that facilitate children's academic and social development, as well as developing and evaluating school-based prevention and intervention programs aimed at improving the quality of interactions between teachers and students.

Donald J. Hernandez, Ph.D., Professor, Sociology Department, 1400 Washington Avenue, Arts and Sciences 351, University of Albany, State University of New York, Albany, NY 12222

Dr. Hernandez received his doctoral degree in sociology from the University of California at Berkeley. Dr. Hernandez is the author of *America's Children: Resources from Family, Government, and the Economy,* the first national research using children as the unit of analysis to document the timing, magnitude, and reasons for revolutionary changes experienced by children since the Great Depression in family composition, parent's education, fathers' and mothers' work, and family income and poverty. He recently directed a study on the health and adjustment of immigrant children and families at the National Academy of Sciences and Institute of Medicine where he had overall responsibility for the National Research Council report titled *From Generation to Generation: The Health and Well-Being of Children in Immigrant Families* and for the companion volume of research papers titled *Children of Immigrants: Health, Adjustment, and Public Assistance.* His current research includes a study using the Foundation for Child Development's Index of Child Well-Being to explore disparities in child well-being by race-ethnic and immigrant origins.

Sharon Lynn Kagan, Ed.D., Co-director, National Center for Children and Families, Teachers College, Columbia University, 525 West 120th Street, Box 39, New York, NY 10027

Dr. Kagan is the Virginia and Leonard Marx Professor of Early Childhood and Family Policy and Associate Dean at Teachers College, Columbia University in New York. She is a professor adjunct at Yale University and Former President of the National Association for the Education of Young Children and Family Support America. Dr. Kagan is the 2005 recipient of the McGraw-Hill Prize, the 2005 recipient of the James Conant Award from the Education Commission of the States, and the 2004 recipient of the Distinguished Service to American Education award of the Council of Chief State School Officers.

Kristie Kauerz, M.A., Doctoral Candidate, Teachers College, Columbia University, 525 West 120th Street, Box 226, New York, NY 10027

Ms. Kauerz is a doctoral candidate in early childhood education policy at Teachers College, Columbia University, and a graduate research fellow at the National Center for Children and Families. Since 2001, Dr. Kauerz has served as Program Director of early learning for the Education Commission of the States (ECS). Prior to joining ECS, Ms. Kauerz was Director of public policy analysis at the Center for Human Investment Policy at the University of Colorado–Denver. She also worked in Colorado Governor Roy Romer's office as Director of Community Development for families and children. Her research interests include the re-forming of public education for children birth through third grade (P–3 education), the unique role of kindergarten as a link between early learning and early elementary school, and the state policy infrastructure required to establish seamless systems of early care and education. She holds a bachelor's degree in political science from Colorado College in Colorado Springs and a master's degree in international development from American University in Washington, D.C.

Hilary Knipe, Doctoral Candidate, The Pennsylvania State University, 300 Rackley Building, University Park, PA 16802

Ms. Knipe is a pursuing her doctoral degree in education theory and policy at The Pennsylvania State University. She has a bachelor's degree in cognitive science from The Johns Hopkins University. Her research interests center around cognition and formal schooling, particularly the effects of schooling on cognitive capacities and the impacts of changing cognitive abilities on activities outside the school.

Suzanne E. Macartney, M.A., Doctoral Candidate, Sociology Department, 1400 Washington Avenue, Arts and Sciences 351, University of Albany, State University of New York, Albany, NY 12222

Ms. Macartney graduated from Temple University in 1996 with a bachelor's degree in sociology. After working for the Institute for Survey Research in her hometown of Philadelphia, she enrolled in graduate school at the University at Albany, State University of New York, and received her master's degree in 2002. She is working on her dissertation for the Department of Sociology, examining children in immigrant families and their neighborhoods.

Kelly Maxwell, Ph.D., Scientist, FPG Child Development Institute, CB #8180, Chapel Hill, NC 27599

Dr. Maxwell is Clinical Assistant Professor in the School of Education at The University of North Carolina at Chapel Hill. Her research interests include school readiness, prekindergarten policies and practices, and evaluation of early childhood initiatives.

Sara McLanahan, Ph.D., Professor of Sociology and Public Affairs, Woodrow Wilson School of Public and International Affairs, Office of Population Research, Princeton University, 265 Wallace Hall, Princeton, NJ 08544

Dr. McLanahan directs the Bendheim-Thoman Center for Research on Child Wellbeing, is a principal investigator on the Fragile Families and Child Wellbeing Study, and is Editor-in-Chief of *The Future of Children*. Her research interests include family demography, poverty and inequality, and social policy. She has written five books and has had many papers published in peer-reviewed journals.

Samuel J. Meisels, Ed.D., President, Erikson Institute, 420 North Wabash, 6th Floor, Chicago, IL 60611

Dr. Meisels's major area of study is screening and assessment in early childhood.

John M. Pascoe, M.D., M.P.H., Professor of Pediatrics, Chief, General and Community Pediatrics, Boonshoft School of Medicine, Wright State University, The Children's Medical Center of Dayton, One Children's Plaza, Dayton, OH 45404

Dr. Pascoe is a former president of the Ambulatory Pediatric Association and has served on a number of editorial boards including *Pediatrics, Pediatrics in Review,* and *Ambulatory Pediatrics*. He is an associate editor of *Current Problems in Pediatric and Adolescent Health*. Dr. Pascoe served as a member of the National Advisory Group for the Head Start Transition Project, has been a member of the National Head Start Research Conference Program Committee for almost 15 years, and was a member of the national Executive Committee for a Health Resources and Services Administration–funded national medical education project, Undergraduate Medical Education in the 21st Century. Dr. Pascoe serves on the Primary Care Organizations Consortium national steering committee, representing general pediatrics.

C. Cybele Raver, Ph.D., Associate Professor, Director, Center for Human Potential and Public Policy, Harris Graduate School of Public Policy Studies, University of Chicago, 1155 East 60th Street, Chicago, IL 60637

As a developmental psychologist, Dr. Raver focuses on the well-being of children and families, with particular emphasis on predicting success and difficulty among young children in poverty. Dr. Raver's programs of research have considered children's social and emotional development within policy contexts of early educational intervention and welfare reform. She leads the Chicago School Readiness Project, a clustered randomized clinical trial study examining classroom-based interventions supporting preschoolers' school readiness in Head Start classrooms. Dr. Raver has received a number of prestigious federal and foundation grants from organizations such as the National Institutes of Health, the William T. Grant Foundation, and the McCormick Tribune Foundation. Before joining the faculty of the University of Chicago, she was an assistant professor in Cornell University's Department of Human Development. Dr. Raver earned her doctoral degree in developmental psychology from Yale University and her undergraduate degree from Harvard/Radcliffe University.

Sharon Ritchie, Ed.D., Senior Scientist and Co-director, FirstSchool Initiative, FPG Child Development Institute, CB #8180, Chapel Hill, NC 27599

Dr. Ritchie is Co-director of the FirstSchool Initiative at FPG Child Development Institute. Her background is in special education and teacher education. She worked extensively on National Center for Early Development and Learning state pre-kindergarten research and on the National Association for the Education of Young Children accreditation.

Cecilia Elena Rouse, Ph.D., Theodore A. Wells '29 Professor of Economics and Public Affairs, Princeton University, 357 Wallace Hall, Princeton, NJ 08544

Dr. Rouse is Director of the Industrial Relations Section and the Education Research Section at Princeton University. Her primary research and teaching interests are in labor economics with a particular focus on the economics of education. She has studied the economic benefit of community college attendance, evaluated the Milwaukee Parental Choice Program, examined the effects of education inputs on student achievement, and tested for the existence of discrimination in symphony orchestras. Her current research includes studies of Florida's school accountability system and randomized evaluations of the use of computers in schools. She received her doctoral degree from Harvard University.

Ulfat Shaikh, M.D., M.P.H., Assistant Professor of Pediatric, University of California, Davis School of Medicine, 2516 Stockton Boulevard, Suite 335, Sacramento, CA 95817

Dr. Shaikh is an academic general pediatrician and health services researcher at the University of California, Davis School of Medicine. She provides clinical services at the Pediatric Weight Management Clinic and Lactation Clinic at UC Davis Medical Center. She completed medical school at Goa Medical College in India. She has a master's degree in public health from the University of Medicine and Dentistry of New Jersey. She completed her pediatric residency training at Albert Einstein College of Medicine/Bronx-Lebanon Hospital in New York, as well as a primary care faculty development fellowship at Michigan State University.

Radiah Smith-Donald, Doctoral Candidate, Irving Harris School of Public Policy, University of Chicago, 1155 East 60th Street, Chicago, IL 60637

Ms. Smith-Donald's research experience includes infant and early childhood mental health, exposure to risk, and measure development. Her current research focuses on preschool-age children and determining which factors matter most for their later school success.

Steven L. Thorne, Ph.D., Assistant Professor, Department of Linguistics and Applied Language Studies, Associate Director, Center for Language Acquisition, The Pennsylvania State University, 305 Sparks, University Park, PA 16802

Dr. Thorne's research areas include second language acquisition, intercultural communication, Internet-mediated communication, and developmental neuroscience. He received his doctoral degree from the University of California at Berkeley.

Jonathan Tudge, Ph.D., Professor, Department of Human Development and Family Studies, University of North Carolina at Greensboro, Post Office Box 26170, Greensboro, NC 27402

Dr. Tudge is a visiting professor at the Institute of Psychology, Federal University of Rio Grande do Sul, Brazil. He completed his undergraduate and master's degrees in England and his doctoral degree in human development and family studies at Cornell University. His research examines cultural-ecological aspects of young children's development across a number of different societies, particularly focusing on the years prior to and immediately following the entry to school.

FOREWORD

Early childhood education is at a crossroads. Continuing along the path of the status quo means focusing on programs from birth to age 5 and getting children ready for K–12 school, Following another path means adapting to changes in organized learning experiences for young children and seeking to integrate such programs with what happens during the early elementary school years—what we call PK–3, the first level of a seamless P–16 educational system. Educators who follow the second path recognize that, at some point in the 21st century, American public education will begin with 3-year-olds.

This transformation of the American public education system will not happen overnight. The two ideas of kindergarten and high school as integral parts of a universal education system in America were introduced around the end of the 19th century. High schools were more uniformly implemented than kindergartens, and kindergarten, even today, is not available to students in all school districts. But with high school now a regular fixture in public education, ideas for having students finish at Grade 10—to enable young people to pursue advanced vocational education or higher education—are being coupled with ideas for beginning the public education system at age 3.

These ideas reflect scientific advances regarding the impressive learning capacities of infants and young children, especially during the first 5 years of life, and the criticality of nurturing capacities for children's educational success in the years immediately following.

School Readiness and the Transition to Kindergarten in the Era of Accountability provides a road map for the second path and recognizes the need to cross-fertilize the ideas that have traditionally undergirded early education on one end and early elementary education—kindergarten through 3rd grade—on the other. Contrary to what some believe, we and the authors of this book do not envision pushing the current elementary school curriculum and pedagogy down into pre-K classrooms—although that danger, admittedly, is present. Rather, we share a focus on both development and learning content across the PK–3 years by infusing respect for and knowledge of children's development into the K–12 system and integrating early literacy and numeracy curricula into the pre-K years.

Research is showing that what we call PK–3—the integration of cognitive and learning motivational skills in aligned educational programs for young children from ages 3 to 8—holds great promise to narrow (not close) the achievement gap between children. Reducing this gap is not the ultimate outcome we seek, but the achievement gap's role in reducing growing social and economic inequalities based on educational inequalities cannot be denied.

What these forward-looking chapters convey is that the path we take will not be easy to navigate. Fortunately, new tools are available to assist in the effort. One of them, the CLASS observational instrument, developed by Pianta and his colleagues and supported by the Foundation for Child Development, is particularly important. Although we know a great deal about schools, educators have been hobbled by having less information about what goes on in classrooms between teachers and students. The CLASS documents the supports that teachers provide for children's learning, the climate they establish in the classroom, and their organization and management of the learning environment. CLASS's use as both a professional development tool and for improving student achievement is very encouraging.

Even if the CLASS were to be implemented in every classroom tomorrow, the pre- and in-service professional development of teachers who can teach children ages 3–8 constitutes central challenges. Currently, all elementary school teachers are prepared in colleges of education. The preparation of many early educators occurs in community colleges—often with problematic articulation issues with 4-year colleges—and in departments outside education schools. Not only are traditions in early and elementary education different, but also separate educational experiences add to the distance between them. In colleges of education, programs typically separate elementary and high school education. PK–3 requires a strategy to assure that teachers are prepared to work with children across the 3–8 age span. If these structural barriers were not formidable enough, knowledge of children's development—which is core to the preparation of early educators—is largely absent from the preparation of elementary educators and school leaders, and delivery of instruction based on knowledge of children's development is the critical attribute of highly qualified PK–3 teachers.

The ideal of a P–16 education system is just that—an ideal. Scattered throughout the country, in individual schools and in a few school districts, strategic superintendents and principals and their staffs recognize that to address the wide gaps between children arriving at the kindergarten door, they must forge partnerships with early education programs in their communities and in their own schools. These school leaders must articulate their vision and provide the resources—including that most precious of resources, *time*—for teachers to do the hard work of aligning standards, curriculum, instruction, and assessment within a grade (horizontal alignment) and across the grades (vertical alignment). In many states and school districts, standards for early education (where they exist) and for elementary education are not aligned. Even when these standards are aligned on paper, many teachers struggle to implement them. What is most encouraging, as we learn about schools and school districts on the pathway to PK–3 schools, is that we see efforts to align standards as coming from thoughtful, innovative educators who are implementing PK–3, often without supportive school district, state, and federal policies in place. As these PK–3 efforts become better known, and as more states and school districts join a movement to implement PK–3 schools, policies to support these broader efforts will be essential.

PK–3 is all about what W.E.B. Du Bois insisted was giving "our children a fairness of start which will equip them with such an array of facts and such an attitude toward truth that they can have a real chance to judge what the world is" (as cited in Darling-Hammond, 2006). Du Bois powerfully argued, "Of all the civil rights for which the world has struggled and fought for 5,000 years, the right to learn is undoubtedly the most fundamental." Children's right to learn must be at the top of our agendas as we work for an educational system that reflects and serves a just and democratic nation.

Ruby Takanishi
President
Foundation for Child Development

Fasaha Traylor
Senior Program Officer
Foundation for Child Development

REFERENCE

Darling-Hammond, L. (2006). Securing the right to learn: Policy and practice for powerful teaching and learning. *Educational Researcher, 35*(7), 13–24.

PREFACE

In nearly every governor's race, big-city mayoral campaign, and federal education initiative, providing early learning and educational experiences that contribute to children's achievement and success in school is presented as a political as well as an economic and social good. It is no longer the case that we debate whether good early childhood education is cost-effective or beneficial to children (although the continued pursuit of evidence on these issues is of great importance) but rather that the central feature shaping public discourse and much of public policy at all levels is how to do early education well.

In many ways, early childhood education is at the forefront of educational reform as states construct and evaluate delivery systems for the equitable distribution of opportunity; as the field addresses the challenge of providing the training and expertise necessary to support the value of early education; and as the public seeks information on the extent to which the delivery system produces desired outcomes for children. In addition, K–12 education policy and practice is now grappling with, and relying on, early childhood education to an unprecedented extent, the strategic use of which is undoubtedly in the interest of not only the United States but a host of other nations as well. It is in the context of early childhood education as leader and as a national asset that this volume is set.

The volume consists of three sections: the first focuses on describing the landscape of early education in terms of the features of programs and policies that drive the experiences children receive and the outcomes such experiences produce; the second section provides a contemporary discussion of developmental processes and domains that figure prominently in our understanding of what it means to be ready for school, particularly in relation to children's capacity to access opportunity in early education settings; and the third section addresses cultural, familial, demographic, and community realities that intersect with learning opportunities in early education programs.

This volume is also being published at a time when the Institute of Education Sciences (IES) has taken a considerable step toward supporting research and development in early education through its new National Center for Research in Early Childhood Education (NCRECE), one of several national centers that IES funds. NCRECE is a collaborative effort involving IES and investigators at the University of Virginia, the University of North Carolina at Chapel Hill, the University of California, Los Angeles, and the University of North Carolina at Greensboro. As the Director of NCRECE, I am pleased to note that this volume is the first in a series of edited volumes that NCRECE will produce over the next several years, each addressing a topic of concern to the education of young children. Over the next several years, we plan to focus attention on topics such as professional development and accountability and we invite input on a range of other issues.

ACKNOWLEDGMENTS

I am very appreciative of the efforts of a number of people with regard to the production of this book, most importantly Martha Cox and Kyle Snow. Martha and Kyle each provided leadership and direction to the production of one of the book's sections and played key roles in the shaping of the volume's content. The editorial and production staff members at Brookes, as always, were responsive and thorough in their work with us, and the quality of their work is manifest throughout this book. As this book now moves into the public arena, I believe I speak for all of the authors in expressing a hope that the book stimulates thinking, planning, and actions that support young children, their families, and their teachers.

—*R.C.P.*

I wish to express appreciation to Bob Pianta for his excellent leadership on this and *The Transition to Kindergarten*. I want to also thank the authors for their thoughtful contributions and the staff at Brookes for a great experience working with a thoroughly professional staff.

—*M.J.C.*

I am grateful for Bob and Martha's leadership and enthusiasm in revisiting a topic that has grown in both the science and the policy arena since publication of the first school readiness book.

—*K.L.S.*

I

EARLY EDUCATION OPPORTUNITIES IN THE UNITED STATES

1

EARLY EDUCATION IN TRANSITION

Robert C. Pianta

This volume is an extension of a previously published book, *The Transition to Kindergarten,* which I co-edited with Martha Cox (Pianta & Cox, 1999) and which was intended at the time to identify and frame issues related to the transition to school. In that volume, we assembled chapters pertaining to conceptual models of transition, evidence of the importance of focusing on transition, and discussions of an assortment of policies and practices that pertained to the transition period. In the final chapter, we speculated about four trends that would focus work in the decade that followed. These trends are a good starting point for this brief introduction to the present volume, and are presented next.

1. There is an emerging conceptual base that integrates developmental psychology and education. This conceptual base, solidly grounded in empirical work, has fueled increasing recognition by educators that 1) the development of young children relies greatly on contexts and 2) the early grades of school are a different, and somewhat critical, period for later school success. Thus, a new conceptual model for understanding the role of the school as a context for development is emerging and will likely influence how educators think about and prepare for the transition to school. . . .

2. The diversity of America's families and school population is increasing rapidly and is likely to be the most pronounced among the younger age groups of children. Challenges of culture, language, family background, and processes and differences in the ways families view schools, all of which are formidable, will be exacerbated by these demographic shifts. These shifts raise issues of how schools will face the challenges of educating a diverse population, how communities work to support families and schools working collaboratively, and how the teacher work force will need to respond to student and family diversity.

3. Public school programs for young children (ages 3 and 4) will continue to increase. Universal prekindergarten programs for 4-year-olds will be the norm, programs for 3-year-olds will be common, and the age for entering school will be 1–2 years earlier than it is now for nearly all American children. . . . Schools will need to be more family-friendly. . . . Transformations of readiness definitions and assessment will also occur as programs are implemented for younger children.

3

4.   A movement for accountability has emerged in American education in response to pressures, political and substantive, from all sides. From one perspective, such a movement holds potential for enhancing the quality of education offered to American children and ensuring their performance at higher levels. Clear communication of expectations, for example, can actually enhance transition processes when these expectations form the basis for constructive communication about a child between home and school and between programs. . . . However, dangers also lurk in the accountability movement. For the most part, this movement has ushered in a rash of new testing and assessment for children of all ages. . . . [that are] not consistent with the emerging conceptual model that underlies most educational practice for young children. Thus, the accountability movement is likely to produce serious tensions for educators interested in this period of transition. (Pianta & Cox, 1999, pp. 363–364)

Our speculations involved the focusing of developmental and education science on the effects of various contextual resources and processes on the development of children's skills. We noted the emerging demographic shifts taking place and judged that early education programs would come to look increasingly diverse in terms of the ethnic backgrounds of and languages spoken by the children in attendance. It was clear at the time that investments in early education programming would increase to the extent that kindergarten would not be the first occasion in which most children would come into contact with a setting in which an adult was trying to teach them new skills that would be valued later. And we noted that the public would want to see a return on this investment. That we were reasonably accurate forecasters is not surprising; these trends were evident to most anyone familiar with the early childhood education policy landscape (Barnett, Robin, Hustedt, & Schulman, 2003; Committee for Economic Development, 2002; U.S. Census Bureau, 2001). What might be surprising to some is the rapidity with which these predictions appeared to become reality.

The expansion of publicly funded prekindergarten programs and the further inclusion of developmental and educational research in early childhood education has given rise to widespread popular support for universal prekindergarten in many states and the emergence of a model of elementary school that extends from preschool to third grade (see Chapter 5). Demographic shifts that pressure early schooling in relation to cultural, linguistic, and economic diversity have occurred far more rapidly than expected, and accountability is firmly entrenched in early childhood policy and practice (see Chapters 2 and 3), whereas 10 years ago, no had one predicted that all Head Start children would be tested or that there would be standards for preschool. These realities provide the context and impetus for this volume's efforts to organize conceptual, policy, and practice initiatives that span early childhood and elementary education.

This volume situates the trends described in *The Transition to Kindergarten* in the realities of early education in contemporary America, less than a decade later. The first section outlines theoretical, policy, and programmatic issues that early childhood education and elementary education have in common. In some sense, these first chapters provide a conceptual and policy bridge between these two sectors of the educational service system. The second section addresses an area of work that was not a focus of the original Pianta & Cox (1999) volume: recent work on domains of child functioning related to performance in school. By including a section on child functioning, we purposefully focused on areas of recent conceptual progress and empirical findings—health, executive functioning, English language learners—in an effort to continue a forward-looking perspective. The third section of the book is devoted to family and community contexts as they relate to a range of issues pertinent to the connection between early childhood and elementary education. Our challenge to the chapter authors was to look forward and, as we did in 1999, to try to forecast the key challenges the field will face and to present solutions if at all possible.

CONTEMPORARY CHALLENGES AND EARLY EDUCATION

This volume will be published at a time of unprecedented interest in identifying, deepening, and exploiting the connections between early childhood and elementary education. There is no longer any question that providing early learning and educational experiences that are *intended* to contribute to children's development of academic, social, and task-oriented skills (or their precursors) is an overarching goal of social and educational policy in the United States today (Barnett et al., 2003; Committee for Economic Development, 2002). The educational and developmental opportunities to which young children are exposed in child care, state-funded prekindergarten programs, Head Start programs, and their homes are leverage points for addressing concerns about K–12 achievement, particularly those related to income and ethnicity or race. Federal, state, and local politicians view providing early learning and educational experiences as a political as well as an economic and social good: universal prekindergarten was on the ballot in California at the time this book went to press, and although the initiative did not pass, advocates contend it is only a matter of time before it does; Virginia may consider a universal prekindergarten program in near-term budget cycles; states and cities are considering new governance and administrative structures out of which to regulate and operate programs for families and young children that integrate social, health, educational, and child care services and funding streams; and an ever-growing number of states and school districts are adopting new and innovative staff development, training, and quality-assurance programs to improve the value of experiences offered to children in early education settings.

The central challenges and concerns of the field are now not only how to provide safe, organized preschool programs to selected groups of children and how to better connect families and schools but also how to offer all preschool children appropriate and effective early educational experiences that are aligned and included with state K–12 standards and reform efforts and that, for some children, provide opportunities for accelerated progress. How to construct delivery systems for the equitable distribution of such experiences, how to ensure the training and expertise necessary to support the value of such experiences, and how to evaluate the extent to which this delivery system is actually responsible for growth in children's skills are the contemporary challenges to scientists and policy makers in early education.

These trends and concerns do not reflect a set of incremental, unrelated shifts in the field. Rather, as anticipated by Bogard & Takanishi (2005) and others (Council of Chief State School Officers, 2002; Gilliam & Zigler, 2001), a complete reconceptualization and redefinition of the loosely regulated, poorly aligned, and chaotically funded collection of opportunities for learning that are offered to children from ages 3 to 8 is taking place. Center-based and family child care, care at home in the family, Head Start, publicly funded prekindergarten programs, kindergarten, and the primary grades of elementary school are slowly being merged and included within a new system of early education and care that increasingly will be publicly funded and more highly regulated (Gilliam & Zigler, 2001). There is no reason to believe this process will not continue.

Although the informal system of early learning and care—composed of Head Start, child care, family day care, and public preschool—has functioned like a school for many years for children in the United States (U.S. Census Bureau, 2001), the pressures of accountability will no doubt force increasing inclusion and formalization. Since the early 1990s, the informal, unintentional nature of learning that takes place in the early learning and care "school" has been challenged by expectations from families, governments, and communities that children meet a set of performance standards, at least by third grade if not sooner. In every way that K–12 education is pressured by accountability, early learning and care opportunities are now under the same set of expectations (Blank, Schulman, & Ewen, 1999; Brown & Scott-Little, 2003) to *intentionally* contribute to children's skill growth in ways that are measurable. I have argued elsewhere that these trends are merely phenotypic expressions of the underlying reality that elementary school starts at age 3 (Pianta, 2005).

A community-based preschool in a YMCA can hardly be described as school if the referent point is the local elementary school building. But in every important way, that conclusion is wrong. Consider that parents think child care (even family-based child care) is school. In the 2000 Current Population Survey, 52% of parents reported that their 3- and 4-year-old children (about 4 million not-yet-5-year-olds) were "in school" (Clifford et al., 2005). A quick glance at the advertisements in many local newspapers each spring reveals that child care is being marketed in terms of its value for improving a child's school readiness, and Amazon.com, specialty stores, web sites for parents, and big box retailers sell billions of dollars worth of educational materials to parents who in turn expose their children as early as the first months of life.

The K–12 establishment views preschool as school and is in fact banking on the dividends expected from early childhood programs to help improve lagging achievement in the era of No Child Left Behind (NCLB) and to meet Adequate Yearly Progress (Committee for Economic Development, 2002; see Chapter 2). Early education and care programs are under pressure from the K–12 establishment and from politicians and regulators to deliver children to kindergarten who are more ready and are, as a consequence, applying standards, accountability assessments, regulation of teacher training, and an assortment of incentives in an effort to ramp up the productivity of this sector of educational services. Like it or not, child care, preschool, home learning environments, and programs for 4-year-olds are being asked to do the same things K–12 does. These settings may not be physically housed in school buildings, but they are school. The debate is no longer whether children should be exposed to early education opportunities but rather how best to leverage these resources in ways that contribute positively both to children's development and to society.

Closing Gaps

Results from the Early Childhood Longitudinal Study–Kindergarten Cohort (ECLS-K), the best national estimate of children's competencies as they enter school, shows that as of 1999, 31% of entering kindergartners were not proficient in recognizing (i.e., naming) letters, and 42% did not demonstrate positive behavior habits associated with successful adjustment in the classroom (West, Denton, & Germino-Hausken, 2000). However, a substantial proportion of that sample of children could read books when they arrived in school. It is also very likely that performance gaps are being underestimated; for example, the ECLS-K evaluates children's readiness skills in terms of very thin estimates of performance in early reading and includes virtually no assessments of math, science, or cognition. In terms of social adjustment of entering kindergartners, kindergarten teachers describe areas of concern that suggest much larger gaps in real-life performance in school than what is reflected in estimates based on national surveys of parents. Teachers describe challenges in social skills, adjustment, and attention that are simply not well estimated in contemporary assays of readiness (Rimm-Kaufman, Pianta, & Cox, 2000). Early childhood education is being asked to close these gaps or at least narrow them. In fact, early education is being asked to *accelerate* the development of the nation's lowest performing children and to contribute positively to the continuing gains of those likely to succeed anyway. And because children from affluent backgrounds often go to better preschools and receive more attention than children from less privileged families, care must be taken so that the early education movement does not actually widen the achievement gaps present at the start of school.

Even under the present circumstances that characterize early education programs, fairly rigorous evidence suggests that the kind of early education experiences to which many children in the United States are being exposed indeed contribute to their readiness for school and are fairly cost-effective in terms of economic returns on investment (Committee for Economic Development, 2002; Council of Chief State School Officers, 2002). On the other hand, if early education in America is to address the serious social and developmental concerns that it is expected to overcome, it will require intellectual, financial, human, and social capital far beyond the amount invested in the contemporary programs and settings that produce significant, but small, effects. In this context, it is imperative that the promise of contemporary early childhood education programs to cost-effectively close the K–12 achievement gap in the near term is not oversold.

The system of early childhood education opportunities, which I am calling *school that starts at three,* is profound in its potential as an asset for promoting the success of the nation's children—it is ubiquitous, it is increasingly systematic and formalized, it appears modestly effective, and it provides a measurable return on the public's investment. But a host of realities confront policy makers, practitioners, and scientists as they attempt to inform and shape this sector of our educational system. What policy levers make programs more effective? How should teachers be trained, and how should the quality of teaching and support for children be raised? Can and should programs be held accountable? If so, how? Can challenges related to equity and access to high-quality education be addressed? These are the central concerns this volume will address.

A High-Quality Program of Early Education

Everyone wants their educational program to be high quality. State and local officials and, to some extent, parents pay a lot of attention to the attributes of programs presumed to reflect or produce quality—per-pupil expenditures; accreditation standards; teacher credentials, degrees, or training; and length of day. Systems of program and school accreditation use some of these factors as metrics for program quality, and point systems for gauging program quality often rely on these indicators (Barnett et al., 2003; Early et al., 2006). Yet, with the exception of full-day programs, very little evidence indicates that these parameters of policy and definitions of program quality or accreditation translate into improved outcomes for children in contemporary early education settings, whether they be prekindergarten programs or the early elementary grades. In fact, the available evidence shows quite clearly that the value of enrollment in preschool is largely determined by the interactions that children have with adults in those settings.

For example, in the 11-state study of prekindergarten conducted by the National Center for Early Development and Learning (NCEDL), Mashburn and colleagues (2006) evaluated whether eight different features of program design used in policy (such as those above) singly or in combination (as in the National Association for the Education of Young Children or National Institute for Early Education Research point systems for program quality) predicted 10 different indicators of children's development measured during the prekindergarten year; importantly, they included as predictors measures of socioemotional and instructional features of child–teacher interactions (Mashburn et al., 2006). In these analyses, none of the distal program quality indicators predicted gains in children's learning; rather, the quality of teachers' interactions with the children accounted for change in performance. If program quality connotes the features responsible for producing children's learning and development, then the metrics favored by politicians, policy makers, and advocates are so far removed from the actual reason behind a program's success that one is inclined to doubt the usefulness of such metrics in policy, program design, or accreditation.

Effective teaching in early childhood education, as in the elementary grades, requires skillful combinations of explicit instruction, sensitive and warm interactions, responsive feedback, and verbal engagement/stimulation intentionally directed to ensure children's learning in a classroom environment that is not overly structured or regimented (e.g., Bowman, Donovan, & Burns, 2000; Pianta et al., 2005). The challenge for policy makers, the public, politicians, and teacher educators is how to grapple with the hard fact that, at present, too little is known about how to produce and distribute effective teachers and teaching in programs serving young children. Discussions of teacher training are too quickly polarized by advocates of "child-centered" approaches and those who argue for teachers to employ specific instructional techniques. Policy makers have to grapple with the reality that assessing *actual* program quality and effectiveness requires spending time observing classrooms and assessing children on something other than the alphabet—efforts that can be expensive and time consuming and the results of which are not easily reduced. Too often, children are not exposed to the types of early education and care experiences that we know will lead to gains in learning, a reality masked by metrics that paint a picture of high quality when it simply may not exist.

The Early School Work Force

Enrollment of 3- and 4-year-olds in early education programs now approaches 70% of the population and is growing annually, pressuring the supply chain for early educators and for evidence-based training of those educators. Universal prekindergarten programs for 4-year-olds will require at least 200,000 teachers, with estimates of 50,000 additional teachers needed by 2020 (Clifford et al., 2005). Unlike K–12, in which the supply chain is regulated by a single-state entity and typically requires a 4-year degree from an accredited institution (or equivalent), training of the early education and care work force is widely distributed and loosely regulated. Growing demand has created problems in relation to supplying staff for expanding programs and also in terms of providing new teachers with appropriate training, staff development, and support to ensure that they create learning opportunities that produce achievement.

Efforts to meet the demand for trained teachers and staff in early education and care settings are moving ahead rapidly, but there is little evidence that accumulating course credits, advancing in terms of degree status (e.g., from associate of arts to bachelor of arts), or attending workshops *directly* contribute to teachers' actual skills in the classroom and to children's achievement (Early et al., in press). In fact, the NCEDL 11-state prekindergarten study demonstrated that even in state-sponsored prekindergarten programs with credentialed teachers with bachelor's degrees, variation in observed curriculum implementation and quality of teaching was enormous, and observed instruction, interaction, and quality of implementation were essentially unrelated to teachers' experience or education (Pianta et al., 2005). Addressing work force concerns in this system requires a rethinking and rebalancing of factors such as incentives, the content and processes of training, and efforts to professionalize the work force and integrate the early education system with K–12.

CONCLUSION

Too few of the students who most need high-quality early education experiences receive them, and the few that do are unlikely to receive them consistently, decreasing the likelihood that benefits will be sustained for children who need consistent supports. In an era of high-stakes testing in which even *young children* may be held to uniform, minimum performance standards, it is disconcerting to note that the system on which the nation is relying to produce such outcomes provides exceptional variability in the nature and quality of actual *opportunities to learn* (see Chapter 4). It seems unreasonable to expect universal levels of minimal performance for students when the opportunities to achieve are so unevenly distributed. These realities about the level and distribution of high-quality early education classrooms in the United States probably reflect the convergence of at least three factors. First, teaching young children is uniquely challenging. Second, many of the publicly funded early education programs that are included in large-scale studies (such as Head Start and state prekindergarten) are composed of a high percentage of children who live below the poverty line and who often need a considerable level of support. Third, the system of early education operates on a shoestring of support—it is often less well funded than K–12 education, classrooms often are housed in trailers or makeshift locations, and teachers describe themselves as alienated from and lacking the supports available in K–12. The degree to which a teacher (or program) can provide gap-closing social and instructional interactions is a product of balancing his or her capacity and skills with the concerns of children in the classroom—an equation that poses serious challenges to policy makers and program administrators interested in making good on the promises of early educational experiences.

REFERENCES

Barnett, W.S., Robin, K.B., Hustedt, J.T., & Schulman, K.L. (2003). *The state of preschool: 2003 state preschool yearbook.* New Brunswick, NJ: National Institute for Early Education Research.

Blank, H., Schulman, K., & Ewen, D. (1999). *Seeds of success: State prekindergarten initiatives, 1998–1999.* Washington, DC: Children's Defense Fund.

Bogard, K., & Takanishi, R. (2005). PK-3: An aligned and coordinated approach to education for children 3 to 8 years old. *Social Policy Report, XIX*(III). Washington, DC: Society for Research in Child Development.

Bowman, B., Donovan, M.S., & Burns, S. (Eds.). (2000). *Eager to learn: Educating our preschoolers.* Washington, DC: National Research Council.

Brown, E.G., & Scott-Little, C. (2003). *Evaluations of school readiness initiatives: What are we learning?* Greensboro, NC: SERVE.

Clifford, R.M., Barbarin, O., Chang, F., Early, D., Bryant, D., Howes, C., et al. (2005). What is prekindergarten? Characteristics of public prekindergarten programs. *Applied Developmental Science, 9*(3), 126–143.

Committee for Economic Development. (2002). *Preschool for all: Investing in a productive and just society.* New York: Author.

Council of Chief State School Officers. (2002). *Ready for success: Five state strategies for expanding effective early childhood education.* Washington, DC: Author.

Early, D., Maxwell, K., Burchinal, M., Alva, S., Bender, R., Bryant, D., et al. (in press). Teachers' education, classroom quality, and young children's academic skills: Results from seven studies of preschool programs. *Child Development.*

Gilliam, W.S., & Zigler, E.F. (2001). A critical meta-analysis of all evaluations of state-funded preschool from 1977 to 1998: Implications for policy, service delivery, and program evaluation. *Early Childhood Research Quarterly, 15*(4), 441–473.

Mashburn, A., Pianta, R., Hamre, B., Downer, J., Barbarin, O., Bryant, D., et al. (2006). *Pre-k program standards and gains in academic and language skills.* Manuscript under review.

Pianta, R. (2005). A new elementary school for American children. *Social Policy Report, 19*(3), 4–5.

Pianta, R.C., & Cox, M.J. (Eds.). (1999). *The transition to kindergarten.* Baltimore: Paul H. Brookes Publishing Co.

Pianta, R., Howes, C., Burchinal, M., Bryant, D., Clifford, R., Early, D., et al. (2005). Features of prekindergarten programs, classrooms, and teachers: Do they predict observed classroom quality and child-teacher interactions? *Journal of Applied Developmental Science, 9*(3), 144–159.

Rimm-Kaufman, S., Pianta, R., & Cox, M. (2000). Teachers' judgments of problems in the transition to kindergarten. *Early Childhood Research Quarterly, 15*(2), 147–166.

U.S. Census Bureau. (2001). *School enrollment of the population 3 to 34 years old, by level and control of school, race, and Hispanic origin: October 1955 to 2000.* Washington, DC: Author.

West, J., Denton, K., & Germino-Hausken, E. (2000). *America's kindergartners.* NCES 2000-070. Washington, DC: National Center for Education Statistics.

2

REACHING FOR THE WHOLE

Integration and Alignment in Early Education Policy

Sharon Lynn Kagan and Kristie Kauerz

Throughout the history of early childhood education in the United States, child care and early education programs have been clearly divided (Bloch, 1987; Cahan, 1989; Kagan, Cohen, & Neuman, 1996). Historically, the term *child care* has been applied to programs that are intended primarily to protect the health and safety of children, from birth through school age, who require custodial care by adults other than their own parents. Child care meets the needs of working parents, regardless of family income. In contrast, *early education* has been used to describe programs that are focused on academic skills, often provided by schools, and offered to children who are 3, 4, and 5 years old. A third strand of early childhood programs, those that provide comprehensive services (e.g., Head Start and Early Head Start), strive to meet both the social service and educational needs of children but often are narrowly targeted to children from birth through age 4 who are most at risk because of low family income. A fourth strand of programs serving children before the age of school entry meet several times a week for several hours only and provide rich socialization opportunities; these often are called nursery schools.

Although these four types of American early care and education programs historically have been characterized by fragmentation and lack of coordination, considerable efforts are being made to overcome these distinctions, with incentives for collaboration now characterizing much early childhood policy. Over the past decade, Head Start–State Collaboration grants, the creation of collaborative councils and administrative structures, and state efforts to promote unified professional development and quality-rating plans have proliferated, exemplifying the movement toward more coordination and integration in early care and education. During the last 5 years, significant policy developments aimed at educationalizing and systematizing early childhood education have been increasing in prevalence. These changes are permeating and changing the nature of the field.

This chapter discusses these trends, providing insight into and evidence of the increasingly educationalized and systematized nature of early care and education. More specifically, this chapter addresses the factors that are accelerating these trends and provides key indicators of these phenomena, using concrete examples from recent policies and practices.

After substantiating the changing early childhood zeitgeist, with its movement toward greater educationalization and systematization, this chapter examines what is simultaneously the driving force of contemporary educational policy and the source of these trends—the accountability movement. This chapter reviews shifts in how accountability is understood in early care and education and proffers that accountability efforts are necessary but insufficient if not done in a systematic and appropriate manner. The chapter closes with a discussion of one critical and often underaddressed aspect of accountability: the alignment of standards, curriculum, and assessment.

THE EDUCATIONALIZATION OF EARLY CARE AND EDUCATION

The educationalization of early care and education is evidenced by a research-driven focus on critical measurements of quality that have traditionally been associated with K–12 education, including teacher certification and quality, leadership, curriculum, and learning standards (National Research Council, 2001; National Research Council and Institute of Medicine, 2000). This chapter demonstrates the educationalization of early care and education through a discussion of increased teacher qualification requirements, curricular effectiveness, and rigorous standards. Importantly, as is true in K–12 education, none of these indicators ensure that children will grow academically or that classroom teaching will be of high quality. They do not guarantee high-quality interactions between teachers and children. Rather, the indicators provide structural supports that increase the possibility that teaching will be effective.

Indicators of Educationalization

Within early care and education is a national movement to raise early learning teacher qualifications for both lead and assistant teachers. This movement rests on research that concludes that early childhood teachers who hold bachelor's degrees (e.g., bachelor of arts, bachelor of science) with specialized training in early childhood education provide better quality learning experiences, which lead to better outcomes, most notably for 3- to 5-year-olds (Barnett, 2003; National Research Council, 2001; Whitebook, 2003). At the federal level, Head Start began raising its standards for teachers by first requiring half of Head Start teachers to acquire an associate of arts degree by 2003; the 2005 reauthorization bill included provisions for half of Head Start teachers to hold a bachelor of arts degree by 2008. At the state level, state-funded prekindergarten programs are now being rated by the National Institute for Early Education Research (NIEER) according to 10 quality factors; 4 of the 10 criteria are related to the qualifications and ongoing professional development of teachers (Barnett, Hustedt, Robin, & Schulman, 2004). Given that many prekindergarten programs now have more stringent personnel qualifications, intense debate is taking place about what constitutes appropriate training and credentialing for teachers of young children (Herzenberg, Price, & Bradley, 2005; Whitebook, Sakai, Gerber, & Howes, 2001). Clearly, the need to ensure the best teachers possible in our nation's early childhood programs has become a central focus of policy makers and researchers alike.

A second indicator of the educationalization of early care and education is the increasing concern with curricular effectiveness, evidenced by the federal government's Preschool Curricula Evaluation Research (PCER) program. The aim of the program is to use scientifically rigorous research to determine whether one or more curricula produce educationally meaningful effects on children's language skills, prereading and premath abilities, cognition, general knowledge, and social competence. The U.S. Department of Education is investing millions of dollars for research universities to conduct randomized experiments that will provide evidence of the impact that each curriculum intervention has on the children it serves. The interest is not only in impacts at the end of the preschool program but also in the longitudinal impacts on children's learning through the end of first grade (U.S. Department of Education, 2002).

Further evidence of the educationalization of early care and education is mounting interest in understanding and supporting the development of children's specific skills, abilities, knowledge, and behaviors. As such, early learning standards—or expectations of what children should know and be able to do—are proliferating across the nation (Scott-Little, Kagan, & Frelow, 2003). As of July 2005, 40 states had early learning standards (although 4 had not yet developed or initiated an author implementation plan and 4 more were revising their existing standards); the remaining 10 states were in the process of developing standards, the last of which was scheduled for completion in December 2006 (Child Care Bureau, 2006). Beyond states are national examples of early learning standards: Head Start has developed the Head Start Child Outcomes Framework, which is intended to guide Head Start programs in their ongoing review of the progress and accomplishments of children in their classrooms. CTB/McGraw-Hill (a subsidiary of The McGraw-Hill Companies), using a team of national experts, also developed national early learning standards for 3- to 5-year-olds that are highly regarded for their vignettes, which help to convert behaviorally driven standards into effective pedagogy (*Pre-Kindergarten Standards: Guidelines for Teaching and Learning,* 2002). These state and national efforts indicate a growing desire to set explicit expectations for children's learning and development.

Although these educationalizing shifts—increased emphasis on teacher qualifications, curricular effectiveness, and learning standards—inform all of early care and education, they are perhaps manifest most clearly in the burgeoning prekindergarten movement that is having an impact on all early childhood policies and practices across the nation. Today, there is a widespread national trend to create and expand prekindergarten programs for 3- and 4-year-old children. More than 40 states have at least one state-administered preschool program that serves children during the 2 years before they enter the formal K–12 education system (Barnett, Hustedt, Robin, & Schulman, 2004). Media coverage of stories related to prekindergarten can be found on a daily basis in national, regional, and local newspapers. State investments in prekindergarten programs have grown by nearly $1 billion, from approximately $1.7 billion in 1998–1999 to $2.54 billion in 2002–2003 (Barnett et al., 2004; Schulman & Blank, 1999). Private investments also have grown, with major national foundations establishing multiyear and multimillion-dollar initiatives devoted to expanding prekindergarten for 3- and 4-year-olds. Without a doubt, the trend toward more and bigger state-based prekindergarten programs is prominent and widespread. Although the expansion of prekindergarten has brought many more opportunities for young children to receive services, it also is a potent reflection of the trends toward the educationalization of early childhood education.

The Roots of Educationalization

The educationalization of early care and education has deep roots. At least four significant aspects of K–12 education in the United States have accelerated the trend toward the educationalization of early childhood education. First is growing concern about issues of equity and access in American society at large, reflected in achievement gaps that exist even as children enter school. Second, the business and corporate world has packaged education as an effective and efficient means to increase the competitiveness of American students in the global marketplace. Thus, American businesses want to gain an educational advantage and, based on early childhood effectiveness data, are committed to fostering it. Third, the ubiquity of and comparatively stable funding for K–12 education have made the notion of preparing children to succeed in school a more palatable frame for advancing an early childhood agenda to policy makers and the public. Fourth, the federal government has exerted a strong influence on state policy to define and measure outcomes of learning, not just for K–12 students but also for young children.

Educationalizing Accelerator #1: Concerns with Stratification of American Society

Racial, ethnic, and socioeconomic gaps in educational achievement have been widely cited throughout the past 30 years and persist today (Education Trust, 2005; Reed, 2001; Schrag, 2003). For example, the 2005 National Assessment of Educational Progress (NAEP) noted that the white–black and white–Hispanic gaps in fourth- and eighth-grade reading scores have not changed significantly since 1992; similarly, large gaps still exist between the performance of children eligible for free or reduced-price school lunch and children from families with higher incomes (Perie, Grigg, & Donahue, 2005). These disparities in achievement among different student subgroups led to major policy efforts to address and close these gaps. The No Child Left Behind (NCLB) Act of 2001 (PL 107-110) is perhaps the most ambitious, the farthest reaching, and the most high-profile policy response. Among other things, NCLB requires every school to measure and report annual academic progress for every student from third through eighth grade. States must produce annual statewide and school district report cards that provide disaggregated data, highlighting any achievement gaps among racial, ethnic, socioeconomic, and disability groups (U.S. Department of Education, 2001). Schools are now held accountable for the progress of *every* student.

Policy makers and practitioners alike have focused their attention on achievement gaps among school-age children for the past half century. Recent research, however, shows that sizable gaps already exist by the time children enter kindergarten, and these inequalities among young children have been less documented, less publicized, and less addressed (Rouse, Brooks-Gunn, & McLanahan, 2005). Before even entering kindergarten, children in the lowest socioeconomic groups have average cognitive scores 60% below the scores of children in the highest socioeconomic groups. This gap is often associated with race and ethnicity; in fact, economic status most closely correlates with educational underachievement (Lee & Burkam, 2002). Evidence spotlighting how the stratification of American society can begin early in children's lives has prompted hearty efforts to confront these disparities, bringing early education to the forefront as a crucial factor that can close achievement gaps.

Educationalizing Accelerator #2: Business Interests in Effectiveness

When *A Nation at Risk* (National Commission on Excellence in Education, 1983) was published, it sounded the alarm that the dismal state of American education was jeopardizing the United States' competitiveness in the global marketplace. This report galvanized the business world to become an active and vocal proponent for education reform. Corporate leaders across the nation used their professional interests to apply business acumen to education. With this clamor from powerful communities and constituents, politicians and policy makers became interested in maximizing and chronicling the competence of all students. They, like their business patrons, hoped that effective interventions would, in the short run, boost America's meager performance on international tests and, in the long run, preserve the nation's global economic status. Education became intimately linked with work force development and sustained economic growth.

During the 1990s, business leaders expanded their interests in education to include young children. National business groups such as the Business Roundtable and the Committee for Economic Development created task forces and work groups that generated position statements on early childhood education (Business Roundtable, 2003; Committee for Economic Development, 2002). In the past 5 years, the business community has presented strong evidence about the economic arguments for investing in early childhood education (Currie, 2001). Using cost-effectiveness studies about the economic benefits of education, the business community, led by important players such as Nobel Prize Laureate Economist Jim Heckman (Carneiro & Heckman, 2003) and the Federal Reserve Bank (Rolnick & Grunewald, 2003), points to early education as a dependable means to advance American education. As such, corporate interests have contributed to the educationalization of early childhood education in the United States.

Educationalizing Accelerator #3: Framing Early Care and Education as School Readiness

Education for children in kindergarten through 12th grade is an assumed right for *all* children in the United States, even though compulsory school age and requirements for school districts to provide kindergarten vary from state to state (Education Commission of the States, 2004). Federal and state funding for K–12 education is also assumed to be a given. Debate is never heard from state legislatures on whether to maintain fourth or eighth grade as guaranteed parts of a child's education. Public education in the United States is viewed as a universal right and, therefore, a durable system available to all children. Because most children will enter this universal system, there is an inherent interest in ensuring that all children are well equipped to thrive and succeed in school. As such, early childhood advocates and policy makers strategically began viewing school readiness as a promising frame through which to earn public support for, and investment in, early childhood programs. The underlying logic is that developmentally appropriate education early in life leads to better education outcomes later (Bredekamp & Copple, 1997). In other words, the early childhood field leveraged the ubiquity and relatively stable public and fiscal support for the institution of public education to further its efforts on behalf of children during the preschool years. If support for K–12 education is widespread, why should similar support not exist for the essential education and learning that occur prior to kindergarten?

This logic is nowhere more evident than in the work of the National Education Goals Panel (NEGP). Convened in 1989, the NEGP's first goal was that "by the year 2000 all children in America will start school ready to learn" (National Education Goals Panel, 1991). Since then, school readiness has become synonymous with national intents for early care and education. The school readiness focus has advanced a radical shift in how early care and education is viewed, from its earlier image as a support for working parents and children's development to a fundamental necessity to ensure that children are ready to succeed in school. Early care and education is no longer seen primarily as a means to care for and nurture children while their parents are at work; neither is early care and education seen as merely the "right" choice to make to nurture children's learning and development. Indeed, recent polling data even suggest that the terms *prekindergarten, pre-K,* and *early learning* are more effective than the term *child care* in building public support for early childhood education efforts (Communications Consortium Media Center, 2005). Thus, both in nomenclature and in emphasis, child care and services for the young are taking on an increased educational orientation.

Educationalizing Accelerator #4: Federal Interest in Outcomes   Recent federal accountability and standards-based policy, according to some scholars, has been the most significant educational reform of the last half century in American education (Goertz, Duffy, & Carlson-LeFloch, 2001). NCLB (PL 107-110), already noted for its attention to achievement gaps among racial, ethnic, and socioeconomic subgroups of students, serves as the cornerstone of the federal government's investment in and vision for accountability in K–12 education. Child or student performance accountability has manifested itself in NCLB and subsequent state-level educational legislation by requiring performance standards, assessments, and their alignment; by calling for the documentation and aggregation of measured results; and, in some cases, by calling for the dispersal of rewards or sanctions on the basis of those results (Barton, 2002; Kagan & Scott-Little, 2004). No longer can program requirements or expenditures be the standard of success, no longer is America satisfied with episodic testing, and no longer are test results shrouded from public review.

So all-encompassing is the federal press for outcomes that it not only is manifest in K–12 education but also is permeating early care and education. Similar to its impact on elementary and secondary education, child or student accountability is affecting both thought and practice related to early childhood education. Some early childhood practices, conventionally regarded as heretical, are becoming standard (Hatch, 2002; Seefeldt, 2005). This sea change—the setting of child-based learning standards, the administration of formal assessments, and the use of results to help children—emanates from diverse policies. First, and actually predating NCLB, the 1998 federal reauthorization of Head Start launched the dissemination and use of the Head Start Child Outcomes Framework, a document that defines 100 specific expectations for children's skills, abilities, knowledge, and behaviors. As further evidence of the federal interest in outcomes, in 2002, President George W. Bush announced his administration's *Good Start, Grow Smart* early childhood initiative, which requires states to develop "voluntary early learning guidelines" (*Good Start, Grow Smart,* 2002) in language and early literacy skills in order to receive Child Care Development Funds (CCDF). So pervasive are these policies and so confounding are their manifestations that a National Early Childhood Accountability Task Force has been established to render clarity and guidance for the field.

These trends—the influence of business to promote the importance of early education for economic competitiveness; the frame of school readiness that positions early care and education as a critical precursor to K–12 schooling; and the federal push to define, measure, and report academic outcomes—have converged to promote the educationalization of American early care and education.

THE SYSTEMATIZATION OF EARLY CARE AND EDUCATION

At the same time that early care and education is becoming increasingly educationalized, it also is becoming more systematized. This is evidenced in increased efforts to institutionalize and formalize partnerships, practices, and policies that support a more comprehensive approach to early childhood education. Increasingly, states are seeking to coordinate and align child care, Head Start, prekindergarten, and other programs and policies that have been traditionally incongruent and categorical. These efforts, although operative over the past 15 years, have gained increasing momentum and are manifest in three distinct ways: the desire to establish an early care and education system, the dedication to expand and raise the quality of subsystems (e.g., professional development systems, quality rating systems [QRSs]), and the growth of intentional efforts to link early childhood with existing social services (e.g., maternal and child health, mental health, family support).

Indicators of Systematization

Early care and education has long been considered a *nonsystem* with disparate funding streams, governance structures, program quality standards, eligibility requirements, and teacher qualifications. Over the past decade, however, researchers and advocates have begun to reach consensus on the core components of an early care and education system (Bruner, Stover Wright, Gebhard, & Hibbard, 2004; Gallagher, Clifford, & Maxwell, 2004; Kagan & Cohen, 1997; Kagan & Rigby, 2003). The Quality 2000 report, *Not by Chance* (Kagan & Cohen, 1997), envisioned what a quality early care and education system for America's young children might look like and succinctly defined its fundamental elements. There is now general agreement that a system of early care and education has eight key components: 1) quality programs; 2) a focus on goals and results for children; 3) parent information and engagement; 4) individual licensing for practitioners in the field; 5) professional preparation and ongoing development for practitioners; 6) facility licensing, enforcement, and accreditation; 7) funding and financing; and 8) governance, planning, and accountability (Kagan & Cohen, 1997). This definition recognizes the inextricable interrelations among early childhood services and infrastructure elements, infrastructure meaning the supports that perform specialized or essential functions for the whole system (e.g., regulation, finance, governance, professional development, quality-assurance mechanisms). These infrastructure pieces are not limited to any single program; indeed, a strong infrastructure is needed by all programs and can bind together traditionally disparate programs and services by providing common standards, reliable funding, and sensible oversight.

Many early childhood policy makers and community leaders across the United States have responded to this report with ambitious efforts to develop systems of early care and education. In many states, the most potent and far-reaching systematization efforts have centered around the establishment and fortification of *sub*systems, comprehensive initiatives that address one or more (but not all) of the components of the overall early care and education system (e.g., high-quality teaching and professional development, program quality and facility licensing). For example, some of the more visible subsystem efforts have been those that strive to improve the quality and transparency of early childhood programs by establishing voluntary QRSs and their related, monetarily driven tiered reimbursement systems (TRSs). Both the QRS and TRS provide opportunities for scores of early care and education programs to assess their program standards and performance via a self-analysis process. Based on the results of the analysis, programs develop plans of improvement and then are evaluated and ranked by external specialists. In the case of the QRS efforts, these rankings may be tied to symbols of success that are widely publicized, giving parents and potential staff a clear indication of the quality of the program. Some states operate under the rubric of TRS, tying state facility licensing and program reimbursements to quality rankings (Stoney, 2004). Beyond program quality subsystems are also promising examples of new governance approaches (e.g., Georgia's Bright From the Start: Department of Early Care and Learning, Massachusetts's State Department of Early Education and Development), new efforts to train and retain qualified personnel (e.g., Connecticut's Charts-A-Course, North Carolina's Child Care Services Association, Inc.), and inventive efforts to make the public aware of these issues (e.g., the Communications Consortium Media Center). These subsystem efforts are compelling steps in the movement toward greater systematization and its correlates, increased program effectiveness, and accountability.

Multiple state-based, multistate, and/or foundation-sponsored initiatives to link systems of care that affect young children are further evidence of the systematization of early care and education. In these efforts, the system focus extends beyond early care and education to include early intervention, health care, mental health, family support, and K–12 education. One of the most notable linked systems efforts, which is now in all 50 states and the District of Columbia, is the State Early Childhood Comprehensive System (SECCS) grant program funded by the Maternal and Child Health Bureau (MCHB) in the U.S. Department of Health and Human Services. The purpose of these grants is for states to plan, develop, and ultimately implement collaborations and partnerships to support families and communities to raise children who are healthy and ready to learn at school entry. To do this, each state must address five systems that the MCHB has identified as critical to children's overall health and well-being: 1) access to health insurance and medical homes that provide comprehensive physical and child development services for all children, including children with special health care needs; 2) mental health services and services that address children's social-emotional development; 3) early care and education/child care that supports children's early learning, health, and development of social competence from birth to age 5; 4) parenting education; and 5) comprehensive family support services. Linked system efforts recognize that many systems already have an impact on young children's health, well-being, and ability to succeed in school and in life.

The Roots of Systematization

In the early childhood field, "building a system" has become a popular catch phrase and a prevalent arena for change. As with the educationalization of early care and education, this systematization did not emerge unexpectedly or without impetus. Rather, the press for systematization has grown out of, and has been accelerated by, two primary conditions in the early childhood field: a deep concern about the declining quality of programs and an understanding of the connections between direct services and infrastructure.

Systematization Accelerator #1: Concerns About Poor Program Quality

Since the advent of Head Start and other preschool programs for disadvantaged children in the 1960s and 1970s, a vast number of empirical studies have been undertaken to determine both the short- and long-term effects of these programs on the learning and development of young children. The research demonstrates that some programs are more effective in producing advanced language, math, and social skills for children in the short term as well as reduced grade repetition and special education placements over the long term (Campbell, Miller-Johnson, Sparling, & Pungello, 2001; Peisner-Feinberg et al., 1999;

Reynolds, Temple, Robertson, & Mann, 2001). Longitudinal studies of high-quality interventions show payoffs to both program participants and taxpayers—in economic productivity, crime reduction, and health status—decades after the initial preschool experience (Reynolds, Temple, Robertson, & Mann, 2002; Schweinhart et al., 2005). Although the methodological rigor of the studies varies, these programs share certain characteristics: They have qualified teaching staff, low teacher–child ratios, small class sizes, curriculum content and learning processes that encourage school-related skills and knowledge, intense and coherent programming, and collaborative relationships with parents (National Institute of Child Health and Human Development Early Child Care Research Network, 2002; National Research Council, 2001).

Unfortunately, whereas one body of research demonstrates the effectiveness of high-quality programs in producing positive child outcomes, another clearly indicates how few of the programs available to America's children and families are of high quality. Indeed, in national or multistate studies, state-funded prekindergarten programs, Head Start programs, and community-based child care all have been shown to have, at worst, disappointingly low and, at best, highly variable levels of program quality (*Head Start FACES: Longitudinal Findings,* 2001; Helburn, 1995; National Institute of Child Health and Human Development Early Child Care Research Network, 1998; Pianta et al., 2005). The importance of quality programs to yield sustained positive outcomes for children is disputable, but so, too, is the knowledge that many public and private early care and education programs are not of high quality. This disparity has encouraged national efforts to look beyond program variables and instead concentrate on systemic variables that influence the nature and quality of individual programs. The system, rather than the program, has become an additional focus for quality enhancement.

Systematization Accelerator #2: Understanding the Interconnectedness of Direct Services and Infrastructure

The available range of solid data implies that American educators know how to produce quality early childhood programs that yield positive outcomes for children. Less encouragingly, the same data imply that such high-quality programs are available only to a handful of children. As public concern about the quality of programs has grown, so has an understanding that simply infusing more money into the provision of direct services to young children and their families is inadequate. If investments are made in direct services without a commensurate investment in the infrastructure that supports coordination and sustainability, program quality—and, therefore, child outcomes—falling far short of expectations should be no surprise. In fact, *Not by Chance* (Kagan & Cohen, 1997), which defines what an early care and education system might look like, suggests that if even one of the eight system components is taken away, the system cannot function as a whole.

Underinvestment in the infrastructure is a problem in normal times; the situation is exacerbated by the significant program expansion that presently characterizes the field. More and more programs are forced to compete for scarce supports, including quality personnel and space, making the need for systematization and coordination even greater. For example, significant program expansion is evoking high rates of personnel turnover and disagreements over the comparative effectiveness of diverse delivery systems (Whitebook & Sakai, 2003). In this case, systemic planning for the educational preparation, ongoing professional development, career ladders, and wage structure for those who work with young children is essential. These critical infrastructural issues are not exclusive to any particular program or sector. Here, the infrastructure, rather than the provision of direct services, has become an additional focus for quality enhancement. Systematization and a focus on infra-structure can help resolve the fragmentation that characterizes early care and education (Kagan & Neuman, 2003).

The educationalization and systematization of early care and education may be neces-sary to yield the kind of outcomes that early childhood education can potentially provide for all children. Educationalization and systematization can address these issues, but only if they are well managed; otherwise, the current expansion of programs and the rush to raise both child and program standards could evoke a system that is even more disorganized and inequitable.

ACCOUNTABILITY: THE CORE OF EDUCATIONALIZATION AND SYSTEMATIZATION

Turning from the indicators and roots of the trends toward educationalization and system-atization, we now address the element that binds and undergirds both: accountability. Ac-countability not only is the contemporary driving force of educationalization and systematization but also is a requisite component and a necessary correlate to the success of both trends and subsequently to the success of early education in the future. Educational-ization is about producing outcomes that will enable all young children to be excited, com-petent learners and to be ready for school. Systematization is about producing an effective and cost-efficient system that will yield the kind of high-quality programs and services needed to produce positive outcomes for children.

If the ultimate goal is to meet the holistic needs of young children competently, com-prehensively, and compassionately, clear standards of what children should know and be able to do, and aligned curricula that address these standards, are needed. These standards, in turn, should be aligned with assessments of children's achievements. Similarly, develop-ment of high-quality programs, program standards, or specifications of what the programs should do and provide, and periodic, aligned assessments of program efficacy in meeting these standards is needed. In other words, effective child standards, curricula, and assess-ments are needed to achieve effective educationalization of early care and education. Pro-gram standards and ways of measuring the efficacy of those programs, as well as their contributions to the total system, are necessary to achieve effective systemization. Account-ability has the power to transform services for young children, but haphazard and poorly de-fined accountability could destroy decades of efforts on behalf of young children.

Historically, considerable attention has been devoted to fostering early childhood pro-gram accountability. Such attention has taken the form of state regulations, program per-formance standards (e.g., Head Start's performance standards), and program accreditation efforts. For instance, in 2006, the National Association for the Education of Young Chil-dren (NAEYC) introduced a new accreditation program that raised the national bar for early education program standards. Today, exciting efforts to establish program standards and commensurate systems of assessment of program quality are taking new forms in the shape of the QRS and TRS efforts discussed previously. In contrast, less work has been done on child-based accountability. And much of what has been done takes its cue from K–12 education. For example, results from federally mandated, state-administered tests under

NCLB are being released across the nation, spiking intense public scrutiny of the value and validity of child-based accountability, not only for children in elementary and secondary schools but also for those in early childhood settings. As a result, a focus on child accountability is timely because many states interested in setting up child-based accountability systems in early childhood are seeking guidance. Thus, the importance and timeliness lead us to focus on child accountability as an essential policy tool. This emphasis, however, does not minimize the importance of further reflection on, and analysis of, the need for increased and improved program accountability in early care and education.

Child Accountability in Early Care and Education: Paradigm Shifts in Standards, Curricula, and Assessments

New child accountability efforts, without question, are evoking major shifts in how early childhood education is conceptualized and carried out. Specifically, paradigm shifts are occurring in the way early childhood standards, curricula, and assessments are viewed. One critical ingredient affecting the value of accountability is alignment. Before understanding the conceptual and practical relationship of alignment to child-based accountability, an understanding of these paradigm shifts is necessary.

Standards: The Shift from Evoking to Specifying What Children Should Know and Be Able to Do   For more than a century, early childhood pedagogy has emphasized recognizing the uniqueness of each child. What children learned was to be shaped by their interests with no standard (much less standardized) set of learning expectations specified (Elkind, 1998, 2003; Katz, 2003; McClellan & Katz, 2001). Children's natural and often fluctuating interests were the focus, leading to learning that was highly individualized and flexible. What children learned was to be evoked from their interests and inclinations, with the goal of exciting them about learning, knowledge, and inquiry.

The advent of the accountability movement has turned these precepts on end. Rather than individualizing expectations for each child, standards are becoming universalized. Rather than evoking learning goals from children's ever-changing interests, standards are being prespecified. Highly revered concepts such as the "invented curriculum" and the "teachable moment" that begin with and focus on the child are being replaced by strategies that accommodate the child but give precedence to prescription. Early learning standards that specify what children know and are able to do are not, as they are in K–12 education, merely a specification of tacitly existing learning goals. In early childhood education, goals and standards shift the starting point of educational pedagogy from the child to the content. Although they alter the basic starting point and the fundamental premise of the centrality of the individual child, early learning standards are taking root, shifting a century-old way of thinking about how young children should be educated.

Curriculum: The Shift from Broad to Focused Learning   Traditionally, the purpose of curricula has been to advance comprehensive child development, which is manifest in skills and competencies that are important both in and of themselves and that are linked to children's long-term success (Kagan, Moore, & Bredekamp, 1995). Throughout the evolution of early childhood education curricula, three beliefs have prevailed:

1) children are competent and eager learners whose natural curiosity allows for rich learning experiences; 2) children learn in an active way so that learning in a specific subject area (e.g., math, science, language) ideally takes place within the context of child-generated experiences (e.g., cooking, gardening, constructing); and 3) children need exposure to all domains of development—physical and motor, language, cognitive, and social and emotional—so that no single domain takes precedence over any other. As noted earlier, the search for effective curricula persists, with the federal government funding randomized clinical trials to compare various curriculum models.

Amid this quest to achieve better outcomes for young children and to help close the achievement gap is growing momentum to shift from a focus on all domains of development to those that promote a greater emphasis on literacy, language, and quantitative skills. Such a shift in focus is manifest formally in new guidelines directing programs to focus more heavily on these areas (Olfman, 2003). Early educators report feeling pressure to stress academic curricular areas from kindergarten teachers who, in turn, report pressure from primary teachers to concentrate on a more limited range of subject areas (Wesley & Buysee, 2003). Some early educators contend that this is shifting the balance of what is taught and what is learned in early childhood programs, once again significantly altering decades of accepted practice.

Assessment: The Shift from Informal Assessment to Formal Assessments and Testing
Early childhood education has long been committed to informal assessment as a means of individualizing instruction. The very absence of prescribed standards had meant that teachers had a special responsibility to be knowledgeable about each child's learning status and to be certain that children were receiving a balanced exposure to all domains of development. Historically, early childhood educators have been trained in observing and recording young children's behaviors, with the intent of using that information to modify classroom practice. Until a decade ago, wide-scale assessments of young children were almost unheard of outside of large-scale research studies. However, increased attention on the importance of child outcomes has created a demand for more formal assessments, especially within most publicly funded preschool and kindergarten programs (Scott-Little, Kagan, & Clifford, 2003). Even though such assessments are increasingly required for program funding, the possibility that assessment results might be used for program evaluation and other high-stakes accountability purposes has raised considerable concern in the early childhood community.

These concerns have several foundations. First, there is a concern that such formal testing is not appropriate for young children. In the quest for valid, reliable measures, test developers have tended to rely on instruments that are norm referenced and group administered. For older children, this approach may work well, particularly when it is accompanied by performance measures that yield greater insight into a child's more nuanced capacities and thoughts. For younger children, however, norm-referenced, group-administered assessments are inappropriate for many reasons. Young children's learning patterns are highly episodic, making a one-time assessment a poor reflection of children's knowledge. Young children's comparatively short attention spans also tend to make them poor test takers (Kagan & Scott-Little, 2004); their capacities and knowledge are better captured in less formal settings (Scott-Little, Kagan, & Clifford, 2003). Moreover, younger children are often wary of unfamiliar adults, making the introduction of a visiting tester a formidable challenge for the comfortable, accurate assessment of young children (Shepard, Kagan, & Wurtz, 1998).

A second major concern about the movement toward formal testing involves the nature of the testing instruments themselves and their appropriateness for young children (Shepard, 1994). Younger children from increasingly diverse cultural backgrounds are entering the early education system, rendering narrowly prescribed assessment strategies inappropriate to 21st-century populations. Furthermore, standardized tests tend to focus on language and literacy (Zaslow & Halle, 2003); consider the prevalence of instruments that assess vocabulary, receptive language, lexical organization, word diversity, social use of language, phonology, and print concepts. Far fewer instruments have been created to assess children's social and emotional development and the ways in which they approach learning (e.g., curiosity, motivation)—domains that are often considered the basis of early childhood education. Because only a limited number of valid tests address all of the domains valued by early childhood educators, the shift from informal assessment to more formal testing is of grave concern. Such concern is exacerbated by the increased use of inappropriate tests in early childhood settings. The field of early childhood education is at an important juncture—as pressures to produce data on child outcomes have increased, programs have moved toward more formal testing and assessments.

ALIGNMENT: THE MISSING ACCOUNTABILITY INGREDIENT

The national press for child-based accountability has led to the important shifts noted previously. However, calls for accountability have often failed to mention the alignment that is necessary to make accountability worthwhile. Specifically, the alignment of standards, curriculum, and assessment is both the crucial ingredient of accountability and the missing element from both discourse and practice.

This failure to align standards, curricula, and assessment is not new. In early childhood education, curriculum and assessment have traditionally been undertaken as separate disciplines, studied by different scholars and funded by different agencies or sponsors. Curriculum development was typically led by early childhood educators and seen as the responsibility of departments of education. Assessments, on the other hand, were developed by developmental and cognitive psychologists and testing experts who were intellectually grounded in psychology and assessment. Because the two groups rarely came together, what was being assessed did not necessarily have any relation to what was being taught. For their part, programs and schools routinely adopted new curricula without considering assessment, or they implemented a new assessment system without considering the curriculum. In early childhood theory and practice, curriculum and assessment were worlds apart.

Despite their shorter legacy in the field, standards suffer from the same segmentation. In many cases, early learning standards have been developed in isolation from existing curricula and assessments. Some suggest this is good because the standards will be fresher and will lay the groundwork for refining the existing curricula and assessments. Others suggest that the task of curriculum and assessment development is so arduous that the lack of correspondence with the new standards is likely to produce pedagogical discontinuities for some time to come (Barton, 2004). This problem is compounded by the additional challenge of programs being asked to implement more than one set of standards. In some states, early childhood programs that combine Head Start funding with state funding are routinely subject to both the state standards and Head Start's Child Outcomes Framework. Inconsistencies among standards, curriculum, and assessment continue to characterize American early childhood education.

Focusing on standards, curriculum, and assessment has propelled policy makers and practitioners to think about improving children's learning experiences. However, as important as each of these three components is, attending to each independently is insufficient. A systemic and systematic approach to accountability is needed. In early childhood education, very little attention has been paid to the alignment of standards, curriculum, and assessments. This inattention to a systematic approach to accountability could prove to be the fatal flaw in the nation's efforts to educationalize and systematize early care and education.

Defining Alignment

The term *alignment,* as it applies to content and comprehensive alignment, means "falling into line"; it connotes the coordination of self-contained parts or elements (e.g., the wheels of a car need to be in alignment for the car to run effectively). Alignment in education refers to the degree of a correspondence regarding the content of early learning standards, curricula, and assessment so that the three components work together toward the common goal of educating students effectively (LaMarca, Redfield, Winter, Bailey, & Despriet, 2000). In early childhood education, content alignment refers to the degree of consistency in the early learning standards, curricula, and assessment used with a specific group of children (typically, preschool-age children and kindergartners).

The premise is that alignment of standards, curricula, and assessments enables more effective teaching processes and, in turn, more positive child outcomes. Alignment reflects the imperative to reach for the whole of a child's classroom experience. An explicit correspondence of what is expected, what is taught, and what is evaluated both provides the foundation for an effective education system and is critical to educational success. Without such alignment, standards, curriculum, and assessments—no matter how excellent each element is in its own right—run the risk of contradicting one another, thereby minimizing the collective impact. Indeed, alignment has been regarded as the essential element of an effective education system (Consortium for Policy Research in Education, 1991; Newman, 1993; Porter, 2002).

Different Types of Alignment

Alignment is composed of two subtypes: horizontal and vertical. *Horizontal alignment* refers to the alignment of standards, curriculum, and assessment within a given age cohort. For example, we can have horizontal alignment at prekindergarten occurring when the standards, curriculum, and assessments being used for a group of preschool-age children are aligned.

Despite its importance, horizontal alignment has received surprisingly little attention in early childhood education, with two notable exceptions. Head Start's Child Outcomes Framework is specifying standards and a corresponding requirement for all programs to assess children on the indicators included in the framework. The second notable, national effort to align child accountability efforts in early childhood has been advanced by curriculum developers working to promote the importance of alignment. For example, the Creative Curriculum (Dodge, Colker, & Heroman, 2002) includes standards, lesson plans, and an aligned assessment that is being used in many early childhood programs. Assessment developers have also created state-specific assessments that are tied to each state's own content standards. However, these efforts notwithstanding, horizontal alignment remains largely unaddressed.

In addition to horizontal alignment, a second kind of alignment is also important for young children: vertical alignment. *Vertical alignment* refers to the synchronicity of standards, curricula, and assessments between age cohorts. For example, early learning standards for preschoolers (specifically, 4-year-old children) might be compared with those for kindergartners, understanding that continuity of standards across age levels is essential if optimum development is to be promoted. Similarly, the content of the curricula at prekindergarten and kindergarten can be compared, and assessment instruments also can be examined for their vertical alignment. Vertical alignment, then, refers to the correspondence of ideas and content as children progress from one grade and age to the next. The idea is that the standards, curricula, and assessments used in prekindergarten settings will be targeted at an age range somewhat below those used in kindergarten. At the same time, the two age levels will have consistency or continuity in terms of the subject matter and developmental areas included. With good vertical alignment, the prekindergarten and kindergarten standards, curricula, and assessments will fit together and build on one another.

Until recently, vertical alignment had been addressed primarily by focusing on transition activities (e.g., parent–child visits to a kindergarten classroom) and structural linkages between prekindergarten and kindergarten (e.g., administrative coordination across programs). Recent research and initiatives, however, are providing more nuanced understandings of vertical alignment and are bringing increased attention to pedagogical alignment. For example, the PK–3 movement is focusing on the period from (pre)kindergarten to grade 3 to ensure that what children experience in their learning environment throughout this period builds on what they experienced in the prior grade and prepares them for what they will encounter in the following grade (Bogard & Takanishi, 2005; Kauerz, 2006). Efforts to vertically align standards also are increasingly evident in states that directly link their early learning standards to K–12 standards (Scott-Little, Kagan, & Frelow, 2003).

Examining Alignment in Early Childhood Education: A Pilot Study

The absence of information about horizontal and vertical alignment in early childhood education is especially problematic now because of heightened accountability and expectations for preschool education, the expansion of early childhood education nationally, and the emergence of a P–16 (prekindergarten through college) movement. Early childhood educators and leaders, parents, policy makers, and the general public need to have a better understanding of 1) what is going on related to alignment within preschools and within kindergarten, 2) what is going on related to alignment between preschools and kindergartens, and 3) what is being done under the rubric of transition efforts. To address these questions, a small pilot study was carried out in four diverse communities in one state.

Method and Limitations   Although different in their density, population makeup, wealth, and geography, the communities all had made a significant investment in promoting the transition from prekindergarten to kindergarten. In some cases, the sites had received special funding for this purpose; in other cases, the sites were participating in large-scale efforts that listed a smooth prekindergarten-to-kindergarten transition among the stated components of their efforts. For each of the four sites, the design called for six documents to be collected: early learning standards, curricula, and assessment for prekindergarten and kindergarten. The documents were analyzed according to a procedure developed in a national study of early learning standards that examined the breadth of the items (e.g., how many learning domains were covered) and the depth of the items (e.g., to what extent or how deeply each domain was covered) (Scott-Little, Kagan, & Frelow, 2003). Interrater reliability reached 90%. Statistical analyses were conducted, with data reverified and reanalyzed. In addition, informal discussions were held with individuals responsible for implementing the demonstration efforts.

Because this was a pilot study, there was no opportunity to visit classrooms or examine the degree of implementation of the standards, curricula, assessments, or their alignment. The communities in one state, however diverse, may not be generalizable to other states. Also, the coding procedure did not address one-to-one correspondence of the items; rather, it examined the extent to which the domains were addressed by the individual items.

Horizontal Alignment Findings　The analysis of the four sites' documents consistently revealed greater horizontal alignment in prekindergarten than in kindergarten. Three of the four prekindergarten sites had complete alignment among the standards, curriculum, and assessments, whereas none of the kindergarten sites demonstrated such alignment. Deeper analysis indicated that the sites that used a packaged curriculum in prekindergarten were likely to show the greatest alignment because the curriculum developers tended to align their curriculum with a set of standards, then develop assessments based on the standards. In prekindergarten programs that used the state's prekindergarten framework for standards and assessments, alignment was also great. By contrast, kindergarten sites that developed their own curriculum tended to align it with the district's standards, but these standards were not aligned with the assessments. This finding raises serious questions about the internal consistency of kindergarten programs.

Vertical Alignment Findings　No vertical alignment was found in any of the four districts selected for their commitment to transitions. That is, prekindergarten standards were not aligned with kindergarten standards in any site, nor were the prekindergarten curricula aligned with the kindergarten curricula. Moreover, the prekindergarten and kindergarten assessments were not aligned in any site. In these districts, transition efforts seemed to be nonpedagogical in orientation.

Content of the Documents　In all of the sites, the prekindergarten documents more comprehensively addressed all domains of development. At the kindergarten level, two domains were consistently omitted: physical and motor development, and social and emotional development. Even when these two domains were addressed, the kindergarten standards, curriculum, and assessment documents dedicated far less attention to these domains than to others (notably, language and cognition). This noticeable difference may account for the persistent lack of alignment between prekindergarten and kindergarten.

Transition Versus Alignment　Selected because of their involvement in funded efforts that addressed transition, the sites appeared not to address systematically the vertical alignment of their standards, curricula, or assessment documents across the prekindergarten and kindergarten settings. With so much effort devoted to easing children's transition from prekindergarten to kindergarten, how could this be? Informally, individuals noted that they were focusing on efforts that had an impact on structural or functional variables (e.g., transition conferences, cross-program visits). Although some had considered analyzing the links between the prekindergarten and kindergarten curricula, such work had not been done. Analyses of the alignment of standards or assessments between prekindergarten and kindergarten had not been considered.

Discussion   On one hand, these findings are quite positive for prekindergarten settings. Not only were the contents of their standards, curricula, and assessments nicely aligned but also the documents addressed all domains of early learning and development. It should be noted that these findings were consistent regardless of program type (public, private, or federally funded and regulated). On the other hand, the lack of horizontal alignment within kindergarten and the total absence of any vertical alignment between prekindergarten and kindergarten certainly suggest a need for review of the kindergarten programs and for consideration of how greater horizontal and vertical alignment could be achieved. Such a review would help determine whether the findings of this analysis hold true. If they do, attention should be paid to the implementation of alignment efforts, as well as the specification of alignment criteria as a part of the definition of transition efforts. Moreover, technical assistance to support a more inclusive understanding of vertical transition might be developed. Without considered attention to these issues, student outcomes could be compromised.

CONCLUSION

The educationalization and systematization of early care and education has introduced numerous challenges and demands. On the educationalization side, the inevitable trickle-down of K–12 trends needs to be consistent with the established foundations of early childhood education. For example, a narrow assessment of literacy and quantitative skills—similar to that in NCLB's provisions for assessment of third graders—is not acceptable in early childhood education, which has traditionally been dedicated to the whole child. We cannot tolerate free-standing assessments without the requisite alignment of standards, curricula, and assessments. Many of the field's conventional approaches to transitions also may need to be reconsidered. We need to move beyond historical ideas about transitions and reconceptualize them in terms of horizontal and vertical alignment. On the systematization side, not only do direct services need to be expanded and improved but also sound and sustainable infrastructure elements need to be implemented to support the whole system.

Although this chapter focuses on child accountability, child accountability without program accountability would deny the whole. Parents and policy makers deserve to know how children are doing, and they deserve to know how programs are doing. Even more important, young children deserve high-quality early care and education opportunities that embrace and nurture their holistic development. As such, America must continue to reach for the whole by fostering alignment in its early childhood practices and policies.

REFERENCES

Barnett, W.S. (2003). *Better teachers, better preschools: Student achievement linked to teacher qualifications.* New Brunswick, NJ: National Institute for Early Education Research.

Barnett, W.S., Hustedt, J.T., Robin, K.B., & Schulman, K.L. (2004). *The state of preschool: 2004 state preschool yearbook.* New Brunswick, NJ: National Institute for Early Education Research.

Barton, P. (2002). *Staying on course in educational reform.* Princeton, NJ: Educational Testing Service.

Barton, P. (2004). *Unfinished business: More measured approaches in standards-based reform.* Princeton, NJ: Educational Testing Service.

Bloch, M.N. (1987). Becoming scientific and professional: An historical perspective on the aims and effects of early education. In T.S. Popkewitz (Ed.), *The formation of school subjects: The struggle for creating an American institution* (pp. 25–62). London: Falmer Press.

Bogard, K., & Takanishi, R. (2005). PK–3: An aligned and coordinated approach to education for children 3 to 8 years old. *Social policy report: A publication of the Society for Research in Child Development, 19*(3), 1–24.

Bredekamp, S., & Copple, C. (Eds.). (1997). *Developmentally appropriate practice in early childhood programs.* Washington, DC: National Association for the Education of Young Children.

Bruner, C., Stover Wright, M., Gebhard, B., & Hibbard, S. (2004). *Building an early learning system: The ABCs of planning and governance structures.* Des Moines, IA: State Early Childhood Policy Technical Assistance Network, Child & Family Policy Center.

Business Roundtable. (2003). *Early childhood education: A call to action from the business community.* Retrieved October 26, 2005, from http://www.brtable.org/document.cfm/901

Cahan, E.D. (1989). *Past caring: A history of U.S. preschool care and education for the poor, 1820–1965.* New York: National Center for Children in Poverty.

Campbell, F., Miller-Johnson, S., Sparling, J., & Pungello, E. (2001). *Early childhood education: Young adult outcomes from the Abecedarian project.* Chapel Hill, NC: FPG Child Development Institute.

Carneiro, P., & Heckman, J. (2003). *Human capital policy* [IZA Discussion Paper No. 821]. Bonn, Germany: Institute for the Study of Labor.

Child Care Bureau. (2006). Child care and development fund report of state and territory plans, FY 2006–2007. Washington, DC: Author.

Committee for Economic Development. (2002). *Preschool for all: Investing in a productive and just society.* New York: Author.

Communications Consortium Media Center. (2005). *What the polling tells us.* Retrieved September 24, 2005, from http://www.earlycare.org/pollingtellsus2.htm

Consortium for Policy Research in Education. (1991). *Putting the pieces together: Systemic school reform.* New Brunswick, NJ: Rutgers, The State University of New Jersey, Eagleton Institute of Politics.

Currie, J. (2001). Early childhood education programs. *Journal of Economic Perspectives, 15*(2), 213–238.

Dodge, D.T., Colker, L., & Heroman, C. (2002). *The Creative Curriculum for Preschool.* Washington, DC: Teaching Strategies.

Education Commission of the States. (2004). *Kindergarten policies database.* Retrieved August 17, 2006, from www.ecs.org/kindergarten/kindergartendatabase

Education Trust. (2005). *The funding gap 2005: Low-income and minority students shortchanged by most states.* Washington, DC: Author.

Elkind, D. (1998). *Reinventing childhood: Raising and educating children in a changing world.* Rosemont, NJ: Modern Learning Press.

Elkind, D. (2003). Thanks for the memory: The lasting value of true play. *Young Children, 58*(3), 46–50.

Gallagher, J.J., Clifford, R.M., & Maxwell, K. (2004). Getting from here to there: To an ideal early preschool system. *Early Childhood Research and Practice, 6*(1). Retrieved August 17, 2006, from http://ecrp.uiuc.edu/v6n1/clifford.html

Goertz, M., Duffy, M., & Carlson-LeFloch, K. (2001). *Assessment and accountability systems in the 50 states: 1999–2000.* Philadelphia, PA: Consortium for Policy Research in Education.

Good start, grow smart: President Bush's plan to strengthen early learning. (2002). Retrieved October 10, 2005, from http://www.whitehouse.gov/infocus/earlychildhood/earlychildhood.pdf

Hatch, J.A. (2002). Accountability showdown: Resisting the standards movement in early childhood education. *Phi Delta Kappan, 83,* 457–562.

Head Start FACES: Longitudinal findings on program performance, third progress report. (2001). Washington, DC: Commissioner's Office of Research and Evaluation and the Head Start Bureau. Administration on Children, Youth and Families, U.S. Department of Health and Human Services.

Helburn, S.W. (Ed.). (1995). *Cost, quality and child outcomes in child care centers.* Denver: University of Colorado at Denver.

Herzenberg, S., Price, M., & Bradley, D. (2005). *Losing ground in early childhood education: Declining workforce qualifications in an expanding industry, 1979–2004.* Washington, DC: Economic Policy Institute.

Kagan, S.L., & Cohen, N.E. (1997). *Not by chance: Creating an early care and education system for America's children.* New Haven, CT: The Bush Center in Child Development and Social Policy, Yale University.

Kagan, S.L., Cohen, N.E., & Neuman, M.J. (1996). The changing context of American early care and education. In S.L. Kagan & N.E. Cohen (Eds.), *Reinventing early care and education: A vision for a quality system.* San Francisco, CA: Jossey-Bass.

Kagan, S.L., Moore, E., & Bredekamp, S. (Eds.). (1995). *Reconsidering children's early development and learning: Toward shared beliefs and vocabulary.* Washington, DC: National Education Goals Panel.

Kagan, S.L., & Neuman, M.J. (2003). Back to basics: Building an early care and education system. In F. Jacobs, D. Wertlieb, R.M. Lerner (Eds.), *Handbook of applied developmental science: Vol. 2. Enhancing the life chances of youth and families: Contributions of programs, policies, and service systems* (pp. 329–345). Thousand Oaks, CA: Sage.

Kagan, S.L., & Rigby, E. (2003). *Policy matters: Improving the readiness of children for school. Recommendations for state policy.* Washington, DC: Center for the Study of Social Policy.

Kagan, S.L., & Scott-Little, C. (2004). Early learning standards: Changing the parlance and practice of early childhood education. *Phi Delta Kappan, 85*(5), 388–396.

Katz, L. (2003). The right of the child to develop and learn in quality environments. *International Journal of Early Childhood, 35*(1–2), 13–22.

Kauerz, K. (2006). *Ladders of learning: Fighting fadeout by advancing PK–3 alignment.* Washington, DC: New America Foundation.

LaMarca, P.M., Redfield, D., Winter, P.C., Bailey, A., & Despriet, L.H. (2000). *State standards and state assessment systems: A guide to alignment.* Washington, DC: Council of Chief State School Officers.

Lee, V.E., & Burkam, D.T. (2002). *Inequality at the starting gate: Social background differences in achievement as children begin school.* Washington, DC: Economic Policy Institute.

McClellan, D.E., & Katz, L.G. (2001). *Assessing young children's social competence.* Champaign, IL: Eric Clearinghouse on Elementary and Early Childhood Education. (ERIC Document Reproduction Service No. ED450953)

National Commission on Excellence in Education. (1983, April). *A nation at risk: The imperative for educational reform.* Retrieved September 5, 2006, from http://www.ed.gov/pubs/NatAtRisk/index.html

National Education Goals Panel. (1991). *The national education goals report: Building a nation of learners.* Washington, DC: Authors.

National Institute of Child Health and Human Development Early Child Care Research Network. (1998). *The NICHD Study of Early Child Care.* Retrieved August 17, 2006, from http://secc.rti.org

National Institute of Child Health and Human Development Early Child Care Research Network. (2002). Early child care and children's development prior to school entry: Results from the NICHD study of early child care. *American Educational Research Journal, 39*(1), 133–164.

National Research Council. (2001). *Eager to learn: Educating our preschoolers.* Washington, DC: National Academies Press.

National Research Council and Institute of Medicine. (2000). *From neurons to neighborhoods: The science of early childhood development.* Washington, DC: National Academies Press.

Newman, F.M. (1993). Beyond common sense in educational restructuring: The issue of content and linkage. *Educational Researcher, 22*(2), 4–13.

No Child Left Behind (NCLB) Act of 2001, PL 107-110, 115 Stat. 1425, 20 U.S.C. §§ 6301 *et seq.*

Olfman, S. (2003). *All work and no play: How educational reforms are harming our preschoolers.* Westport, CT: Preager.

Peisner-Feinberg, E.S., Burchinal, M., Clifford, R.M., Culkin, M.L., Howes, C., Kagan, S.L., et al. (1999). *The children of the cost, quality, and outcomes study go to school.* Chapel Hill, NC: University of North Carolina at Chapel Hill, FPG Child Development Center.

Perie, M., Grigg, W.S., & Donahue, P.L. (2005). *The nation's report card: Reading 2005* (No. NCES 2006–451). U.S. Department of Education, Institute of Education Sciences, National Center for Education Statistics. Washington, DC: U.S. Government Printing Office.

Pianta, R., Howes, C., Burchinal, M., Bryant, D., Clifford, R.M., Early, D., et al. (2005). Features of pre-kindergarten programs, classrooms, and teachers: Do they predict observed classroom quality and child-teacher interactions? *Applied Developmental Science, 9*(3), 144–159.

Porter, A.C. (2002). Measuring the content of instruction: Uses in research and practice. *Educational Researcher, 31*(7), 3–14.

Pre-kindergarten standards: Guidelines for teaching and learning. (2002, October). Monterey, CA: CTB/McGraw-Hill.

Reed, D.S. (2001). *On equal terms: The constitutional politics of educational opportunity.* Princeton, NJ: Princeton University Press.

Reynolds, A.J., Temple, J.A., Robertson, D.L., & Mann, E.A. (2001). Long-term effects of an early childhood intervention on educational achievement and juvenile arrest: A 15-year follow-up of low-income children in public schools. *Journal of the American Medical Association, 285*(18), 2339–2346.

Reynolds, A.J., Temple, J.A., Robertson, D.L., & Mann, E.A. (2002). Age 21 cost-benefit analysis of the Title I Chicago child–parent centers. *Educational Evaluation and Policy Analysis, 24*(4), 267–303.

Rolnick, A., & Grunewald, R. (2003). Early childhood development: Economic development with a high public return. *Fedgazette.* Retrieved March 4, 2005, from http://minneapolisfed.org/pubs/fedgaz/03-03/earlychild.cfm

Rouse, C., Brooks-Gunn, J., & McLanahan, S. (2005). Introducing the issue. *The Future of Children, 15*(1), 5–14.

Schrag, P. (2003). *Final test: The battle for adequacy in America's schools.* New York: The New Press.

Schulman, K.L., & Blank, H. (1999). *Seeds of success: State prekindergarten initiatives, 1998–1999.* Washington, DC: Children's Defense Fund.

Schweinhart, L.J., Montie, J., Xiang, Z., Barnett, W.S., Belfield, C.R., & Nores, M. (2005). *Lifetime effects: The High/Scope Perry Preschool study through age 40.* Ypsilanti, MI: High/Scope Press.

Scott-Little, C., Kagan, S.L., & Clifford, R.M. (2003). *Assessing the state of state assessments: Perspectives on assessing young children.* Greensboro, NC: SERVE.

Scott-Little, C., Kagan, S.L., & Frelow, V.S. (2003). *Standards for preschool children's learning and development: Who has standards, how were they developed, and how are they used? Executive summary.* Greensboro, NC: University of North Carolina, SERVE.

Scott-Little, C., Kagan, S.L., & Frelow, V.S. (2005). *Inside the content: The breadth and depth of early learning standards. Creating the conditions for success with early learning standards.* Greensboro, NC: University of North Carolina, SERVE.

Seefeldt, C. (2005). *How to work with standards in the early childhood classroom.* New York: Teachers College Press.

Shepard, L.A. (1994). The challenges of assessing young children appropriately. *Phi Delta Kappan, 76*(3), 206–213.

Shepard, L.A., Kagan, S.L., & Wurtz, E. (1998). *Principles and recommendations for early childhood assessments.* Washington, DC: National Education Goals Panel.

Stoney, L. (2004). *Financing quality rating systems: Lessons learned.* Alexandria, VA: United Way of America, Success by Six.

U.S. Department of Education. (2001). *The No Child Left Behind Act of 2001: Executive Summary.* Washington, DC: Author.

U.S. Department of Education. (2002, July 25). *Department awards grants to evaluate preschool curriculums* [Press release]. Retrieved August 17, 2006, from http://www.ed.gov/news/pressreleases/2002/07/07252002.html

Wesley, P.W., & Buysee, V. (2003). Making meaning of school readiness in schools and communities. *Early Childhood Research Quarterly, 18*(3), 351–375.

Whitebook, M. (2003). *Bachelor's degrees are best: Higher qualifications for pre-kindergarten teachers lead to better learning environments for children.* Washington, DC: Trust for Early Education.

Whitebook, M., & Sakai, L. (2003). Turnover begets turnover: An examination of job and occupational instability among child care center staff. *Early Childhood Research Quarterly, 18*(3), 273–293.

Whitebook, M., Sakai, L., Gerber, E., & Howes, C. (2001). *Then and now: Changes in child care staffing, 1994–2000.* Washington, DC, and Berkeley, CA: Center for the Child Care Workforce and Institute of Industrial Relations, University of California.

Zaslow, M., & Halle, T. (2003). Statewide school readiness assessments: Challenges and next steps. In C. Scott-Little, S.L. Kagan, & R.M. Clifford (Eds.), *Assessing the state of state assessments: Perspectives on assessing young children.* Greensboro, NC: University of North Carolina, SERVE.

3

ACCOUNTABILITY IN EARLY CHILDHOOD

No Easy Answers

Samuel J. Meisels

▬▬ ▬▬ ▬▬

Education and social service programs in the first part of the 21st century are dominated by accountability. Publicly at least, politicians, policy makers, journalists, and scholars are focused on outcomes—on what works. For the U.S. Department of Education, this vow to hew to the path of accountability has even been translated into law. President George W. Bush's signature education legislation, the 2001 reauthorization of Title I titled the *No Child Left Behind Act* (NCLB; PL 107–110), made accountability the centerpiece of educational policy and test scores the sole means of demonstrating it. Annual testing in reading and math is required for grades 3–8, and severe consequences, leading even to closures for schools not making adequate yearly progress (AYP) as shown by scores on standardized tests, are spelled out in the legislation. Despite the problems inherent in this law (see Lynn, 2005), including "perverse incentives" that result in lowering rather than raising standards, NCLB has dominated educational practice since its passage (Ryan, 2004). Nearly all discussion of school reform, curriculum models, and novel school governance structures (other than charter schools) has given way to a single-minded attempt to increase students' scores on high-stakes tests.

Accountability pressures also affect programs for children enrolled in preschool and the early elementary grades. Some states have instituted annual kindergarten accountability testing. Others are attempting to link testing in kindergarten to performance of state-funded prekindergarten (pre-k) programs during the previous year. The most extensive use of high-stakes testing has taken place in Head Start, where a biannual standardized test—the *National Reporting System (NRS)* (Administration for Children and Families, 2003)—was first administered in 2003.

In the face of this near-obsession with accountability, educators and policy makers have sought expedient solutions to the complex problems of determining who has learned what, how much they learned, and how well they learned it. Conventional norm-referenced tests enable the ranking and ordering of individuals according to a single, easily understandable metric. But the tests' closed-ended questions do not reward children's natural curiosity, ability to solve problems, or emergent creativity. The tests are unable to describe individual patterns of learning and teaching; they do not give voice to cultural and ethnic differences that may depart from the mainstream; and they have become vested by our educational system with disproportionate power over teachers' decisions regarding curriculum and the utilization of instructional time.

As test scores assume high-stakes properties, they are increasingly viewed not as one datum about student performance, or one source of information about student learning, among many. Rather, they are perceived as sufficient evidence to render decisions about retention, promotion, teachers' expertise, and school success. These are the consequences typically associated with high-stakes testing (Madaus, 1988), despite the well-known fact that important educational decisions should be based on multiple sources of information (Heubert & Hauser, 1999). Because of the limited range of information commonly sampled by high-stakes tests and their closed-ended questions and responses, they can distort the educational process by suggesting that an indicator of learning can stand for the whole of learning (Corbett & Wilson, 1991). In this type of a results-oriented framework, teaching becomes preparation for testing.

Some commentators have gone so far as to say that primarily test-oriented instruction is "anti-educational" (Parini, 2005, p. 10). Such teaching is viewed as

> a kind of unpleasant game that subverts the real aim of education: to waken a student to his or her potential and to pursue a subject of considerable importance without restrictions imposed by anything except the inherent demands of the material. (Parini, 2005, p. 10)

The test-driven perspective may take its greatest toll on young children who have not yet learned to play the "school game." For them, an early introduction to high-stakes testing may influence their long-term attitudes not just about what takes place in schools but about their overall academic capabilities and their sense of self. With the expansion of large-scale testing to preschool and the first few years of formal schooling, the exploration of the implications of applying a testing paradigm designed for older students to those younger than age 8 is essential.

The purpose of this chapter is fourfold. First, the chapter focuses on the reasons behind the growth of accountability testing in preschool and the early grades. An explanation follows about why accountability testing is such a problematic activity in the first 8 years of life. Next, the content and rationale for these tests is illustrated using the NRS as an example. Then, the chapter uses the parameters of program evaluation to explore other means of responding to the major questions that policy makers expect high-stakes testing to provide. Finally, a potentially less problematic design for outcome assessment of young children is introduced.

WHAT POLICY MAKERS WANT TO KNOW ABOUT THE EFFECTIVENESS OF EARLY CHILDHOOD PROGRAMS

Early childhood care and education as we know it today does not have an extremely long history. As detailed elsewhere, the first public kindergarten programs did not appear before the mid-19th century, and research-based programs for children younger than age 5 did not begin until the early 1960s (Bowman, Donovan, & Burns, 2001; Lazar & Darlington, 1982; Meisels & Shonkoff, 2000).

The model programs of the 1960s sought to obtain evidence about how preschool could reverse the cycle of poverty that led to poor education, poor job prospects, and poor parenting (Farran, 2000; Halpern, 2000; Zigler & Valentine, 1979). Reflecting the knowledge base of that time, research sought to link the effectiveness of these programs to growth in IQ test scores of impoverished children, this seen as a first step in changing the life chances of these children (Schweinhart & Weikart, 1980). The psychologist Urie Bronfenbrenner reviewed the data from these programs in a 1974 monograph titled *Is Early Intervention Effective?* His question continues to be posed today, regardless of how many times it has been answered or how often it has been reformulated (see Meisels, 1985; Shonkoff & Phillips, 2000).

Bronfenbrenner's (1974) view was that the family is the most efficacious and economical system for fostering and sustaining the development of the child. The active participation of the child's family is critical to the success of any intervention program, and without family involvement the effects of intervention erode quickly. Involvement of parents has the potential for establishing an ongoing system that can reinforce the effects of a program and that can help sustain them after the program ends. Thus, the family appears to be a key target on which to focus intervention efforts.

But Bronfenbrenner's review, while ahead of its time in its focus on the child as part of a system or network and thus foreshadowing Bronfenbrenner's landmark work on the ecology of human development (Bronfenbrenner, 1979), fell victim to the implied view that children, families, and interventions are relatively homogeneous and uniform. Hence, the title of his monograph, *Is Early Intervention Effective?* rather than *Are Early Interventions Effective?* The lesson since then is that not one question, but many, must be asked. The task is not to find the best intervention for everyone; the goal is to determine the best intervention for this child and family at this time and in this situation.

Policy makers today seem to be ensnared in the same fallacy of searching for uniform solutions to disparate problems. But the questions we hear from them today are somewhat different from Bronfenbrenner's. One issue that emerged at the beginning of the 1990s, when the National Education Goals Panel (NEGP) was active, is derived from the first national goal that all children will be ready for school by the year 2000 (Kagan, 1990). Stated simply, this question is: Are children ready for kindergarten? However, the NEGP resource groups that dealt with this question in the 1990s made it clear that this question has no simple answer. Instead of suggesting a common set of skills that all children must master in order to be considered ready—skills that the familiar technology of testing could readily evaluate—scholars noted that children's differing early experiences and heterogeneous cultural and familial environments render a single test at the outset of school misleading at best (Kagan, Moore, & Bredekamp, 1995; Meisels, 1999). Indeed, as the NEGP groups noted, early childhood development is multi-faceted. It includes the domains of cognition and general knowledge, language and literacy, motor and physical development, socio-emotional development, and approaches to learning. In short, the readiness question cannot be answered easily or quickly, despite policy makers' pressing need for information about how well children are doing in school.

In recent years, public support for pre-k programs has grown dramatically. Previously, the largest public investment in pre-k programs was the federal Head Start program, which today serves more than 900,000 children at a cost in excess of $7 billion. But over the past 10 years, state pre-k programs have grown to where they nearly match Head Start in terms of number of children served (almost 750,000), although the amount of money spent ($2 billion in 2002) is lower than Head Start, in part because pre-k programs rely on so many in-kind contributions from local school districts and other sources that are difficult to tabulate (National Center for Early Development and Learning, 2005; Stipek, 2005). Pre-k programs are now offered by 43 states and the District of Columbia, and more than 10 states either have or are exploring the option of providing universal pre-k services (National Institute for Early Education Research [NIEER], 2005). With the growth of these programs, the readiness for kindergarten question has been sharpened and expanded. Now policy makers are asking two questions that are corollaries of their earlier readiness query: Are children learning, and are public funds being used wisely?

These two questions are extremely important, although the methods used to obtain meaningful answers to them are not obvious. The first question about children's learning goes to the heart of why policy makers have embraced pre-k and other early childhood programs. These programs are provided in part to recognize that the majority of parents are now in the workforce, and safe and sound child care is a necessity to maintain our economy. Beyond this, the United States is facing a prolonged and pernicious achievement gap between white and nonwhite students and between students from economically more advantaged versus less advantaged families. Like the early model preschool programs of the 1960s and the original formulation of Head Start from that same era, pre-k programs today are intended to close this gap, equalize opportunity, and enable our society to derive benefits from and for more of its citizens. The pre-k solution is meant to have an impact on these fundamental inequities. It is no wonder that policy makers are becoming impatient for answers.

This analysis leads directly to the second question, regarding the value of the public investment that these programs represent. The reasoning goes something like this: If the programs are not improving learning—if they are not closing the achievement gap—then how can their cost be justified?

Some might argue that numerous programs are supported by public dollars without proof of their efficacy (e.g., public parks, civic holiday decorations, contemporary birthing innovations). Others could point out that the expectation that program efficacy continue to be demonstrated, even when evidence of effectiveness has already been shown, is higher than is required for other professions. For example, physicians and other health professionals have a great deal of leeway in how they implement interventions for their patients, as long as they follow an established protocol. Similarly, early care and education has a growing list of efficacious experiments and implementations that provide the basis for the work of pre-k professionals (Brooks-Gunn, Fuligni, & Berlin, 2003; Karoly et al., 1998; Meisels & Shonkoff, 2000; Shonkoff & Phillips, 2000). But there is a difference. All health care professionals are trained to a particular level of recognized and acceptable expertise, and their working conditions generally enhance their professional growth and expertise. Most early childhood professionals do not have this background or supportive professional environment (see Hart & Schumacher, 2005). Furthermore, the fact that children differ so greatly from one another in their early experiences, opportunities to learn, genetic inheritance, and family structure, among other variables, only adds to the challenge of evaluating early education outcomes.

In short, the two questions policy makers are asking are reasonable and appropriate. The debate here is not about the questions, although if other changes were made in the preparation and working conditions of early care and education professionals, the insistence on obtaining answers for each local or state situation might possibly diminish. The problem is that the high-stakes methods being proposed to determine if a program is or is not effective are themselves open to question regarding their accuracy, appropriateness, and meaningfulness.

THE ARGUMENT AGAINST HIGH-STAKES TESTING IN EARLY CHILDHOOD

High-stakes testing refers fundamentally to the uses made of test scores, rather than to any particular test or type of test data (Madaus, 1988; Mueller, 2002). To the extent that test information, or any other type of comparative data, is used to make decisions about who should receive rewards or experience sanctions, then that test is considered high-stakes. In early childhood, rewards can take the form of public attention, additional funds for teachers or materials, increased salaries, or improved facilities. Sanctions include holding children back or enrolling them in extra year programs, wresting control of curriculum from teachers, or even program closure (Meisels, 1992).

Although high-stakes testing is common in the K–12 world, it is less frequently encountered in early childhood. Previous examples include the widespread use of the Gesell School Readiness Test (Haines, Ames, & Gillespie, 1980) to determine whether children could enter kindergarten (Shepard & Smith, 1986) and the statewide adoption of an adapted form of the California Achievement Test (CTB; CTB/McGraw-Hill, 1988) to decide if kindergarten children could be promoted to first grade (Meisels, 1989). Of course, the incentive structure of NCLB for third–eighth graders is built entirely around high-stakes testing, with the ultimate sanction being closure of a poor performing school (Ryan, 2004).

Many scholars have expressed misgivings about the use of high-stakes tests as a means of determining a program's overall achievement level (Madaus & Clarke, 2001). Some even claim that it is scientifically indefensible to use the average achievement scores of a school to judge how well a school is performing (Raudenbush, 2005). Raudenbush (2005) points out that "If you want to measure what goes on in a school, you have to develop measures that look at the educational process and practices, not just at children's relative achievement" (p. 11). Conventional high-stakes tests do not measure the quality of the educational practices at a particular school or children's relative rates of learning.

The problems of using high-stakes tests with young children are even more severe. Four reasons stand out for not basing accountability decisions on young children's test taking performance (see Meisels, 1994, and Meisels & Atkins-Burnett, 2006, for a discussion of these and other related points).

Practical Problems of Measurement

Young children are developmentally unreliable test takers. They have a restricted ability to comprehend such assessment cues as verbal instructions, aural stimuli, situational prompts, or written instructions. Furthermore, questions that require complex information-processing skills—giving differential weights to alternative choices, distinguishing recency from primacy, or responding correctly to multistep directions—may cause a child to give the wrong answer. In addition, young children may not be able to control their behavior to meet the demand characteristic of the assessment situation—whether because they are affected by fatigue, boredom, hunger, illness, or anxiety, or simply because they are unable to sit still and attend for the length of time required.

Unintended Consequences

High-stakes tests may result in long-term negative consequences for young children. This follows because the structure of teaching and learning can be affected negatively by focusing on test results, thus resulting in measurement-driven instruction, which can homogenize what might otherwise be a very heterogeneous curriculum. Also included are the potential negative effects on children's sense of self-worth and self-perception that judgments based on test results can convey to children. Rist (1970) described these effects in great detail by noting how both teachers and children were changed by what Rosenthal and Jacobson (1968) called the "Pygmalion effect," when teachers' perceptions are altered by information from tests and other sources external to the classroom, regardless of their accuracy. For young children, the risk is that children will feel stigmatized and be tracked into low-achieving groups that will further confirm their sense of powerlessness and limited potential. Their estimates of their own abilities—their self-perceptions and their motivation and ultimately their achievement—are likely to suffer as a result.

Opportunity to Learn

Children's opportunities to learn differ greatly in early childhood, when no period of common schooling (such as occurs to some extent in K–12) is available to them. *Opportunity to learn* concerns the possibility of children having been taught something before entering the program in which they are enrolled. The range of opportunities to learn in early childhood describes the fundamental differences in society and especially reflects the challenges faced by impoverished and disadvantaged children prior to even arriving at the school door. To assume that a test administered at the outset of school can be used to make valid predictions that may have long-term consequences is to believe that these inequities are virtually immutable. The task of schooling is to begin to overcome these inequities by providing an environment in which children can learn what they have not yet been taught and can begin to achieve. If we ignore differences attributable to opportunity to learn, as conventional accountability measures do, we are begging the fundamental question of what individual children need and how we can fashion a curriculum that is responsive to these needs.

Variability and Predictability

The final argument for not using high-stakes testing in early childhood derives from the extensive variability and change that marks early development. LaParo and Pianta (2000) documented this instability of development in a meta-analysis of 70 longitudinal studies. Their purpose was to study the associations between academic/cognitive and social/behavioral measures in preschool and kindergarten with like measures in first and second grade. They found that only about a quarter of the variance in early academic/cognitive performance was predicted by preschool or kindergarten cognitive status; only 10% or less of the variance in K–grade 2 social/behavioral measures was accounted for by similar measures at preschool or kindergarten. LaParo and Pianta concluded that "instability or change may be the rule rather than the exception during this period" (2000, p. 476). In short, their study shows that tests used to make predictions—even relatively short-term predictions—are insufficiently stable to justify assigning stakes based on them. Given that young children are undergoing significant changes in their first 8 years of life in terms of brain growth, physiology, and emotional regulation, and recognizing that children come into this world with varied inheritance, experience, and opportunities for nurturance, it is not difficult to imagine that a brief snapshot of a child's skills and abilities taken on a single occasion will be unable to capture the shifts and changes in that development. To draw long-term conclusions from such assessments seems baseless.

Kim and Suen (2003) put forth additional research that supports this view. Using hierarchical linear modeling, they reported a validity generalization study of 716 predictive correlation coefficients from 44 studies. Their purpose was to determine if the predictive validity coefficients of early assessments could be used to draw generalized conclusions about later achievement or success in school. The authors posed two questions. First, is it possible that "predictive validity is unique to each early assessment procedure and unique to each specific set of local testing conditions" (Kim & Suen, 2003, p. 548)? This would be the case if predictability was affected by sample characteristics, length of time between prediction and outcome, or the outcome criterion itself. Kim and Suen's second question focused more specifically on statistical artifacts: Are there statistical or measurement errors that potentially prevent us from obtaining reliable predictions of outcomes from early childhood assessments? The errors or statistical artifacts include a range of variabilities concerned with test and criterion unreliabilities, local restricted ranges of scores, and other sampling errors.

Their study answered these questions definitively. Kim and Suen (2003) demonstrated that predictive validity coefficients in early childhood are different in different situations. They pointed out that "the predictive power of any early assessment from any single study is not generalizable, regardless of design and quality of research. The predictive power of early assessments is different from situation to situation" (Kim & Suen, 2003, p. 561). This does not mean that there are no early childhood tests with predictive value. Rather, Kim and Suen's study demonstrates that predictions from early childhood assessments cannot be generalized meaningfully. Even if all adjusted predictive coefficients were averaged in order to obtain a "typical" overall prediction, misleading information could result. This follows because an overall average coefficient conceals unaccounted-for variation and is not therefore representative or meaningful.

Kim and Suen (2003) have shown that if you use a test to demonstrate predictive validity in one situation, and another test in a different situation, assuming that the same thing is being measured in these situations or by these tests is unjustified. Each assessment and each set of conditions needs to be treated as unique. However, this does not imply that individual outcome studies are invalid. Rather, this study contends that early assessments *in general* are not predictive of future performance.

In brief, both Kim and Suen's (2003) and LaParo and Pianta's (2000) studies arrive at conclusions that are very similar, although they get there by different means. They help us to understand the consequences of developmental instability in early childhood development, and they remind us that tests of accountability that overlook this variability have a high likelihood of providing unsubstantiated conclusions. We will now turn to an account of a national test of Head Start children that appears to incorporate nearly all of these problems.

A FAILED EXPERIMENT: THE NRS

A milestone in U.S. educational history took place in the fall of 2003. That year, the largest administration of a single standardized test—the Head Start NRS—was launched. At an estimated total cost in excess of $25 million annually (including direct and indirect costs), approximately 450,000 4-year-olds from every state and nearly every locale in the nation were administered the NRS biannually. This may be the largest test administration in U.S. history. Even the *National Assessment of Educational Progress* (NAEP)—known as the "Nation's Report Card" (Pellegrino, Jones, & Mitchell, 1999)—included no more than 350,000 students in its 2005 administration. Moreover, the NAEP uses a matrix sampling approach so that different students receive different parts of the test at different times. Ultimately, the scores from these separate administrations are combined statistically to provide an overview of the nation's school performance.

The NRS is different. All Head Start children age 4 years and older who speak English or Spanish are administered the entire test biannually. The stated purpose of the test is threefold: 1) to enable programs to engage in self-assessment and improvement, 2) to target needed training and technical assistance efforts, and 3) to monitor programs' performance in order to determine if public funding should be continued (Administration for Children and Families [ACF], 2003).

The test is a classically top-down policy initiative in which high-level government officials directed U.S. Department of Health and Human Services (HHS) and ACF bureaucrats to put the test in place post haste. The decision to create such a test was announced less than a year before it was implemented. In only 9 months, it was developed and piloted on a small number of children and programs, 30,000 teachers or their surrogates were trained, and the test was manufactured and sent out to the field in record time. For example, the assessments that became part of the 22,625-child Early Childhood Longitudinal Study- Kindergarten cohort required more than 3 years of development, piloting, and extensive field testing and analysis before they were considered ready for widescale use (West, Denton, & Germino-Hausken, 2000).

When the NRS was announced, many in the field urged that if the test had to be given, only a sample of children in Head Start be tested. But the HHS administrators wanted to test the population, not a sample, for the reason that without testing every child in every program, answering the efficacy or accountability question about those programs would be impossible. In short, HHS wanted answers to the two questions raised previously: Are children learning, and are public funds being used wisely?

HHS eventually funded a small-scale evaluation of the test, but very little oversight was devoted to the preparation or implementation of the assessment. A technical work group charged to advise the contractor who developed the test and the government officials who had responsibility for implementing it was impaneled. But the work group was not given an opportunity to review the test items before they went to the field in the fall of 2003.

To some extent, the test items are a parody of a well-developed standardized test despite the fact that during a visit to a Virginia Head Start program in July 2003, President Bush said that "we would be defeating the purpose of accountability before we even began it if we . . . give standardized tests to 4-year-olds" (Goldstein & Strauss, 2003). The methodology used here is not much different from that employed in NCLB. Although individually administered, the NRS is fundamentally a high-stakes test that relies extensively on multiple-choice items. The test is composed of five subtests, including two language screeners to determine if the child is English- or Spanish-speaking, and tests of vocabulary (derived from the *Peabody Picture Vocabulary Test,* Dunn & Dunn, 1997), letter-naming skills, and early math skills.

Much has been made of the culture- and class-specific nature of the vocabulary chosen from the Peabody Picture Vocabulary Test—such words as *swamp, vase, awarding,* and *horrified*—and of the problems with the Spanish language test (see Meisels & Atkins-Burnett, 2004). Also of great concern is the linguistic burden and psychometric construction of the math items that assume that Head Start 4-year-olds can attribute causality, do subtraction, use standard metric units, and understand the subjunctive case. Even the letter-naming task on the test is misconceived and reflects a lack of understanding about what rapid letter naming teaches us about young children's skills in early literacy. These problems were not corrected throughout the life of this test, though. Because of public outcry, congressional complaints, and prodding from members of the technical work group, the problems became less egregious.

In May 2005, the problems with the NRS were highlighted in a report to Congress by the U.S. General Accounting Office (GAO, 2005). In a monograph titled *Further Development Could Allow Results of New Test to Be Used for Decision Making,* the GAO concluded that

> As of February 2005, [the] Head Start Bureau had not conducted certain analyses on NRS results to establish the validity and some aspects of the reliability of the assessment. . . . The NRS by itself does not provide sufficient information to draw conclusions about the effects of Head Start grantees on children's outcomes—information that would support use of the NRS for Head Start grantee accountability. (2005, pp. 23, 26)

In short, after a year of study that included 12 site visits to Head Start programs in five states, a review of data and documents, interviews with multiple informants, and advice from three national experts, the GAO found the NRS to produce data that are suspect and to have potentially harmful unintended consequences. As the report noted,

> There is a concern that local Head Start programs will alter their teaching practices and curricula based on their participation in the NRS. . . . At least 18% of grantees changed instruction during the first year to emphasize areas covered in the NRS. (2005, pp. 19–20)

High-stakes tests—and although not yet used for high-stakes purposes, the NRS was designed, among other things, to be such a test—change instruction. This problem accompanies such tests at all levels of administration (Herman, 2004; Johnson & Johnson, 2002; McNeil, 2002). In early childhood, however, and in particular in Head Start, high-stakes testing may have a more pernicious effect than among older students.

Because the Head Start work force contains fewer than 30% of teachers with a bachelor's degree and, as of 2003, only 27% who hold even an associate's degree (Hart & Schumacher, 2005), many teachers in Head Start will likely alter their teaching to conform to the pedagogical model implicit in this test. Without more training, these teachers will not be able to critically analyze what is being asked of them and their children; this state of affairs was documented by the GAO report.

As is the case with other high-stakes examinations, the NRS implies a model of pedagogy (Elmore, 2004; Kornhaber & Orfield, 2001). It is a model of passive reception, of pouring into a vessel knowledge and skills that are needed for competence rather than recognizing learning as active and teaching as a joint process of interaction between child and adult. An active view of learning, fundamentally based on enhancing relationships between teachers, children, and challenging materials, is nowhere to be seen in the NRS test, although Head Start has been committed to a constructivist outlook on teaching for many years (Zigler & Muenchow, 1992). Yet, when teachers know that the results of a test will be used to make decisions that may affect their program's continuation and other elements they value, they are sorely tempted to begin teaching to the test. Not only does this lead to a great deal of what is called measurement-driven instruction (Darling-Hammond & Rustique-Forrester, 2005) between the fall and spring administrations but also it raises the possibility of "gaming" the system by arranging for children to score low in the fall and then make marked progress by the spring. After all, most of the testing is done by teachers or others who are part of the program and who themselves will be affected by the NRS scores. The potential impact of this test on 3-year-olds as their teachers spend a year preparing them to identify vocabulary words, name letters, and solve counting and measuring tasks also can not be overlooked.

In brief, the pedagogical model implicit in the test is highly questionable for young children. But an even more invidious problem emerges from the overall rationale for the NRS. This rationale is associated with the discussion of the achievement gap mentioned earlier.

Policy makers in Washington and elsewhere have long recognized that impoverished children, and in particular, children enrolled in Head Start, do not start school with skills equivalent to those from more affluent backgrounds (Haskins & Rouse, 2005; Lee & Burkham, 2002). As noted previously, these policy makers believe that if Head Start were doing its job, this discrepancy—this incipient achievement gap—would be eliminated. This argument is, of course, very familiar. When Head Start was originally proposed by President Lyndon B. Johnson, it was intended to reverse the cycle of poverty and bring equity to school achievement, despite children's inequitable life circumstances (Zigler & Muenchow, 1992). At first, many believed that this type of inoculation against the snares and traps of poverty could be overcome by just an 8-week summer Head Start program.

How will the NRS help us overcome the inequities of poverty? The answer implicit in the NRS is by demonstrating which programs are successful and which are not, so that poorly performing programs can be improved or eliminated and high-performing programs can be rewarded (Horn, 2003). Those who propound this accountability model are fond of likening the NRS or other accountability tests to a quality-assurance or quality-control system such as those used, for example, in manufacturing automobiles. Craig Ramey, chairman of the technical work group that advised Head Start about the test said, "If you were the head of any industry . . . you would have a quality assurance system in place to determine how your product is faring in terms of quality. . . . The Head Start test is just another quality assurance program" (Rimer, 2003, p. A23).

Although this country is very good at building factories, constructing assembly lines, and devising high-tech methods for producing goods; it has not been very successful at translating this expertise into educational endeavors. As Malcolm Gladwell put it, "If schools were factories, America would have solved its education problem long ago"(Gladwell, 2003).

Why is the production model a poor fit for early education? One reason is that schools are not factories, children are not raw materials, and early care and education programs are anything but homogeneous stamping plants. The variables that educators work with are much more variegated and difficult to control than glass, steel, and production schedules.

Children enter preschool dramatically different one from the other. Just because nearly all of the children in Head Start are impoverished does not mean that they all are the same—and these differences go far beyond variation in geography, language, or ethnicity. Children also differ from one another in terms of inheritance, culture, experience, and many other factors. Moreover, as noted earlier, development is not linear, especially in the first 5–8 years of life.

Simply put, the NRS was a failure not only because it tapped a narrow sample of children's skills, not only because a single purpose was never clearly specified, not only because it failed to conform to professional standards of test development, and not only because of its potential for changing Head Start to a "skill and drill" curriculum. It was a failure because it ignored the complexity of early development that teaches us that no single indicator can assess a child's skills, achievements, or personality.

For these reasons and others, the House of Representatives passed an amendment to the Head Start reauthorization bill in September 2005 to suspend the administration of the NRS until further information can be obtained about it from a panel of the National Academy of Sciences. Although the potential harm to children, teachers, and programs that could be done by the NRS was not halted because the Senate did not pass the House version of the Head Start reauthorization, the NRS stands as a cautionary tale or paradigmatic illustration of the use of accountability testing in the early childhood years. No brief test of young children's achievement administered in a summative way can capture the complexity of pre-k children's growth. Just as a single facet of a reflective surface can never provide an accurate reflection of a complex phenomenon, so a one-dimensional early childhood test of achievement will give a distorted image of what it is intended to measure. The following section discusses a proposal for evaluating children's growth and learning in early education programs that may avoid the problems of the NRS and similar assessments.

NO EASY ANSWERS: ACCOUNTABILITY AND EVALUATION

Wade Horn, the assistant secretary of HHS and one of the architects of the NRS, said the following about the test: "I can't for the life of me understand why anyone would think it's a bad idea to assess whether a program is progressing in crucial academic areas" (Friel, 2005, p. 541). Horn's comment is well taken: There is nothing inherently wrong or mistaken about trying to find out how well a program is achieving its goals. Indeed, from a public policy perspective, this information is critically important to have. The problem is that giving a test—especially, the NRS—appears not to be the best way to obtain this kind of information.

Such an effort to learn about program effectiveness and program quality runs contrary to current research. Numerous studies point to a very similar set of variables that define program quality (National Institute of Child Health and Human Development [NICHD] Early Child Care Research Network [ECCRN], 2000; Pianta et al., 2005). They include low child–staff ratios; training of staff in early childhood development; provision of continuing professional development; use of practices that are developmentally appropriate; high levels of positive interaction between children and staff; continuity and competitive salaries and working conditions for staff; and the creation of a safe, caring environment and one that encourages strong parental involvement. This is how quality is assessed—not through measuring vocabulary, letter knowledge, and early math skills. To assume otherwise is to assume a homogeneity of children and programs such that differences in outcomes will yield unambiguous information about program quality. Such a belief is unfounded.

In order to learn about the impact of the kinds of variables listed above, one cannot rely simply on a test of child outcomes or any other collection of unidimensional accountability data. Rather, a design for a program evaluation is needed, but one that does not preclude child outcomes.

Accountability calls for information about whether something happened. For example, was something taught or learned and how much was mastered? Evaluation data enable us to make inferences about why something happened. For example, why did this child learn more than that child, or why did this technique work better than that one? Accountability is close in concept to monitoring or documentation, whereas evaluation bears some resemblance to research into root causes of a phenomenon. Evaluation goes beyond the collection of child outcomes to include examination of variations in children, families, teachers, and programs that may help explain differences in those outcomes. In short, in program evaluation, the overall goal is to understand exactly what a program did and how it accomplished its purposes (Gilliam & Leiter, 2003).

In order to explain why a particular program works for a specific child under certain circumstances, evaluation data must be collected on both structural and dynamic characteristics of the early childhood setting. Structural variables are those that represent formal features of early care and education programs that can be specified quantitatively and are often regulated by policy, such as class sizes and child–staff ratios. Dynamic factors are concerned with qualitative assessments of how teachers, staff, and children interact with one another on a regular basis and include an analysis of curriculum as well as teacher–child interactions. Finally, a whole range of demographic variables needs to be considered about the child and family as well as the teacher's background. These variables might include the child's age, gender, race/ethnicity, primary language, family socioeconomic status, special needs, and previous out-of-home experiences. For the family, socioeconomic status; neighborhood characteristics; home environment; maternal mental health; and mother's age, education, and employment would need to be explored. In addition, teachers' age, gender, race, level of formal schooling, training in early childhood, amount and type of professional development, and teaching history would need to be known. Without this information, researchers and policy makers may fall into the trap of assuming that one size program fits all children, all parents, all teachers, and all communities.

For an evaluation design to be useful to policy makers, however, more needs to be known than just the structural and dynamic dimensions of a program. The impact of the program on children is also critical to know. The challenge is to accomplish this without incurring the numerous unintended consequences described earlier in this chapter.

One way of approaching this task is by using an assessment that is based on item response theory (IRT), a statistical procedure used for constructing tests and assessments. Such tests are intended to describe levels or patterns of growth, ability, or developmental achievement (Thorndike, 1999; Wright, 1999). They can be used as individually administered assessments that provide information about a child's relative position on a specific developmental path ordered by difficulty.

As with virtually any other evaluative measure, IRT-based instruments are not immune to being used for high-stakes purposes. In order to minimize the potential for abuse and distortion, in this approach, individual child scores would not be reported. Parents would receive an aggregated profile concerning the achievements of the children in their child's program. To learn more about their own child's accomplishments and areas in need of development, parents would meet with their child's teacher to obtain detailed information about the child's skills, accomplishments, and social-emotional characteristics. Information of this kind is available from instructional assessments that can provide diagnostic information about the child's learning. Such information also can be reported to and analyzed for policy makers (Meisels et al., 2003).

Unlike other tests, IRT-based assessments can be administered without necessarily narrowing the curriculum. Those who develop IRT-based tests try to determine whether different items represent estimates of the same level of achievement. In this way, different sets of items that may all provide similar information to different children can be administered. In short, although it is essential that individual items are developmentally meaningful, they do not have the unique importance or status that is ascribed to items on other norm- or criterion-referenced tests. Consequently, they do not have the same potential to narrow the curriculum.

The importance of this is twofold: 1) this approach may minimize teaching to the specific items of the test because they do not have the same value or meaning as on conventional tests and the test item bank may simply contain more items than in a conventional test, and 2) change in children's skills can be assessed using a metric that describes a position on a developmental path, rather than strictly a position in a normative group. This enables a focus on reporting children's relative progress over time (known as a *value-added metric*) rather than simply on achievement at the end of the program. To the extent that children can be grouped demographically according to comparability of background and to stratify the structural and dynamic program evaluation data according to program types and resources, it should be possible to draw conclusions about changes in developmental level or cognitive skills that are associated with the program itself.

Another important property of an assessment based on this model is that item difficulties can be tailored to the child's level of development, thus permitting more accurate measurement as well as minimizing the frustration levels for younger children and for children with special needs. This tailoring of item difficulty to the child's level of development minimizes floor and ceiling effects in cross-sectional, but more important, longitudinal studies. Ideally, as exemplified by the Early Childhood Longitudinal Study-Kindergarten Cohort (West et al., 2000), a two-stage, adaptive design would be used in which a child would first take a brief routing test to target his or her current level of functioning and assign him or her to a low-, mid-, or high-level second-stage test. Then, on another occasion, the child would be administered the second-stage test, which would permit a much more extensive review of his or her skills within that range of difficulty.

Although constructed differently from the model described previously, several early childhood assessments based on IRT already exist (see Berry, Bridges, & Zaslow, 2004, and Kochanoff, 2003, for suggestions and reviews). Some of these instruments can be incorporated into evaluation designs, although the risk that their results will be misused and that they will become high-stakes assessments exists if they do not meet the other criteria presented earlier. After all, IRT was utilized in the development of the NRS, although many of the other features described here (e.g., large item bank, buffers against test-driven instruction, adaptive administration, sampling rather than census) were overlooked. No statistical technique, no matter how sophisticated, will solve all of the problems of high-stakes testing with young children. No statistical or psychometric technique is immune to misuse. Virtually all of the problems of classical norm-referenced testing described earlier can be ascribed to IRT as well, unless safeguards are put in place. But, if used as proposed, this plan will answer the policy makers' first question: Are children learning?

The second question—Are public funds being used wisely?—can also be answered by this approach because the information about structural and dynamic features of the programs will enable analyses to be conducted of a variety of program elements, pedagogical techniques, and child outcomes. In this way, determining if particular aspects of the program, or the child and family background, are more or less strongly associated with child outcomes is possible. This not only indicates if the program works but also indicates for whom it works best under which combination of circumstances. For example, a program evaluation may show that certain approaches to teaching reading are most successful with children from certain backgrounds. Evaluation data can also help in tailoring specific programs for parents and particular in-service for teachers. The task here is to answer the overall question of program effectiveness by opening the black box of program operations and connecting these data to information about children, families, teachers, and children's achievements.

CONCLUSION

Accountability can have a meaningful role in early childhood if it is not monolithic in concept or high-stakes in implementation. Too often, policy makers and practitioners confuse means and ends when they discuss accountability. Tests and assessments are the means—or more accurately, are among the means—that can be used to demonstrate accountability. But such measures are not sufficient to render a valid decision about whether a program is realizing its promise or achieving its goals. Assessments are administered for a wide variety of reasons, from screening to diagnosis and instructional planning to achievement testing. Not just any assessment makes sense in an accountability logarithm. And when high stakes are added to the equation, even more perturbations are generated. No summative test administered to individual children can indicate how well a program or school is performing overall unless something is first known about the background of the participants in that program (teachers, children, and families) and what the practices and processes of the program consist of. Added to this are the unique developmental features of early childhood, features that call into question the predictions that can be made from achievement tests early in life.

This chapter argues that high-stakes tests are of limited utility with young children and may even result in misleading conclusions and potentially damaging unintended consequences. In their place, I recommend conducting a program evaluation on a sample of children and classrooms in order to provide a comprehensive picture of what children are learning, how they are being taught and by whom, and what the social context and resources of the program and families are. Evaluations based on a sample of children, teachers, and classrooms can provide useful and usable information that can answer fundamental questions about children's learning and the value of the public's investment in those programs.

Policy makers are notoriously unhappy with complex answers to apparently simple questions. Unfortunately, the questions discussed here—Are children learning? Are public funds being used wisely?—yield meaningful answers only when they reflect the complex phenomena they are intended to explicate. Simple answers that are flawed are of little value when compared with reliable data that are based on a comprehensive picture of how children are developing and what role programs play in that development. Although there are no easy answers to accountability in early childhood, the promise of embracing complexity is that more children will succeed because the information needed to improve their programs will be available.

REFERENCES

Administration for Children and Families. (2003, June 6). *Information memorandum: Description of the NRS child assessment.* Retrieved September 28, 2003, from http://www.headstartinfo.or/publications/im03_07.htm

Berry, D.J., Bridges, L.J., & Zaslow, M.J. (2004). *Early childhood measures profiles.* Washington, DC: Child Trends.

Bowman, B.T., Donovan, M.S., & Burns, M.S. (Eds.). (2001). *Eager to learn: Educating our preschoolers.* Washington, DC: National Academies Press.

Bronfenbrenner, U. (1974). *Is early intervention effective?* Washington, DC: Office of Human Development.

Bronfenbrenner, U. (1979). *The ecology of human development.* Cambridge: Harvard University Press.

Brooks-Gunn, J., Fuligni, A.S., & Berlin, L.J. (Eds.). (2003). *Early child development in the 21st century: Profiles of current research initiatives.* New York: Teachers College Press.

Corbett, H.D., & Wilson, B.L. (1991). *Testing, reform, and rebellion.* Norwood, NJ: Ablex.

CTB/McGraw-Hill. (1988). *California Achievement Test, Grade K.* (Georgia ed.). Monterey, CA: Author.

Darling-Hammond, L., & Rustique-Forrester, E. (2005). The consequences of student testing for teaching and teacher quality. In J.L. Herman & E.H. Haertel (Eds.), *Uses and misuses of data for educational accountability and improvement, 104th yearbook of the National Society for the Study of Education* (Part II, pp. 289–319). Malden, MA: Blackwell.

Dunn, L.M., & Dunn, L.M. (1997). *Peabody Picture Vocabulary Test—Third Edition (PPVT—III).* Circle Pines, MN: American Guidance Service.

Elmore, R.F. (2004). Conclusion: The problem of stakes in performance-based accountability systems. In S.H. Fuhrman & R.F. Elmore (Eds.), *Redesigning accountability systems for education* (pp. 274–296). New York: Teachers College Press.

Farran, D.C. (2000). Another decade of intervention for children who are low income or disabled: What do we know now? In J.P. Shonkoff & S.J. Meisels (Eds.), *Handbook of early childhood intervention* (2nd ed., pp. 510–548). New York: Cambridge University Press.

Friel, B. (2005, February 19). Scrutiny mounts for Head Start. *National Journal, 37*(8), 539–541.

General Accounting Office. (2005). *Head Start: Further development could allow results of new test to be used for decision making.* Washington, DC: Author.

Gilliam, W.S., & Leiter, V. (2003). Evaluating early childhood programs: Improving quality and informing policy. *Zero to Three, 23*(6), 6–13.

Gladwell, M. (2003). Making the grade. *New Yorker.* Retrieved September 30, 2005, from http://*www.newyorker.com/printables/talk/030915ta_talk-gladwell:*

Goldstein, A., & Strauss, V. (2003, July 8). Bush spells out Head Start changes. *Washington Post,* p. A02.

Haines, J., Ames, L.B., & Gillespie, C. (1980). *The Gesell Preschool Test Manual.* Lumberville, PA: Modern Learning Press.

Halpern, R. (2000). Early intervention for low income children and families. In J.P. Shonkoff & S.J. Meisels (Eds.), *Handbook of early childhood intervention.* (2nd ed., pp. 361–686). New York: Cambridge University Press.

Hart, K., & Schumacher, R. (2005). *Making the case: Improving Head Start teacher qualifications requires increased investment.* Washington, DC: Center for Law and Social Policy, Head Start Series, Paper No. 1.

Haskins, R., & Rouse, C. (2005). Closing achievement gaps. *The future of children* (Policy brief). Washington, DC: Brookings Institution and Princeton University.

Herman, J.L. (2004). The effects of testing on instruction. In S.H. Fuhrman & R.F. Elmore (Eds.), *Redesigning accountability systems for education* (pp. 141–166). New York: Teachers College Press.

Heubert, J.P., & Hauser, R.M. (Eds.). (1999). *High stakes: Testing for tracking, promotion, and graduation.* Committee on Appropriate Test Use. Washington, DC: National Academies Press.

Horn, W.F. (2003). Improving Head Start: A common cause. *Head Start Bulletin, 76,* 5–6.

Johnson, D.D., & Johnson, B. (2002). *High stakes: Children, testing, and failure in American schools.* Lanham, MD: Rowman & Littlefield Publishers, Inc.

Kagan, S.L. (1990). Readiness 2000: Rethinking rhetoric and responsibility. *Phi Delta Kappan, 72,* 272–279.

Kagan, S.L., Moore, E., & Bredekamp, S. (1995). *Reconsidering children's early development and learning: Toward common views and vocabulary.* Washington, DC: National Education Goals Panel.

Karoly, L.A., Greenwood, P.W., Everingham, S.S., Hoube, J., Kilburn, M.R., Rydell, C.P., et al. (1998). *Investing in our children: What we know and don't know about the costs and benefits of early childhood interventions.* Santa Monica, CA: RAND.

Kim, J., & Suen, H.K. (2003). Predicting children's academic achievement from early assessment scores: A validity generalization study. *Early Childhood Research Quarterly, 18,* 547–566.

Kochanoff, A.T. (Ed.). (2003). *Report of the Temple University forum on preschool assessment: Recommendations for Head Start.* Philadelphia, PA: Temple University.

Kornhaber, M.L., & Orfield, G. (2001). High-stakes testing policies: Examining their assumptions and consequences. In G. Orfield & M.L. Kornhaber (Eds.), *Raising standards or raising barriers? Inequality and high-stakes testing in public education* (pp. 1–18). New York: The Century Foundation Press.

LaParo, K.M., & Pianta, R.C. (2000). Predicting children's competence in the early school years. A meta-analytic review. *Review of Educational Research, 70*(4), 443–484.

Lazar, I., & Darlington, R. (1982). Lasting effects of early education: A report from the Consortium for Longitudinal Studies. *Monographs of the Society for Research in Child Development, 47*(2–3, Serial No. 195).

Lee, V.E., & Burkham, D.T. (2002). *Inequality at the starting gate: Social background differences in achievement as children begin Kindergarten.* Washington, DC: Economic Policy Institute.

Lynn, R.L. (2005). *Fixing the NCLB accountability system* (CRESST Policy Brief 8). Los Angeles: UCLA Center for the Study of Evaluation.

Madaus, G.F. (1988). The influence of testing on the curriculum. In N. Tanner & K.J. Rehage (Eds.), *Critical issues in curriculum: Eighty-seventh yearbook of the national society for the study of education* (pp. 83–121). Chicago, IL: University of Chicago Press.

Madaus, G.F., & Clarke, M. (2001). The adverse impact of high-stakes testing on minority students: Evidence from one hundred years of test data. In G. Orfield & M.L. Kornhaber (Eds.), *Raising standards or raising barriers? Inequality and high-stakes testing in public education* (pp. 85–106). New York: The Century Foundation Press.

McNeil, L.M. (2002). *Contradictions of school reform: Educational costs of standardized testing.* New York: Routledge.

Meisels, S.J. (1985). The efficacy of early intervention: Why are we still asking this question? *Topics in Early Childhood Special Education, 5,* 1–11.

Meisels, S.J. (1989). High stakes testing in kindergarten. *Educational Leadership, 46,* 16–22.

Meisels, S.J. (1992). Doing harm by doing good: Iatrogenic effects of early childhood enrollment and promotion policies. *Early Childhood Research Quarterly, 7,* 155–174.

Meisels, S.J. (1994). Designing meaningful measurements for early childhood. In B.L. Mallory & R.S. New (Eds.), *Diversity in early childhood education: A call for more inclusive theory, practice, and policy* (pp. 205–225). New York: Teachers College Press.

Meisels, S.J. (1999). Assessing readiness. In R.C. Pianta & M.J. Cox (Eds.), *The transition to kindergarten* (pp. 39–66). Baltimore, MD: Paul H. Brookes Publishing Co..

Meisels, S.J., & Atkins-Burnett, S. (2004). The Head Start national reporting system: A critique. *Young Children, 59*(1), 64–66.

Meisels, S.J., & Atkins-Burnett, S. (2006). Evaluating early childhood assessments: A differential analysis. In K. McCartney & D. Phillips (Eds.), *Handbook of early childhood development* (pp. 533–549). Oxford: Blackwell Publishing.

Meisels, S.J., Atkins-Burnett, S., Xue, Y., Nicholson, J., Bickel, D.D., & Son, S. (2003). Creating a system of accountability: The impact of instructional assessment on elementary children's achievement test scores. *Education Policy Analysis Archives, 11*(9). Retrieved September 30, 2005, from http://epaa.asu.edu/epaa/v11n9

Meisels, S.J., & Shonkoff, J.P. (2000). Early childhood intervention: A continuing evolution. In J.P. Shonkoff & S.J. Meisels (Eds.), *Handbook of early childhood intervention* (2nd ed., pp. 3–33). New York: Cambridge University Press.

Mueller, J. (2002). Facing the unhappy day: Three aspects of the high stakes testing movement. *Kansas Journal of Law and Public Policy, 11,* 201–278.

National Center for Early Development and Learning. (2005). Pre-k education in the states. *Early Developments, 9*(1).

National Institute of Child Health and Human Development Early Child Care Research Network. (2000). Characteristics and quality of child care for toddlers and preschoolers. *Applied Developmental Science, 4*(3), 116–135.

National Institute for Early Education Research. (2006). *The state of preschool: 2005 state preschool yearbook.* Rutgers University: Author.

Parini, J. (2005). *The art of teaching.* New York: Oxford.

Pellegrino, J.W., Jones, L.R., & Mitchell, K.J. (Eds.). (1999). *Grading the nation's report card: Evaluating NAEP and transforming the assessment of educational progress.* Washington, DC: National Research Council.

Pianta, R., Howes, C., Burchinal, M., Bryant, D., Clifford, R., Early, D., et al. (2005). Features of pre-kindergarten programs, classrooms, and teachers: Do they predict observed classroom quality and child-teacher interactions? *Applied Developmental Science, 9*(3), 144–159.

Raudenbush, S. (2005). Newsmaker interview: How NCLB testing can leave some schools behind. *Preschool Matters, 3*(2), 11–12.

Rimer, S. (2003, October 29). Now, standardized tests in Head Start. *New York Times,* p. A23.

Rist, R.C. (1970). Student social class and teacher expectations: The self-fulfilling prophecy in ghetto education. *Harvard Educational Review, 40*(3), 411–451.

Rosenthal, R., & Jacobson, L. (1968). *Pygmalion in the classroom.* New York: Holt, Rinehart & Winston.

Ryan, J.E. (2004). The perverse incentives of the No Child Left Behind Act. *New York University Law Review, 79*(3), 932–989.

Schweinhart, L., & Weikart, D. (1980). *Young children grow up: The effects of the Perry preschool program on youths through age 15* (Monograph No. 7). Ypsilanti, MI: High/Scope Educational Research Foundation.

Shepard, L.A., & Smith, M.L. (1986). Synthesis of research on school readiness and kindergarten retention. *Educational Leadership, 44,* 78–86.

Shonkoff, J.P., & Phillips, D.A. (Eds.). (2000). *Neurons to neighborhoods: The science of early childhood development.* Committee on Integrating the Science of Early Childhood Development. Washington, DC: National Academies Press.

Stipek, D. (2005). Early childhood education at a crossroads. *Harvard Education Letter (Special issue), 21*(4).

Thorndike, R.M. (1999). IRT and intelligence testing: Past, present, and future. In S.E. Embretson & S.L. Hershberger (Eds.), *The new rules of measurement: What every psychologist and educator should know* (pp. 17–36). Mahwah, NJ: Lawrence Erlbaum Associates.

West, J., Denton, K., & Germino-Hausken, E. (2000). *America's kindergartens: Findings from the Early Childhood Longitudinal Study, Kindergarten class of 1998–99, Fall 1998.* Washington, DC: U.S. Department of Education, Office of Educational Research and Improvement.

White House Press Release. (2003, July 7). *President discusses strengthening Head Start.* Retrieved December 12, 2005, from http://www.whitehouse.gov/news/releases/2003/07/20030707-2.html

Wright, B.D. (1999). Fundamental measurement for psychology. In S.E. Embretson & S.L. Hershberger (Eds.), *The new rules of measurement: What every psychologist and educator should know* (pp. 65–104). Mahwah, NJ: Lawrence Erlbaum Associates.

Zigler, E.E., & Muenchow, S. (1992). *Head Start: The inside story of America's most successful educational experiment.* New York: Basic Books.

Zigler, E.E., & Valentine, J. (Eds.). (1979). *Project Head Start: A legacy of the war on poverty.* New York: The Free Press.

4

LEARNING OPPORTUNITIES IN PRESCHOOL AND EARLY ELEMENTARY CLASSROOMS

Bridget K. Hamre and Robert C. Pianta

Accountability reform has placed individual schools and teachers in the spotlight by requiring evidence of their ability to produce student achievement. This spotlight has directed the attention of policy makers and school administrators to what is happening *inside* the classroom—what experiences are students having in classrooms, and how do these experiences help explain the successes and failures of teachers and schools within this new accountability system? Illumination of the daily experiences of the youngest students—those in preschool to third-grade classrooms—is of particular interest given well-publicized evidence supporting positive long-term effects and cost-effectiveness of early education (Barnett, 1996; Ramey & Ramey, 1998; Reynolds, Temple, Robertson, & Mann, 2002; Masse & Barnett, 2002) and the importance of the early years of schooling in predicting positive academic trajectories (Bogard & Takanishi, 2005; Entwisle & Hayduck, 1988; Hamre & Pianta, 2001). Unfortunately, few reliable methods exist of determining which classroom experiences promote academic success and positive social development across the preschool to third-grade period.

There are several reasons for the lack of a clearly articulated message about the learning opportunities that really matter for young children. First, research in early childhood and elementary education has progressed somewhat independently, resulting in the use of different theoretical frameworks and language. Phrases such as "quality teaching" and "developmentally appropriate practice" can take on very different meanings depending on the context in which they are used (e.g., Bredekamp & Copple, 1997; Darling-Hammond, 1997; NCES, 2003). Second, the lack of consensus regarding the goals of early childhood and elementary education makes it difficult to clearly define the strategies teachers might use to meet those goals. Questions about how to effectively teach early literacy versus how to support social development are likely to get different, often conflicting, answers. Nowhere is this more apparent than in current debates regarding preschool curriculum and learning standards, as policy makers try to balance the push for academic content with appropriate consideration of children's developmental abilities and needs (Neuman & Roskos, 2005). A third factor impeding a clearly articulated message about effective learning opportunities is the high degree of variability in children's schooling experiences prior to kindergarten entry, with children attending a wide range of programs, including Head Start; state-funded preschool; private, for-profit, and nonprofit child care centers; and family child care (National Institute of Child Health and Human Development Early Child Care Research Network [NICHD ECCRN], 2000). Variability in early childhood settings makes synthesis about effective practice within this early childhood time frame challenging (Fuller, Kagan, & Loeb, 2004) and confounds efforts to integrate these findings with those from early elementary classrooms. Finally, prior to 2000, few studies were available to provide national-level data on children's actual experiences in these settings. Devising plans for improving classrooms without knowledge of their current condition is difficult.

In the past few years, these unsolved problems have been addressed to the extent that a synthesis of research is possible. Certainly, a great deal of debate remains regarding the most effective teaching practices, but there are many areas of converging evidence and consensus. Furthermore, given the increasing integration of practice and research across the preschool to third-grade period (Bogard & Takanishi, 2005) and the availability of large, national-level data on what actually happens in classrooms during this critical period (Early, Barbarin, Bryant, et al., 2005; NICHD ECCRN, 2002, 2005), a synthesis of information on children's learning opportunities in the early years of schooling can inform policy, guide future research efforts, and contribute to attempts to improve early childhood and elementary classrooms at scale. To this end, the goals of this chapter include 1) defining *learning opportunities* and describing the assumptions on which this definition is based; 2) providing a context for understanding children's learning opportunities, including a summary of descriptive data on how young children spend their time in U.S. preschool to third-grade classrooms; 3) introducing the *CLASS Framework for Children's Learning Opportunities,* a theoretically driven and empirically supported conceptual framework for understanding children's experiences in the early years of schooling; 4) synthesizing research on the nature and quality of these learning opportunities as observed in more than 3,000 U.S. classrooms from preschool through third grade; and 5) briefly discussing implications of these findings for researchers, policy makers, administrators, and teacher-educators.

DEFINING AND UNDERSTANDING CHILDREN'S EXPOSURE TO LEARNING OPPORTUNITIES

The conceptualization of learning opportunities presented in this chapter builds on recent advances in the integration of educational research with systems and bioecological theories of development (Pianta, 2006). Learning opportunities are defined as *a set of theoretically driven dimensions of interactions between adults and children with empirically supported links to children's social, emotional, and academic development.* Other frequently used terms, such as *quality teaching* (Fenstermacher & Richardson, 2005; Koster, Brekelmans, & Korthagen, 2005; NICHD ECCRN, 2005; Pianta, Howes, Burchinal, et al., 2005) and *effective practice* (Astleitner, 2005; Muijs, Campbell, & Kyriakides, 2005; Yates, 2005) may be subsumed under this definition of learning opportunities. This conceptualization of learning opportunities is based on the following assumptions, each discussed briefly next:

1. Children are most directly influenced through *proximal processes,* their daily interactions with adults and peers (Bronfenbrenner & Morris, 1998).

2. The formation and refinement of knowledge about children's learning opportunities must proceed through an iterative process of *theoretically driven* research linking specific types of proximal processes with specific child outcomes.

3. The environments in which learning opportunities occur are *unique developmental settings* requiring adequate knowledge of and attendance to the realities of children's experiences in classrooms and schools.

Proximal Processes: Opportunities to Learn Versus Opportunities to Teach

Bronfenbrenner and Morris (1998) advanced the notion that *proximal processes*—interactions that take place between children and their environment over time—serve as the primary mechanism for children's development. This theory, as applied to schooling, suggests that classroom interactions between adults and children should be a primary focus of study when seeking to understand children's development in school contexts (Pianta, 2006). Examples of proximal processes in classrooms include teachers' interactions with students around behavior management, questioning and feedback during instruction, and teachers' facilitation of peer interactions.

In this view, the effects of more distal features of classrooms and schools, such as school climate and curriculum, although potentially important to students' development, are largely mediated through and/or moderated by classroom interactions. The case of curriculum provides an example of both mediation and moderation. A school may adapt a new math curriculum based on strong evidence that it promotes student learning. The presence of this curriculum in classrooms may provide an excellent opportunity for teachers to transmit knowledge to students, but the actual transmission occurs during instructional interactions within the classroom (mediation). Furthermore, the actual transmission is constrained, or moderated, by other components of the classroom environment. If students feel uncomfortable or disconnected from the social environment in the classroom, or if classroom management is so poor that students find it hard to attend to instruction, the potential effects of the curriculum are unlikely to be realized.

These more distal features of the environment may be better conceptualized as providing opportunities to teach rather than opportunities to learn. Early childhood education and elementary settings need to optimize these opportunities to teach by providing well-validated curricula, creating positive school environments, encouraging parent participation, and providing teachers with sufficient professional development supports. However, the ultimate effect of these opportunities to teach on children's growth are transmitted primarily through opportunities to learn in the classroom.

Theory-Driven Conceptualization

Consistent with a developmental approach to understanding classrooms, research on proximal processes that affect young children must be driven by theory on children's development (Magnussun & Stattin, 1998; Pianta, 2006). This chapter integrates findings from a range of academic disciplines that have developed theories about the mechanisms through which learning opportunities promote positive outcomes for students. This more mechanistic approach has the potential to produce an ongoing cycle of hypothesis generation and testing, with successful iterations of theory-building leading to the design and evaluation of interventions in schools and, ultimately, improvement of educational systems at scale (Pianta, 2006). Successful research programs based on developmental theory can inform educational practice as well as advance new theories and models for typical and atypical child development (e.g., Alexander & Entwisle, 1988; Conduct Problems Prevention Research Group, 1999; Cook, Murphy, & Hunt, 2000; Eccles & Roeser, 1998; Howes, Galinsky, & Kontos, 1998; Ladd & Burgess, 1999; Morrison & Connor, 2002; Ramey, Campbell, Burchinal, Skinner, Gardner, & Ramey, 2000; Stevenson & Lee, 1990).

Classrooms as Unique Developmental Settings

One must be careful, however, not to assume that developmental theories can be blindly applied to classroom settings. Most developmental theories, particularly theories on younger children, are produced through the study of children in home settings. Although basic developmental processes are assumed to exist across contexts, classrooms offer complexities without family or home equivalents. For example, in families, feedback is typically given to children during one-to-one interactions. In classrooms, children receive feedback from a much broader array of sources, such as one-to-one interactions with multiple teachers, whole-group lessons in which they listen to feedback given to other students, and peer interactions during structured and unstructured classroom activities. Furthermore, classrooms are often directed toward very different goals and are responsive to different pressures than are family environments. Developmentally informed, school-based research must therefore pay explicit attention to the realities of school and classroom settings.

EPIDEMIOLOGICAL STUDIES OF CLASSROOMS

Medical science relies heavily on epidemiological studies to help determine the most effective and efficient pathways to intervention. Epidemiological studies provide data on the prevalence of disease, as well as the prevalence of factors that may contribute to the development of disease (e.g., television watching and fast food contributing to childhood obesity). These studies have helped pinpoint geographic areas and ages in which children are most likely to be exposed to these factors, helping to target intervention and prevention efforts. Until the past decade, however, no parallel studies were available for school-based researchers interested in population-level data on children's exposure to particular classroom practices known to relate to academic success or failure. Two large national studies conducted over the past 10 years provide some of the first epidemiological data on U.S. classrooms (NICHD ECCRN, 2002, 2005; Early et al., 2005). Together, they describe the content and quality of children's experiences in more than 3,000 classrooms across the United States of America. Neither study is nationally representative, and one has been criticized for its failure to adequately sample low-income and minority families (Johnson, Jaeger, Randolph, et al., 2003); however, the stories these studies tell of children's experiences in early childhood and elementary classrooms provide a starting point for those interested in school-based research and intervention. They are unique in offering a national-level picture of classrooms, based on actual observations over time; as such, these studies are referenced throughout this chapter for data on children's experiences in the early years of schooling. Each of these studies is described briefly, including important sampling and methodological information to provide a context for interpretation of the results.

The NICHD and NCEDL studies represent an important advance in our understanding of learning opportunities in the early years of schooling; however, several factors limit the ability to draw conclusive inferences about *changes* in children's experiences over time including differences in measures and observation procedures. Therefore, any inferences drawn about changes over time were made conservatively and should be interpreted with caution.

The NICHD Study of Early Child Care and Youth Development

The NICHD Study of Early Child Care and Youth Development (NICHD SECCYD) is a longitudinal national study initiated in 1989 to examine associations between child care experiences and developmental outcomes among approximately 1,300 children. As children entered elementary school, researchers expanded the initial aims of the study to include a comprehensive examination of children's experiences in classrooms. The classroom observations discussed in this chapter were conducted when children were in first and third grade, using qualitative ratings and behavioral sampling from the Classroom Observation System (COS; NICHD ECCRN, 2002, 2005) Detailed information on the study and COS are available on the NICHD SECCYD web site (http://secc.rti.org).

National Center for Early Development and Learning Multi-State Preschool Study and State-Wide Early Education Programs Study

The National Center for Early Development and Learning (NCEDL) has conducted two major studies of state-funded preschool programs aimed at understanding variations among preschool programs and examining how these variations relate to children's academic and social development through first grade: the six-state Multi-State Study of Preschool (MS), and the five-state State-Wide Early Education Programs (SWEEP) study (Early et al., 2005). When combined, these two studies provide observational data on more than 700 preschool and 800 kindergarten classrooms across the United States of America. Classrooms were observed using a variety of measures to capture the content and quality of learning opportunities and materials available to children in these environments, including the Early Childhood Environment Rating Scale (ECERS-R; Harms, Clifford, & Cryer, 1998), Classrooms Assessment Scoring System (CLASS; Pianta, La Paro, & Hamre, 2004), and Emerging Academics' Snapshot (Ritchie, Howes, Kraft-Sayre, & Weiser, 2001). More information about these studies can be found on the NCEDL web site (http://www.fpg.unc.edu/~ncedl) and in several published articles (see Clifford et al., 2005; Early et al., 2005; Pianta, et al., 2005).

HOW DO YOUNG STUDENTS SPEND THEIR TIME IN CLASSROOMS?

Before examining children's learning opportunities as defined by the nature and quality of children's interactions in the classroom, the context in which these opportunities occur needs to be better understood. To this end, the NICHD SECCYD and NCEDL MS/SWEEP studies provide a wealth of descriptive data on young students' experiences on a typical day of school. The results of these studies are discussed next and summarized in Table 4.1, including a summary of observational methodology to aid in interpretation.

Instructional Time

At the most basic level, opportunities to learn occur when children are exposed to instructional activities, regardless of content or quality. According to these studies, however, young children spend considerable time in classrooms *not* exposed to any type of instruction. Across studies and grades, observers recorded the proportion of time spent on a variety of academic subject areas. These subject areas were inclusive of all major areas of curriculum and broadly defined. For example, in the NCEDL MS/SWEEP studies, observers recorded the amount of time students spent in reading, oral language and phonemic awareness activities, writing, math, science, social studies, aesthetics, and fine and gross motor activities (Early et al., 2005). These areas were broadly defined such that time spent in dramatic play, block areas, coloring with markers, talking with teachers about things outside of school, and singing songs were all included in one of these areas. Yet, during the full preschool day in half-day programs (or until nap time in full-time programs) the average preschool student spent 42% of his or her time engaged in none of these activities (Early et al., 2005). What were students doing during this time? Much of the time (22%) was spent engaged in routine activities such as transitioning, waiting in line, washing hands, and so forth. Some time (11%) was also spent in meals and snacks (Early et al., 2005). Importantly, routine, meal, and snack times could be included as instructional time if, for example, teachers read a book during snack time or had the students recite a familiar poem during a transition. But few preschool teachers appear to take advantage of these strategies for getting the most out of students' time in the classroom.

Students continue to spend a significant portion of their time in noninstructional activities during elementary school, but this time decreases from preschool to third grade (see Table 4.1). These observations typically occurred during the most productive months of schooling, purposely avoiding the beginning- and end-of-year and holiday period to try to capture typical school days. Thus, when considered across the year, these findings may actually underestimate the amount of noninstructional time to which young children are exposed.

Literacy and Language Arts

When examining the content of what children are doing during instructional times, a clear pattern emerges in which literacy and language arts activities predominate and increase rather dramatically from preschool to kindergarten and first grade. On average, preschoolers in the NCEDL studies spent about 20% of the day engaged in literacy and language arts activities (Early et al., 2005). This was distributed among reading (8%), phonemic awareness (4%), oral language (7%), and writing (2%) activities. By kindergarten, the average student in the NCEDL MS study spent 28% of his or her day in these types of activities (Hamre, La Paro, Locasale-Crouch, & Pianta, 2006). The proportion of time spent in literacy and language arts was even higher (60%) in the NICHD ECCRN (2002) first-grade classrooms, although unlike in the other grades, these observations occurred only during the first 3 hours of school,

Table 4.1. Time spent in early childhood and elementary classrooms: Results from NICHD SECCYD and NCEDL multi-state and SWEEP studies

	Public preschool	Kindergarten	First grade	Third grade
Source	MS/SWEEP[a]	MS[b]	SECCYD[c]	SECCYD[d]
Number of classrooms	701	746	827	780
Year(s)	2001–2002 and 2003–2004	2002–2003	1998	2000
Time of day sampled	All day in half-day programs; until nap in full day programs	Entire day except recess, lunch, and nap	First 3 hours (excluded recess and lunch)	Start of day for 6 hours (excluded recess and lunch)
Percent of time spent[e] in:				
Literacy/language arts	.21	.28	.62	.48
Math	.06	.11	.14	.24
Science	.08	.03	.04	.05
Social studies	.13	.06	.02	.05
Music/art	.09	.09	.10	.03
Noninstructional time[f]	.42	.40	.17	.18
Large/whole group	.23	.38	.51	.55
Small group	.06	.11	.06	.06

[a]Source: Early et al., 2005.
[b]Source: Hamre, La Paro, et al., 2006.
[c]Source: NICHD ECCRN, 2003.
[d]Source: NICHD ECCRN, 2005.
[e]Measurement differed across studies. For more complete information on measurement, consult the referenced citation.
[f]Noninstructional time included snack, management and transition times for preschool and kindergarten years, social and transition time for first grade, and transition and management for third grade.

a time when many teachers focus on this area. Nonetheless, evidence clearly shows that, consistent with a considerable push from local, state, and federal reading initiatives, young students are spending much of their day exposed to early literacy and language activities.

Math and Science

Despite increasing interest in exposing young children to high-quality math and science instruction (Ginsburg & Golbeck, 2004; Sarama & Clements, 2002; Starkey, Klein, & Wakeley, 2004), young children are not consistently exposed to math or science. Children in preschool classrooms spend an average of 6% of their day engaged in math activities. As with literacy and language arts, time spent in math increases from preschool to third grade, with students spending an average of one-quarter of their time in third-grade classrooms on math (NICHD ECCRN, 2005). In contrast, across grades the typical young student is rarely exposed to science instruction and the proportion of time spent on science actually decreases from preschool to third grade (Early et al., 2005; Hamre, La Paro, et al., 2006; NICHD ECCRN, 2002, 2005). As reported by NICHD ECCRN (2005), during a typical 6-hour school day, the average third-grade student spends just 18 minutes on science.

Instructional Settings

An examination of the settings in which this instructional content is delivered suggests that by first grade, students spend the majority of their time in whole group instruction (NICHD ECCRN, 2002), a fairly dramatic shift from preschool in which students spend an average of just 23% of time in whole group instruction (Early et al., 2005). Across grades, teachers rarely use small groups as a format for instruction (NICHD ECCRN, 2002). Data from the NCEDL MS study offer a unique opportunity to look at shifts in students' experiences in this domain during the transition between preschool and kindergarten (Hamre, La Paro, et al., 2006). This study followed the same group of students from preschool to kindergarten and used very similar methodology, making it easier to draw conclusions about children's experiences across time. In preschool classrooms, observers started at the beginning of the day and watched until the end of the day in half-day programs and nap time in whole day programs. In kindergarten, observers watched for the whole day with the exception of lunch and recess.

As presented in Figure 4.1, young children experience a substantial shift from preschool to kindergarten in the ways in which they are instructed. Children have significantly less time in free choice or center play and spend substantially more time in whole group instruction. These data provide direct evidence of the shift toward more formalized instruction from preschool to kindergarten that has been the focus of much debate (Gronlund, 2001; Rimm-Kaufman & Pianta, 2005).

Variability in Experiences

These findings paint a picture of how young children spend their time in early childhood and elementary classrooms. The average student spends significant time engaged in center-

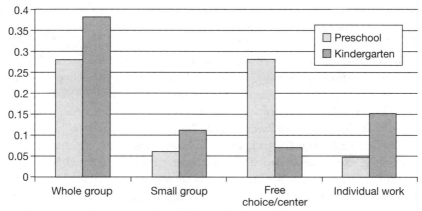

Figure 4.1.   Percent of time observed in instructional settings in preschool and kindergarten. (Sources: Early et al., 2005; Hamre, La Paro, et al., 2006.) *Note:* Preschool classrooms were observed for the whole day (half-day programs) or until nap (full-day programs); kindergarten classrooms were observed for the full day excluding recess, lunch, and nap time.

based play during preschool and more time in whole group instruction as he or she progresses through elementary school, particularly in the area of language arts. Across grades, students spent a great deal of time in noninstructional activities. However, one point these studies have made abundantly clear is that one should not assume that these average experiences can be interpreted as typical. Rather, within each study is a high degree of variability among students in the ways in which they spend their time. For example, in first grade the average student spent 14% of their first 3 hours in math instruction (NICHD ECCRN, 2002); however, this ranged from classrooms that spent no time on math to classrooms that spent 83% of the observation on math activities. The variability in students' experiences is evident across grades and subject areas and is mirrored in the discussion of the *quality* of children's learning opportunities that follows. These findings, although informative, provide only a foundation for understanding children's experiences in the early years of schooling. The sections explore the nature and quality of children's interactions with adults and peers from preschool to third grade.

CLASS FRAMEWORK FOR CHILDREN'S LEARNING OPPORTUNITIES IN EARLY CHILDHOOD AND ELEMENTARY CLASSROOMS

The remainder of this chapter presents the CLASS Framework for Children's Learning Opportunities in Early Childhood and Elementary Classrooms (CLASS Framework) as a guide to reviewing research on children's experiences in the early years of school. This theoretically-driven framework draws directly from the *Classroom Assessment Scoring System* (CLASS; Pianta et al., 2004), an observational measure of classroom quality for preschool to third-grade classrooms. The CLASS Framework describes three broad domains of classroom interactions as well as descriptions of more specific dimensions within each broad domain (see Table 4.2). Consistent with the assumptions discussed above, the CLASS Framework focuses on proximal processes in the classroom and was derived from basic, theory-driven research on classroom environments and many years of research on effective teaching practices. Indeed, despite the frequent debates that draw attention to areas of dispute (Educational Testing Service, 2004; Fallon, 2003; Lasley, Siedentop, & Yinger, 2006), there is general consensus on many of the ingredients of effective teachers and supportive classroom environments (e.g., Brophy, 1986; Brophy & Good, 1986; Dwyer, 1994).

The dimensions of learning opportunities described within the CLASS Framework are not new. In fact, the CLASS Framework shares much with other descriptions of classroom quality put forth in the educational literature (e.g., Brophy & Good, 1986; Pressley, Roehrig, & Raphael, 2003; Soar & Soar, 1979). The CLASS Framework is, however, unique in its theoretical grounding, empirical validation, and inclusion of early childhood and elementary classroom settings. Furthermore, this structure for organizing interactions between teachers and children has been validated across multiple samples (Hamre, Mashburn, Pianta, & Downer, 2006). Thus, the CLASS Framework is intended to help organize a broad range of research in a way that fits natural variation in actual classrooms and suggests terminology that may be helpful for heuristic purposes as the science of classroom process effects moves forward.

The CLASS Framework suggests that, within the school environment, students' academic and social development is most directly affected by interactions in the classroom described as emotional supports, classroom organization, and instructional supports. A brief description of the dimensions of learning opportunities within each domain is provided in Table 4.2. The following sections provide an overview of each broad domain of learning opportunities, including a synthesis of the theoretical foundations on which they are based. Within each domain, the individual dimensions of learning opportunities (e.g., teacher sensitivity, concept development) are reviewed by providing an overview of the types of teacher–student interactions included in the dimension and empirical evidence of the dimension's significance in predicting children's development. Finally, for each broad domain, national-level research on the extent to which these learning opportunities are available to students from preschool to third grade is summarized. It is beyond the scope of this chapter to provide an exhaustive review of research in any one area. Rather, the following sections are intended to synthesize and organize findings and provide illustrative examples of relevant work. When possible, readers are referred to available reviews specific to particular dimensions.

Emotional Supports

Children's social and emotional functioning in the classroom is increasingly recognized as an indicator of school readiness (Blair, 2002; Denham & Weissberg, 2004; Raver, 2004), a potential target for intervention (Greenberg, Weissberg, O'Brien, et al., 2003; Zins, Bloodworth, Weissberg, & Walberg, 2004) and even a student outcome that might be governed by a set of standards similar to those for academic achievement (Illinois State Board of Education, 2004). Children who are more motivated and connected to others in the early years of schooling are much more likely to establish positive trajectories of development in both social and academic domains (Hamre & Pianta, 2001; Ladd et al., 1999; Pianta et al., 1995; Silver et al., 2005). Teachers' abilities to support social and emotional functioning in the classroom are therefore central to any conceptualization of effective classroom practice.

Table 4.2. CLASS Framework for early childhood and elementary classroom quality

Area	Dimension	Description
Emotional support	Classroom climate	Reflects the overall emotional tone of the classroom and the connection between teachers and students. Considers the warmth and respect displayed in teachers' and students' interactions as well as the degree to which they display enjoyment and enthusiasm during learning activities.
	Teacher sensitivity	Encompasses teachers' responsivity to students' concerns and awareness of students' levels of academic and emotional functioning. The highly sensitive teacher helps students see adults as a resource and creates an environment in which students feel safe and free to explore and learn.
	Regard for student perspectives	The degree to which the teachers' interactions with students and classroom activities place an emphasis on students' interests, motivations, and points of view, rather than being very teacher driven. This may be demonstrated by teachers' flexibility within activities and respect for students' autonomy to participate in and initiate activities.
Classroom organization	Behavior management	Encompasses teachers' ability to use effective methods to prevent and redirect misbehavior by presenting clear behavioral expectations and minimizing time spent on behavioral issues.
	Productivity	Considers how well teachers manage instructional time and routines so that students have the maximum number of opportunities to learn. Not related to the quality of instruction but to teachers' efficiency.
	Instructional learning format	The degree to which teachers maximize students' engagement and ability to learn by providing interesting activities, instruction, centers, and materials. Considers the manner in which the teachers facilitate activities so that students have opportunities to experience, perceive, explore, and use materials.
Instructional support (general)	Concept development	The degree to which instructional discussions and activities promote students' higher order thinking skills rather than focusing on rote and fact-based learning.
	Quality of feedback	Considers teachers' feedback focused on expanding learning and understanding (formative evaluation), not correctness or the end product (summative evaluation).
	Language modeling	The quality and amount of teachers' use of language-stimulation and language-facilitation techniques during individual, small-group, and large-group interactions with children. Components of high-quality language modeling include self- and parallel talk, open-ended questions, repetition, expansion/extension, and use of advanced language.

59

Two broad areas of developmental theory guide much of the work on emotional support in classrooms, specifically attachment theory (Ainsworth, Blehar, Waters, & Wall, 1978; Bowlby, 1969; Pianta, 1999) and self-determination theory (Connell & Wellborn, 1991; Ryan & Deci, 2000; Skinner & Belmont, 1993). Attachment theorists posit that when parents provide emotional support and a predictable, consistent, and safe environment, children become more self-reliant and are able to take risks as they explore the world because they know that they have an adult who will be there to help them if they need it (Bowlby, 1969; Ainsworth et al., 1978). This theory has been broadly applied to and validated in school environments (Birch & Ladd, 1998; Hamre & Pianta, 2001; Howes, Hamilton & Matheson, 1994; Lynch & Cicchetti, 1992; Pianta, 1999). Self-determination (or self-systems) theory (Connell & Wellborn, 1991; Ryan & Deci, 2000; Skinner, Zimmer-Gembeck, & Connell, 1998) suggests that children are most motivated to learn when adults support their need to feel competent and autonomous and encourage them to develop positive relationships with others. Related work by Wentzel (1999, 2002) suggests that students who see teachers as supportive are more likely to pursue goals valued by teachers, such as engagement in aca-demic activities. Building from these two theoretical backgrounds are three dimensions of emotional support in the classroom: classroom climate, teacher sensitivity, and regard for student perspectives.

Classroom Climate   Classrooms are, by their very nature, social places. Teachers and children laugh and play together, share stories about their lives outside of the classroom, and work together to create an environment in which all learning occurs. The classroom climate can be described along positive and negative dimensions. Positive climate encompasses the degree to which students experience warm caring relationships with adults and peers and enjoy the time they spend in the classroom. Negative climates are those in which students experience frequent yelling, humiliation, or irritation in interactions with teachers and peers.

The aspect of climate that has been studied most extensively in the past 10 years is the nature and quality of teachers' relationships with students. There is strong evidence for the salience of student–teacher relationships as an important context for children's development (for review, see Pianta, Hamre, & Stuhlman, 2003); student–teacher relationships are associated with children's peer competencies (e.g., Birch & Ladd, 1998; Howes, et al., 1994; Howes, 2000) and trajectories toward academic success or failure (Birch & Ladd, 1996, 1998; Hamre & Pianta, 2001; Ladd et al., 1999; Pianta et al., 1995; Silver et al., 2005; van Ijzendoorn, Sagi, & Lambermon, 1992). Evidence indicates that certain teachers have tendencies to develop more positive relationships, across multiple students in their classroom, than do others (Hamre, Pianta, Downer, & Mashburn, in press; Mashburn, Hamre, Downer, & Pianta, 2005). Children in classrooms with higher composite levels of teacher support have higher levels of peer acceptance and classroom engagement than do their peers in less supportive classrooms, even after controlling for individual levels of teacher support (Hughes, Shang, & Hill, 2006).

Peer relations are also important. Children who experience peer rejection or victimization in the early years of schooling are likely to have continued problems as they mature, including social difficulties and academic failure (Asher, Parkhurst, Hymel, & Williams, 1990; Buhs & Ladd, 2001; Cassidy & Asher, 1992; Ladd, Kochenderfer, & Coleman, 1997; Ladd & Troop-Gordon, 2003). Furthermore, evidence shows that children in preschool classrooms characterized by poor peer relationships are more likely to display significant aggression and disruptive behavior in second grade, even after controlling for individual variation in peer functioning (Howes, 2000).

Teacher Sensitivity　　Teachers need to provide more than a warm and caring social environment. They must be attuned and responsive to the individual cues and needs of students in their classrooms, a dimension of teaching referred to here as *teacher sensitivity.* Highly sensitive teachers, through their consistent and responsive interactions, help students see adults as a resource and create environments in which students feel safe and free to explore and learn (Pianta et al., 2004). Highly sensitive teaching requires teachers to attend to, process, and respond to a lot of information simultaneously. For example, during whole group instruction, a sensitive teacher may, within quick succession, notice some children not paying attention, see that one child is frustrated because he doesn't understand her questions, and observe a sad look on a child she knows is generally very happy and engaged. The sensitive teacher not only notices these subtle cues from students but also knows her students well enough to respond in ways that help alleviate their problems. She may, for example, change the tone of her voice to re-engage those students not participating, take a quick moment to restate her question in simpler language, and make a mental note to check in with the sad student at recess. In contrast, an insensitive teacher may completely miss these subtle cues or respond in ways that aggravate, rather than alleviate, students' problems.

Students in classrooms with sensitive teachers are more engaged and self-reliant in the classroom and have lower levels of mother-reported internalizing problems than do those with less sensitive teachers (NICHD ECCRN, 2003; Rimm-Kaufman et al., 2002). Sensitive teaching is important not just to social outcomes but to academic outcomes as well. For example, among a group of preschoolers, those who experienced more responsive teacher interactions in preschool displayed stronger vocabulary and decoding skills at the end of first grade (Connor, Son, & Hindman, 2005).

Regard for Students' Perspectives　　The final dimension of emotional support is the degree to which classrooms and interactions are structured around the interests and motivations of the teacher, versus those of the students. In some classrooms, teachers frequently ask for students' ideas and thoughts, follow students' lead, and provide opportunities for students to have a formative role in the classroom. In these classrooms, students not only are allowed to talk but also are actively encouraged to talk to one another (Pianta et al., 2004). At the other end of the continuum are classrooms in which teachers follow very scripted plans for how the day should run, show little flexibility or response to students' interests and motivations, and provide few opportunities for students to express their thoughts or to assume responsibility for activities in the classroom. Teachers in these classrooms may also be very controlling of student movement, requiring, for example, students to sit quietly on the rug with their legs crossed and hands in their laps for long periods of time.

The early childhood field, in particular, has emphasized the importance of child-focused classroom environments, as reflected in the recommendations for practice from the National Association for the Education of Young Children (Bredekamp & Copple, 1997). Empirical support for these recommendations comes from work showing that young children report more positive feelings about school, display more motivation, and are more engaged when they experience more child-focused and autonomy-supportive instruction (de Kruif, McWilliam, Ridley, & Wakeley, 2000; Gutman & Sulzby, 2000; Pianta et al., 2002; Valeski & Stipek, 2001), whereas children in more teacher-directed classrooms have higher levels of mother-reported internalizing problems (NICHD ECCRN, 2003). Some findings, however, suggest that the optimal level of teacher control may vary depending on factors such as learning objectives (Brophy & Good, 1986; Soar & Soar, 1979) and grade (Valeski & Stipek, 2001).

Evidence for Children's Exposure to Emotionally Supportive Classrooms   The NICHD SECCYD and NCEDL MS/SWEEP studies provide unique data on the extent to which dimensions of emotional support are available to young children across the early years of schooling (see Table 4.3). The measurement differed slightly between studies, with MS/SWEEP studies using the CLASS instrument (Pianta et al., 2004) and the SECCYD using the COS instruments (NICHD ECCRN, 2002, 2005), but the descriptions of what constituted each dimension (e.g., teacher sensitivity) remained relatively stable. In each case, observers made ratings on a 1–7 scale (1–2 low; 3–5 mid; 6–7 high). Readers are referred to documentation from those studies for more complete descriptions.

As displayed in Table 4.3, across the early years of schooling, the average child in these studies was exposed to emotional supports at the high end of the mid-range as described by these scales (Early et al., 2005; Hamre, La Paro, et al., 2006; NICHD ECCRN, 2002, 2005). Classrooms offered relatively positive classroom climates, characterized by warm and supportive teacher–child and peer interactions. The average student was very unlikely to engage in negative interactions with peers or teachers. For example, based on time-sampling data, third-grade children were observed in negative interactions in fewer than one percent of observed intervals (NICHD ECCRN, 2005). Teachers in these studies were moderately sensitive, and most early childhood and elementary classrooms appear to have fairly high regard for student perspective. This was measured by *overcontrol* in all studies, which is largely a reverse of the Regard for Student Perspectives Dimension (Pianta et al., 2004).

A few other findings are notable. First, despite the generally positive emotional climates, the degree of variability is significant. For example, in the NICHD SECCYD study in first grade, a small proportion of classrooms had notably poor emotional supports. Among the 827 classrooms, 9% had classroom environments at the very low end of positive climate and 7% were at the low end of sensitivity (NICHD ECCRN, 2003). Importantly, across studies these descriptions reflect the average of ratings made during several observation intervals across the school day. Thus, these classrooms with averages in the low range are characterized by consistently low levels of emotional support. Second, despite an emphasis in early childhood and elementary education on facilitating peer connections, classroom observations suggest that teachers rarely make use of peer collaboration as an instructional tool. In third grade, students were observed in collaborative or cooperative work with peers in fewer than 5% of observed intervals.

Classroom Organization

Classroom organization is a broad domain of classroom processes related to the organization and management of students' behavior, time, and attention in the classroom (Emmer & Strough, 2001). Classrooms function best, and provide the most opportunities to learn,

Table 4.3. Average ratings (on 1–7 scale) of learning opportunities in early childhood and elementary classrooms using CLASS (MS/SWEEP) and COS (SECCYD) measures

	Public preschool	Kindergarten	First grade	Third grade
Source	MS/SWEEP[a]	MS[b]	SECCYD[c]	SECCYD[d]
Number of classrooms	694	885	827	780
Year(s)	2001–2002 and 2003–2004	2002–2003	1998	2000
Time of day sampled	All day in half-day programs; until nap in full-day programs	Entire day except recess, lunch, and nap	First 3 hours (excluding recess and lunch)	Start of day for 6 hours (excluding recess and lunch)
Emotional Support				
Positive climate	5.27 (.87)	5.17 (.77)	5.36 (1.27)	5.07 (.76)
Negative climate	2.38 (1.59)	1.88 (.76)	1.58 (1.06)	1.17 (.47)
Teacher sensitivity	4.70 (.96)	4.69 (.89)	5.33 (1.14)	4.94 (1.01)
Overcontrol	2.38 (1.59)	1.88 (.76)	2.31 (1.46)	2.57 (1.37)
Classroom organization				
Behavior management	4.97 (.97)	5.21 (.80)	5.03 (1.31)	n/a
Productivity	4.49 (.91)	4.67 (.78)	n/a	4.90 (.97)
Instructional learning formats	3.90 (1.13)	4.11 (.87)	n/a	n/a
Instructional support				
Concept development	2.09 (.88)	2.11 (.77)	3.13 (1.54)[e]	2.11 (.78)[f]
Quality of feedback	2.03 (.96)	1.84 (.66)	3.24 (1.52)	n/a

[a]Source: Early et al., 2005.
[b]Source: Hamre, La Paro, et al., 2006.
[c]Source: NICHD ECCRN, 2003.
[d]Source: NICHD ECCRN, 2005.
[e]Coded as instructional conversation.
[f]Coded as richness of instructional methods.
Note: Measurement differed across studies. For more complete information on measurement, consult the referenced citation.

when students are well behaved, consistently have things to do, and are interested and engaged in learning tasks (Pianta et al., 2004). The theoretical underpinnings of this domain include work by developmental psychologists interested in children's self-regulatory skills (Blair, 2003; Raver, 2004), ecological psychologists examining the extent to which these skills are determined by various setting and interactive contexts (Kounin, 1970), and constructivist theories on engaging young children in learning (Bowman & Stott, 1994; Bruner, 1996; Rogoff, 1990; Vygotsky, 1978). The term *self-regulated learning* (Schunk, 2005; Sperling, Howard & Staley, 2004) is often used to refer to the regulatory skills in classrooms and is defined as, "an active constructive process whereby learners set goals for their learning and then attempt to monitor, regulate, and control their cognition, motivation, and behavior, guided and constrained by their goals and the contextual features in the environment" (Pintrich, 2000, p. 453). As emphasized by Pintrich (2000), in work by ecological psychologists (e.g., Kounin, 1970) and numerous process-product researchers (Anderson, Evertson, & Emmer, 1980; Emmer & Strough, 2001; Sanford & Evertson, 1981; Soar & Soar, 1979), the development and expression of these regulatory skills is highly dependent on the classroom environment. At the simplest level, this work suggests that students are better regulated in well-regulated classroom environments. The CLASS Framework suggests three dimensions of this classroom-level regulation: Behavior Management, Productivity, and Instructional Learning Formats.

Behavior Management   Behavior management is a term often applied to a broad spectrum of classroom management strategies, including teachers' abilities to engage students and make constructive use of time. Within the CLASS Framework, behavior management is defined more narrowly as practices intended to *promote positive behavior* and *prevent or terminate misbehavior* in the classroom. There is general consensus around a set of practices associated with more positive student behavior including 1) providing clear and consistent behavioral expectations; 2) monitoring the classroom for potential problems and proactively preventing problems rather than being reactive; 3) efficiently redirecting minor misbehavior before it escalates; 4) using positive, proactive strategies such as praising positive behavior rather than calling attention to misbehavior; and 5) spending a minimal amount of time on behavior management issues (Emmer & Strough, 2001; Pianta et al., 2004). At the low end of this dimension, classrooms are chaotic with very few consistently enforced rules and a great deal of student misbehavior.

Most of the research on behavior management was conducted by process-product researchers in the 1970s and 1980s with studies consistently showing that classrooms with positive behavior management tend to have students who make greater academic progress (Good & Grouws, 1977; Soar & Soar, 1979). Intervention studies suggest that teachers who adopt these types of practices after training are more likely than teachers in control groups to have students who are engaged and learning (Emmer & Strough, 2001; Evertson, Emmer, Sanford, & Clements, 1983; Evertson & Harris, 1999). Surprisingly, researchers have yet to examine the extent to which these specific behavioral strategies are associated with the more recent concept of self-regulated learning behaviors, although prior work would suggest clear linkages.

Productivity   In productive classrooms, teachers not only are effective managers of behavior but also are well organized, spend a minimal amount of time on basic management activities such as taking attendance or passing out and collecting homework, and are prepared for instructional activities so that little time is lost in transition. A highly productive classroom may resemble a well-oiled machine in which everyone in the classroom seems to know what is expected of him- or herself and how to go about doing it (Pianta et al., 2004). In contrast, when teachers do not efficiently manage time, students may spend extraordinary amounts of time looking for materials, waiting for the next activity, or simply sitting around.

Early work by process–product researchers focused attention on the importance of time management, providing consistent evidence that students are most engaged in productive classrooms and that this engagement is, in turn, directly associated with student learning (Brophy & Evertson, 1976; Coker, Medley, & Soar, 1980; Good & Grouws, 1977; Stallings, 1975; Stallings, Cory, Fairweather, & Needels, 1978). Several more recent studies suggest that productive teachers spend more time creating efficient routines at the beginning of the school year and that this early investment pays off for students and teachers by enabling them to spend less time in transition and more time in child-managed activities later in the school year (Bohn, Roehrig, & Pressley, 2004; Cameron, Connor, & Morrison, 2005).

Instructional Learning Formats   For students to learn, not only must they have something to do but also they must be effectively engaged and interested in the instructional activities provided to them (Yair, 2000). Although many of the other dimensions described in the CLASS Framework are hypothesized to have an indirect effect on student engagement, instructional learning formats focus directly on the extent to which teachers provide interesting activities, instruction, centers, and materials and facilitate activities so that students are actively engaged in instructional opportunities. Consistent with constructivist theories that guide much of early childhood practice (Bowman & Stott, 1994; Bruner, 1996; Rogoff, 1990; Vygotsky, 1978), in which teachers provide high-quality learning formats, students are not just passively engaged in learning but are active participants in it. In classrooms low on this dimension, teachers may rely on one format, typically lecture, and fail to provide materials and activities that will keep students engaged. A classroom's placement along this dimension is not solely contingent on the type of instruction or number of materials a teacher uses but rather how effectively the teacher is able to use instruction and materials to engage students (Rimm-Kaufman, La Paro, Downer, & Pianta, 2005). For example, a classroom of 4-year-olds may be mesmerized by an effective whole group lesson or, alternately, can be minimally engaged during center time if the centers are not interesting and adults are not actively facilitating to scaffold children's play-based learning (Bodrova & Leong, 2003).

Evidence for Children's Exposure to Effectively Managed Classrooms
As with emotional supports, findings from the NICHD SECCYD and NCEDL MS/SWEEP studies suggest that the average student is exposed to classroom management of mid-range quality. Across studies, ratings on behavior management scales were toward the high end of the mid-range (see Table 4.3), suggesting that teachers, on average, use a mix of proactive and reactive behavior management strategies and spend limited amounts of time on behavior management (Early et al., 2005; Hamre, La Paro, et al., 2006; NICHD ECCRN, 2002, 2005). In third grade, for example, the average child was disciplined by his or her teacher, individually or as a part of a group, in only 2% of observed intervals (NICHD ECCRN, 2005). Consistent with the instructional time use data reported above, classrooms in these studies were moderately productive, providing children with instructional activities during most of

the day but with substantial time spent in management, transition, and other noninstructional activities. Ratings on instructional learning formats, or the degree to which teachers use effective strategies to engage children, are somewhat lower in preschool and kindergarten (see Table 4.3), the only time points at which this dimension was measured through qualitative ratings. Frequency data from third grade provide commensurate evidence on student engagement. The average third grader was observed to be at least passively engaged in instructional activities for an average of 67% of observed intervals across the school day (not including lunch and recess), a percentage consistent with the moderate ratings made on qualitative scales. More active engagement was much more infrequent (NICHD ECCRN, 2005).

INSTRUCTIONAL SUPPORTS

The previous sections discussed the ways in which classrooms' provision of nurturing and supportive emotional environments and clear and consistent organizational systems may provide young students with opportunities to learn. These two broad areas set the stage for what most consider the main goal of schooling—to educate children. The assessment of effective learning opportunities requires attending to the nature and quality of instructional interactions in the classroom. Instructional methods in early childhood and elementary classrooms have been put in the spotlight in recent years as the result of three interrelated factors. First, evidence of the significance and malleability of children's early learning, as highlighted by the White House Summit on Early Childhood Cognitive Development in the summer of 2001, is increasing. Second, more effort has been placed on the translation of cognitive science, learning, and developmental research to educational environments. For example, the exemplary work of the National Research Council series *How Students Learn* (Donovan & Branstord, 2005) summarizes research across disciplines to emphasize how specific teaching strategies can enhance young children's learning (Bransford et al., 1999). A third force is a shift in expectations for the academic outputs of early education and elementary classrooms (Neuman & Roskos, 2005). Third grade marks the first point at which young children are tested under the No Child Left Behind (NCLB) Act of 2001 (PL 107-110), placing extraordinary pressure on teachers to adequately prepare students for these tests. As more preschools are moved into elementary schools, this push-down of testing and standards is occurring across the preschool to third-grade years (Neuman & Roskos, 2005).

The theoretical foundation for the CLASS conceptualization of instructional supports comes primarily from research on children's cognitive and language development (e.g., Catts, Fey, Zhang, & Tomblin, 1999; Fujiki, Brinton, & Clarke, 2002; Romberg, Carpenter, & Dremock, 2005; Taylor et al., 2003; Vygotsky, 1991; Wharton-McDonald, Pressley, & Hampston, 1998). This literature highlights the distinction between simply learning facts and gaining usable knowledge that is based on learning how facts are interconnected, organized, and conditioned across one another (Bransford et al., 1999; Mayer, 2002). A child's cognitive and language development is contingent on the opportunities adults provide to express existing skills and scaffold more complex ones (Davis & Miyake, 2004; Skibbe, Behnke, & Justice, 2004; Vygotsky, 1991). The development of metacognitive skills, or the awareness and understanding of one's thinking processes, is also critical to children's academic development (Veenman, Kok, & Blöte, 2005; Williams, Blythe, & White, 2002). As with the other CLASS domains, interactions between adults and children are the key mechanism through which these opportunities are provided to children in the early years of schooling. Thus, CLASS instructional supports do not focus on the content of curriculum or learning activities but rather on the ways in which teachers implement these to effectively support cognitive and academic development.

The CLASS Framework further differentiates between general and content-specific instructional supports. General instructional supports are those that are relevant and observable across grades and content areas, including concept development, quality of feedback, and language modeling (see Table 4.2). Content-specific instructional supports, in contrast, describe strategies for teaching students particular skills and knowledge such as reading, math, or science. The definition of high-quality content-specific instructional supports is much more contingent on intended learning goals and therefore may be more variable from grade to grade and even within grade depending on the skills and background of students (Morrison & Connor, 2002; Torgesen, 2002). It is beyond the scope of this chapter to describe evidence for content-specific instructional supports in detail; therefore, the next section focuses on general supports and provides a brief overview of content-specific instructional supports, referring readers to related work for more information.

General Instructional Supports

Concept Development   Concept development describes the instructional behaviors, conversations, and activities that teachers use to help stimulate students' higher order thinking skills (Pianta et al., 2004). In an extension of Bloom and colleagues' *Taxonomy of Educational Objectives* (Bloom, Engelhart, Furst, Hill, & Krathwohl, 1956), Mayer (2002) offered a helpful description of the teaching and learning practices associated with the development of these skills. According to Mayer (2002), learning requires not only the acquisition of knowledge (retention) but also the ability to obtain and apply this knowledge in new situations (transfer). Teachers can facilitate this transfer process by providing students with opportunities to understand (build connections between new and previous knowledge), apply (use procedures and knowledge to help solve new problems) analyze (divide information into meaningful parts), evaluate (make conclusions based on criteria or standards), and create (put pieces of knowledge together to produce new ideas). Importantly, at the high end of this dimension, teachers are opportunists who not only plan activities in ways that will stimulate higher order thinking but also take advantage of the moment-to-moment opportunities within their daily interactions to push students toward deeper thinking. All of these processes are in contrast to what is observed in classrooms low on concept development in which there is a focus on remembering facts or simple tasks in which students must recognize or recall information.

Teachers who use concept development practices tend to have students who make greater achievement gains (Romberg et al., 2005; Taylor et al., 2003; Wharton-McDonald, Pressley, & Hampston, 1998). As noted by Brophy (1986), greater achievement gains do not require that all of a teacher's questions are higher level questions but rather that teachers use higher level questions in balance to help focus student attention on the process of learning rather than solely on the product. In one recent study, Taylor and colleagues (2003) examined the role of these teacher practices in reading development among children in 88 high-poverty classrooms (1st to 5th grade) across the United States. They observed in classrooms three times over the course of the year and examined growth in a randomly selected nine students per classroom. Their observations consisted of mixed methods in which they collected quantitative information on the types and frequency of questions used by teachers, as well as detailed qualitative information on teacher practices. Results suggested that children in classrooms in which teachers emphasized higher order thinking skills through questioning and activities, displayed more reading growth over the course of the year.

Quality of Feedback   In order to get the most benefit from the instructional opportunities described above, students need feedback about their learning. Feedback is a term used in education to refer to a broad range of teachers' interactions with students in which the teacher provides some information back to the student about his or her performance or effort. Research on feedback has typically focused on praise (Brophy & Evertson, 1976; Stallings, 1975), behavioral feedback (citations), or attributional feedback, in which teachers make statements to students attributing their performance to either ability (e.g., "You did this well because you are a good reader") or effort (e.g., "You did this well because you worked hard") (Burnett, 2003; Dohrn & Bryan, 1994; Mueller & Dweck, 1998). Although the CLASS Framework definition includes these forms of feedback, the focus is on *instructional feedback* or feedback that provides students with specific information about the content or process of learning. High-quality feedback is described as communications from teachers that provide students with specific information about not only whether they are correct (Brophy, 1986) but also how they might get to the correct answer. Teachers providing high-quality feedback provide frequent feedback loops, or back and forth exchanges in which a teacher responds to an initial student comment by engaging with the student, or group of students, in a sustained effort to reach deeper understanding (Pianta et al., 2004). An example of a feedback loop occurred during the following exchange as a preschool class discussed a book on shadows:

Teacher:	What do you think made this shadow?
Various children:	A thing. A boy. A girl. A girl and a doll.
Teacher:	Hmm. Hannah, why do you think it's a girl?
Hannah:	The arm.
Teacher:	Well, but don't boys have arms, too?
Hannah:	And the hair.
Teacher to class:	What do you notice about the hair?
Cordesia:	It's a girl's hair.
Teacher:	But how do you know?
Various children:	Pony tails. Long. It is long hair.
Teacher:	Oh, so you think it is a girl because she has long ponytails? Let's turn the page and find out.

Most research on feedback has focused on quantity rather than quality. For example, within a group of elementary, middle, and secondary Kentucky schools, those identified as successful in reducing the achievement gap between White and African American students had teachers who were more likely to provide frequent corrective and immediate feedback to students (Meehan et al., 2003). The most direct evidence for the effect of quality of feedback on student learning comes from work conducted as a part of the NICHD and NCEDL studies. In these studies, instructional composites that included the quality of concept development and feedback offered in classrooms, were associated with gains in literacy and language across the preschool and kindergarten years (Howes et al., 2005) and a closing of the achievement gap among first-grade students coming from disadvantaged backgrounds (Hamre & Pianta, 2005).

Language Modeling   Children's ability to navigate the instructional and social opportunities in classrooms is dependent in large part on their language skills (Catts, Fey, Zhang, & Tomblin, 1999; Fujiki, Brinton, & Clarke, 2002). Language Modeling describes the degree to which teachers engage students in conversations that promote the development of specific language skills such as social language and pragmatics (Ninio & Snow, 1999; Whitehurst, Falco, Lonigan, et al., 2002), vocabulary (Justice, 2002; Penno, Wilkinson, & Moore, 2002), and narrative skills (Catts, Fey, Zhang, & Tomblin, 1999; Zevenbergen, Whitehurst, & Zevenbergen, 2003). In classrooms offering high levels of language modeling, teachers often converse with students, ask many open-ended questions, repeat or extend children's responses, and use a variety of words, including more advanced language that is explicitly linked to words the students already know. Although teacher and student talk in these classrooms is mixed, teachers have a clear and intentional effort to promote children's language use, including explicit attempts to facilitate peer conversations (Justice, Mashburn, Hamre, & Pianta, 2006; Pianta et al., 2004). At the low end, classrooms are dominated by teacher talk, and children's utterances are rarely attended or responded to in any meaningful way.

Children exposed to high-quality language modeling, at home and at school, display more positive language development (Catts et al., 1999; Justice, 2002; Ninio & Snow, 1999; Penno et al., 2002; Reese & Cox, 1999; Schuele, Rice, & Wilcox, 1995; Whitehurst et al., 1988; Zevenbergen, et al., 2003) which, in turn, is associated with more positive social adjustment (Hempel & Siperstien, 1990; Pianta & Nimetz, 1991) and greater reading abilities (Catts et al., 1999). In one example of research on part of language modeling, specifically using advanced language, Justice, Meier, and Walpole (2005) tested the degree to which kindergarten children's exposure to new words through storybook reading led to increases in vocabulary. Results suggest that when children are explicitly introduced to new words through providing a definition (e.g., a marsh is a very wet place where there are wetlands covered with grasses) and using the new word in a supportive context (e.g., we took a boat through the marsh and we saw lots of birds and alligators), they show greater vocabulary development relative to a comparison group (Justice et al., 2005). In contrast, simple exposure to new words through book reading was not associated with significant vocabulary gains.

Evidence for Children's Exposure to General Instructional Supports   In stark contrast to findings on emotional supports and classroom management, evidence consistently shows that students are exposed to low-quality instructional supports in early childhood and elementary classrooms. Across studies and grades, average scores on scales measuring concept development and feedback are in the low range (see Table 4.3). As with any rating system, placement on the continuum of instructional supports entirely depends on the metric and definitions used. To aid in interpretation of these findings, Table 4.4 provides an overview of the definitions of low, moderate, and high concept development as defined by the CLASS measure (Pianta et al., 2004). As exemplified by this table, the average preschool and kindergarten classroom, rated as about a two on this dimension (Early et al., 2005; Hamre, La Paro, et al., 2006), offers a consistent focus on rote learning, few opportunities for students to engage in analysis and reasoning, and a failure to link current learning to previously learned concepts or relate information to students' lives. Findings based on these ratings from preschool and kindergarten

Table 4.4. Description of low-, moderate-, and high-concept development using the CLASS framework

	Low (1, 2)	Moderate (3, 4, 5)	High (6, 7)
Higher order thinking[a] and and cognition versus rote learning[b]	Activities and discussions in this classroom focus on getting students to give the correct answer or other forms of rote learning or recitation	Activities and discussions in this classroom sometimes focus on getting students to give the right answer and other times on developing higher order thinking skills and cognition.	Activities and discussions in this classroom consistently and intentionally focus on developing higher order thinking skills and cognition.
Analysis and reasoning	The teacher does not use discussions and activities that encourage analysis and reasoning, such as sequencing, compare/contrast, and problem solving.	The teacher occasionally uses discussions and activities that encourage analysis and reasoning, such as sequencing, compare/contrast, and problem solving.	The teacher often uses discussions and activities that encourage analysis and reasoning, such as sequencing, compare/contrast, and problem solving.
Hypothesis testing	The teacher fails to use discussions and activities that promote prediction, experimentation, and brainstorming.	The teacher occasionally uses discussions and activities that promote prediction, experimentation, and brainstorming.	The teacher often uses discussions and activities that promote prediction, experimentation, and brainstorming.
Integration with previous concept	The teacher fails to link current activities to previous concepts or activities—concepts are presented independent of students' previous learning.	The teacher sometimes links current activities to previous concepts or activities and at other times presents concepts independent of students' previous learning.	The teacher consistently links current activities to previous concepts or activities.
Connections to the real world	The teacher does not relate concepts to the real world of students' lives.	The teacher makes some attempts to relate concepts to the real world of students' lives.	The teacher consistently relates concepts to the real world of students' lives.

[a]Higher order thinking skills include (but are not limited to) understanding, interpreting, classifying, analyzing, evaluating, and problem solving.
[b]Rote learning focuses on memorization of material and facts as well as repetitive practice of basic skills.

are corroborated by data from time-sampling methods in third-grade classrooms, which revealed that students are exposed to rote learning (compared with analysis and inference) at a ratio of 13:1 (NICHD ECCRN, 2005). National data on language modeling are not available, but in a recent geographically and economically diverse statewide sample, the typical state-funded preschool program offered language supports at a similarly low level (Justice et al., 2006).

The ability to examine shifts in instructional support across grades is severely constrained by inconsistency in measurement of instructional dimensions within and across studies, but conservative interpretation of available evidence suggests that there are no dramatic increases in instructional quality from preschool to third grade (Early et al., 2005; k-report; NICHD ECCRN, 2002, 2005). Thus, across the early grades of school, children are rarely exposed to teaching strategies intended to stimulate higher order thinking and rarely get feedback beyond being told that they are correct or incorrect. Consistent with findings in the other domains of learning opportunities, there is a high degree of variability in children's exposure to instructional supports across studies (NICHD ECCRN, 2002, 2005).

Content-Specific Instructional Supports

Content-specific instructional supports are those intended to promote a specific content area such as early literacy, reading, math, or science. Brief summaries of work on early literacy/reading and math are provided next. As noted previously, however, it is beyond the scope of this chapter to discuss content-specific instructional supports in great detail, and readers are referred to reviews of findings elsewhere.

Early Literacy, Reading, and Language Arts Instructional Support   After a long debate among researchers and practitioners about whole language versus phonics-based reading instruction, there is general consensus that a balanced approach to reading and early literacy instruction—offering explicit instruction in the areas of phonetics, fluency, reading comprehension, oral language, spelling, and writing (Juel & Minden-Cupp, 2000; Foorman, Francis, Fletcher, Schatschneider, & Mehta, 1998; Torgesen, 2002) within a meaningful context (Lane, Pullen, Eisele, & Jordan, 2002; Wadlington, 2000)—produces the greatest academic gains (National Reading Panel [NRP], 2000; Snow, Burns, & Griffin, 1998; Strickland, Snow, Griffin, Burns, & McNamara, 2002). Several seminal works have pulled together research on reading development and teaching to provide teachers and other practitioners with comprehensive, research-based information on effective practice (NRP, 2000; Snow, Burns, & Griffin, 1998; Strickland, Snow, Griffin, Burns, & McNamara, 2002). Although reaching this consensus may not have been easy, the fields of early literacy and reading research offer a model for ways in which research on learning and teaching can inform one another (Lyon, 2002; NRP, 2000; Snow, Burns, & Griffin, 1998; Torgesen, 2002).

Math and Science Instructional Support   Although there is much less knowledge and consensus about the most appropriate instructional supports for math and science instruction in the early years of school, several researchers have developed frameworks suggesting ways to develop effective curricula and teaching practices in this area (Clements, 2004; Donovan & Bransford, 2005; Ginsburg & Golbeck, 2004; NRC, 2005). Two reports from the National Research Council, based on a review of the best available evidence, lay a foundation for future work in this area. *Adding It Up* (NRC, 2001) defined five interrelated areas of mathematical development for elementary-age children: conceptual understanding, procedural fluency, strategic competence, adaptive reasoning, and productive disposition. As a part of the *How Students Learn* series (Donovan & Bransford, 2005), specific teaching principles were mapped onto these student goals, including engaging students' preconceptions, teaching factual knowledge and conceptual frameworks, and encouraging a metacognitive approach to enable student monitoring. Within each principle, more specific teaching strategies are provided. These principles and teaching strategies, as applied to early childhood and elementary classrooms, form the basis for future research in young children's mathematical learning.

Evidence for Children's Exposure to Content-Specific Instructional Supports   Although there is a dearth of national-level information on the quality of content-specific instruction in early childhood and elementary classrooms, three consistent findings suggest the unlikelihood that young children are consistently being exposed to high-quality, content-specific instructional supports in the classroom. First, as discussed previously, in all areas except reading, children are rarely exposed to any content-specific instruction, regardless of quality (Early et al., 2005; Hamre, La Paro, et al., 2006; NICHD ECCRN, 2002, 2005). Second, there is a high degree of variability in curricula used among early childhood and elementary teachers (Early et al., 2005), and very few available curricula in areas such as math, reading, and science have strong empirical support (Whitehurst, 2003). Finally, evidence indicates that early childhood and elementary teachers lack content knowledge, particularly in the areas of math and science, making it unlikely that they can effectively teach these areas (Appleton, 2003; Baroody & Coslick, 1998; Garbett, 2003). Although these findings are consistent with the assumption of low quality of content-specific instructional supports, national-level data are needed to provide more definitive information on children's exposure to these important learning opportunities in early childhood and elementary classrooms.

CHILDREN'S EXPOSURE ACROSS DOMAINS OF LEARNING OPPORTUNITIES

Simply describing distributions of the classroom quality dimensions along a 1–7 scale fails to adequately convey a picture of the overall classroom environments that students are likely to experience in the early years of school. Several investigators have used a statistical procedure called cluster analysis to identify descriptive profiles of classrooms, looking across the various dimensions to see how they tend to co-occur, or cluster, in large national samples of classrooms. (LoCasale-Crouch et al., in press; Stuhlman & Pianta, 2006). Among a sample of 676 state-funded preschool classrooms in the NCEDL MS and SWEEP studies, five core profiles were empirically identified and validated (see Figure 4.2). Approximately 15% of the classrooms displayed consistently high levels of emotional support and classroom organization and relatively high (compared to the mean) levels of instructional support. At the other extreme, nearly 19% of classrooms had low levels across all three domains. The rest of classrooms fell into three profiles characterized by ratings falling between the high and low-quality profiles. These findings are consistent with those reported by Stuhlman and Pianta (2005) in a sample of first-grade classrooms from the NICHD SECC and provide strong evidence that across the United States, early education and elementary classrooms are far from a standardized intervention and that young children are exposed to dramatically different daily classroom interactions depending on where they go to school.

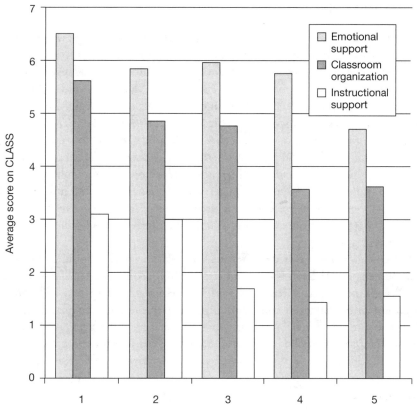

Figure 4.2. Profiles of classroom learning opportunities in state-funded preschool programs. (Source: LoCasale-Crouch et al., 2006.)

REFINING MODELS OF LEARNING OPPORTUNITIES

As described using the CLASS Framework, strong and consistent evidence shows that, on average, children are exposed to moderate levels of emotional support and classroom organization and relatively low levels of instructional support during the early years of school. Yet, a key component of bioecological theory as discussed by Bronfenbrenner and Morris (1998) is the understanding that the ultimate results of processes, such as classroom learning opportunities, are dependent on a complex interaction of those processes with characteristics of the people involved, the setting or context, and time. Assuming that the learning opportunities described previously operate in the same way for all students, teachers, or classrooms would be inconsistent with the principles on which the CLASS Framework is based. Rather, they describe general classroom processes involved in children's early development and thereby form the basis of numerous examinations of this complex process-person-context-time model (Bronfenbrenner & Morris, 1998) as applied to classroom and school settings. Questions stemming from this work may offer insights into larger developmental theories (Pianta, 2006) and have many potential implications for the ways in which findings on classroom processes are translated into practice. The following section highlights a few examples of research into the ways in which children's response to particular learning opportunities depends on characteristics of themselves, their cultural context, and time.

Individualized Supports

Questions of moderation are embedded in all educational research: For whom do particular types of classroom interactions matter most? Are different types of interactions needed to produce optimal development for different types of children? In the instructional arena, there is strong evidence of moderation. For example, Morrison and Connor (2002) demonstrated that children at risk of reading difficulties at the beginning of first grade (identified on the basis of test scores) benefited from high levels of teacher-directed explicit language instruction—the more teacher-directed, explicit instruction they received, the higher were their word decoding skills at the end of first grade. In contrast, teacher-directed explicit instruction made no difference in decoding skills for children with already high skills on this dimension upon school entry. Highly skilled children made the strongest gains in classrooms with more child-led, literacy-related activities. These findings have been replicated in preschool (Connor, 2005) and third-grade (Connor, Morrison, & Petrella, 2004) classrooms.

Moderating effects are evident in social processes as well (Hamre & Pianta, 2005; Ladd & Burgess, 2001; Rimm-Kaufman et al., 2002). For example, Rimm-Kaufman et al. (2002) examined whether teacher sensitivity predicted kindergarten children's behavior for groups of socially bold and wary children, with the bold children demonstrating high levels of off-task behavior and negative interactions with peers and teachers. Although teachers' sensitivity and child classroom behavior had no relation among the socially wary children, socially bold children who had more sensitive teachers were more self-reliant and displayed fewer negative and off-task behaviors than did bold children with less sensitive teachers.

Cultural Variation

Teaching is embedded in a cultural context, and this context may shape the meaning of observed behaviors (Rogoff, 2003). One good example of this comes from work by Inagaki, Morita, & Hatano (1999), who examined mathematics lessons in Japanese and American elementary classrooms. They found significant differences in the ways in which teachers provided feedback during discussions, with Japanese teachers much more likely to ask students to explain their thinking (when correct or incorrect) as a way of providing feedback to others and American teachers much more likely to give directive feedback. The effectiveness of these differing feedback strategies depended on the cultural context to the extent that children in the Japanese classrooms were more accustomed to listening to and learning from peers than were American students (Bransford et al., 1999). Of course, these variations occur *within* cultures as well, as highlighted by Johnson and colleagues (2003) in their commentary on studying the effects of child care on children of color. For example, these authors suggested that one aspect of quality that is not typically measured in studies of early childhood environments, but which may be critical to the positive development of young children of color, is the degree to which family values and practices and those experienced by children in out-of-home environments are consistent. More research is greatly needed into ways in which cultural backgrounds may moderate the effects of learning opportunities on children's development.

Developmental Changes

Refinement of the CLASS Framework also requires greater attention to developmental changes across the early childhood and elementary period. A 4-year-old's cognitive and social abilities are very different from those of an 8-year-old, and these changes are likely to have important implications for the provision of learning opportunities across this time period. Although the CLASS dimensions were developed with the intention of describing classroom processes that may be important across the early grades of school, important questions remain about the ways in which these processes may operate differently for older and younger children. For example, the degree to which autonomy support may facilitate student motivation and engagement may change as children mature, and although evidence suggests that instructional supports are important across the preschool to third-grade period, the threshold for what is necessary to promote academic development (e.g., a 3 versus a 5 on a 7-point scale) may vary across grades.

IMPLICATIONS

NCLB has focused attention on students' learning opportunities throughout their school careers, but classroom interactions in the early years of school may be particularly critical because of their potential to change trajectories of children's school careers (Entwisle, Alexander, & Olson, 2005; Hamre & Pianta, 2005). The learning opportunities described previously, if broadly available, could be viewed as a mechanism for increasing student achievement at scale. Unfortunately, when learning opportunities are defined in this way, as the provision of consistent access to high-quality interactions with teachers across the early years of schooling, the odds are stacked against students actually getting the classroom supports necessary for their success. In nearly every study that includes a large number of classrooms, the degree of variability in the quality of classroom experience and interactions is notable (Early et al., 2005; NICHD ECCRN, 2002, 2005). This variability permeates all types of classrooms, those in public and private schools and those in suburban, rural, and inner-city districts.

The problems of inconsistent exposure to high quality classrooms are compounded by clear evidence of inequity—students from disadvantaged backgrounds are more likely to be exposed to poor quality classroom supports (Pianta et al., 2005). Further troubling is evidence that even the student lucky enough to experience a high-quality classroom one year is very unlikely to be systematically exposed to high quality over a period of years (NICHD ECCRN, 2005). Thus, the current state of early childhood and elementary education falls far short of providing a systematic intervention—too few of the students who are in greatest need of high-quality learning opportunities receive them and the few that do are unlikely to receive them consistently.

For policy makers and educational administrators, the findings reviewed here, particularly related to low levels of instructional quality and inconsistent exposure to learning opportunities, could spark an interest in finding solutions that focus on raising and leveling the quality of learning opportunities available to children in preschool and elementary school. Although we have a lot to learn about how to do this most effectively, we do know that it will require more than just changing policies, such as increasing teacher educational requirements or decreasing class sizes. Across the studies reviewed in this chapter are small, if any, effects of teacher qualifications on observed classroom quality, and most important, there continues to be a high degree of variability in classroom quality even when observing in classrooms where teachers have the highest levels of education and experience and work with small numbers of high-income children (Mashburn et al., 2005; NICHD ECCRN, 2005; Pianta et al., 2005). Some programs, however, are explicitly integrating research on learning opportunities into policy and professional development systems. Two such programs are described briefly below to illustrate novel approaches to this challenge—one that focuses on making changes at the policy level and another that focuses on new systems of professional development for teachers. Readers should be cautioned that these programs are new and, although based on research, have yet to produce empirical evidence of effectiveness. However, they are good examples of the ways in which basic research can be applied to and tested within school-based settings.

On the policy side, the creators of the universal preschool program Los Angeles Universal Preschool (LAUP) have built classroom observations into the rating system used to provide funding. To be eligible for funding under LAUP, preschool centers must receive at least 3 stars in a 5-star system for rating the quality of preschool programs. Ratings of observed quality are included as one piece of this 5-star system and thus policy makers are directly regulating classroom interactions rather than simply relying on proxies such as teacher degree status or student–teacher ratios. Similar programs are available across the United States, including Georgia's Standards of Care program and Arkansas's School-Age Quality Initiative Project.

Another novel solution is being tested in a randomized control study conducted at the University of Virginia (Downer, Kraft-Sayre, & Pianta, 2006). Teachers in this project have access to a web site (MyTeachingPartner.com) offering hundreds of video examples of real teachers implementing high-quality classroom interactions illustrating CLASS Framework dimensions. Teachers in randomly selected districts are also supported by consultants who view and edit videotape from the teachers' classrooms, place it on a secure web site for teachers to view, respond to a series of prompts, and then meet with teachers via web-based video conference software. The edited video and prompts highlight interactions in the classroom exemplifying positive examples of CLASS Framework dimensions, as well as areas for improvement. The hypothesis of this work is that focusing professional development resources on teachers' actual interactions with children and implementation of activities, guided by validated indicators of those interactions, is in the end a more powerful tool for changing those interactions than is requiring them to take a course or attend a workshop.

CONCLUSION

Clearly, much still needs to be learned about the nature of children's experiences in the early years of schooling and how best to maximize these experiences for all children. The framework presented in this chapter lays the foundation for a body of empirical work that may help refine knowledge on children's learning opportunities. However, the simple accumulation of knowledge is insufficient to help children and teachers in U.S. schools. As theories of development in classroom contexts advance, researchers are greatly needed who are able to collaborate effectively with schools to translate this research into practical, at-scale interventions and then submit these interventions to rigorous evaluation. Only through this ongoing collaboration of researchers, policy makers, and practitioners can the knowledge we have about children's experiences during these critical early years of schooling actually make a difference.

REFERENCES

Ainsworth, M.D., Blehar, M.C., Waters, E., & Wall, D. (1978). *Patterns of attachment: A psychological study of the strange situation.* Hillsdale, NJ: Lawrence Erlbaum Associates.

Alexander, K.L., & Entwisle, D.R. (1988). Achievement in the first 2 years of school: Patterns and processes. *Monographs of the Society for Research in Child Development, 53*(2), 157.

Anderson, L., Evertson, C., & Emmer, E. (1980). Dimensions in classroom management derived from recent research. *Journal of Curriculum Studies, 12,* 343–356.

Appleton, K. (2003). How do beginning primary school teachers cope with science? Toward an understanding of science teaching practice. *Research in Science Education, 33,* 1–25.

Asher, S.R., Parkhurst, J.T., Hymel, S., & Williams, G.A. (1990). Peer rejection and loneliness in childhood. In S.R. Asher & J.D. Coie (Eds.), *Peer rejection in childhood* (pp. 253–273). New York: Cambridge University Press.

Astleitner, H. (2005). Principles of effective instruction—General standards for teachers and instructional designers. *Journal of Instructional Psychology, 32*(1), 3–8.

Barnett, W.S. (1996). *Lives in the balance: Age 27 benefit-cost analysis of the High/Scope Perry Preschool Program.* Ypsilanti, MI: High/Scope Press.

Baroody, A.J., & Coslick, R.T. (1998). *Fostering children's mathematical power. An investigative approach to k–8 mathematics instruction.* New Jersey: Lawrence Erlbaum Associates.

Birch, S.H., & Ladd, G.W. (1996). Interpersonal relationships in the school environment and children's early school adjustment. In K. Wentzel, & J. Juvonen (Eds.), *Social motivation: Understanding children's school adjustment* (pp. 199–225). New York: Cambridge University Press.

Birch, S.H., & Ladd, G.W. (1998). Children's interpersonal behaviors and the teacher–child relationship. *Developmental Psychology, 34,* 934–946.

Blair, C. (2002). School readiness: Integrating cognition and emotion in a neurobiological conceptualization of children's functioning at school entry. *American Psychologist, 57*(2), 111–127.

Blair, C. (2003). Behavioral inhibition and behavioral activation in young children: Relations with self-regulation and adaptation to preschool in children attending Head Start. *Developmental Psychobiology, 42*(3), 301–311.

Bloom, B.S., Engelhart, M.D., Furst, E.J., Hill, W.H., & Krathwohl, D.R. (1956). *Taxonomy of educational objectives: The classification of educational goals. Handbook 1: Cognitive domain.* New York: David McKay.

Bodrova, E., & Leong, D.J. (2003). The importance of being playful. *Educational Leadership, 60,* 50–53.

Bogard, K., & Takanishi, R. (2005). PK–3: An aligned and coordinated approach to education for children 3 to 8 years old. *Social Policy Report: A publication of the Society for Research in Child Development, 19*(3), 1–24.

Bohn, C.M., Roehrig, A.D., & Pressley, M. (2004). The first days of school in the classrooms of two more effective and four less effective primary-grades teachers. *Elementary School Journal, 104*(4), 269–287.

Bowlby, J. (1969). *Attachment and loss, vol. 1: Attachment.* New York: Basic Books.

Bowman, B., & Stott, F. (1994). Understanding development in a cultural context: The challenge for teachers. In B. Mallory & R. New (Eds.), *Diversity and developmentally appropriate practices: Challenges for early childhood education* (pp. 19–34). New York: Teachers College Press.

Bransford, J., Brown, A.L., & Cocking, R.R. (1999). *How people learn: Brain, mind, experience, and school.* Washington, DC: National Academies Press.

Bredekamp, S., & Copple, C. (Eds.). (1997). *Developmentally appropriate practice in early childhood programs* (Rev. ed.). Washington, DC: National Association for the Education of Young Children.

Bronfenbrenner, U., & Morris, P.A. (1998). The ecology of developmental processes. In W. Damon & R.M. Lerner (Eds.), *Handbook of child psychology: Vol. 1. Theoretical models of human development* (5th ed., pp. 993–1029). New York: John Wiley & Sons.

Brophy, J. (1986). Teacher influences on student achievement. *American Psychologist, 41*(10), 1069–1077.

Brophy, J., & Evertson, C. (1976). *Learning from teaching: A developmental perspective.* Boston, MA: Allyn and Bacon.

Brophy, J.E., & Good, T.L. (1986). Teacher behavior and student achievement. In M.C. Wittrock (Ed.), *Handbook of research on teaching* (3rd edition, pp. 328–375). New York: Macmillan.

Bruner, J. (1996). *The culture of education.* Cambridge, MA: Harvard University Press.

Buhs, E.S., & Ladd, G.W. (2001). Peer rejection as antecedent of young children's school adjustment: An examination of mediating processes. *Developmental Psychology, 37,* 550–560.

Burnett, P.C. (2003). The impact of teacher feedback on student self-talk and self-concept in reading and mathematics. *Journal of Classroom Interaction, 38*(1), 11–16.

Cameron, C.E., Connor, C.M., & Morrison, F.J. (2005). Effects of variation in teacher organization on classroom functioning. *Journal of School Psychology, 43*(1), 61–85.

Cassidy, J., & Asher, S.R. (1992). Loneliness and peer relations in young children. *Child Development, 63,* 350–365.

Catts, H.W., Fey, M.E., Zhang, X., & Tomblin, J.B. (1999). Language basis of reading and reading disabilities: Evidence from a longitudinal investigation. *Scientific Studies of Reading, 3*(4), 331–361.

Clements, D. (2004). Curriculum research: Toward a framework for research based curricula. A presentation made at the Annual Meeting of AERA, San Diego, CA.

Clifford, R.M., Barbarin, O., Chang, F., Early, D., Bryant, D., Howes, C., et al. (2005). What is pre-kindergarten? Characteristics of public pre-kindergarten programs. *Applied Developmental Science, 9*(3), 126–143.

Coker, H., Medley, D.M., & Soar, R.S. (1980). How valid are expert opinions about effective teaching? *Phi Delta Kappan, 62*(2), 131–134, 149.

Conduct Problems Prevention Research Group. (1999). Initial impact of the Fast Track prevention trial for conduct problems: II. Classroom effects. *Journal of Consulting and Clinical Psychology, 67,* 648–657.

Connell, J.P., & Wellborn, J.G. (1991). Competence, autonomy, and relatedness: A motivational analysis of self-system processes. In R. Gunnar & L.A. Sroufe (Eds.), *Minnesota Symposia on Child Psychology* (Vol. 23, pp. 43–77). Hillsdale, NJ: Lawrence Erlbaum Associates.

Connor, C.M. (2005). *Individual students' differences in response to preschool literacy instruction: Effects on vocabulary, alphabet and letter-word recognition skill growth.* A presentation made at the Society for the Scientific Study of Reading, Toronto, Canada.

Connor, C.M., Morrison, F.J., & Petrella, J. (2004). Effective reading comprehension instruction: Examining child by instruction interactions. *Journal of Educational Psychology, 96*(4), 682–698.

Connor, C.M., Son, S., & Hindman, A.H. (2005). Teacher qualifications, classroom practices, family characteristics, and preschool experience: Complex effects on first graders' vocabulary and early reading outcomes. *Journal of School Psychology, 43*(4), 343–375.

Cook, T.D., Murphy, R.F., & Hunt, H.D. (2000). Comer's School Development Programs in Chicago: A theory-based evaluation. *American Educational Research Journal, 37*(2), 535–597.

Darling-Hammond, L. (1997). *Doing what matters most: Investing in quality teaching.* New York: National Committee on Teaching and America's Future.

Davis, E.A., & Miyake, N. (2004). Explorations of scaffolding in complex classroom systems. *Journal of the Learning Sciences, 13*(3), 265–272.

de Kruif, R.E.L., McWilliam, R.A., Ridley, S.M., & Wakeley, M.B. (2000). Classification of teachers' interaction behaviors in early childhood classrooms. *Early Childhood Research Quarterly, 15*(2), 247–268.

Denham, S.A., & Weissberg, R.P. (2004). Social-emotional learning in early childhood: What we know and where to go from here. In E. Chesebrough, P. King, T.P. Gullotta, & M. Bloom (Eds.), *A blueprint for the promotion of prosocial behavior in early childhood* (pp. 13–50). New York : Kluwer Academic/Plenum Publishers.

Dohrn, E., & Bryan, T. (1994). Attribution instruction. *Teaching Exceptional Children, 26*(4), 61–63.

Donovan, M.S., & Bransford, J.D. (2005). *How students learn: History, mathematics, and science in the classroom.* Washington, DC: National Academies Press.

Downer, J.T., Kraft-Sayre, M.E., & Pianta, R.C. (2006). *Ongoing, collaborative professional development with early childhood educators: Is it feasible to implement at-scale?* Manuscript submitted for publication.

Dwyer, C.A. (1994). *Development of the knowledge base for the Praxis III: Classroom performance assessments assessment criteria.* Princeton, NJ: Educational Testing Service.

Early D., Barbarin, O., Bryant, D., Burchinal, M., Chang, F., Clifford, R., et al. (2005). *Prekindergarten in eleven states: NCEDL's multistate study of pre-kindergarten and study of state-wide early education programs.* Retrieved December 1, 2005, from http://www.fpg.unc.edu/NCEDL/pdfs/SWEEP_MS_summary_final.pdf

Eccles, J., & Roeser, R. (1998). School and community influences on human development. In M.H. Bornstein & M.E. Lamb (Eds.), *Developmental psychology: An advanced textbook* (4th edition, pp. 503–554). Mahwah, NJ: Lawrence Erlbaum Associates.

Educational Testing Service. (2004). *Where we stand on teacher quality. An issue paper from ETS.* Retrieved February 15, 2006, from http://ftp.ets.org/pub/corp/position_paper.pdf

Emmer, E.T., & Strough, L. (2001). Classroom management: A critical part of educational psychology, with implications for teacher education. *Educational Psychologist, 36*(2), 103–112.

Entwisle, D.R., Alexander, K.L., & Olson, L.S. (2005). First grade and educational attainment by age 22: A new story. *American Journal of Sociology, 110*(5), 1458–1502.

Entwisle, D.R., & Hayduk, L.A. (1988). Lasting effects of elementary school. *Sociology of Education, 61,* 147–159.

Evertson, C., & Harris, A. (1999). Support for managing learning-centered classrooms: The classroom organization and management program. In H.J. Freiberg (Ed.), *Beyond behaviorism: Changing the classroom management paradigm* (pp. 59–74). Boston: Allyn & Bacon.

Evertson, C., Emmer, E., Sanford, J., & Clements, B. (1983). Improving classroom management: An experiment in elementary classrooms. *Elementary School Journal, 84,* 173–188.

Fallon, D. (2003). *Case study of a paradigm shift (The value of focusing on instruction).* Retrieved November 13, 2005, from http://www.ecs.org/clearinghouse/49/00/4900.htm

Fenstermacher, G.D., & Richardson, V. (2005). On making determinations of quality in teaching. *Teachers College Record, 107*(1), 186–213.

Foorman, B.R., Francis, D.J., Fletcher, J.M., Schatschneider, C., & Mehta, P. (1998). The role of instruction in learning to read: Preventing reading failure in at-risk children. *Educational Psychology, 90*(1), 37–55.

Fujiki, M., Brinton, B., & Clarke, D. (2002). Emotion regulation in children with specific language impairment. *Language, Speech, & Hearing Services in Schools, 33,* 102–111.

Fujiki, M., Brinton, B., Morgan, M., & Hart, C.H. (1999). Withdrawn and sociable behavior of children with language impairment. *Language, Speech, and Hearing Services in Schools, 30,* 183–195.

Fuller, B., Kagan, S.L., & Loeb, S. (2004). Child care quality: Centers and home settings that serve poor families. *Early Childhood Research Quarterly, 19*(4), 505–527.

Garbett, D. (2003). Science education in early childhood teacher education: Putting forward a case to enhance student teacher's confidence and competence. *Research in Science Education, 33,* 467–481.

Ginsburg, H.P., & Golbeck, S.L. (2004). Thoughts on the future of research on mathematics and science learning and education. *Early Childhood Research Quarterly, 19*(1), 190–200.

Good, T., and Grouws, D. (1977). Teaching effects: A process-product study of fourth grade mathematics classrooms. *Journal of Teacher Education, 28,* 49–54.

Greenberg, M.T., Weissberg, R.P., & O'Brien, M.U. (2003). Enhancing school-based prevention and youth development through coordinated social, emotional, and academic learning. *American Psychologist, 58*(6–7), 466–474.

Gronlund, G. (2001). Rigorous academics in preschool and kindergarten? Yes! Let me tell you how. *Young Children, 56,* 42–43.

Gutman, L.M., & Sulzby, E. (2000). The role of autonomy-support versus control in the emergent writing behaviors of African-American kindergarten children. *Reading Research & Instruction, 39*(2), 170–183.

Hamre, B.K., La Paro, K.M., LoCasale-Crouch, J., Pianta, R.C., Bryant, D.M., Early, D.M., et al. (2006). Children's experiences in kindergarten and stability from the preschool year. Manuscript submitted for publication.

Hamre, B.K., Mashburn, A., Pianta, R.C., Downer, J. (2006). *Building and validating a theoretical model of classroom effects on over 4,000 classrooms.* Manuscript submitted for publication.

Hamre, B.K., & Pianta, R.C. (2001). Early teacher–child relationships and the trajectory of children's school outcomes through eighth grade. *Child Development, 72*(2), 625–638.

Hamre, B.K., & Pianta, R.C. (2005). Can instructional and emotional support in the first grade classroom make a difference for children at risk of school failure? *Child Development, 76*(5), 949–967.

Hamre, B.K., Pianta, R.C., Downer, J.T., & Mashburn, A.J. (in press). Teachers' perceptions of conflict with young students: Looking beyond problem behaviors. *Social Development.*

Harms, T., Clifford, R.M., & Cryer, D. (1998). *Early childhood environment rating scale* (Rev. ed). New York: Teachers College Press.

Hempill, L., & Siperstien, G.N. (1990). Conversational competence and peer response to mildly retarded children. *Journal of Educational Psychology, 82*(1), 1–7.

Howes, C. (2000). Social-emotional classroom climate in child care, child–teacher relationships and children's second grade peer relations. *Social Development, 9,* 191–204.

Howes, C., Burchinal, M., Pianta, R., Bryant, D., Early, D., Clifford, R., et al. (2005). *Ready to learn? Children's pre-academic achievement in pre-kindergarten programs.* Manuscript submitted for publication.

Howes, C., Galinsky, E., & Kontos, S. (1998). Child care caregiver sensitivity and attachment. *Social Development, 4,* 44–61.

Howes, C., Hamilton, C.E., & Matheson, C.C. (1994). Children's relationships with peers: Differential associations with aspects of the teacher–child relationship. *Child Development, 65,* 253–263.

Hughes, J.W., Zhang, D., & Hill, C.R. (2006). Peer assessment of normative and individual teacher–student support predict social acceptance and engagement among low-achieving children. *Journal of School Psychology, 43,* 447–463.

Illinois State Board of Education. (2004). *Illinois learning standards: Social/emotional learning (SEL).* Retrieved February 16, 2006, from http://www.isbe.net/ils/social_emotional/standards.htm

Inagaki, K., Morita, E., & Hatano, G. (1999). Teaching-learning of evaluative criteria for mathematical arguments through classroom discourse: A cross-national study. *Mathematical Thinking and Learning, 1*(2), 93–111.

Johnson, D.J., Jaeger, E., Randolph, S.M., Cauce, A.M., Ward, J., & the NICHD Early Child Care Research Network. (2003). Studying the effects of early child care experiences on the development of children of color in the United States: Towards a more inclusive research agenda. *Child Development, 74,* 1227–1244.

Juel, C., & Minden-Cupp, C. (2000). Learning to read words: Linguistic units and instructional strategies. *Reading Research Quarterly, 35,* 492–498.

Justice, L.M. (2002). Word exposure conditions and preschoolers' novel word learning during shared storybook reading. *Reading Psychology, 23*(2), 87–106.

Justice, L., Mashburn, A.J., Hamre, B.K., & Pianta, R.C. (2006). *Exemplary language and literacy instruction in the pre-kindergarten classroom: Contributions of teacher qualification and experience.* Manuscript submitted for publication.

Justice, L.M., Meier, J., & Walpole, S. (2005). Learning new words from storybooks: An efficacy study with at-risk kindergartners. *Language, Speech, and Hearing Services in Schools, 36,* 17–32.

Koster, B., Brekelmans, M., & Korthagen, F. (2005). Quality requirements for teacher educators. *Teaching and Teacher Education, 21*(2), 157–176.

Kounin, J.S. (1970). *Discipline and group management in classrooms.* New York: Holt, Rinehart and Winston.

Ladd, G.W., Birch, S.H., & Buhs, E.S. (1999). Children's social and scholastic lives in kindergarten: Related spheres of influence? *Child Development, 70,* 1373–1400.

Ladd, G.W., & Burgess, K.B. (1999). Charting the relationship trajectories of aggressive, withdrawn, and aggressive/withdrawn children during early grade school. *Child Development, 70,* 910–929.

Ladd, G.W., & Burgess, K.B. (2001). Do relational risks and protective factors moderate the linkages between childhood aggression and early psychological and school adjustment? *Child Development, 72,* 1579–1601.

Ladd, G.W., Kochenderfer, B.J., & Coleman, C.C. (1997). Classroom peer acceptance, friendship, and victimization: Distinct relational systems that contribute uniquely to children's school adjustment? *Child Development, 68,* 1181–1197.

Ladd, G.W., & Troop-Gordon, W. (2003). The role of chronic peer difficulties in the development of children's psychological adjustment problems. *Child Development, 74,* 1325–1348.

Lane, H.B., Pullen, P.C., Jordan, L., & Eisele, M. (2002). Preventing reading failure: Phonological awareness assessment and instruction. *Preventing School Failure, 46,* 101–111.

Lasley, T.J., Siedentop, D., & Yinger, R. (2006). A systematic approach to improving teacher quality: The Ohio Model. *Journal of Teacher Education, 57,* 13–21.

LoCasale-Crouch, J., Konold, T., Pianta, R., Howes, C., Burchinal, M., Bryant, D., et al. (in press). Profiles of observed classroom quality in state-funded pre-kindergarten programs and association with teacher, program, and classroom characteristics. *Early Childhood Research Quarterly.*

Lynch, M., & Cicchetti, D. (1992). Maltreated children's reports of relatedness to their teachers. In R.C. Pianta (Ed.), *Relationships between children and non-parental adults: New directions in child development* (pp. 81–108). San Francisco: Jossey-Bass.

Lyon, G.R. (2002). Reading development, reading difficulties and reading instruction: Educational and public health issues. *Journal of School Psychology, 40,* 3–6.

Magnusson, D., & Stattin, H. (1998). Person-context interaction theory. In W. Damon & R.M. Lerner (Eds.), *Handbook of child psychology; Vol. 1. Theoretical models of human development* (5th ed., pp. 685–760). New York: Wiley.

Mashburn, A.J., Hamre, B.K., Downer, J.T., & Pianta, R.C. (in press). Teacher and classroom characteristics associated with teachers' ratings of pre-kindergartners' relationships and behaviors. *Journal of Psychoeducational Assessment.*

Masse, L.N., & Barnett, W.S. (2002). *A benefit-cost analysis of the Abecedarian Early Childhood Intervention.* New Brunswick, NJ: National Institute for Early Education Research, Rutgers University.

Mayer, R.E. (2002). Rote versus meaningful learning. *Theory into Practice, 41,* 226–233.

Meehan, B.T., Hughes, J.N., & Cavell, T.A. (2003). Teacher–student relationships as compensatory resources for aggressive children. *Child Development, 74,* 1145–1157.

Morrison, F.J., & Connor, C.M. (2002). Understanding schooling effects on early literacy: A working research strategy. *Journal of School Psychology, 40,* 493–500.

Mueller, C., & Dweck, C. (1998). Praise for intelligence can undermine children's motivation and performance. *Journal of Personality & Social Psychology, 75*(1), 33–52.

Muijs, D., Campbell, J., & Kyriakides, L. (2005). Making the case for differentiated teacher effectiveness: An overview of research in four key areas. *School Effectiveness and School Improvement, 16*(1), 51–70.

National Institute of Child Health and Human Development Early Child Care Research Network. (2000). Characteristics and quality of child care for toddlers and preschoolers. *Applied Developmental Science, 4,* 116–135.

National Institute of Child Health and Human Development Early Child Care Research Network. (2002).The relation of first grade classroom environment to structural classroom features, teacher, and student behaviors. *The Elementary School Journal, 102,* 367–387.

National Institute of Child Health and Human Development Early Child Care Research Network. (2003). Social functioning in first grade: Prediction from home, child care and concurrent school experience. *Child Development, 74,* 1639–1662.

National Institute of Child Health and Human Development Early Child Care Research Network. (2005). A day in third grade: A large-scale study of classroom quality and teacher and student behavior. *The Elementary School Journal, 105,* 305–323.

National Reading Panel. (2000). *Teaching children to read: An evidence-based assessment of the scientific research literature on reading and its implications for reading instruction.* Washington, DC: National Institute of Child Health and Human Development.

National Research Council. (2001). *Adding it up: Helping children learn mathematics.* Washington, DC: Center for Education.

National Research Council. (2005). *Mathematics and scientific development in early childhood: A workshop summary.* Washington, DC: The National Academies Press.

Neuman, S.B., & Roskos, K. (2005). The state of state pre-Kindergarten standards. *Early Childhood Research Quarterly, 20*(2), 125–145.

Ninio, A., & Snow, C.E. (1999). The development of pragmatics: Learning to use language appropriately. In W.C. Ritchie & T.K. Bhatia (Eds.), *Handbook of child language acquisition* (pp. 347–383). San Diego: Academic Press.

No Child Left Behind Act of 2001, PL 107-110, 115 Stat. 1425, 20 U.S.C. §§ 6301 *et seq.*

Penno, J.F., Wilkinson, I.A., & Moore, D.W. (2002). Vocabulary acquisition from teacher explanation and repeated listening to stories: Do they overcome the Matthew Effect? *Journal of Educational Psychology, 94*(1), 23–33.

Pianta, R.C. (1999). *Enhancing relationships between children and teachers.* Washington, DC: American Psychological Association.

Pianta, R.C. (2006). Teacher–child relationships and early literacy. In D. Dickinson & S. Newman (Eds.), *Handbook of Early Literacy Research* (Vol. II, pp. 149–162). New York: The Guilford Press.

Pianta, R.C, Hamre, B., & Stuhlman, M. (2003). Relationships between teachers and children. In W. Reynolds and G. Miller (Eds.), *Comprehensive Handbook of Psychology: Vol. 7. Educational Psychology* (pp. 199–234). Hoboken, NJ: John Wiley & Sons.

Pianta, R.C., Howes, C., Burchinal, M., Bryant, D., Clifford, R., Early, C., et al. (2005). Features of pre-kindergarten programs, classrooms, and teachers: Do they predict observed classroom quality and child–teacher interactions? (3), 144–159.

Pianta, R.C., La Paro, K.M., & Hamre, B.K. (2004). *Classroom assessment scoring system (CLASS).* Unpublished measure, University of Virginia.

Pianta, R.C., La Paro, K.M., Payne, C., Cox, M.J., & Bradley, R. (2002). The relation of kindergarten classroom environment to teacher, family, and school characteristics and child outcomes. *Elementary School Journal, 102*(3), 225–238.

Pianta, R.C., & Nimetz, S.L. (1991). Relationships between children and teachers: Associations with classroom and home behavior. *Journal of Applied Developmental Psychology, 12*(3), 379–393.

Pianta, R.C., Steinberg, M.S., & Rollins, K.B. (1995). The first two years of school: Teacher–child relationships and deflections in children's classroom adjustment. *Development and Psychopathology, 7,* 295–312.

Pintrich, P.R. (2000). The role of goal orientation in self-regulated learning. In M. Boekaerts, P.R. Pintrich, and M. Zeidner (Eds.), *Handbook of self-regulation* (pp. 451–502). San Diego: Academic Press.

Pressley, M., Roehrig, A., Raphael, L., Dolezal, S., Bohn, K., Mohan, L., et al. (2003). Teaching processes in elementary and secondary education. In W.M. Reynolds & G.E. Miller (Eds.), *Comprehensive handbook of psychology: Vol. 7. Educational psychology* (pp. 153–175). New York: Wiley.

Ramey, C.T., Campbell, F.A., Burchinal, M., Skinner, M.L., Gardner, D.M., & Ramey, S.L. (2000). Persistent effects of early intervention on high-risk children and their mothers. *Applied Developmental Science, 4,* 2–14.

Ramey, C.T., & Ramey, S.L. (1998). Early intervention and early experience. *American Psychologist, 53,* 109–120.

Raver, C.C. (2004). Placing emotional self-regulation in sociocultural and socioeconomic contexts. *Child Development, 75*(2), 346–353.

Reese, E., & Cox, A. (1999). Quality of adult book reading affects children's emergent literacy. *Developmental Psychology, 35*(1), 20–28.

Reynolds, A.J., Temple, J.A., Robertson, D.L., & Mann, E.A. (2002). Age 21 cost-benefit analysis of the Title I Chicago Child–Parent Centers. *Educational Evaluation and Policy Analysis, 24*(4), 267–303.

Rimm-Kaufman, S.E., Early, D.M., & Cox, M.J. (2002). Early behavioral attributes and teachers' sensitivity as predictors of competent behavior in the kindergarten classroom. *Journal of Applied Developmental Psychology, 23*(4), 451–470.

Rimm-Kaufman, S.E., La Paro, K.M., Downer, J.T., & Pianta, R.C. (2005). The contribution of classroom setting and quality of instruction to children's behavior in the kindergarten classroom. *Elementary School Journal, 105,* 377–394.

Rimm-Kaufman, S.E., & Pianta, R.C. (2005). Family–school communication in preschool and kindergarten in the context of a relationship-enhancing intervention. *Early Education and Development, 16,* 287–316.

Ritchie, S., Howes, C., Kraft-Sayre, M., & Weiser, B. (2001). Emerging academics snapshot. Unpublished measure. University of California at Los Angeles.

Rogoff, B. (1990). *Apprenticeship in thinking: Cognitive development in social context.* New York: Oxford University Press.

Rogoff, B. (2003). *The cultural nature of human development.* New York: Oxford University Press.

Romberg, T.A., Carpenter, T.P., & Dremock, F. (2005). *Understanding mathematics and science matters.* Mahwah, NJ: Lawrence Erlbaum Associates.

Ryan, R.M., & Deci, E.L. (2000). Self-determination theory and the facilitation of intrinsic motivation, social development, and well-being. *American Psychologist, 55,* 68–78.

Sanford, J., & Evertson, C. (1981). Classroom management in a low SES junior high: Three case studies. *Journal of Teacher Education, 32*(1), 34–38.

Sarama, J., & Clements, D.H. (2002). Building blocks for young children's mathematical development. *Journal of Educational Computing Research, 27*(1–2), 93–110.

Schuele, C.M., Rice, M.L., & Wilcox, K.A. (1995). Redirects: A strategy to increase peer interactions. *Journal of Speech and Hearing Research, 38,* 1319–1333.

Schunk, D.H. (2005). Self-regulated learning: The educational legacy of Paul R. Pintrich. *Educational Psychologist, 40*(2), 85–94.

Silver, R.B., Measelle, J., Essex, M., & Armstrong, J.M. (2005). Trajectories of externalizing behavior problems in the classroom: Contributions of child characteristics, family characteristics, and the teacher–child relationship during the school transition. *Journal of School Psychology, 43,* 39–60.

Skibbe, L., Behnke, M., & Justice, L.M. (2004). Parental scaffolding of children's phonological awareness skills: Interactions between mothers and their preschoolers with language difficulties. *Communication Disorders Quarterly, 25*(4), 189–203.

Skinner, E.A., & Belmont, M.J. (1993). Motivation in the classroom: Reciprocal effects of teacher behavior and student engagement across the school year. *Journal of Educational Psychology, 85,* 571–581.

Skinner, E.A., Zimmer-Gembeck, M.J., & Connell, J.P. (1998). Individual differences and the development of perceived control. *Monographs of the Society for Research in Child Development, 63*(2–3), v–220.

Snow, C., Burns, M.S., & Griffin, P. (Eds.). (1998). *Preventing reading difficulties in young children.* Washington, DC: National Academies Press.

Soar, R., & Soar, R. (1979). Emotional climate and management. In P. Peterson & H. Walberg (Eds.), *Research on teaching: Concepts, findings, and implications* (pp. 97–119). Berkeley, CA: McCutchan.

Sperling, R.A., Howard, B.C., & Staley, R. (2004). Metacognition and self-regulated learning constructs. *Educational Research and Evaluation, 10*(2), 117–139.

Stallings, J. (1975). Implementation and child effects of teaching practices in Follow Through classrooms. *Monographs of the Society for Research in Child Development, 40*(7–8), Serial No. 163.

Stallings, J., Cory, R., Fairweather, J., & Needels, M. (1978). *Early childhood education classroom evaluation.* Menlo Park, CA: SRI International.

Starkey, P., Klein, A., and Wakeley, A. (2004). Enhancing young children's mathematical knowledge through a pre-kindergarten mathematics intervention. *Early Childhood Research Quarterly, 19*(1), 99–120.

Stevenson, H.W., & Lee, S.Y. (1990). Contexts of achievement: A study of American, Chinese, and Japanese children. *Monographs of the Society for Research in Child Development, 55*(1–2), 123.

Strickland, D., Snow, C.E., Griffin, P., Burns, M.S., & McNamara, M. (2002). *Preparing our teachers: Opportunities for better reading instruction.* Washington, DC: Joseph Henry Press.

Stuhlman, M.W., & Pianta, R.C. (2006). *Profiles of quality in first grade classrooms: A pattern oriented approach.* Manuscript submitted for publication.

Taylor, B.M., Pearson, P.D., Peterson, D.S., & Rodriguez, M.C. (2003). Reading growth in high-poverty classrooms: The influence of teacher practices that encourage cognitive engagement in literacy learning. *The Elementary School Journal, 104,* 3–28.

Torgesen, J.K. (2002). The prevention of reading difficulties. *Journal of School Psychology, 40,* 7–26.

Valeski, T.N., & Stipek, D.J. (2001). Young children's feelings about school. *Child Development, 72*(4), 1198–1213.

Van Ijzendoorn, M.H., Sagi, A., & Lambermon, M.W.E. (1992). The multiple caretaker paradox: Some data from Holland and Israel. In R.E. Pianta (Ed.), *New Directions in Child Development: Vol. 57. Relationships between children and non-parental adults* (pp. 5–24). San Francisco: Jossey-Bass.

Veenman, M.V.J., Kok, R., & Blöte, A.W. (2005). The relation between intellectual and metacognitive skills in early adolescence. *Instructional Science, 33*(3), 193–211.

Vygotsky, L.S. (1978). *Mind and society: The development of higher mental processes.* Cambridge, MA: Harvard University Press.

Vygotsky, L.S. (1991). Genesis of the higher mental functions. In P. Light, S. Sheldon, & M. Woodhead (Eds.), *Learning to think* (pp. 32–41). Florence, KY: Taylor & Frances/Routledge.

Wadlington, E. (2000). Effective language arts instruction for students with dyslexia. *Preventing School Failure, 44,* 61–65.

Wentzel, K.R. (1999). Social-motivational processes and interpersonal relationships: Implications for understanding motivation at school. *Journal of Educational Psychology, 91,* 76–97.

Wentzel, K.R. (2002). Are effective teachers like good parents? Teaching styles and student adjustment in early adolescence. *Child Development, 73*(1), 287–301.

Wharton-McDonald, R., Pressley, M., & Hampston, J.M. (1998). Literacy instruction in nine first-grade classrooms: Teacher characteristics and student achievement. *Elementary School Journal, 99*(2), 101–128.

Whitehurst, G. (2003). *The Institute of Education Sciences: New wine and new bottles. Presentation at the annual meeting of the American Educational Research Association, Chicago.*

Whitehurst, G.J., Falco, F.L., Lonigan, C.J., Fischel, J.E., DeBaryshe, B.D., Williams, W.M., et al. (2002, June). Practical intelligence for school: Developing metacognitive sources of achievement in adolescence. *Developmental Review, 22*(2), 162–210.

Williams, W.M., Blythe, T., & White, N. (2002). Practical intelligence for school: Developing metacognitive sources of achievement in adolescence. *Developmental Review, 22*(2), 162–210.

Yair, G. (2000). Educational battlefields in America: The tug-of-war over students' engagement with instruction. *Sociology of Education, 73,* 247–269.

Yates, G.C.R. (2005). "How obvious": Personal reflections on the database of educational psychology and effective teaching research. *Educational Psychology, 25*(6), 681–700.

Zevenbergen, A., Whitehurst, G.J., & Zevenbergen, J.A. (2003). Effects of a shared-reading intervention on the inclusion of evaluative devices in narratives of children from low-income families. *Journal of Applied Developmental Psychology, 24*(1), 1–15.

Zins, J.E., Bloodworth, M.R., Weissberg, R.P., and Walberg, H. (2004). The scientific base linking social and emotional learning to school success. In J.E. Zins, R.P. Weissberg, M.C. Wang, & H.J. Walberg (Eds.), *Building academic success on social and emotional learning: What does the research say?* (pp. 3–22). New York: Teachers College Press.

5

FIRSTSCHOOL

A New Vision for Education

Sharon Ritchie, Kelly Maxwell, and Richard M. Clifford

Previous chapters have addressed the reconceptualization of transitions, the increased emphasis on the early years of schooling, the move toward alignment, and the rethinking of accountability. This chapter outlines the purpose, rationale, conceptual model, fundamentals, and components of FirstSchool, an innovative, comprehensive plan for the education of children ages 3–8 years (Bogard, 2003). FirstSchool aspires to promote and support public school efforts to become more responsive to the needs of an increasingly younger, more diverse population of children. Making a real difference in the lives of all young children requires rethinking public education in complex and meaningful ways that optimize expertise, broaden the knowledge base, and challenge any practices that sustain inequity.

PURPOSE AND RATIONALE

Early education in the United States is changing in ways that provide unique opportunities regarding the beginning of school and the potential to influence practice. By the end of the 20th century, an estimated nearly 1 million children were entering kindergarten prior to the traditional entry age (Clifford, Early, & Hills, 1999). This number equals roughly one fourth of all children in this age cohort in the United States. The time is rapidly approaching that, for all intents and purposes, school will start a year earlier than it did between the 1980s and 1990s. Currently, 38 states offer prekindergarten services to at least some 4-year-olds (Barnett, Hustedt, Robin, & Schulman, 2006), and universal preschool is finding footing throughout the nation (American Federation of Teachers, 2002; Committee for Economic Development, 2002; Council of Chief State School Officers, 1999; Espinosa, 2002; Foundation for Child Development, 2001; National Education Association, 2003; Trust for Early Education, n.d.; U.S. Conference of Mayors, 2004). These programs will likely grow over the next decade to the point that school for 3- and 4-year-olds will be a viable choice for all families. Before these programs for young children become fully developed and implemented, the early education establishment must thoughtfully plan with schools and the broader community to be ready to meet the needs of young children. During this time of change, there is a choice of whether to simply add to the existing organizational structure and practice of schools or to use this opportunity to reexamine early education in the United States (Foundation for Child Development, 2003). The former option will likely fail to address the full range of needs of these youngest members of the educational system; decades of attempts at school reform have repeatedly demonstrated that change is difficult once practices are set in place. Rather, a new vision is needed.

Most children develop substantial oral language skills by age 3, and by the time they reach third grade, schools expect them to be relatively competent in written language. Because success beyond third grade is highly dependent on children's skills in writing and understanding written language, children's early school experiences should ensure that they have optimal opportunities to become highly competent readers and writers. Schools typically increase and alter expectations for children at about age 7 or 8, which underscores the need to prepare both children and schools for this shift in emphasis.

Language and literacy, however, cannot be the only focus. Teachers of young children must also facilitate the development of critical thinking skills and provide opportunities to develop knowledge, skills, and concepts in math, science, social studies, creative expression, and technology. Children must develop physically, socially, and emotionally and become increasingly competent in practices that will keep them healthy and safe. These are all critical tasks for children's early school years.

FirstSchool will provide a new vision for early education. The evidence regarding quality practices for young children, publicly funded prekindergarten, and the achievement gap that continues as children move through school defines both the strength and the challenges in creating this new vision. The strength lies in the decades of research that have provided the field of early education with solid information on quality practices for young children (e.g., Campbell, Ramey, Pungello, Sparling, & Miller-Johnson, 2002; Peisner-Feinberg et al., 2001; Reynolds, Temple, Robertson, & Mann, 2002; Schweinhart, Barnes, & Weikart, 1993). The similarity in criteria for quality described in position papers for state and national early learning and performance standards and national standards indicates much agreement about what constitutes the enriched learning environments, positive teacher–child relationships, and instructional approaches that make learning meaningful for children and support them as they grow and develop (National Association for the Education of Young Children, 2005; National Association of State Boards of Education, 1988; National Education Association, 2003; National Education Goals Panel, 1998; Scott-Little, Kagan, & Frelow, 2005). This knowledge provides professionals with the foundation for their work and is the source of their vision:

> FirstSchool is a learning community in which development and education of 3- to 8-year-old children is at the heart of everything we do. Every child has a right to a successful, enjoyable, high quality FirstSchool experience that fosters intellectual, physical, emotional, and social well-being, and optimizes learning and development. In partnership with families and communities, FirstSchool accepts responsibility for preparing each child for a lifetime of learning, in school and beyond. (FirstSchool, n.d.)

The same field of research that has demonstrated the importance of safe, healthy, and positive environments, stimulating curricula, and a broad range of instructional practices for young children has also documented how many children—especially children who live in poverty and are African American or Latino—do not get a fair shake. Indeed, they are not having a successful, enjoyable, high-quality first school experience (Barbarin, 2002; Brooks-Gunn,

Klebanov, & Duncan, 1996; Lee & Burkam, 2002; Smith, Brooks-Gunn, & Klebanov, 1997). School must grow and change from a place that honors and benefits some children—usually those who look and act like their teachers and who have access by virtue of race and socioeconomic status to the culture of schooling (Delpit, 1995)—to a place that benefits all. School must become a place where *all* children develop the knowledge, skills, and confidence necessary to be active citizens in a diverse, democratic society; where many more children learn how to read and write by grade 3; where those vulnerable to failure are better received and served; and where a child's sense of wonder, curiosity, and desire to learn is fostered.

One of the most immediate challenges to rethinking the early school years is in effectively translating knowledge into practice. Studies of early education practice show the difficulties in moving from highly successful experimental programs (Campbell et al., 2002; Schweinhart et al., 1993) to moderate-size (Reynolds et al., 2002) or large-scale implementation of programs (Clifford et al., 2005; Pianta et al., 2005) designed to serve children and families during the preschool and early school periods. We may be able to define quality, but current practices, regulations, and funding levels are not ensuring high-quality programs. School days for children, especially minority children and those who live in poverty, are characterized by low global quality, low levels of meaningful or reciprocal interactions between children and teachers, and low levels of child engagement in meaningful activities (Clifford et al., 2005; Early et al., 2005). The need to identify and understand which practices lead to higher quality experiences for all children and to eliminate disparities presents a challenge: to consider the multiple, interactive factors that either support or hinder the translation of knowledge into practice (Burchinal & Cryer, 2003).

An additional challenge is found in the poor coordination of the educational experiences of young children between the ages of 3 and 8 years. At this time, the differences between elementary education and early childhood education are far greater than the similarities. For the most part, the systems have different funding streams, disparate pay scales, incongruent education and training, and unrelated national support. Little effort on the part of either system facilitates the transition of children from one to the other (Early, Pianta, Taylor, & Cox, 2001). This divide between early childhood programs and elementary education separates teacher knowledge and values into different and often conflicting camps. The challenge is to create an educational system that unites the best practices of both into a coordinated continuum of learning and care. Following the recommendations of Bogard and Takanishi (2005), FirstSchool will align standards, curricula, and assessment practices across the early grades to investigate how learning experiences can be systematically organized to complement and reinforce one another in support of more positive outcomes for children.

CONCEPTUAL MODELS

Conceptual models are essential guides for the FirstSchool effort. Committees concerned with the multiple components of quality education are developing guiding principles and establishing their theoretical and empirical basis. The common principles, detailed in the next section, are fundamental to all components of FirstSchool. FirstSchool likely will not rely on a distinctly new conceptual model but, rather, on the integration and expansion of existing models to provide a theoretical road map. Within the year, a broad conceptual model of successful schools will be developed. This model will include the common principles, as well as those specific to different aspects of FirstSchool and will draw from many areas, including systems change literature, developmental systems theory, sociocultural and cognitive theories, and the concepts of constructivism and social justice. This conceptual model is currently emerging.

The FirstSchool planning process itself is guided by theoretical models, especially the ideas of Vygotsky (1986) and Dewey (1989). Vygotsky's ideas on the contribution of social interaction to learning have powerful implications for the planning process. A collaborative process enables the people working together to co-construct contexts in which knowledge comes from the best available scientific research as well as the wisdom and values of the multiple and varied partners. This is an inquiry model—a way to learn what other people believe and to struggle for common understandings to broaden the collective intellect. The challenge to this work is in establishing trust among people who differ in many elements in which the power of status, race, and gender usually dictate outcomes. Breaking this pattern requires a commitment to moving slowly, reflecting on various practices, listening carefully, and integrating the ideas of all partners in a significant and discernible manner.

Dewey's work is important because it encourages collaborators to operate as members of a community, actively pursuing interests in cooperation with others, and simultaneously cautions against the pitfall of merely accepting the status quo. His work encourages the challenging of educational traditions through a dialectical process in which grappling with conflicting ideas provides increased access to diverse thoughts. FirstSchool's success depends on the commitment to inclusive practices that embrace and value differences.

The next section describes ideas that are fundamental to the FirstSchool conceptual model and that will be evident throughout the planning, implementation, and evaluation of FirstSchool.

FIRSTSCHOOL FUNDAMENTALS

The valuing of positive relationships, a commitment to dialogue, the use of innovation and evidence, the contribution of context to content, and an unremitting attention to equity are fundamental to the work of FirstSchool.

Positive Relationships

Positive relationships are central to all aspects of the planning, implementation, and evaluation of FirstSchool. For both children and adults, the cognitive and social development that promotes learning occurs in an interactive context (Pianta & Walsh, 1996; Vygotsky, 1986). FirstSchool is conscientiously and consistently working to establish positive prosocial environments characterized by mutually reciprocated relationships, respect, and cooperative work (Wesley & Buysse, 2001). Developing relationships takes time and attention to become genuine. Commitment to positive relationships developed through dialogue and attention to equity does not allow for shortcuts or missteps and implies an unwavering faithfulness to this basic premise.

Commitment to Dialogue

"Dialogue implies talk between people. . . . It is a humanizing form, one that challenges and resists domination. The give and take makes struggling together for meaning a powerful experience in self definition and self discovery." (Ladson-Billings, 1994)

Dialogue, a vital factor in all FirstSchool phases, is essential to learning and to the development of shared values and beliefs. The challenge is to establish relationships, build trust, and design the infrastructure necessary to support give-and-take conversations among diverse groups of people and on various topics throughout each phase of FirstSchool. This commitment to dialogue is important not just for adults but also for children. It is easy to say and even believe that all constituents' opinions are encouraged and valued, but it is difficult to generate discussions in which everyone feels adequate and important to the task when the group members vary in status, age, class, race, and expertise and are governed by a history of mistrust.

Another potential dilemma is that reform and restructuring efforts are traditionally initiated by people who believe they already know all of the answers. Not having answers implies disorganization, chaos, and incompetence. On the contrary, FirstSchool does not (and does not want to) have all of the answers at the outset. Instead, it is important to pose questions, initiate conversations, and listen to a broad range of people with differing ideas, experiences, and values. In this increasingly disparate nation, the knowledge and experiences of people from different cultures, socioeconomic levels, and geographic regions will provide advantages for navigating the complexities of schools and schooling. Diversity of thought is a vital asset.

Evidence and Innovation

FirstSchool has the opportunity, born of time and enhanced by partnership, to blend evidence with innovation. The challenge is to remain grounded in research while thinking creatively about continuing questions. The evidence-based practice approach used by FirstSchool is a decision-making process that integrates the best available research evidence with family and professional wisdom and values. At the heart of this definition, representing the most dramatic shift from previous thinking, is the notion that evidence-based practice is essentially a process requiring practitioners to identify, evaluate, and interpret the evidence and apply it to solve problems about practice (Buysse & Wesley, in press). The *Journal of Early Intervention* provides guidelines for the use of innovative practice. It defines *innovative* models, programs, techniques, or practices "as those that focus on valued outcomes, are based on sound theory and relevant research, and offer new approaches to address effectively challenges faced by the field" (2006). The journal defines *promising* models, programs, techniques, or practices as those that have well-formulated and coherent procedures and preliminary evidence demonstrating potential effectiveness. FirstSchool will contribute to the knowledge base of the field through the investigation of multiple unanswered issues. The evaluation phase will be characterized by research methodology that illustrates the effects of difference on success in school and on how specific efforts to address these issues may result in positive change for children.

Equity

The path toward increased equity in educational processes and outcomes is multifaceted. Equity throughout the planning stage of FirstSchool means involving a wide range of people in decision making; encouraging everyone to participate in the dialogue, addressing any gaps, and recognizing and questioning assumptions; and, most important, ensuring that each child receives what he or she needs to be successful. Equity in the implementation of FirstSchool requires a social justice perspective, paying particular attention to inequalities associated with race, social class, language, and gender. FirstSchool views social justice as transformative—founded on the principle that theory and practice are joined as *praxis*. Democracy not only is taught but also lives within the classroom, the school, and the community.

Contribution of Context to Content

FirstSchool's work is wide ranging. It is essential to think both locally and nationally, balancing the specificity of a model with the flexibility of a framework in which children's FirstSchool experiences are conceived within the broader context of culture and community. Local models allow for the recognition and negotiation of local assets and needs. The national framework enables identification of primary components of success, both in terms of process and content, that apply across communities. Working at both levels simultaneously emphasizes the importance of context when determining which aspects of FirstSchool are essential to the program's philosophy and goals and which are contingent on the local community.

Of course, the local work of FirstSchool is situational. The core participants have been highly invested in their work, adequate time and funds have been available, and the program has benefited from access to the resources of a university and a research institute dedicated to quality practices for young children. Other communities may not have these same assets. For FirstSchool to be a viable option for communities across the nation, its design must limit the degree to which reforms can be imposed from the outside; such a design would recognize the important differences in implementation that are linked to particular contexts (Datnow, 2000) as well as the importance of engaging the community in the work. Local experiences in the development process of a FirstSchool model site might be just as important as the content of the framework itself. FirstSchool will begin piloting aspects of FirstSchool in two local districts in 2007. Initial work will include the integration of preschool children and families into the local K-5 model and aligning the curriculum, instructional practices, and environments between pre-K and kindergarten to promote a smooth and appropriate transition (Bogard & Takanishi, 2005). Negotiations are under way to partner with a local district to build a model facility to be completed in 2010.

FIRSTSCHOOL COMPONENTS

The starting point for FirstSchool is determining how to fully integrate preschool into elementary schools and to rethink early school experience. Planning groups are addressing nine issues that are critical to moving forward with this agenda. Members of the planning groups include parents, teachers of young children both in and out of public school, administrators and directors, child care community representatives, teacher educators, researchers, and other community leaders. A significant challenge of the current work is to sustain a holistic view of FirstSchool. Although separate descriptions of the nine issues and committee tasks are described briefly next, many issues will cut across the components. The authors of this chapter are developing multiple ways to help groups approach similar issues from different perspectives and to keep participants apprised of all progress and major decisions. As FirstSchool evolves, additional groups may be created.

Business

To make FirstSchool work in the real world, it is essential to determine how to finance a school that combines children eligible for funding for public education with large numbers of children not eligible for such support. In most states, children below the legal age of entry into kindergarten may not be supported by funds from the state general education fund. Although many states offer prekindergarten funding for some children, only a handful of states have attempted to make prekindergarten services available to all children. When funding is available, it is often not sufficient to operate a high-quality program that would meet the standards of FirstSchool. Additional financial and operational concerns involve financing the part of the program for all children that operates before and after school and during holidays and vacation periods to accommodate the needs of working families. The business committee is developing a business plan describing the financial resources available to all children in the 3- to 8-year-old range and detailing how those resources can be used to support a high-quality program for all children. The first task will be to develop a plan that is unique to the model site. This plan will form the basis for creation of a model business plan that will be made available to state and local agencies across the country working to create a FirstSchool model.

Coordinated School Health and Wellness

To benefit from education and maintain quality of life, children, staff, and families in the FirstSchool community need to be as healthy as possible. FirstSchool will use a national model of coordinated school health and wellness that incorporates the components of family, school, and community partnerships; health education and life skills; healthy and safe environments; health services; nutrition; physical education and activity; social and emotional well-being; and staff wellness. The committee is concerned with health protection, disease, and injury prevention and health promotion. The concerns of this committee will inform and be informed by designs and plans from many committees: The facilities committee must ensure an environment that promotes health and safety; the families, communities, and outreach committee will help determine schools' responsibilities (and part of that conversation includes what services should be available for families); the curriculum and instruction committee will integrate the health, nutrition, and safety practices in daily learning; and the professional development committee will prepare teachers to be aware of and responsive to the health, safety, and mental health concerns of children and families.

Curriculum and Instruction

FirstSchool is dedicated to the structural, curricular, and pedagogical continuity of children's early education experiences. The curriculum and instruction committee is developing a framework that builds on local and national work to align standards and curriculum and that attend to both developmental domains and content areas. Although this area has merited much attention in the last few years, most of the work has focused either on early childhood or elementary curriculum, with no efforts to align and coordinate an approach that would span the 3- to 8-year-old period and account for children's developmental characteristics and abilities (Griffith, 1996; Kagan & Neuman, 1998; National Association of State Boards of Education, 1988; National Education Goals Panel, 1998; Pianta & Cox, 1999). The FirstSchool framework will outline the learning objectives across the 3- to 8-year-old period and describe instructional strategies for effectively teaching young children. The framework is guided by 10 principles. The first five—all children are capable; children are constructors of their own knowledge; teachers, parents, and peers co-construct knowledge and broaden learning; context contributes to content; and positive relationships are central to children's success—derive broadly from fundamental assumptions about human nature and social structure. The last five—use of wide-ranging and varied approaches; access to a curriculum that maximizes potential; contribution of assessment practices to individual growth and progress as well as the growth of the classroom community; purposeful and intentional practices; and a commitment to lifelong learning—derive more narrowly from the particular conditions and concerns of early childhood education.

Diversity

Instead of focusing on the traditional divisions of language, culture, and special needs, the diversity committee is addressing the diversity of learners in general. This intentional move away from a deficit view of children who are "different" recognizes diversity as the primary descriptor for the current population of young children. About 45% of children under 5 are ethnically or linguistically diverse, and this trend is expected to grow (U.S. Census Bureau, 2004). Diverse learners also include young children with developmental disabilities; those at risk for learning, social, emotional, or behavioral problems; and those with gifts, talents, or exceptional potential. Most children reflect one or more of these notions of diversity. Careful thought in deciding how best to use both financial and human resources to ensure equity of access for all children and families underlies the committee's work to ensure that each child in FirstSchool succeeds. FirstSchool will advance the field's understanding of diversity issues in early education such as bilingual education, early intervention, culturally responsive practices, and inclusion.

Evaluation and Research

Evaluation is an essential component of FirstSchool. The primary work of the evaluation and research committee is to 1) design an evaluation of the process of planning and implementing FirstSchool and 2) design an overall evaluation of the effectiveness of FirstSchool in reaching its primary goals. Evaluating the planning and implementation process will provide valuable lessons to other communities interested in FirstSchool or PK–3 ideas. This committee will provide guidance on gathering the scientific data needed to evaluate FirstSchool, using data in a constructive way to support reflection and change, and conducting research that follows the FirstSchool guiding principles.

Facilities

School buildings are generally not designed for young children and their families. Ideally, FirstSchool would be implemented in a facility designed specifically to serve children 3–8 years old. When implementing a local demonstration site, FirstSchool will design and oversee the construction of a state-of-the-art facility for the education and care of children ages 3–8. Fundamentally, the FirstSchool physical environment will support all aspects of children's development and learning, provide for teachers' needs and comfort, be accessible to families and community members, and serve as a research and training facility. Moving beyond essentials, FirstSchool will use this opportunity to take a fresh, cutting-edge view of environments that are welcoming, flexible, environmentally sound, and sustainable and that demonstrate respect and regard for families, teachers, and children in all details.

Families, Communities, and Outreach

The families, communities, and outreach committee has two main goals: 1) to build strong partnerships with families and other community members, and 2) to communicate effectively about FirstSchool, locally and nationally. This committee will provide leadership to help engage families and communities in decision making and planning processes that will lead to strong, sustainable relationships among schools, families, and others in the community. The committee will explore questions such as "In what ways is education a societal and shared responsibility, where families and community members along with schools are accountable for the development of the children in their care?" and "What does it mean for families to be involved in their children's education?"

Professional Development

Teachers who are well prepared to work more effectively with all children are key to the success of FirstSchool. This requires moving beyond traditional methods of preparation toward efforts to understand and appreciate diversity and to broaden teachers' skills. This requires professional development focused on developing culturally responsive practitioners with the ability to recognize multiple ways of thinking and multiple definitions of important knowledge; support a wide range of cultural perspectives and practices; and justify using social interaction as the primary medium of instruction (Oakes & Lipton, 2003). The urgency of integrating cultural knowledge and competence into all aspects of teacher preparation is fueled by the disparity between early childhood personnel and the children they teach. Fundamental to the long-term success of FirstSchool is teacher preparation and professional development that unite best practices of elementary and early childhood education, promote interdisciplinary collaboration and communication among education professionals (Early et al., 2006), and align models of preservice and in-service education. Success in these areas calls for sweeping changes in teacher education, professional development, curricula, assessment, and pedagogy.

Transitions

Effective transition policies and practices are essential to a successful, coordinated school experience for children and their families (Ramey & Ramey, 1999). The transitions committee will provide guidance in how best to support children and families as they move into, out of, and within FirstSchool. This committee will also consider the effect of FirstSchool on larger systems of services for children and policies that affect transitions at the federal, state, and local levels. The conceptual model promotes an approach to transition that views children as adaptable and able to develop and engage maximally, including during times of transition; ensures that teachers and family members have the skills and knowledge to sustain children through transitions; and makes sure that structures are in place within the school organization and in the community that support smooth transitions.

FirstSchool's most immediate task is to clearly identify which fundamental principles of FirstSchool are not negotiable and which can evolve in the context of larger education reform. With input from committee members and through processes that include wider segments of the population, FirstSchool is making progress toward a more solid, better articulated identity.

CONCLUSION

Public education in the United States began largely as an educational opportunity for predominantly White boys who were enrolled at about age 6 when their fathers moved from farm work to industrial and commercial enterprise. Gradually, school expanded to serve both boys and girls, and the standard number of years of schooling increased with the inclusion of kindergarten as the beginning point for most children and the notion of full access to school through 12th grade. In the 20th century, schools further expanded to serve children of color more equitably and to serve children with disabilities. Previously, both of these groups had been either denied access to public schools or provided substandard educational opportunities. By the end of the 20th century, equal access to public education for children from about 5 to 18 years of age was mostly achieved, although still problematic.

For a variety of reasons, including those addressed earlier in this chapter, this pattern of expansion of public education has shifted yet again to encompass still younger children. For all intents and purposes, U.S. public education is moving toward a model in which most children will begin school at about age 4 and possibly age 3 in the foreseeable future.

This expansion will entail major new financial investments—estimates are in the tens of billions in yearly operational costs plus many billions in new construction (Barnett & Masse, 2003). Yet, as indicated in this chapter, little has been done to plan for this huge shift in the work of public schools. FirstSchool is one effort to fill this void.

The intricacies of the idea of FirstSchool merely scratch the surface of possibility; FirstSchool is predicated as the ideal place to start. Change is slow, but it is made of small and relentless steps. As Margaret Mead said, "Never doubt that a small group of thoughtful, committed citizens can change the world. Indeed it's the only thing that ever has" (Warner, 1992).

REFERENCES

American Federation of Teachers. (2002). *At the starting line: Early childhood education programs in the 50 states.* Washington, DC: Author.

Barbarin, O. (2002). African-American males in kindergarten. In J.U. Gordon (Ed.), *The African-American male in American life and thought* (pp. 1–12). New York: Nova Science Publishers.

Barnett, W.S., Hustedt, J.T., Robin, K.B., & Schulman, K.L. (2006). *The state of preschool: 2005 state preschool yearbook.* New Brunswick, NJ: National Institute for Early Education Research.

Barnett, W.S., & Masse, L.N. (2003). Funding issues for early childhood education and care program. In D. Cryer & R.M. Clifford (Eds.), *Early childhood education and care in the USA* (pp. 137–165). Baltimore: Paul H. Brookes Publishing Co.

Bogard, K. (2003). *Mapping the P-3 continuum (MAP): P-3 as the foundation of education reform.* New York: Foundation for Child Development. Retrieved October 11, 2004, from www.ffcd.org/ourwork/f-index.html

Bogard, K., & Takanishi, R. (2005). PK-3: An aligned and coordinated approach to education for children 3 to 8 years old. *Social Policy Report, 19*(3).

Brooks-Gunn, J., Klebanov, P., & Duncan, G. (1996). Ethnic differences in children's intelligence test scores: Role of economic deprivation, home environment, and maternal characteristics. *Child Development, 67,* 396–408.

Burchinal, M.R., & Cryer, D. (2003). Diversity, child care quality, and developmental outcomes. *Early Childhood Research Quarterly, 16,* 475–497.

Buysse, V., & Wesley, P.W. (Eds.). (in press). *Evidence-based practice in the early childhood field.* Washington, DC: ZERO TO THREE.

Campbell, F.A., Ramey, C.T., Pungello, E.P., Sparling, J., & Miller-Johnson, S. (2002). Early childhood education: Young adult outcomes from the Abecedarian Project. *Applied Developmental Science, 6,* 42–57.

Clifford, R.M., Barbarin, O., Chang, F., Early, D., Bryant, D., Howes, C., et al. (2005). What is pre-kindergarten? Characteristics of a public system of pre-kindergarten services in six states. *Applied Developmental Science, 9*(3), 126–143.

Clifford, R., Early, D.M., & Hills, T. (1999). Almost a million children in school before kindergarten. *Young Children, 54*(5), 48–51.

Committee for Economic Development. (2002). *Preschool for all: Investing in a productive and just society.* New York: Author.

Council of Chief State School Officers. (1999). *Early childhood and family education: New realities, new opportunities, A council policy statement.* Washington, DC: Author.

Datnow, A. (2000). Power and politics in the adoption of school reform models. *Educational evaluation and policy analysis, 22*(4), 357–374.

Delpit, L. (1995). *Other people's children: Cultural conflict in the classroom.* New York: The New Press.

Dewey, J. (1989). Democracy and education. In J. Dewey (Ed.), *John Dewey: The middle works, 1899–1924* (Vol. 9). Carbondale, Illinois: Southern Illinois University Press. (Original work published 1916)

Early, D., Barbarin, O., Bryant, D., Burchinal, M., Chang, F., Clifford, R., et al. (2005). *Pre-kindergarten in eleven states: NCEDL's multi-state study of pre-kindergarten & study of state-wide early education programs (SWEEP)* (NCEDL Working Paper). Chapel Hill: The University of North Carolina, FPG Child Development Institute, NCEDL. Retrieved February 15, 2006, from http://www.fpg.unc.edu/~ncedl/pdfs/SWEEP_MS_summary_final.pdf

Early, D.M., Bryant, D., Pianta, R., Clifford, R., Burchinal, M., Ritchie, S., et al. (2006). Are teacher education, major, and credentials related to classroom quality and children's academic gains in pre-kindergarten? *Early Childhood Research Quarterly.*

Early, D.M., Pianta, R.C., Taylor, L.C., & Cox, M.J. (2001). Transition practices: Findings from a national survey of kindergarten teachers. *Early Childhood Education Journal, 28*(3), 199–206.

Espinosa, L.M. (2002). High quality preschool: Why we need it and what it looks like. *Preschool Policy Matters* (Policy Brief No. 1). New Brunswick, NJ: National Institute for Early Education Research.

FirstSchool. (n.d.). *Vision.* Available from the FPG Child Development Institute web site, http://www.fpg.unc.edu/~firstschool/newvision.cfm

Foundation for Child Development. (2001). *Toward early education for all.* New York: Author.

Foundation for Child Development. (2003). *First things first: Prekindergarten is the starting point for education reform.* New York: Author.

Griffith, J. (1996). Relation of parental involvement, empowerment, and school traits to student academic performance. *Journal of Educational Research, 90,* 33–41.

Journal of Early Intervention. (2006). *Guidelines for authors of articles dealing with innovative practices.* Retrieved from http://alliedhealth.lsuhsc.edu/jei

Kagan, S.L., & Neuman, M.J. (1998). Lessons from three decades of transition research. *The Elementary School Journal, 98*(4), 365–379.

Ladson-Billings, G. (1994). *The dreamkeepers: Successful teachers of African-American children.* San Francisco: Jossey-Bass.

Lee, V.E., & Burkam, D.T. (2002). *Inequality at the starting gate: Social background differences in achievement as children begin school.* Washington, DC: Economic Policy Institute.

National Association for the Education of Young Children. (2005). *NAEYC accreditation standards and criteria.* Washington, DC: Author.

National Association of State Boards of Education. (1988). *Right from the start: The report of the NASBE task force on early childhood education.* Alexandria, VA: Author.

National Education Association. (2003, July 4). *News release: NEA delegates call for universal pre-kindergarten and full day kindergarten.* Retrieved October 20, 2004, from http://www.nea.org/newsreleases/2003/nr030704b.html

National Education Goals Panel. (1998). *Ready schools.* Washington, DC: Author.

Oakes, J., & Lipton, M. (2003). *Teaching to change the world* (2nd ed.). New York: McGraw-Hill.

Peisner-Feinberg, E.S., Burchinal, M.R., Clifford, R.M., Culkin, M.L., Howes, C., Kagan, S.L., et al. (2001). The relation of preschool quality to children's cognitive and social developmental trajectories through second grade. *Child Development, 72*(5), 1534–1553.

Pianta, R.C., & Cox, M.J. (1999). The changing nature of the transition to school: Trends for the next decade. In R.C. Pianta & M.J. Cox (Eds.), *The transition to kindergarten* (pp. 363–379). Baltimore: Paul H. Brookes Publishing Co.

Pianta, R., Howes, C., Burchinal, M., Bryant, D., Clifford, R., Early, D., et al. (2005). Features of pre-kindergarten programs, classrooms, and teachers: Do they predict observed classroom quality and child-teacher interactions? *Applied Developmental Science, 9*(3), 144–159.

Pianta, R.C., & Walsh, D.J. (1996). *High risk children in schools.* New York: Routledge.

Ramey, C.T., & Ramey, S.L. (1999). Beginning school for children at risk. In R.C. Pianta & M.J. Cox (Eds.), *The transition to kindergarten* (pp. 217–251). Baltimore: Paul H. Brookes Publishing Co.

Reynolds, A.J., Temple, J.A., Robertson, D.L., & Mann, E.A. (2002). Age 21 cost-benefit analysis of the Title I Chicago child-parent centers. *Educational Evaluation and Policy Analysis, 24*(4), 267–303.

Schweinhart, L.J., Barnes, H.V., & Weikart, D.P. (1993). *Significant benefits: The High/Scope Perry Preschool study through age 27.* (Monographs of the High/Scope Educational Research Foundation, 10). Ypsilanti, MI: High/Scope Press.

Scott-Little, C., Kagan, S.L., & Frelow, V.S. (2005). *Inside the content: The depth and breadth of early learning standards.* University of North Carolina at Greensboro: SERVE Center for Continuous Improvement.

Smith, J.R., Brooks-Gunn, J., & Klebanov, P.K. (1997). Consequences of living in poverty for young children's cognitive and verbal ability and early school achievement. In G. Duncan & J. Brooks-Gunn (Eds.), *Consequences of growing up poor* (pp. 132–189). New York: Russell Sage Foundation.

Trust for Early Education. (n.d.). *Mission statement.* Retrieved October 11, 2004, from http://www.trustforearlyed.org/TEE_Mission.aspx

U.S. Census Bureau. (2004). *Hispanic and Asian Americans increasing faster than overall population.* Retrieved February 15, 2006, from http://www.census.gov/Press-Release/www/releases/archives/race/001839.html

U.S. Conference of Mayors. (2004). *Quality pre-kindergarten for all* (Adopted resolution, 72nd annual meeting, Boston, MA). Retrieved October 28, 2004, from http://usmayors.org/uscm/resolutions/72nd_conference/education_02.asp

Vygotsky, L. (1986). *Thought and language.* Cambridge, MA: The MIT Press.

Warner, C. (Ed.). (1992). *The last word: A treasury of women's quotes.* Englewood Cliffs, NJ: Prentice Hall.

Wesley, P.W., & Buysse, V. (2001). Communities of practice: Expanding professional roles to promote reflection and shared inquiry. *Topics in Early Childhood Special Education, 21*(2), 114–123.

II

Domains of Developmental Functioning in the P-3 Years

6

HEALTH AND NUTRITION AS A FOUNDATION FOR SUCCESS IN SCHOOL

John M. Pascoe, Ulfat Shaikh, Shalini G. Forbis, and Ruth A. Etzel

Educators, parents, and policy makers share an increasing awareness of the impact of elementary school students' health and physical well-being on their ability to learn. Several states have already initiated programs that include health concerns/concepts into their curricula, and the early evaluation data are encouraging (Center for Health and Health Care in Schools, 2003). Although the methodology is challenging for research examining the association between children's health and their school performance, recent findings suggest that hunger has an adverse effect on children's learning (Weinreb et al., 2002) and that school-based breakfast programs may enhance a child's ability to learn (e.g., Simeon & Grantham-McGregor, 1989). Another recent study from Los Angeles found that children from poor neighborhoods who were exposed to higher levels of ambient air toxins displayed decreased school performance after controlling for socioeconomic status and demographic covariates (Pastor, Sadd, & Morello-Forsch, 2004). Chronic threats to children's health as diverse as asthma (Anderson et al., 2005), obesity (Howard & Potts-Datema, 2005) and child maltreatment (Veltman & Browne, 2001; Zolotor et al., 1999) have all been linked to lower school performance.

Physical health and well-being encompass a broad array of physical, biological, and environmental factors that influence child development. A full review of the range of possible factors is beyond the scope or intent of this chapter (cf. Currie, 2005). Rather, this chapter addresses several broad child health issues related to children's learning abilities: children's nutrition, including micronutrients, obesity, and hunger and food insufficiency; children's physical environment, especially exposure to environmental toxins; and childhood ongoing medical conditions.

NUTRITIONAL FACTORS AFFECTING THE SUCCESS OF SCHOOL-AGE CHILDREN

Good dietary practices appear to promote optimal cognitive development and performance in children. In children with good nutritional status, it is unclear whether significant additional benefits are provided by acute dietary changes. In malnourished children, correction of identifiable nutrient deficiencies can improve or completely correct cognitive and behavioral impairments. These findings are described more fully in this section. Regarding the impact of nutrition on children's adaptation to school, the research community is divided as to the appropriate level of analysis. It is typically assumed that understanding the impact of nutrition on child development requires a consideration of both the quantity of food and its quality. As a result, the literature tends to focus either on eating behavior habits and the availability of food or on the nutritional composition of the food that is ingested. In recent years, an apparent epidemic of obesity in the United States has led to increased attention on the consequences (as well as causes) of childhood obesity. In the school context, attention is also focused on programs designed to provide or encourage breakfast, as well as school approaches to provide nutritional food to students (and remove less nutritious food choices). Efforts such as nutrition and health education interventions are relatively recent, and data are limited on their impact on school outcomes. Data are available, however, concerning the importance of breakfast for young children.

Breakfast Intake/Omission

Poor classroom performance may be related to not consuming breakfast (Abalkhail & Shawsky, 2002; Chandler, Walker, Connolly, & Grantham-McGregor, 1995; Connors & Blouin, 1983; Dickie & Bender, 1982; Michaud, Musse, Nicholas, & Mejean, 1991; Pollitt, Leibel, & Greenfield, 1981; Simeon & Granthem-McGregor, 1989; Wyon, Abrahamsson, Jartelius, & Fletcher, 1997). Part of the challenge in understanding the role of breakfast in young children's school outcomes is that the effects on cognition of skipping breakfast can vary depending on the task performed as well as the child's intelligence quotient (IQ), age, and nutritional status (Pollitt et al., 1981; Pollitt, Cueto, & Jacoby, 1998; Pollitt, Lewis, Graza, & Schulman, 1982; Powell, Walker, Chang, & Grantham-McGregor, 1998). Positive effects of breakfast consumption on academic performance tend to be more pronounced in children who have been malnourished compared with adequately nourished children (Chandler et al., 1995; Pollitt et al., 1998; Richter, Rose, & Griesel, 1997; Simeon & Grantham-McGregor, 1989). Eating breakfast has been shown to improve cognitive function on the day it is eaten (Simeon & Grantham-McGregor, 1989). Wyon et al. (1997) in Sweden demonstrated that children who consumed breakfast with higher caloric intake (20% of recommended daily values) scored higher on mathematical, creativity, and physical endurance tests than children who consumed lower energy breakfast (less than 10% of recommended daily values).

The data on the importance of breakfast prompted the development of school breakfast programs, which are shown to improve attendance rates, tardiness, behavior habits, attention, academic performance, and cognitive functioning (Edward & Evers, 2001; Meyers, Sampson, Weitzman, Rogers, & Kayne, 1989; Murphy, Pagano, et al., 1998). Students who are nutritionally at risk and who experience a reduction in nutritional risk following the implementation of school breakfast programs demonstrate improved attendance and grades (Kleinman, Hall, & Green, 2002). A drawback of school breakfast programs is the possibility of duplicating breakfast eaten at home, thus contributing to excessive caloric intake. Some of the evidence of the long-term benefits of consuming breakfast on cognition, memory, or school learning in well-nourished children is unconvincing. School children who consume breakfast in school show improved height, weight, and school attendance compared with children who do not receive breakfast in school (Powell et al., 1998).

Food Insufficiency and Hunger

Part of the rationale and motivation for school lunch and breakfast programs is that some school children come from homes in which food is not easily available or is lacking in nutritional value. Chronic undernutrition as reflected by low height, weight, and head circumference for age is associated with low scores on standardized math and language achievement tests (Hall, Khanh, & Son, 2001; Ivanovic et al., 1992; Mukudi, 2003). Hungry children and children at risk of being hungry are more likely to have poor scores on academic achievement tests, grade repetition, impaired psychosocial functioning, hyperactivity, and absenteeism than nonhungry children (Alaimo, Olson, & Frongillo, 2001; Murphy, Wehler, et al., 1998; Upadhyay, Agarwal, & Agarwal, 1989). Even intermittent food insufficiency in low-income children is associated with academic underachievement, aggression, and anxiety (Kleinman, Murphy, & Little, 1998; Murphy, Wehler, et al., 1998). Well-timed snacks and foods that minimize fluctuations in blood glucose levels can optimize cognitive ability because the brain is sensitive to short-term fluctuations of glucose supply (Benton et al., 2003). Ingestion of carbohydrate-rich food improves attention, short-term memory, problem-solving ability, and arithmetic ability, especially during demanding mental tasks (Benton, Brett, & Brain, 1987; Donohoe & Benton, 1999; Kennedey & Scholey, 2000).

Micronutrients

As noted previously, food insufficiency concerns the availability of food in general. The quality of food, regardless of its availability, is also of concern, although the risks associated with specific micronutrient deficiencies and general supplementation protocols have not received as much attention in the United States as in developing nations and/or nations with chronic malnutrition issues.

Children with iron-deficiency anemia have reduced cognitive performance, academic achievement, health status, and school attendance (Abalkhail & Shawsky, 2002; Grantham-McGregor, & Ani, 2001; Halterman, Kaczorowski, Aligne, Auinger, & Szilagyi, 2001; Hutchinson, Powell, Walker, Chang, & Grantham-McGregor, 1997; Lynn & Harland, 1998; Sungthong, Mo-suwan, & Chongsuvivatwong, 2002; Walker, Grantham-McGregor, Himes, Williams, & Duff, 1998). Data on academic achievement and cognition in children with nonanemic iron-deficiency are less convincing (Bruner, Joffe, Duggan, Casella, & Brandt, 1996; Sungthong et al., 2002). Otero, Aguirre, Porcayo, and Fernandez (1999) demonstrated that children with iron deficiency have lower IQs than children with typical iron levels. Moreover, electroencephalograms of children with iron deficiency have slower activity, possibly related to central nervous system impairment (Abalkhail & Shawsky, 2002; Otero et al., 1999). Iron-deficiency anemia places children at an academic disadvantage unless the deficiency is corrected by supplementation (Pollitt, 1997). Treatment of iron-deficiency anemia has been shown to improve achievement test scores, IQ, cognitive performance, and memory (Pollitt, 1997; Seshadri & Gopaldas, 1989). In a study conducted in South Africa, oral supplementation with a combination of iron, iodine, and beta carotene improved cognitive function related to short-term memory and reduced missed school days caused by respiratory and diarrhea disease (van Stuijvenberg et al., 1999).

Iodine deficiency has been shown to impair cognition and motor skills in childhood, whereas the treatment of iodine deficiency produces improvements in IQ test scores (Bautista, Barker, Dunn, Sanchez, & Kaiser, 1982; Sankar, Rai, & Pulger, 1994). In a randomized controlled trial, Chinese children supplemented with a combination of zinc and other micronutrients showed improvement in motor skills, attention, concept formation, and abstract reasoning (Sandstead, Penland, & Alcock, 1998). Other studies demonstrated no improvement in cognition and academic performance (Cavan et al., 1993; Gibson et al., 1989).

Data on general supplementation show greater consistency in its lack of general impact. Researchers in the United States and in Europe have demonstrated the lack of benefit of vitamin and mineral supplements in enhancing academic and cognitive performance in healthy children with adequate nutritional status (Crombie et al., 1990; Nelson, Naismith, Burley, Gatenby, & Geddes, 1990; Schoenthaler, Amos, Doraz, & Kelly, 1991; Schoenthaler & Bier, 1999; Schoenthaler, Bier, Young, Nichols, & Jansenns, 2000). However, if a child has a poor diet with micronutrient deficiencies, supplementation with the deficient nutrient or a low-dose vitamin–mineral supplement may improve IQ test scores (Benton & Buts, 1990; Eysenck & Schoenthaler, 1997; Nelson, 1992; Schoenthaler et al., 2000). These enhancements were selectively seen in tests of nonverbal intelligence (Benton & Roberts, 1988).

Obesity

Increased attention is being paid to obesity among young children (for a review, see Krishnamoorthy, Hart, & Jelalian, 2006), especially as its prevalence in the population appears to increase (e.g., Ogden et al., 2006; Ogden, Flegal, Carroll, & Johnson, 2002). The prevalence of overweight (defined as body mass index [BMI] for age at the 95th percentile or greater; see Dietz and Robinson, 1998, for a discussion about the use of BMI as an index for overweight and at-risk for overweight) has increased by epidemic proportions in the United States since the 1970s (e.g., Ogden et al., 2002, 2006; Strauss & Pollack, 2001). Using data from the National Health and Nutrition Survey (NHANES) for 2003–2004, Ogden et al. (2006) found 13.9% of preschool-age children and 18.8% of school-age children (ages 6–11) to be obese. In both age groups, Ogden et al. (2006) noted an upward trend that, although not statistically significant, does mark continued increases in prevalence across the study years considered and across gender and race/ethnic groups. Wang and Dietz (2002) estimated a national economic burden attributable to pediatric obesity (children ages 6–17) of $127 million (in 2001 U.S. dollars).

Compared with children of typical weight, overweight children score lower on intelligence and achievement tests and may have a lower range of interests, poorer capacity for social adaptation, and a higher likelihood of being placed in remedial classes (Campos, Sigulem, Moraes, Escrivao, & Fisberg, 1996; Datar, Sturm, & Magnabosco, 2004; Li, 1995;

Strauss & Pollack, 2003; Tershakovec, Weller, & Gallagher, 1994). Overweight children are also at risk for sleep disturbances due to obstructive sleep apnea, which, in turn, may contribute to impaired attention, learning problems, and school failure (Schechter, 2002; Slyper, 1998). Socioeconomic and behavioral factors may play a role in this relationship, and being overweight could possibly be a marker of lower scores on achievement tests (Datar et al., 2004). Overweight children are at risk for reduced school attendance because of health-related issues and may also be at current and future risk for behavior problems, low self-esteem, and depression (Datar & Sturm, 2004; Mustillo et al., 2003; Schwimmer, Burwinkle, & Varni, 2003).

In response to trends in the incidence of obesity, schools have undertaken a range of programs to promote healthy eating and physical activity (for reviews, see Campbell, Waters, O'Meara, & Summerbell, 2001; Krishnamoorthy et al., 2006; Story, Kaphingst, & French, 2006). Students in schools with coordinated obesity-prevention programs have lower rates of overweight, more nutritious diets, and more physical activity than students from schools without similar programs (Veugelers & Fitzgerald, 2005). The consumption of sodas and other sugar-sweetened beverages increases the risk of obesity, and the inclusion of healthy food choices in school vending machines may be a strategy to prevent and reduce obesity (Harnack, Stang, & Story, 1999; Ludwig, Peterson, & Gortmaker, 2001). The American Academy of Pediatrics (AAP), Committee on School Health (2004) has issued a policy statement advising school districts to restrict child access to soda in school, and the U.S. General Accounting Office (GAO; 2003) has encouraged schools to support more nutritious options for children. Indeed, although schools are moving to eliminate soda from their campuses in favor of water, milk, and fruit juices, many schools struggle with revenue losses associated with the elimination of soft drinks from vending machines (e.g., Nestle, 2000; Zorn, 1999). The Center for Science in the Public Interest (2006) surveyed school food policies across the states and concluded that although progress was being made, more than half of the states did not have guidelines to ensure that food and beverages available to children at school were high in nutritional value.

Hyperactivity

Concerns about the nutrition in children's diets have not only focused on weight and obesity; in the 1970s and 1980s, concern about children's diet was focused on the purported role of certain foods, notably those high in sugar, in the development of hyperactivity. Studies at the time suggested associations between sugar intake and hyperactivity and impulsivity (Crook, 1974; Prinz & Riddle, 1986; Prinz, Roberts, & Hantman, 1980; Rapp, 1978). However, the ingestion of glucose or sucrose has not been shown to have a causal relationship with the presence or severity of attention-deficit/hyperactivity disorder (ADHD; Ferguson, Stoddart, & Simeon, 1986; Roshon & Hagen, 1989; Wolraich, Milich, Stumbo, & Schultz, 1985). Furthermore, active children possibly consume more sugar to provide for their higher energy requirements (Deheeger, Rolland-Cachera, & Fontvieille, 1997). Some data suggest an inverse relationship between activity and sucrose/glucose ingestion (Behar, Rapaport, Adams, Berg, & Cornblath, 1984; Saravis, Schachar, Zlotkin, Leiber, & Anderson, 1990). Still, because the educational impact of ADHD can be profound (e.g., Zentall, 1993), there is continued attention on the physiological mechanisms that may be influenced by diet.

A child's nutritional profile provides an important consideration of child health at school entry. Still, the literature base is quite limited, especially considering that studies performed with U.S. children may be of less relevance to children in other, particularly developing, economies. In general, children appear remarkably resilient to minor disparities in nutrition until such disparities extend to full-scale nutrient deficiencies.

EFFECTS OF THE PHYSICAL ENVIRONMENT

For many school-age children, the physical environment presents numerous risks to their physical health as well as their learning abilities as they enter school (Evans, 2004). Although a full review of the entire range of environmental risks is beyond the scope of this chapter, several environmental factors are noteworthy because of their implications in child physical health as well as consistent associations with school-related outcomes. Several of these environmental factors are presented here.

Noise

Although one can reasonably assume that schools often present a noisy environment for children, the emerging literature on the impact of exposure to chronic high-noise environments emphasizes the important distinction between low-level (or ambient) noise and noise that reaches even modest decibel (dB) levels. Noise levels greater than 60 dB not only are intrusive and annoying but also can interfere with cognitive activities. High noise levels (e.g., airport operations) reliably interfere with reading acquisition (Evans, 2004; Evans & Lepore, 1993) and oral language skills (Evans & Maxwell, 1997). The presence of high levels of background noise may present additional risks to children with ADHD, who may have difficulty focusing on important information rather than on background noise (Zentall, 1993). In an experimental study, Maxwell and Evans (2000) showed negative effects on prereading skills, problem solving, and motivation to learn. Although some evidence suggests that children may adapt to the noise level of their environment, with children from chronic high-noise settings performing better on tasks performed in high-noise settings and children from low-noise settings performing better on tasks in quieter settings (Hambrick-Dixon, 1986; Heft, 1979), evidence also shows that this adaptation fades over time so that children from chronic high-noise environments do show decreased performance compared with children from quieter backgrounds (e.g., Cohen, Evans, Stokols, & Krantz, 1986). Chronic noise exposure may also lead to persistent minimal sensorineural hearing loss (Etzel, 2003a). In school-age children, minimal sensorineural hearing loss has been associated with poor school performance and social and emotional dysfunction (Bess, Dodd-Murphy, & Parker, 1998).

Indoor Air Pollution

Air quality and pollution has long been studied by environmental scientists and epidemiologists, who have attributed a range of effects to long-term exposure to pollution. In the last 20 years, scientists have begun to focus on the quality of indoor air, with concerns rising about the need for providing for higher quality air and better ventilation in schools. A recent review of the literature (Mendell & Heath, 2005) linked a range of indicators of poor air quality to student outcomes. Lewis, Snow, Farris, Smerdon, Cronen, and colleagues (2000), reported that approximately one quarter of school administrators reported unsatisfactory ventilation systems in public elementary school, and 18% reported indoor air quality as unsatisfactory in elementary schools.

Commonly studied indoor air pollutants include sidestream smoke (or secondhand smoke) and a range of biological pollutants. Exposure to sidestream smoke has been associated with poor performance on several cognitive tests administered in the third National Health and Nutrition Examination Survey (Yolton, Dietrich, Auinger, Lanphear, & Hornung, 2005). Researchers compared sidestream smoke exposure and performance on four cognitive tests among 4,399 nonsmoking children ages 6–16. The team examined math skills, visual perception of spatial relationships, recognition of printed words, and short-term memory. Eighty-four percent of participants had detectable cotinine, a reliable biomarker of smoke exposure. The researchers showed that children with 3–15 ng/mL of cotinine, the category of greatest exposure, scored about 10% below the least exposed group in reading, math, and spatial relations, although no differences were found between exposure groups in the short-term memory of children in this study. Although regulations prohibiting smoking in schools and many public indoor spaces have existed for quite some time, dramatically reducing children's exposure to secondhand smoke, children may still be exposed in their homes and in automobiles.

In addition to smoke, children may be exposed to a wide range of airborne biological pollutants. Sources of biological pollutants include outdoor air, human occupants who shed viruses and bacteria, animal dander on children's clothing, insects and other arthropods that shed allergens, and damp indoor surfaces and water reservoirs (e.g., humidifiers) in which bacteria and molds can grow. Molds may produce mycotoxins, fungal metabolites with toxic effects ranging from short-term irritation to immunosuppression (Etzel, 2002, 2003b). Mycotoxins are contained on some mold spores that can enter the body through the respiratory tract. Concentrations are often higher indoors than outdoors, and excessive exposure can lead to toxic or allergic reactions (Etzel, 2001). These high concentrations, combined with prolonged exposure throughout a school day, may lead directly to the development of chronic health problems such as respiratory infections that would likely increase absenteeism, as well as indirectly by exacerbating existing medical conditions such as asthma.

Lead

Although banned from nearly all manufactured products for many years, environmental lead exposure continues to be chronic, especially for children living in poverty and/or those living in urban areas. Ingestion of lead from deteriorating paint is a major source of lead exposure for children ages 6 and younger. Blood-lead levels typically peak at about age 2 and then fall without intervention (Lanphear et al., 2002). The AAP, Committee on Environmental Health (2005), uses 10 µg/dL as the concentration of concern. Exposure to lead has been associated with subclinical effects on hearing (Schwartz & Otto, 1991) and balance (Bhattacharya, Shukla, Bornschein, Dietrich, & Keith, 1990). Lead causes cognitive impairment, measured by IQ tests. The strength of this association and its time course are characteristic (Pocock, Smith, & Baghurst, 1994). Some studies have used tooth or bone lead, which are thought to represent integrated, possibly lifetime, exposure measures. Teachers reported that students with elevated tooth-lead levels were more inattentive, hyperactive, disorganized, and less able to follow directions (Needleman et al., 1979; Sciarillo, Alexander, & Farrell, 1992). Further follow-up of these children with elevated blood-lead levels showed higher rates of failure to graduate from high school, reading disabilities, and greater absenteeism in the final year of high school (Needleman, Schell, Bellinger, Leviton, & Allred, 1990). Elevated bone-lead concentrations are associated with increased attentional dysfunction, aggression, and delinquency (Needleman, Riess, Tobin, Biesecker, & Greenhouse, 1996).

Among young children, lead exposure has most frequently been studied as a detriment to general intelligence as measured by IQ tests (for a review, see Pocock et al., 1994). Much of this literature has examined childhood IQ test scores at around the time of school entry (i.e., 5–7 years) among children with blood-lead levels exceeding AAP limits. These studies have reliably shown a decline in IQ test scores with increased lead levels (e.g., Baghurst et al., 1992; Ernhart, Morrow-Tlucak, Wolf, Super, & Drotar, 1989; Needleman and Gatsonis, 1990; Pocock et al., 1994; Schwartz, 1994; Wasserman et al., 1997). Still, recent evidence suggests that exposure to lead below the AAP threshold is associated with IQ test score disparities among children (e.g., Bellinger & Needleman, 2003; Canfield et al., 2003). For example, Canfield et al. (2003) reported declines in IQ test scores in relation to increasing levels of blood-lead levels. Indeed, they found that IQ test scores declined 7.4 points (nearly one standard deviation) as lead levels increased from 1 to 10 µg/dl. The rate of change in IQ test scores was most dramatic as exposure to lead increased, with the most pronounced effect due to lead found at its lowest levels. The linear relation between blood-lead level and IQ test scores has made the establishment of an empirically derived threshold challenging. However, Lanphear et al. (2005) drew from their pooled analysis of data from 1,333 children enrolled in any of seven previously reported longitudinal prospective studies of children exposed to lead to argue that exposures of 7.4 µg/dl were sufficient to create significant reduction in IQ scores. Similarly, in children 6–16 years old, a relationship between blood-lead concentration at the time of testing and decreased scores on reading and arithmetic test scores is apparent, including those whose blood-lead concentrations by then are less than 5 µg/dL (Lanphear, Dietrich, Auinger, & Cox, 2000). Canfield, Gendle, and Cory-Slechta (2004) further specified the effects of lead exposure on $5^1/_2$-year-old children, noting detrimental effects of lead exposure on working memory and a range of executive functioning measures, even after controlling for child IQ test scores in the analysis (see also Stiles and Bellinger, 1993).

Pesticide Exposure

Increased application has made pesticides—including insecticides, herbicides, fungicides, rodenticides, fumigants, and insect repellents—ubiquitous in the environment. The mechanism by which these substances kill pests often is similar to that which harms or kills human beings. These compounds can be toxic to children. Because they are present in food, medications, homes, schools, and parks, children frequently may be exposed.

Some evidence suggests delayed or chronic neurotoxicity associated with pesticide exposure during nervous system development. Although plasticity is inherent in the development of the nervous system in the infant and child, toxic exposures during the brain growth spurt may exert subtle, permanent effects on the structure and function of the brain. Animal studies have demonstrated periods of vulnerability to neurotoxicants during early life. Single, relatively modest doses of organophosphate, pyrethroid, or organochlorine pesticides during the brain growth spurt in rodents lead to permanent changes in muscarinic receptor levels in the brain and behavioral changes into adulthood (Ahlbom, Fredriksson, & Eriksson, 1994, 1995). Recent evidence suggests that acetylcholinesterase may play a direct role in axonal outgrowth and neuronal differentiation (Brimijoin & Koenigsberger, 1999). The widely used organophosphate pesticides chlorpyrifos and diazinon, which are suspected neuroteratogens, have been banned by the United States Environmental Protection Agency (EPA) for general use. These chemicals inhibit deoxyribonucleic acid synthesis in neuronal and glial cells (Qiao, Seidler & Slotkin, 2001).

Some investigators have hypothesized that exposure to neurotoxicants during early life may result in atypical behavioral traits such as hyperactivity, decreased attention span, and neurocognitive deficits (Schettler, Stein, Reich, & Valenti, 2000). One observational study in children from a region in Mexico with intensive pesticide use found a variety of developmental delays compared with otherwise similar children living in a region in which fewer pesticides were used. The children were similar in growth and physical development. However, significant delays were noted among the exposed children in physical stamina, gross and fine hand–eye coordination, short-term memory, and ability to draw a person (Guillette, Meza, Aquilar, Soto, & Garcia, 1998).

In summary, a child's physical environment offers many potential health and developmental risks. Some disparities at school entry, however, may be attributable to environmental exposures. As noted, the environmental factors discussed here have been shown to have effects across large subpopulations of children, in many cases at extremely low levels of exposure. Entry into school marks an important environmental event in the life of a child in that each child's earlier exposures, which are largely beyond the control of school systems, intersect with the possibility of exposure within schools.

PEDIATRIC CHRONIC ONGOING MEDICAL CONDITIONS AND THE TRANSITION INTO ELEMENTARY SCHOOL

About one third of school-age children have some form of ongoing medical condition (Newacheck et al., 1998). Using data from 1994, Newacheck et al. (1998) reported that 18% of U.S. children (approximately 12.6 million) had some form of ongoing medical condition that required additional services. Such conditions account for an additional 52 million missed days of school for children with ongoing medical conditions compared with healthy children. Currie (2005) summarized the range of ways in which ongoing medical conditions may affect children's school readiness, including lost time due to medical attention or illness, possible side effects of treatment, alterations in biophysical systems (possibly including neurological systems), and impacts on the child's relationships with parents, peers, and teachers. Ongoing medical conditions pose a potential threat to child school readiness, both directly and indirectly. For children with ongoing medical conditions such as asthma, diabetes, or seizure disorders, the transition into elementary school requires communication among school personnel, teachers, parents, and health care providers.

For most children entering school, the school's role in their health is generally restricted to ensuring that a child's immunizations are complete and that the child has received a physical examination by a pediatrician (e.g., Lyons, Stanwyck, & McCauley, 2004; Orenstein & Hinman, 1999). However, federal and state policies allow for a range of exemptions to mandatory vaccinations, including exemptions for religious or philosophical objections on the part of children, and for medical contraindications, although Orenstein and Hinman (1999) reported that fewer than 1% of children nationally have such exemptions. Salmon et al. (2005) reported that exemption status is greatly influenced by school policies and practices; thus, considerable variability exists across geographic areas in the extent to which students are vaccinated, a pattern also evident among children younger than school age (Smith, Chu, & Barker, 2004). However, for children who arrive at the school door with ongoing medical conditions, the school becomes a de facto partner (with parents, pediatricians, other medical specialists, and so forth) in addressing the child's serious health concerns. A failure in this partnership would surely be detrimental to the child's physical health and would likely contribute to a range of academic challenges.

For children with ongoing medical conditions, communication among primary caregivers of the child, health care providers (specifically primary care providers and any key subspecialists), and school staff (including school health services, teachers, and other school personnel) is key to facilitating the transition to elementary school (AAP, Committee on Children with Disabilities, 1999; Sexson & Madan-Swain, 1993). Prior to school entry, an evaluation for appropriate placement is necessary. Children with specific diagnoses such as Type I diabetes mellitus may require injections throughout the school day as well as checks of blood sugar levels. During the early elementary years, this may require a school nurse to be on-site throughout the school day to facilitate care. Diagnoses that involve learning disabilities may also require early involvement of school psychologists to facilitate appropriate classroom placements as well as individual education plans (IEPs; AAP, Committee on Children with Disabilities, 2000). Optimizing a child's ability to participate in school to facilitate educational attainment and to improve socialization skills is of paramount importance. Children with ongoing medical conditions have higher rates of repeating grades and are also more likely to be placed in special education classrooms (Gortmaker, Walker, Weitzman, & Sobol, 1990).

Role of Schools in Managing Child Ongoing Medical Conditions

Education of school personnel about the ongoing medical condition of a child will facilitate integration of the child into school (AAP, Committee on Children with Disabilities, Committee on School Health, 1990). Education should encompass knowledge about the specific disease and its management: the nature of illness and the child's prognosis, the treatment prescribed and possible side effects, information regarding what the child knows about the disease and what he or she calls the condition, what the child and parents would like other classmates and school personnel to know about the condition, and regular updates about medically related appointments (Sexson & Madan-Swain, 1993). Education regarding the condition will help teachers understand the limitations while enabling them to challenge the child to achieve his or her potential (AAP, Committee on Children with Disabilities, Committee on School Health, 1990). Schools frequently do not have nurses available all day, every day, so medical preparations, especially for children with ongoing medical conditions, should involve teachers and/or other school personnel. Barrett (2001) showed the utility of school nurses providing some training and preparation for classroom teachers, but this study focused on acute emergency response rather than on responding to the concerns of children with ongoing medical conditions (e.g., responding to a seizure).

Many children with ongoing medical conditions need medication administered during school hours, either on a routine basis (such as medications for ADHD) or in response to symptoms (such as albuterol inhalers for children with asthma). Developing communication plans is important to ensure that teachers, school nurses, and other personnel who may oversee or administer medications for children are educated about the appropriate storage and administration of the medications (AAP, Committee on School Health, 2003). In addition, these individuals should know the adverse effects of the medication, when and for what symptoms they should administer medications, and when they should utilize 911.

Finally, facilitating or providing emergency care for children with ongoing medical conditions is an important facet of care for these children during the school day. Although such preparations are important for all children in the event of a medical emergency, children with ongoing medical conditions are more likely to experience an emergency, and the nature of their illness may require more exhaustive preparations than would be required for otherwise healthy children. In a survey of 675 school nurses, Olympia, Wan, and Avner (2005) found nurses and their schools generally prepared to deal with medical emergencies. In their study, 86% of nurses reported that their schools had emergency medical response plans in place, although nearly one third (35%) of schools never practiced implementing their plans. According to Olympia et al. (2005), nurses were generally confident in their capacity to handle medical emergencies. Following guidance from the AAP and the American Heart Association, 81% percent of schools had asthma care plans for asthmatics, 90% had diabetic response plans for diabetic children, and 86% of schools had specific plans for children with special needs (Olympia et al., 2005).

Asthma

Asthma is the most common ongoing medical condition of childhood. Approximately 12% of children have been given an asthma diagnosis at some time in their lives (Dey, Schiller, & Tai, 2004). According to the National Asthma Education and Prevention Program (2000), asthma accounts for approximately 10 million missed days of school (approximately three times the number of days missed by children without asthma). Specific effects of asthma on school-related competencies have been examined, resulting in a somewhat mixed literature. However, most of the studies that have shown few effects of asthma on child outcomes have been conducted in the context of efforts to examine the effects of asthma-managing therapies (e.g., Annett et al., 2000), in which the child's asthma, although diagnosed, is under control. Studies that examined asthma including cases that are less well controlled, however, have shown effects on behavioral problems and self-control (e.g., Butz et al., 1995; Calam et al., 2003; Gutstadt et al., 1989). In a study of parents with children in kindergarten, Halterman, Montes, et al. (2001) found that parents with asthmatic children reported lower school readiness than parents of nonasthmatic children and were more likely to report their children as needing extra help with learning.

The most important step in caring for these students is correctly identifying a child's asthma and having the necessary information and supplies at hand. The provision of an asthma action plan for school personnel can aid in the care of children with asthma during the school day. The child's primary care physician completes the action plan. As noted previously, Olympia et al. (2005) reported that four of five schools have such plans in place. This individualized plan provides information on 1) the early warning signs of asthma, 2) what medications the student uses and how they should be used based on the child's symptoms, and 3) when to call 911. In conjunction with the action plan, all children should have "rescue" medications available during the school day to treat acute asthma symptoms. If the child is deemed able to correctly self-administer his or her rescue medication (typically Albuterol, either as an inhaler or via aerosol machine), then allowing the child to carry his or her medication will facilitate relief of symptoms and increase the likelihood of use when necessary. This assessment should be completed by the physician in conjunction with the child's parents. For children not able to carry their inhalers, inhalers should be readily available for administration at all times (AAP, Committee on School Health, 2003). Schools should also insist that the inhaler is provided with a spacer, a valved holding chamber that increases the delivery of medication to the lungs, increasing the medication's effectiveness in relieving the asthma symptoms (Rubin & Fink, 2003).

The United States EPA, Indoor Environments Division Office of Air and Radiation (2000), recommends that school buildings and classrooms be assessed for common asthma triggers, particularly for children who need their rescue inhaler during the school day on a regular basis. Checklists to assist with the assessment are available through the EPA. Some common triggers include dust mites, chalk dust, animals, strong odors (e.g., perfumes, chemicals, paint), and exercise.

The third component of managing asthma in schools is education of teachers, coaches, school health personnel, and other staff members who may be responsible for medications when health personnel are not available (National Asthma Education and Prevention Program, 2000). Components of education should include signs of an asthma episode, how to respond to the episode, and information about side effects of asthma rescue medicines. In addition, coaches should receive education about exercise-induced asthma and techniques to prevent symptoms during exercise.

Through communication among parents, school staff, and the child's health care provider, a child's asthma should be optimally managed to maximize participation in all aspects of school with minimal days absent. Sapien, Fullerton-Gleasen, and Allen (2004) found that even brief but direct training in the management of asthma helped increase teachers' confidence in managing asthma-related crises in the classroom.

Allergies

Allergies are extremely common among young children. Currie (2005) cited data from the 2002 National Health Interview Survey indicating that 10.3% of children suffer from hay fever, 12.3% have respiratory allergies, and 11.3% have other allergies, including food and medicinal, although variability in reporting makes exact prevalence estimation difficult. Allergic symptoms include nasal congestion, nasal drainage, sneezing, itchy and watery eyes, and itchy nose. The most common allergens include pollens from trees, grasses, and weeds; molds, including outdoor molds (which are seasonal in colder climates) and indoor molds (which can manifest as year-round symptoms); animal dander; dust mites; and cockroaches. Because of their nature, many allergens can be controlled through air-quality control and ventilation.

Important considerations in the classroom include what plants will be grown in the classroom and whether animals should be kept in a classroom. If any plants or animals are kept in a classroom and a child continually has symptoms (e.g., a runny nose, sneezing), the offending agent should be identified and removed from the classroom. If the classroom has no pets or plants, evaluating the classroom for molds may identify a source for the allergies. Symptoms experienced by children can interfere with their ability to pay attention or fully participate in classroom activities. In addition, certain medications used to treat allergies can cause symptoms such as drowsiness, which also may impede classroom performance. If increased drowsiness is noted in a child with allergies, communication with the parent may aid in medication selection by the child's health care provider.

Another area of concern is anaphylaxis, or serious allergic reactions. Although these reactions can potentially occur following exposure to any substance, the most common causes are foods (e.g., tree nuts, peanuts, shellfish), drugs, or certain bee venoms. These are critical allergic reactions that may begin as mild cases of hives (known as *urticaria*) that progress to wheezing, swelling of tissues in the throat and mouth, difficulty breathing, abdominal cramps, and, eventually, loss of consciousness and slow heart rate. Anaphylaxis usually occurs within 30 minutes of exposure to the substance if injected (e.g., bee venom) or within 2 hours if ingested (e.g., food).

Once a child is diagnosed as allergic to one of the above substances, school personnel, including teachers, health personnel, and others, must be informed (American Academy of Allergy, Asthma and Immunology Board of Directors, 1998). Appropriate school personnel should also be involved in education about the allergy and on how to avoid the offending agent (such as what prepared foods to avoid or how to avoid insect stings). A plan should be formulated to respond to an anaphylactic reaction, and all personnel involved with the child should understand the plan (AAP, Committee on School Health, 2003). In addition, children who are developmentally ready should carry a prescribed self-administered epinephrine kit when deemed appropriate. Each child's primary teacher also should be instructed in use of the kit, and school staff responsible for medication administration should receive similar instruction. These children should be encouraged to wear MedicAlert bracelets to identify the allergy. These bracelets help facilitate expeditious treatment. However, the degree to which these recommendations have been implemented in schools is not entirely clear (e.g., Rhim & McMorris, 2001).

Diabetes

Diabetes is one of the most common ongoing medical conditions present in school-age children, with approximately 1 in 400–500 children having a form of diabetes (National Diabetes Education Program, 2005). Diabetes in childhood usually is Type 1 diabetes, in which the insulin-producing cells in the body are destroyed, leaving the person dependent on insulin injections for life (unlike those with Type 2 diabetes). Management of diabetes includes monitoring of blood glucose levels, healthy eating, and physical activity. Because Type 1 diabetic children are taking insulin shots, they also are at risk of hypoglycemia (low blood sugar levels), so these children and their teachers must be prepared to identify and respond to the symptoms of hypoglycemia.

The National Diabetes Education Program (2003), a collaborative effort jointly sponsored by the National Institutes of Health and the U.S. Centers for Disease Control and Prevention with the support of more than 200 organizations, has developed a guide that provides education and information for various school personnel. In addition, it provides tools to ensure that correct medical information is shared with all concerned parties and that accurate communication of the child's concerns during the school day occurs. The family and the health care providers who manage the child's diabetes develop the medical management plan. In addition, an emergency plan assists school personnel in recognizing both hypoglycemia and hyperglycemia (high blood sugar levels) and in correctly responding to both of these urgent conditions. School nurses should be highly involved in coordinating medical care for the child throughout the school day, which may include checking blood sugar levels as well as the potential provision of insulin shots.

Epilepsy/Seizure Disorders

There are many different seizure disorders, with approximately 3%–5% of children experiencing some form of seizure. Epilepsy, a disorder of spontaneous recurrent seizures not related to fevers, is seen in approximately 4–6 children per 1,000 (Haslam, 1997). Controlling seizures without adverse effects is the goal; however, this can be difficult to achieve for some children. These adverse effects range from severe physiological symptoms, such as liver toxicity, to a range of potentially serious behavioral issues, such as hyperactivity, irritability, and aggressive behavior habits. Most children who experience seizures are of typical intelligence, although learning disabilities are more common than in the general population. Therefore, the academic progression of these children should be closely monitored, and evaluation should occur in a timely manner if concerns arise.

Many of the considerations necessary for the medical management of children with seizures are similar to those mentioned in previous sections. These include identification of children with this condition and communication among parent, health care provider, school health staff, and teachers as to the children's condition and level of functioning. Staff should be educated about the seizure type and what physical manifestations are common for the student's type of seizure disorder. In addition, completing a seizure action plan that will detail the appropriate responses to a seizure event is helpful (sample forms are available at the Epilepsy Foundation web site, School Nurse Program, www.epilepsyfoundation.org). These action plans provide information on how to place the child for his or her safety, when and if medications should be administered, and when to call 911. For most children who have a seizure disorder without other medical conditions, their only limitations are that they cannot swim or bathe unattended. In addition, these children should wear a helmet when riding bicycles. Otherwise, if they are physically able and their seizures are well controlled, they should be allowed to participate fully in gym and other school activities (AAP, 2001).

Special issues must be considered for children with ongoing medical conditions during the transition into school; however, through thoughtful management and preparation for the concerns of children with ongoing medical conditions, children's educational outcomes can be improved and their participation in school activities can be optimized. A common concern regarding any child with ongoing medical conditions is that the child's school and family must work in concert to manage the child's academic progress as well as his or her physical well-being.

CONCLUSION

This chapter has summarized the impact of several broad child health issues on children's ability to learn. Adequate nutrition; a quiet, toxin-free environment; and appropriate treatment of childhood ongoing medical conditions all play an important role in ensuring that young children arrive in school each morning ready to learn. As data continue to accumulate on the relation between children's health and their school performance, educators, parents, and policy makers should use these findings to collaborate and create community-based interventions (Devlin & Asay, 2005) that will improve children's school performance (Goldfeld & Oberklaid, 2005). When considering that young children spend nearly half of their waking hours (and even more if they are involved in wraparound or after-school programs) in the classroom, addressing the health and physical well-being of children as they enter school involves a partnership between parents and schools, just as addressing child academic development requires a partnership between parents and teachers. To be successful, such partnerships need to be informed by the best science available.

REFERENCES

American Academy of Allergy, Asthma and Immunology Board of Directors. (1998). Anaphylaxis in schools and other child care settings. *Journal of Allergy and Clinical Immunology, 102,* 173–176.

Abalkhail, B., & Shawsky, S. (2002). Prevalence of daily breakfast intake, iron-deficiency anaemia, and awareness of being anaemic among Saudi school students. *International Journal of Food Science and Nutrition, 53,* 519–528.

Ahlbom, J., Fredriksson, A., & Eriksson, P. (1994). Neonatal exposure to a type-I pyrethroid (bioallethrin) induces dose-response changes in brain muscarinic receptors and behaviour in neonatal and adult mice. *Brain Research, 645,* 318–324.

Ahlbom, J., Fredriksson, A., & Eriksson, P. (1995). Exposure to an organophosphate (DFP) during a defined period in neonatal life induces permanent changes in brain muscarinic receptors and behaviour in adult mice. *Brain Research, 677,* 13–19.

Alaimo, K., Olson, C.M., & Frongillo, E.A.J. (2001). Food insufficiency and American school-aged children's cognitive, academic and psychosocial development. *Pediatrics, 108*(1), 44–53.

American Academy of Pediatrics (AAP), Committee on Children with Disabilities. (1999). Care coordination: Integrating health and related systems of care for children with special health needs. *Pediatrics, 104,* 978–981.

American Academy of Pediatrics (AAP), Committee on Children with Disabilities. (2000). Provision of educationally-related services for children and adolescents with chronic diseases and disabling conditions. *Pediatrics, 105,* 448–451.

American Academy of Pediatrics (AAP), Committee on Children with Disabilities, Committee on School Health. (1990). Children with Health Impairments in Schools. *Pediatrics, 86,* 636–638.

American Academy of Pediatrics (AAP), Committee on Environmental Health. (2005). Lead exposure in children: Prevention, detection, and management. *Pediatrics, 116,* 1036–1046.

American Academy of Pediatrics (AAP), Committee on Pediatric Emergency Medicine. (1999). Emergency preparedness for children with special health care needs. *Pediatrics, 104,* e53.

American Academy of Pediatrics (AAP), Committee on School Health. (2003). Guidelines for the administration of medication in school. *Pediatrics, 112,* 697–699.

American Academy of Pediatrics (AAP), Committee on School Health. (2004). Soft drinks in schools. *Pediatrics, 113,* 152–154.

American Academy of Pediatrics, Committee on Sports Medicine and Fitness. (2001). Medical conditions affecting sports participation. *Pediatrics, 107*(5), 1205–1209.

Anderson, E.W., Valerio, M., Liu, M., Jones Benet, D., Joseph, C., Brown, B., et al. (2005). Schools' capacity to help low-income, minority children to manage asthma. *The Journal of School Nursing, 21*(4), 236–242.

Annett, R.D., Aylward, E.H., Lapidus, J., Bender, B.G., DuHamel, T., & the Childhood Asthma Management Program. (2000). Neurocognitive functioning in children with mild and moderate asthma in the Childhood Asthma Management Program. *Journal of Allergy and Clinical Immunology, 105,* 717–724.

Baghurst, P.A., McMichael, A.J., Wigg, N.R., Vimpani, G.V., Robertson, E.F., Roberts, R.J., et al. (1992). Environmental exposure to lead and children's intelligence at the age of seven years: The Port Pirie Cohort Study. *New England Journal of Medicine, 327,* 1279–1284.

Barrett, J.C. (2001). Teaching teachers about school health emergencies. *Journal of School Nursing, 17,* 316–322.

Bautista, A., Barker, P.A., Dunn, J.T., Sanchez, M., & Kaiser, D.L. (1982). The effects of oral iodized oil on intelligence, thyroid status, and somatic growth in school-age children from an area of endemic goitre. *American Journal of Clinical Nutrition, 35,* 127–134.

Behar, D., Rapaport, J.L., Adams, A.A., Berg, C.K., & Cornblath, M. (1984). Sugar challenge testing with children considered behaviorally "sugar-active." *Nutrition and Behavior, 1,* 277–288.

Bellinger, D.C., & Needleman, H.L. (2003). Intellectual impairment and blood lead levels. *New England Journal of Medicine, 349,* 500–502.

Benton, D., Brett, V., & Brain, P.F. (1987). Glucose improves attention and reaction to frustration in children. *Biological Psychology, 24,* 95–100.

Benton, D., & Buts, J.P. (1990). Vitamin/mineral supplementation and intelligence. *Lancet, 335,* 1158–1160.

Benton, D., & Roberts, G. (1988). Effects of multivitamin and mineral supplementation on intelligence of a sample of school children. *Lancet, 1,* 140–143.

Benton, D., Ruffin, M.P., Lassel, T., Nabb, S., Messaoudi, M., Vinoy, S., et al. (2003). The delivery rate of dietary carbohydrates affects cognitive performance in both rats and humans. *Psychopharmacology, 166,* 86–90.

Bess, F.H., Dodd-Murphy, J., & Parker, R.A. (1998). Children with minimal sensorineural hearing loss: Prevalence, educational performance, and functional status. *Ear and Hearing, 19,* 339–354.

Bhattacharya, A., Shukla, R., Bornschein, R.L., Dietrich, K.N., & Keith, R. (1990). Lead effects on postural balance of children. *Environmental Health Perspectives, 89,* 35–42.

Brimijoin, S., & Koenigsberger, C. (1999). Cholinesterases in neural development: New findings and toxicologic implications. *Environmental Health Perspectives, 107* (Suppl. 1), 59–64.

Bruner, A.B., Joffe, A., Duggan, A.K., Casella, J.F., & Brandt, J. (1996). Randomized study of cognitive effects of iron supplementation in non-anaemic iron-deficient adolescent girls. *Lancet, 348,* 1789–1792.

Butz, A.M., Malveaux, F.J., Eggleston, P., Thompson, L., Huss, K., Kolodner, K., et al. (1995). Social factors associated with behavioral problems in children with asthma. *Clinical Pediatrics, 34,* 581–590.

Calam, R., Gregg, L., Simpson, B., Morris, J., Woodcock, A., & Custovic, A. (2003). Childhood asthma, behavior problems, and family functioning. *Journal of Allergy and Clinical Immunology, 112,* 499–504.

Campbell, K., Waters, E., O'Meara, S., & Summerbell, C. (2001). Interventions for preventing obesity in childhood: A systematic review. *Obesity Review, 2,* 149–157.

Campos, A.L., Sigulem, D.M., Moraes, D.E., Escrivao, A.M., & Fisberg, M. (1996). Intelligence quotient of obese children and adolecents by the Weschler scale. *Revista de Saúde Pública, 30*(1), 85–90.

Canfield, R.L., Gendle, M.H., & Cory-Slechta, D.A. (2004). Impaired neuropsychological functioning in lead-exposed children. *Developmental Neuropsychology, 26,* 513–540.

Canfield, R.L., Henderson, C.R., Cory-Slechta, D.A., Cox, C., Jusko, T.A., & Lanphear, B.P. (2003). Intellectual impairments in children with blood lead concentrations below 10 µg per deciliter. *New England Journal of Medicine, 348,* 1517–1526.

Cavan, K.R., Gibson, R.S., Grazioso, C.F., Isalgue, A.M., Ruz, M., & Solomons, N.W. (1993). Growth and body composition of periurban Guatemalan children in relation to zinc status: A longitudinal zinc intervention trial. *American Journal of Clinical Nutrition, 57,* 344–352.

Center for Health and Health Care in Schools. (2003). *Improving academic performance by meeting student health needs.* Retrieved January 19, 2006, from http://www.healthinschools.org/education.asp

Center for Science in the Public Interest. (2006). *School foods report card.* Washington, DC: Author.

Chandler, A.M.K., Walker, S.P., Connolly, K., & Grantham-McGregor, S.M. (1995). School breakfast improves verbal fluency in under-nourished Jamaican children. *Journal of Nutrition, 125,* 894–900.

Clifford, R., Early, D.M., & Hills, T. (1999). Almost a million children in school before kindergarten. *Young Children, 54*(5), 48–51.

Cohen, S., Evans, G.W., Stokols, D., & Krantz, D.E. (1986). *Behavior, health, and environmental stress.* New York: Plenum.

Connors, C.K., & Blouin, A.G. (1983). Nutritional effects on behaviour in children. *Journal of Psychiatric Research, 17,* 198–201.

Crombie, I.K., Todman, J., McNeill, G., Florey, C.D., Menzies, I., & Kennedy, R.A. (1990). Effect of vitamin supplementation on verbal and non-verbal reasoning of school children. *Lancet, 335,* 744–747.

Crook, W.G. (1974). An alternative method of managing the hyperactive child. *Pediatrics, 5,* 46–56.

Currie, J. (2005). Health disparities and gaps in school readiness. *The Future of Children, 15,* 117–138.

Datar, A., & Sturm, R. (2004). Childhood overweight and parent- and teacher-reported behavior problems: Evidence from a prospective study of kindergartners. *Archives of Pediatric and Adolescent Medicine, 158*(8), 804–810.

Datar, A., Sturm, R., & Magnabosco, J.L. (2004). Childhood overweight and academic performance: National study of kindergartners and first-graders. *Obesity Research, 12*(1), 58–68.

Deheeger, M., Rolland-Cachera, M.F., & Fontvieille, A.M. (1997). Physical activity and body composition in 10 year old French children: Linkages with nutritional intake? *International Journal of Obesity and Related Metabolic Disorders, 21,* 372–379.

Devlin, L.M., & Asay, M.K. (2005). Rising student health needs require a school safety net. *North Carolina Medical Journal, 66*(2), 152–154.

Dey, A.N., Schiller, J.S., & Tai, D.A. (2004). Summary health statistics for U.S. children: National Health Interview Survey, 2002. *National Center for Health Statistics, Vital Health Statistics, 10,* 1–78.

Dickie, N.H., & Bender, A.E. (1982). Breakfast and performance in school children. *British Journal of Nutrition, 48,* 483–496.

Dietz, W.H., & Robinson, T.N. (1998). Use of the body mass index as a measure of overweight in children and adolescents. *Journal of Pediatrics, 132,* 191–193.

Donohoe, R.T., & Benton, D. (1999). Cognitive function is susceptible to the level of blood glucose. *Psychopharmacology, 145,* 378–385.

Edward, H.G., & Evers, S. (2001). Benefits and barriers associated with participation in food programs in three, low-income Ontario communities. *Canadian Journal of Dietetic Practice and Research, 62,* 76–81.

Ernhart, C.B., Morrow-Tlucak, M., Wolf, A.W., Super, D., & Drotar, D. (1989). Low level lead exposure in the prenatal and early preschool periods: Intelligence prior to school entry. *Neurotoxicology and Teratology, 11,* 161–170.

Etzel, R.A. (2001). Indoor air pollutants in homes and schools. *Pediatric Clinics of North America, 48,* 1153–1165.

Etzel, R.A. (2002). Mycotoxins. *Journal of the American Medical Association, 287,* 425–427.

Etzel, R.A. (Ed.). (2003a). *Pediatric environmental health.* Elk Grove Village, IL: American Academy of Pediatrics, Committee on Environmental Health.

Etzel, R.A. (2003b). Stachybotrys. *Current Opinions in Pediatrics, 15,* 103–106.

Evans, G.W. (2004). The environment of childhood poverty. *American Psychologist, 59,* 77–92.

Evans, G.W., & Lepore, S.J. (1993). Non-auditory effects of noise on children: A critical review. *Children's Environments, 19,* 31–51.

Evans, G.W., & Maxwell, L. (1997). Chronic noise exposure and reading deficits: The mediating effects of language acquisition. *Environment and Behavior, 29,* 638–656.

Eysenck, H.J., & Schoenthaler, S. (1997). Raising IQ level by vitamin and mineral supplementation. In R.J. Sternberg & E.L. Grigorenko (Eds.), *Intelligence, heredity and environment* (pp. 363–392). Cambridge, UK: Cambridge University Press.

Ferguson, H.B., Stoddart, C., & Simeon, P.G. (1986). Double blind challenge studies of behavioral and cognitive effects of sucrose-aspartame ingestion in normal children. *Nutrition Reviews, 44,* 144–150.

Gibson, R.S., Vanderkooy, P.D., MacDonald, A.C., Goldman, A., Ryan, B.A., & Berry, M. (1989). A growth-limiting, mild zinc-deficiency syndrome in some South Ontario boys with low height percentiles. *American Journal of Clinical Nutrition, 49,* 1266–1273.

Goldfeld, S.R., & Oberklaid, F. (2005). Maintaining an agenda for children: The role of data in linking policy, politics and outcomes. *The Medical Journal of Australia, 183*(4), 209–211.

Gortmaker, S.L., Walker, D.K., Weitzman, M., & Sobol, A.M. (1990). Chronic conditions, socioeconomic risks and behavioral problems in children and adolescents. *Pediatrics, 85,* 267–276.

Grantham-McGregor, S., & Ani, C. (2001). A review of studies on the effect of iron deficiency on cognitive development in children. *Journal of Nutrition, 131*(2S-2), 649S–666S.

Guillette, E.A., Meza, M.M., Aquilar, M.G., Soto, A.D., & Garcia, I.E. (1998). An anthropological approach to the evaluation of preschool children exposed to pesticides in Mexico. *Environmental Health Perspectives, 106,* 347–353.

Gutstadt, L.B., Gillette, J.W., Mrazek, D.A., Fukuhara, J.T., LaBrecque, J.F., & Strunk, R.C. (1989). Determinants of school performance in children with chronic asthma. *American Journal of Diseases in Children, 143*(4), 471–475.

Hall, A., Khanh, L.N., & Son, T.H. (2001). An association between chronic undernutrition and educational test scores in Vietnamese children. *European Journal of Clinical Nutrition, 55,* 801–804.

Halterman, J.S., Kaczorowski, J.M., Aligne, C.A., Auinger, P., & Szilagyi, P.G. (2001). Iron deficiency and cognitive achievement among school-aged children and adolescents in the United States. *Pediatrics, 107*(6), 1381–1386.

Halterman, J.S., Montes, G., Aligne, C.A., Kaczorowski, J.M., Hightower, D., & Szilagyi, P.G. (2001). School readiness among urban children with asthma. *Ambulatory Pediatrics, 1,* 201–205.

Hambrick-Dixon, P.J. (1986). Effects of experimentally imposed noise on task performance of black children attending day care centers near elevated subway tracks. *Developmental Psychology, 22,* 259–264.

Harnack, L., Stang, J., & Story, M. (1999). Soft drink consumption among U.S. children and adolescents: Nutritional consequences. *Journal of the American Dieticians Association, 99,* 436–441.

Haslam, R.H. (1997). Nonfebrile seizures. *Pediatrics in Review, 18*(2), 39–49.

Heft, H. (1979). Background and focal environmental conditions of the home and attention in young children. *Journal of Applied Social Psychology, 9,* 47–69.

Howard, T., & Potts-Datema, W. (2005). Obesity and student performance at school. *Journal of School Health, 75*(8), 291–295.

Hutchinson S.E., Powell, C.A., Walker, S.P., Chang, S.M., & Grantham-McGregor, S.M. (1997). Nutrition, anaemia, geohelminth infection, and school achievement in rural Jamaican primary school children. *European Journal of Clinical Nutrition, 51,* 729–735.

Ivanovic, D., Vasquez, M., Aguayo, M., Ballester, D., Marambio, M., & Zacarias, I. (1992). Educational achievement and food habits of Chilean elementary and high school graduates. *Archives of Latinoamerican Nutrition, 42,* 9–14.

Kennedey, D.O., & Scholey, A.B. (2000). Glucose administration, heart rate and cognitive performance: Effects of increasing mental effort. *Psychopharmacology, 149,* 63–71.

Kleinman, R.E., Hall, S., & Green, H. (2002). Diet, breakfast, and academic performance in children. *Annals of Nutrition and Metabolism, 46*(Suppl. 1), 24–30.

Kleinman, R.E., Murphy, J.M., & Little, M. (1998). Hunger in children in the United States: Potential behavioral and emotional correlates. *Pediatrics, 101*(1), e3.

Krishnamoorthy, J.S., Hart, C., & Jelalian, E. (2006). The epidemic of childhood obesity: Review of research and implications for public policy. *Social Policy Report, 20,* 3–17.

Lanphear, B.P., Dietrich, K.N., Auinger, P., & Cox, C. (2000). Cognitive deficits associated with blood lead concentrations of 10 mg/dL in U.S. children and adolescents. *Public Health Reports, 115,* 521–529.

Lanphear, B.P., Hornung, R., Ho, M., Howard, C.R., Eberly, S., & Knauf, K. (2002). Environmental lead exposure during early childhood. *Journal of Pediatrics, 140,* 40–47.

Lanphear, B.P., Hornung, R., Khoury, J., Yolton, K., Baghurst, P., Bellinger, D.C., et al. (2005). Low-level environmental lead exposure and children's intellectual function: An international pooled analysis. *Environmental Health Perspectives, 113,* 894–899.

Lewis, L., Snow, K., Farris, E., Smerdon, B., Cronen, S., & Kaplan, J., et al. (2000). *Condition of America's public school facilities: 1999* (NCES 2000-032). Washington, DC: U.S. Department of Education, National Center for Education Statistics.

Li, X. (1995). A study of intelligence and personality in children with simple obesity. *International Journal of Obesity and Related Metabolic Disorders, 19*(5), 355–357.

Ludwig, D.S., Peterson, K.E., & Gortmaker, S.L. (2001). Relation between consumption of sugar-sweetened drinks and childhood obesity: A prospective, observational analysis. *Lancet, 357,* 505–508.

Lynn, R., & Harland, P. (1998). A positive effect of iron supplementation on the IQ's of iron deficient Children. *Personality and Individual Differences, 24,* 883–885.

Lyons, B., Stanwyck, C., & McCauley, M. (2004). Vaccination coverage among children entering school: United States, 2003-04 school year. *Morbidity and Mortality Weekly Report, 53,* 1041–1044.

Maxwell, L.E., & Evans, G.W. (2000). The effects of noise on pre-school children's pre-reading skills. *Journal of Environmental Psychology, 20,* 91–97.

Mendell, M.J., & Heath, G.A. (2005). Do indoor air pollutants and thermal conditions in schools influence student performance? A critical review of the literature. *Indoor Air, 15,* 27–52.

Meyers, A.F., Sampson, A.E., Weitzman, M., Rogers, B.L., & Kayne, H. (1989). School breakfast program and school performance. *Archives of Pediatrics and Adolescent Medicine, 143,* 1234–1239.

Michaud, C., Musse, N., Nicholas, J.P., & Mejean, L. (1991). Effects of breakfast size on short-term memory, concentration, mood and blood glucose. *Journal of Adolescent Health, 12,* 53–57.

Mukudi, E. (2003). Nutrition status, education participation, and school achievement among Kenyan middle-school children. *Nutrition, 19,* 612–616.

Murphy, J.M., Pagano, M.E., Nachmani, J., Sperling, P., Kane, S., & Kleinman, R.E. (1998). The relationship of school breakfast to psychosocial and academic functioning: Cross-sectional and longitudinal observations in an inner-city school sample. *Archives of Pediatric and Adolescent Medicine, 152,* 899–907.

Murphy, J.M., Wehler, C.A., Pagano, M.E., Little, M., Kleinman, R.E., & Jellinek, M.S. (1998). Relationship between hunger and psychosocial functioning in low-income American children. *Journal of the American Academy of Child and Adolescent Psychiatry, 37,* 163–170.

Mustillo, S., Worthman, C., Erkanli, A., Keeler, G., Angold, A., & Costello, E.J. (2003). Obesity and psychiatric disorder: Developmental trajectories. *Pediatrics, 111,* 851–859.

National Asthma Education and Prevention Program. (2000). *Pediatric asthma: Promoting best practice— A guide for managing asthma in children.* Milwaukee, WI: American Academy of Allergy, Asthma & Immunology.

National Diabetes Education Program. (2003). *Helping the student with diabetes succeed: A guide for school personnel.* Washington, DC: U.S. Department of Health and Human Services.

National Diabetes Education Program. (2005). *Overview of diabetes in children and adolescents: A fact sheet from the National Diabetes Education Program.* Retrieved from http://www.ndep.nih.gov/ diabetes/youth/youth_FS.htm, 11/2/2005

Needleman, H.L., & Gatsonis, C.A. (1990). Low-level lead exposure and the IQ of children: A meta-analysis of modern studies. *Journal of the American Medical Association, 263,* 673–678.

Needleman, H.L., Gunnoe, C., Leviton, A., Reed, R., Peresie, H., Maher, C., et al. (1979). Deficits in psychological and classroom performance of children with elevated dentine lead levels. *New England Journal of Medicine, 300,* 689–695.

Needleman, H.L., Riess, J., Tobin, M., Biesecker, G., & Greenhouse, J. (1996). Bone lead levels and delinquent behavior. *Journal of the American Medical Association, 275,* 363–369.

Needleman, H.L., Schell, A., Bellinger, D., Leviton, A., & Allred, E.N. (1990). The long-term effects of exposure to low doses of lead in childhood: an 11-year follow-up report. *New England Journal of Medicine, 322,* 83–88.

Nelson, M. (1992). Vitamin and mineral supplementation and academic performance in schoolchildren. *Proceedings of the Nutrition Society, 51,* 303–313.

Nelson, M., Naismith, D.J., Burley, V., Gatenby, S., & Geddes, N. (1990). Nutrient intakes, vitamin-mineral supplementation, and intelligence in British schoolchildren. *British Journal of Nutrition, 64*(1), 13–22.

Nestle, M. (2000). Soft drink "pouring rights": Marketing empty calories to children. *Public Health Reports, 115,* 308–319.

Newacheck, P.W., Strickland, B., Shonkoff, J.P., Perrin, J.M., McPherson, M., McManus, M., et al. (1998). An epidemiologic profile of children with special health needs. *Pediatrics, 102,* 117–123.

Ogden, C.L., Carroll, M.D., Curtin, L.R., McDowell, M.A., Tabak, C.J., & Flegal, K.M. (2006). Prevalence of overweight and obesity in the United States, 1999–2004. *Journal of the American Medical Association, 295,* 1549–1555.

Ogden, C.L., Flegal, K.M., Carroll, M.D., & Johnson, C.L. (2002). Prevalence and trends in overweight among U.S. children and adolescents, 1999–2000. *Journal of the American Medical Association, 288,* 1728–1732.

Olympia, R.P., Wan, E., & Avner, J.P. (2005). The preparedness of schools to respond to emergencies in children: A national survey of school nurses. *Pediatrics, 116,* 738–745.

Orenstein, W.A., & Hinman, A.R. (1999). The immunization system in the United States: The role of school immunization laws. *Vaccine,17*(Suppl. 3), S19–S24.

Otero, G.A., Aguirre, D.M., Porcayo, R., & Fernandez, T. (1999). Psychological and electroencephalographic study in school children with iron deficiency. *International Journal of Neuroscience, 99,* 113–121.

Pastor, M., Sadd, J.L., & Morello-Forsch, R. (2004). Reading, writing, and toxics: Children's health, academic performance, and environmental justice in Los Angeles. *Environment & Planning C: Government & Policy, 22*(2), 271–290.

Pocock, S.J., Smith, M., & Baghurst, P. (1994). Environmental lead and children's intelligence: A systematic review of the epidemiological evidence. *British Medical Journal, 309,* 1189–1197.

Pollitt, E. (1997). Iron deficiency and educational deficiency. *Nutrition Review, 55*(4), 133–141.

Pollitt, E., Cueto, S., & Jacoby, E.R. (1998). Fasting and cognition in well- and under-nourished school children: A review of three experimental studies. *American Journal of Clinical Nutrition, 67*(Suppl.), 779S–784S.

Pollitt, E., Leibel, R.L., & Greenfield, D. (1981). Brief fasting, stress and cognition in children. *American Journal of Clinical Nutrition, 34,* 1526–1533.

Pollitt, E., Lewis, N.L., Graza, C., & Schulman, R.J. (1982). Fasting and cognitive function. *Journal of Psychiatric Research, 17*(2), 169–174.

Powell, C.A., Walker, S.P., Chang, S.M., & Grantham-McGregor, S.M. (1998). Nutrition and education: A randomized trial of the effects of breakfast in rural primary school children. *American Journal of Clinical Nutrition, 68,* 873–879.

Prinz, R.J., & Riddle, D.B. (1986). Association between nutrition and behavior. *Nutrition Review, 44,* 151–158.

Prinz, R.J., Roberts, W.A., & Hantman, E. (1980). Dietary correlates of hyperactive behavior in children. *Journal of Consulting and Clinical Psychology, 47,* 760–769.

Qiao, D., Seidler, F.J., & Slotkin, T.A. (2001). Developmental neurotoxicity of chlorpyrifos modeled in vitro: Comparative effects of metabolites and other cholinesterase inhibitors on DNA synthesis in PC12 and C6 cells. *Environmental Health Perspectives, 109,* 909–913.

Rapp, D.J. (1978). Does diet affect hyperactivity? *Journal of Learning Disabilities, 11,* 383–389.

Rhim, G.S., & McMorris, M.S. (2001). School readiness for children with food allergies. *Annals of Allergy, Asthma, and Immunology, 86,* 172–176.

Richter, L.M., Rose, C., & Griesel, R.D. (1997). Cognitive and behavioral effects of a school breakfast. *South African Medical Journal, 87,* 93–100.

Roshon, M.S., & Hagen, R.L. (1989). Sugar consumption, locomotion, task orientation, and learning in preschool children. *Journal of Abnormal Child Psychology, 17,* 349–357.

Rubin, B.K., & Fink, J.B. (2003). The delivery of inhaled medication to the young child. *Pediatric Clinics of North America, 50*(3), 717–731.

Salmon, D.A., Omer, S.B., Moulton, L.H., Stokley, S., deHart, M.P., Lett, S., et al. (2005). Exemptions to school immunization requirements: The role of school-level requirements, policies, and procedures. *American Journal of Public Health, 95,* 436–440.

Sandstead, H.H., Penland, J.G., & Alcock, N.W. (1998). Effects of repletion with zinc and other micronutrients on neuropsychological performance and growth of Chinese children. *American Journal of Clinical Nutrition, 68*(Suppl. 2), 470S–475S.

Sankar, R., Rai, B., & Pulger, T. (1994). Intellectual and motor functions in school children from severely iodine deficient regions in Sikkim. *Indian Journal of Pediatrics, 61,* 231–236.

Sapien, R.E., Fullerton-Gleasen, L., & Allen, N. (2004). Teaching school teachers to recognize respiratory distress in asthmatic children. *Journal of Asthma, 41,* 739–743.

Saravis, S., Schachar, R., Zlotkin, S., Leiber, L.A., & Anderson, G.H. (1990). Aspartame: Effects on learning, behavior and mood. *Pediatrics, 86,* 75–80.

Schechter, M.S.; Section on Pediatric Pulmonology, Subcommittee on Obstructive Sleep Apnea Syndrome. (2002, April). Diagnosis and management of childhood obstructive sleep apnea syndrome. *Pediatrics, 109*(4), e69.

Schettler, T., Stein, J., Reich, J., & Valenti, M. (2000). *In harm's way: Toxic threats to child development.* Cambridge, MA: Greater Boston Physicians for Social Responsibility.

Schoenthaler, S.J., Amos, S.P., Doraz, W.F., & Kelly, J.W. (1991). Controlled trial of vitamin-mineral supplementation on intelligence and brain function. *Personality and Individual Differences, 12,* 343–350.

Schoenthaler, S.J., & Bier, I.D. (1999). Vitamin-mineral intake and intelligence: A macrolevel analysis of randomized controlled trials. *Journal of Alternative and Complementary Medicine, 5,* 125–134.

Schoenthaler, S.J., Bier, I.D., Young, K., Nichols, D., & Jansenns, S. (2000). The effect of vitamin-mineral supplementation on the intelligence of American schoolchildren: A randomized, double-blind, placebo-controlled trial. *Journal of Alternative and Complementary Medicine, 6,* 31–35.

Schwartz, J. (1994). Low-level lead exposure and children's IQ: A meta-analysis and search for a threshold. *Environmental Research, 65,* 42–55.

Schwartz, J., & Otto, D. (1991). Lead and minor hearing impairment. *Archives of Environmental Health, 46,* 300–305.

Schwimmer, J.B., Burwinkle, T.M., & Varni, J.W. (2003). Health-related quality of life of severely obese children and adolescents. *Journal of the American Medical Association, 289,* 1813–1819.

Sciarillo, W.G., Alexander, G., & Farrell, K.P. (1992). Lead exposure and child behavior. *American Journal of Public Health, 82,* 1356–1360.

Seshadri, S., & Gopaldas, T. (1989). Impact of iron supplementation on cognitive functions in preschool and school-aged children: the Indian experience. *American Journal of Clinical Nutrition, 50,* 675–686.

Sexson, S.B., & Madan-Swain, A. (1993). School reentry for the child with chronic illness. *Journal of Learning Disabilities, 26,* 115–125.

Simeon, T., & Grantham-McGregor, S. (1989). Effects of missing breakfast on the cognitive functions of school children with differing nutritional status. *American Journal of Clinical Nutrition, 49,* 646–653.

Slyper, A.H. (1998). Childhood obesity, adipose tissue distribution, and the pediatric practitioner. *Pediatrics, 102*(1), e4.

Smith, P.J., Chu, S.Y., & Barker, L.E. (2004). Children who have received no vaccines: Who are they and where do they live? *Pediatrics, 114,* 187–195.

Stiles, K.M., & Bellinger, D.C. (1993). Neuropsychological correlates of low-level lead exposure in school-age children: A prospective study. *Neurotoxicology and Teratology, 15,* 27–35.

Story, K., Kaphingst, K., & French, S. (2006). The role of schools in obesity prevention. *The Future of Children, 16*(1), 109–142.

Strauss, R.S., & Pollack, H.A. (2001). Epidemic increase in childhood overweight, 1986–1998. *Journal of the American Medical Association, 286,* 2845–2848.

Strauss, R.S., & Pollack, H.A. (2003). Social marginalization of overweight children. *Pediatric and Adolescent Medicine, 157,* 746–752.

Sungthong, R., Mo-suwan, L., & Chongsuvivatwong, V. (2002). Effects of haemoglobin and serum ferritin on cognitive function in school children. *Asian and Pacific Journal of Clinical Nutrition, 11*(2), 117–112.

Tershakovec, A.M., Weller, S.C., & Gallagher, P.R. (1994). Obesity, school performance and behavior of black, urban elementary school children. *International Journal of Obesity and Related Metabolic Disorders, 18*(5), 323–327.

United States Environmental Protection Agency, Indoor Environments Division Office of Air and Radiation. (2000). *IAQ tools for schools: Managing asthma in the school environment* (EPA 402-K-00-003). Washington, DC: Author.

Upadhyay, S.K., Agarwal, K.N., & Agarwal, D.K. (1989). Influence of malnutrition on social maturity, visual motor coordination and memory in rural school children. *Indian Journal of Medical Research, 90,* 320–327.

U.S. General Accounting Office. (2003). *School lunch program: Efforts needed to improve nutrition and encourage healthy eating* (03-056). Washington, DC: Author.

van Stuijvenberg, M.E., Kvalsvig, J.D., Faber, M., Kruger, M., Kenoyer, D.G., & Benade, A.J. (1999). Effects of iron, iodine, and beta-carotene fortified biscuits on the micronutrient status of primary school children: A randomized controlled trial. *American Journal of Clinical Nutrition, 69,* 497–503.

Veltman, M.W.M., & Browne, K.D. (2001). Three decades of child maltreatment research: Implications for the school years. *Trauma, Violence, & Abuse, 2,* 215–239.

Veugelers, P.J., & Fitzgerald, A.L. (2005). Effectiveness of school programs in preventing childhood obesity: A multilevel comparison. *American Journal of Public Health, 95,* 432–435.

Walker, S.P., Grantham-McGregor, S.M., Himes, J.H., Williams, S., & Duff, E.M. (1998). School performance in adolescent Jamaican girls: Associations with health, social and behavioral characteristics, and risk factors for dropouts. *Journal of Adolescent Health, 21,* 109–122.

Wang, G., & Dietz, W.H. (2002). Economic burden of obesity in youths aged 6 to 17 years: 1979–1999. *Pediatrics, 109,* 81–86.

Wasserman, G.A., Liu, X., Lolocono, N.J., Factor-Litvak, P., Kline, J.K., Popovac, D., et al. (1997). Lead exposure and intelligence in 7-year-old children: The Yugoslavia Prospective Study. *Environmental Health Perspectives, 105,* 956–962.

Weinreb, L., Wehler, C., Perloff, J., Scott, R., Hosmer, D., Sagor, L., et al. (2002). Hunger: Its impact on children's health and mental health. *Pediatrics, 110*(4), e41.

Wolraich, M., Milich, R., Stumbo, P., & Schultz, F. (1985). Effects of sucrose ingestion on the behavior of hyperactive boys. *Pediatrics, 106,* 675–682.

Wyon, D.P., Abrahamsson, L., Jartelius, M., & Fletcher, R.J. (1997). An experimental study of the effects of energy intake at breakfast on the test performance of 10-year-old children in school. *International Journal of Food Science and Nutrition, 48,* 5–12.

Yolton, K., Dietrich, K., Auinger, P., Lanphear, B.P., & Hornung, R. (2005). Exposure to environmental tobacco smoke and cognitive abilities among U.S. children and adolescents. *Environmental Health Perspectives, 113,* 98–103.

Zentall, S.S. (1993). Research on the educational implications of attention deficit hyperactivity disorder. *Exceptional Children, 60,* 143–153.

Zolotor, A., Kotch, J., Dufort, V., Winsor, J., Catellier, D., & Bou-Saada, I. (1999). School performance in a longitudinal cohort of children at risk of maltreatment. *Maternal and Child Health Journal, 3*(1), 19–27.

Zorn, R.L. (1999). The great cola wars: How one district profits from the competition for vending machines. *American School Board Journal, 186,* 31–33.

7

THE ROLES OF EMOTION REGULATION AND EMOTION KNOWLEDGE FOR CHILDREN'S ACADEMIC READINESS

Are the Links Causal?

C. Cybele Raver, Pamela W. Garner, and Radiah Smith-Donald

C hildren experience a host of emotion-eliciting situations in their early schooling environments with opportunities for raucous laughter, righteous anger, and considerable anxiety (Schutz & DeCuir, 2002). Children face the anxiety of separation from their caregivers, are expected to make friends among a large group of peers, and must earn the trust and respect of adult authorities (Aber & Baker, 1990; Cryer et al., 2005). Children also face major expectations for their compliance, attentiveness, and impulse control, and violating those expectations may lead to frustration for both teachers and children (Gilliom, Shaw, Beck, Schonberg, & Lukon, 2002). Learning itself, with so many moments of getting things right or wrong, can be exhilarating or frustrating; it is also simply boring at times. Although classrooms trigger a wide range of emotions for both children and adults, relatively little is known about whether young children's emotional competence or difficulty makes much difference to their chances of academic success.

Increasingly, an emerging literature on young children's school readiness has begun to address these questions. As evidenced by a large body of research literature and by state and federal educational standards, researchers and policy makers alike have long been concerned with broad-band indicators of emotional competence as an important educational goal (Administration for Children & Families [ACF], 2000; Raver & Zigler, 1997; Rimm-Kaufman, Pianta, & Cox, 2000; Ross, Powell, & Elias, 2002; Shonkoff & Meisels, 2000; Zigler, Gilliam, & Jones, 2006). Emotional competence is a multifaceted construct that refers to children's knowledge of emotion and to their efforts to regulate their emotional experiences in their social exchanges with others (Saarni, 1988). This chapter discusses emotional competence in these two domains (emotion regulation and emotion knowledge) and then considers research findings on whether skills such as children's ability to handle and interpret emotions are causally related to children's academic achievement.

Do more emotionally well-regulated children have greater opportunities for learning? Conversely, do children who have a more difficult time regulating their anxiety or frustration and who misidentify others' emotions have fewer opportunities to learn? If so, is it due to regulatory and cognitive processes that take place within the child, or to social processes that take place around the child in his or her classroom, or to some combination of both psychobiological and interpersonal processes that make learning more difficult? This chapter explores these questions, examining a number of innovative areas of research in developmental and social psychology and developmental neuroscience that may offer some promising answers. This chapter will also outline ways that prevention and intervention programs targeting children at risk for poor academic, behavioral, and emotional outcomes may provide more conclusive answers to causal questions regarding the links between children's emotional competence and their opportunities to learn.

WHY WOULD EMOTIONS MATTER FOR LEARNING? A BRIEF OVERVIEW OF HYPOTHESIZED MECHANISMS

Consistently, results of large nationally representative samples of young children suggest that individual differences in children's socioemotional skills are moderately related to their early cognitive achievement, with correlation coefficients of the association of these two broad domains of competence in the .25–.40 range (Duncan, Claessens, & Engel, 2005; Gershoff, Aber, Raver, & Lennon, 2007). Measures of children's emotional, behavioral, and social skills in early childhood have repeatedly been found to be associated with children's later competence in adulthood (as indicated, for example, by years of completed schooling or wages earned), leading to increased interest in early investments in these domains of "human capital" and "noncognitive skills" (Carniero & Heckman, 2003). Longitudinal research consistently demonstrates that children's emotional dysregulation is predictive of problematic school performance in elementary school and early school dropout (Miller, Gouley, Seifer, Dickstein, & Shields, 2004; Nelson, Martin, Hodge, Havill, & Kamphaus, 1999). In contrast, emotional competence has figured prominently in the prediction of children's success in first grade (Agostin & Bain, 1997). A complex set of hypothesized mechanisms might underlie this association.

The first and probably the simplest hypothesis is a noncausal one. A skeptical reader might argue that children's emotional competence does not causally support or constrain learning but that the two domains of children's developing skill covary because of some underlying neuropsychological or contextual factor that predicts both domains of development. Specifically, a third set of unmeasured characteristics (of children or environments) may be responsible for the covariance often reported between children's emotional competence and their academic performance. Following this line of reasoning, findings that children suffer academically under teachers who maintain emotionally negative classroom climates could be interpreted as resulting from the placement of less emotionally and cognitively skilled children in classrooms that reflect, rather than shape, children's emotional skills and learning. This hypothesis will be addressed more fully later in this chapter with an examination of statistical and research design approaches that would provide more persuasive evidence of causal links between emotions and learning. Whenever possible, experimental studies will be reviewed to provide compelling evidence of the extent to which children's and teachers' emotions may support or impede learning.

Next, an alternative set of hypotheses that highlight multiple possible mechanisms of influence will then be reviewed. The first of these hypotheses, which posits a set of neurobiological mechanisms, considers ways that children's cognitive, attentional, and emotional systems may be biobehaviorally linked (Blair, 2002; see Chapter 8). The second hypothesized mechanism views the child as a social actor who makes attributions regarding situations, people, and events in the classroom and selects behavioral responses to the challenges that unfold. A third hypothesized mechanism involves the ecological context of learning: The emotional climates that teachers foster may limit or facilitate the amount of learning that children can pursue. The fourth and fifth hypothesized mechanisms underscore transactions between children and teachers, examining ways that children's acquisition of cognitively oriented material is scaffolded by adults and peers in fundamentally social contexts, replete with positive and negative emotions that might promote or inhibit those opportunities for learning. Classroom environments could serve as mediators or as moderators of children's opportunities to learn. The evidence supporting these hypothesized mechanisms is reviewed, and ways that these mechanisms can be tied together and rigorously tested is discussed.

Children's Emotion Regulation as a Support or Obstacle to Learning

Temperament research suggests that children come to school with relatively stable biobehavioral profiles of emotional reactivity and regulation (Calkins & Keane, 2004; Fox, Henderson, Rubin, Calkins, & Schmidt, 2001; Lopez, Vazquez, & Olson, 2004). Some children are more vulnerable to negative emotions, anxiety, or anger than other children (Gunnar & Donzella, 2004). For example, some children are prone to be fearful, avoidant, and socially reticent in new or stressful social situations (Kagan, Reznick, & Snidman, 1988). These children show signs of hypervigilance as well as heightened limbic reactivity during novel or ambiguous situations. Other children approach novel situations with either a dispositionally positive or negative emotional profile (Blair, Peters, & Granger, 2004; Lopez et al., 2004). Classroom environments present complex challenges for young children's abilities to modulate their arousal, as indicated by physiological measures of reactivity such as cortisol (Gunnar, Sebanc, Tout, Donzella, & van Dulmen, 2003; Lopez et al., 2004). Temperamentally inhibited children who generally show higher basal levels of cortisol have been found to avoid peer interactions when introduced into new classroom settings and to show smaller increases in cortisol than less inhibited children. In contrast, less inhibited children, who appear to have a higher threshold of arousal and greater tolerance for novelty, show lower basal levels of cortisol but greater increases in cortisol as they engage in more peer interactions that involve greater stress (Lopez et al., 2004). Research findings suggest that, for both groups of children, the anterior cingulate cortex region of children's brains appears to kick into high gear to cognitively control emotion (Aksan & Kochanska, 2004; Lewis & Steiben, 2004). Children's recruitment of visual attention and cognitions, referred to as *effortful control,* play a central part in models of emotional self-regulation (Posner & Rothbart, 2000). Effortful control comprises "the child's capacity to inhibit a dominant response and initiate a subdominant response" in which children must "modulate impulsive responding according to varying situational demands" (Olson, Sameroff, Kerr, Lopez, & Wellman, 2005, p. 26). Children who have difficulty marshalling these same cognitive skills are vulnerable to undercontrol of negative emotion and a higher probability of later psychopathology (Moffitt, Caspi, Rutter, & Silva, 2002; Olson et al., 2005).

In short, newly emerging neurobiopsychological evidence supports the hypothesis that children's cognitions play a role in regulating emotion. Does evidence exist that the converse is true, with children's emotion regulation playing a role in children's cognitive processing and/or acquisition of new information through encoding, memory, or recall? The brief answer is a qualified "yes." Experimental research has repeatedly demonstrated that adults and children demonstrate better recall for emotional stimuli than for nonemotional stimuli (Cahill & McGaugh, 1998; Davidson, Luo, & Burden, 2001). Following basic U-shaped models of physiological arousal and performance outlined almost a century ago (Yerkes & Dodson, 1908), experimental exposure to moderate levels of emotional and physiological arousal leads individuals to maintain greater attentional focus and to encode and recall a greater number of details of an event. In contrast, high levels of negative emotional arousal are associated with difficulties attending to and retrieving that information (Lench & Levine, 2005; Tomaka, Blascovitch, Kelsey, & Leitten, 1993). Paralleling these findings, Blair, Granger, and Razza (2005) concluded in their review of experimental research on cortisol and cognition that although moderate increases in cortisol are associated with improvements in cognitive tasks, high levels of cortisol are associated with lower cognitive performance in a number of studies.

Similarly, experimental research also suggests that new, potentially threatening situations or stimuli that are introduced to the learning environment can interfere with cognitive performance. Individuals have been found to quickly shift and allocate their attention and their information processing away from the problem-solving situation and toward the stimulus to assess its valence, relevance, and relative risks or dangers. Experimentally induced exposure to highly negative arousing stimuli or information typically lowers individuals' speed and accuracy when they are asked to solve unfamiliar cognitively oriented problems (Lang, 1995; Schimmack, 2005; Steele & Aronson, 1995). Although fewer studies include young children in applied learning contexts, correlational studies with children suggest that experiences of high negative arousal may interfere with at least some children's ability to encode and remember information (Quas, Bauer, & Boyce, 2004). The implications of the experimental and nonexperimental studies reviewed previously are that children who experience high levels of negative emotional arousal may have a more difficult time attending to cognitively oriented information and may have more trouble encoding and recalling that information. For example, children who experience high negative emotional arousal may have a more difficult time when asked to name or remember cognitively oriented details such as the names of letters and the sounds that they make.

In contrast, positive emotions have repeatedly been found to facilitate learning and effort when individuals are given difficult problems to solve (for reviews, see Henderlong & Lepper, 2002; Isen, 2000; and Izard, 2002). According to motivational and goal appraisal theories of emotion, children's positive emotions have been argued to facilitate children's work effort and their persistence in completing academic-related tasks (Ford, 1992; Lazarus, 1991; Schutz & Davis, 2000). Children who are able to remain curious and engaged in the work of school and to maintain positive feelings in the face of academic challenges tend to have higher school performance and standardized test scores than other children (Lepper, Corpus, & Iyengar, 2005).

The concern that more cognitively competent children might report higher enjoyment of the work involved in learning has led psychologists to implement experimental paradigms to test the effects of positive emotions and praise on children's problem-solving abilities and attentiveness (for reviews, see Henderlong & Lepper, 2002; Isen, 2000; and Lang, 1995). Theories of motivation and emotion have also proposed that positive affect may improve cognitive problem solving, facilitate the recall of affectively neutral and positive information, and improve the decision-making strategies used by individuals during ongoing cognitive tasks (Estrada, Young, & Isen, 1994; Isen, Daubman, & Nowicki, 1987; Isen & Shalker, 1982). Some research with older children has helped support the hypothesis that feelings such as pride, shame, or guilt may indirectly influence academic achievement, either by promoting children's persistence in the face of challenging learning tasks or by leading children to disengage from such tasks and, ultimately, from the active pursuit of learning (Boekaerts, 1993, 2002; Lewis, 1993; Pekrun, Goetz, Titz, & Perry, 2002). In short, emotions may play a key role in supporting or hindering children's attentional and motivational processes and information processing.

Emotions Knowledge as a Support or an Obstacle to Learning

In addition to managing their emotions, young children develop increasing competence in being able to identify, label, and communicate about emotions. Beginning sometime in the second year of life, children begin to use what psychologists call *internal state language* to describe their own and others' feelings, concerns, and desires. At this point in development, internal state language plays an important self-regulatory function and helps young children label their own emotional states, thus contributing to their ability to rein in their emotional displays (Bretherton, Fritz, Zahn-Waxler, & Ridgeway, 1986; Brown & Dunn, 1991). Interpersonally, internal state language may also reflect young children's early moral awareness and understanding of others (Brown & Dunn, 1991; Garner, 2003). For older preschoolers, researchers have focused on how and when children begin to understand and label their own and others' emotional expressions as well as when they are able to identify normative reactions to emotion-eliciting situations. Children's knowledge of emotional expressions encompasses their ability to comprehend verbal labels for facial displays of emotion, whereas children's emotion situation knowledge relates to their skills in interpreting contextual cues of emotion. Emotion situation knowledge is often considered a more advanced understanding of emotions because facial expressions are sometimes difficult to interpret and do not always reflect one's true feelings (Arsenio, Cooperman, & Lover, 2000; Barth & Bastiani, 1997; Garner & Estep, 2001; Garner, Jones, & Miner, 1994; Michalson & Lewis, 1985).

Children's skill in understanding emotion improves with age; children understand the facial expressions and situational determinants of happiness, sadness, and anger before they learn about the facial and situational cues of other primary emotions such as fear and surprise (Denham & Couchoud, 1990, 1991). Children's emotion knowledge also appears to be influenced by other individual characteristics such as socioeconomic status (SES) and child gender (e.g., Bosacki & Moore, 2004; Pons, Harris, & de Rosnay, 2004; Walden & Smith, 1997). For example, researchers studying African American preschoolers diverse in SES and parenting backgrounds found that these children were especially accurate at identifying facial and situational cues of fear (Walden & Smith, 1997). Other research has indicated that preschoolers from low-income households tend to not perform as well as children from higher income households on measures of emotion understanding (Cutting & Dunn, 1999). These differences may diminish, however, when these children are asked to identify the emotions of their friends rather than those of a hypothetical other (e.g., Weimer, 2005).

Difficulty in emotion knowledge may be especially problematic for children characterized as having trouble regulating their negative emotions and their behavior. Research with preschool- and early elementary school–age children has shown that children who are prone to anger and aggression are less able to identify the causes of emotions than other children (Barth & Bastiani, 1997; Bohnert, Crnic, & Lim, 2003; Schultz, Izard, & Ackerman, 2000). Aggressive children may have more angry emotional events stored in memory; consequently, they may be less able to turn their attention away from these events when processing new information. Aggressive and anxious individuals have been found to demonstrate a greater negative interpretation bias toward anger-eliciting events, and the biases of aggressive individuals tend to be more pervasive (Wenzel & Lystad, 2005). Children who are exposed to higher levels of parental negative emotional expressiveness have been found to be less accurate in identifying emotions than children in less negative households (Gottman, Katz, & Hooven, 1996; Raver & Spagnola, 2002). Two additional studies have found that girls who are more aggressive are also less accurate in their perceptions of anger in others (Fine, Trentacosta, Izard, Mostow, & Campbell, 2004; Garner, Dunsmore, & Southam-Gerow, in press). Such biases appear to have significant ramifications for children's social experience in classroom settings, in which preschool children's misperception of anger has been associated with a higher likelihood of rejection, aggression, and victimization by peers (Izard & Ackerman, 2000; Garner & Lemerise, in press).

Does a child's knowledge of his or her own and others' feelings help or hinder his or her ability to learn? Certainly, children who have greater overall verbal skills will likely do better on measures of emotion knowledge and score higher on vocabulary tests. Past researchers have tried to guard against the confounding factors introduced by children's language ability, making sure to include it as a statistical control (Cassidy, Werner, Rourke, Zubernis, & Balaraman, 2003). An alternate hypothesis is that children's knowledge of their own and others' emotions indirectly affects their experiences of their learning environment, in which the social contexts of learning may seem baffling and upsetting to a child who has difficulty reading emotional cues. For more emotionally astute children who are skilled at reducing their own and their peers' negative feelings, the classroom may be a more easily navigable, positive environment. In short, the role of emotion knowledge in predicting children's noncognitive learning is likely to be indirect, with children's social status and social behavior in the classroom likely to serve as key mediating mechanisms (Birch & Ladd, 1997, 1998). To help create democratic classrooms and positive school environments, teachers and students regularly rely on emotion-based language and behavior to create dialogue about the appropriate ways to express emotions in the school setting and to negotiate conflict among peers (Dunn, Brown, & Beardsall, 1991; Elias, Arnold, & Hussey, 2003).

Teachers' Emotions as a Support or an Obstacle to Learning

One concern might be that children are not the source but rather the recipients of the challenges that classrooms pose. It has been hypothesized that inadequate quality of care in early educational and child care classrooms can contribute to some children's emotional and behavioral problems and underdeveloped cognitive skills (Hamre & Pianta, 2005; Peisner-Feinberg et al., 1999). As indicated by the studies reviewed next, research suggests that teachers can play a key buffering role for some higher risk children by helping to place them on a positive emotional and educational trajectory. At the same time, evidence also points to specific emotional self-regulatory problems that might negatively affect how much teachers can teach.

A growing literature in educational research considers how teachers develop ongoing relationships with students and help children feel attached to their schools as institutions, to learning as a process, and to their own identities as learners (Battistich, Solomon, Watson, & Schaps, 1997; Gest, Welsh, & Domitrovich, 2005). With older children, research has focused extensively on children's sense of "school attachment," which has been defined as "the extent to which students feel that they are embedded in and part of their school communities" (Johnson, Crosnoe, & Elder, 2001). This term serves as an important theoretical bridge, linking schooling research with the extensive attachment literature that examines parents' behavior within the home. As with the literature on parenting, much educational research on student attachment focuses on the interpersonal and emotional dimensions of teachers' behavior toward the class as a whole and toward specific students to predict how much students will learn in their classrooms (Brophy & Kher, 1986; Wentzel, 2002).

Research suggests that teachers differ considerably in the degree of warmth, sensitivity, and positive emotional tone they demonstrate with their students in both preschool and early elementary school (Hamre & Pianta, 2005; NICHD Early Child Care Research Network, 2003; Sutton, 2004). The importance of teacher emotionality for children's learning is supported by work demonstrating that positively expressive adults may be especially good at encouraging children's involvement and on-task learning behavior (Hyson & Cone, 1989). The hypothesis that adults' emotional communications may have an impact on children's learning and performance has been supported by experimental research in which 4- and 5-year-olds demonstrated better recall for activities in which their mothers had expressed warmth than for activities in which their mothers had expressed irritation (Dunsmore, Halberstadt, Eaton, & Robinson, 2005). Importantly, children appeared to demonstrate greater procedural memory for activities in which their mothers' experimentally manipulated emotional expressions were consistent with their typical expressive style. The implications of this research are particularly important when considering the role of teachers' emotional communications in school contexts and the ways that children must learn and remember new information learned within those school contexts.

Teacher–child closeness has also been positively associated with young children's reading ability (Burchinal, Peisner-Feinberg, Pianta, & Howes, 2002). A positive teacher–child relationship is hypothesized to impact a child's involvement with the teacher and to encourage positive exploration of the classroom (Dolezal, Welsh, Pressley, & Vincent, 2003; NICHD Early Child Care Research Network, 2003). In contrast, dependency and conflict in teacher–student relationships are associated with children's school avoidance and poor academic performance, whereas teacher–child closeness predicts school liking and self-directedness (Birch & Ladd, 1997). Just as children are hypothesized to bring differing styles of emotional competence to the classroom, teachers have been found to bring their dispositions and emotional styles to bear on their instruction.

In related work, emotions have been implicated in theories of classroom management. For example, researchers believe that creating an environment that is conducive to learning depends, in large part, on the teacher's ability to generate and implement appropriate strategies for maintaining behavioral and emotional order in the classroom (Doyle, 1990). In fact, it has been argued that a teacher's inability to deal with negative child behavior such as teasing, name calling, and aggression can interfere with educational instruction during both structured and unstructured classroom activities (Arnold, McWilliams, & Arnold, 1998). Teachers are expected to manage large numbers of young children in their classrooms (NICHD Early Child Care Research Network, 2003; Rimm-Kaufman, La Paro, Downer, & Pianta, 2005), often with little support or training in effective methods of classroom management. Classroom management theorists highlight the importance of positive teacher–student relationships and teachers' use of strategies that minimize disruptive classroom behavior and facilitate on-task behavior (Jones, 1996; Kellam, Ling, Merisca, Brown, & Ialongo, 1998). Research adopting this perspective has focused on varied constructs such as teacher personality, classroom seating arrangements, teacher organization and planning skills, and student involvement in developing classroom rules (Anderson, Evertson, & Brophy, 1979; Good & Grouws, 1979; Lambert, 1994; Soar & Soar, 1977). Conceptual frameworks for understanding the role of emotion in the development of social competence are also relevant to these issues (Halberstadt, Denham, & Dunsmore, 2001; Saarni, 1988). High levels of teacher criticism and low levels of warmth are hypothesized to lower young children's motivation and interest in classroom activities (Daley, Renyard, & Sonuga-Barke, 2005). Although it might seem obvious that an angry, frustrated teacher will be less effective than a teacher who can maintain an even keel, a teacher's negative mood could inhibit learning in a number of ways.

First, Pianta and colleagues have made a clear case for the ways that teachers maintain internal working models of their relationships with students, aiming to provide discipline and emotional support as well as instruction to children (Stuhlman & Pianta, 2002). Teachers' narratives about their relationships with students provide a window into the intense, emotional world of classrooms. Teachers discussed more positive feelings about children who were independently observed to express positive emotions in the classroom, and teachers discussed more negative feelings about children who were independently observed to be more emotionally negative (Stuhlman & Pianta, 2002). In an extensive body of observational research, Pianta and colleagues have shown how teacher practices can be best characterized along the two dimensions of instructional support and emotional support (Pianta, La Paro, & Hamre, 2005; Pianta, La Paro, Payne, Cox, & Bradley, 2002).

Second, ethnographic research on classroom processes often yield rich descriptions of teachers' efforts to structure positive emotional climates. For example, in a qualitative study of young children in child care settings (Ahn, 2005a, 2005b), teachers skillfully incorporated emotionally focused instruction into everyday contexts by helping children identify feelings of distress with words, labeling children's positive displays, scaffolding children's social problem solving and conflict management, and complimenting children for positive, caring behavior toward others (Ahn, 2005a). Teachers helped children manage negative emotions by using empathy, reassurance, and distraction. In both cases, teachers' strategies encouraged emotional competence in children and strengthened teacher–child relationships; the teachers demonstrated that they were aware, concerned, and invested in the children's school success.

Third, Hamre and Pianta (2005) reviewed extensive correlational evidence that children do better in classrooms characterized by positive emotional climates than in less supportive classrooms. Research on preschoolers' perceptions of a typical school day suggests that children are well aware that teachers can be "mean" (Wiltz & Klein, 2001). Within such an attachment-oriented framework, children with emotionally negative teachers have been found to like school less and to be less attached to their schools.

Finally, adults' feelings of anger, frustration, and exasperation are likely to limit their ability to marshal their time and attention toward instruction. Observational research suggests that many teachers become emotionally dysregulated while managing their classrooms (Arnold et al., 1998). Teachers face a large array of task demands and have relatively little autonomy and support. In addition to instruction, they are expected to monitor child safety, maintain positive relationships among children, and fill out reports for accountability purposes (Peters & Rutte, 2005). Research on occupational stress suggests that teachers face considerable psychological strain (Peters & Rutte, 2005). This problem is exacerbated when teachers must repeatedly contend with children's disruptive behavior (Arnold et al., 1998; Kellam et al., 1998). Children may learn less in classrooms in which teachers are harsh and emotionally negative because children's resulting distress may inhibit their own learning and motivation, and teachers' distress may limit the amount of instruction that they can provide.

Transactional Models of Emotion and Learning: Classroom Quality as a Mediator

As is clear from the previous sections, both children and adults bring emotional dispositions, regulatory skills, and competence into the classroom. A third hypothesis is that the interactions between children and teachers represent a transactional system that can result in mutual positive regard and supportive exchange or, conversely, a mixture of teacher frustration and child negativity and disruptiveness. Paralleling the research literatures on the role of emotions for adult teaching and child learning, a third research literature has burgeoned on the role of individual differences in children's emotional self-regulation and emotion knowledge in predicting positive relationships among teachers and peers. Children who handle emotions in prosocial (as opposed to antisocial) ways appear to build more positive relationships with peers and with teachers; such relationships can serve as a "source of provisions" that either help or hurt children's chances of doing well academically in school (Ladd, Birch, & Buhs, 1999, p. 1,375). Children who have difficulty managing anger and anxiety might have difficulty being accepted by classmates and teachers (Kuperschmidt & Coie, 1990; Shores & Wehby, 1999), participate less in the classroom, and do less well academically, even after controlling for children's preexisting cognitive skills (DeRosier, Kuperschmidt, & Patterson, 1994; Ladd et al., 1999). Similarly, children who are more skillful at interpreting emotional expressions, correctly identifying the causes and consequences of emotions, and taking appropriate steps to quell negative emotions tend to be more socially accepted by peers (Denham & Couchoud, 1990; Fabes, Eisenberg, Hanish, & Spinrad, 2001; Field & Walden, 1982; Garner, Jones, & Miner, 1994; Nowicki & Duke, 1992). The limited research in this area has shown that emotion knowledge may make children more outgoing with peers and more likely to receive help, support, and comfort from their peers (Cassidy et al., 2003; Cutting & Dunn, 1999; Garner & Estep, 2001; Garner, Jones, & Miner, 1994; Garner, Jones, & Palmer, 1994). Conversely, children who lack an adequate level of emotion knowledge are more likely to respond with nonconstructive behavior habits and emotions when angry, thereby escalating peer conflict (Garner & Estep, 2001). For children with difficulties in emotion regulation and emotion knowledge, the risk of long-term school problems is not simply about popularity; children who are disliked report liking school less and have lower school attendance (Berndt & Keefe, 1995; Birch & Ladd, 1997; Murray & Greenberg, 2000).

Finally, some studies point to the ways that children's low levels of emotional competence are associated with clinical levels of internalizing and externalizing problems, which in turn are associated with lower academic achievement. Problems in regulating emotion expressions are a frequent cause for referral of young children to psychological services (Greenberg, Kusche, & Speltz, 1991). Children with low levels of emotion knowledge are more likely to have internalizing behavior problems; this has been demonstrated both concurrently and longitudinally, even after statistically controlling for income level, verbal ability, and prior internalizing problems (Schultz, Izard, Ackerman, & Youngstrom, 2001; Fine, Izard, Mostow, Trentacosta, & Ackerman, 2003). A deficiency in the ability to identify the normative responses to emotion-eliciting situations may be linked to internalizing symptoms, thus fostering loneliness and depression (e.g., Fine et al., 2003). This is problematic because experimental research suggests that children perform better and learn more when working collaboratively with a peer than when working alone (Fawcett & Garton, 2005; Garton & Pratt, 2001; King, Staffieri, & Adelgais, 1998). Moreover, internalizing problems may increase the likelihood, even among young children, of being victimized by peers (Egan & Perry, 1998; Garner & Lemerise, in press; Owens, Slee, & Shute, 2000).

TRAJECTORIES OF CHANGE: THE POTENTIALLY MODERATING ROLE OF CLASSROOM QUALITY FOR CHILDREN WITH FEWER EMOTIONAL COMPETENCIES

Children develop more effective emotional regulatory skills in the company of supportive adults and other socially competent children than in classrooms that provide low levels of emotional support (Hamre & Pianta, 2005). Findings from more than 1,000 children enrolled in the NICHD Study of Early Child Care suggest that the achievement gap between children facing high risk versus low risk was significantly reduced when children facing high functional risk were enrolled in classrooms offering high emotional support (Hamre & Pianta, 2005, p. 30). A second study found that having a conflict-laden relationship with a teacher was associated with an escalation of externalizing behavior problems for those children at higher risk (Silver, Measelle, Armstrong, & Essex, 2005). In short, children's emotional self-regulatory skills and their learning may be further helped or hindered by the environments that are shaped by other members of the classroom. Classroom climates are fostered by children's peers as well as their teachers; classrooms with high levels of peer victimization, bullying, and antisocial behavior are associated with decreases in children's social competence and increases in children's behavioral problems, net of children's initial levels of adjustment at school entry (Aber, Jones, Brown, Chaudry, & Samples, 1998; Hoglund & Leadbeater, 2004; Kellam et al., 1998). Structuring supportive classrooms may play an important moderating function in shifting children from negative educational trajectories to more positive ones. For example, if children who are vulnerable to regulatory difficulty are given additional support in better-managed classrooms, they may have increased opportunities to develop greater effortful control. That support might come from teachers and peers in well-organized classrooms with positive emotional climates, from parents assisting children with emotional difficulty at school, from clinical or prevention-oriented programs, or from all of the above (see Dumas, Prinz, Smith, & Laughlin, 1999; Raver, 2004; Stormshak, Ried, & Webster-Stratton, Reid, & Hammond, 2004).

A few investigators have highlighted how positive classroom climates can support children's emotional and behavioral competence, whereas negative classroom climates can exacerbate children's emotional and behavioral difficulty (Hughes, Cavell, Meehan, Zhang, & Collie, 2005). Some studies have examined the extent to which a child's chances for school success versus vulnerability to school difficulty depend on biobehavioral predisposition to negative emotionality as well as sensitive, warm, and positive relationships with the other key members of his or her social environment (Hamre & Pianta, 2005; Quas et al., 2004; Silver et al., 2005; Mezzacappa, Kindlon, Saul, & Earls, 1998). For example, Boyce and colleagues suggest that children's physiologically based reactivity only serves as a risk factor for negative outcomes when the environment is stressful. In contrast, "When the environment is nurturing and supportive, high reactivity would enhance children's ability to attend to and engage in the environment, thus potentially leading to associated benefits." (Quas et al., 2004, p. 798). Some results have supported this hypothesis, demonstrating how highly reactive children face greater risk of negative educational and socioemotional outcomes only when placed in low-quality classrooms in which teachers were harsh, negative, and unsupportive (Gunnar et al., 2003; Hamre & Pianta, 2005). Similarly, children who are prone to negative reactivity may process social information in faulty ways and make hostile attributions about others' intentions only when situations are objectively unsupportive. Work by Bar-Haim, Fox, VanMeenen, & Marshall (2004) echoes this hypothesis. In this light, interventions should be most effective in supporting positive cognitive and emotional outcomes for those children who function with significant vulnerability. This serves as one of the primary rationales for providing targeted intervention in addition to universal prevention when supporting young children's learning through emotionally and behaviorally focused intervention efforts, as will be discussed below.

PLACING THESE MODELS IN CONTEXTS THAT INCLUDE RACE/ETHNICITY, GENDER, AND SES

Developmental models of school readiness must be squarely placed in multiple ecological contexts, taking into account children's membership in multiple groups defined by race and ethnicity, gender, and SES. One approach is to ask whether models of children's emotional competence and academic achievement fit similarly or differently at the levels of measurement and of proposed mechanisms (see Knight & Hill, 1998; Raver et al., 2007). Regarding measurement, assessments tapping children's and teachers' emotional competence have often been assumed to work similarly for boys and girls, for ethnic minority children as well as ethnic majority children, and for children and teachers in underresourced schools in lower income neighborhoods as well as more advantaged schools (Raver & Zigler, 1997). However, little research has been conducted on whether measures of children's effortful control and teachers' maintenance of positive emotional climates maintain factorial invariance across these different ecological contexts. This is a fruitful area for future research; measures in cognitive and socioemotional development that are appropriate for use with children from underrepresented groups have not always been readily available.

Although this remains an issue, there has been encouraging work by John Fantuzzo and colleagues, who have designed several measures developed specifically for use with low-income preschoolers and their families (e.g., Bulotsky-Shearer & Fantuzzo, 2004;

Fantuzzo, Sekino, & Cohen, 2004). Work in the chapter authors' (and other) laboratories has emphasized the importance of validating direct assessments of emotional self-regulation, emotion knowledge, and outcome measures of competence for ethnic minority preschool-age children in low-income and middle-income socioeconomic contexts (for examples, see Blair et al., 2005; Garner, Jones, & Miner, 1994; Garner & Spears, 2000; Raver, Blackburn, Bancroft, & Torp, 1999; Smith-Donald, Raver, Hayes, & Richardson, 2005). In addition, considerable established measurement equivalence is still lacking, which would help prevent faulty assumptions regarding the generalizability of "general process" models and methods to children who inhabit differing socioeconomic and sociocultural contexts (Knight & Hill, 1998).

A mounting body of evidence suggests that poverty-related stressors place children at significant risk for higher externalizing and internalizing behavior problems as well as lower academic achievement, at least partially mediated by emotional regulatory processes (Bolger, Patterson, Thompson, & Kuperschmidt, 1995; Schultz et al., 2001; Shaw, Vondra, Hommerding, Keenan, & Dunn, 1994). Cumulative and persistent exposure to poverty-related adversity has been significantly associated with children's heightened emotional reactivity and greater difficulties with regulation (Caspi, Taylor, Moffitt, & Plomin, 2000; Cicchetti & Rogosch, 2001; Gunnar, 2000). Work on the neurodevelopmental systems involved in children's recognition of emotion suggests that the development of those processes may be substantially affected by exposure to high levels of early adversity (Pollak, 2003). High levels of family disruption, including housing instability, marital conflict, and parental job loss, have specifically been found to be associated with indications of greater emotional regulatory difficulty for young children; such findings have significant implications for the underresourced educational settings serving a higher proportion of children facing these stressors (Ackerman, Kogos, Youngstrom, Schoff, & Izard, 1999; Conduct Problems Prevention Research Group, 2002; Hoglund & Leadbeater, 2004).

Research highlighting additional child and family characteristics as moderators suggests a broadened definition of risk; several studies have shown that teachers have more negative relationships with boys than with girls (Birch & Ladd, 1998; Mantzicopoulos Neuharth-Pritchett, 2003) and are more likely to mention problems regarding compliance in their narratives about boys than about girls (Stuhlman & Pianta, 2002). Children's aggressive behavior and social competence in the classroom also have an impact on the quality of the relationship between teachers and children (Blankemeyer, Flannery, & Vazsonyi, 2002); boys are viewed as more aggressive than girls, and girls are reported as more socially competent (e.g., Loeber & Hay, 1997). As a result, teachers may have more positive interactions with girls and more negative interactions with boys. These differences in the classroom behavior of boys and girls may also negatively affect teachers' ratings of boys' school-related competence.

For the most vulnerable of children, understanding linkages between social and emotional competence and school-related outcomes is especially important. A growing body of work on samples of ethnically and economically diverse children indicates that approximately 20% of preschoolers evidence moderate to clinically significant social and emotional difficulties (Pianta & Caldwell, 1990). Low-income children are at significant risk for emotion regulation problems (Bolger et al., 1995; Campbell, Shaw, & Gilliom, 2000; Gilliom et al., 2002); for many of these children, this pattern of behavior is apparent by school entry (Keenan, Shaw, Walsh, Delliquadri, & Giovanelli, 1997). These difficulties seem to be correlated with learning and attentional problems (Lavigne et al., 1996).

INNOVATIVE APPROACHES TO TESTING THE CAUSAL ROLE OF EMOTIONS FOR CHILDREN'S LEARNING

As discussed earlier, a simple counterhypothesis is that some set of omitted variables may be the source of covariance among child emotional competencies and children's academic gains (for a more extensive discussion, see Duncan et al., 2005). However, there is no easy way to rule out the possibility that a few simple characteristics of children or of environments (such as children's general ability to process information or community-level poverty coupled with low-quality educational settings) are at work when examining the covariance between children's emotional competence and their school success. In past work, the chapter authors and other researchers have argued that random assignment experimental intervention designs (often used in clinical and social policy research) and fixed-effects designs (capitalizing on change over time) could profitably be applied to more clearly test these hypothesized causal linkages (e.g., NICHD Early Child Care Research Network & Duncan, 2003; Howe, Reiss, & Yuh, 2002; Raver, 2004).

One nonexperimental approach addresses the problem of omitted variable bias by controlling for potentially confounding characteristics that are not expected to vary over time. Specifically, research using fixed-effects designs assumes that if a confound (or omitted variable) is stable and unlikely to change over time, then regressing intraindividual changes in a given outcome on intraindividual changes in a set of predictors will reduce the likelihood that the observed associations between the outcome and predictors is due to that third, troublesome, confounding variable (Raver, 2004). This approach is increasingly being used to more rigorously test whether change in a given dependent variable (e.g., children's problem behavior) can be modeled as a function of change in a given predictor (e.g., increases versus decreases in interparental conflict over time; Cui, Conger, & Lorenz, 2005; Cummings, Goeke-Morey, & Dukewich, 2001).

Some analyses of a nationally representative sample of young children transitioning from kindergarten to the end of first grade have considered whether children's gains in academic achievement were best predicted by changes in their literacy and math skills (labeled *hard skills*) or by their gains in socioemotional skills (labeled *soft skills*; Duncan et al., 2005). Results from this study suggested that children's learning trajectories were more strongly predicted by hard skills such as reading and math, with children's soft skills such as aggression and getting along with peers predicting only a small proportion of the variance in learning over time (Duncan et al., 2005). These findings have important policy implications and represent a stark contrast to the mounting correlational evidence supporting the role of children's soft skills in models of early learning. How can these findings be reconciled?

Relying on adults' reports on a small number of items for each domain of socioemotional competence (four to five items in each domain), one concern might be that the Duncan et al. (2005) estimates of change in children's socioemotional development contain a good deal of measurement error, with relatively low discriminant validity. The result might be that the explanatory power of such estimators may be low because of the relatively crude psychometric properties of the measures used. That said, even considering the relatively small effect size estimates of children's emotional and behavioral skills in predicting children's achievement scores, these findings can still be viewed as good news when placed in perspective. These findings suggest that children's gains in emotional and behavioral development in kindergarten predict relatively small increments in later academic achievement, even after controlling for a host of other characteristics, including children's initial levels of academic and behavioral skills. In addition, children's literacy gains in kindergarten predict somewhat larger increments in later academic achievement, with estimated effect sizes also relatively modest at best. In many ways, this makes sense; few emotions researchers would argue that children would learn much academic content if they were in well-managed classrooms with, nonetheless, little to no effort on the part of teachers to read to or help children with writing, early math, or other learning objectives. There is considerable consensus that emotions-focused curricula will not be an effective cure-all to children's academic problems and that emotions curricula represent an important complement to, but not a reasonable substitute for, instruction in literacy and learning activities.

In short, this methodological approach holds great promise in answering the question of whether emotional regulatory skills are causally linked to children's academic achievement. But the inclusion of carefully validated, directly assessed measures of children's language and learning skills must be matched by investigators' inclusion of more comprehensive, direct assessments of children's emotional regulation and emotion knowledge before the field can take full advantage of this methodological approach.

Experimental studies can also provide the opportunity to experimentally test causal hypotheses in ecologically valid contexts (Howe et al., 2002). Izard (2002) pointed out that despite interest in children's antisocial and aggressive behavior, few interventions have targeted emotional mechanisms, treating emotions as "epiphenomena" of cognitive processes such as deficient social information-processing problems (p. 797). Some reviews of interventions have suggested greater attention to emotions (Howe et al., 2002; Raver, 2004), and the rise of randomized trial interventions represents welcome opportunity to test causal claims. Specifically, the case that emotions "matter" for learning is likely to be conservatively tested if interventions targeting emotional processes are found to have a significant impact on learning outcomes. A number of studies representing good examples of such work are outlined briefly next.

Because it appears to be such a robust and critical factor in children's educational experiences, a number of theoretically driven, randomized prevention and intervention trials have tried to modify children's emotional self-regulation skills and emotion knowledge skills. By randomly assigning children and classrooms to programs that specifically target change in children's knowledge of emotions, teachers' ability to manage emotional climate, and children's ability to regulate their emotions, researchers can experimentally test how these multiple pathways can produce positive impacts on young children's long-term chances for school success. As an experimental test of the role of this developmental mechanism, intervention-oriented research offers an important complement to experimental laboratory research with lower risk populations (Gennetian, Morris, Bos, & Bloom, 2005).

INTERVENTIONS TARGETING EMOTIONAL COMPETENCE

Psychophysiological research and social psychological research suggest that there may be considerable plasticity in both the neurological systems involved in emotion regulation and in the attributions and beliefs that children hold regarding their interpretation of others' emotions (Davidson, 2003; Davidson et al., 2003). Unfortunately, interventions aimed at increasing children's emotion competence rarely identify the unique roles of children's emotion regulation skills, their emotion knowledge, and teachers' provision of emotionally supportive classroom environments as distinguishable targets of intervention (Izard, 2002). The discussion next, reviewing several interventions that have been conducted using randomized clinical trial (RCT) design, is structured within the framework of the multiple hypothesized mechanisms outlined earlier in this chapter.

One strategy for supporting children's emotional competence has been to develop classroom curricula for preschools and child care settings that specifically focus on teaching children to handle and interpret emotions in prosocial ways. Across a small number of studies, these programs have been shown to be moderately effective in teaching children about emotions. In one study, children's participation in an affective intervention program led to increases in emotion knowledge and a decrease in the expression of negative emotions in the preschool classroom (Izard, Trentacosta, King, & Mostow, 2004). In separate work, Izard and colleagues (2001) found that emotion knowledge was an independent, positive predictor of academic competence and that it mediated the association between receptive language skills and academic outcomes. Another group of researchers demonstrated that emotion knowledge is a positive predictor of young children's teacher-rated school adjustment and adaptation (Shields, Dickstein, Seifer, Giusti, Dodge-Magee, & Spritz, 2001). One drawback may be that children's understanding of emotions may make them more sensitive to teacher criticism (Cutting & Dunn, 2002).

Interventions that focus on the transactional model of emotion competence and school success treat the classroom or the school as a whole to impact students' social, academic, and emotion competence. Promoting Alternative Thinking Skills (PATHS) is a school-based prevention program that has been shown to improve students' social skills and behavior regulation in both urban and rural schools. PATHS gives teachers a concrete curriculum to help children develop emotion knowledge, emotion regulation, behavior regulation, and social skills. However, the benefits of the program are vulnerable to design implementation. When the program was evaluated in an effectiveness study, the gains across all PATHS students were no longer observed (Kam, Greenberg, & Walls, 2003). Significant gains were apparent only when teachers followed the PATHS curriculum reliably within schools that had programmatic support from the principal.

The Second Step program is another curriculum-based prevention approach used in preschool classrooms. It aims to decrease disruptive behavior and increase socially competent behavior habits by supporting emotion competence and behavioral regulation and by reorienting children away from aggressive behavior (Frey, Nolen, Van Schoiack-Edstrom, & Hirschstein, 2005). The program is implemented by teachers and is incorporated into the framework of the school classroom using concrete lessons. In addition, teachers are expected to apply the general principles when appropriate throughout the day to further reinforce program goals. Following an RCT design administered to second and fourth graders, intervention students were observed to use prosocial problem-solving strategies more often and aggressive strategies less often (Frey, Hirschstein, et al., 2005). Students in classrooms with the Second Step curriculum were also reported to exhibit a significant decrease in antisocial behavior compared with control children after 1 year of intervention. The impact was especially large for students with high baseline ratings of antisocial behavior. The same impact on antisocial behavior habits was not observed during the second year of intervention. However, teacher-reported social competence showed significant increases for intervention children during both the first and second years of the intervention.

In addition, a number of RCT-designed studies have targeted children's emotional knowledge and social cognition as a means of reducing bullying. Studies with older children have found significant success in changing children's normative beliefs about anger and aggressive behavior habits and in lowering the incidence of bullying on school playgrounds (Frey, Hirschstein, et al., 2005; Hoglund & Leadbeater, 2004). Investigators unfortunately do not report academic outcomes; it would be intriguing to know whether children with higher propensity for victimization by peers would show improved academic achievement as the likelihood of being bullied decreased. Similarly, it would be important to learn whether children with higher propensity to bully others would show academic improvement or greater school liking.

It is important to place intervention research that focuses on universal approaches using classroom curricula within stage-salient and complex developmental contexts. For example, Izard (2002) pointed out a key, theoretically driven insight: Emotions are activated in different ways, for different children, with higher or lower proneness to impulsivity and negative emotionality. Izard (2002) warned that children's anger and distress may be easily triggered through a process that is both rapid and nonconscious. This "raises questions about the use of the 'stop-and-think' cognitive-behavioral techniques in dealing with intense on-line emotion in young, impulsive children" (p. 806). Because cognitive-behavioral techniques take time and must be implemented in an orderly, multistep process, they may be less effective with young children who may be more impulsive. Izard (2002) and others have pointed out the need for intervention approaches that give children simple, behaviorally oriented tools with which to actively manage and modulate both positive and negative emotions.

To date, much research on child-level interventions focuses on children deemed to be at risk of significant behavior problems. Children are selected into programs as a result of parents' reports of child difficulties, often in combination with teachers' reports or observation by program staff. Selected children are then randomly assigned to control and intervention groups. Intervention and prevention programs at this level often incorporate methods in which children's parents, teachers, and peers use group discussion and applied situations.

As one example of this multicomponent approach targeting children at higher risk for emotional and behavioral difficulty, Webster-Stratton and colleagues have assembled an intervention program titled The Incredible Years and have assessed its efficacy across multiple studies (Hartman, Stage, & Webster-Stratton, 2003; Reid, Webster-Stratton, & Hammond, 2003; Webster-Stratton et al., 2004). The program is designed for children 4–8 years old who are referred for aggression or oppositional behavior problems without other severe problems (e.g., cognitive delay or history of psychosis). It includes child training (in group sessions) with a focus on socioemotional skills, teacher training to bolster teachers' classroom management skills, and parent training for help with parenting skills, parental conflict resolution, and encouraging children's scholastic performance. Children who were exposed to one, two, or all three of the interventions described previously were observed to be less oppositional at home and at school and exhibited better social skills with their peers than children in the control group (Webster-Stratton et al., 2004).

Similarly, the Early Risers Program (August, Lee, Bloomquist, Realmuto, & Hektner, 2004; August, Realmuto, Hektner, & Bloomquist, 2001) focused heavily on improving children's emotional-behavioral adjustment and provided social skills training—including Dinosaur School from Webster-Stratton and colleagues' The Incredible Years program—

to help children at risk be more successful in school and at home. The program was evaluated in two stages: an efficacy study and an effectiveness study. The efficacy study showed improvements in socioemotional domains and academic domains, with an effect size of .26 (August et al., 2001). Although the investigators' subsequent effectiveness study replicated findings for the intervention's socioemotional impacts, the academic achievement effects were not observed under "real-world conditions" (i.e., when services were provided by community practice providers). Post hoc analyses suggested that child participation (as measured through total hours of program attendance) was a significant predictor of children's gains in academic achievement. Furthermore, this finding differed for boys and girls, with level of participation being more important for boys' improved academic performance than for girls. These findings indicate the need for methods to encourage and sustain intervention participation when programs are moved from the research world to the real world.

"Fast Track" represents a third example of a randomized prevention trial targeted at "early starters" (Conduct Problems Prevention Research Group, 2002). Children were recruited in kindergarten and selected into the trial based on teacher and parent report of aggressive behavior habits and conduct problems. The 3-year prevention program included structured training sessions in which children had the opportunity to learn and practice effective methods of communication and emotion competence skills including managing conflicts and understanding emotions. One-to-one play sessions with peers provided additional opportunities to hone skills of emotion regulation, emotion knowledge, social problem solving, and other social skills. In addition, Fast Track used parent groups, parent–child sessions, and home visits to support the child-level interventions. Teachers were trained to incorporate a social and emotional development curriculum (PATHS, described previously), which was then administered to all children in classrooms with target children. In fourth grade, after 3 years of intervention, children in the intervention group were rated higher than children in the control group on a measure of social preference and were also less likely to socialize with children identified as trouble makers (Conduct Problems Prevention Research Group, 2002). One challenge for making causal claims from this intervention is that children were also given support on early reading. That said, it represents an important model of multicomponent emotion-oriented intervention.

Little work has examined interventions targeting teachers' emotional competence with the goal of improving children's school readiness. One possible avenue is stress management. Teachers face a number of stressors; they handle children who come to preschool from a range of differing home backgrounds, with a range of different temperaments, and different ability levels within the same classroom. They work to advance all children to the appropriate grade level and, therefore, must find room for flexibility within structured curricula. In addition, they juggle parents' demands and administrative rules and procedures, often in settings that lack sufficient resources. A number of school consultation models suggest that teachers and classrooms benefit when mental health consultants take a program-focused approach, working to help teachers deal with their own emotions and with techniques of stress management. But, to date, few RCT-designed interventions report helping teachers deal with their own emotions with techniques of stress management.

Combining some of these more structurally oriented approaches, the Positive Action program is a prevention program with both classroom-based and schoolwide components (Flay & Allred, 2003). The classroom-based curriculum focuses on a number of domains theorized to contribute to positive behavior, including positive self-concept, socioemotional adjustment, self-regulation, and social skills. The program also has elements that aim to involve parents and the surrounding community. It has been implemented in a variety of elementary schools over the years. Retrospective review of the program in more than 65 schools demonstrated that Positive Action schools had significantly fewer incidents of violence and suspensions than non–Positive Action schools (Flay & Allred, 2003). In addition, it is one of the few interventions based on noncognitive skills to examine academic achievement as an outcome measure. Students in intervention schools performed 45% better on two standardized tests of academic achievement (reading and general achievement) than students in control schools.

Academic improvement was also an outcome measure for the Unique Minds School Program (UMSP), a socioemotional intervention (Linares et al., 2005) developed for urban public schools. UMSP is designed for elementary school children and uses teacher training and a classroom-based curriculum. In addition, the curriculum provides concrete strategies for carrying the socioemotional focus over to academic tasks and generalizing the classroom lessons to nonclassroom settings. Preliminary evaluation of the UMSP offers promising results with intervention students demonstrating significant advantage on socioemotional and academic outcome measures.

The results of these programs are consistent—children's understanding of their own and others' emotions, their ability to regulate their emotions, and their social skills can be improved through processes of child training, parent training, teacher training, and school-wide prevention programs. Program implementation and ongoing participation are key to the success of these interventions. One major innovation is that some randomized prevention and intervention trials have included multiple types of child outcome measures, including indicators of children's biobehavioral reactivity as well as indicators of children's effortful control, recognition of emotions, and social problem solving to identify both the neurophysiological and behavioral processes that may be affected by intervention (see Brotman, Gouley, Klein, Castellanos, & Pine, 2003; Fisher, Gunnar, Chamberlain, & Reid, 2000). In our view, the biggest stumbling block to testing the impact of emotional competence on children's academic readiness is that most evaluation studies of emotion-focused intervention and prevention programs do not directly assess academic outcomes. Practically speaking, it may be that a major benefit of these interventions—one of great interest to parents and policy makers, among others—is going unobserved. From a theoretical perspective, valuable information on the causal impacts of children's emotional competence on their school success cannot be established if academic outcomes are not available from these innovative studies.

CONCLUSION

Researchers and policy makers committed to improving young children's chance of early school success have a rich experimental tradition as well as a remarkable body of observational research from which to draw as they test evidence-based practices that target children's emotional competence and academic gains. This chapter has highlighted the ways that both types of research can be integrated to better understand how innovative educational initiatives might work in real-world contexts. Longitudinal research clearly shows that children's experiences in the classroom are framed by complex social and emotional systems involving neurobiological and affective processes, interpersonal processes, and institutional processes. The findings culled from both types of research highlight the need for multivariate models that capture this complexity across the contexts of home, school, and playground, and also across time.

It is also clear that children's social, emotional, and behavioral adjustment are important domains of school readiness in their own right. Even if there were no association between children's socioemotional outcomes and their cognitively oriented outcomes, the extent of children's risk levels of emotional and behavioral difficulty, peer rejection, and dislike of school would be of grave concern. A child's abilities to regulate negative emotions and to skillfully interpret the emotions of others are key skills for the transition to school that clearly predict important future benchmarks of well-being. That said, policy makers, educators, and research scientists often have focused on the association between children's emotional competence and their academic achievement in the hope that children's chances of academic success might be supported by implementation of curricula, training, and classroom reforms that support children's early emotional competence.

Although there have been relatively few studies in this area, some progress has been made in establishing a link between emotional competence and academic achievement in the past several years. For instance, children's effortful control and understanding of emotions have been identified as unique predictors of cognitive and language competence (e.g., Cook, Greenberg, & Kusche, 1994; Izard et al., 2001). In addition, children with higher emotion knowledge scores seem to remain more focused and on task in the face of emotional challenges in the classroom than other children (Nelson et al., 1999). Experimental evidence also shows that programs aimed at teaching school-age children socioemotional skills lead to increased cognitive performance, improved classroom climate, and decreased behavior problems (Cook et al., 1994; Flay & Allred, 2003; Greenberg & Kusche, 1998; Linares et al., 2005).

Alongside such optimism, a few words of caution and concern are necessary. Effect sizes from studies of emotional competence as a predictor of children's later school success are often small; studies that try to guard against the threat of omitted variable bias yield estimates that are even smaller. Evidence suggests that children's early emotional gains in a given year do not necessarily serve as a magic-bullet solution to close gaps in children's long-term academic achievement. Some research highlights the relatively low level of instruction and the relatively negative emotional climate of classrooms in later elementary years (Pianta, Howes, et al., 2005). Given this sanguine perspective on elementary education, expecting children's short-term emotional gains to innoculate them from later academic difficulty if those same children are enrolled in elementary school classrooms that lack adequate emotional and academic support is unreasonable.

There are several additional obstacles to building a more persuasive and rigorous case that children's emotional skills matter for early academic achievement (Raver, 2004; Raver & Zigler, 1997). First, more precise measures of children's emotional regulation and emotional knowledge that are developed in conjunction with the specific tasks and challenges that young children face in the context of school would help. Such measures should be held to the same standards of discriminant validity and cross-race/ethnic equivalence that cognitively oriented measures must meet. Second, the field lacks research on the impact of teachers' ability to maintain emotionally supportive classrooms on teachers' instruction, as well as students' learning. Both the developmental and educational sciences would benefit from more observational and more experimental research on the emotionally linked mechanisms that can constrain teaching and learning.

Third, intervention research is sometimes inconsistent about which components of theory are being tested. Emotionally and behaviorally focused intervention would benefit from more careful specification of the theoretical frameworks driving intervention and from routine reporting of academic achievement outcomes. Bolder steps need to be considered by investigators in both basic and applied domains of emotions research to design and implement RCT-designed interventions to both inform theory and provide policy makers with clearer guidance on which aspects of children's school readiness are most amenable to change and offer the highest likelihood of significant payoff. Analyzing the relations between children's emotional competence and their academic achievement requires a large investment of time and effort and a complex, multilayered approach that considers child, family, neighborhood, teacher, and other school-related characteristics. However, through such a complex approach, both policy and theory in early education will make the largest strides.

REFERENCES

Aber, J.L., & Baker, A.J.L. (1990). Security of attachment in toddlerhood: Modifying assessment procedures for joint clinical and research purposes. In M.T. Greenberg, D. Cicchetti, & E.M. Cummings (Eds.), *Attachment in the preschool years.* Chicago, IL: University of Chicago Press.

Aber, J.L., Jones, S.M., Brown, J.L., Chaudry, N., & Samples, R. (1998). Resolving conflict creatively: Evaluating the developmental effects of a school-based violence prevention program in neighbourhood and classroom context. *Development and Psychopathology, 10,* 187–213.

Ackerman, B.P., Kogos, J., Youngstrom, E., Schoff, K., & Izard, C. (1999). Family instability and the problem behaviors of children from economically disadvantaged families. *Developmental Psychology, 35,* 258–268.

Administration for Children & Families (ACF). (2000). *Head Start child outcomes framework.* Retrieved September 12, 2005, from www.headstartinfo.org/pdf/im00_18a.pdf

Agostin, T.M., & Bain, S.K. (1997). Predicting early school success with developmental and social skills screeners. *Psychology in the Schools, 34,* 219–228.

Ahn, H.J. (2005a). Child care teachers' strategies in children's socialization of emotion. *Early Child Development and Care, 175,* 49–61.

Ahn, H.J. (2005b). Teachers' discussions of emotion in child care centers. *Early Childhood Education Journal, 32,* 237–242.

Aksan, N., & Kochanska, G. (2004). Links between systems of inhibition from infancy to Preschool years. *Child Development, 75,* 1477–1490.

Anderson, L., Evertson, C., & Brophy, J. (1979). An experimental study of effective teaching in first grade reading groups. *Elementary School Journal, 79,* 193–223.

Arnold, D.H., McWilliams, L., & Arnold, E.H. (1998). Teacher discipline and child misbehavior in day care: Untangling causality with correlational data. *Developmental Psychology, 34,* 276–287.

Arsenio, W.F., Cooperman, S., & Lover, A. (2000). Affective predictors of preschoolers' aggression and peer acceptance: Direct and indirect effects. *Developmental Psychology, 36,* 438–448.

August, G.J., Lee, S.S., Bloomquist, M.L., Realmuto, G.M., & Hektner, J.M. (2004). Maintenance effects of an evidence-based prevention innovation for aggressive children living in culturally diverse urban neighborhoods: The Early Risers Effectiveness Study. *Journal of Emotional and Behavioral Disorders, 12,* 194–205.

August, G.J., Realmuto, G.M., Hektner, J.M., & Bloomquist, M.L. (2001). An integrated components preventive intervention for aggressive elementary school children: The Early Risers Program. *Journal of Consulting and Clinical Psychology, 69,* 614–626.

Bar-Haim, Y., Fox, N.A., VanMeenen, K.M., & Marshall, P.J. (2004). Children's narratives and patterns of cardiac reactivity. *Developmental Psychobiology, 44,* 238–249.

Barth, J.M., & Bastiani, A. (1997). A longitudinal study of emotion recognition and preschool children's social behavior. *Merrill-Palmer Quarterly, 43,* 107–128.

Battistich, V., Solomon, D., Watson, M., & Schaps, E. (1997). Caring school communities. *Educational Psychologist, 32,* 137–151.

Berndt, T.J., & Keefe, K. (1995). Friends' influence on adolescents' adjustment to school. *Child Development, 66,* 1312–1329.

Birch, S.H., & Ladd, G.W. (1997). The teacher–child relationship and children's early school adjustment. *Journal of School Psychology, 35,* 61–79.

Birch, S.H., & Ladd, G.W. (1998). Children's interpersonal behaviors and the teacher–child relationship. *Developmental Psychology, 34,* 934–946.

Blair, C. (2002). School readiness: Integrating cognition and emotion in a neurobiological conceptualization of children's functioning at school entry. *American Psychologist, 57,* 111–127.

Blair, C., Granger, D., & Razza, R.P. (2005). Cortisol reactivity is positively related to executive function in preschool children attending Head Start. *Child Development, 76,* 554–567.

Blair, C., Peters, R., & Granger, D. (2004). Physiological and neuropsychological correlates of approach/withdrawal tendencies in preschool: Further examination of the behavioral inhibition system/behavioral activation system scales for young children. *Developmental Psychobiology, 45,* 113–124.

Blankemeyer, M., Flannery, D.J., & Vazsonyi, A.T. (2002). The role of aggression and social competence in children's perceptions of the child–teacher relationship. *Psychology in the Schools, 39,* 293–304.

Boekaerts, M. (1993). Anger in relation to school learning. *Learning and Instruction, 3,* 269–280.

Boekaerts, M. (2002). Toward a model that integrates motivation, affect, and learning. In L. Smith, C. Rogers, & P. Tomlinson (Eds.), *Development and motivation: Joint perspectives* (pp. 173–189). Leicester, England: British Psychological Society.

Bohnert, A.M., Crnic, K.A., & Lim, K.G. (2003). Emotional competence and aggressive behavior in school-age children. *Journal of Abnormal Child Psychology, 31,* 79–91.

Bolger, K.E., Patterson, C.J., Thompson, W.W., & Kuperschmidt, J.B. (1995). Psychosocial adjustment among children experiencing persistent and intermittent family economic hardship. *Child Development, 66,* 1107–1129.

Bosacki, S.L., & Moore, C. (2004). Preschoolers' understanding of simple and complex emotions: Links with gender and language. *Sex Roles, 50,* 659–675.

Bretherton, I., Fritz, J., Zahn-Waxler, C., & Ridgeway, D. (1986). Learning to talk about emotions: A functionalist perspective. *Child Development, 55,* 529–548.

Brophy, J., & Kher, N. (1986). Teacher socialization as a mechanism for developing student motivation to learn. In R.S. Feldman (Ed.), *The social psychology of education: Current research and theory* (pp. 257–288). New York: Cambridge University Press.

Brotman, L.M., Gouley, K.K., Klein, R.G., Castellanos, F.X., & Pine, D.S. (2003). Children, stress and context: Integrating basic, clinical and experimental prevention research. *Child Development, 74,* 1053–1057.

Brown, J.R., & Dunn, J. (1991). 'You can cry mum': The social and developmental implications of talk about internal states. *British Journal of Developmental Psychology, 9,* 237–256.

Bulotsky-Shearer, R., & Fantuzzo, J. (2004). Adjustment scales for preschool intervention: Extending validity and reliability and relevance across multiple perspectives. *Psychology in the Schools, 41,* 725–736.

Burchinal, M.R., Peisner-Feinberg, E., Pianta, R., & Howes, C. (2002). Development of academic skills from preschool through second grade: Family and classroom predictors of developmental trajectories. *Journal of School Psychology, 40,* 415–436.

Cahill, L., & McGaugh, J.L. (1998). Mechanisms of emotional arousal and lasting declarative memory. *Trends in Neuroscience, 21,* 294–299.

Calkins, S., & Keane, S.P. (2004). Cardiac vagal regulation across the preschool period: Stability, continuity, and implications for childhood adjustment. *Developmental Psychobiology, 45,* 101–112.

Campbell, S.B., Shaw, D.S., & Gilliom, M. (2000). Early externalizing behavior problems: Toddlers and preschoolers at risk for later maladjustment. *Development and Psychopathology, 12,* 467–488.

Carniero, P., & Heckman, J.J. (2003). Human capital policy. In J.J. Heckman & A.B. Krueger (Eds.), *Inequality in America: What role for human capital policies?* (pp. 77–240). Boston: MIT Press.

Caspi, A., Taylor, A., Moffitt, T.E., & Plomin, R. (2000). Neighborhood deprivation affects children's mental health: Environmental risks identified in genetic design. *Psychological Science, 11,* 338–342.

Cassidy, K.W., Werner, R.S., Rourke, M., Zubernis, L.S., & Balaraman, G. (2003). The relationship between psychological understanding and positive social behaviors. *Social Development, 12,* 198–221.

Cicchetti, D., & Rogosch, F.A. (2001). Diverse patterns of neuroendocrine activity in maltreated children. *Development and Psychopathology, 13,* 677–693.

Conduct Problems Prevention Research Group. (2002). Using the Fast Track randomized prevention trial to test the early-starter model of the development of serious conduct problems. *Development and Psychopathology, 14,* 925–943.

Cook, E.T., Greenberg, M.T., & Kusche, C.A. (1994). The relations between emotional understanding, intellectual functioning, and disruptive behavior problems in elementary-school–aged children. *Journal of Abnormal Child Psychology, 22,* 205–219.

Cryer, D., Wagner-Moore, L., Burchinal, M., Yazejian, N., Hurwitz, S., & Wolery, M. (2005). Effects of transitions to new child care classes on infant/toddler distress and behavior. *Early Childhood Research Quarterly, 20,* 37–56.

Cui, M., Conger, R.D., & Lorenz, F.O. (2005). Predicting change in adolescent adjustment from change in marital problems. *Developmental Psychology, 41,* 812–823.

Cummings, E.M., Goeke-Morey, M.C., & Dukewich, T.L. (2001). The study of relations between marital conflict and child adjustment: Challenges and new directions for methodology. In J.H. Grych & F.D. Fincham (Eds.), *Interparental conflict and child development: Theory, research and applications* (pp. 39–63). New York: Cambridge University Press.

Cutting, A.L., & Dunn, J. (1999). Theory of mind, emotion understanding, language, and family background: Individual differences and interrelations. *Child Development, 70,* 853–865.

Cutting, A., & Dunn, J. (2002). The cost of understanding other people: Social cognition predicts young children's sensitivity to criticism. *Journal of Child Psychology and Psychiatry, 43,* 849–860.

Daley, D., Renyard, R., & Sonuga-Barke, E.J.B. (2005). Expressed emotion in teachers of children with and without behavioural difficulties. *British Journal of Educational Psychology, 75,* 25–35.

Davidson, D., Luo, A., & Burden, M.J. (2001). Children's recall of emotional behaviors, emotional labels, and non-emotional behaviors: Does emotion enhance memory? *Cognition and Emotion, 15,* 1–26.

Davidson, R.J. (2003). Affective neuroscience and psychophysiology: Toward a synthesis. *Psychophysiology, 40,* 655–665.

Davidson, R.J., Kabat-Zinn, J., Schumacher, J., Rosenkranz, M., Muller, D., Santorelli, S.F., et al. (2003). Alterations in brain and immune function produced by mindfulness meditation. *Psychosomatic Medicine, 65,* 564–570.

Denham, S.A., & Couchoud, E.A. (1990). Young preschoolers' understanding of emotions. *Child Study Journal, 20,* 171–192.

Denham, S.A., & Couchoud, E.A. (1991). Social-emotional predictors of preschoolers' responses to adult negative emotion. *Journal of Child Psychology and Psychiatry, 32,* 595–608.

DeRosier, M., Kuperschmidt, J.B., & Patterson, C.J. (1994). Children's academic and behavioral adjustment as a function of chronicity and proximity of peer rejection. *Child Development, 65,* 1799–1813.

Dolezal, S.E., Welsh, L.M., Pressley, M., & Vincent, M.M. (2003). How nine third-grade teachers motivate student academic engagement. *Elementary School Journal, 103,* 239–269.

Doyle, W. (1990). Classroom management techniques. In O.C. Moles (Ed.), *Student discipline strategies: Research and practice* (pp. 113–127). Albany: State University of New York Press.

Dumas, J.E., Prinz, R.J., Smith, E.P., & Laughlin, J. (1999). The EARLY ALLIANCE Prevention Trial: An integrated set of interventions to promote competence and reduce risk for conduct disorder, substance abuse, and school failure. *Clinical Child and Family Psychology Review, 2,* 37–53.

Duncan, G.J., Claessens, A., & Engel, M. (2005). *The contributions of hard skills and socio-emotional behavior to school readiness* (Working paper WP-05-01). Evanston, IL: Institute for Policy Research, Northwestern University. Retrieved September 16, 2005, from www.northwestern.edu/ipr/publications/workingpapers/wpabstracts05/wp0501.html

Dunn, J., Brown, J., & Beardsall, L. (1991). Family talk about feeling states and children's later understanding of others' emotions. *Developmental Psychology, 27,* 448–455.

Dunsmore, J.C., Halberstadt, A.G., Eaton, K.L., & Robinson, M.L. (2005). Mothers' typical and event-specific positive expressions influence children's memory of events. *Social Development, 14,* 339–360.

Egan, S.K., & Perry, D.G. (1998). Does low self-regard invite victimization? *Developmental Psychology, 34,* 299–309.

Elias, M., Arnold, H., & Hussey, C.S. (2003). Introduction: EQ, IQ, and effective learning and citizenship. In M. Elias & H. Arnold (Eds.), *EQ + IQ = best leadership practices for caring and successful schools* (pp. 3–10). Thousand Oaks, CA: Corwin Press.

Estrada, C., Young, M., & Isen, A. (1994). Positive affect influences creative problem solving and reported source of practice satisfaction in physicians. *Motivation and Emotion, 18,* 285–299.

Fabes, R.A., Eisenberg, N., Hanish, L.D., & Spinrad, T.L. (2001). Preschoolers' spontaneous emotional vocabulary: Relations to likeability. *Early Education and Development, 12,* 11–27.

Fantuzzo, J., Sekino, Y., & Cohen, H. (2004). An examination of the contributions of interactive peer play to salient classroom competencies for urban Head Start children. *Psychology in the Schools, 41,* 323–336.

Fawcett, L.M., & Garton, A.F. (2005). The effect of peer collaboration on children's problem-solving ability. *British Journal of Educational Psychology, 75,* 157–169.

Field, T., & Walden, T.A. (1982). Production and discrimination of facial expressions by preschool children. *Child Development, 53,* 1299–1311.

Fine, S.E., Izard, C.E., Mostow, A.J., Trentacosta, C.J., & Ackerman, B.P. (2003). First grade emotion knowledge as a predictor of fifth grade self-reported internalizing behaviors in children from economically disadvantaged families. *Development and Psychopathology, 15,* 331–342.

Fine, S.E., Trentacosta, C.J., Izard, C.E., Mostow, A.J., & Campbell, J.L. (2004). Anger perception, caregivers' use of physical discipline, and aggression in children at risk. *Social Development, 13,* 213–228.

Fisher, P.A, Gunnar, M.R., Chamberlain, P., & Reid, J.B. (2000). Preventive intervention for maltreated preschool children: Impact on children's behavior, neuroendocrine activity, and foster parent functioning. *Journal of the American Academy of Child & Adolescent Psychiatry, 39,* 1356–1364.

Flay, B.R., & Allred, C.G. (2003). Long-term effects of the Positive Action program. *American Journal of Health Behavior, 27,* S6–S21.

Ford, M.E. (1992). *Motivating humans: Goals, emotions and personal agency beliefs.* Newberry Park, CA: Sage.

Fox, N.A., Henderson, H.A., Rubin, K., Calkins, S.D., & Schmidt, L.A. (2001). Continuity and discontinuity of behavioral inhibition and exuberance: Psychophysiological and behavioral influences across the first 4 years of life. *Child Development, 72,* 1–21.

Frey, K.S., Hirschstein, M.K., Snell, J.L., Van Schoiack-Edstrom, L., MacKenzie, E.P., & Broderick, C.J. (2005). Reducing playground bullying and supporting beliefs: An experimental trial of Steps to Respect Program. *Developmental Psychology, 41,* 479–491.

Frey, K.S., Nolen, S.B., Van Schoiack-Edstrom, L., & Hirschstein, M.K. (2005). Effects of a school-based social-emotional competence program: Linking children's goals, attributions, and behavior. *Journal of Applied Developmental Psychology, 26,* 171–200.

Garner, P.W. (2003). Child and family correlates of toddlers' emotional and behavioral responses to a mishap. *Infant Mental Health Journal, 24,* 580–596.

Garner, P.W., Dunsmore, J., & Southam-Gerow, M. (in press). Mother–child conversations about emotions: Linkages to child aggression and prosocial behavior. *Social Development.*

Garner, P.W., & Estep, K.M. (2001). Emotional competence, emotion socialization, and young children's peer-related social competence. *Early Education and Development, 12,* 29–48.

Garner, P.W., Jones, D.C., & Miner, J.L. (1994). Social competence among low-income preschoolers: Emotion socialization practices and social cognitive correlates. *Child Development, 65,* 622–637.

Garner, P.W., Jones, D.C., & Palmer, D.J. (1994). Social cognitive correlates of preschool children's sibling caregiving behavior. *Developmental Psychology, 30,* 905–911.

Garner, P.W., & Lemerise, E. (in press). The roles of behavioral adjustment and conceptions of peers and emotions in preschool children's peer victimization. *Development and Psychopathology.*

Garner, P.W., & Spears, F.M. (2000). Emotion regulation in low-income preschoolers. *Social Development, 9,* 246–264.

Garton, A.F., & Pratt, C. (2001). Peer assistance in problem-solving. *British Journal of Developmental Psychology, 19,* 307–318.

Gennetian, L.A., Morris, P.A., Bos, J.M., & Bloom, H.S. (2005). Constructing instrumental variables from experimental data to explore how treatments produce effects. In H.S. Bloom (Ed.), *Learning more from social experiments: Evolving analytic approaches* (pp. 75–114). New York: Russell Sage Foundation.

Gershoff, E.T., Aber, J.L., Raver, C.C., & Lennon, M.C. (2007). Income is not enough: Incorporating material hardship into models of income associations with parent mediators and child outcomes. *Child Development, 78.*

Gest, S.D., Welsh, J.A., & Domitrovich, C.E. (2005). Behavioral predictors of change in social relatedness and liking school in elementary school. *Journal of School Psychology, 43,* 281–301.

Gilliom, M., Shaw, D., Beck, J.E., Schonberg, M.A., & Lukon, J.L. (2002). Anger regulation in disadvantaged preschool boys: Strategies, antecedents, and the development of self-control. *Developmental Psychology, 38,* 222–235.

Good, T.L., & Grouws, D.A. (1979). The Missouri Mathematics Effectiveness Project: An experimental study in fourth-grade classrooms. *Journal of Educational Psychology, 71,* 355–362.

Gottman, J.M., Katz, L.F., & Hooven, C. (1996). Parental meta-emotion philosophy and the emotional life of families: Theoretical models and preliminary data. *Journal of Family Psychology, 10,* 243–268.

Greenberg, M.T., & Kusche, C.A. (1998). Preventive interventions for school-age deaf children: The PATHS curriculum. *Journal of Deaf Studies and Deaf Education, 3,* 49–63.

Greenberg, M.T., Kusche, C.A., & Speltz, M. (1991). Emotional regulation, self-control, and psychopathology: The role of relationships in early childhood. In D. Cicchetti & S.L. Toth (Eds.), *Internalizing and externalizing expressions of dysfunction* (pp. 21–55). Mahwah, NJ: Lawrence Erlbaum Associates.

Gunnar, M.R. (2000). Early adversity and the development of stress reactivity and regulation. In C.A. Nelson (Ed.), *The effects of adversity on neurobehavioral development: Minnesota symposium on child psychology* (Vol. 31, pp. 163–200). Mahwah, NJ: Lawrence Erlbaum Associates.

Gunnar, M.R., & Donzella, B. (2004). Tympanic membrane temperature and emotional dispositions in preschool-aged children: A methodological study. *Child Development, 75,* 639–650.

Gunnar, M.R., Sebanc, A.M., Tout, K., Donzella, B., & van Dulmen, M.M. (2003). Peer rejection, temperament, and cortisol activity in preschoolers. *Developmental Psychobiology, 43,* 343–358.

Halberstadt, A.G., Denham, S.A., & Dunsmore, J.C. (2001). Affective social competence. *Social Development, 10,* 79–119.

Hamre, B.K., & Pianta, R.C. (2005). Can instructional and emotional support in the first-grade classroom make a difference for children at risk of school failure? *Child Development, 76,* 949–967.

Hartman, R.R., Stage, S.A., & Webster-Stratton, C. (2003). A growth curve analysis of parent training outcomes: Examining the influence of child risk factors (inattention, impulsivity, and hyperactivity problems), parental and family risk factors. *Journal of Child Psychology and Psychiatry, 44,* 388–398.

Henderlong, J., & Lepper, M.R. (2002). The effects of praise on children's intrinsic motivation: A review and synthesis. *Psychological Bulletin, 128,* 774–795.

Hoglund, W.L., & Leadbeater, B.J. (2004). The effects of family, school and classroom ecologies on changes in children's social competence and emotional and behavioral problems in first grade. *Developmental Psychology, 40,* 533–544.

Howe, G.W., Reiss, D., & Yuh, J. (2002). Can prevention trials test theories of etiology? *Development and Psychopathology, 14,* 673–694.

Hughes, J.N., Cavell, T.A., Meehan, B.T., Zhang, D., & Collie, C. (2005). Adverse school context moderates the outcomes of selective interventions for aggressive children. *Journal of Consulting and Clinical Psychology, 73,* 731–736.

Hyson, M., & Cone, J. (1989). Giving form to feeling: Emotions research and early childhood education. *Journal of Applied Developmental Psychology, 10,* 375–399.

Isen, A.M. (2000). Some perspectives on positive affect and self-regulation. *Psychological Inquiry, 11,* 184–187.

Isen, A.M., Daubman, K.A., & Nowicki, G.P. (1987). Positive affect facilitates creative problem solving. *Journal of Personality and Social Psychology, 52,* 1122–1131.

Isen, A.M., & Shalker, T.E. (1982). The effect of feeling state on evaluation of positive, neutral, and negative stimuli: When you "accentuate the positive," do you "eliminate the negative"? *Social Psychology Quarterly, 45,* 58–63.

Izard, C.E. (2002). Translating emotion theory and research into preventive interventions. *Psychological Bulletin, 128,* 796–824.

Izard, C.E., & Ackerman, B.P. (2000). Motivational, organizational, and regulatory functions of discrete emotions. In M. Lewis & J.M. Haviland-Jones (Eds.), *Handbook of emotions* (2nd ed., pp. 253–322). New York: Guilford Press.

Izard, C.E., Fine, S., Schultz, D., Mostow, A.J., Ackerman, B.P., & Youngstrom, E.A. (2001). Emotion knowledge as a predictor of social behavior and academic competence in children at risk. *Psychological Science, 12,* 18–23.

Izard, C.E., Trentacosta, C.J., King, K.A., & Mostow, A.J. (2004). An emotion-based prevention program for Head Start children. *Early Education and Development, 15,* 407–422.

Johnson, M.K., Crosnoe, R., & Elder, G.H. (2001). Students' attachment and academic engagement: The role of race and ethnicity. *Sociology of Education, 74,* 318–340.

Jones, V. (1996). Classroom management. In J. Sikula (Ed.), *Handbook of research on teacher education* (2nd ed., pp. 503–521). New York: Simon & Schuster.

Kagan, J., Reznick, J.S., & Snidman, N. (1988). Biological bases of childhood shyness. *Science, 240,* 167–171.

Kam, C., Greenberg, M.T., & Walls, C.T. (2003). Examining the role of implementation quality in school-based prevention using the PATHS curriculum. *Prevention Science, 4,* 55–63.

Keenan, K., Shaw, D.S., Walsh, B., Delliquadri, E., & Giovanelli, J. (1997). DSM-III-R disorders in preschool children from low-income families. *Journal of the American Academy of Child & Adolescent Psychiatry, 36,* 620–627.

Kellam, S.G., Ling, X., Merisca, R., Brown, C.H., & Ialongo, N. (1998). The effect of the level of aggression in the first grade classroom on the course and malleability of aggressive behavior into middle school. *Development and Psychopathology, 10,* 165–186.

King, A., Staffieri, A., & Adelgais, A. (1998). Mutual peer tutoring: Effects of structuring tutorial interaction to scaffold peer learning. *Journal of Educational Psychology, 90,* 134–152.

Knight, G.P., & Hill, N.E. (1998). Measurement equivalence in research involving minority adolescents. In V.C. McLoyd & L. Steinberg (Eds.), *Studying minority adolescents: Conceptual methodological, and theoretical issues* (pp. 183–210). Mahwah, NJ: Lawrence Erlbaum Associates.

Kuperschmidt, J.B., & Coie, J.D. (1990). Preadolescent peer status, aggression, and school adjustment as predictors of externalizing problems in adolescence. *Child Development, 61,* 1350–1362.

Ladd, G.W., Birch, S.H., & Buhs, E.S. (1999). Children's social and scholastic lives in kindergarten: Related spheres of influence? *Child Development, 70,* 1373–1400.

Lambert, N.M. (1994). Seating arrangements in classrooms. *The International Encyclopedia of Education, 9,* 5355–5359.

Lang, P.J. (1995). The emotion probe: Studies of motivation and attention. *American Psychologist, 50,* 372–385.

Lavigne, J.V., Gibbons, R.D., Christoffel, K.K., Arend, R., Rosenbaum, D., Binns, H., et al. (1996). Prevalence rates and correlates of psychiatric disorders among preschool children. *Journal of the American Academy of Child & Adolescent Psychiatry, 35,* 204–214.

Lazarus, R.S. (1991). *Emotion and adaptation.* New York: Oxford University Press.

Lench, H.C., & Levine, L.J. (2005). Effects of fear on risk and control judgments and memory: Implications for health promotion messages. *Cognition & Emotion, 19,* 1049–1069.

Lepper, M.R., Corpus, J.H., & Iyengar, S.S. (2005). Intrinsic and extrinsic motivational orientations in the classroom: Age differences and academic correlates. *Journal of Educational Psychology, 97,* 184–196.

Lewis, M. (1993). Self-conscious emotions: Embarrassment, pride, shame, and guilt. In M. Lewis & J.M. Haviland (Eds.), *Handbook of emotions* (pp. 563–573). New York: Guildford Press.

Lewis, M.D., & Steiben, J. (2004). Emotion regulation in the brain: Conceptual issues and directions for developmental research. *Child Development, 75,* 371–376.

Linares, L.O., Rosbruch, N., Stern, M.B., Edwards, M.E., Walker, G., Abikoff, H.B., et al. (2005). Developing cognitive-social-emotional competencies to enhance academic learning. *Psychology in the Schools, 42,* 405–417.

Loeber, R., & Hay, D. (1997). Key issues in the development of aggression and violence from childhood to early adulthood. *Annual Review of Psychology, 48,* 371–410.

Lopez, N.L., Vazquez, D.M., & Olson, S.L. (2004). An integrative approach to the neurophysiological substrates of social withdrawal and aggression. *Development and Psychopathology, 16,* 69–93.

Mantzicopoulos, P., & Neuharth-Pritchett, S. (2003). Development and validation of a measure to assess Head Start children's appraisals of teacher support. *Journal of School Psychology, 41,* 431–451.

Mezzacappa, E., Kindlon, D., Saul, J.P., & Earls, F. (1998). Executive and motivational control of performance task behavior, and autonomic heart-rate regulation in children: Physiologic validation of 2-factor solution inhibitory control. *Journal of Child Psychology and Psychiatry, 39,* 525–531.

Michalson, L., & Lewis, M. (1985). What do children know about emotions and when do they know it? In M. Lewis & C. Saarni (Eds.), *The socialization of emotions* (pp. 117–139). New York: Plenum.

Miller, A.L., Gouley, K.K., Seifer, R., Dickstein, S., & Shields, A. (2004). Emotions and behaviors in the Head Start classroom: Associations among observed dysregulation, social competence, and preschool adjustment. *Early Education and Development, 15,* 147–165.

Moffitt, T., Caspi, A., Rutter, M., & Silva, P. (2002). Sex differences in antisocial behaviour: Conduct disorder, delinquency and violence in the Dunedin longitudinal study. *Psychological Medicine, 32,* 1475–1476.

Murray, C., & Greenberg, M.T. (2000). Children's relationship with teachers and bonds with school. An investigation of patterns and correlates in middle childhood. *Journal of School Psychology, 38,* 423–445.

Nelson, B., Martin, R.P., Hodge, S., Havill, V., & Kamphaus, R. (1999). Modeling the prediction of elementary school adjustment from preschool temperament. *Personality and Individual Differences, 26,* 687–700.

NICHD Early Child Care Research Network. (2003). Social functioning in 1st grade: Associations with earlier home and child care predictors and with current classroom experiences. *Child Development, 74,* 1639–1662.

NICHD Early Child Care Research Network, & Duncan, G. (2003). Modeling the impacts of child care quality on children's preschool cognitive development. *Child Development, 74,* 1454–1475.

Nowicki, S., & Duke, M.P. (1992). The association of children's nonverbal decoding abilities with their popularity, locus of control, and academic achievement. *Journal of Genetic Psychology, 153,* 385–393.

Olson, S.L., Sameroff, A.J., Kerr, D.C.R., Lopez, N.L., & Wellman, H.M. (2005). Developmental foundation of externalizing problems in young children: The role of effortful control. *Development and Psychopathology, 17,* 25–45.

Owens, L., Slee, P., & Shute, R. (2000). "It hurts a hell of a lot . . . ": The effects of indirect aggression on teenage girls. *School Psychology International, 21,* 359–376.

Peisner-Feinberg, E., Burchinal, M., Clifford, R., Culkin, M., Howes, C., Kagan, S., et al. (1999). The children of the cost, quality, and outcome study go to school (Executive summary). Chapel Hill, NC: FPG Child Development Center.

Pekrun, R., Goetz, T., Titz, W., & Perry, R. (2002). Academic emotions in students' self-regulated learning and achievement: A program of qualitative and quantitative research. *Educational Psychologist, 37,* 67–68.

Peters, M.A., & Rutte, C.G. (2005). Time management behavior as a moderator for the job demand-control interaction. *Journal of Occupational Health Psychology, 10,* 64–75.

Pianta, R.C., & Caldwell, C.B. (1990). Stability of externalizing symptoms from kindergarten to first grade and factors related to instability. *Development and Psychopathology, 2,* 247–258.

Pianta, R., Howes, C., Burchinal, M., Bryant, D., Clifford, R., Early, D., et al. (2005). Features of pre-kindergarten programs, classrooms, and teachers: Do they predict observed classroom quality and child–teacher interactions? *Applied Developmental Science, 9,* 144–159.

Pianta, R.C., La Paro, K.M., & Hamre, B.K. (2005). *Classroom Assessment Scoring System (CLASS).* Unpublished measure, University of Virginia.

Pianta, R.C., La Paro, K.M., Payne, C., Cox, M.J., & Bradley, R. (2002). The relation of kindergarten classroom environment to teacher, family, and school characteristics and child outcomes. *Elementary School Journal, 102,* 225–238.

Pollak, S.D. (2003). Experience-dependent affective learning and risk for psychopathology in children. In J.A. King, C.F. Ferris, and I.I. Lederhendler (Eds.), *Roots of mental illness in children. Annals of the New York Academy of Sciences* (pp. 102–111). New York: New York Academy of Sciences.

Pons, F., Harris, P., & de Rosnay, M. (2004). Emotion comprehension between 3 and 11 years: Developmental periods and hierarchical organization. *European Journal of Developmental Psychology, 1,* 127–152.

Posner, M.I., & Rothbart, M.K. (2000). Developing mechanisms of self-regulation. *Development and Psychopathology, 12,* 427–441.

Quas, J.A., Bauer, A., & Boyce, W.T. (2004). Physiological reactivity, social support, and memory in early childhood. *Child Development, 75*(2), 797–814.

Raver, C.C. (2004). Placing emotional self-regulation in sociocultural and socioeconomic contexts. *Child Development, 75,* 346–353.

Raver, C.C., Blackburn, E., Bancroft, M., & Torp, N. (1999). Relations between effective emotional self-regulation, attentional control, and low-income preschoolers' social competence. *Journal of Early Education and Development, 10,* 333–350.

Raver, C.C., Gershoff, E.T., & Aber, J.L. (2007). Testing equivalence of mediating models of income, parenting, and school readiness for White, Black, and Hispanic children in a national sample. *Child Development, 78.*

Raver, C.C., & Spagnola, M. (2002). When my mommy was angry, I was speechless: Children's perceptions of maternal emotional expressiveness within the context of economic hardship. *Marriage and Family Review, 34,* 63–88.

Raver, C.C., & Zigler, E.F. (1997). Social competence: An untapped dimension in evaluating Head Start's success. *Early Childhood Research Quarterly, 12,* 363–385.

Reid, M.J., Webster-Stratton, C., & Hammond, M. (2003). Follow-up of children who received the Incredible Years intervention for oppositional-defiant disorder: Maintenance and prediction of 2-year outcome. *Behavior Therapy, 34,* 471–491.

Rimm-Kaufman, S.E., La Paro, K.M., Downer, J.T., & Pianta, R.C. (2005). The contribution of classroom setting and quality of instruction to children's behavior in kindergarten classrooms. *Elementary School Journal, 105,* 377–394.

Rimm-Kaufman, S.E., Pianta, R.C., & Cox, M.J. (2000). Teachers' judgments of problems in the transition to kindergarten. *Early Childhood Research Quarterly, 15,* 147–166.

Ross, M.R., Powell, S.R., & Elias, M.J. (2002). New roles for school psychologists: Addressing the social and emotional learning needs of students. *School Psychology Review, 31,* 43–52.

Saarni, C. (1988). Emotional competence: How emotions and relationships become integrated. *Nebraska Symposium on Motivation, 36,* 115–182.

Schimmack, U. (2005). Attentional interference effects, emotional pictures: Threat, negativity, or arousal? *Emotion, 5,* 55–66.

Schultz, D., Izard, C.E., & Ackerman, B.P. (2000). Children's anger attributional bias: Relations to family environment and social adjustment. *Social Development, 9,* 284–301.

Schultz, D., Izard, C.E., Ackerman, B.P., & Youngstrom, E.A. (2001). Emotion knowledge in economically disadvantaged children: Self-regulatory antecedents and relations to social difficulties and withdrawal. *Development and Psychopathology, 13,* 53–67.

Schutz, P.A., & Davis, H.A. (2000). Emotions and self-regulation during test taking. *Educational Psychologist, 35,* 243–256.

Schutz, P.A., & DeCuir, J.T. (2002). Inquiry on emotions in education. *Educational Psychologist, 37,* 125–135.

Shaw, D.S, Vondra, J.I., Hommerding, K.D., Keenan, K., & Dunn, M. (1994). Chronic family adversity and early child behavior problems: A longitudinal study of low income families. *Journal of Child Psychology and Psychiatry, 35,* 1109–1122.

Shields, A., Dickstein, S., Seifer, R., Giusti, L., Dodge-Magee, K., & Spritz, B. (2001). Emotional competence and early school adjustment: A study of preschoolers at risk. *Early Education and Development, 12*(1), 73–96.

Shonkoff, J.P., & Meisels, S.J. (Eds.). (2000). *Handbook of early childhood intervention* (2nd ed.). New York: Cambridge University Press.

Shores, R.E., & Wehby, J.H. (1999). Analyzing the classroom social behavior of students with EBD. *Journal of Emotional and Behavioral Disorders, 7,* 194–199.

Silver, R.B., Measelle, J.R., Armstrong, J.M., & Essex, M.J. (2005). Trajectories of classroom externalizing behavior: Contributions of child characteristics, family characteristics, and the teacher–child relationship during school transition. *Journal of School Psychology, 43,* 39–60.

Smith-Donald, R., Raver, C.C., Hayes, T., & Richardson, B. (2005). *Preliminary construct and concurrent validity of the Preschool Self-Regulation Assessment (PSRA) for field-based research.* Unpublished manuscript.

Soar, R., & Soar, R. (1977). Emotional climate and management. In P. Petersen & H. Walberg (Eds.), *Research on teaching: Concepts, findings, and implications* (pp. 97–119). Berkeley, CA: McCutchan.

Steele, C.M., & Aronson, J. (1995). Stereotype threat and the intellectual test performance of African Americans. *Journal of Personality and Social Psychology, 69,* 797–811.

Stuhlman, M., & Pianta, R.C. (2002). Teachers' narratives about their relationships with children: Associations with behavior in classrooms. *School Psychology Review, 31,* 148–163.

Sutton, R.E. (2004). Emotional regulation goals and strategies of teachers. *Social Psychology of Education,7,* 379–398.

Tomaka, J., Blascovitch, J., Kelsey, R.M., & Leitten, C. (1993). Subjective, physiological, and behavioral effects of threat and challenge appraisal. *Journal of Personality and Social Psychology, 65,* 248–260.

Walden, T.A., & Smith, M.C. (1997). Emotion regulation. *Motivation and Emotion, 21,* 7–25.

Webster-Stratton, C., Reid, M.J., & Hammond, M. (2004). Treating children with early-onset conduct problems: Intervention outcomes for parent, child, and teacher training. *Journal of Clinical Child and Adolescent Psychology, 33,* 105–124.

Weimer, A. (2005). False belief, emotion understanding, and social skills among Head Start and non-Head Start children. *Early Education and Development, 16,* 341–366.

Wentzel, K.R. (2002). Are effective teachers like good parents? Teaching styles and student adjustment in early adolescents. *Child Development, 73,* 287–301.

Wenzel, A., & Lystad, C. (2005). Interpretation biases in angry and anxious individuals. *Behavior Research and Therapy, 43,* 1045–1054.

Wiltz, N.W., & Klein, E.L. (2001). "What do you do in child care?" Children's perceptions of high and low quality classrooms. *Early Childhood Research Quarterly, 16,* 209–236.

Yerkes, R.M., & Dodson, J.D. (1908). The relationship of strength of stimulus to rapidity of habit-formation. *Journal of Comparative Neurology of Psychology, 18,* 459–482.

Zigler, E., Gilliam, W.S., & Jones, S.M. (2006). *A vision for universal preschool education.* New York: Cambridge University Press.

8

A DEVELOPMENTAL NEUROSCIENCE APPROACH TO THE STUDY OF SCHOOL READINESS

Clancy Blair, Hilary Knipe, Eric Cummings,
David P. Baker, David Gamson, Paul Eslinger, and Steven L. Thorne

This chapter examines the applicability of work in developmental neuroscience to the study of school readiness. The turn of the 21st century has seen tremendous growth in neuroscience research. Advances in brain imaging have greatly enhanced knowledge of brain structure and function, and a variety of research, both human and nonhuman, has substantially increased understanding of genetic, neural, and physiological contributions to developing cognitive and social competence. Given this growth, however, can neuroscience contribute meaningfully to the study of school readiness? Arguably, it can in a number of ways. By reviewing several relevant literatures and presenting some of our work, this chapter can help to set the stage for the application of developmental neuroscience to specific issues in school readiness research and to child study more generally.

This chapter presents a specific approach that we have used in the study of school readiness that focuses on an aspect of cognitive development referred to as *executive function* (EF). The chapter examines issues in the definition of EF, also referred to as *fluid cognitive functioning* or *working memory,* broadly defined, and its relation to aspects of cognition and behavior that are at the core of child-centered approaches to school readiness. In doing so, the chapter describes research in neuroscience relevant to the development of EF in early childhood and examines the effects of early experience on brain development and neural and physiological functioning relevant to EF. This primarily includes an examination of work investigating the neural substrate of EF and the extent to which this work may provide insight into a number of questions concerning influences on readiness such as those associated with parenting and early care.

The first author's research and scholarly activities are supported, in part, by National Institute of Child Health and Human Development grant numbers R03 HD39750 and P01 HD39667. All authors acknowledge support from the Spencer Foundation.

This chapter is dedicated to the memory of Gilbert Gottlieb (1929–2006).

The chapter then turns to a specific area of school readiness and early learning—the development of proficiency in mathematics—and to work examining the neural substrate of number sense and basic mathematical ability. Following this, the chapter will detail ways in which EF is related to mathematical ability and how the study of EF has informed our research on the development of mathematical ability as an aspect of school readiness.

The chapter concludes with future directions for a developmental neuroscience approach to the study of school readiness and with thoughts on possible curricular innovations and training programs to promote school readiness. This concluding section describes work suggesting the trainabililty of EF abilities and considers some expectations regarding effects of such training on school readiness and early math learning and achievement.

DEFINING SCHOOL READINESS

School readiness can mean different things to different people. As a phenomenon of interest to scholars and parents of varying backgrounds, school readiness has proven to be something of a dynamic entity, the definition of which can, and perhaps should, be suited to a variety of concerns. Although somewhat obvious and intuitive from a practical standpoint, empirical definition of school readiness has been quite challenging. This is because the correspondence between the overarching or universal construct of readiness and the individual differential measures employed to indicate that construct is far from perfect. It is quite logical in societies that place a premium on the formal education of children to state that children should enter school ready for the demands that will be made of them. However, determining the nature of those demands and the characteristics and abilities required of children to meet those demands has resulted in an epistemological gridlock.

To some extent, readiness must be seen as a function of decisions made by the socially defined institution of schooling. To another, however, it must reflect the characteristics and abilities of young children as fostered by parenting and early care experiences. Determining where the balance lies between the demands of the institution and the characteristics of the child has been the subject of many a parent–teacher conference and is the source of ongoing discussion among scholars and policy makers interested in studying and promoting school readiness. As a result, there is no single overarching definition of readiness but, rather, a universal readiness construct to which a variety of differential indicators have been brought to bear.

To list just a few, these indicators include preliteracy abilities, behavioral self-regulation, social skills, general cognitive ability, and language ability (perhaps the whole gamut of child developmental study) on the child side of the equation. On the school environment side of the equation, teacher practices and abilities, administrative policies, availability of high-quality preschool experiences, and priorities for early educational progress are just a few of the factors that have been considered as aspects of the multidimensional matrix of school readiness. Each aspect of the matrix of readiness provides a potentially viable entry point for the study of the phenomenon. However, no single approach can adequately encompass its overall nature. As a result, readiness exists in the abstract and is a valuable part of the educational landscape. However, it is an abstraction without a single well-defined set of indicators that can be universally applied.

SCHOOL READINESS: A SYSTEMS VIEW

Although many approaches to readiness have focused either on specific child- or school-related factors, a number of investigators have approached readiness using a developmental systems framework. In a systems framework, examination of the development of a given skill important for readiness occurs in tandem with the study of classroom quality, early learning experiences, and relationships with peers and teachers (Mashburn & Pianta, 2006). Within the framework, readiness is a function of the interaction of the child with the resources, social and material, of the institution and the resulting enhancement or constraint of social and cognitive development that this interaction provides.

The developmental neuroscience approach that we use in our work on EF and early math learning is best understood within this systems view of readiness. It considers the child within social context and provides specific expectations regarding early development and learning trajectories for diverse children within various family, classroom, and school settings. This approach to school readiness and early school success considers readiness as an emergent outcome of the interaction between child and environmental characteristics and is consistent with an overarching developmental science approach to child development (e.g., Cairns, Elder, & Costello, 1996). One of the goals of this chapter is to describe a program of research on readiness that is consistent with developmental science principles and that provides some specific expectations regarding relations among early experience, emerging EF, and the development of academic ability, particularly mathematical ability.

EXECUTIVE FUNCTION, DEVELOPMENTAL NEUROSCIENCE, AND SCHOOL READINESS

As developmental psychologists and educational theorists interested in young children's early progress in school, our work has focused on the integration of cognitive and emotional functioning in young children and the ways in which child characteristics and early care and schooling influences affect the development of this integration (Blair, 2002). As a part of this work, we have focused primarily on aspects of cognition that go under the general heading of EF (Diamond, 2002; Zelazo & Müller, 2002) and are similar if not identical to constructs studied in the psychological literature under the terms executive attention (Posner & Rothbart, 2000), working memory (WM; Baddeley, 1992), and working memory capacity (Engle, 2002). Generally speaking, EF denotes flexible and adaptive cognitive control in the face of various types of information processing and social-emotional demand. More specifically, EF refers to cognitive or supervisory processes associated with the active maintenance of information in working memory, the appropriate shifting and sustaining of attention among goal-relevant aspects of a given task or problem, and the inhibition of prepotent or extraneous information and responding within a given task context (Miyake, Friedman, Emerson, Witzki, & Howerter, 2000). In particular, these effortful cognitive processes are distinct from those associated with relatively automatic cognitive processing and retrieval from long-term store of previously well-learned or crystallized information. Examples of such crystallized knowledge include language ability, vocabulary, and reading ability as well as basic knowledge, such as knowledge of arithmetic facts (e.g., $2 + 2 = 4$, the times tables).

Although EF is only one aspect of readiness, close examination of EF can provide a valuable perspective on the systems approach to readiness and early progress in school. Indeed, if, for the purposes of argument, one were to consider the acquisition of crystallized knowledge a primary objective of schooling, EF could be considered important for the knowledge acquisition that schooling conveys. That is, if the cognitive control processes that characterize EF support knowledge acquisition, then the promotion of EF is an important, although not exclusive, focus for research on school readiness. Thus, EF might underlie the development of readiness to learn. However, the developmental science approach to school readiness that we use in our work suggests that although EF may be important for knowledge acquisition, the role of EF in the definition and study of school readiness and early school success is more complex than the preceding argument would imply.

Specifically, although EF may contribute to the organization of information and the planning and problem-solving processes that support learning in classroom environments, the development of the cognitive processes that comprise EF are also a central focus of schooling in their own right. They characterize aspects of cognition, analogous to critical thinking skills, the development of which is a primary objective of high-quality education. In addition to conveying information, an overarching goal of schooling is to foster the self-regulation of cognition and behavior important for learning: identifying the components of a given problem or task, identifying and organizing the steps required to solve the problem or complete the task, and executing those steps to reach the desired goal. In this, EF describes aspects of cognition associated with self-regulated learning that support the development of a sense of self as an efficacious learner (Rothbart & Jones, 1998) and an intrinsic motivational orientation known to be important for later achievement (Dweck, 1986).

A LONGITUDINAL STUDY OF EF AND SCHOOL ADAPTATION

At the outset, two issues can serve as the focus of research efforts on EF as an aspect of school readiness. The first concerns the extent of the relation between EF and general cognitive ability and the second concerns the relation of EF to the development of aspects of social-emotional functioning known to be important for school readiness (Ladd, Birch, & Buhs, 1999). Prior work indicates that the cognitive abilities that comprise EF are distinct from but highly similar to general intelligence (Blair, 2006) and that although EF plays some role in the development of social-emotional competence (Hughes & Ensor, 2005), it is largely distinct from aspects of social-emotional self-regulation. Limited work, however, has examined the specific relation of EF to general intelligence and to social-emotional development within the context of school readiness. Our work with children in Head Start, the U.S. federal preschool program for children from low-income homes, indicates a relation of EF to early math and reading ability in kindergarten that is independent of both general intelligence and social-emotional competence (Blair & Razza, in press). Following 141 children from Head Start into kindergarten, we found that a peg-tapping measure of the inhibitory control aspect of EF (Diamond & Taylor, 1996), which requires children to inhibit a prepotent response tendency while remembering and executing the rule for correct responding, was uniquely associated with measures of early mathematics and literacy ability. Furthermore, we observed that the inhibitory control aspect of EF assessed both in Head Start and in kindergarten demonstrated a particularly strong relation with mathematics ability in kindergarten. These relations were present over and above those associated with measures of fluid intelligence (e.g., the Raven Colored Progressive Matrices test, Raven, 1956), crystallized verbal intelligence (the Peabody Picture Vocabulary Test, Dunn & Dunn, 1997), and aspects of social-emotional development, including false-belief understanding and teachers' reports of an aspect of child temperament referred to as *effortful control.*

As expected, our measures of EF, fluid and verbal intelligence, and social-emotional behavior were moderately correlated. However, each tended to account for unique variance in either early math or literacy outcomes. Specifically, whereas the peg-tapping measure of the inhibitory control aspect of EF was related to early math as well as indicators of emerging literacy, phonemic awareness and letter knowledge, Raven's matrices test was uniquely related to math and phonemic awareness but not letter knowledge. The vocabulary measure was uniquely related only to letter knowledge. For aspects of social-emotional development, we found that both false-belief understanding and teacher-reported effortful control were uniquely related to both math ability and letter knowledge but not to phonemic awareness.

Our findings relating EF to early academic abilities for children from low-income homes are similar to those of others examining EF in children from typical-income homes both in preschool and the early elementary grades. This is particularly so for math ability. For example, a prior study with preschoolers found that measures of the inhibitory control and working memory aspects of EF were uniquely related to math ability (Espy et al., 2004). Furthermore, these investigators found that the inhibitory control aspect of EF demonstrated a robust relation to math ability that remained strong after controlling for general intelligence and other relevant covariates. Similarly, a study with 7-year-old children found that measures of working memory, inhibitory control, and attention shifting accounted for unique variance in math ability in first grade, again controlling for general intelligence (Bull & Scerif, 2001).

DEVELOPMENTAL NEUROSCIENCE OF EF

As an aspect of developing self-regulation important for school readiness, our approach to the study of EF has been to consider the construct at multiple levels, from the neural to the social, and to propose a developmental systems model relating EF to early learning and progress in school. This approach follows the general psychobiological model developed by Gilbert Gottlieb (1991) and illustrated in Figure 8.1. The model presents bidirectional relations among genetic, physiological, behavioral, and environmental levels of influence on psychological development and suggests that processes occurring at one level are influenced by processes at all others. Specifically, using the model, we are interested in ways in which aspects of genetic background and neural and physiological processes important for EF may both affect and be affected by children's psychological development, experiences in school, and interactions with parents, peers, and teachers. Furthermore, the model recognizes the need to place development within context and, to the extent possible, to consider home, school, and community characteristics that may alter bidirectional relations among genetic, physiological, and psychological influences on development.

To begin at the level of neural and physiological processes, numerous studies using functional magnetic resonance imaging (fMRI) or positron emission tomography (PET) have indicated a role for specific regions of the prefrontal cortex (PFC) in the execution of tasks that can be considered dependent on cognitive processes associated with EF (Smith & Jonides, 2003). For example, in a widely used task, the "n-back" working memory task, the individual is presented a sequential series of letters or a single figure in various locations and must determine whether the current letter or location is the same as that presented one, two, or three letters or locations before (resulting in one, two, or three back conditions of the task). Results from imaging studies using the n-back and similar types of tasks requiring a constant updating of information present converging evidence of increased activity in the dorsal lateral area of the PFC, the anterior cingulate cortex (ACC), ventral medial PFC, superior and inferior parietal cortex, and the striatum (Braver et al., 1997; Gray, Chabris, & Braver, 2003; Rypma, Prabhakaran, Desmond, Glover, & Gabrieli, 1999). Common regions of activation across tasks appear to indicate a cortical network that is active in response to tasks that require the integration of various EF processes (Duncan & Owen, 2000; Prabhakaran, Smith, Desmond, Glover, & Gabrieli, 1997).

Although there are common regions of activation across diverse tasks, there are also distinctions among areas activated by different aspects of various tasks. In particular, examination of tasks that make heavy demands on inhibitory control and the resolution of cognitive interference have indicated a primary role for the ACC (Bush, Luu, & Posner, 2000; MacDonald, Cohen, Stegner, & Carter, 2000; Ridderinkhof, van den Wildenberg, Segalowitz, & Carter, 2004). These studies suggest the ACC is central to the detection of error and the initiation of cognitive control in response to conflict or error (Carter et al., 1998; Ridderinkhof et al., 2004). These relations are in keeping with anatomical and functional studies of the ACC, indicating that the ACC is an intermediary between prefrontal cortical structures associated with the maintenance of information in working memory and limbic structures associated with emotionality, autonomic nervous system function, and the stress response (Allman, Hakeem, Erwin, Nimchinsky, & Hof, 2001; Paus, 2001).

Studies of brain activation associated with the cognitive processes that underlie EF raise several points relevant to the developmental neuroscience approach to school readiness. First, because most brain-imaging studies of EF have been conducted with healthy adults, there are questions of whether findings from studies of adult brains are applicable to research on child development. However, imaging studies conducted with children in the range that can be assessed using MRI (usually a lower bound of about 7 or 8 years of age) reveal patterns of activation that are similar to, but more widespread than, those seen in adults (Casey et al., 1995, 1997; Rivera, Reiss, Eckert, & Menon, 2005; see also Bunge, Ochsner, Desmond, Glover, & Gabrieli, 2001). Furthermore, the study of age-related change in brain activation in response to working memory tasks suggests that the cortical network supporting EF matures gradually. For example, examination of brain activation using fMRI in response to a visual-spatial working memory task revealed specific age-related increases in activation in the frontal and parietal cortices (Klingberg, Forssberg, & Westerberg, 2002). Indeed, maturation of the parieto-frontal network was shown to be associated with age-related increases in white matter density supporting faster neural conductivity in this working memory circuit (Olesen, Nagy, Westerberg, & Klingberg, 2003).

A second point of particular interest for the developmental neuroscience approach to the study of EF and school readiness is the indication from the adult literature that levels of PFC activation in response to working memory tasks exhibit a quadratic, inverse U relation to memory load. Specifically, examination of changes in brain activation in response to increasing working memory load, that is, from one to two to three back versions of the task, indicate a capacity constraint such that when a given capacity set point is exceeded, lower (rather than higher) levels of PFC activation are observed (Callicott et al., 1999; Goldberg et al., 1998; Rypma et al., 1999). Consistent with this point, studies that have imaged tasks that are relatively easy for adults but more difficult for children have indicated increased activity in frontal and striatal regions associated with EF in children relative to adults (Durston et al., 2002; Eslinger et al., 2006; Rivera et al., 2005).

A third and somewhat overarching point central to the developmental neuroscience approach to school readiness relates to findings indicating that the ACC is composed of divisions that are preferentially activated by cognitive and emotional stimulation. Studies examining activation in the ACC in response to interference resolution demonstrate reciprocal relations between the emotional and cognitive divisions in response to cognitive tasks and to tasks containing some affective content (Bush et al., 2000; Drevets & Raichle, 1998). This aspect of ACC function indicates that brain structures that subserve EF are integrated with brain structures of the limbic system that subserve emotion and stress responses. This prefrontal corticolimbic interconnectivity underlies the give and take between cognition and emotion and influences the ability to regulate one's behavior. In combination, prefrontal, limbic, and brainstem structures integrate cognitive, emotional, and autonomic responses to stimulation. The primary implication of such reciprocal innervation and regulation is that cognitive processes associated with EF directly influence and, most important for present purposes, are influenced by emotional arousal and autonomic responses to stimulation (de Kloet, Oitzl, & Joels, 1999; Gray, Braver, & Raichle, 2002; Kaufman & Charney, 2001). A traditional view of reasoning or executive cognitive ability as distinct from or liable only to disruption from emotion has been replaced by a model in which cognitive and emotional responses work in concert to organize patterns of behavior (Davidson, 2002; Van Eden & Buijs, 2000). Studies in adult populations examining the intentional reappraisal of emotional arousal and the cognitive regulation of emotion have indicated the reciprocal nature of activity in prefrontal and limbic brain regions (Mayberg et al., 1999; Ochsner, Bunge, Gross, & Gabrieli, 2002). During periods of negative affect, increased limbic and emotional ACC and decreased prefrontal and cognitive ACC activations have been observed. With reappraisal of negative emotion and recovery from sadness and depression, however, prefrontal and cognitive ACC activation is increased and limbic and emotional ACC activation is decreased.

From the perspective of the theoretical model presented in Figure 8.1, the findings of brain imaging work described above suggest the need to carefully consider influences on developing emotionality and emotion regulation as they relate to the development of prefrontal corticolimbic neural circuitry that supports EF. The role of emotional arousal in brain imaging studies of cognition helps to illustrate a central point of the developmental neuroscience approach to school readiness, namely that high levels of negative emotional reactivity and chronic stress are likely to adversely influence the development of EF and behavioral self-regulation important for school readiness. Although studies using fMRI are not feasible for preschool- and early school–age children (due to the requirement that participants in imaging research remain still for long periods of time), imaging findings in older children and adults suggest a meaningful developmental neuroscience model of experiential influences on the development of neural systems that support self-regulation abilities important for school readiness. As suggested in Figure 8.1, processes external to the child at the family, school, and social levels are likely to affect emotional arousal and stress-related processes that will facilitate (at optimal levels) or inhibit (at extremely low or high levels) neural and physiological development that supports the early development of EF and social-emotional self-regulation abilities important for school readiness.

Although admittedly speculative, given principles of experience-dependent synaptic plasticity and a developmental psychobiological theoretical orientation, early care and educational experiences conceivably shape, to some extent, the development of synaptic connectivity among

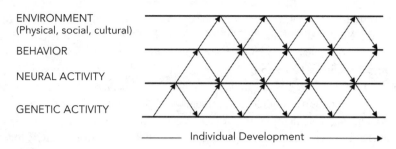

ENVIRONMENT
(Physical, social, cultural)

BEHAVIOR

NEURAL ACTIVITY

GENETIC ACTIVITY

⟵——— Individual Development ———⟶

Figure 8.1. General psychobiological model. (From Gottlieb, G. [1991]. Experiential canalization of behavioral development. *Developmental Psychology, 27,* 4–13; reprinted by permission).

structures associated with emotional reactivity and executive cognitive control. In effect, early experience may influence the balance between emotional reactive and effortful cognitive responses to stimulation in ways that may bias cognitive and social developmental trajectories toward or away from the types of self-regulation skills and goal-directed behavior required of children in school settings. In caregiving and early educational settings that are inconsistent in their expectations for children's behavior or demand highly regimented or routinized responding, children would conceivably begin to exhibit patterns of prefrontal corticolimbic reciprocity that would be weighted toward emotional reactivity and external regulation rather than cognitive control and internally directed self-regulation. In contrast, caregiving environments that provide appropriate structure and consistency may allow for increased autonomy and the development of self-regulation that facilitates executive cognitive processing and supports self-regulated learning.

However, rather than attribute an overarching influence on development to external factors, relations between emotional reactive and effortful cognitive aspects of child functioning need to be considered with an eye to individual differences. At the ascending genetic and neural levels of influence in the model presented in Figure 8.1, individuals are understood to vary in levels of emotional reactivity and levels of general cognitive abilities. Genes involved in the regulation of neurotransmitters important for prefrontal cortical functioning, particularly the catecholamines, dopamine (Diamond, Briand, Fosella, & Gehlbach, 2004; Egan et al., 2001; Fan, Fossella, Sommer, Wu, & Posner, 2003) and serotonin (Hariri et al., 2002), are an important source of influence on neural processes that underlie EF and emotional and stress reactivity. Individual differences in the working memory aspect of EF have in part been related to a single nucleotide polymorphism of the catechol-o-methyl-transferase (COMT) gene, the val[108/158]met polymorphism. This polymorphism determines the enzymatic action of the gene in inactivating dopamine. Individuals with the valine (val) allele of this polymorphism exhibit more rapid dopamine inactivation and reduced working memory ability. Furthermore, the methionine (met) version of the allele is unique to humans and those who carry this allele inactivate dopamine in the PFC less rapidly. Similarly, individual differences in emotional reactivity and impulse regulation have been associated with the short form of a polymorphism in the serotonin transporter gene. Individuals with the short form allele exhibit higher levels of neuronal reactivity to fear-invoking stimuli (Hariri et al., 2002), and individuals with the short form who experience adverse rearing conditions may exhibit higher levels of impulsivity and problems with stress regulation (Suomi, 2003). As well, numerous behavioral genetic studies using twin and adoption study methodologies indicate heritability for personality and for general cognitive ability, although the specific source and mechanism of that influence remains to be determined (Plomin, DeFries, McClearn, & McGuffin, 2001).

It is also necessary to recognize the reciprocal nature of influences in the model, particularly with respect to emotional arousability and early stress processes. Nonhuman animal models indicate that early caregiving experiences influence gene expression and the development of brain structures and functions (Kinnunen, Keonig, & Bilbe, 2003; Lemaire, Koehl, Le Moal, & Abrous, 2000; Lyons, Afarian, Schatzberg, Sawyer-Glover, & Moseley, 2002; Sanchez, Hearn, Do, Rilling, & Herndon, 1998) that are important for the regulation of the stress response (Francis, Caldji, Champagne, Plotsky, & Meaney, 1999) and the development of cognitive and behavioral self-regulation. In rodents, high levels of maternal competence (defined as high levels of licking and grooming and a style of nursing known as arched back nursing) are associated with gene expression that promotes regulation of the hypothalamic–pituitary–adrenal (HPA) axis response to stress and promotes learning and memory processes associated with effective HPA regulation (Liu, Diorio, Francis, & Meaney, 2000; Meaney, 2001; Weaver et al., 2004).

Application of the model linking early life experience with reactivity to stress and cognitive and social development is a priority for child development research. In one step in this process, we have demonstrated a relation between the HPA response to stress and EF in preschool children from low-income homes (Blair, Granger, & Razza, 2005) and are conducting studies to link this relation to aspects of early experience. In our study with preschoolers, children who exhibited a flexible stress response characterized by moderate up-regulation and down-regulation of the HPA axis in response to mild stress exhibited higher levels of EF and were rated by teachers as better regulated in the classroom. This work is consistent with a variety of work in children and adults indicating relations among HPA axis function and aspects of cognitive and behavioral regulation (Erickson, Drevets, & Schulkin, 2003; Gunnar, Tout, de Haan, Pierce, & Stansbury, 1997). Evidence indicating the relation of HPA function to developing cognitive and social competence provides an important link between early care experiences and the development of aspects of cognition and behavior important for school readiness.

EF AND EDUCATION

A developmental neuroscience approach to the study of EF that focuses on cognition–emotion interaction and self-regulation yields a perspective on child readiness for school that is highly consistent with child-centered or progressive beliefs about early care and education. The approach suggests that child-centered practices in preschool and early elementary education can yield more optimal educational outcomes than those that employ more traditional information dissemination or "back to basics" educational practices. Progressive approaches to education intentionally foster the critical thinking skills that are dependent on EF and that are associated with an intrinsic motivational orientation. If improvements in self-regulation and critical thinking skills are more likely to yield greater learning and school engagement, then the developmental neuroscience approach can inform school readiness research and provide insight into the types of early educational practices that are likely to be most productive. A central tenet of the child-centered, progressive approach to education is that knowledge acquisition occurs more effectively when children are engaged and using the cognitive abilities that characterize EF. If such engagement is taken to represent bona fide as opposed to rote learning, it may be possible to characterize this engagement and learning at the physiological and neural levels as well as the psychological level. This characterization would associate bona fide learning with an optimal state of physiological arousal that supports the long-term synaptic potentiation (LTP) through which learning transpires at the neural level. Although such a relation and characterization of learning requires much further work, the study of cellular functioning in the PFC indicates that moderate levels of dopamine and glucocorticoid receptor occupation indicative of optimal arousal are associated with greater working memory ability (Goldman-Rakic, Muly, & Williams, 2000) and synaptic LTP (de Kloet et al., 1999). Although studies are needed to directly test the optimal arousal hypothesis in the study of learning in school environments, a neuroscientifically grounded model of best educational practices does seem realizable.

Research on the developmental neuroscience of EF can provide support for a progressive, child-centered approach to education. One answer to the question "ready for what?" in the study of school readiness is that children should be ready to benefit from education that promotes learning through discovery and through emerging autonomy and self-regulation skills. Within a child-centered approach to early elementary education, an emphasis on the development of EF is appropriate as a focus for school readiness research. However, it is important to also focus on skill building as an aspect of schooling and to consider the neuroscientific basis for developing proficiency in domains of knowledge that are acquired in school. One educational subject area with clear links to developing EF and also a considerable body of neuroscientific research to inform this EF-based approach is mathematics.

DEVELOPMENTAL NEUROSCIENCE OF MATHEMATICAL ABILITY

Knowledge of the neural basis for specific aspects of mathematical cognition is well advanced and provides insight into what is developing at the neural level as children become proficient in mathematics. Of primary interest are widely replicated findings indicating the role of the brain's parietal lobe in number processing and in the representation of quantity. In particular, three parietal circuits have been identified, each with a specific relation to mathematical cognition. One segment of the parietal lobe, the horizontal segment of the intraparietal sulcus (HIPS), has been shown to be active bilaterally (on both sides of the brain) whenever number processing occurs. Activity in the HIPS in response to quantity has been seen in a number of species and across a wide variety of human cultures, suggesting that this area of the parietal lobe may represent an evolutionarily determined "number line in the head" that provides the basis for intuitive understanding of quantity. In contrast, the left angular gyrus of the parietal cortex is thought to be associated with a more general verbal representation of quantity. Increasing activation in this region is seen in response to mathematical tasks requiring greater verbal processing of information and retrieval of mathematical information from long-term memory (i.e., multiplication facts). Similar to the left angular gyrus, bilateral activation in a region of the parietal cortex behind and above the HIPS, referred to as the posterior superior parietal lobule, has been seen in response to number comparison, counting, and simple calculation problems and is thought to represent the contribution of general attentional orienting and visual-spatial working memory to mathematical cognition (Dehaene, Piazza, Pinel, & Cohen, 2003).

Consistent with the contribution of verbal and spatial–attentional components of the parietal cortex to mathematical cognition are findings indicating activation of a prefrontal–parietal cortical circuit in response to math tasks requiring calculation. Using fMRI and PET with adults, activation in the prefrontal–parietal cortical circuit has been observed in response to simple calculation problems (Burbaud et al., 1995; Zago et al.,

2001). Furthermore, activation detected in this network in response to simple calculation overlaps with activation seen in response to attentional control and language-based working memory problems (Simon et al., 2004) and also with visual-spatial working memory (Klingberg, Forssberg, & Westerberg, 2002). This work provides evidence at the neural level for a relation between aspects of EF and basic mathematical ability. Indeed, perhaps the strongest evidence for the role of prefrontal–parietal network in number processing is provided by evidence from nonhuman primates. Single-cell recording from prefrontal and parietal neurons indicates neurons in both areas of the brain that are selectively tuned to specific numerosities and that appear to communicate information in a posterior to anterior direction (Neider, 2005; Neider & Miller, 2004).

Evidence in Children

Although there is evidence for parietal–prefrontal neural connectivity in brain imaging studies of calculation with adults, limited research has addressed this overlap in the neural basis for EF and mathematical cognition in young children. Knowledge of the developmental integration of the neural networks that underlie EF and early mathematical ability may have valuable implications for school readiness research and for understanding variation in learning problems in young children. Basic developmental work suggests the presence of a rudimentary quantitative ability early in life (Feigenson, Dehaene, & Spelke, 2004), and brain imaging (Cantlon, Brannon, Carter, & Pelphrey, 2006) and electroencephalographic recording (Temple & Posner, 1998) studies suggest that immediate processing of quantity is similar in young children and adults. These findings indicate similarity in one aspect of mathematical cognition in children and adults, presumably that associated with the immediate processing of quantity as indicated by activity of the HIPS. Given this similarity, however, it is unclear whether educational experiences to which young children are routinely exposed are geared toward the development and strengthening of the parietal–prefrontal network associated with EF and basic mathematical ability. A developmental fMRI study of the neural response to basic calculation problems (single digit addition and subtraction problems with no solution greater than nine) indicated that young children exhibited increased activity relative to adolescents in frontal and striatal regions associated with EF. In contrast, adolescents exhibited greater parietal activation associated with more efficient and less effortful processing of numbers (Rivera et al., 2005).

To address the relation of educational experience to neural activity associated with mathematical cognition, our research group has been using fMRI to examine brain activation in response to specific types of math problems routinely encountered by young children in the early elementary grades. These problem types, suggested by a historical review of the math curriculum for young children in U.S. schools (described next), included basic numerical addition and subtraction problems, addition and subtraction problems using coins, and also pattern-completion problems. Both the coin-calculation problems and pattern-completion problems are highly similar to types of problems that are in widespread use in the mathematics curriculum of the early elementary grades in the United States. With 16 participants between ages 8 and 19 years, findings indicated that all three types of problems were associated with activation in parietal, frontal, and striatal regions. Of greatest interest were findings indicating that age was negatively correlated with activations occurring in frontal and striatal regions and positively correlated with activation in the parietal cortex in the region of the intraparietal sulcus. These findings suggest that pattern-completion and coin-calculation exercises, both of which are well represented in the mathematics curriculum of the early elementary grades, are associated with activation of cortical structures that underlie mathematical cognition and EF. Generally speaking, the findings of our brain-imaging work suggest that standard types of math activities routinely encountered by young children in the early elementary grades are associated with the activation of the parietal–prefrontal network thought to underlie mathematical cognition. The correlation of brain activation with age in our studies suggests that change over age in response to basic math exercises is associated with increasing bilateral superior parietal activation that is also seen in response to attentional and spatial working memory tasks and known to be active in response to mathematics problems (Dehaene, Molko, Cohen, & Wilson, 2004; Zago et al., 2001). Our data suggest that educational activities and practices geared toward strengthening EF, such as child-centered educational experiences, as well as practice on pattern completion and similar types of tasks, will help to strengthen the neural substrate associated with self-regulation abilities as well as math ability and achievement.

Evidence in the Curriculum: Historical Analysis

The study of relations among EF, the neural substrate supporting mathematical cognition, and mathematics education in our fMRI experiments is based on historical review of changes during the 20th century in the math curriculum in the early elementary grades in the United States. Specifically, one aspect of the approach to the study of school readiness and developing math ability outlined previously has been to ask what types of cognitive processes are required of children as they enter kindergarten and the early elementary grades. In terms of math education during the 20th century, the answer to this question is that children have been exposed increasingly to activities that require the application of EF skills (Blair, Gamson, Thorne, & Baker, 2005).

During the course of the 20th century, the typical mathematics curriculum in schools in the United States changed radically, from introducing simple mathematical processes such as counting and numeracy in the first or second grade during the 1920s, to introducing kindergartners in the late 20th century to relational reasoning, pattern-solving skills and concepts fundamental to geometry. Changes to the early elementary math curriculum over time have been characterized by an increased emphasis on problems that require little automatized, crystallized knowledge and that, in some instances, are designed almost exclusively to exercise executive cognitive functions. A related trend has been the practice of introducing in increasingly lower elementary grades geometric concepts dependent on visual-spatial working memory that had historically been reserved for introduction at later grades.

The executive cognitive demand of the math curriculum has been assessed through a systematic analysis of the textbooks identified as modal texts by scholars of the mathematics curriculum during the three periods that represent significant shifts in the content and pedagogy of mathematics instruction in elementary schools (Gamson, Cummings, & Knipe, 2006). During these time periods—the Progressive era (approximately 1876–1957), the New Math era (approximately 1957–1972), and the years following the 1983 release of the U.S. Department of Education report, *A Nation at Risk*—the content and pedagogy of elementary school mathematics were heavily influenced by changes in psychology and learning theory, curriculum design, and advances in mathematics, facilitated by social and political changes exerting pressure on formal processes of schooling (for a more detailed discussion of the historical influences on the mathematics curriculum, see Gamson et al., 2006).

1. Count the boys on the bench. How many boys?
2. Count the girls on the bench. How many girls?
3. Count all the girls in the picture. How many?
4. Count all the children in the picture. How many children?
5. Count the windows in your school room. How many?
6. Count the panes in each window. How many?
7. Count the pictures in the room. How many?
8. Count the rows of seats. How many?
9. Count the seats in each row. How many?
10. Count the blackboard erasers. How many?

Figure 8.2a. Counting exercises for young children from the early 20th century. (From Harris, A.V.S., & Waldo, L.M. [1911]. *First journeys in numberland.* Chicago: Scott Foresman; reprinted by permission.)

The first math texts written specifically for first or second grade appeared in the early 1910s and 1920s. Previously, very little math instruction was offered until after second grade, and math texts were rarely used before third grade (National Education Association, 1895). The goal of mathematics instruction was that "By the end of the sixth grade the child should be able to carry out the four fundamental operations with integers and with common and decimal fractions accurately and with a fair degree of speed" (National Committee on Mathematical Requirements, 1923, p. 6). Generally, educators in the early decades of the 20th century considered the acquisition of literacy a prerequisite for math instruction; one early text mentions that math instruction should begin in the middle of the fourth year (Smith, Luse, & Morss, 1929a, 1929b). Items in these texts (especially in the first third of any given book, but often throughout) rarely make demands of EF abilities and focus on rote counting and the application of previously learned algorithms. Figure 8.2a and 8.2b provide representative samples of the activities asked of students in two books from the early 1900s. In Figures 8.2a and 8.2b, colorful pictures serve as platforms for counting practice. In both examples, the task is designed simply for counting practice. Almost all of the books examined from this time period (1911–1930) begin with basic counting and numeracy exercises and progress to concrete exercises such as associating the numeral 6 with a quantity of six objects and understanding the ordinal and cardinal properties of numbers. Measurement, addition, and subtraction follow, with large portions of the text devoted to word problems and drills, as in Figures 8.3 and 8.4.

Progressive era texts emphasized the use of algorithms and mechanical rote learning habits for problem solution, with little focus on conceptual understanding of the properties of mathematical processes. For example, sections of texts were dedicated to "adding five to a number," or "working with threes," in which students were drilled in counting by five and in using threes in addition and subtraction problems (see Figure 8.3 for a sample of such problems). As a result of the amount of drill exercises present in the text and extended focus on basic counting and numeracy, these early mathematics texts for elementary schools cover between 20 and 40 discrete mathematical concepts.

AT THE CIRCUS

Four
4

Five
5

Count the big balloons.
Count the little balloons.
Find 4 funny men.
Find 5 big elephants.

Figure 8.2b. Counting exercises for young children from the early 20th century. (From Peet, H.E., & Clapp, F.L. [1930]. *Number games and stories.* Boston: Houghton Mifflin; reprinted by permission.)

The content of these early texts indicates the expectations of school readiness that educators had at the time for students entering schools. During this period, public school enrollments increased dramatically, reflecting dual trends of foreign immigration and the internal migration of rural people to urban areas. Many of the children entering school, especially the rural migrants, were likely to come from families who had little or no prior schooling themselves. In addition, enrollments in the relatively few kindergartens available were low, and the kindergarten curriculum was primarily focused on behavioral, not academic, issues of school readiness (Tyack & Cuban, 1995).

By the late 1950s, enrollment figures had stabilized, and increasing numbers of children entering school came from families that had at least been exposed to elementary education. The cognitive demand of texts from the early 1950s increased slightly through the Progressive era texts, but a greater increase was seen after the reforms supported by the National Defense Education Act of 1958. Concerns about progressive education's perceived lack of academic rigor and American students' ability to compete with the Soviet Union were exac-

Tell what number is left:

1. 12	17	13	16	14	18	15	18
<u>1</u>	<u>4</u>	<u>2</u>	<u>3</u>	<u>2</u>	<u>4</u>	<u>3</u>	<u>1</u>

2. 16	15	17	15	16	18	13	14
<u>4</u>	<u>5</u>	<u>1</u>	<u>4</u>	<u>2</u>	<u>7</u>	<u>1</u>	<u>3</u>

3. 19	17	17	18	15	16	19	18
<u>6</u>	<u>2</u>	<u>6</u>	<u>3</u>	<u>2</u>	<u>1</u>	<u>2</u>	<u>5</u>

Figure 8.3. Rote learning exercises typically used in math education for young children in the early to mid-20th century. (From Harris, A.V.S., & Waldo, L.M. [1911]. *First journeys in numberland.* Chicago: Scott Foresman; reprinted by permission.)

1. John made dolls from candles, pipes, clothespins, nuts, and corncobs. He made pigs from lemons. He sold them to his playmates for toy money.

2. He charged 3 cents admission to the tent where the dolls and the pigs were on sale.

3. Frank bought a pipe doll for 7 cents. What did his admission and the doll cost?

4. Ada bought a 5 cent nut doll. The doll and her admission cost ____ cents.

5. Mary bought a candle doll for 4 cents. The doll and admission cost her ____ cents.

6. Lily bought a clothespin doll for 3 cents. The doll and admission cost her ____ cents.

7. Tom bought a lemon pig, which cost 6 cents. His admission and the pig cost him ____ cents.

1. Read the number in blue.

   1, 2,   4, 5,   7, 8,

2. 3 + 3 = ___   3 + 7 = ___
   3 + 5 = ___   3 + 6 = ___
   3 + 4 = ___   3 + 2 = ___

3. 3 + ___ = 10   3 + ___ = 7
   3 + ___ = 6   3 + ___ = 9
   3 + ___ = 8   3 + ___ = 5

4. ___ + 7 = 10   ___ + 4 = 7
   ___ + 3 = 6   ___ + 6 = 9
   ___ + 7 = 8   ___ + 2 = 5

5. $\begin{array}{cccccccccc} 3 & 3 & 5 & 3 & 7 & 8 & 10 & 6 & 9 & 7 \\ +3 & +4 & +3 & +6 & +3 & -3 & -3 & -3 & -3 & -3 \\ \hline \end{array}$

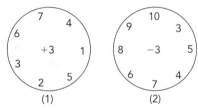

(1)   (2)

6. Put 3 with each number around circle (1).

7. Take 3 from each number around circle (2)

Figure 8.4. Word problems used in math education for young children in the early 20th century. (From Smith, D.E., Luse, E.M., & Morss, E.L. [1929b]. *Walks and talks in numberland.* Boston: Ginn and Company; reprinted by permission.)

erbated after the launch of the Sputnik spacecraft. These concerns led to close scrutiny of the pedagogy and content of the curriculum in general and mathematics in particular. Several university-sponsored mathematics reform groups began to formulate curricular responses to the weaknesses in mathematics instruction.

The collective work of these groups became known as "the New Math." Instead of focusing on drills and rote memorization of algorithms to establish the proper habits of mathematical problem solving, advocates of the New Math argued that instruction should begin with understanding mathematical properties. In the New Math model, "memorization, when it does occur, follows meaning" (Barker, Curran, & Metcalf, 1964, p. iii). For example, the first-grade math texts published by the School Mathematics Study Group began with set theory, using arbitrary symbols before any numbers are introduced. Once computational skills were introduced, the stress on increasing students' mathematical understanding translated into practices such as teaching the commutative (a + b = b + a) and associative ([a + b] + c = a + [b + c]) properties of numbers to children. New Math materials also introduced components of mathematical concepts in early elementary grades that traditionally had not been introduced until secondary level schools, such as geometry, integers, coordinates, and rational numbers; naming and understanding the basic properties of simple geometric shapes began in kindergarten (Barker et al., 1964).

Although the overall influence of New Math reforms in their purest form is a matter of debate in educational circles, math books after 1960 show evidence of the incorporation of New Math tenets, however moderated. For example, among the textbooks reviewed in this chapter, set theory was not included in any elementary texts prior to 1960 but was included in all of the sampled texts after this date, appearing somewhere between the first and third

1 two = ?

2 twos = ?

3 twos = ?

4 twos = ?

5 two = ?

6 two = ?

Painting Eggs

Multiplying with Twos

Each child in Ann's room painted 2 eggs.

1. Find picture A. This shows how many eggs were painted by one child.

2. Which picture shows the number of eggs painted by 2 children? 3 children? 4 children? 5 children? 6 children?

3. For each of the pictures A, B, C, D, E, and F, tell:
   a. how many groups of twos you see.
   b. how many eggs there are.

4. Why is each picture of the eggs above an array pattern? Now let us write some problems about the columns of eggs in the array patterns above. Suppose each column shows you the number of eggs painted by each child. Then two columns of eggs will show you the number of eggs painted by two children. Which picture shows that each child painted:
5 eggs?   3 eggs?   6 eggs?   1 egg?   4 eggs?   2 eggs?

5. For each of pictures A, B, C, D, E, and F, tell:
   a. how many eggs were painted by each child.
   b. how many eggs were painted by 2 children.

6. How did we use the Law of Order for Multiplication in this lesson?

Figure 8.5. Math exercises for young children that exercise executive function. (From Brueckner, L.J., Merton, E.L., & Grossnickle, F.E. [1963]. *Moving ahead in arithmetic: Books 3–6.* New York: Holt, Rinehart and Winston; reprinted by permission.)

grades. Material requiring more abstract problem-solving skills and involving executive cognitive demand, patterns, and pattern-completion activities, for example, appeared with more regularity. After this date, texts were much more likely to ask elementary students to think like mathematicians, that is, to think more conceptually about the problems they were solving (Walmsley, 2003). Figures 8.5, 8.6, and 8.7 provide examples of representative problems requiring the direct application of executive cognitive skills. Texts from the end of the century show an even greater emphasis on executive cognitive problem-solving skills and strategies, the conceptual understanding of mathematical properties, and critical thinking. There is less emphasis in these texts on algorithmic procedures or repeated exercises in simple computation. The executive cognitive demand of the material in these texts is greater than in math texts from previous time periods. A representative pattern completion exercise from a 1991 textbook task is presented in Figure 8.8.

EVIDENCE IN THE CURRICULUM: CODING EXECUTIVE COGNITIVE DEMAND

To document the extent of change in the math curriculum in the United States both as an aspect of a changing historical emphasis in the teaching of math to young children as

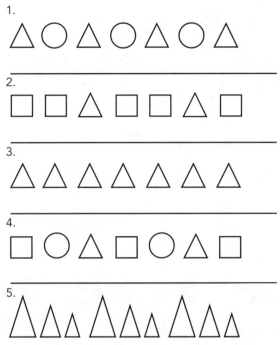

Figure 8.6. Math exercises for young children that exercise executive function. (From Clark, C.H., Beatty, L.S., Payne, J.N., & Spooner, G.A. [1966]. *Let's begin: Elementary mathematics—Primer.* New York: Harcourt, Brace & World; reprinted by permission.)

well as an aspect of school readiness, we developed a coding scheme to assess the executive cognitive demand of the math curriculum for the early elementary grades. This coding scheme assists in determining the types of cognitive processes that the math urriculum makes of children as they enter school and progress through the early elementary grades. Although curricular materials cannot tell the complete story of what goes on in classrooms and what children are actually taught (Cohen, 1990; Lampert, 1985), decontextualized analysis of materials is necessary to assess and understand the cognitive demands placed on children in school mathematics. The empirical strength of this strategy is that it relies on features of the problems and materials themselves to determine cognitive demand rather than using error rates or response times to approximate the complexity or difficulty of an item. Each problem sampled is carefully analyzed to determine the cumulative demands placed on the problem solver's working memory, attention shifting, inhibitory control, and general knowledge resources.

In measuring the executive cognitive demand of traditional number and operation-oriented mathematics problems, working memory demands include information that must be held in mind during any given step or across steps and the number of operations or steps involved. For more visually and spatially oriented problems, the number of attributes or characteristics a figure varies on, the number of figures in an array or pattern, and the physical distance (in degrees, or linear measure) that a figure rotates or moves determine the working memory load of a problem. Attention-shifting demand is operationalized as the number of items, categories, or concepts among which the problem solver must distribute attention.

166   Blair et al.

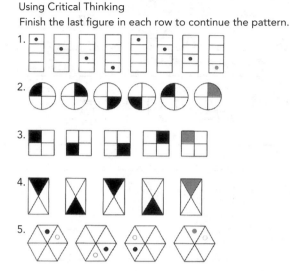

Using Critical Thinking
Finish the last figure in each row to continue the pattern.

Figure 8.7. Representative pattern-completion exercises from a first-grade textbook. (From Eicholz, R.E., O'Daffer, P.G., Fleener, C.R., Young, S.L., Charles, R.I., & Barnett, C.S. [1991]. *Addison-Wesley mathematics, Grade 2* (Vol. 2). Menlo Park, CA: Addison-Wesley; reprinted by permission.)

Attention-shifting demands include such tasks as shifting between digits, operands, or iterations of a process or between known information and needed information. Inhibitory control demand is operationalized in traditional numerical and operational math as the cumulative number of times that the problem solver must select or infer the correct operation or information and the number of pieces of distracting or unnecessary information the problem solver must ignore. In the case of pattern solving or visual-spatial problems, inhibitory control demand depends on the number of distracter figures and attributes, the size of the array or length of the pattern, and the number of attributes the problem solver must selectively choose from to solve the problem.

As noted previously, one problem type that became increasingly prevalent during the late 20th century for young children entering school involves visual-spatial working memory. Typical examples of these pattern-completion problems for young children are seen in Figures 8.7 and 8.8. An interesting feature of these problems is that unlike basic arithmetic problems, which vary significantly in difficulty with level of external support and as crystallized

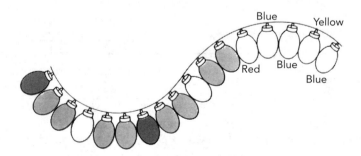

Figure 8.8. A representative pattern completion exercise from a second grade textbook. (From Eicholz, R.E., O'Daffer, P.G., Fleener, C.R., Young, S.L., Charles, R.I., & Barnett, C.S. [1991]. *Addison-Wesley mathematics, Grade 2* (Vol. 2). Menlo Park, CA: Addison-Wesley; reprinted by permission.)

knowledge increases, these problems are rarely made easier with provision of pencil and paper or any type of automatized knowledge. In much the same way, these problems are largely unaffected by teachers who instruct students in rigid and rote-based mathematics because there are no simple algorithms for their solution.

LINKING CURRICULUM CONTENT AND TEACHING MODE WITH COGNITIVE FUNCTIONING

An important but unmeasured aspect of the study of the cognitive demand of early elementary math education as presented in textbooks is that the way any curriculum is enacted will vary from teacher to teacher. Although curricular analysis can provide only a limited representation of actual classroom experience, the analysis presented in this chapter provides a platform for examining the effects of teaching style and other classroom and school factors on the cognitive demand of the enacted curriculum. The abstracted measure of cognitive demand of the curriculum is the starting point from which a teacher could either increase or decrease the cognitive demand of classroom activity by encouraging or discouraging such things as conceptual understanding, flexible thinking, and multiple solution strategies, or selecting to teach (or not teach) selected content within curricular materials.

Just as the presentation style of the content in textbooks indicates the intent and potential cognitive demand of that particular curriculum, the presentation and questioning style of teachers can have an impact on the cognitive demands placed on students and the development of EF in school-age children. Teachers play an important role in promoting executive cognitive skills in the mathematics classroom because different teachers could teach the same mathematical content in very different ways. An illustrative example is addition. One could easily teach students only the relatively simple, highly mechanical process of adding and carrying across all digits of the operands and focus on basic drills and memorization of facts. On the other hand, students might learn from their teacher that they can manipulate objects to see and feel addition of small numbers or that addition of large addends is easier when the numbers are split into their hundreds, tens, and ones components, or even that they can use approximation strategies to come close to a solution, then use simple addition to find an exact answer. Although the end result is the same—students learn to add—the quality of the experience and the underlying cognitive development are very different. Using multiple strategies teaches students to think flexibly, represent quantities or problems in multiple ways, and evaluate and select strategies that best fit the particular context. This, in turn, helps students develop and refine EF skills in a way that teaching rote mathematical facts is not designed to do.

Empirical identification of the types of cognitive skills related to math proficiency can provide the basis for balanced assessment and evaluation tools and a better understanding of children's progress or delay in developing mathematical abilities. An issue that looms over all aspects of educational policy and theory, school readiness included, concerns the role of assessment and the use of standardized testing to track educational progress and achievement. Identification of the EF demand of mathematics problem solving can help to provide an a priori empirical basis for determining the level of complexity of math activities to which children are exposed at any given level of content knowledge. This is an alternative to item-based approaches in which error rates are used as a proxy for complexity under the assumption that more complex problems will result in more errors and longer response times. Item-based analyses, however, do not explain *what* is more complex or where the demand comes from. In some cases, complexity is attributed to a hierarchy of content complexity in which more advanced material is inherently more complex, but such a theory cannot account for low complexity (i.e., low-level content) problems with high error rates.

CONCLUSION

The developmental neuroscience approach presented in this chapter is supported by a variety of evidence but requires additional empirical support before its applicability to the study of school readiness, specifically, and issues in educational research, more generally, can be fully evaluated. The developmental science approach on which this work is based has been endorsed in the field of child study as having considerable utility for addressing the complex nature of various phenomena (Cairns et al., 1996; Shonkoff & Phillips, 2000). It will likely prove valuable for the study of school readiness. In the specific instance of school readiness, the approach proposes pathways of influence from expectations for children as embedded in the curriculum, to conceptions of readiness and readiness practices, to neurological and cognitive development in children.

At the center of this application of neuroscience to the study of school readiness is EF. The overlapping executive cognitive functions of working memory, inhibitory control, and attention shifting are seen as potentially foundational aspects of readiness, although their relations to crystallized knowledge and aspects of social development and behavioral self-regulation important for school readiness remain to be fully addressed. A focus on EF in the study of school readiness is consistent with research indicating positive relations of intrinsic motivation and self-regulated learning to later school achievement. It may be that efforts to promote EF early in schooling can lead to improved educational outcomes that are associated with increased intrinsic motivation and greater self-regulation in learning.

One way that EF is being promoted in young children is through everyday exercises in the math curriculum of the early elementary grades. The study of the neural basis of mathematical cognition in adults and children suggests that the pattern-completion and visual-spatial reasoning activities that children have increasingly encountered in math education in the late 20th and early 21st centuries are in fact associated with the activation of prefrontal and parietal cortical structures believed to be important for proficiency in math.

One of the large unanswered questions in the relation of EF to math education and educational progress in young children concerns the actual implementation of the curriculum by teachers in the classroom. Educational theorists espousing a progressive approach to early childhood education strongly advocate classroom practices that encourage children to be engaged and active learners, acquiring knowledge through classroom activities with minimal direct instruction from the teacher. Such a progressive approach seems consistent with a developmental neuroscience understanding of school readiness and early school progress based on EF. However, the specific relation of EF to such an approach and the extent to which the early math curriculum may exemplify a progressive child-centered approach remains to be determined. Math particularly seems to be an aspect of the curriculum in which progressive discovery-based teaching methods may prove effective in encouraging interest and promoting learning. However, the extent to which such teaching methods do or do not promote the type of math achievement that standards-based educators consider the yardstick of effective teaching will, no doubt, remain controversial and a topic of intense concern to many.

In addition to the need for work examining the promotion of EF skills through progressive, discovery-based methods of teaching, it is also desirable to examine the extent to which direct training of EF skills may be associated with improvements in EF and academic ability. Although direct training of EF is perhaps anathema to progressive approaches to educational practice, such an attempt is recommended by training studies indicating cognitive benefits associated with repetitive game-like practice on computer-based EF tasks. In studies with both children and adults, including children with attention-deficit/hyperactivity disorder (ADHD), training on some of the cognitive skills that comprise EF has been shown to improve those cognitive skills, to improve behaviors associated with those skills, and to induce increased activity in the neural substrate supporting those skills and behaviors (Klingberg et al., 2002; Olesen, Westerberg, & Klingberg, 2004; Rueda, Rothbart, McCandliss, Saccomanno, & Posner, 2005). An important direction for future research on this type of training concerns the replication of effects with diverse samples of typically developing children and examination of the generalizability of any effects of training to aspects of cognition, such as math learning and achievement.

Finally, with respect to the developmental neuroscience approach to school readiness, the sociological perspective implicit in this approach should be reiterated. Although many changes in pedagogy and child development that support an interest in EF and school readiness are consistent, underneath these are deeper changes that have fundamentally transformed school and its role in society (Tyack & Cuban, 1995). The relatively rapid and inexorable extension of formal education to nearly every corner of the globe has resulted in the ascension of formal schooling as arguably the most influential modern sociological process affecting the context of human development (Meyer, 1977). A revolution in education has come about in the past 150 years that continues to this day. It is a revolution in the form of widespread schooling for primary and secondary school, and increasingly now for higher education, for larger and larger proportions of cohorts of children and youth. In a very short time, human society all over the world went from providing only limited schooling for the masses while saving advanced educational opportunity for elite students, to the idea and now common practice of schooling all children and youth. The standard of how much schooling it takes for one to be considered an educated person has steadily risen with every generation. Educational credentials and curricular specialties are essential for the modern labor market. Increasingly, education stratifies the marriage market, sets lifestyles, yields civic participation, and has an impact on health and longevity more than any other characteristic of individuals. Children in most places around the world grow up in a schooled society. It is no wonder that long schooling careers are increasingly seen as a normative aspect of growing up in modern society. Consequently, investment by parents in children's long-term development and chances for social status are now almost solely limited to investment in schooling in terms of parental assistance, strategic planning, and capital (Baker & LeTendre, 2005). Seen this way, the ability to prepare children for this powerful and transforming institution takes on large meaning for society.

The dimensions of the educational revolution have major consequences for understanding school readiness and the cognitive demands of the modern school. A crucial idea driving the educational revolution is that children can only become fully developed adults through lengthy and successful school careers. And the major currency of successful schooling is academic achievement, a task that has gotten more demanding over time within schools. By spreading the time-consuming and common activity of going to school, this worldwide educational revolution has brought massive attention to certain types of human capabilities, making them seem as if they were always central human capabilities; in other words, the educational revolution has made it natural for so many to focus on cognitive skills and academic achievement as never before in human history. For the some 200,000 years of modern homo sapiens' existence, the human experience has been about thinking capabilities, but, until just recently, most human existence was a predominantly physical one in which the reified, abstract thinking that is now required in school was not common, useful, or even valued. Of course, this is no longer the case. Indeed, the answer to the question "ready for what?" in the study of school readiness can be construed in very broad terms. At root, however, there are certain key elements of readiness in the development of EF that help to set the stage for the fostering of self-regulated and intrinsically motivated learning and that are key components of the socially defined educational process.

REFERENCES

Allman, J.M., Hakeem, A., Erwin, J., Nimchinsky, E., & Hof, P. (2001). The anterior cingulate cortex: The evolution of an interface between emotion and cognition. *Annals of the New York Academy of Sciences, 935,* 107–117.

Baddeley, A. (1992). Working memory. *Science, 255,* 556–559.

Baker, D., & LeTendre, G. (2005). *National differences, global similarities: World culture and the future of mass schooling.* Palo Alto, CA: Stanford University Press.

Barker, C.M., Jr., Curran, H., & Metcalf, M. (1964). *The "new" math: For teachers and parents of elementary school children.* Palo Alto, CA: Fearon.

Blair, C. (2002). School readiness: Integrating cognition and emotion in a neurobiological conceptualization of child functioning at school entry. *American Psychologist, 57,* 111–127.

Blair, C. (2006). How similar are fluid cognition and general intelligence? A developmental neuroscience perspective on fluid cognition as an aspect of human cognitive ability. *Behavioral and Brain Sciences, 29,* 109–125.

Blair, C., Gamson, D., Thorne, S., & Baker, D. (2005). Rising mean IQ: Cognitive demand of mathematics education for young children, population exposure to formal schooling, and the neurobiology of the prefrontal cortex. *Intelligence, 33,* 93–106.

Blair, C., Granger, D., & Razza, R.P. (2005). Cortisol reactivity is positively related to executive function in preschool children attending Head Start. *Child Development, 76,* 554–567.

Blair, C., & Razza, R.P. (in press). Relating effortful control, executive function, and false-belief understanding to emerging math and literacy ability in kindergarten. *Child Development.*

Braver, T.S., Cohen, J.D., Nystrom, L.E., Jonides, J., Smith, E., & Noll, D. (1997). A parametric study of prefrontal cortex involvement in human working memory. *Neuroimage, 5,* 49–62.

Brueckner, L.J., Merton, E.L., & Grossnickle, F.E. (1963). *Moving ahead in arithmetic: Books 3–6.* New York: Holt, Rinehart and Winston.

Bull, R., & Scerif, G. (2001). Executive functioning as a predictor of children's mathematics ability: Inhibition, switching, and working memory. *Developmental Neuropsychology, 19,* 273–293.

Bunge, S.A., Ochsner, K.N., Desmond, J.E., Glover, G.H., & Gabrieli, J.D.E. (2001). Prefrontal regions involved in keeping information in and out of mind. *Brain, 124,* 2074–2086.

Burbaud, P., Degreze, P., Lafon, P., Franconi, J., Bouligand, B., Bioulac, B., et al. (1995). Lateralization of prefrontal activation during internal mental calculation: A functional magnetic imaging study. *Journal of Neurophysiology, 74,* 2194–2200.

Bush, G., Luu, P., & Posner, M.I. (2000). Cognitive and emotional influences in the anterior cingulate cortex. *Trends in Cognitive Sciences, 4,* 215–222.

Cairns, R.B., Elder, G.H., & Costello, E.J. (1996). *Developmental science.* New York: Cambridge University Press.

Callicott, J., Matay, V., Bertolino, A., Finn, K., Coppola, R., Frank, J., et al. (1999). Physiological characteristics of capacity constraints in working memory as revealed by functional MRI. *Cerebral Cortex, 9,* 20–26.

Cantlon, J.F., Brannon, E.M., Carter, E.J., & Pelphrey, K.A. (2006). Functional imaging of numerical processing in adults and 4-year-old children. *Public Library of Science Biology, 4,* e125.

Carter, C., Braver, T., Barch, D., Botvinik, M.M., Cohen, J.D., & Noll, D.C. (1998). Anterior cingulate cortex, error detection, and the online monitoring of performance. *Science, 280,* 747–749.

Casey, B.J., Castellanos, F.X., Giedd, J.N., Marsh, W.L., Hamburger, S.D., Schubert, A.B., et al. (1997). The role of the anterior cingulate in automatic and controlled processes: A developmental neuroanatomical study. *Developmental Psychobiology, 30,* 61–69.

Casey, B.J., Cohen, J.D., Jezzard, P., Turner, R., Noll, D.C., Trainor, R.J., et al. (1995). Activation of prefrontal cortex in children during a nonspatial working memory task with functional MRI. *Neuroimage, 2,* 221–229.

Clark, C.H., Beatty, L.S., Payne, J.N., & Spooner, G.A. (1966). *Let's begin: Elementary mathematics—Primer.* New York: Harcourt, Brace & World.

Cohen, D.K. (1990). A revolution in one classroom: The case of Mrs. Oublier. *Educational Evaluation and Policy Analysis, 12,* 327–345.

Davidson, R.J. (2002). Anxiety and affective style: Role of prefrontal cortex and amygdala. *Biological Psychiatry, 51,* 68–80.

de Kloet, E.R., Oitzl, M.S., & Joels, M. (1999). Stress and cognition: Are corticosteroids good or bad guys? *Trends in Neuroscience, 22,* 422–426.

Dehaene, S., Molko, N., Cohen, L., & Wilson, A. (2004). Arithmetic and the brain. *Trends in Neurobiology, 14,* 218–224.

Dehaene, S., Piazza, M., Pinel, P., & Cohen, L. (2003). Three parietal circuits for number processing. *Cognitive Neuropsychology, 20,* 487–506.

Diamond, A. (2002). Normal development of the prefrontal cortex from birth to young adulthood: Cognitive functions, anatomy, and biochemistry. In D.T. Stuss & R.T. Knight (Eds.), *Principles of frontal lobe function* (pp. 466–503). New York: Oxford University Press, USA.

Diamond, A., Briand, L., Fossella, J., & Gehlbach, L. (2004). Genetic and neurochemical modulation of prefrontal cognitive functions in children. *American Journal of Psychiatry, 161,* 125–132.

Diamond, A., & Taylor, C. (1996). Development of an aspect of executive control: Development of the abilities to remember what I said and to "do as I say, not as I do." *Developmental Psychobiology, 29,* 315–334.

Drevets, W.C., & Raichle, M.E. (1998). Reciprocal suppression of regional cerebral blood flow during emotional versus higher cognitive processes: Implications for interactions between emotion and cognition. *Cognition and Emotion, 12,* 353–385.

Duncan, J., & Owen, A.M. (2000). Common regions of the human frontal lobe recruited by diverse cognitive demands. *Trends in Neurosciences, 23,* 475–483.

Dunn, L.W., & Dunn, L.M. (1997). *Peabody Picture Vocabulary Test-Revised (PPVT-R).* Circle Pines, MN: American Guidance Service.

Durston, S., Thomas, K.M., Yang, Y., Uluğ, A.Z., Zimmerman, R.D., & Casey, B.J. (2002). A neural basis for the development of inhibitory control. *Developmental Science, 5,* F9–F16.

Dweck, C.S. (1986). Motivational processes affecting learning. *American Psychologist, 41,* 1040–1048.

Egan, M.F., Goldberg, T.E., Kolachana, B.S., Callicott, J.H., Mazzanti, C.M., Straub, R.E., et al. (2001). Effect of COMT val[108/158]met genotype on frontal lobe function and risk for schizophrenia. *Proceedings of the National Academy of Sciences, USA, 98,* 6917–6922.

Eicholz, R.E., O'Daffer, P.G., Fleener, C.R., Young, S.L., Charles, R.I., & Barnett, C.S. (1991). *Addison-Wesley mathematics, Grade 2* (Vol. 2). Menlo Park, CA: Addison-Wesley.

Engle, R.W. (2002). Working memory capacity as executive attention. *Current Directions in Psychological Science, 11,* 19–23.

Erickson, K., Drevets, W., & Schulkin, J. (2003). Glucocorticoid regulation of diverse cognitive functions in normal and pathological emotional states. *Neuroscience and Biobehavioral Reviews, 27,* 233–246.

Eslinger, P., Blair, C., Wang, J., Lipovsky, B., Realmuto, J., Baker, D., Thorne, S., Gamson, D., Zimmerman, E., Yang, Q., & Rohrer, L. (2006). *A developmental functional magnetic resonance imaging study of neural systems subserving relational reasoning in childhood and adolescence.* Manuscript submitted for publication.

Espy, K., McDiarmid, M., Kwik, M., Stalets, M., Hamby, A., & Senn, T. (2004). The contribution of executive functions to emergent mathematics skills in preschool children. *Developmental Neuropsychology, 26,* 465–486.

Fan, J., Fossella, J., Sommer, T., Wu, Y., & Posner, M.I. (2003). Mapping the genetic variation of executive attention onto brain activity. *Proceedings of the National Academy of Sciences, USA, 100,* 7406–7411.

Feigenson, L., Dehaene, S., & Spelke, E. (2004). Core systems of number. *Trends in Cognitive Sciences, 8,* 307–314.

Francis, D.D., Caldji, C., Champagne, F., Plotsky, P.M., & Meaney, M.J. (1999). The role of corticotropin-releasing factor-norepinephrine systems in mediating the effects of early experience on the development of behavioral and endocrine responses to stress. *Biological Psychiatry, 46,* 1153–1166.

Gamson, D., Cummings, E., & Knipe, H. (2006). *The fall and rise of intellectual rigor: The case of school mathematics, 1890–2000.* Paper presented at the Annual Meeting of the American Educational Research Association, April 10, 2006, San Francisco, CA.

Goldberg, T., Berman, K., Fleming, K., Ostrem, J., Van Horn, J., Esposito, G., et al. (1998). Uncoupling cognitive workload and prefrontal cortical physiology: A PET rCBF study. *Neuroimage, 7,* 296–303.

Goldman-Rakic, P., Muly, E.C., & Williams, G.V. (2000). D1 receptors in prefrontal cells and circuits. *Brain Research Reviews, 31,* 295–301.

Gottlieb, G. (1991). Experiential canalization of behavioral development. *Developmental Psychology, 27,* 4–13.

Gray, J.R., Braver, T.S., & Raichle, M. (2002). Integration of cognition and emotion in lateral prefrontal cortex. *Proceedings of the National Academy of Sciences, USA, 99,* 4115–4120.

Gray, J.R., Chabris, C.F., & Braver, T.S. (2003). Neural mechanisms of general fluid intelligence. *Nature Neuroscience, 6,* 316–322.

Gunnar, M.R., Tout, K., de Haan, M., Pierce, S., & Stansbury, K. (1997). Temperament, social competence, and adrenocortical activity in preschoolers. *Developmental Psychobiology, 31,* 65–85.

Hariri, A.R., Mattay, V., Tessitore, A., Kolachana, B., Fera, F., Goldman, D., et al. (2002). Serotonin transporter genetic variation and the response of the human amygdala. *Science, 297,* 400–403.

Harris, A.V.S., & Waldo, L.M. (1911). *First journeys in numberland.* Chicago: Scott Foresman.

Hughes, C., & Ensor, R. (2005). Executive function and theory of mind in 2-year-olds: A family affair? *Developmental Neuropsychology, 28,* 645–668.

Kaufman, J., & Charney, D. (2001). Effects of early stress on brain structure and function: Implications for understanding the relationship between child maltreatment and depression. *Development and Psychopathology, 13,* 451–471.

Kinnunen, A.K., Keonig, J.I., & Bilbe, G. (2003). Repeated variable prenatal stress alters pre- and postsynaptic gene expression in the rat frontal pole. *Journal of Neurochemistry, 86,* 736–748.

Klingberg, T., Forssberg, H., & Westerberg, H. (2002). Training of working memory in children with ADHD. *Journal of Clinical and Experimental Neuropsychology, 24,* 781–791.

Ladd, G., Birch, S., & Buhs, E. (1999). Children's social and scholastic lives in kindergarten: Related spheres of influence? *Child Development, 70,* 1373–1400.

Lampert, M. (1985). How do teachers manage to teach? Perspectives on problems in practice. *Harvard Educational Review, 55,* 178–194.

Lemaire, V., Koehl, M., Le Moal, M., & Abrous, D.N. (2000). Prenatal stress produces learning deficits associated with an inhibition of neurogenesis in the hippocampus. *Proceedings of the National Academy of Sciences, USA, 97,* 11032–11037.

Liu, D., Diorio, J., Francis, D.D., & Meaney, M.J. (2000). Maternal care, hippocampal neurogenesis, and cognitive development in rats. *Nature Neuroscience, 3,* 799–806.

Lyons, D.M., Afarian, H., Schatzberg, A.F., Sawyer-Glover, A., & Moseley, M.E. (2002). Experience-dependent asymmetric variation in primate prefrontal morphology. *Behavioral and Brain Research, 36,* 51–59.

MacDonald, A.W., Cohen, J.D., Stegner, V.A., & Carter, C.S. (2000). Dissociating the role of dorsolateral prefrontal cortex and anterior cingulate cortex in cognitive control. *Science, 288,* 1835–1838.

Mashburn, A.J., & Pianta, R.C. (2006). Social relationships an school readiness. *Early Education and Development, 17,* 151–176.

Mayberg, H.S., Liotti, M., Brannan, S.K., McGinnis, S., Mahurin, R.K., Jerabek, P.A., et al. (1999). Reciprocal limbic-cortical function and negative mood: Converging PET findings in depression and normal sadness. *American Journal of Psychiatry, 156,* 675–682.

Meaney, M.J. (2001). Maternal care, gene expression, and the transmission of individual differences in gene expression across generations. *Annual Review of Neuroscience, 24,* 1161–1192.

Meyer, J.W. (1977). The effects of education as an institution. *American Journal of Sociology, 83,* 55–77.

Miyake, A., Friedman, N.P., Emerson, M.J., Witzki, A.H., & Howerter, A. (2000). The unity and diversity of executive functions and their contributions to complex "frontal lobe" tasks: A latent variable analysis. *Cognitive Psychology, 41,* 49–100.

National Committee on Mathematical Requirements. (1923). *The reorganization of mathematics in secondary education.* New York: The Mathematical Association of America.

National Education Association. (1895). *Report of the Committee of Fifteen on Elementary Education.* New York: The National Education Association.

Neider, A. (2005). Counting on neurons: The neurobiology of numerical competence. *Nature Reviews: Neuroscience, 6,* 177–190.

Neider, A., & Miller, E. (2004). A parietal-frontal network for visual numerical information in the monkey. *Proceedings of the National Academy of Sciences, USA, 101,* 7457–7462.

Ochsner, K.N., Bunge, S.A., Gross, J.J., & Gabrieli, J.D.E. (2002). Rethinking feelings: An fMRI study of the cognitive regulation of emotion. *Journal of Cognitive Neuroscience, 14,* 1215–1229.

Olesen, P.J., Nagy, Z., Westerberg, H., & Klingberg, T. (2003). Combined analysis of DTI and fMRI data reveals a joint maturation of white and gray matter in a fronto-parietal network. *Cognitive Brain Research, 18,* 48–57.

Olesen, P., Westerberg, H., & Klingberg, T. (2004). Increased prefrontal and parietal activity after training of working memory. *Nature Neuroscience, 7,* 75–79.

Paus, T. (2001). Primate anterior cingulate cortex: Where motor control, drive, and cognition interface. *Nature Reviews: Neuroscience, 2,* 417–424.

Peet, H.E., & Clapp, F.L. (1930). *Number games and stories.* Boston: Houghton Mifflin.

Plomin, R., DeFries, J.C., McClearn, G.E., & McGuffin, P. (2001). *Behavioral genetics* (4th ed.). New York: Worth.

Posner, M., & Rothbart, M. (2000). Developing mechanisms of self-regulation. *Development and Psychopathology, 12,* 427–441.

Prabhakaran, V., Smith, J.A.L., Desmond, J.E., Glover, G.H., & Gabrieli, J.D.E. (1997). Neural substrates of fluid reasoning: An fMRI study of neocortical activation during performance of the Raven's Progressive Matrices Test. *Cognitive Psychology, 33,* 43–63.

Raven, J.C. (1956). *Colored Progressive Matrices Test.* San Antonio, TX: The Psychological Corporation.

Ridderinkhof, K., van den Wildenberg, W., Segalowitz, S., & Carter, C.S. (2004). Neurocognitive mechanisms of cognitive control: The role of prefrontal cortex in action selection, response inhibition, performance monitoring, and reward-based learning. *Brain and Cognition, 56,* 129–140.

Rivera, S.M., Reiss, A.L., Eckert, M.A., & Menon, V. (2005). Developmental changes in mental arithmetic: Evidence for increased functional specialization in the left inferior parietal cortex. *Cerebral Cortex, 15,* 1779–1790.

Rothbart, M., & Jones, L. (1998). Temperament, self-regulation, and education. *School Psychology Review, 27,* 479–491.

Rueda, R., Rothbart, M., McCandliss, B., Saccomanno, L., & Posner, M. (2005). Training, maturation, and genetic influences on the development of executive attention. *Proceedings of the National Academy of Sciences, 102,* 14931–14936.

Rypma, B., Prabhakaran, V., Desmond, J.E., Glover, G.H., & Gabrieli, J.D.E. (1999). Load dependent roles of frontal brain regions in the maintenance of working memory. *Neuroimage, 9,* 216–226.

Sanchez, M.M., Hearn, E.F., Do, D., Rilling, J.K., & Herndon, J.G. (1998). Differential rearing affects corpus callosum size and cognitive function of rhesus monkeys. *Brain Research, 812,* 38–49.

Shonkoff, J., & Phillips, D. (Eds.). (2000). *From neurons to neighborhoods.* Washington DC: National Academies Press.

Simon, O., Kherif, F., Flandin, G., Poline, J.B., Riviere, D., Mangin, J.F., et al. (2004). Automatized clustering and functional geometry of human parietofrontal networks for language, space, and number. *Neuroimage, 23,* 1192–1202.

Smith, D.E., Luse, E.M., & Morss, E.L. (1929a). *The problem and practice arithmetics: First book.* Boston: Ginn and Company.

Smith, D.E., Luse, E.M., & Morss, E.L. (1929b). *Walks and talks in numberland.* Boston: Ginn and Company.

Smith, E., & Jonides, J. (2003). Executive control and thought. In L. Squire, F. Bloom, S. McConnell, J. Roberts, N. Spritzer, & M. Zigmond (Eds.), *Fundamental neuroscience* (2nd ed., pp. 1377–1394). New York: Academic Press.

Suomi, S. (2003). Gene-environment interactions and the neurobiology of social-conflict. *Annals of the New York Academy of Sciences, 1008,* 132–139.

Temple, J., & Posner, M. (1998). Brain mechanisms of quantity are similar in 5-year-old children and adults. *Proceedings of the National Academy of Sciences, USA, 95,* 7836–7841.

Tyack, D., & Cuban, L. (1995). *Tinkering toward utopia: A century of public school reform.* Cambridge: Harvard University Press.

Van Eden, C.G., & Buijs, R.M. (2000). Functional neuroanatomy of the prefrontal cortex: Autonomic interactions. In H. Uylings, C. Van Eden, J. De Bruin, M. Feenstra, & C. Pennartz (Eds.), *Progress in brain research, vol. 126. Cognition, emotion and autonomic responses: The integrative role of the prefrontal cortex and limbic structures* (pp. 49–62). Amsterdam: Elsevier.

Walmsley, A.L.E. (2003). *A history of the "new mathematics" movement and its relationship with current mathematical reform.* Lanham, MD: University Press of America.

Weaver, I., Cervoni, N., Champagne, F., Alessio, A., Sharma, S., Seckl, J., Dymov, S., Szyf, M., & Meaney, M. (2004). Epigenetic programming by maternal behavior. *Nature Neuroscience, 7,* 847–854.

Zago, L., Pesenti, M., Mellet, E., Crivello, F., Mazoyer, B., & Tzourio-Mazoyer, N. (2001). Neural correlates of simple and complex mental calculation. *Neuroimage, 13,* 314–327.

Zelazo, P.D., & Müller, U. (2002). Executive function in typical and atypical development. In U. Goswami (Ed.), *Handbook of childhood cognitive development* (pp. 445–469). Oxford, UK: Blackwell.

9

ENGLISH-LANGUAGE LEARNERS AS THEY ENTER SCHOOL

Linda M. Espinosa

Internationally, it is estimated that there are as many children who grow up learning two languages as who grow up learning one (Reyes & Moll, in press). In the United States, the number of young children whose home language is not English (English-language learners [ELLs]) has been increasing steadily over the past 3 decades. Approximately 20% of the school-age population speaks a language other than English at home; between 14 and 16% of all children speak Spanish as their home language (Reyes & Moll, in press), and another 4–6% speak a language other than Spanish. Within the younger K–5 population of ELLs, the majority (76%) speak Spanish and are considered Latino/Hispanic (Capps, Fix, & Reardon-Anderson, 2003).

The Latino/Hispanic population is the largest and fastest growing ethnic minority group in the United States (U.S. Census Bureau, 2004). There are now more Latinos (almost 40 million) than African Americans (almost 39 million) or any other ethnic group, and they represent about 14% of the total population in the nation. Because of immigration trends and child-bearing rates of Latina women, the number of Latino children as a proportion of all young children also has been steadily increasing. Hispanics make up about 22% of all children under the age of 5 (Calderon, Gonzalez, & Lazarin 2004). It has been estimated that by 2050, the number of Latino children under 5 will increase by 146% and that the number of Hispanic and Black children under age 5 will outnumber non-Hispanic White children, resulting in a country in which children who have traditionally been classified as racial/ethnic minorities will become the majority group.

These demographic shifts are even more concentrated in some publicly funded early childhood programs and local communities. During the 2002–2003 program year, 27% of children enrolled in Head Start did not speak English as their home language. Of these, the vast majority were from Spanish-speaking homes, with 139 other language groups also reported (Head Start Bureau, 2004a). In California, approximately 45% of the 5-year-old children entering kindergarten in the public schools in 2004–2005 were children whose primary home language was not English, with most of these children (82%) being Spanish speaking (California Department of Education, 2005). Within Los Angeles County, these estimates are even higher; more than 55% of the 5-year-olds entering kindergarten in 2004–2005 were children whose primary home language was not English, and 88% were from Spanish-speaking homes (California Department of Education, 2005). These demographic shifts are increasingly altering the fabric of early education and will certainly influence future state and federal educational policies.

School readiness among ELL children, and particularly Latino ELL children from low-income homes, is a major concern for educational policy makers at the state and federal levels (Pew Hispanic Research Center, 2004). The need to understand and promote effective teaching practices and educational policies for young ELLs is urgent for several reasons: 1) there is an explosion of young children who live in homes in which English is not spoken, and the rate is expected to continue increasing (National Center for Education Statistics [NCES] 2003; U.S. Census Bureau, 2004), and 2) children who have limited fluency in English when they enter school are at greater risk for reading difficulties and low academic achievement levels (Regalado, Goldenberg, & Appel, 2001). Young Latino children who speak Spanish in the home are also much more likely to be from low-socioeconomic status (SES) households and score significantly behind their English-speaking peers on measures of language, early literacy, and mathematics at kindergarten entry (Espinosa, Laffey & Whittaker, 2006). An additional cause for concern is that recent program evaluation data indicate that some early childhood programs may not be as effective for Spanish-speaking children as for English-speaking children (Head Start Bureau, 2004b).

A growing and convincing body of research indicates that well-designed and carefully implemented early intervention programs that are culturally and linguistically responsive can improve the educational achievement of children from diverse linguistic and cultural backgrounds and help to reduce this achievement gap before kindergarten (Barnett, 1995; Gormley & Gayer, 2003; Winsler, Diaz, Espinosa, & Rodriguez, 1999). Therefore, it is important for the early childhood profession to have a clear understanding of the developmental characteristics of young ELLs and of how children successfully learn a second language so that educators can design and provide high-quality learning environments for children who are in the process of acquiring English as their second language.

This chapter provides an overview of the developmental profiles of ELLs at kindergarten entry, their unique cultural and linguistic strengths and learning concerns, and examples of promising programs and instructional approaches that have been linked to positive long-term educational outcomes. Finally, educational policies are suggested at the classroom, local, and state levels to support the research findings reported.

WHO ARE ELL CHILDREN?

Children whose home language is not English or who primarily speak a language other than English in the home are considered ELLs. They are also frequently described as linguistic minority (LM) students or linguistically diverse students. LM or ELL children vary greatly as a group; the country of origin, recency of immigration, SES of the family, and specific home language all influence a child's progress in English acquisition and academic achievement. As a child acquires a second language, one language may be more dominant because the child is using that language more than the other at a particular point in time. Frequently, children demonstrate a language imbalance as they progress toward bilingualism.

In the nationally representative study of more than 22,000 children who entered kindergarten in 1998, the Early Childhood Longitudinal Study of Kindergarten Children (ECLS-K), 68% of the children were classified as English speaking and 18.1% were classified as LM children (Espinosa et al., 2006). Almost 13% of the total sample were classified as Spanish speaking, with 2.7% identified as Asian speaking and 2% as speaking a European language. The majority of the language minority children were in the two lowest quintiles for household SES (52%); most remarkably, 80% of the Spanish speakers who were judged to be the least fluent in English were in the lowest two SES quintiles (Espinosa et al., 2006). This means that Spanish-speaking children who are learning English as a second language during the preschool years are the most likely of all preschool children to live in poverty and have a mother or guardian without a high school education. These data are similar to other studies that show that non–English-proficient children are about twice as likely to live in poverty as English-proficient children in grades K–5 and that only about 50% have parents with a high school education (Capps et al., 2003).

Recent immigrant households and undocumented individuals are the most likely to have limited English fluency, low levels of formal education, and low family incomes (Crosnoe & Lopez-Gonzalez, 2005). The majority of recent immigrants who are not fluent in English are from Mexico and speak Spanish. These dramatic increases in linguistic diversity during the early childhood years have implications for the composition, professional preparation, and training of the work force as well as improved instructional and assessment approaches that are better suited to this growing population.

WHO AND WHERE ARE YOUNG LATINOS?

The Latino/Hispanic population makes up about 22% of all children under the age of 5 (Calderon, Gonzalez, & Lazarin, 2004; U.S. Census Bureau, 2004). Latinos in the United States, although sharing some common characteristics, are in fact a diverse cultural group. The largest percentage of Hispanics are of Mexican American descent (66%), followed by Central and South American (15%), Puerto Rican (9%), Cuban (4%), and other Hispanic (6%). Although Hispanics in the United States are united by a common language background (Spanish), they vary considerably based on their country of origin, time and reasons for migration, amount and type of education received in home country, SES, English-language fluency, and how they have been received within the United States (Portes & Rumbaut, 2001).

People of Mexican origin make up the largest percentage of Latinos in the United States as well as the largest group of new immigrants. Wide variations exist in educational level, occupational status, and income within the Mexican American community. Although some Mexican Americans actively work in agricultural occupations (e.g., migrant farm laborers), the majority now work in industrial and service sectors. Puerto Ricans experience the lowest SES of the major Latino groups in the United States. Historically, impoverished Puerto Ricans have emigrated to the urban northeast because of limited employment opportunities in Puerto Rico. In the last 2 decades, Puerto Rican professionals seeking improved job opportunities have emigrated to Florida and Texas as well as the northeast (Portes & Rumbaut, 2001).

The majority (83%) of Hispanics live in 10 states: California, Arizona, Texas, New Mexico, Colorado, Illinois, Florida, New Jersey, New York, and Washington. Although Latinos continue to have a large and growing presence in these 10 states, they are also dispersing to states in the Southeast and Midwest. In the last decade, North Carolina, Arkansas, and Georgia have experienced the largest increases in Latino children under the age of 4 (417, 392 and 342%, respectively) of all the states in the United States (Calderon, 2004). Increasingly, Hispanic immigrants are also settling in rural areas of the Midwest, creating new demands on the educational, social, and health services of small communities (Hernandez, 2004).

ENGLISH-LANGUAGE LEARNERS AND KINDERGARTEN TRANSITION

The concept of school readiness usually includes skills of the child, factors in the family and home environment, and characteristics of the educational and community systems available to the child and family, that is, "ready child, ready school" (Child Trends, 2003). Certain aspects of the child's developmental status such as emergent literacy skills, approaches to learning, and social competence at kindergarten entry have been identified as important to school readiness and predictors of future academic success (Kagan, Moore, & Bredekamp, 1995). Several features of the home learning environment have been shown to contribute positively to children's readiness skills. In particular, "family characteristics such as maternal education and parents' caregiving practices were the strongest predictors of child outcomes" (Burchinal, Peisner-Feinberg, Pianta, & Howes, 2000, p. 431). For English-speaking populations, the parents' or caregiver's amount and type of language interactions have been shown to influence the child's language development and emergent literacy skills during the preschool years (Dickinson & McCabe, 2001). Little corollary research documents the exact relations between adult language (first or second) and young children's emergent bilingualism or long-term academic success (Genesee, Paradis, & Crago, 2004).

The extent of the child's school readiness as assessed at kindergarten entry almost always includes some measure of language ability. The two largest national studies of children's language abilities prior to kindergarten entry, the ECLS-K and the Head Start National Reporting System (NRS), both assess limited aspects of the child's language development in English or, if the child does not pass a short English-language screener and speaks Spanish at home, in Spanish. No other home languages are assessed in these large national studies. In the ECLS-K, the child's Spanish fluency was assessed at only one point in time, whereas in the NRS (an ongoing biannual assessment in Head Start), if Spanish is the language of assessment at the initial fall testing, the child is assessed in Spanish and English during the spring testing (Head Start Bureau, 2004a). Analysis of these two national data sets reveals that young Latino ELLs at school entry are more likely than White or African American peers to live in low-income homes (Espinosa et al., 2006) with both parents and with a mother who is less likely to work outside the home (Crosnoe & Lopez-Gonzalez, 2005). Low-income Hispanic children in the ECLS-K sample also scored more than half of a standard deviation below the national average in math and reading achievement at kindergarten entry (Lee & Buram, 2002). These achievement disparities persist as children who are not native English speakers continue to have substantially lower levels of educational achievement including high school completion and college enrollment rates than their peers from English-only backgrounds (Gandara, Rumberger, Maxwell-Jolly, & Callahan, 2003; Rumberger, 2004).

When the ECLS-K data are disaggregated according to which language is spoken in the home (English, European, Asian, or Spanish) and according to the SES of the home, the discrepancies in the initial achievement scores as well as the amount of growth over time are greatly reduced (Espinosa et al., 2006). The LM children from European- or Asian-language–speaking households were much less likely to live in low-SES homes and had school achievement scores that were comparable with—and in some cases exceeded—their English-speaking peers. Within the classification of language minority status, there is great diversity:

> The general language status definition masks distinctions within the LM cohort; more Spanish speaking homes are in the lowest SES and Spanish speaking homes have the largest representation in the LM sample. Asian speaking homes have lower SES than English speaking homes but also have a greater percentage of high SES homes. In general LM children from European speaking homes have the highest SES of all the language types. In addition, one of the most striking features of the ECLS-K data on LM children reveals that Spanish-speaking children who score below the cutoff for the English OLDS test are overwhelmingly found in the first or second quintile of SES (80%). These are children who do not have basic fluency in English, speak mostly Spanish in the home, and are living in poor or near poor households. Although this analysis did not ask about their fluency in Spanish, their home language, that is one of the questions that needs to be asked. We know that these children are living in reduced economic circumstances and have not mastered simple English vocabulary, we do not know the level of their first language development. (Espinosa et al., 2006, p. 49)

In addition, this analysis of the ECLS-K data set by language type revealed that when compared as a group, the LM children scored below their native English-speaking peers on math and reading assessments, but when compared by language type, the findings are more nuanced.

> In general, . . . children from European and Asian speaking homes do as well or better than their English speaking counterparts. Children from Spanish speaking homes are behind all other language groups. The difference is pronounced when the achievement scores of the Spanish speaking children who score lower than the cutoff are compared to the English speaking children or to the Spanish speaking children who score above the cutoff score. (Espinosa et al., 2006, p. 52)

Clearly, the economic and educational resources of the family influence the child's academic knowledge at kindergarten entry; the finding that the vast majority of the children who had limited English fluency and spoke Spanish at home were also living in reduced economic circumstances leads to a question about their native language fluency. Based on other research of the language learning opportunities and overall language development of children living in poverty (Hart & Risley, 1995), it is quite possible that these Spanish-speaking children are also behind in their native language abilities. Other research shows that low-income Spanish-speaking children growing up in the United States score below their monolingual peers in both Spanish and English on standardized tests of language ability (Head Start Bureau, 2004b; Tabors, Roach, & Snow, 2001). The extant research suggests that the long-term achievement of ELL children is influenced greatly by the circumstances of their early learning environment, not just by their status as dual-language learners; others have concluded that, all things being equal, children have no difficulty acquiring two languages during the preschool years and will benefit from becoming bilingual (Genesee et al., 2004). However, all things are rarely equal. Thus, it is important to remember that there is great diversity within the U.S. ELL population; ELLs vary in the home language they speak, the age at which they were first exposed to English, their fluency in both their first language and English, and the level of family and community resources available to them.

Nevertheless, by the common standards through which educational success is measured—that is, math and reading standardized achievement test scores, high school completion, higher education enrollment, and English-language fluency—Latino ELLs are, as a group, behind even before they begin formal schooling.

Some have suggested that differences in initial achievement can be explained by SES and language background (Rumberger & Anguiano, 2004); others propose sociocultural explanations such as subtractive segmented assimilation (Portes & Rumbaut, 2001), intense community poverty, limited access to high-quality preschool programs, mainstream bias, negative stereotyping, and narrow definitions of academic achievement (Suarez-Orozco, Suarez-Orozco, & Doucet, 2003). Others have argued that Hispanic and other children from ethnic and linguistic minority families are unfairly compared with White children according to standards that have been designed for a White population (Valencia, 2000). This has been commonly referred to as a "deficit model" that does not recognize the strengths and abilities of non-White children and fails to capitalize on the knowledge and cultural resources Latino children bring to school (Cortez & Cortez, 2004; Crosnoe & Lopez-Gonzalez, 2005; Garcia-Coll, Meyer, & Brillon, 1995).

The important consideration for educators and policy makers in this climate of accountability and consequences for failing to make achievement goals in English is the role of language and culture in school success. Is a child from a Mexican American immigrant family that speaks Spanish in the home necessarily "at risk" for school failure? What are the talents, resources, and strengths of this young child and his or her family? How can early education programs recognize, support, and expand the "funds of knowledge" (Moll, 1991, p. 201) that young Latinos bring into the school?

SOCIAL-EMOTIONAL DEVELOPMENT AND RESILIENCY

A considerable body of research underscores the critical nature of children's social and emotional development to their long-term school and life success (Ravler & Zigler, 1997; Shonkoff & Phillips, 2000; Wentzel & Asher, 1995). This research points to children's ability to positively build relationships with peers and adults as critical to their academic success. Specifically, research suggests that preschool children who learn to regulate their emotions in prosocial ways and control negative emotions do better in school (Blair, 2003). If young children can pay attention, follow directions, and get along with others, they are more likely to be accepted by their peers and teachers and succeed academically. When teachers view children positively, especially at-risk children, they are more likely to give them opportunities to participate and perceive them as having academic ability (Espinosa & Laffey, 2003; Rist, 2000).

Young children who are in the process of acquiring English as a second language face additional social-emotional challenges in the preschool setting. "Affective filter" is the term Krashen and Terrell (1983) have used to refer to the constellation of negative emotional and motivational factors that may interfere with a child's ability to learn a second language efficiently. Such factors include anxiety, self-consciousness, boredom, embarrassment, fear, and so forth. According to Krashen and Terrell, when a child's affective filter is aroused, the child will shut down and not actively engage in the process of learning English. Krashen and Terrell claimed that learners with high motivation, self-confidence, a good self-image, and a low level of anxiety are better equipped for success in second-language acquisition. Low motivation, low self-esteem, and debilitating anxiety can combine to raise the affective filter and form a mental block that prevents developmentally appropriate language-learning opportunities from being processed and used for English acquisition. In other words, when the filter is on, it impedes language acquisition. On the other hand, positive affect is necessary, but not sufficient on its own, for language acquisition to take place (Krashen & Terrell, 1983).

Researchers have found a consistent relation between various forms of anxiety and language proficiency in all situations, formal and informal, with school-age children. This is an important point when considering the role of social-emotional development for young Latinos because their emotional state as well as their social skills can affect their English-language acquisition and ultimate school success.

Clearly, the emotional and social health of young ELL children is important to their school adjustment and academic achievement. According to multiple measures of family risk factors (e.g., poverty, immigrant status, English-language fluency, access to mental and physical health services), Latino ELL children would appear to be at greater risk than their White and non-Hispanic peers. However, when Robert Crosnoe (2005) analyzed kindergarten teachers' ratings of Mexican immigrant children's level of internalizing and externalizing symptoms, he found that children from Mexican immigrant families had lower levels of internalizing and externalizing symptoms than both their White and African American peers. These two variables from the ECLS-K data set refer to the degree to which kindergarten teachers observed signs of internalizing symptoms (e.g., anxiety, sadness) or externalizing symptoms (e.g., anger, fighting) in the child. In essence, the teachers rated the children of Mexican immigrant families at kindergarten entry as more socially and emotionally competent than their peers from similar backgrounds. This is remarkable given the multiple risk factors associated with the Mexican immigrant families and the finding that these children were rated as having more physical health complications than their African American and White peers. Crosnoe and Lopez-Gonzalez (2005) concluded that

> These children tend to be mentally healthier than some of their peers and no less mentally healthy than their other peers at the start of kindergarten. If mental health is related to subsequent learning trajectories, then this mental health advantage could turn out to be an academic resource. (p. 38)

It is possible that the Hispanic cultural emphasis on family cohesiveness, respect, and moral development that Mexican immigrant families bring with them to the United States may provide a foundation of social security for young Latinos. Although Mexican immigrant families were characterized by low SES, high degrees of poverty, and lack of medical insurance, they also were more likely to have a two-parent family structure. Latino families have been characterized as sharing a set of values that include familia/familism (family centeredness), respeto (respect), carino (nurturance), responsibilidad (personal sense of responsibility), and educacion (formal education) (Delgado-Gaitan, 2004; Valdes, 1996). The Hispanic emphasis on family loyalty, solidarity, and mutual obligations has been recognized for decades (Espinosa, 1995; Rothenberg, 1995). The focus on the "familia" is one of the most striking values of the Latino culture. It promotes strong connections to both the immediate and the extended family. This value has been found consistently across the majority of Latino families regardless of country of origin, acculturation, and SES (Bulcroft, Carmody, & Bulcroft, 1996; Fuligini, Tseng, & Lam, 1999; Rueschenberg & Buriel, 1995). Included in this belief is the expectation that the family will be the major source of both instrumental and emotional support as well as the collective base of loyalty and solidarity (Negy & Woods, 1992). This family stability, combined with traditional Hispanic cultural values of the family as the primary socializing influence for children (Manning, 2004), could create a safe and secure early care environment for children from Mexican immigrant families.

This observed social-emotional strength of young Latinos may be a potential source of resilience that school personnel should recognize, support, and enhance. Because young Mexican immigrant children are judged to be at least as, if not more, intra- and interpersonally competent than their peers, something about Hispanic child-rearing practices has promoted these children's ability to control their emotions and get along with others at school entry—two highly prized social competencies for school success (Boyd et al., 2005). Hispanic parents who are influential and who have the capacity to support their children's emotional security and social competence often face barriers to meaningful school involvement, and their culturally preferred ways of supporting their children's achievement may not be consistent with traditional school expectations (Lopez, 2001). This represents a great, untapped resource for young Latinos, schools, and social programs (Espinosa, 1995).

SOCIAL-EMOTIONAL DEVELOPMENT AND BILINGUALISM

Because many young ELL children speak a language other than English in the home and enter early group care/educational settings that use English as the language of instruction, it is important to know how the development of bilingualism or the acquisition of English and the potential loss of home language affect the child's social competence. Sociocultural theory posits that individual development is embedded within and shaped by social interaction and that knowledge is created by the interactions between teachers and students. The concepts, perspectives, and cognitive constructs that an individual develops are produced by shared social activities, values, and discussions. Studying the cultural and linguistic characteristics of the children, teachers, and peers can provide a better understanding of the relationships among language, culture, and cognitive development (Garcia, 2005).

A young child's development of language proficiency depends highly on the cultural context of his or her early child rearing; the earliest interactions between a child and the people around him or her communicate to the child what types of language are valued, when one should talk, and how to use language as a tool for thinking. Because children have learned these language skills in the highly specific cultural contexts of their homes, they must learn new communicative strategies in school settings. When linguistically diverse children enter school, they often encounter classroom cultures that differ markedly from their familiar home culture. Children who are not native English speakers face many challenges because the language they have used to form their cognitive structures and gain control over their cognitive processes is no longer dominant. The social and cognitive skills that have been developed through the use of one language and cultural context may no longer apply to this new setting. This linguistic and cultural disconnect, from a sociocultural perspective, would then place the child at risk for interrupted cognitive development and poor academic achievement (Diaz & Klinger, 1991).

For young children, language development and learning about one's own culture are closely linked. "Culture and linguistic identity provide a strong and important sense of self and family belonging, which in turn supports a wide range of learning capabilities, not the least of which is learning a second language" (Garcia, 1991, p. 2).

Families vary considerably in the ways in which they socialize their young children into language and literacy use. For young children from culturally and linguistically diverse groups, their early socialization experiences and the accompanying values acquired in their home and community environments frequently are not those celebrated by the school setting and used as the basis for academic learning and achievement. These discrepancies between the learning culture of the home and that of the school result in cultural discontinuity for the child; this discontinuity can create a vulnerability for that child (Garcia, 1993; McGhee & Richgels, 1996). Children who experience cultural discontinuity between the home and school are more likely to have a negative perception of self as learner, reader, writer, and speaker (Garcia, 1993). Many have argued for learning and teaching contexts that are socioculturally and linguistically meaningful for all learners, but such contexts are most critical for the youngest students (Sanchez, 1999). It is important to remember that young children have formed culturally shaped expectations and attitudes for when they are supposed to talk, for whom they should talk to, and for what type of language is appropriate in different contexts. When the cultural expectations of the home and school vary markedly, the child may initially feel some discomfort and anxiety in the school setting. Although most researchers agree that children can learn to successfully navigate two different cultures, school personnel need to be aware of the values and practices of the child's home environment to design classroom practices that support the child's successful transition.

Some intriguing research on the effects of bilingualism has been conducted by Bialystok (2001) in Toronto, Canada. Bialystok provided compelling evidence that young bilinguals have an advantage over monolingual children when performing tasks that require voluntary selective attention. Bilinguals are better able to inhibit irrelevant or misleading information when processing cognitive tasks such as classifying or sorting or developing certain aspects of early literacy. Bialystok attributed this advantage to the need for young bilingual children to actively discriminate between languages during everyday communication and instructional activities. This voluntary inhibition of irrelevant information and focusing of attention on the demands of the task could be theoretically linked to the linguistic processing abilities that are necessary for the development of self-regulation. The ability to use language as a tool to think through the relevant features of a task and then sort or discard information that may interfere with successful completion of the task is a cognitive skill that may also be central to social competence. Although further research is needed to determine whether an empirical link exists between the ability to discriminate between languages and the ability to self-regulate and select appropriate behavior habits, it suggests another rationale for promoting bilingualism in young children.

For young Latino children who are ELLs, the relationship between their social-emotional development and personality characteristics and English acquisition is reciprocal: Their individual social competencies and personality traits influence their progress in English acquisition, and the instructional methods used to teach them English influence their long-term social and cognitive development.

Eventually, all children will need to learn the mainstream patterns of discourse they will encounter as they progress through the schooling system (Delpit, 1988); however, with supportive policies and practices, school personnel can increase students' chances of academic success if the school environment fosters school–home continuity. Improving continuity between home and school requires culturally responsive curricula and pedagogy. Culturally responsive approaches include the students' histories, language, early experiences, and values in the classroom activities and instruction that is "consistent with the students' own cultures and aimed at improving academic learning" (Au, 1993, p. 13).

HOW DO CHILDREN LEARN A SECOND LANGUAGE?

It is commonly assumed that preschool-age children can just pick up a second language without much effort or systematic teaching. However, becoming proficient in a language is a complex, demanding process that can take many years. As with any type of learning, children will vary enormously in the rate at which they learn a first and a second language. The speed of language acquisition is attributable to factors both within the child and in the child's learning environment. The child's personality, aptitude for languages, interest, and motivation interact with the quantity and quality of language inputs and opportunities for use to influence the rate and eventual fluency levels.

Simultaneous Versus Sequential Second Language Acquisition

Barry McLaughlin and his colleagues (1995) made a distinction between children who learn a second language simultaneously or sequentially. When a child learns two languages simultaneously, for instance, before 3 years of age, the developmental pathway is similar to how monolingual children acquire language. In fact, the majority of young children in the world successfully learn two languages (or more) from the first years of life (Reyes & Moll, in press). However, there is some disagreement in the literature about whether bilingualism results in a rate of vocabulary development slower than that of children learning a single language. As children are acquiring two languages and becoming bilingual, it is typical for one language to dominate.

The language development of children who learn a second language after 3 years of age, or *sequentially*, follows a different progression and is highly sensitive to characteristics of the child as well as the language-learning environment. At this point, the basics of the child's first language have been learned. They know the structure of one language but now must learn the specific features, grammar, vocabulary, and syntax of a new language. According to Tabors and Snow (1994), sequential second-language acquisition follows a four-stage developmental sequence:

1. *Home language use.* When a child has become competent in one language and is introduced into a setting in which everyone is speaking a different language—for instance, an ELL child entering an English-dominant preschool classroom—the child will frequently continue to speak his or her home language even when others do not understand. This

period can be short (e.g., a few days), but in some cases the child will persist in trying to get others to understand him or her for months.

2. *Nonverbal period.* After young children realize that speaking their home language will not work, they enter a period during which they rarely speak and use nonverbal means to communicate. This is a period of active language learning for the child; he or she is busy learning the features, sounds, and words of the new language (receptive language) but not verbally using the new language to communicate. This is an extremely important stage of second-language learning that may also last a long time or be brief. Any language assessments conducted during this stage of development may result in misleading information that underestimates the child's true language capacity.

3. *Telegraphic and formulaic speech.* The child is now ready to start using the new language and does so through telegraphic speech that involves the use of formulas. This is similar to a monolingual child who is learning simple words or phrases (content words) to express whole thoughts. For instance, a child might say "me down" to indicate he or she wants to go downstairs. Formulaic speech refers to unanalyzed chunks of words or sometimes even syllables strung together that are repetitions of what the child has heard. For example, Tabors (1997) reported that ELLs in the preschool she studied frequently used the phrase "lookit" to engage others in their play. These are phrases the children had heard from others that helped to achieve their social goals, even though the children probably did not know the meaning of the two words and were only repeating familiar sounds that were functionally effective.

4. *Productive language.* Now the child is starting to go beyond telegraphic or formulaic utterances to create his or her own phrases and thoughts. Initially, the child may use very simple grammatical patterns such as "I wanna play," but over time he or she will gain control over the structure and vocabulary of the new language. Errors in language usage are common during this period because the child is experimenting with the new language and learning its rules and structure.

As with any developmental sequence, the stages are flexible and not mutually exclusive. McLaughlin and colleagues (1995) described the process as waves "moving in and out, generally moving in one direction, but receding, then moving forward again" (pp. 3–4).

Sequential bilingual children may have somewhat different patterns of development than monolingual children in certain aspects of language development in the short term. This may include vocabulary, early literacy skills, and interpersonal communication. Young ELLs frequently know fewer vocabulary words in both English and their home language than monolingual children. This may be due to the limited memory capacity of young children or limited exposure to a rich and varied vocabulary. If a child speaks one language in the home and is learning English at preschool, he or she may also know some words in one language and not the other. For instance, the child may have learned the English words *recess, chalk,* and *line* at school without having learned the corresponding words in Spanish because there was no need or opportunity to do so in the home. However, when the total number of words the child knows in both languages is considered together, it is generally comparable with the number and range of vocabulary words monolingual children know.

Code Switching/Language Mixing

It is important for early childhood educators to understand that *code switching* (switching languages for portions of a sentence) and *language mixing* (inserting single items from one language into another) are typical aspects of second-language acquisition. This does not mean that the child is confused or cannot separate the languages. The main reason that children mix the two languages in one communication is because they lack sufficient vocabulary in one or both languages to fully express themselves. Research has shown that even proficient adults mix their languages to convey special emphasis or establish cultural identity (Garcia, 2003). In any case, code switching or language mixing is a typical and natural part of second-language acquisition that parents and teachers should not be concerned about. The goal must always be on enhancing communication rather than enforcing rigid rules about which language can be used at a given time or under certain circumstances.

Young children who have regular and rich exposure to two languages during the early childhood years can successfully become bilingual. Most research concludes that there are no negative effects of bilingualism on the linguistic, cognitive, or social development of children, and there may even be some general advantages in these areas of development (Bialystok, 2001; Genesee et al., 2004). Simultaneous bilingualism follows a path similar to monolingual development; sequential second-language acquisition occurs in a predictable series of stages or waves. Typically, at any given time, one language may dominate depending on the amount of time spent in each language. As early childhood programs become increasingly diverse, teachers will need to understand the process of second-language acquisition and how to adapt their expectations and instruction accordingly. Increased understanding will lead to improved methods that will promote the learning and achievement of young children who are learning English as a second language.

Young children who successfully learn English seem to possess certain social skills (Valdes, 1996; Wong Fillmore, 1976). These social abilities appear to affect the rate at which preschool-age children acquire English:

1. Join groups and pretend to understand what is going on even if you do not; this is a "fake it till you make it" approach toward communicating in a new language.

2. Use the limited language ability you have to give the impression that you can speak English. This will motivate other children to continue to interact with you.

3. Find friends who will help you learn English. The English-speaking friend will provide opportunities to practice the new language as well as the social motivation to keep trying.

Social confidence, an outgoing personality, and the willingness to take risks all appear to facilitate a young child's rapid English acquisition in a preschool setting (Tabors, 1997). But what are the consequences on a child's social development of learning English while losing the ability to communicate in the home language?

Home Language Loss

When preschool children learn two languages, they are learning two cultures. For Latino children who speak Spanish in the home, the second language they learn, English, is the dominant, mainstream language and corresponds to the more powerful White culture that is evident in U.S. classrooms. Many researchers have documented the fragility of a child's home language and cultural practices when such language and practices are not highly valued or mainstream. Genesee et al. (2004) cautioned that "dual language children are particularly at risk for both cultural and linguistic identity displacement" (p. 33). They further argued that

> Erasing a child's language or cultural patterns of language use is a great loss for the child. Children's identities and senses of self are inextricably linked to the language they speak and the culture to which they have been socialized. They are, even at an early age, speakers of their languages and members of their cultures. Language and culture are essential to children's identities. All of the affectionate talk and interpersonal communication of their childhoods and family life are embedded in their languages and cultures. (p. 33)

Other researchers have linked loss of home language with poor long-term academic outcomes (Oller & Eilers, 2002; Slavin & Cheung, 2005). Slavin and Cheung (2005) reviewed all of the experimental studies on reading instruction for ELLs and concluded that teaching reading in the child's home language and English at different times of the day leads to the best reading outcomes. They went on to explain why this may be a resolution to the bilingual debate:

> Proponents of bilingual education want to launch English language learners with success while maintaining and valuing the language they speak at home. Opponents are concerned not so much about the use of the native language but about delaying the use of English. (p. 275)

Thus, early instruction in both languages can promote both goals and can also be used as the foundation of a two-way bilingual program that promotes Spanish acquisition for English-only children.

Oller and Eilers (2002) studied the impact of bilingualism and school instructional variables on language and literacy outcomes in 952 students (grades K–5) in Miami-Dade County, Florida. They included for analysis the SES of the family, the language spoken at home, and the instructional method of the school. Children were assessed in both Spanish and English on a wide array of standardized and more open-ended language and reading measures. For monolingual English-speaking children who were instructed in only English, "differences favoring monolinguals were relatively large at kindergarten (K) or second grade, but notably smaller or absent by fifth grade, suggesting that bilingual children's abilities were improving relative to monolingual peers across the elementary years" (p. 282). For Spanish-speaking children learning English, they concluded,

> Thus, it seems inevitable to conclude that two-way education as opposed to English Immersion showed few if any long-term advantages or disadvantages with regard to language and literacy in English, but that two-way education showed significant advantages for bilingual children in acquisition of language and literacy in Spanish. (p. 285)

An unexpected finding of their research was that

> Spanish appears to be losing ground rapidly in the Hispanic communities of Miami. . . . Data based on observations of usage of language in classrooms and hallways indicated a strong preference among Hispanic children for speaking English when given the choice, regardless of age or language background at home. (p. 291)

Wong Fillmore (1976) also documented the loss of language and cultural patterns among U.S. immigrant populations. Wong Fillmore described the pain and personal sense of loss that she experienced as a Chinese immigrant when she lost the ability to communicate with family members and described the sense of shame associated with Chinese cultural practices.

The important point to keep in mind for young ELL children is that their home language and cultural practices are fragile and susceptible to dominance by the English language and mainstream culture. The consequences of learning English too early without systematic support for the home language are certainly detrimental socially and culturally, and recent evidence points to negative long-term academic outcomes.

The literature on bilingual education has repeatedly reported linguistic, cognitive, metalinguistic, and, frequently, early literacy advantages for children who successfully become bilingual. Many conceptual, literacy, and language skills clearly transfer from the child's first language to English. However, many questions remain unanswered as to the impact of social class, degree of similarity of home language and English, and bilingual education for very young children who have not yet developed proficiency in their first language. When ELL children from low-SES families enter U.S. early childhood programs, what are the costs of adding English when their native language abilities are significantly delayed? How much native language fluency is necessary before adding a second language? Does this vary by individual child characteristics and the resources of the program? Although there are clearly social, economic, and cultural benefits to becoming bilingual and biliterate, the research has yet to conclusively describe the methods for achieving this goal for all children within the constraints of current staffing and program resources. In addition, the current state and federal mandates emphasize the importance of rapid English acquisition and standardized testing in English by third grade. This has resulted in increased pressure for early childhood programs to get children ready for English-only K–12 programs.

Nevertheless, a consensus of researchers in bilingual education and language acquisition recognizes that the following propositions have strong empirical support and implications for how early childhood programs prepare ELL children for successful transitions to formal schooling (Genesee et al., 2004):

1. Native-language instruction does not slow the acquisition of English.

2. Well-developed skills in the child's home language are associated with high levels of long-term academic achievement.

3. Bilingualism is a valuable skill for individuals and for the country.

PRESCHOOL AND ENGLISH-LANGUAGE LEARNERS

In this era of explicitly defined learning expectations by grade level, frequent testing, public reporting, and punitive consequences for failure, the years before formal schooling are receiving heightened attention. Research has consistently shown that 3- and 4-year-olds who attend a quality preschool are more successful in kindergarten and beyond, both academically and socially, and that children who are at risk for school failure are more strongly influenced by the quality of preschool (Barnett, 1995; Magnuson, Ruhm, & Waldfogel, 2004).

Preschool-age Latino children are the least likely of any ethnic/racial group to enroll in preschool or child care in the nation. For example, across all racial groups, close to half of California's children ages 3–5 are enrolled in preschool/child care (47%), whereas only 37% of Latinos ages 3–5 are similarly enrolled (Lopez & de Cos, 2004). When Latino preschoolers live in a linguistically isolated household in which no one over the age of 14 speaks English fluently, the enrollment rate further drops to 32%. In contrast, about 50% of Asian children in California attend preschool/child care irrespective of the ability of people older than 14 to speak English fluently. The language of the home appears to differentially affect participation in group care and education during the preschool years.

The reasons behind differential participation rates need to be more clearly understood before effective policies can be designed; however, some data suggest that Latino children attend preschool/child care at lower rates because of lack of access and financial constraints, not because of any cultural reluctance among Hispanics and Latinos to enroll their children in group care settings (Fuller, 2005; Hernandez, 2004). In fact, some early care programs in California that serve primarily Hispanic ELLs are consistently overenrolled and have long waiting lists (Espinosa & Lessar, 1996). A recent study in Chicago further supports this conclusion: "Latina mothers needing child care generally viewed child care centers favorably; the fact that few Latinos used child care centers is because affordable center care is not available in their neighborhoods" (Illinois Facilities Fund, 2003, p. 4).

PROMISING MODELS AND INSTRUCTIONAL APPROACHES FOR PRESCHOOL ELLS

Family Literacy Programs

The ECLS-K data indicate that Hispanic/Latino ELL children are less likely to be read to frequently or told stories or engaged in early literacy activities in the home (Denton & West, 2002; Espinosa et al., 2006). Because the home literacy environment has a significant influence on the child's vocabulary development (Senechal, Le Fevre, Hudson, & Lawson, 1996), and reading books to children positively influences their overall literacy development, enhancing home literacy activities with culturally and linguistically responsive strategies is an important goal. Some research shows that young Latina mothers who participated in home-visiting programs increased their enjoyment of and amount of time spent in early literacy activities (Espinosa & Lessar, 1996).

Preschool Programs Serving ELL Children

In California, several studies of the impact of a publicly funded bilingual preschool program on children's home language, in addition to their acquisition of English, provided support for the positive influence of a bilingual preschool on children's overall language and cognitive development (Rodriguez, Diaz, Duran, & Espinosa, 1995; Winsler, Diaz, Espinosa, & Rodriguez, 1999). Children enrolled in the high-quality bilingual preschool program were compared with a matched monolingual Spanish-speaking comparison group. The authors of both studies described the preschool program as being truly bilingual, with equal amounts of instructional time spent in Spanish and English, and as high quality, with a well-defined curriculum and ongoing assessment. Children enrolled in the bilingual preschool showed enhanced development in both Spanish and English acquisition over the comparison group. This sample of low-income, Spanish-speaking ELL children was advancing toward balanced bilingualism while gaining mastery over the linguistic structures of two languages and learning the academic skills identified as important to school readiness.

A Kickoff to Kindergarten (KTK) program in San Mateo County, California, is also showing promising results for ELL children (Child Trends, 2003). This program serves more than 1,200 children in 60 elementary schools across nine school districts in San Mateo County. It offers 4–6 weeks of summer instruction to children prior to kindergarten entry. Although not all sites are able to provide bilingual instruction, all ELL children are provided with support and assistance in their home language. On measures of school readiness, the ELL children showed the largest gains in communication and language skills.

The Tulsa, Oklahoma, universal pre-k program has also shown impressive results for children from all racial, ethnic, and SES groups. The Hispanic children enrolled in the program experienced the largest percentage gains in letter- and word-identification tasks, spelling, and applied problem-solving tasks. It should be noted that the number of Hispanic children who were ELL was not reported, the assessments were all done in English, and little was reported about the content of the curriculum. Nevertheless, Hispanic preschool children who attended the Tulsa, Oklahoma, pre-k program experienced significant gains in early literacy and math skills that will improve their chances of long-term academic success. The program evaluators of the Tulsa, Oklahoma, pre-k program attribute the larger than expected gains to the high quality of the teaching staff, salary equity with elementary school teachers, and classrooms that tended to emphasize developmentally appropriate instruction.

The Parent Institute for Quality Education (PIQE), which has programs in California and Texas, provides outreach services to low-income, ethnically diverse parents to help them learn the skills they need to successfully work with the institutions their children will attend. Latino parents are taught how to navigate the school system and become partners with school personnel to acquire the necessary services and support for their children and families. An evaluation by the Rand Corporation in 2004 concluded that parents were highly satisfied with the services they received, including the parenting classes offered by PIQE and the preschool education (Parent Institute for Quality Education, 2004). The PIQE classes appear to have a positive impact on parents participating in the program, helping them to be more effective advocates for their children and have a positive influence on their children's school-related behavior habits.

RECOMMENDATIONS FOR PRACTICE AND POLICY

Young ELL Latino children have social, cultural, and linguistic strengths that have been identified in the research literature. In addition, they are typically raised in families that have long traditions of family cohesion, stability, and moral values. They frequently have the potential to become bilingual, which is an asset in this global society. Unfortunately, these strengths and sources of resiliency are most often not recognized and enhanced in the early school setting. The following points for policy makers and recommendations for practitioners should help educators capitalize on the talents of a vulnerable population and enrich the social fabric for everyone.

Classroom Practices

1. Get to know the culture of the child and family. Early childhood teachers can promote school–home continuity by understanding the customs, values, and aspirations of the child's family. This is especially critical when the teacher and the child are from different racial, ethnic, cultural, and linguistic backgrounds.

2. Build on the language capacities of the children. When ELL children enter an English-dominant preschool or kindergarten classroom, they already know much about the structure, syntax, and function of their home language. Much of this knowledge will transfer to their English fluency and should be incorporated into daily classroom activities. Just because a child does not know a concept in English does not mean he or she does not know the concept.

3. Extend the language abilities of school personnel. By teaching all school personnel to correctly speak a few words of each child's home language, programs can affirm and recognize the value of languages other than English. Place a high priority on hiring qualified teachers who are fluent in the children's home language and reflect the culture/ethnicity of the children served.

4. Engage the parents of ELL children and incorporate their talents, skills, and interests into the curriculum. Parents who speak languages other than English and who have diverse cultural practices can enhance the richness and textures of classrooms.

5. Enlist the resources of the community. Many senior community residents can share their language and cultural history with children. The local small businesses, religious centers, and social organizations can offer background information and connect young children to their diverse customs.

6. Celebrate the unique contributions of Hispanics/Latinos. The family and social customs that frame Latino culture can enhance early childhood programs and communities if they are understood and embraced by school personnel.

State and Local Policies

1. Promote dual-language instruction and the development of bilingualism whenever possible. To promote long-term social competence and academic achievement, school policies should support ongoing development of the child's home language as well as English acquisition. The research solidly supports bilingualism for ELL children; if this is beyond the capacity of the school program, then policies should, at a minimum, explicitly support maintenance of the home language through family and community resources.

2. Require that all early childhood staff serving ELL children understand the process of first- and second-language development, assessment of dual-language learners, and instructional strategies that capitalize on the language strengths of young ELL children. This will probably require additional preservice courses as well as ongoing staff development on these topics.

3. Require that all early childhood staff are cross-culturally competent and able to establish positive relationships with families from diverse linguistic and cultural backgrounds.

4. Recruit and retain additional early childhood staff at all levels who are representative of the cultural and linguistic backgrounds of the children served by the programs. The first priority should always be to employ staff who are highly qualified and have excellent supervision, teaching, and assessment abilities; however, more talented early childhood professionals who are bilingual and bicultural will need to be identified, trained, and promoted into positions of responsibility.

5. Continually monitor the growth and achievement of young ELL children. This is a growing proportion of the U.S. early childhood population that possesses talents and strengths as well as multiple language resources and that is susceptible to persistent low performance if not well understood and competently educated. For the future of U.S. ELL children and families as well as the country's social and economic institutions, educational policies need to reflect what is known about promoting success for young dual-language learners.

REFERENCES

Au, K.H. (1993). *Literacy instruction in multicultural settings.* New York: Harcourt Brace.

Barnett, W.S. (1995). Long-term effects of early childhood programs on cognitive and school outcomes. *The Future of Children, 5,* 25–50.

Bialystok, E. (2001). *Bilingualism in development: Language, literacy & cognition.* New York: Cambridge University Press.

Blair, C. (2003). *Self-regulation and school readiness.* Champaign, IL: ERIC Clearinghouse on Elementary and Early Childhood Education. (ERIC Document Reproduction No. ED477640)

Boyd, J., Barnett, S., Bodrova, D., Leong, J., Gomby, D., & Robin, K. (2005, March). Promoting children's social and emotional development through preschool. *National Institute for Early Education Research (NIEER) Policy Report.*

Bulcroft, R., Carmody, D., & Bulcroft, K. (1996). Patterns of parental independence giving to adolescents: Variations by race, age, and gender of child. *Journal of Marriage and the Family, 58*(4), 866–883.

Burchinal, M.R., Peisner-Feinberg, E., Pianta, R., & Howes, C. (2000). Development of academic skills from preschool through second grade: Family and classroom predictors. *Journal of School Psychology, 40*(5), 415–436.

Calderon, M., Gonzalez, R., & Lazarin, M. (2004). *State of Hispanic America 2004.* Washington, DC: National Council of La Raza.

California Department of Education. (2005). *Fact book.* Sacramento, CA: Author.

Capps, R., Fix, M., & Reardon-Anderson, J. (2003). *Children of immigrants show slight reduction in poverty, hardship* (Working paper). Washington, DC: Urban Institute.

Child Trends. (2003). *Naturally occurring patterns of school readiness: How the multiple dimensions of school readiness fit together.* Paper presented at the biennial meeting of the Society for Research in Child Development (SRCD), Tampa, FL.

Cortez, J., & Cortez, A. (2004). Effective higher education recruitment strategies: Findings from a research study of San Antonio College. *IDRA Newsletter.*

Crosnoe, R., & Lopez-Gonzalez, L. (2005). Immigration from Mexico, school composition, and adolescent functioning. *Sociological Perspectives, 48,* 1–24.

Delgado-Gaitan, C. (2004). *Involving Latino families in schools: Raising student achievement through home–school partnerships.* Thousand Oaks, CA: Corwin Press.

Delpit, L.D. (1988). The silenced dialogue: Power and pedagogy in educating other people's children. *Harvard Educational Review, 58,* 280–298.

Denton, K., & West, J. (2002). *Children's reading and mathematics achievement in kindergarten and first grade* (NCES 2002-125). Washington, DC: U.S. Department of Education, National Center for Education Statistics.

Diaz, R.M., & Klinger, C. (1991). Towards an exploratory model of the interaction between bilingualism and cognitive development. In E. Bialystok (Ed.), *Language processing in bilingual children* (pp. 140–185). New York: Cambridge University Press.

Dickinson, D.K., & McCabe, A. (2001). Bringing it all together: The multiple origins, skills and environmental supports of early literacy. *Learning Disabilities Research and Practice, 16*(4), 186–202.

Espinosa, L. (1995). *Hispanic involvement in early childhood programs.* Champaign, IL: ERIC Clearinghouse on Elementary and Early Childhood Education. (ERIC Document Reproduction No. ED382412)

Espinosa, L.M., & Laffey, J.M. (2003). Urban primary teacher perceptions of children with challenging behaviors. *Journal of Children & Poverty, 9*(2), 23–44.

Espinosa, L., Laffey, J., & Whittaker, T. (2006). *Language minority children analysis: Focus on technology use* (Final report). CRESST Line/National Center for Education Statistics.

Espinosa, L., & Lessar, S. (1996). Family focus for school success: An early intervention program in Redwood City. *Thrust for Educational Leadership, 23*(7), 12–15.

Fuligini, A.J., Tseng, V., & Lam, M. (1999). Attitudes toward family obligations among American adolescents with Asian, Latin American, and European backgrounds. *Child Development, 70,* 1030–1044.

Fuller, B. (2005). *Mapping the availability of center-based care in Latino communities.* Paper presented at the technical work group meeting of the National Task Force on Hispanic Children and Early Education, Tuscon, AZ.

Gandara, P., Rumberger, R., Maxwell-Jolly, J., & Callahan, R. (2003). English learners in California schools: Unequal resources, unequal outcomes. *Education Policy Analysis Archives, 11*(36). Retrieved January 2, 2006, from http://epaa.asu.edu/epaa/v11n36/v11n36.pdf

Garcia, E.E. (1991). Caring for infants in a bilingual child care setting. *Journal of Educational Issues of Language Minority Students, 9,* 1–10.

Garcia, E.E. (1993). The education of linguistically and culturally diverse children. In B. Spodek (Ed.), *Handbook of research on the education of young children* (pp. 372–384). New York: Macmillan.

Garcia, E.E. (2003). *Student cultural diversity: Understanding and meeting the challenge.* Boston: Houghton Mifflin.

Garcia, E.E. (2005). *Teaching and learning in two languages: Bilingualism and schooling in the United States.* New York: Teachers College Press.

Garcia-Coll, C., Meyer, E., & Brillon, L. (1995). Ethnic and minority parenting. In M. Bornstein (Ed.), *Handbook of parenting, Vol. 2. Biology and ecology of parenting* (pp. 189–209). Mahwah, NJ: Lawrence Erlbaum Associates.

Genesee, F., Paradis, J., & Crago, M.B. (2004). *Dual language development and disorders: A handbook on bilingualism and second language learning.* Baltimore: Paul H. Brookes Publishing Co.

Gormley, W.T., & Gayer, T. (2003). *Promoting school readiness in Oklahoma: An evaluation of Tulsa's pre-k program* (Research policy paper). Washington, DC: Public Policy Institute, Georgetown University.

Hart, B., & Risley, T.R. (1995). *Meaningful differences in the everyday experience of young American children.* Baltimore: Paul H. Brookes Publishing Co.

Head Start Bureau. (2004a). *Head Start National Reporting System* (Final report on fall 2003 assessment results). Washington, DC: Author.

Head Start Bureau. (2004b). *Head Start Program Information Report for 2002–2003.* Washington, DC: Author.

Hernandez, D.J. (2004). Demographic change and the life circumstances of immigrant families. *The Future of Children, 5*(3), 145–160.

Illinois Facilities Fund. (2003). *Latino families and child care preferences in metropolitan Chicago.* Chicago: Author.

Kagan, S.L., Moore, E., & Bredekamp, S. (Eds.). (1995). *Reconsidering children's early development and learning: Toward common views and vocabulary* (Report of the National Education Goals Panel, Goal for Technical Planning Group). Washington, DC: U.S. Government Printing Office.

Krashen, S., & Terrell, T. (1983). *The natural approach: Language acquisition in the classroom.* Upper Saddle River, NJ: Prentice Hall.

Lee, V., & Buram, D. (2002). *Inequality at the starting gate: Social background differences in achievement as children begin school.* Washington, DC: Economic Policy Institute.

Lopez, E., & de Cos, P. (2004). Preschool and childcare enrollment in California (Report No. 04-003). Sacramento, CA: California Research Bureau.

Lopez, G. (2001). The value of hard work: Lessons on parent involvement from an (im)migrant household. *Harvard Education Review,* 416–437.

Magnuson, K.A., Ruhm, C., & Waldfogel, J. (2004). *Does prekindergarten improve school preparation and performance?* (Working Paper No. 10452). Cambridge, MA: National Bureau of Economic Research.

Manning, L. (2004). *Diversity within: A typology of first-generation Mexican parenting.* Unpublished dissertation proposal, University of Missouri-Columbia.

McGhee, L.M., & Richgels, D.J. (1996). *Literacy beginnings: Supporting young readers and writers.* Boston: Allyn & Bacon.

McLaughlin, B., Blanchard, A., & Osanai, Y. (1995). Assessing language development in bilingual preschool children. *NCELA Program Information Guide Series, 22.* Retrieved January 2, 2006, from http://www.ncela.gwu.edu/pubs/pigs/pig2.htm

Moll, L.C. (1991). Literacy learning: A community mediated approach. In S. Silvern (Ed.), *Literacy through family, community, and social interaction* (pp. 201–215). Greenwich, CT: JAI Press.

National Center for Education Statistics. (2003). *Status and trends in the education of Hispanics.* Washington, DC: Author.

Negy, C., & Woods, D. (1992). The importance of acculturation in understanding research with Hispanic-Americans. *Hispanic Journal of Behavioral Sciences, 14,* 224–247.

Oller, K.D., & Eilers, R.E. (Eds.). (2002). *Language and literacy in bilingual children.* New York: Multilingual Matters.

Parent Institute for Quality Education. (2004). *Annual report.* San Diego: Author.

Pew Hispanic Research Center. (2004). *Latino youth and the pathway to college.* Washington, DC: Author.

Portes, A., & Rumbaut, R.G. (2001). *Legacies: The story of the immigrant second generation.* Berkeley: University of California.

Ravler, C.C., & Zigler, E.F. (1997). Social competence: An untapped dimension in evaluating Head Start's success. *Early Childhood Research Quarterly, 12,* 363–385.

Regalado, M., Goldenberg, C., & Appel, E. (2001). *Reading and early literacy* (Policy Brief No. 11). Los Angeles: UCLA Center for Healthier Children, Families and Communities.

Reyes, I., & Moll, L.C. (in press). Bilingualism and Latinos. In Ilan Stavans (Ed.), *Encyclopedia Latina: History, culture, and society in the United States.* New York: Grolier.

Rist, R. (2000). Student social class and teacher expectations: The self-fulfilling prophesy in ghetto education. *Harvard Education Review, 70*(3), 266–301. (Original work published 1970)

Rodriguez, J., Diaz, R., Duran, D., & Espinosa, L. (1995). The impact of bilingual preschool education on the language development of Spanish-speaking children. *Early Childhood Research Quarterly, 10,* 475–490.

Rothenberg, A. (1995). *Understanding and working with parents and children from rural Mexico.* Menlo Park, CA: The CHC Center for Child and Family Development Press.

Rueschenberg, E., & Buriel, R. (1995). Mexican American family functioning and acculturation: A family systems perspective. In A.M. Oadukka (Ed.), *Hispanic Psychology* (pp. 15–42). Thousand Oaks, CA: Sage.

Rumberger, R. (2004). Why students drop out of school. In G. Orfield (Ed.), *Dropouts in America: Confronting the graduation rate crisis.* Cambridge, MA: Harvard Education Press.

Rumberger, R., & Anguiano, A. (2004). *Understanding and addressing the California Latino achievement gap in early elementary school* (Working paper 2004-01). Santa Barbara, CA: University of California, Santa Barbara.

Sanchez, S.Y. (1999). Learning from the stories of culturally and linguistically diverse families and communities. A sociohistorical lens. *Remedial and Special Education, 20*(6), 351–359.

Senechal, M., Le Fevre, J., Hudson, E., & Lawson, P. (1996). Knowledge of storybooks as a predictor of young children's vocabulary. *Journal of Educational Psychology, 88,* 520–536.

Shonkoff, J.P., & Phillips, D.A. (Eds.). (2000). *From neurons to neighborhoods: The science of early childhood development.* Washington, DC: National Academies Press.

Slavin, R.E., & Cheung, A. (2005). A synthesis of research on language of reading instruction for English language learners. *Review of Educational Research, 75*(2), 247–281.

Suarez-Orozco, C., Suarez-Orozco, M., & Doucet, F. (2003). The academic engagement and achievement of Latino youth. In J. Banks & C. McGhee-Banks (Eds.), *Handbook of multicultural education* (2nd ed., pp. 420–437). New York: Jossey-Bass.

Tabors, P.O. (1997). *One child, two languages: A guide for preschool educators of children learning English as a second language.* Baltimore: Paul H. Brookes Publishing Co.

Tabors, P.O., Roach, K.A., & Snow, C.E. (2001). Home language and literacy environment: Final results. In D.K. Dickinson & P.O. Tabors (Eds.), *Beginning literacy with language: Young children learning at home and school* (pp. 111–148). Baltimore: Paul H. Brookes Publishing Co.

Tabors, P.O., & Snow, C.E. (1994). English as a second language in preschool programs. In F. Genesee (Ed.), *Educating second language children: The whole child, the whole curriculum, the whole community* (pp. 103–125). Cambridge, MA: Cambridge University Press.

U.S. Census Bureau. (2004). Hispanics and Asian Americans increasing faster than overall population. *United States Department of Commerce news.* Retrieved June 14, 2004, from http://www.census.gov/Press-Release/www/releases/archives/race/001839.html

Valdes, G. (1996). *Con respeto: Bridging the distances between culturally diverse families and schools. An ethnographic portrait.* New York: Teachers College Press.

Valencia, R. (2000). Inequalities and the schooling of minority students in Texas. *Hispanic Journal of Behavioral Sciences, 22,* 445–459.

Wentzel, K., & Asher, S. (1995). The academic lives of neglected, rejected, popular, and controversial children. *Child Development, 66,* 754–763.

Winsler, A., Diaz, R.M., Espinosa, L., & Rodriguez, J.L. (1999). When learning a second language does not mean losing the first: Bilingual language development in low-income, Spanish-speaking children attending bilingual preschool. *Child Development, 70*(2), 349–362.

Wong Fillmore, L. (1976). *The second time around: Cognitive and social strategies in second language acquisition.* Unpublished doctoral dissertation, Stanford University, Palo Alto, CA.

10

INTEGRATIVE VIEWS OF THE DOMAINS OF CHILD FUNCTION

Unifying School Readiness

Kyle L. Snow

The concept of school readiness has evolved during the past few decades from its introduction in the National Education Goals Panel (NEGP; 1997) to recent efforts to define it (e.g., Ackerman & Barnett, 2005; Kagan, 1990; Snow, 2006b). Despite some debate about the details, the general conceptualization is that school readiness encompasses those skills and knowledge associated with success in school (e.g., Crnic & Lamberty, 1994), a definition rendered questionable by the very mixed success that school readiness tests have in predicting school outcomes (e.g., Carlton & Winsler, 1999; La Paro & Pianta, 2001). In a social and educational policy context, the general parameters of school readiness were laid out by the National Education Goals Panel (1997) and included physical well-being and motor development, social and emotional development, approaches toward learning, communication and language usage, and cognition and general knowledge. These were made more concrete and specific with the reauthorization of Head Start as the School Readiness Act of 2005 (S1107; H.R.2123), which specified the primary expectations for Head Start children on entering kindergarten: language knowledge and skills, including oral language and listening comprehension; prereading knowledge and skills, including phonological awareness, print awareness, print skills, and alphabetic knowledge; premathematics knowledge and skills, including aspects of classification, seriation, number, spatial relations, and time; cognitive abilities related to academic achievement; social and emotional development related to early learning, school success, and sustained academic gains; and, in the case of limited–English-proficient children, progress toward acquisition of the English language while making meaningful progress toward the knowledge, skills, and abilities expected for English-speaking children.

Portions of this chapter are from Snow, K. (2006a, June 27). Disentangling components of school readiness. In D.J. Armor (Chair), *Measuring readiness of Head Start children.* Symposium conducted at Head Start's 8th National Research Conference, Washington, DC.

In a practical sense, definitions need to be examined as they arise among a number of stakeholders in a child's development, including standards established by state education agencies, teachers, and parents. Neuman and Roskos (2005) reported that, as of 2005, 43 states had developed early education standards, up from 16 in 2000, and Scott-Little, Kagan, and Frelow (2006) conducted content analyses on 46 standards. These standards vary greatly in their specifications, definitions, and alignment (Neuman & Roskos, 2005; Scott-Little, Kagan, & Frelow, 2003, 2006). In the broadest terms, however, state standards blend expectations set forth in the NEGP and those expressed in federal legislation. They tend to reflect a view of independence among components, which is notable because components included in definitions of school readiness may vary in the degree to which they are influenced by instruction. For example, in examining a broad range of child competencies often considered in definitions of school readiness during the first 2 years of schooling, Christian, Morrison, Frazier, and Massetti (2000) noted that the nature and timing of growth differed considerably across skills during the time period and concluded that these skills are therefore independent, even if correlated. Furthermore, Christian et al. (2000) noted that growth in any specific domain could be divided into schooling effects and non-schooling effects and that the degree to which growth could be attributable to instruction was itself a variable that differentiated domains of functioning. Similarly, in analyzing long-term data from the Abecederian Project, Campbell, Pungello, Miller-Johnson, Burchinal, and Ramey (2001) noted that differences between project participants and control children were maintained throughout their years in school; participation in school following Abecederian did not mediate or moderate the effects of the intervention.

When kindergarten teachers have been asked to identify important skills for children to have as they enter school, they tend to focus on social and emotional aspects of school readiness rather than preacademic skills (see, e.g., Dockett & Perry, 2003; Hains, Fowler, Schwartz, Kottwitz, & Rosenhoetter, 1989; Heaviside & Farris, 1993; Lin, Lawrence, & Gorrell, 2003). Recent studies of teacher expectations, however, have noted an increasing emphasis on preacademic skills (Wesley & Buysse, 2003), especially among teachers of low-income children (Wright, Diener, & Kay, 2000) and teachers from minority groups (Heaviside & Farris, 1993; Piotrkowski, Botsko, & Matthews, 2000). In contrast, parental views of school readiness differ dramatically from those of their children's teachers (Diamond, Reagan, & Bandyk, 2000; West, Germino-Hausken, & Collins, 1995). In general, parents are more focused on preacademic skills, such as knowing letters and numbers. This focus on preacademic skills is the most prevalent among parents from low-income homes and those with less education (Piotrkowski, 2004; Piotrkowski et al., 2000; West et al., 1995).

There are no coherent theories about how components of school readiness fit together, and few account for multiple competencies simultaneously. The literature predominantly comprises either descriptive studies or papers that argue for parity among components, especially those calling for more attention to socioemotional factors (Raver, 2002) and emotional competence (e.g., Denham et al., 2003), a trend also noted among state standards (Scott-Little et al., 2006). One result of the lack of clear theory coupled with extensive data from descriptive studies is that there is "a veritable laundry list" of interrelated skills for which the nature of relationships has not been extensively examined (Snow, 2006b, p. 19).

Across diverse stakeholder and researcher definitions, two features emerge. First, school readiness comprises multiple skill sets and capacities, which vary within the population. Second, these skills and capacities are both independent and interrelated. To date, the research literature has focused predominantly on the first of these themes—identifying key competencies, demonstrating variation within the population, and describing these at school entry, including the identification of precursors and later outcomes. The second theme, examining interrelations of key school readiness components, has been less frequently explored. It is not the intent of this chapter to account for all interrelationships, at all levels of analysis, for all constructs implicated in school readiness (e.g., components of early literacy or early math) but, rather, to focus on relationships across domains (e.g., math's relationship to language). In addition, for the purposes of this chapter, except where indicated by data, the domains of school readiness considered are drawn from federal legislation (e.g., Head Start) rather than NEGP, and consideration is given to children's school readiness rather than schools' readiness for children (Emig, Moore, & Scarupa, 2001).

FRAMEWORK FOR CONSIDERING INTERRELATIONSHIPS

Before discussing the various interrelationships that are theorized or empirically shown to exist among components of school readiness, several caveats are in order. First, this chapter focuses primarily on relationships among variables, most of which are quantified through correlation or similar analyses. It is therefore necessary to briefly revisit concerns that correlation does not equal causation. When considering that two components of school readiness are related, it is conceivable that A causes B, that B causes A, or that a third factor, C, causes both of the observed variables. Few studies discussed here include designs that specifically address issues of causality. Second, for the purposes of much of this chapter, school readiness components generally considered to be socioemotional or cognitive in nature are considered, whereas (with one exception) child health is excluded (but see Chapter 6). This is primarily due to limitations in the extant literature. Finally, there are two temporal dimensions along which to consider interrelationships among aspects of school readiness. The first is a consideration of contemporaneous relations among domains. At any given point in time (e.g., the year before kindergarten, kindergarten entry or completion, first-grade entry, and so forth), how do domains of school readiness relate? Such single-point estimates are frequently considered when examining the effects of programs designed for young children and in kindergarten-screening regimens and typically rely on between-subject research designs. The second temporal dimension considers interrelationships over time. Such an approach considers the simultaneous development of multiple school readiness components over time and typically relies on a within-subject design. This chapter primarily focuses on contemporaneous relations, although developmental dimensions are discussed next.

CONTEMPORANEOUS RELATIONSHIPS
AMONG SCHOOL READINESS DOMAINS

In this context, contemporaneous relationships are considered to be those that exist at a relatively restricted moment of convergence, which may be as long as the initial weeks or months of school entry, or as brief as the period of time during which a child is being assessed or, possibly, even the moment-to-moment behavior habits of children. The general theme is that these relationships occur temporally in ways that make any discussion of causality, developmental precedent, or order speculative at best. From a practical standpoint, understanding contemporaneous relationships may have the greatest impact on instruction and assessment because these occur within reasonably defined temporal windows within which teachers work. For example, a given teacher's approach to instruction is typically limited to the academic year during which the student is in that classroom, so understanding interrelations as they occur throughout the school year is of more importance to the teacher; however, understanding how these relationships arise and change over time may be of more importance to those interested in developing early learning standards and aligning them with existing educational standards (Bogard & Takanishi, 2005).

BIVARIATE RELATIONSHIPS

The literature includes numerous efforts to correlate child competence in one area with competence in another area. This is especially the case in large-scale studies, such as the Early Childhood Longitudinal Study–Kindergarten (ECLS-K) cohort, in which domain-specific subtests are developed and administered to all children. In ECLS-K, for example, numerous cross-domain correlations are noted (Denton & Germino-Hausken, 2000). In the direct child assessment from the ECLS-K kindergarten-year data, reading and mathematics scores are highly correlated ($r = .79$), and general knowledge is correlated with both reading ($r = .60$) and mathematics ($r = .65$), although parental measures of child social competence are not correlated with cognitive outcomes, and dimensions of social skills rated by teachers show few, weak correlations with the cognitive measures (for all measures, $r < .25$). Ratings of child approaches to learning (discussed next) were also correlated with child cognitive measures (for all measures, $r = .30$). Importantly, in many studies such as the ECLS-K and other descriptive studies, the presence of correlations across domains, although documented, is not explicitly explored, and there tends to be no specific theoretical model or underlying hypothesis behind the relationships. Next, two bivariate relations are more fully discussed. Each has both data and underlying theory.

Behavior Regulation and Literacy

The relationship between behavioral control and reading has received a great deal of attention in the literature, although the nature of the relationship remains somewhat unclear (McGee & Share, 1988; Spira & Fischel, 2005), primarily because of methodological limitations across studies (see Hinshaw, 1992). Spira and Fischel (2005) presented four possible models relating the two domains: reading problems may cause behavioral problems, behavioral problems may cause reading difficulties, reading difficulties and behavioral problems in school may have a common antecedent or set of antecedents, and the relationship is bidirectional. To date, some data support all of these possibilities. However, recent data are overcoming some of the methodological limitations of their predecessors by using longitudinal designs (e.g., Miles & Stipek, 2006; Rabiner, Coie, & Conduct Problems Prevention Research Group, 2000), using multidimensional measures of behavior habits and behavior control (e.g., Agostin & Bain, 1997; Fantuzzo, Bulotsky, McDermott, Mosca, & Lutz, 2003), or placing behavior control within a larger context of social skills (e.g., Doctoroff, Greer, & Arnold, 2006). Despite an inability to specify the causal patterns involved, this body of research demonstrates a relationship connecting behavioral control (primarily indicated by lack of control), behavioral problems, and/or reading outcomes. However, two serious limitations remain. First, without specifying causal pathways, the most efficient interventions—those that take advantage of any underlying linkages across domains—cannot be developed or implemented with any clear expectation for success. Second, because the literature is based primarily on behavioral problems, it is not yet clear whether behavioral control can improve reading outcomes for children who are at risk of reading difficulties.

Math, Reading, and Language

There is an intuitive connection between math and reading skills in that number words are considered to be a bridge between the two. The reporting of correlations between reading and math, as noted, seems to support this belief. Still, several researchers have noted that number words may be distinct from other words in important ways so that what would appear to be a bridge may actually be a third, separate category of functioning, or at least a component within mathematical competence (see Lipton & Spelke, 2006; Musolino, 2004; Sarnecka & Gelman, 2004; Wynn, 1992). As a result, the existence and nature of this relationship is a matter of some debate (Gelman & Butterworth, 2005).

Research with adults shows that language impairment and math disabilities (e.g., dyscalculia) are independent (Cappelletti, Butterworth, & Kopelman, 2001; Rossor, Warrington, & Cipolotti, 1995) and that different brain regions are involved in language processing and a range of mathematical skills (Cipolotti & van Harskamp, 2001), suggesting independence. Importantly, these studies rely on adult data and often reflect relative end points in domain development. It may be that relationships not present in adults are evident earlier in development and represent a relegation of skill sets into different systems in their developed state.

Mix, Huttenlocher, and Levine (2002) and Carey (2004) have each assigned a causal role to language in children's acquisition of number concepts. Carey's (2001, 2004) approach acknowledges a distinction between children's understanding of very small quantities and their acquisition of understanding of larger numbers. The critical distinction occurs when children start to map quantities onto quantitative words, such as *few, many,* and so forth. In Carey's accounting, children can exhibit competence with higher quantities without language, but the system of counting words is crucial in manipulating numbers that are beyond very small quantities. However, research in cultures that do not have the same specificity in number words has shown that mathematical problem solving (in this case, comparing quantities) is not hindered by the lack of appropriate number words (Gordon, 2004). So, it would appear that language skills and numerical competence are not, by necessity, related. However, the presence of such correlations among American school children may be reflective of a particular cultural context within which young children receive explicit instruction in number words and their use.

MEDIATING RELATIONSHIPS

Some relationships among domains of child competence may occur not because the two are directly related but because of a third factor that contributes to competence in multiple areas. In such cases, the relationships among domains would be mediated through this third factor. In this section, two areas of competence—executive function and attention control—and approaches to learning are used to illustrate the potentially complex mediational relationships that can exist among other domains of child competency at school entry and through the early grades.

Executive Function and Attention

Although there is no consensus about the exact nature of executive function and its components (e.g., Blair, Zelazo, & Greenberg, 2005; Lyon & Krasnegor, 1996; Pennington, 1997; see also Chapter 8), the role of executive function in early childhood development has become a matter of intense speculation and theory building (Blair, 2002). In general, executive functioning reflects a child's abilities to mobilize and control his or her cognitive resources, so inhibition, attention control, and memory processes are all implicated in the process, and these are seen as permeating a broad range of child competencies. There are data relating executive function to mathematical outcomes (e.g., Bull & Scerif, 2001; Espy et al., 2004; McLean & Hitch, 1999) in young and school-age children. Among young children, executive functioning has been related to theories of mind tasks (for a review, see Perner & Lang, 1999). However, few data indicate the role of executive functioning in other school-related outcomes (but see St. Clair-Thompson & Gathercole, 2006).

A broad literature indicates that poor attentional control and executive functioning skills are a risk factor for poor academic performance (Cantwell & Satterfield, 1978; Palisin, 1986) as well as a risk for learning disabilities (Holborow & Berry, 1986; Horn & Packard, 1985) and poor social skills (Campbell, Pierce, March, Ewing, & Szumowski, 1994; Eisenberg et al., 2000). To date, much of this literature focuses on children with attention problems, including attention-deficit/hyperactivity disorder. However, analysis conducted by the National Institute of Child Health and Human Development (NICHD) Early Child Care Research Network (2003) focused on a normative population using multiple measures of attentional processes and other domains of child functioning. They reported that two attentional processes measured at preschool—sustained attention and inhibition of impulsive responding—predicted language, academic achievement, and social outcomes during the transition to school. The effect sizes, although statistically significant, were small but evident after controlling for a range of potential confounding variables, including sociodemographic factors.

Approaches to Learning

The phrase "approaches to learning" is used here to capture a broad range of skills that children bring with them to school that may influence how they approach classroom and/or learning activities. The broad range of terms used in the literature to capture this construct includes such ideas as attentiveness to the teacher, persistence, attitude, resilience in the face of error, and other learning-specific skills. Conceptually, "approaches to learning" is similar to "learning style," although it includes some degree of social skills, even if in a limited way (cf. Stott, Green, & Francis, 1983).

Cooper and Farran (1988, 1991) first introduced the concept of work-related skills as a distinct form of social skills. Work-related skills include paying attention to directions, participating in groups, and focusing on classroom tasks. Cooper and colleagues (Cooper & Speece, 1988; Speece & Cooper, 1990) have shown positive relations between work-related skills and later academic achievement, and Bronson, Tivnan, and Seppanen (1995) showed a relationship with kindergarten outcomes. Cooper and Speece (1988) also showed a relationship between poor work-related skills and children's referrals for special education. In a descriptive longitudinal study of children entering school from preschool, McClelland, Morrison, and Holmes (2000) showed that having stronger work-related social skills acted as a buffer against sociodemographic risk in predicting short-term learning outcomes.

McWayne, Fantuzzo, and McDermott (2004) examined a number of dimensions of approaches to learning in urban Head Start children. Using a number of measures to tap possible aspects of child approaches to learning, McWayne et al. (2004) identified three stable factors within approaches to learning: general classroom competence, including cognitive and social skills; specific approaches to learning, including motivation, persistence, and positive attitudes toward learning; and interpersonal problems, including disruptive behavior habits and poor attitudes toward learning. McWayne et al. (2004) then applied cluster analysis to generate a number of profiles based on children's scores. These profiles differentiated children's scores on an early learning screening test, with results indicating that general classroom competence and specific approaches to learning were associated with early academic success. Fantuzzo, Perry, and McDermott (2004) also found three dimensions within the Preschool Learning Behavior Scale (PLBS; McDermott, Green, Francis, & Stott, 2000) in a low-income sample of children. Using the PLBS, factor analysis revealed scales for competence motivation, attention/persistence, and attitude, all of which were related to child language measures. A focus on these skill sets has important implications for intervention because data show that these skills can be taught to children as they enter school (Schaefer & McDermott, 1999).

Finally, Onatsu-Arvilommi and Nurmi (2000) explored the role of task avoidance and task focus in academic outcomes during the transition to school. This study is notable because its longitudinal nature allowed the authors to draw some conclusions about causal directions. Briefly, children with high task avoidance had poorer reading skills (with no effect on mathematics) even after controlling for earlier reading. However, children with poor reading and math skills at school entry showed increases in task avoidance during the year, and this change was evident during the first months of the first year, leading the authors to conclude that the first months of the school year are critical for children's development or adoption of particular learning styles that also relate to later outcomes.

CLUSTER ANALYSIS AND GROUPING

A small number of studies have examined multiple components of school readiness simultaneously. Although researchers have long looked for patterns in their data to describe groupings (e.g., Cronbach & Gleser, 1953), the use of cluster analysis is a cutting-edge technique for examining a complex set of variables among a sample of children to determine the degree to which subsamples can be identified with common attributes that are homogeneous within one group while also creating heterogeneous groups (Aldenderfer & Blashfield, 1984). To be fully realized, the results of cluster analysis should create internally consistent groups that are dissimilar from equally internally consistent groups; these clusters should provide for the range of all variables included in the cluster solution, and resultant clusters should be replicable (see McDermott, 1998). Such techniques have been shown to provide powerful descriptive and diagnostic purposes in a number of assessment contexts (e.g., Morris, Blashfield, & Satz, 1981), including those applied to young children (e.g.,

Glutting, McDermott, & Konold, 1997; Konold, Glutting, & McDermott, 1997), but they have been applied only recently in the study of school readiness.

Konold and Pianta (2005) applied cluster analysis to a group of cognitive and social developmental measures among 54-month-old children in the NICHD Study of Early Child Care and Youth Development (SECCYD). The three cognitive measures were drawn from direct child assessments using the memory-for-sentences and incomplete-words subtests from the Woodcock-Johnson Revised Tests of Cognitive Ability (Woodcock & Johnson, 1989) and the omission errors scale from the Continuous Performance Test (CPT; Mirsky, Anthony, Duncan, Ahearn, & Kellam, 1991). The three social measures included were externalizing behavior problems taken from the Child Behavior Checklist (Achenbach, 1991), social skills measured using the Social Skills Rating System (SSRS; Gresham & Elliott, 1990), and positive engagement, measured through observation of 15 minutes of semistructured play between a parent (typically the mother) and a child. Konold and Pianta reported six stable clusters (listed using their labels and reported incidence rates in the sample):

Attention problems (10%)—generally average on all scales, but elevated omission error scores

Low cognitive ability (7%)—lowest scores on cognitive measures, average social skills, slightly elevated omission error scores

Low to average social and cognitive skills (20%)—somewhat lower social skills than average, and low to average cognitive skills

Social and externalizing problems (17%)—moderately low social skills but elevated externalizing behavior habits, lowest levels of positive engagement, with average cognitive scores and slightly elevated omission error scores

High social competence (24%)—above-average social skills, including highest ratings of social skills and lowest level of externalizing behavior habits, and average cognitive skills

High cognitive ability and mild externalizing (22%)—highest scores on cognitive measures, with some elevation in externalizing behavior habits

Colvig-Amir, Liu, and Mobilio (2005) surveyed the kindergarten teachers in Santa Clara County (CA) using an instrument designed to provide data on the relative proficiency levels of children on 20 items drawn from the framework provided by the NEGP. Using cluster analytic techniques on data reported for 943 children, Colvig-Amir et al. (2005) identified four stable clusters. They noted that "the four-cluster solution produced the most logical, clear-cut, and meaningful differentiation between various groupings of children" (p. 31). In constructing the data for these analyses, Colvig-Amir et al. averaged teacher reports on child behavior habits in each of the five domains identified by the NEGP as critical for school readiness: physical well-being and motor development, social and emotional development, approaches toward learning, communication and language usage, and cognition and general knowledge. These clusters and the estimated prevalence in Santa Clara County were described as follows (using their descriptors):

All stars (48%)—This group was reported as near or at proficiency in all five NEGP domains.

Needs prep (11%)—This group was reported as not quite progressing in attaining any of the five NEGP domains.

Social stars (15%)—Children rated high on emotional and social development, physical well-being, and motor development but were not as prepared in communication and language usage and cognition and general knowledge domains.

Focused on the facts (26%)—Children are nearly proficient in cognition and general knowledge but below proficiency in other areas.

Hair, Halle, Terry-Humen, and Calkins (2003)[1] took a similar approach, based on the NEGP, in examining clusters among children. Hair et al. (2003) examined child competency using data from the ECLS-K cohort in four domains: health, social and emotional functioning, emergent literacy, and general cognitive functioning. These authors collapsed scores in each domain in ways similar to Colvig-Amir et al. (2005), using proficiency scores derived from raw data provided by direct assessment of children and parent and teacher reports, then constructing clusters based on risk relative to kindergarten children's expected levels of proficiency. Hair et al. (2003) identified four clusters (their descriptors and estimated prevalence):

Health risk (9.0%)—Children were nearly 2.5 standard deviations below the population mean in aspects of physical health, including ratings of general health, body-mass index, and fine and gross motor skills and were within 0.5 standard deviations of the mean on other domains.

Social and emotional risk (14.4%)—Children scored nearly two standard deviations below the mean in areas such as self-control, social interaction, and behavior problems and within one standard deviation of the mean on other domains.

Language or cognitive risk (37.2%)—Children scored greater than 0.5 standard deviations below the mean on skills such as emergent writing and reading and problem solving, classifying, and sorting.

Low risk (39.4%)—Children scored greater than the mean in all areas and were nearly one standard deviation above the mean in the language and cognition measures.

Despite the differing study samples, measures, and even frameworks (NEGP versus others), these three studies converge in some of their findings. First, each study identified a sizeable "ready for school" group that meets most or all expectations. These clusters carry both expected predictive relations (when tested) and sociodemographic predictors based on the literature. Second, blended-strength (or risk) clusters have differences in their readiness in social versus cognitive domains. Finally, cluster membership was differentiated by a number of demographic variables, including maternal education and family income (variably measured), although each study provided a different number of demographic correlates in their design and reporting of findings.

DEVELOPMENTAL RELATIONSHIPS AMONG SCHOOL READINESS DOMAINS

The relationships noted previously occur at a given period of time and would likely be evidenced in cross-sectional as well as longitudinal studies. However, some relationships among constructs can best be understood by taking a developmental perspective that virtually requires

---

[1]This work has been further expanded in Hair, Halle, Terry-Humen, and Calkins, 2006.

longitudinal research designs to become apparent. In the context of this chapter, the developmental frame is applied across domains, rather than within domains; for the latter, there is already an extensive literature.

DEVELOPMENTAL CONVERGENCE

One way to consider developmental convergence has been used in the study of resilience (e.g., Ayoub & Fischer, 2006), which considers that the range of child competencies have developmental trajectories that may or may not intercept. A large body of data demonstrates the developmental trajectories of some component skills of school readiness, such as literacy (Neuman & Dickinson, 2001; Snow, Burns, & Griffin, 1998), whereas the developmental trajectories of other components, such as math, are less well studied (Clements, Sarama, & DiBiase, 2004; Kilpatrick, Swafford, & Findell, 2001). If component skills are considered independently, developmental trajectories can be identified and mapped onto each other. Doing so would likely reveal that these growth curves may or may not intersect. For skills with nonintersecting parallel trajectories, assumingly they are likely to be independent. For skills with nonintersecting, nonparallel trajectories, relationships may or may not exist. For skills with intersecting trajectories, the point of intersection possibly reflects a point of convergence. When these skills intersect at the same time that the resulting combined skill is assessed, a strong convergent relationship is apparent, especially if, rather than intersecting, the curves fuse into a single trajectory, possibly reflecting a new skill set. In addition, as numerous chapters in Sameroff and Haith (1996) indicate, the time of school entry is one of broad developmental change (the 5- to 7-year shift), which may exert additional pressures on independent developmental trajectories to converge. The examples given next illustrate this last case of intersecting trajectories that then become fused into a new skill set.

FOURTH-GRADE SLUMP

First observed by Chall, Jacobs, and Baldwin (1990), the "fourth-grade slump" defines an apparently emerging discrepancy between children who previously had been scoring equally on reading tests but who, when assessed in fourth grade, scored differently along patterns related to demographic risk factors (for a review, see Hirsch, 2003). In other words, despite broad differences in background, children tested prior to fourth grade tended to score comparably well (in Chall et al.'s 1990 data); yet, when tested in fourth grade, differences in performance appeared and became larger throughout the remainder of school. Shortly after these data appeared, potential explanations were explored, with the general consensus suggesting that the slump manifests in fourth grade because of changes in how reading is assessed between third and fourth grade, making a discrepancy more visible than it was previously, although discrepancies earlier could also be found if investigated appropriately. Around fourth grade, reading assessments become more heavily focused on reading comprehension rather than the early literacy and decoding skills tapped by earlier reading measures. Nagy and Scott (2000) argued that reading comprehension is strongest when the reader knows as much as 90%–95% of the words in the text, and Sticht, Beck, Hauk, Kleiman, and James (1974) argued that oral language comprehension places an upper limit on reading comprehension; all of these researchers have suggested a strong role for vocabulary in reading comprehension. Reading comprehension is thus the result of two converging skills: decoding a text (a set of preliteracy skills that is well discussed in the literature) and vocabulary. By the middle of elementary school, a typically developing child will have acquired most of the skills that contribute to decoding (e.g., phonemic awareness, sound–letter mapping, and so forth), so the developmental trajectory will generally be flat. In contrast, vocabulary growth continues, and over time, initial differences in vocabulary dramatically increase (Graves, Brunetti, & Slater, 1982; Hart & Risley, 1995). The result is that reading comprehension emerges as an additional skill set (through convergence of decoding and vocabulary).

MATH WORD PROBLEMS

One point of convergence that may be specific to assessment strategies is in childhood math assessments that contain word problems as part of the assessment. As with reading comprehension, word problems represent a convergence of multiple individual skills, in this case, children's understanding of numbers, basic operations, and language. To solve a typical word problem, a child must be able to extract the relevant information concerning quantity and determine the operation necessary to solve the problem. Although most word problems included in childhood assessments are not complex (they tend to contain reasonably transparent operations and little, if any, distracting numerical information), the task demands are such that children with poor reading skills but strong quantitative skills may score lower than children with better reading skills and comparable math skills. Indeed, O'Neill, Pearce, and Pick (2004) found that children's narrative skills in preschool predicted math scores 2 years later.

DEVELOPMENTAL SYNERGY

Although some relationships may result in convergence with the resulting implications for a third domain of development, some relationships arise developmentally and reflect an acceleration effect on one of the related domains. In this context, development within a given domain of competence continues even as it exerts an apparent effect on other domains, creating a widening of discrepancies in one skill based on discrepancies in another. The most often-cited example of this is the purported Matthew effect due to reading skill, but similar discrepancies can also be seen in the impact of social skills over time. Each of these is discussed briefly here.

MATTHEW EFFECT

Although initially used by Walberg and Tsai (1983) in describing young adult educational outcomes, the Matthew effect in education has become most closely associated with Stanovich's (1986) usage in describing the long-term differentiation that occurs between skilled and unskilled readers. According to this model, children with strong reading skills come to more advanced reading tasks and tasks that require strong reading to perform, better equipped than their poorer reading peers so that performance differences are seen not only in reading but also across a range of cognitive skills, including mathematics, science, and general knowledge. Indeed, Chall (1996) argued that during the development of read-ing skills, children go through a transition between learning to read and reading to learn. Presumably, children with stronger reading skills are in a better position to use reading as a means of learning in other areas.

Despite the strength of the argument made by Stanovich (1986) and its prima facie va-lidity, research exploring the Matthew effect is mixed, with some studies showing support (e.g., Bast & Reitsma, 1998; Luyten, Cremers-van, Wees, & Bosker, 2003) and some stud-ies unable to find such an effect (e.g., Aarnoutse & van Leeuwe, 2000) or finding an effect but attributing it to some other factor (e.g., Shaywitz et al., 1995). Indeed, in Shaywitz et al. (1995), a more general cognitive feature, IQ test score, was shown as having a broad ef-fect on child outcomes in reading and other domains.

SOCIAL SKILLS

As noted previously, social competence, especially behavioral control, has been examined in relation to contemporaneous cognitive functioning in children. However, some lit-erature suggests an additional synergistic effect of social skills on cognitive outcomes. Mashburn and Pianta (2006) recently provided an integrative model of school readiness in which the teachers, peers, and family with whom the child has relationships serve as mediators during the early years of school. Similarly, Ladd, Herald, and Kochel (2006) have presented a model of early school transitions that focuses on child acquisition of so-cial school entry tasks, which can be supported by relationships with peers and teachers. Both of these models represent the culmination of many years of research on the impor-tance of peer relationships and child–teacher relationships in supporting a child's transi-tion to school.

Ladd and colleagues (Ladd, 1989, 1990; Ladd, Kochenderfer, & Coleman, 1996; Ladd & Price, 1987) have focused on children's capacity to form close friendships with peers, leading to peer acceptance in the classroom, which then serves to support the child's engagement in school and emerging academic achievement (see also Wentzel, 1999). Evi-dence suggests that the quality of peer relationships contributes to a range of social and be-havioral skills that support children's classroom learning (e.g., Coolahan, Fantuzzo, Mendez, & McDermott, 2000; Fantuzzo & McWayne, 2002). More recently, Ladd, Birch, and Buhs (1999) have simultaneously considered the roles of peer relationships and child–teacher relationships in creating the most optimum context in which children can learn.

Pianta and colleagues have tended to focus on child–teacher relationships as mecha-nisms that support early academic achievement (e.g., Hamre & Pianta, 2001; Pianta, 1997, 2000; Pianta, Steinberg, & Rollins, 1995; Pianta & Stuhlman, 2004; see also Birch & Ladd, 1997) and as a protective mechanism for children at risk for school difficulties (e.g., Hamre & Pianta, 2005). In this model, the more a child establishes close, conflict-free relationships with teachers, the more adequately the child will acquire skills taught in school, maximiz-ing the impact of instruction and deriving the most benefit from school.

These two bodies of research, although focused on different relationship partners for the young child, converge on several conclusions. First, positive relationships promote pos-itive outcomes or protect against other risk factors. Negative relationships are seen as threats to other outcomes. Importantly, however, child relationships during early schooling are dynamic; that is, each year brings a new teacher with whom the child may bond. Yet, early relationships also have the potential to influence both the opportunities for and nature of later relationships. This appears to be the case especially for peer relationships. Positive social skills lead to peer acceptance, and status among peers is reasonably stable across the early school years. As a result, relationships, especially among peers, have tremendous potential influence throughout the young child's academic life. The extent to which the nature of the child–teacher relationship may be amenable to intervention through professional development appears to be an important avenue for exploring the wider impact of relatively focused intervention.

IMPLICATIONS OF INTERRELATIONSHIPS AND FUTURE RESEARCH

Considering concurrent interrelationships, there are several implications for current practice and policies during children's transition to school. One immediate implication of these relationships is that current assessment strategies, which seek to quantify competency in specific areas, may be imposing (or assuming) an independence that does not exist. For example, if there is a relationship between mathematical competency and reading skill, the use of a reading-dependent measure to assess mathematics (e.g., using words problems) will confound mathematical problem solving with reading ability. Likewise, extremely long assessments may result in confounding performance for children with poor attention control or regulation skills, even though the content of the assessment (e.g., vocabulary) may be a strength. This conundrum has been recognized by the field and has generated two different responses. One argument is for "pure" assessments that minimize the potential confounding of domains through instrument design. This is an extension of classical assessment design through which scales are derived based on the relative strength of relationships among common items against other items, typically on other scales. So, for example, with instruments such as the Woodcock-Johnson (Woodcock & Johnson, 1989), subtests generally have very strong internal consistency, but the field has come to accept as reasonable some correlations among the subtests. A number of recent efforts have focused on the development of multidimensional measures specific to domains of school readiness (e.g., Atkins, Kelly, & Morrison, 2001; Crooks & Peters, 2005; Lutz, Fantuzzo, & McDermott, 2002). An alternative approach is to develop an assessment with a goal not to create independent scores for competencies but, rather, to apply assessments in naturally occurring contexts in which the domains of school readiness and achievement would be intertwined. Such approaches are advocated by a push toward authentic assessment (Meisels, 1994; Neisworth & Bagnato, 2004). Hirsh-Pasek, Kochanoff, Newcombe, and de Villiers (2005) called for assessments that focus on processes evidenced by child behavior habits, which may cross predefined construct boundaries.

The existence of these relationships validates and extends constructivist approaches to education that each child brings to school a unique set of attributes. However, this view is attenuated by research suggesting that although children vary, it is not necessary to drill down to individual student differences in tailoring instruction for children with differing skill sets. Rather, as shown in the cluster studies outlined previously, at least as far as identified school readiness skills are concerned, there is a finite set of group characteristics into which nearly all children fall. Although there is certainly variation within these groups, the analysis demands that cohesion within the group be stronger than cohesions to others, and thus there is a strong base of commonality that can be identified and potentially targeted with different instructional approaches. Children who are strong academically but less strong socially would benefit most from instruction that fosters social skill acquisition, coupled with more academic instruction. Similarly, children with strong social skills but relatively weaker academic skills may be delivered instruction in ways that capitalize on their strengths in support of their weaknesses. Of course, either of these strategies would require the identification of instructional strategies appropriate for children with differing characteristics.

CONCLUSION

It must be noted that many, but not all, of the studies cited in this chapter come from intervention studies, either targeted (such as efforts to address behavioral problems) or broad (such as Head Start), and the nature of interrelationships may be affected by intervention. Although intervention studies, especially randomized trials, hold the greatest strength in explanatory power, they may also enhance or suppress relationships among school readiness domains, especially to the extent that interventions are targeted at populations with sociodemographic characteristics that are associated with school readiness domains. This leads to two potentially fruitful avenues for additional work. First, more normative studies are needed to examine naturally occurring interrelationships, especially those that may arise among diverse populations of children. Second, intervention studies that target one of two or more related domains can identify the degree to which change in one domain has crossover effects on its correlates. To the degree to which these crossover effects can be documented, the current zeitgeist favoring complex, integrated interventions may prove less effective than more strategically employed interventions. The results of the cluster analyses described previously suggest that different types of interventions may prove to be more effective when delivered to children with differing skill sets. This is intuitively appealing, but data are still needed to clarify how students should be grouped to receive different types of interventions.

Finally, despite many acknowledgments that domains of school readiness are interrelated, the body of empirical study on many of these relationships is limited. Future efforts using more innovative designs and measurement strategies are needed to more fully explore the relations among domains. In particular, studies using cluster analysis and similar approaches are needed to replicate existing findings and to expand them by considering the degree to which cluster membership is stable over time and the degree to which cluster membership is affected by different types of intervention. Additional data on these relationships are beginning to surface from genetic studies (e.g., Dickens, 2005; Hohnen & Stevenson, 1999; Petrill, Deater-Deckard, Thompson, Dethome, & Shatschneider, 2006), and as the emerging field of educational neuroscience (e.g., Ansari & Coch, 2006; Noble, Tottenham, & Casey, 2005; Posner & Rothbart, 2005) starts to map domains of competence to brain structure and function, even more data on interrelationships will certainly add to the discourse. This chapter is intended as an initial effort at considering how domains of school readiness are or may be related and, it is hopeful, will prompt many more questions than it purports to answer. It is time for the field to move beyond acknowledging interrelations in favor of description, explanation, and translation into practice and policy.

REFERENCES

Aarnoutse, C., & van Leeuwe, J. (2000). Development of poor and better readers during the elementary school. *Educational Research and Evaluation, 6,* 251–278.

Achenbach, T. (1991). *Manual for the Child Behavior Checklist/4-18 and 1991 profile.* Burlington, VT: University of Vermont, Department of Psychiatry.

Ackerman, D.J., & Barnett, W.S. (2005). *Prepared for kindergarten: What does "readiness" mean?* New Brunswick, NJ: National Institute for Early Education Research.

Agostin, T.M., & Bain, S.K. (1997). Predicting early school success with developmental and social skills screeners. *Psychology in the Schools, 34,* 219–228.

Aldenderfer, M.S., & Blashfield, R.K. (1984). *Cluster analysis.* Beverly Hills, CA: Sage.

Ansari, D., & Coch, D. (2006). Bridges over troubled waters: Education and cognitive neuroscience. *Trends in Cognitive Sciences, 10,* 146–151.

Atkins, D.H., Kelly, K.T., & Morrison, G.S. (2001). Development of the child evaluation measure: An assessment of children's learning across disciplines and in multiple contexts. *Educational and Psychological Measurement, 61,* 505–511.

Ayoub, C.C., & Fischer, K.W. (2006). Developmental pathways and intersections among domains of development. In K. McCartney & D. Phillips (Eds.), *Blackwell handbook on early childhood development* (pp. 62–82). Malden, MA: Blackwell.

Bast, J., & Reitsma, P. (1998). Analyzing the development of individual differences in terms of Matthew effects in reading: Results from a Dutch longitudinal study. *Developmental Psychology, 34,* 1373–1399.

Birch, S.H., & Ladd, G.W. (1997). The teacher–child relationship and children's early school adjustment. *Journal of School Psychology, 35,* 61–79.

Blair, C. (2002). School readiness as propensity for engagement: Integrating cognition and emotion in a neurobiological conceptualization of child functioning at school entry. *American Psychologist, 57,* 111–127.

Blair, C., Zelazo, P.D., & Greenberg, M.T. (2005). The measurement of executive function in early childhood. *Developmental Neuropsychology, 28,* 561–571.

Bogard, K., & Takanishi, R. (2005). PK–3: An aligned and coordinated approach to education for children 3 to 8 years old. *Social Policy Reports, 19*(3), 3–21.

Bull, R., & Scerif, G. (2001). Executive functioning as a predictor of children's mathematics ability: Inhibition, switching, and working memory. *Developmental Neuropsychology, 19,* 273–293.

Bronson, M.B., Tivnan, T., & Seppanen, P.S. (1995). Relations between teacher and classroom activity variables and the classroom behaviors of prekindergarten children in Chapter I funded programs. *Journal of Applied Developmental Psychology, 16,* 253–282.

Campbell, F.A., Pungello, E.P., Miller-Johnson, S., Burchinal, M., & Ramey, C.T. (2001). The development of cognitive and academic abilities: Growth curves from an early childhood education experiment. *Developmental Psychology, 37,* 231–242.

Campbell, S.B., Pierce, E.W., March, C.L., Ewing, L.J., & Szumowski, E.K. (1994). Hard-to-manage preschool boys: Symptomatic behavior across contexts and time. *Child Development, 65,* 836–851.

Cantwell, D.P., & Satterfield, J.H. (1978). The prevalence of academic underachievement in hyperactive children. *Journal of Pediatric Psychology, 3,* 168–171.

Cappelletti, M.N., Butterworth, B., & Kopelman, M. (2001). Spared numerical abilities in a case of semantic dementia. *Neuropsychologia, 39,* 1224–1239.

Carey, S. (2001). Cognitive foundations of arithmetic: Evolution and ontogenesis. *Mind & Language, 16,* 37–55.

Carey, S. (2004). Bootstrapping and the origin of concepts. *Daedelus,* 59–68.

Carlton, M.P., & Winsler, A. (1999). School readiness: The need for a paradigm shift. *School Psychology Review, 28,* 338–352.

Chall, J.S. (1996). *Stages of reading development* (2nd ed.). Fort Worth, TX: Harcourt Brace.

Chall, J.S., Jacobs, V.A., & Baldwin, L.E. (1990). *The reading crisis: Why poor children fall behind.* Cambridge, MA: Harvard University Press.

Christian, K., Morrison, F.J., Frazier, J.A., & Massetti, G. (2000). Specificity in the nature and timing of cognitive growth in kindergarten and first grade. *Journal of Cognition and Development, 1,* 429–448.

Cipolotti, L., & van Harskamp, N. (2001). Disturbances of number processing and calculation. In R.E. Berndt (Ed.), *Handbook of neuropsychology* (pp. 305–334). Amsterdam: Elsevier.

Clements, D., Sarama, J., & DiBiase, A.M. (Eds.). (2004). *Engaging young children in mathematics: Findings of the 2000 national conference on standards for preschool and kindergarten mathematics education.* Mahwah, NJ: Lawrence Erlbaum Associates.

Colvig-Amir, L., Liu, D., & Mobilio, L. (2005). *Assessing school readiness in Santa Clara County: Results from the 2004 school readiness assessment project.* San Jose, CA: Applied Survey Research. Retrieved June 12, 2005, from http://www.appliedsurveyresearch.org/mainmenu.shtml

Coolahan, K., Fantuzzo, J., Mendez, J., & McDermott, P. (2000). Preschool peer interactions and readiness to learn: Relationships between classroom peer play and learning behaviors and conduct. *Journal of Educational Psychology, 92,* 458–465.

Cooper, D.H., & Farran, D.C. (1988). Behavioral risk factors in kindergarten. *Early Childhood Research Quarterly, 3,* 1–19.

Cooper, D.H., & Farran, D.C. (1991). *The Cooper-Farran Behavioral Rating Scale.* Brandon, VT: Clinical Psychology Publishing Company.

Cooper, D.H., & Speece, D.L. (1988). A novel methodology for the study of children at risk for school failure. *The Journal of Special Education, 22,* 186–198.

Crnic, K., & Lamberty, G. (1994, April). Reconsidering school readiness: Conceptual and applied perspectives. *Early Education and Development, 5*(2), 99–105.

Cronbach, L., & Gleser, G. (1953). Assessing similarity between profiles. *Psychological Bulletin, 50,* 456–473.

Crooks, C.V., & Peters, R.D. (2005). Predicting academic difficulties: Does a complex, multidimensional model outperform a unidimensional teacher rating scale? *Canadian Journal of Behavioural Science, 37,* 170–180.

Denham, S., Blair, K., DeMulder, E., Levitas, J., Sawyer, K., Auerbach-Major, S., et al. (2003). Preschool emotional competence: Pathway to social competence? *Child Development, 74,* 238–256.

Denton, K., & Germino-Hausken, E. (2000). *America's kindergartners* (NCES 2000-070). Washington, DC: U.S. Department of Education, National Center for Education Statistics.

Diamond, K.E., Reagan, A.J., & Bandyk, J.E. (2000). Parents' conceptions of kindergarten readiness: Relationships with race, ethnicity, and development. *The Journal of Educational Research, 94,* 93–100.

Dickens, W.T. (2005). Genetic differences in school readiness. *The Future of Children, 15,* 55–69.

Dockett, S., & Perry, B. (2003). The transition to school: What's important? *Educational Leadership, 60*(7), 30–33.

Doctoroff, G.L., Greer, J.A., & Arnold, D.H. (2006). The relationship between social behavior and emergent literacy among preschool boys and girls. *Applied Developmental Psychology, 27,* 1–13.

Eisenberg, N., Guthrie, I.K., Fabes, R.A., Shepard, S., Losoya, S., Murphy, B.C., et al. (2000). Prediction of elementary school children's externalizing problem behaviors from attentional and behavioral regulation and negative emotionality. *Child Development, 71,* 1367–1382.

Emig, C., Moore, A., & Scarupa, H.J. (2001). *School readiness: Helping communities get children ready for school and school ready for children.* Washington, DC: Child Trends.

Espy, K.A., McDiamind, M.M., Cwik, M.F., Stalets, M.M., Hamby, A., & Senn, T.E. (2004). The contribution of executive functions to emergent mathematical skills in preschool children. *Developmental Neuropsychology, 26,* 465–486.

Fantuzzo, J., Bulotsky, R., McDermott, P., Mosca, S., & Lutz, M.N. (2003). A multivariate analysis of emotional and behavioral adjustment and preschool educational outcomes. *School Psychology Review, 32,* 185–203.

Fantuzzo, J., & McWayne, C. (2002). The relationship between peer-play interactions in the family context and dimensions of school readiness for low-income preschool children. *Journal of Educational Psychology, 94,* 79–87.

Fantuzzo, J., Perry, M.A., & McDermott, P. (2004). Preschool approaches to learning and their relationship to other relevant classroom competencies for low-income children. *School Psychology Quarterly, 19,* 212–230.

Gelman, R., & Butterworth, B. (2005). Number and language: How are they related? *Trends in Cognitive Sciences, 9,* 6–10.

Glutting, J.J., McDermott, P.A., & Konold, T.R. (1997). Ontology, structure and diagnostic benefits of a normative subtest taxonomy from the WISC-III standardization sample. In D.P. Flanagan, J.L. Genshaft, & P.L. Harrison (Eds.), *Contemporary intellectual assessment: Theories, tests, and issues* (pp. 349–372). New York: Guilford.

Gordon, P. (2004). Numerical cognition without words: Evidence from Amazonia. *Science, 306,* 496–499.

Graves, M.F., Brunetti, G.J., & Slater, W.H. (1982). The reading vocabularies of primary-grade children of varying geographic and social backgrounds. In J.A. Harris & L.A. Harris (Eds.), *New inquiries in reading research and instruction* (pp. 99–104). Rochester, NY: National Reading Conference.

Gresham, F., & Elliott, S. (1990). *Social skills rating system.* Circle Pines, MN: American Guidance Service.

Hains, A.H., Fowler, S.A., Schwartz, I.S., Kottwitz, E., & Rosenhoetter, S. (1989). A comparison of preschool and kindergarten teacher expectations for school readiness. *Early Childhood Research Quarterly, 4,* 75–88.

Hair, E.C., Halle, T., Terry-Humen, E., and Calkins, J. (2003). *Naturally occurring patterns of school readiness: How the multiple dimensions of school readiness fit together.* Paper presented at the 2003 biennial meeting for the Society for Research in Child Development, Tampa, FL.

Hair, E., Halle, T., Terry-Humen, E., Lavelle, B., & Calkins, J. (2006). Children's school readiness in the ECLS-K: Predictions to academic, health, and social outcomes in first grade. *Early Childhood Research Quarterly, 21*(4), 431–454.

Hamre, B.K., & Pianta, R.C. (2001). Early teacher–child relationships and the trajectory of children's school outcomes through eighth grade. *Child Development, 72,* 625–638.

Hamre, B.K., & Pianta, R.C. (2005). Can instructional and emotional support in the first-grade classroom make a difference for children at risk for school failure? *Child Development, 76,* 949–967.

Hart, B., & Risley, T.R. (1995). *Meaningful differences in the everyday experience of young American children.* Baltimore, MD: Paul H. Brookes Publishing Co.

Heaviside, S., & Farris, S. (1993). *Public school kindergarten teachers' views on children's readiness for school.* Washington, DC: National Center for Educational Statistics.

Hinshaw, S. (1992). Externalizing behavior problems and academic underachievement in childhood and adolescence: Causal relationships and underlying mechanisms. *Psychological Bulletin, 111,* 127–155.

Hirsch, E.D., Jr. (2003, Spring). Reading comprehension requires knowledge—of words and the world. *American Educator,* 10–29.

Hirsh-Pasek, K., Kochanoff, A., Newcombe, N.S., & de Villiers, J. (2005). Using scientific knowledge to inform preschool assessment: Making the case for "empirical validity." *Social Policy Report, 19*(1), 3–19.

Hohnen, B., & Stevenson, J. (1999). The structure of genetic influences on general cognitive, language, phonological, and reading abilities. *Developmental Psychology, 35,* 590–603.

Holborow, P.L., & Berry, P.S. (1986). Hyperactivity and learning disabilities. *Journal of Learning Disabilities, 19,* 426–431.

Horn, W.F., & Packard, T. (1985). Early identification of learning problems: A meta-analysis. *Journal of Educational Psychology, 77,* 597–607.

Kagan, S.L. (1990). Readiness 2000: Rethinking rhetoric and responsibility. *Phi Delta Kappan, 72,* 272–279.

Kilpatrick, J., Swafford, J., & Findell, B. (Eds.). (2001). *Adding it up.* Washington, DC: National Academies Press.

Konold, T.R., Glutting, J.J., & McDermott, P.A. (1997). The development and applied utility of a normative aptitude-achievement taxonomy for the Woodcock-Johnson Psycho-Educational Battery-Revised. *The Journal of Special Education, 31,* 212–232.

Konold, T.R., & Pianta, R.C. (2005). Empirically-derived, person-oriented patterns of school readiness in typically-developing children: Description and prediction to first-grade achievement. *Applied Developmental Science, 9,* 174–187.

Ladd, G.W. (1989). Children's social competence and social supports: Precursors to early school adjustment? In B. H. Schneider, G. Attili, J. Nadel, & R. Weissberg (Eds.), *Social competence in developmental perspective* (pp. 271–291). Amsterdam: Kluwer.

Ladd, G.W. (1990). Having friends, keeping friends, and being liked by peers in the classroom: Predictors of children's early school adjustment? *Child Development, 61,* 1081–1100.

Ladd, G.W., Birch, S.H., & Buhs, E.S. (1999). Children's social and scholastic lives in kindergarten: Related spheres of influence? *Child Development, 70,* 1373–1400.

Ladd, G.W., Herald, S.L., & Kochel, K.P. (2006). School readiness: Are there social prerequisites? *Early Education and Development, 17,* 115–150.

Ladd, G.W., Kochenderfer, B.J., & Coleman, C.C. (1996). Friendship quality as a predictor of young children's early school adjustment. *Child Development, 67,* 1103–1118.

Ladd, G.W., & Price, J.M. (1987). Predicting children's social and school adjustment following the transition from preschool to kindergarten. *Child Development, 58,* 1168–1189.

La Paro, K.M., & Pianta, R.C. (2001). Predicting children's competence in the early school years: A meta-analytic review. *Review of Educational Research, 70,* 443–484.

Lin, H.-L., Lawrence, F.R., & Gorrell, J. (2003). Kindergarten teachers' views of children's readiness for school. *Early Childhood Research Quarterly, 18,* 225–237.

Lipton, J.S., & Spelke, E.S. (2006). Preschool children master the logic of number words meanings. *Cognition, 98,* B57–B66.

Lutz, M.N., Fantuzzo, J., & McDermott, P. (2002). Multidimensional assessment of emotional and behavioral adjustment problems of low-income preschool children: Development and initial validation. *Early Childhood Research Quarterly, 17,* 338–355.

Luyten, H., Cremers-van, L.M.C.M. Wees, & Bosker, R.J. (2003). The Matthew effect in Dutch primary education: Differences between schools, cohorts, and pupils. *Research Papers in Education, 18*(2), 167–195.

Lyon, G.R., & Krasnegor, N.A. (Eds.). (1996). *Attention, memory, and executive function.* Baltimore: Paul H. Brookes Publishing Co.

Mashburn, A.J., & Pianta, R.C. (2006). Social relationships and school readiness. *Early Education and Development, 17,* 151–176.

McClelland, M.M., Morrison, F.J., & Holmes, D.L. (2000). Children at risk for early academic problems: The role of learning-related social skills. *Early Childhood Research Quarterly, 15,* 307–329.

McDermott, P.A. (1998). MEG: Megacluster analytic strategy for multistage hierarchical groupings with relocations and replications. *Educational and Psychological Measurement, 58,* 677–686.

McDermott, P.A., Green, L.F., Francis, J.M., & Stott, D.H. (2000). *Preschool Learning Behaviors Scale.* Philadelphia: Edumetric and Clinical Science.

McGee, R., & Share, D.L. (1988). Attention deficit disorder-hyperactivity and academic failure: Which comes first and what should be treated? *Journal of the American Academy of Child and Adolescent Psychiatry, 27,* 318–325.

McLean, J.F., & Hitch, G.J. (1999). Working memory impairments in children with specific arithmetic learning difficulties. *Journal of Experimental Clinical Psychology, 74,* 240–260.

McWayne, C.M., Fantuzzo, J.W., & McDermott, P.A. (2004). Preschool competency in context: An investigation of the unique contribution of child competencies to early academic success. *Developmental Psychology, 40,* 633–645.

Meisels, S.J. (1994). Designing meaningful measurements for early childhood. In B.L. Mallory & R.S. New (Eds.), *Diversity in developmentally appropriate practices* (pp. 202–222). New York: Teachers College Press.

Miles, S.B., & Stipek, D. (2006). Contemporaneous and longitudinal associations between social behavior and literacy achievement in a sample of low-income elementary school children. *Child Development, 77,* 103–117.

Mirsky, A.F., Anthony, B.J., Duncan, C.C., Ahearn, M.B., & Kellam, S.G. (1991). Analysis of elements of attention: A neuropsychological approach. *Neuropsychology Review, 2,* 109–145.

Mix, K.S., Huttenlocher, J., & Levine, D. (2002). *Quantitative development in infancy and early childhood.* Oxford, UK: Oxford University Press.

Morris, R., Blashfield, R., & Satz, P. (1981). Neuropsychology and cluster analysis: Potentials and pitfalls. *Journal of Clinical Neuropsychology, 3,* 79–99.

Musolino, J. (2004). The semantics and acquisition of number words: Integrating linguistic and developmental perspectives. *Cognition, 93,* 1–41.

Nagy, W.E., & Scott, J. (2000). Vocabulary processes. In M. Kamil, P. Mosenthal, P.D. Pearson, & R. Barr (Eds.), *Handbook of reading research* (Vol. 3). Mahwah, NJ: Lawrence Erlbaum Associates.

National Education Goals Panel. (1997). *Getting a good start in school.* Washington, DC: Author.

Neisworth, J.T., & Bagnato, S.J. (2004). The mismeasure of young children: The authentic assessment alternative. *Infants and Young Children, 17,* 198–212.

Neuman, S.B., & Dickinson, D. (2001). *Handbook of early literacy research.* New York: Guilford Press.

Neuman, S.B., & Roskos, K. (2005). The state of state pre-kindergarten standards. *Early Childhood Research Quarterly, 20,* 125–145.

NICHD Early Child Care Research Network. (2003). Do children's attention processes mediate the link between family predictors and school readiness? *Developmental Psychology, 39,* 581–593.

Noble, K.G., Tottenham, N., & Casey, B.J. (2005). Neuroscience perspectives on disparities in school readiness and cognitive achievement. *The Future of Children, 15,* 71–89.

Onatsu-Arvilommi, T., & Nurmi, J.-E. (2000). The role of task-avoidant and task-focused behaviors in the development of reading and mathematical skills during the first school year: A cross-lagged longitudinal study. *Journal of Educational Psychology, 92,* 478–491.

O'Neill, D.K., Pearce, M.J., & Pick, J.L. (2004). Preschool children's narratives and performance on the Peabody Individualized Achievement Test-Revised: Evidence of a relationship between early narrative and later mathematical ability. *First Language, 24,* 149–183.

Palisin, H. (1986). Preschool temperament and performance on achievement tests. *Developmental Psychology, 22,* 766–770.

Pennington, B.F. (1997). Dimensions of executive functions in normal and abnormal development. In N.A. Krasnegor, G.R. Lyon, & P.S. Goldman-Rakic (Eds.), *Development of the prefrontal cortex: Evolution, neurobiology, and behavior* (pp. 265–281). Baltimore: Paul H. Brookes Publishing Co.

Perner, J., & Lang, B. (1999). Development of theory of mind and executive control. *Trends in Cognitive Science, 3,* 337–344.

Petrill, S.A., Deater-Deckard, K., Thompson, L.A., Dethorne, L.S., & Shatschneider, C. (2006). Genetic and environmental effects of serial naming and phonological awareness on early reading outcomes. *Journal of Educational Psychology, 98,* 112–121.

Pianta, R.C. (1997). Adult–child relationship processes and early schooling. *Early Education and Development, 8,* 11–26.

Pianta, R.C. (2000). *Enhancing relationships between children and teachers.* Washington, DC: American Psychological Association.

Pianta, R.C., Steinberg, M., & Rollins, K. (1995). The first two years of school: Teacher–child relationships and deflections in children's school adjustment. *Development and Psychopathology, 7,* 295–312.

Pianta, R.C., & Stuhlman, M.W. (2004). Teacher–child relationships and children's success in the first years of school. *School Psychology Review, 33,* 444–458.

Piotrkowski, C.S. (2004). A community-based approach to school readiness in Head Start. In E. Zigler & S.J. Styfco (Eds.), *The Head Start debates* (pp. 129–142). Baltimore: Paul H. Brookes Publishing Co.

Piotrkowski, C.S., Botsko, M., & Matthews, E. (2000). Parents' and teachers' beliefs about children's school readiness in a high-need community. *Early Childhood Research Quarterly, 15,* 537–558.

Posner, M.I., & Rothbart, M.K. (2005). Influencing brain networks: Implications for education. *Trends in Cognitive Science, 9,* 99–103.

Rabiner, D., Coie, J.D., & Conduct Problems Prevention Research Group. (2000). Early attention problems and children's reading achievement: A longitudinal investigation. *Journal of the American Academy of Child and Adolescent Psychiatry, 39,* 859–867.

Raver, C.C. (2002). Emotions matter: Making the case for the role of young children's emotional development for early school readiness. *Social Policy Reports, 16*(3), 3–18.

Rossor, M.N., Warrington, E.K., & Cipolotti, L. (1995). The isolation of calculation skills. *Journal of Neurology, 242,* 78–81.

Sameroff, A., & Haith, M. (Eds.). (1996). *The five to seven year shift: The age of reason and responsibility.* Chicago: University of Chicago Press.

Sarnecka, B., & Gelman, S. (2004). Six does not just mean a lot: Preschoolers see number words as specific. *Cognition, 92,* 329–352.

Schaefer, B.A., & McDermott, P.A. (1999). Learning behavior and intelligence as explanations for children's scholastic achievement. *Journal of School Psychology, 37,* 299–313.

Scott-Little, C., Kagan, S.L., & Frelow, V.S. (2003). *Standards for preschool children's learning and development: Who has standards, how were they developed, and how are they used?* Greensboro, NC: SERVE. Retrieved June 23, 2005, from www.serve.org/ELO

Scott-Little, C., Kagan, S.L., & Frelow, V.S. (2006). Conceptualization of readiness and the content of early learning standards: The intersection of policy & research? *Early Childhood Research Quarterly, 21,* 153–173.

Shaywitz, B.A., Holford, T.R., Holahan, J.M., Fletcher, J.M., Stuebing, K.K., Francis, D.J., et al. (1995). A Matthew effect for IQ but not for reading: Results from a longitudinal study. *Reading Research Quarterly, 30,* 894–906.

Snow, C., Burns, M.S., & Griffin, P. (1998). *Preventing reading difficulties in young children.* Washington, DC: National Academies Press.

Snow, K. (2006a, June 27). Disentangling components of school readiness. In D.J. Armor (Chair), *Measuring readiness of Head Start children.* Symposium conducted at Head Start's 8th National Research Conference, Washington, DC.

Snow, K.L. (2006b). Measuring school readiness: Conceptual and practical considerations. *Early Education and Development, 17,* 7–41.

Speece, D.L., & Cooper, D.H. (1990). Ontogeny of school failure: Classification of first-grade children. *American Educational Research Journal, 27,* 119–140.

Spira, E.G., & Fischel, J.E. (2005). The impact of preschool inattention, hyperactivity, and impulsivity on social and academic development: A review. *Journal of Child Psychology and Psychiatry, 46,* 755–773.

Stanovich, K.E. (1986). Matthew effects in reading: Some consequences of individual differences in the acquisition of literacy. *Reading Research Quarterly, 21,* 360–407.

St. Clair-Thompson, H., & Gathercole, S.E. (2006). Executive functions and achievements in school: Shifting, updating, inhibition, and working memory. *The Quarterly Journal of Experimental Psychology, 59,* 745–759.

Sticht, T.G., Beck, L.J., Hauk, R.N., Kleiman, G.M., & James, J.H. (1974). *Auding and reading: A developmental model.* Alexandria, VA: Human Resources Research Organization.

Stott, D.H., Green, L.F., & Francis, J.M. (1983). Learning style and school attainment. *Human Learning, 2,* 61–75.

Walberg, H.J., & Tsai, S. (1983). Matthew effects in education. *American Educational Research Journal, 54,* 87–112.

Wentzel, K.R. (1999). Socio-emotional processes and interpersonal relationships: Implications for understanding motivation in school. *Journal of Educational Psychology, 91,* 76–97.

Wesley, P.W., & Buysse, V. (2003). Making meaning of school readiness in schools and communities. *Early Childhood Research Quarterly, 18,* 351–375.

West, J., Germino-Hausken, E., & Collins, M. (1995). *Readiness for kindergarten: Parent and teacher beliefs* (Statistics in brief). Washington, DC: National Center for Education Statistics.

Woodcock, R.W., & Johnson, M.B. (1989). *Woodcock-Johnson–Revised Tests of Cognitive Ability.* Chicago: Riverside.

Wright, C., Diener, M., & Kay, S.C. (2000). School readiness of low-income children at-risk for school failure. *Journal of Children & Poverty, 6,* 99–117.

Wynn, K. (1992). Addition and subtraction by human infants. *Nature, 358,* 749–750.

III

FAMILIES
AND
COMMUNITIES

11

DEMOGRAPHIC TRENDS AND THE TRANSITION YEARS

Donald J. Hernandez, Nancy A. Denton, and Suzanne E. Macartney

The success of children during the transition to kindergarten and the early grades of school is influenced by a wide range of social, economic, and educational circumstances experienced by children and their families. During the past 150 years, but especially since World War II, children's lives have been completely transformed by revolutionary changes in the factors mentioned previously (Hernandez, 1993, 1994, 2005). More recently, during the past 3 decades, rapid growth in the number of children in immigrant families (i.e., families with at least one immigrant parent) has become an additional demographic force leading to both rapid change and increasing diversity in the lives of children. This demographic transformation presents enormous new challenges and opportunities for policies and programs to ensure the educational success of all children.

This chapter begins with an overview of childhood poverty because limited economic resources constrain educational opportunities for many children. It then portrays demographic changes that underlie the emergence of a new American majority of which more than half of children will be members of race-ethnic minorities by about 2030. Next, it discusses important strengths that children experience in many immigrant and American-born families. The chapter then turns to challenges confronting many parents and families. Finally, additional challenges (e.g., limited parental education, high poverty rate) and opportunities (e.g., using bilingual skills to improve the competitiveness of the United States in the global economy) for children are discussed. The focus is on young children ages 0–8 years, particularly those in immigrant and race-ethnic minority families who are experiencing the greatest challenges. Except where another source is cited, results presented in this chapter are based

The authors wish to thank Ruby Takanishi for wise counsel, Jared Bernstein and his colleagues at the Economic Policy Institute for providing their basic budget estimates in electronic format and for their path-breaking research, and Charles T. Nelson for his indispensable advice in navigating the Current Population Survey data collection, files, and tax estimates. For computer assistance, we are indebted to Hui-Shien Tsao. Finally, the authors wish to thank the William and Flora Hewlett Foundation for supporting research that provided a basis for this chapter, as well as the Russell Sage Foundation and the Population Reference Bureau.

Items with Ruggles et al. (2004), as the source were calculated by the chapter authors from data collected by the United States Census 2000 using the IPUMS 5% microdata file created by Ruggles et al. (2004). These items are original to this chapter, not the U.S. Census Bureau or Ruggles et al. (2004).

218 Hernandez, Denton, & Macartney

on new analyses of data from U.S. Census 2000 using the Integrated Public Use Microdata Series (IPUMS) 5% microdata file prepared by Ruggles et al. (2004).

OVERVIEW OF CHILD POVERTY

Children in families with low incomes experience negative consequences for both cognitive functioning and school achievement compared with other children, particularly during the formative preschool and early elementary school years. Furthermore, extensive research has documented that the negative consequences of poverty are greater than the effects of the mother's education or of living in a one-parent family (Duncan & Brooks-Gunn, 1997; McLoyd, 1998). However, young children in various race-ethnic groups differ enormously in their exposure to poverty in the United States (see Appendix Table 11.1). Among Whites and Asians, 1 in 10 (9%–10%) young children ages 0–8 were found to be officially poor in Census 2000. Official poverty rates are much higher for other groups, doubling to 1 in 5 (19%) for Native Hawaiian and other Pacific Islander young children, climbing higher to 1 in 4 (26%) for Hispanic young children, and reaching a peak of about 1 in 3 (31%–33%) for Black and American Indian young children. (The official poverty thresholds in 1999 were $16,895 income for a family of four with two children and $13,423 income for a family of three with two children.)

As discussed in detail later in this chapter, however, scholars and others have extensively criticized the official poverty measure for underestimating the level of economic need in the United States (Citro & Michael, 1995; Hernandez, Denton, & Macartney, in press-a). An alternative baseline basic budget poverty measure, which takes into account the local costs of food, housing, other necessities, and transportation for parents to commute to work, indicates that poverty levels for Whites and Asians are 12%–17%, but 26% of Native Hawaiians and other Pacific Islanders are basic budget poor, and this jumps to 37%–41% for Hispanics, Blacks, and American Indians.

However, the baseline basic budget poverty measure is itself limited because it does not take into account the cost for child care/early childhood education, which is essential for many working parents and which can have important beneficial consequences for the educational success of children in elementary school and beyond. It also does not take into account the cost of health insurance, which can ensure timely access to preventive health care and to medical care for acute and chronic conditions, which, in turn, can affect the capacity of children to function effectively in school. A more comprehensive basic budget poverty measure that includes these costs classifies about one third (31%–33%) of White and Asian young children as poor, compared with one half to two thirds (51%–66%) of young children who are Hispanic, Black, American Indian, or Native Hawaiian or other Pacific Islander. Thus, many young children in the United States, particularly if they are race-ethnic minorities, do not have access to economic resources that are important for their cognitive development and academic success.

These differences in poverty are taking on new meaning in light of the enormous increase during the past 4 decades in the number of race-ethnic minority persons who are immigrating to the United States. Children and parents in immigrant families often confront additional barriers and challenges to educational and economic success because of circumstances associated with immigration from another country; perhaps most notable are the barriers posed by limited proficiency in the English language. More than 40% of Hispanic

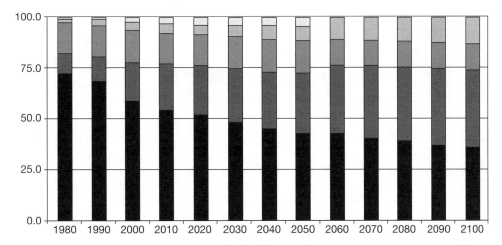

Figure 11.1. Percent of U.S. children ages 0–8 in specified race/ethnic groups, 1980–2100. (*Key:* ▨ American Indian [2000–2050 with Native Hawaiian and other Pacific Islander]; ▤ Asian/Native Hawaiian and other Pacific Islander [2000–2050 Asian alone, 2060–2100 includes American Indian]; ■ Black, Non-Hispanic; ■ Hispanic; ■ White, Non-Hispanic; *Sources:* U.S. Bureau of the Census, 1990, 2000, 2004.)

young children and more than 30% of Asian children live in families with a father or mother who is limited English proficient (see Appendix Table 11.1).

Immigration and the diverse countries of origin of children in immigrant families also are important because they are leading to the creation of a new American majority in which race-ethnic minorities will together constitute more than half of the population. The nature and implications of this demographic transformation are explored in the next section. Then, this chapter turns to a detailed discussion of the social, economic, and educational circumstances of children in specific race-ethnic and immigrant-origin groups.

THE NEW AMERICAN MAJORITY

The proportion of young children who are non-Hispanic White is projected by the U.S. Census Bureau to fall steadily in the future, dropping below 50% within 25 years (see Figure 11.1). The projections through 2050 in Figure 11.1 take into account the much larger Hispanic population identified in Census 2000. Projections and estimates for other years are from an earlier series released by the U.S. Census Bureau on January 13, 2000, and were based on the count of Hispanics in Census 1990. The corresponding rise of the new American majority does not, however, reflect the emergence of a single numerically dominant group but, rather, a mosaic of diverse race-ethnic groups from around the world. By 2030, the projections indicate that among all children, the proportions will be 26% Hispanic; 16% Black; 5% Asian; and 4% Native American, Hawaiian, or other Pacific Islander.

The Role of Immigration

Immigration and births to immigrants and their descents are the demographic forces driving this historic transformation. A century ago, an enormous wave of immigration brought

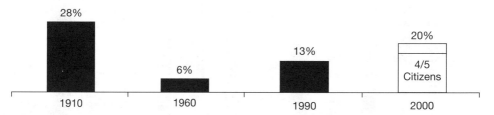

Figure 11.2.   Percent of children in immigrant families: 1910, 1960, 1990, and 2000. (*Source:* For 1910, 1960, and 1990 results, Hernandez & Darke, 1999; for 2000 results, Ruggles et al., 2004.)

many newcomers to the United States, and by 1910, more than one fourth of all children (28%) lived in immigrant families with at least one foreign-born parent (see Figure 11.2). Immigration plummeted during the era of the world wars and the Great Depression, and by 1960 only 6% of children lived in immigrant families. Beginning around 1965, a second great wave of immigration began sweeping across the United States, and the proportion of children in immigrant families climbed to 13% in 1990 and to 20% in 2000. In fact, between 1990 and 1997 alone, the number of children in immigrant families grew by 47%, compared with only 7% for U.S.-born children with U.S.-born parents (Hernandez & Charney, 1998). Thus, by 2000, one of every five children lived in immigrant families.

The past century also saw an enormous shift in the global origins of immigrants. In 1910, 97% of children in immigrant families had parents from Europe (87%) or Canada (10%), but this fell to only 14% by 2000 (see Figure 11.3; Hernandez & Darke, 1999). At the beginning of the 21st century, 62% of children in immigrant families had origins in Latin America, 22% had origins in Asia, and 2% had origins in Africa (see Appendix Table 11.2). Within these regions, the origins of children in immigrant families are quite diverse (Hernandez, 2004; Hernandez, Denton, & Macartney, in press-a).

Implications for All Americans

The emergence of race-ethnic minorities as the majority population is occurring most rapidly among children. In 2030, the baby-boom generation—born between 1946 and 1964—will be in the retirement ages of 66–84 years old. The Census Bureau's projections indicate that by 2030, 72% of older adults will be non-Hispanic White, compared with only 56% for working-age adults and 49% for young children (see Figure 11.4). As a result, as the growing elder population of the predominantly White baby-boom generation reaches retirement age, it will increasingly depend for its economic support during retirement on the productive activities and civic participation (e.g., voting) of working-age adults who are members of racial and ethnic minorities. Many of these working-age adults will, as children, have grown up in immigrant families. Although the year 2030 may seem far into the future, it is important to remember that children ages 0–8 in 2006 will be in the prime working ages of 24–32 in 2030. Immigrant and race-ethnic minority children of today will be providing economic resources to support the mainly non-Hispanic White baby boomers throughout their years of retirement. Therefore, the primary focus of this chapter is on circumstances of children in immigrant and race-ethnic minority groups.

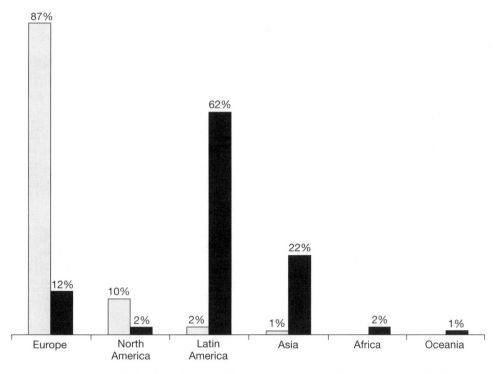

Figure 11.3.   Percent of children in immigrant families by region of origin, 2000. (*Key:* ▨ 1910, ■ 2000. *Source:* For 1910 results, Hernandez & Darke, 1999, for 2000 results, Ruggles et al., 2004.)

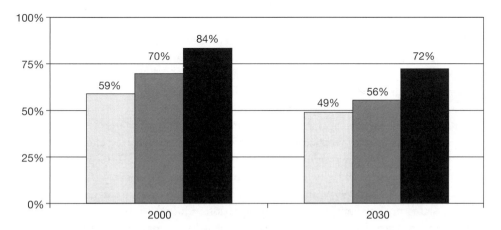

Figure 11.4.   Estimates and projected percent of Non-Hispanic Whites by age, 2000 and 2030. (*Key:* ▨ 0–8 years, ▨ 18–64 years, ■ 65 years and older. *Source:* U.S. Census Bureau, 2004.)

Geographic Spread of Children
in Immigrant and Race-Ethnic Minority Families

Young children in race-ethnic minority and immigrant families are highly concentrated in a few states but also spread widely across many states (see Appendix Table 11.3). Just five states—California, Texas, New York, Florida, and Illinois—account for 52% of race-ethnic minority young children and an even larger 64% of young children in immigrant families. In these states, 23%–49% of all young children live in immigrant families, and 41%–67% are race-ethnic minorities (see Appendix Table 11.4). However, in an additional seven states and the District of Columbia, at least 20% live in immigrant families and the proportion is at least 10% in an additional 15 states, many of which are in the Midwest (Kansas, Minnesota, Nebraska) and the south (Arkansas, Georgia, North Carolina, Virginia). Similarly, race-ethnic minority children constitute at least one half of all young children in five states (Arizona, California, Hawaii, New Mexico, and Texas) and the District of Columbia, at least 40% in an additional 10 states, and at least 25% in an additional 15 states. Thus, young children in immigrant families account for at least 10% of young children in 27 states (and the District of Columbia), and race-ethnic minority young children account for at least 25% of young children in 30 states (and the District of Columbia).

Generational and Citizenship
Status of Young Children in Immigrant Families

The overwhelming majority of young children in immigrant families are U.S. citizens because they were born in the United States. The proportion is 87% overall and 80% or more for nearly all of the countries and regions of origin discussed in this chapter (see Appendix Table 11.5). The proportions are slightly lower at 76% for Japan, 78% for Korea, and 60% for the former Soviet Union. Thus, all children in immigrant families have at least one immigrant parent, but the vast majority of young children in immigrant families are citizens. Although adult immigrants are increasingly likely to become U.S. citizens the longer they live in this country, many children in immigrant families lived in mixed-citizenship–status families with at least one citizen (often the child him- or herself) and one noncitizen (often a parent and sometimes other siblings).

The 1996 welfare reform drew a sharp distinction in eligibility criteria between citizens and immigrant noncitizens. For the first time, noncitizens became ineligible for important public benefits and services. As a consequence, noncitizen parents of young children who are not eligible for specific public benefits may be unaware of their children's eligibility, or they may be hesitant to contact government authorities on behalf of their children for fear of jeopardizing their own future opportunities to become citizens (Capps, Kenney, & Fix, 2003; Fix & Passel, 1999; Fix & Zimmermann, 1995; Hernandez & Charney, 1998; Zimmermann & Tumlin, 1999). In total, 64% of young children in immigrant families live in mixed-status nuclear families, and the proportions are highest among young children with origins in Mexico and Central America (75%–76%), followed by the Dominican Republic, Haiti, Cambodia, Laos, and the Hmong and Blacks from Africa (59%–68%; see Appendix Table 11.6). As shown later in this chapter, young children in immigrant families from these countries not only are most likely to live in mixed-citizenship–status nuclear families but also are among the groups with the highest poverty rates and, therefore, among those most in need of public benefits and services.

FAMILY STRENGTHS

Most young children live in families with two parents, and they often live with grandparents, other relatives, or nonrelatives in the home who provide nurturance or economic resources to children and their families.

Parents in the Home

Children living with two parents tend, on average, to be somewhat advantaged in their educational success compared with children in one-parent families (Cherlin, 1999; McLanahan & Sandefur, 1994). Young children in immigrant families from many regions are equally or more likely than Whites in native families (85%) to have two parents in the home (including stepparents and the cohabiting partners of parents). This includes young children with origins in Mexico, South America, Cuba, all major origin countries and regions in Asia, as well as Europe, and Whites from Africa (see Appendix Table 11.7). The proportions are nearly as high for young children in immigrant families from Central America and Blacks from Africa (81%–82%). Only among young children with origins in Cambodia and Caribbean Islands other than Cuba does the proportion fall to a lower range of 66%–74%. The proportions of young children living with two parents are also in about the same range for most race-ethnic minorities in native families: 63%–77%. Only two groups experience lower rates: at 52% for mainland-origin Puerto Ricans (children and parents born in one of the 50 states or the District of Columbia) and 43% for Blacks in native families. Thus, large majorities of young children in most immigrant and native groups benefit from having two parents in the home, although significant portions of all groups (at least 5%–10%) at any given time live with only one parent.

Siblings in the Home

The presence of brothers or sisters in a child's home can be beneficial but also a liability. Siblings provide companionship that may last a lifetime, but they also must share available family resources. Insofar as the time and finances of parents are limited, they must be spread more thinly in larger families than in smaller ones. Hence, aside from any benefits they experience, children in larger families, other things equal, tend to experience less educational success and to complete fewer years of schooling than children with fewer siblings (Blake, 1985, 1989; Hernandez, 1986).

Dependent siblings living at home are most likely to be sharing available resources. Young children in various groups differ substantially in the proportion living in large families with four or more siblings, ages 0–17, in the home (see Appendix Table 11.7). Young Hmong children in immigrant families are most likely to live in such large families (70%), followed by those with origins in Mexico, Haiti, Cambodia, Laos, Thailand, Iraq, Israel/Palestine, and Blacks from Africa (20%–35%). Young children in Native Hawaiian and other Pacific Islander families also often live in families this large (20%), whereas at least 13% live in families with four or more siblings among young children in native families who are Black, island-origin Puerto Rican (child or at least one parent born in Puerto Rico), mainland-origin Puerto Rican, Mexican, or American Indian, or in immigrant families from Central America, Vietnam, Pakistan/Bangladesh, Afghanistan, or the former Soviet Union. Thus, children with these race-ethnic groups and with these immigrant origins are more likely than others to experience both the benefits and the constraints of having many siblings in the home.

Grandparents, Other Relatives, and Nonrelatives in the Home

Grandparents, other relatives, and nonrelatives in the homes of young children can provide important nurturing, child care, and/or economic resources to families with young children. Most race-ethnic minority and immigrant groups are at least twice as likely as Whites in native families or in immigrant families from Europe and Canada to have a grandparent in the home (see Appendix Table 11.7). The proportion is 6% for these White groups compared with 13% for island-origin Puerto Ricans and 15%–23% for all other native race-ethnic minority groups. The proportion with a grandparent in the home is also between 11% and 24% of young children in most immigrant groups, with the exceptions only of those with origins in Japan, Israel/Palestine, and both Blacks and Whites from Africa.

Some groups also are likely to have other adult relatives age 18 or older in the home (see Appendix Table 11.7). The proportion is no more than 9% among Whites and Asians in native families and among nine immigrant origin groups, but this jumps to 20%–29% for young children in immigrant families who are from Central America, Dominican Republic, Haiti, Jamaica and other English-speaking Caribbean Islands, Cambodia, Laos, Thailand, Vietnam, and Afghanistan or who are Blacks from Africa or Hmong, and further to 33% for those from Mexico. Nonrelatives also are common among many of the groups with large numbers of other adult relatives, ranging between 5% and 7% for all native race-ethnic minority groups and between 5% and 15% for young children from Mexico, Central America, Dominican Republic, Haiti, Cambodia, Laos, and Vietnam and who are Blacks from Africa, as well as a few who are from other places (see Appendix Table 11.7).

Thus, many groups with large numbers of siblings also are especially likely to have grandparents, other relatives, or nonrelatives in the home who may be nurturing and providing child care for young children, as well as sharing economic resources with the children and their families. This is particularly likely to be the case for children in immigrant families from Mexico and Central America.

Parents' Commitment to Paid Work

Parents' paid work is the primary source of income for most children (Hernandez, 1993). The vast majority of young children with a father in the home have fathers who worked for pay during the past year (Appendix Tables 11.8a–11.8d). The proportion is at least 90% for most native and immigrant groups. The proportion is only slightly lower at 82%–85% for Blacks and island-origin Puerto Ricans in native families and for young children in immigrant families who are Hmong or from Dominican Republic, Iraq, or the Indochinese countries of Cambodia, Laos, or Thailand.

A majority of young children living with their mothers also have mothers who work for pay to support the family. The proportion among native race-ethnic groups ranges from 60% for island-origin Puerto Ricans to 78% for Blacks. Young children in immigrant families least likely to have a working mother are from Pakistan/Bangladesh (33%), Japan (39%), and Mexico, Afghanistan, Iraq, and Israel/Palestine (44%–48%). Among other immigrant groups, a majority have working mothers, and the highest rates (70% or more) are found among young children from Haiti, Jamaica, other English-speaking Caribbean countries; China; and the Philippines and children who are Blacks from Africa.

Many young children also live in homes with adult workers in addition to parents. Least likely to have such workers in the home (4%–8%) are Whites in native families; young children in immigrant families from Japan, Korea, Taiwan, Iran, Israel/Palestine, and Europe/Canada; and Whites from Africa. But the proportion is 15% or more among young children in native-born families who are Mexican and other Hispanic/Latino, Native Hawaiian and other Pacific Islander, as well as among children in immigrant families from Mexico and Central America (27%), most of the Caribbean (17%–19%), South America (19%), and all of the groups with Indochinese origins (15%–21%).

Thus, young children in both native and immigrant families live with fathers and mothers who are strongly committed to working for pay to support their families, and many native and immigrant groups also are likely to have additional adult workers in the home. It is especially noteworthy that among young children in immigrant families from Mexico, the largest immigrant group, 93% have working fathers. In addition, although they are among the groups least likely to have a working mother (48%), they are substantially more likely than all other native and immigrant groups, except Central Americans, to have another adult worker in the home, at 27% (compared with the next highest proportions of 21%–22% for only four other groups). In fact, young children in immigrant families from Mexico, along with those from Central America and the Philippines, are most likely to have three or more adult workers in the home (10%–11%) and to have four or more adult workers in the home (8%); see Appendix Table 11.9). Clearly, young children live in families with strong work ethics, regardless of their race-ethnicity or immigrant origins.

CHALLENGES CONFRONTING PARENTS AND FAMILIES

Most young children from native race-ethnic and immigrant groups live in strong families with two parents who are working to support their needs. Many, however, also have parents who cannot find full-time year-round work. Limited parental education and English-language skills can lead not only to part-time work and low pay, but also to high levels of family poverty. This section discusses these challenges, which have important consequences for the educational success of young children.

Parent Not Working Full-Time Year-Round

Despite the strong work ethic of parents, many young children live with fathers who cannot find full-time year-round work (see Appendix Tables 11.8a–11.8d). Among young

White children, 16% have fathers who do not work full-time year-round, the lowest level of any native or immigrant group. For other native race-ethnic minority groups (except Asians), the proportions range between 26% and 36%. At least 25% of young children in 18 of 31 immigrant groups also have fathers who do not work full-time year-round. The proportion is 30%–38% for four native groups (Blacks; island-origin Puerto Ricans; Native Hawaiian and other Pacific Islanders; American Indians) and for 13 immigrant groups from Latin America (Mexico, Central America), the Caribbean (Dominican Republic, Haiti), Indochina (the Hmong, Cambodia, Laos, Thailand), and West Asia (Pakistan/Bangladesh, Afghanistan, Iraq), as well as the former Soviet Union and those who are Blacks from Africa. For these young children, the proportion with a father not working full-time year-round approaches or exceeds twice the level experienced by Whites in native families.

Young children are much more likely to have mothers than fathers who do not work full-time year-round, no doubt in part because mothers often have greater responsibility for the day-to-day care of children than do fathers. However, a large number of dependent siblings in the home is not necessarily a strong indication of the amount that mothers work. The nine immigrant groups with the largest number of siblings include three with very low proportions (18%–21%) of mothers working full-time year-round (Mexico, Iraq, Israel/ Palestine), four with high proportions (38%–45%) of mothers working full-time (Haiti, Cambodia, Laos, Blacks from Africa), and two (the Hmong, Thailand) with intermediate proportions (32%–33%).

Parents' Low-Wage Work

Low hourly wages are most common among groups with high proportions of fathers not working full-time year-round (see Appendix Table 11.9). Among the 13 immigrant groups for whom 30%–38% have fathers not working full-time year-round, 8 experienced proportions of at least 35% with fathers earning below twice the value of the minimum wage, which amounts to $10.30 per hour (Mexico, Central America, Dominican Republic, Haiti, the Hmong, Laos, Afghanistan, Iraq). No additional immigrant group experienced this high level of father's low-wage work. Similarly, three of the four native groups with many fathers not working full-time year-round also had high proportions earning less than $10.30 per hour (Blacks, island-origin Puerto Ricans, American Indians). Among every other immigrant and native group with many fathers not working full-time year-round, at least 24% had fathers earning less than twice the minimum wage. The corresponding proportion for young Whites in native families is 19%. Not surprisingly, the groups with high proportions of fathers who have low hourly wages also have high proportions (usually in the range of 50%–70%) of mothers with low hourly earnings. Thus, lack of full-time year-round work for fathers goes hand in hand with low hourly earning for fathers and mothers in 18 immigrant and native groups.

Parents' Educational Levels

Limited parental educational attainments are common among young children in groups with fathers who often do not work full-time year-round and/or parents who often earn less than twice the federal minimum hourly wage. The proportions with fathers in the home in which the father is not a high school graduate for young children in native families is only 6%–10% for Asians and Whites, but 19% for Blacks and 21%–25% for mainland-origin Puerto Ricans, Mexicans, and American Indians (see Appendix Table 11.10). The level is similar for young children in immigrant families from Cuba (22%), Thailand (24%), and Vietnam (28%). Thirty-five percent of young island-origin Puerto Ricans have fathers not completing high school, nearly the level experienced by young children in immigrant families (38%–43%) who are Hmong or from Dominican Republic, Cambodia, Laos, and Iraq. Still higher, compared with the preceding groups, the proportion with a father not graduating from high school rises for young children in immigrant families to 54% for Central America and 67% for Mexico.

Among the groups with high proportions of fathers not working full-time year-round, only those from the former Soviet Union and Blacks from Africa are similar to White natives in the low proportion of fathers who have not graduated from high school (9%–10%). Although the proportions in these two groups with fathers earning less than $10.30 per hour (24%–26%) are higher than among native Whites (19%), this is less than the levels experienced by young children in other groups (29%–49%) who have high proportions of fathers not working full-time year-round.

Especially striking is that fathers of young children in many groups have not entered, let alone graduated from, high school. The proportion with fathers completing only 8 years of school or fewer is 9%–20% for island-origin Puerto Ricans and for young children in immigrant families from Haiti, Thailand, Vietnam, and Iraq, but 24% for Laos, 30%–31% for Central America and the Hmong, and 40% for Mexico. Results for mothers are broadly similar to those for fathers and are not discussed here but are presented in Appendix Table 11.10. It has long been known that children whose parents have completed fewer years of school tend, on average, to complete fewer years of school and to obtain lower paying jobs when they reach adulthood (Blau & Duncan, 1967; Featherman & Hauser, 1978; Sewell & Hauser, 1975; Sewell, Hauser, & Wolf, 1980).

Parents whose education does not extend beyond the elementary level may be especially limited in the knowledge needed to help their children succeed in school. Immigrant parents often have high educational aspirations for their children (Hernandez & Charney, 1998; Kao, 1999; Rumbaut, 1999), but they may have little knowledge about the U.S. educational system, particularly if they have themselves completed only a few years of school. Parents who have completed few years of schooling may, therefore, be less comfortable with the education system, less able to help their children with school work, and less able to effectively negotiate with teachers and the educational system. It may be especially important, therefore, for educators to focus special attention on the needs of island-origin Puerto Rican children and on children in immigrant families from Mexico and Central America, the Dominican Republic and Haiti, Indochina, and Iraq because these children are especially likely to have parents who have completed only a few years of school.

Parents' Limited English Proficiency

Parents with limited English skills are less likely to find well-paid, full-time, year-round employment than English-fluent parents, and they may be less able to help their children with school subjects taught in English. Because many early education centers and other institutions do not provide Spanish-language outreach to such parents, parents may also be cut off from getting access to programs important for their young children. Groups of young children with large proportions of limited–English-proficient parents also often are ones with limited parental education, high proportions not working full-time year-round, and high proportions earning low wages.

For example, the highest proportions with a limited–English-proficient father are for young children in immigrant families who are Hmong or from Mexico (69%–73%) and for those from Central America, Dominican Republic, Cambodia, Laos, and Vietnam (59%–64%; see Appendix Table 11.11). Very high proportions with a limited–English-proficient father also are experienced by young children in immigrant families from China (51%) and from Haiti, South America, Korea, Taiwan, Thailand, Afghanistan, Iraq, and the former Soviet Union (41%–47%). Many, although not all, of these regions also have high proportions of young children with parents who do not work full-time year-round, have low hourly earnings, or have limited educational attainments. Results for mothers are generally similar (see Appendix Table 11.11). Because some young children live with one parent who is limited English proficient and a second who is English fluent, the proportions with both parents limited English proficient are modestly lower (usually by 5%–15%) for all groups.

Linguistically Isolated Households

Some young children with limited–English-proficient parents have older siblings, other relatives, or other adults in the home who are fluent in English. The U.S. Census Bureau refers to households that do not include any English-fluent people older than age 13 as linguistically isolated households. At least one fourth of young children in immigrant families from most of the countries/regions presented in this chapter live in linguistically isolated households (see Appendix Table 11.11). The primary exceptions are children with origins in Cuba (20%); Jamaica and other English-speaking Caribbean countries (1%); and India, Iran, Israel/Palestine, and Europe other than the former Soviet Union and who are both Whites and Blacks from Africa (10%–15%). At least one fourth of young children from most other regions live in linguistically isolated households, and this rises from the preceding groups to 39%–49% for young children in immigrant families from Mexico, Central America, Dominican Republic, China, and Vietnam and who are Hmong. Children in these families may be largely isolated from English-speaking society and institutions.

Family Poverty

Children with poverty-level incomes often lack resources for decent housing, food, clothing, books, other educational resources, child care/early education, and health care. Children from low-income families also tend to experience a variety of negative developmental outcomes, including less success in school, lower educational attainments, and lower incomes during adulthood (Duncan & Brooks-Gunn, 1997; McLoyd, 1998; Sewell & Hauser, 1975). In fact, as noted previously, parental income has a greater influence on children's ability and academic achievements than do a mother's education level or living in a one-parent family (Duncan & Brooks-Gunn, 1997).

The official poverty rate is the measure most commonly used to assess economic need in the United States. However, this official measure has come under increasing criticism because it has been updated since 1965 only for inflation (but not for increases in the real standard of living) and because it does not take into account the local cost of living, which varies greatly across the United States (Citro & Michael, 1995; Hernandez, Denton, & Macartney, in press-a). To provide a more complete picture of economic need for young children, results are presented for the official measure and for two alternatives that take into account federal taxes and the local cost of various goods and services (Bernstein, Brocht, & Spade-Aguilar, 2000; Boushey, Brocht, Gundersen, & Bernstein, 2001; Hernandez, Denton, & Macartney, in press-a).

Young race-ethnic minority children in native families (except Asians) are two to four times more likely than Whites in native families to be officially poor (see Appendix Tables 11.12a–11.12f). The official poverty rate climbs from 9% for Whites and Asians in native families to 18%–22% for young children in native Mexican and Native Hawaiian and other Pacific Islander families, to 27%–30% for American Indians and mainland-origin Puerto Ricans, to a high of 35%–36% for Blacks and island-origin Puerto Ricans (see Figure 11.5). Young children in immigrant families also experience rates at this level if they are Hmong (36%); if they are from Mexico, Dominican Republic, or Cambodia (31%–32%); if they are from Central America, Haiti, Laos, Thailand, Pakistan/Bangladesh, Afghanistan, Iraq, or Israel/Palestine; or if they are Blacks from Africa (19%–28%; see Figure 11.6).

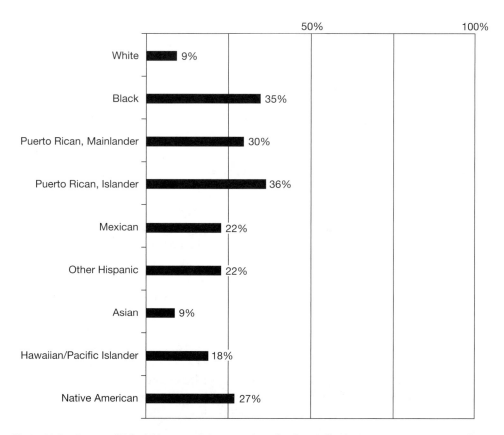

Figure 11.5. Percent of U.S. children ages 0–8 in native-born families in official poverty, 2000. (*Source:* Ruggles et al., 2004.)

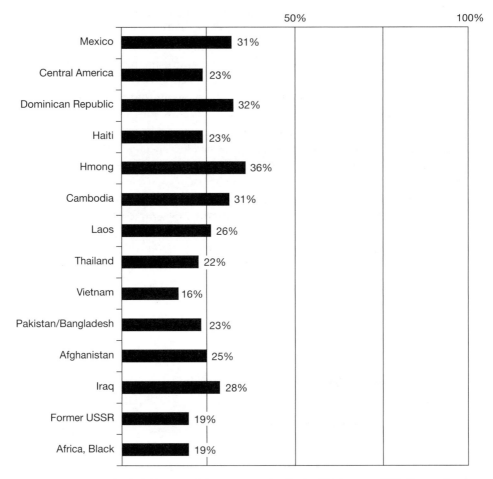

Figure 11.6. Percent of U.S. children ages 0–8 in immigrant families in official poverty, 2000. (*Source:* Ruggles et al., 2004.)

Thus, not surprisingly, official poverty rates are quite high among young children in most native race-ethnic minority groups and in most immigrant groups that experience low parental education, high parental limited English proficiency, high proportions with fathers not working full-time year-round, and/or high proportions with parents earning low hourly wages. Not all race-ethnic minority groups experience such high official poverty rates, but the vast majority of the groups that do experience high official poverty are race-ethnic minorities in native or immigrant families. The official poverty rate for Whites in native families is 9%, whereas the gaps separating these groups from Whites in native families range from 9% to 27%.

The first alternative measure of economic need presented here is the baseline basic budget poverty rate, which takes into account the local cost of food; housing; transportation for parents to commute to work; and other necessities such as clothing, personal care items, household supplies, telephone, television, school supplies, reading materials, music, and toys. The monthly cost in 1999 of decent, safe housing for a family with two parents and two children was, for example, $1,167 in San Francisco compared with $500 in Fresno, California (Boushey, Brocht, Gundersen, & Bernstein, 2001). The second more comprehensive basic budget poverty measure also takes into account the local cost of child care/early childhood education and health care, although it may somewhat overestimate the effect of the cost of child care/early childhood education and underestimate the effect of health care costs (Hernandez, Denton, & Macartney, in press-a).

The baseline basic budget poverty measure for young White children in native families is somewhat higher than the official rate (12% versus 9%), whereas the increases are somewhat larger for other native groups and for most other immigrant groups (see Figures 11.7 and 11.8). Thus, the gap in poverty separating White natives from the high-poverty native race-ethnic minority and immigrant groups expands from the range of 9%–27% using the official measure to 15%–33% for various groups using the baseline basic budget poverty rate.

The estimates based on the more comprehensive basic budget poverty measure tend to increase the gaps between Whites and most other groups by a similar amount, and the rates are quite high. The comprehensive basic budget poverty rate suggests that about 31% of young native White children are impoverished, taking into account the cost of child care/early childhood education and health care, whereas the rates for most native race-ethnic minority groups and high-poverty immigrant groups are in the 48%–82% range. In European countries, young children have access to nearly universal preschool and national health insurance programs, but this is not the case in the United States. Comparable

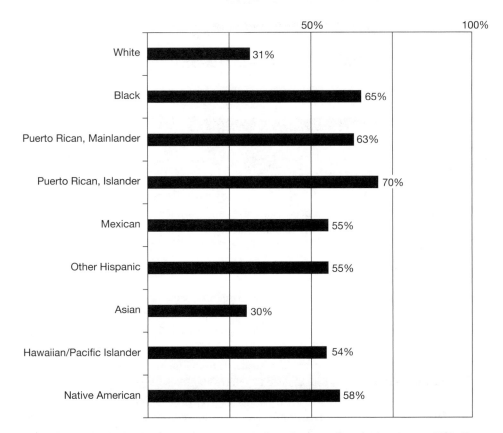

Figure 11.7. Percent of U.S. children ages 0–8 in native-born families in basic budget poverty, 2000. (*Source:* Ruggles et al., 2004.)

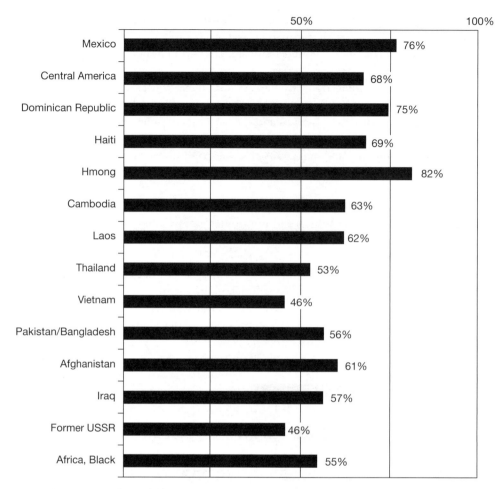

Figure 11.8. Percent of U.S. children ages 0–8 in immigrant families in basic budget poverty, 2000. (*Source:* Ruggles et al., 2004.)

poverty rates for children ages 0–17 are 2%–10% in the six European countries of Belgium, Denmark, Finland, France, Germany, and Sweden (Hernandez, Denton, & Macartney, 2006, in press-a; UNICEF, 2005).

Housing-Cost Burden

Limited income, combined with high housing costs, can force families to spend extraordinary portions of their incomes on housing. A household is defined as experiencing moderate housing-cost burden if it devotes at least 30% but less than 50% of its income to paying for housing (including utilities), whereas severe housing-cost burden is defined as paying 50% or more for housing (Bureau of the Census, 1994; Millennial Housing Commission, 2002). One fourth of young White children in native families (25%) experience moderate or severe housing-cost burden (see Appendix Table 11.13). The proportion is much higher for most native race-ethnic minority groups and most immigrant groups with high poverty rates, in the range of 34%–57%. Among the groups with the highest proportions experiencing moderate or severe housing-cost burden are several that tend to be concentrated in the high-cost New York metropolitan region: mainland and island-origin Puerto Ricans, at 45% and 47%, respectively, and young children in immigrant families from the Dominican Republic (50%) and Haiti (48%). The two groups experiencing the very highest proportions of moderate or severe housing-cost burden are young children in immigrant families from Iraq (52%) and Afghanistan (57%).

Overcrowded Housing

Overcrowded housing can make it difficult for a child to find a place to do homework and can also have negative consequences for behavioral adjustment and psychological health (Evans, Saegert, & Harris, 2001; Saegert, 1982). Young children are characterized in this chapter as living in overcrowded housing if they live in a home with more than one person per room (Bureau of the Census, 1994). Young Whites in native families are least likely to live in overcrowded housing, at 8% (see Appendix Table 11.13). Rates of overcrowding are at least twice as high for every other race-ethnic and immigrant group distinguished in this chapter, with the lone exception of children in immigrant families from Europe and Canada, which, at 14%, fall slightly short of double the White native rate. The rate of overcrowding exceeds 40% for 13 immigrant groups and Native Hawaiian and other Pacific Islanders.

Not surprisingly, the highest rates of overcrowding are for immigrant groups with very high poverty rates from Mexico (69%) and Central America (61%), Dominican Republic (49%), and Haiti (47%), as well as from Indochinese groups (45–80%), Pakistan/Bangladesh (53%), Afghanistan (42%), and Blacks from Africa (47%). These groups typically have high proportions of grandparents, other adult relatives, and/or nonrelatives in the home. These other household members can be a mixed blessing. On the one hand, they can provide important nurturing, child care, and financial resources for young children and their parents. But they can also contribute to overcrowding, with negative consequences for behavioral adjustment, psychological health, and access to quiet study space.

CHALLENGES AND OPPORTUNITIES FOR YOUNG CHILDREN

Beyond the major family strengths experienced by young children and key challenges confronting these children and their parents, several other circumstances pose additional challenges or notable opportunities. These pertain to the English language skills of young children, their enrollment in pre-K/nursery school, their housing situations, and their health insurance.

Young Children's English-Language Skills

The limited proficiency in English of many children in immigrant families may act as a barrier to success in English-only schools for these children. Overall, 36% of young children ages 5–8 in immigrant families are limited English proficient (see Appendix Table 11.11). The highest proportions are for young Hmong children (70%) and for young children in immigrant families from Mexico (52%); from Cambodia, Laos, and Vietnam (45%–46%); and from Central America, the Dominican Republic, and China (38%–42%). Between 30% and 35% also are limited English proficient if their origins are in Japan, Thailand,

Pakistan/Bangladesh, Afghanistan, and the former Soviet Union. Among native groups, children most likely to be limited English proficient are island-origin Puerto Ricans (30%) and mainland-origin Puerto Ricans and Mexicans (10%–12%). Most of these groups also are especially likely to live in poverty and to suffer from challenging circumstances discussed earlier in the chapter. Of course, the proportions of limited English proficiency are quite low for young children in immigrant families from some countries, particularly if English is widely spoken in the origin country—including Jamaica and other English-speaking Caribbean Islands (2%), Philippines, Europe other than the former Soviet Union (10%–11%), India, Iran, and Israel/Palestine—and for both Blacks and Whites from Africa (14%–20%).

Although many young children in immigrant families are limited English proficient, the same proportion (36%) speak a language other than English at home but also speak English very well (see Appendix Table 11.11). Thus, many young children in immigrant families are well positioned to become fluent bilingual speakers. The highest proportions (45%–54%) are found for young children in immigrant families from Central America, Cuba, Dominican Republic, South America, Taiwan, India, Pakistan/Bangladesh, Afghanistan, Iran, Iraq, and other West Asian countries. Even among young children in immigrant families from Mexico, which has the second-highest proportion of limited English proficiency (52%), a large 38% of these children speak Spanish at home but also speak English very well. Thus, with appropriate support from schools for both languages, these children might become proficient in both languages. Bilingual speakers are a valuable national resource for the United States in the increasingly competitive global economy.

Young Children's Pre-K/Nursery School Enrollment

Young children with origins in various regions and family migration circumstances experience quite different pre-K/nursery school enrollment rates (see Appendix Tables 11.14 and 11.15). The pre-K/nursery school enrollment rate for Whites in native families is 37% at age 3 and 61% at age 4. Four groups of young children in native families experience rates nearly this high or higher at ages 3 and/or 4 (Blacks, mainland-origin Puerto Ricans, Asians, and Native Hawaiian or other Pacific Islanders), as do young children in immigrant families from Haiti, Jamaica, other English-speaking Caribbean Islands, South America, several (mainly East) Asian countries, and former Soviet Union and other Europe/Canada and who are both Blacks and Whites from Africa.

But young children who experience much lower pre-K/nursery school enrollment rates include those in native families who are Mexican, island-origin Puerto Rican, or American Indian, and those in immigrant families from Mexico, Central America, Dominican Republic, Indochina, Pakistan/Bangladesh, and Iraq. The pre-K/nursery school enrollment rate gap between these groups and Whites in native families ranges between 4% and 21% at age 3, and these gaps rise to 5%–36% at age 4.

What accounts for the low enrollment rates of some groups? One possible reason sometimes cited, particularly for Hispanic immigrants, is more familistic cultural values leading parents to prefer that their children be cared for at home rather than in formal educational settings by nonrelatives (Liang, Fuller, & Singer, 2000; Takanishi, 2004; Uttal, 1999). But alternative explanations include the following socioeconomic or structural factors (Hernandez, Denton, & Macartney, in press-b).

First, cost can be an insurmountable barrier for poor families. Because of limited funding, most low-income families eligible for child care assistance do not receive such assistance (Mezey, Greenberg, & Schumacher, 2002). Second, parents with extremely limited educational attainments may not be aware that early education programs are important and are used by most highly educated parents to foster their children's educational success. Third, in immigrant neighborhoods with many non-English speakers, there may be too few openings in early education programs to accommodate the demand (Hill-Scott, 2005). Fourth, even if spaces are available, access may be limited for parents who are not proficient in English because programs may not reach out to parents in their home language (Matthews & Ewen, 2006). Fifth, parents may hesitate to enroll their children in programs that are not designed and implemented in a culturally competent manner, especially if teachers lack a minimal capacity to communicate with children in their home language (Holloway, Fuller, Rambaud, & Eggers-Pierola, 1997; Shonkoff & Phillips, 2000).

Recent research indicates that socioeconomic or structural influences, especially family poverty, mother's education, and parental occupation, account for most or all of the enrollment gap separating children in immigrant and native Mexican families and children in immigrant families from Central America and Indochina from White children in native families (Hernandez, Denton, & Macartney, in press-b). Depending on the age and the group, socioeconomic and structural factors account for at least half and perhaps all of the enrollment gap, whereas cultural influences account for no more than 14% of the gap for the Mexican groups, no more than 39% of the gap for the Central Americans, and no more than 17% for the Indochinese.

These results may be surprising, especially for the Hispanics, but it is important to note that these estimates are consistent with the strong commitment to early education in contemporary Mexico, where universal enrollment at age 3 will become obligatory in 2008–2009 (OECD Directorate for Education, 2006). In fact, in 2002–2003, 63% of children age 4 in Mexico were enrolled in preschool, the same as the proportion for White children in native families in Census 2000 (OECD Directorate for Education, 2006; see Appendix Table 11.14). Insofar as preschool is less costly in Mexico than in the United States, and insofar as poverty for the Mexican immigrant group in the United States is quite high, it is not surprising that the proportion enrolled in school for the immigrant Mexican group at age 4 in the United States at 45% is substantially lower than the age 4 enrollment in Mexico at 63%.

In summary, familistic cultural values are sometimes cited as a plausible explanation for lower early education enrollment rates among children in immigrant families than among White children in native families, but recent research indicates that socioeconomic and structural influences can account for at least 50% and for some groups essentially all of the gap. Early education programs have been found to promote school readiness and educational success in elementary school and beyond (Gormley, Gayer, Phillips, & Dawson, 2005; Haskins & Rouse, 2005; Lynch, 2004). Research suggests that children with low family incomes and limited English proficiency may be most likely to benefit from early education programs (Gormley & Gayer, 2005; Takanishi, 2004), but children in several groups challenged by these circumstances are less likely than Whites and the other groups noted above to be enrolled in early education programs. Insofar as the socioeconomic and structural barriers can account for much or all of the lower enrollment in early education programs for these groups, public policies could be developed and implemented to assure access to early education for these children.

Home Ownership and Residential Stability

Home ownership represents a financial investment in and personal commitment to the local community. Although 40% of young children in immigrant families have a parent who has lived in the United States for fewer than 10 years (see Appendix Table 11.6), young children in immigrant families live in families with rates of home ownership and residential stability that are not greatly different from young children in native families. Two thirds of young children in native families live in homes owned by their parents or the head of the household compared with one half of young children in immigrant families, but much of this difference disappears when groups with similar income levels are compared (see Appendix Table 11.13). For example, the proportion of young children in native families living in owned homes is 70%–75% for Whites and Asians but 30%–45% for Blacks, mainland and island-origin Puerto Ricans, and Native Hawaiians and other Pacific Islanders and 52%–55% for Mexicans and American Indians. Among young children in immigrant families with high poverty rates, the proportions in owned homes are 37%–46% for those from Mexico, Central America, Haiti, Pakistan/Bangladesh, and Cambodia and who are the Hmong and Blacks from Africa and 51%–56% for those with origins in Laos, Thailand, Afghanistan, and the former Soviet Union; this rises to 61% for young children in immigrant families from Iraq. Thus, many young children in immigrant families live with parents who are making strong financial commitments to their local communities through the purchase of their own homes.

Young children in immigrant and native families also have similar rates of residential mobility, 58% and 54%, respectively (see Appendix Table 11.6). There is little variation across groups. Among young children in native families, the proportion of various race-ethnic groups moving in the past 5 years ranges between 51% and 64%. Similarly, among young children in immigrant families, the proportion of most country-of-origin groups moving in the past 5 years ranged between 43% and 64% with only three exceptions: children with origins in Japan, Pakistan/Bangladesh (67%–68%), and the former Soviet Union (72%). Thus, migration rates for young children indicate that immigrant and native families have broadly similar commitments to staying in (or moving from) their local communities. Children in various groups are broadly similar in the challenges presented by changes in residence and the opportunities available to those who remain in their communities for longer periods of time.

Young Children Not Covered by Health Insurance

Young children and their families require good health to succeed in school and in work. Although Census 2000 does not measure health insurance coverage, good health and access to health care are of such importance that health insurance coverage estimates for a more restricted set of race-ethnic and immigrant origin groups are presented here based on the authors' calculations from the U.S. Census Bureau's Current Population Survey for 1998–2000. One in 10 young children in native families who are White, Asian, or American Indian (10%–11%) are not covered by health insurance (either private or public), but this rises to 14%–16% for other native race-ethnic groups. The proportion for children in immigrant families from the former Soviet Union and Yugoslavia is fairly low at 11%, but this jumps to 17% for those from Indochina, 19% for Blacks from Africa, 20% for the Dominican Republic,

26% for Central America, 32% for Mexico, and 38% for Haiti. Thus, many young children in immigrant families from countries of origin with high U.S. poverty rates are not covered by health insurance, jeopardizing their physical health and their capacity to fully realize their educational potential.

CONCLUSION

Among many features of children's lives influencing their success during the transition into and through the early school years, two critical factors are poverty and country of origin. The economic resources available in a family determine their access to decent housing, food, clothing, books and other educational resources, child care/early education, and health care. Children of immigrants live in families in which one or both parents may have only limited exposure to the U.S. educational system and to other features of U.S. culture that parents in native families can draw upon to facilitate their children's school success. The challenges posed by these circumstances can be compounded for children who live both in poverty and in immigrant families, and associated factors can place additional difficulties in the paths of these children, particularly if they are members of race-ethnic or cultural minority groups that confront social and economic discrimination or segregation.

Statistics presented in this chapter document the extent to which young race-ethnic minority children in native families (e.g., Blacks, Hispanics, American Indians, Native Hawaiian and other Pacific Islanders) experience circumstances that can impede their educational success compared with Whites and Asians, including high poverty rates, limited parental education, and, especially for Hispanics and American Indians, lower rates of pre-K/nursery school enrollment. Hispanics in native families also experience substantial levels of limited English proficiency.

However, this chapter has focused particularly on children in immigrant families because they are leading the creation of a new American majority in which race-ethnic minorities will together constitute more than half the population. First- and second-generation young children with immigrant origins in three sets of countries often experience poverty, low parental educational attainments, limited English proficiency, and other factors that can slow their educational progress.

The first set includes Mexico, Central America, Dominican Republic, and Haiti, all in the western hemisphere. Most of these children are Hispanic or Black, and they constitute 53% of all children in immigrant families. Despite higher levels of parental education and English fluency, Black children in immigrant families from Africa also experience high poverty, and they account for an additional 2% of children in immigrant families. Although Spanish is the official language of Dominican Republic, most Dominicans are at least partly of African origin. Altogether, about 6% of children in immigrant families are Blacks from Africa or are from Dominican Republic or Haiti.

Indochina encompasses a second set of origins for children who experience low parental education levels, high rates of poverty, and limited English proficiency (Cambodia, Laos, Thailand, Vietnam, and the Hmong). Immigration for these families was set in motion by much more traumatic events (related to the war in Vietnam) than for better-situated Asian immigrants from countries such as China, India, Japan, Korea, or the Philippines.

The third set consists of four nations: Iraq, Afghanistan, Pakistan, and Bangladesh. Most children in immigrant families from Iraq and Afghanistan are classified as White in Census

2000, whereas most from Pakistan or Bangladesh are classified as Asian. Perhaps more important in the cultural context of the United States, these countries of origin are almost universally Muslim. Children in immigrant families from these four nations also experience relatively high rates of poverty and limited English proficiency, although low parental education levels are especially common only for children with origins in Iraq. Taken together, children with origins in these four countries account for about 1.5% of all young children in immigrant families.

Despite these challenges, children in immigrant families from these (and most other) countries of origin also benefit from important strengths. Most live in two-parent families, and many have additional adults in the home who can supplement the care and nurturance provided by parents. The vast majority of homes also have fathers working for pay to support their families, and many have working mothers and/or other adult workers in the home supporting the family. Nevertheless, many of these children have parents who earn low hourly wages, many live in overcrowded housing, and children in immigrant families from these countries experience comparatively low rates of pre-K/nursery school enrollment.

It is important to reemphasize that as members of the predominantly White baby-boom generation will soon begin entering their years of retirement, and by 2030 they will be 66–84 years old, they also will increasingly depend for their support on the economic productivity of an increasingly Hispanic and non-White labor force, many of whom grew up in immigrant families. Young children ages 0–8 in immigrant families in 2006 will be in the prime working ages of 24–32 in 2030.

Most children in immigrant families benefit from living in two-parent families with a strong work ethnic. But parental educational attainments are low and poverty rates are high for more than a dozen countries of origin, which, together, include substantially more than one half of young children in immigrant families. These children are among those least likely to be enrolled in pre-K/nursery schools that could facilitate a successful transition to kindergarten and the early grades of school. The educational success of children in immigrant families, the vast majority of whom are U.S. citizens by birth, is important not only to these children and their parents but to all Americans. Public policies and programs fostering children's success are critical to the future of our nation.

REFERENCES

Bernstein, J., Brocht, C., & Spade-Aguilar, M. (2000). *How much is enough? Basic family budgets for working families.* Washington, DC: Economic Policy Institute.

Blake, J. (1985). Number of siblings and educational mobility. *American Sociological Review, 50*(1), 84–94.

Blake, J. (1989). *Family size and achievement.* Berkeley, CA: University of California Press.

Blau, P.M., & Duncan, O.D. (1967). *The American occupational structure.* New York: Wiley.

Boushey, H., Brocht, C., Gundersen, B., & Bernstein, J. (2001). *Hardships in America: The real story of working families.* Washington, DC: Economic Policy Institute.

Capps, R., Kenney, G., & Fix, M. (2003). Health insurance coverage of children in mixed-status immigrant families. *Snapshots of America's Children, 12.* Retrieved March 2, 2006, from http://www.urban.org/publications/310886.html

Cherlin, A.J. (1999). Going to extremes: Family structure, children's well-being, and social sciences. *Demography, 36*(4), 421–428.

Citro, C.F., & Michael, R.T. (1995). *Measuring poverty: A new approach.* Washington, DC: National Academies Press.

Duncan, G.J., & Brooks-Gunn, J. (Eds.). (1997). *Consequences of growing up poor.* New York: Russell Sage Foundation.

Evans, W.G., Saegert, S., & Harris, R. (2001). Residential density and psychological health among children in low-income families. *Environment and Behavior, 33*(2), 165–180.

Featherman, D.L., & Hauser, R.M. (1978). *Opportunity and change.* New York: Academic Press.

Fix, M., & Passel, J. (1999). *Trends in noncitizens' and citizens' use of public benefits following welfare reform: 1994–97.* Washington, DC: The Urban Institute.

Fix, M., & Zimmerman, W. (1995). When should immigrants receive benefits? In I.V. Sawhill (Ed.), *Welfare reform: An analysis of the issues.* Washington, DC: The Urban Institute.

Gormley, W.T., & Gayer, T. (2005). Promoting school readiness in Oklahoma: An evaluation of Tulsa's pre-k program. *Journal of Human Resources, 40*(3), 533–558.

Gormley, W.T., Jr., Gayer, T., Phillips, D., & Dawson, B. (2005). The effects of universal pre-k on cognitive development. *Developmental psychology, 41*(6), 872–884.

Haskins, R., & Rouse, C. (2005, Spring). Closing achievement gaps [Policy brief]. *The Future of Children,* 1–7. Available from http://www.futureofchildren.org/usr_doc/Policy_Brief__SPRING_2005pdf.pdf

Hernandez, D.J. (1986). Childhood in sociodemographic perspective. In R.H. Turner & J.F. Short, Jr. (Eds.), *Annual review of sociology* (Vol. 12, pp. 159–180). Palo Alto, CA: Annual Reviews.

Hernandez, D.J. (1993). *America's children: Resources from family, government, and the economy.* New York: Russell Sage Foundation.

Hernandez, D.J. (1994, Spring). Children's changing access to resources: A historical perspective. *Social Policy Report, VII*(1), 1–23. Available from Society for Research in Child Development, University of Michigan, 3131 S. State Street, Suite 302, Ann Arbor, MI 48108; 734-998-6578.

Hernandez, D.J. (2004). Demographic change and the life circumstances of immigrant families. *The Future of Children, Special Issue on Children of Immigrants, 14*(2), 17–47.

Hernandez, D.J. (2005). Changes in the demographics of families over the course of American history. In J. Heymann & C. Beem (Eds.), *Unfinished work: Building equality and democracy in an era of working families* (pp. 13–35). New York: The New Press.

Hernandez, D.J., & Charney, E. (Eds.). (1998). *From generation to generation: The health and well-being of children in immigrant families.* Washington, DC: National Academies Press.

Hernandez, D.J., & Darke, K. (1999). Socioeconomic and demographic risk factors and resources among children in immigrant and native-born families: 1910, 1960, 1990. In D.J. Hernandez (Ed.), *Children of immigrants: Health, adjustment, and public assistance* (pp. 19–125). Washington, DC: National Academies Press.

Hernandez, D.J., Denton, N.A., & Macartney, S.E. (in press-a). Child poverty in the U.S.: A new family budget approach with comparison to European countries. In H. Wintersberger, L. Alanen, T. Olk, & J. Qvortrup (Eds.), *Children's economic and social welfare.* Odense: University Press of Southern Denmark.

Hernandez, D.J., Denton, N.A., & Macartney, S.E. (in press-b). Early education programs: Differential access among young children in newcomer and native families. In M. Waters & R. Alba (Eds.), *The next generation: Immigrant youth and families in comparative perspective.* Ithaca, NY: Cornell University Press.

Hill-Scott, K. (2005). *Facilities technical report.* Los Angeles: First 5 LA.

Holloway, S.D., Fuller, B., Rimbaud, M.F., & Eggers-Pierola, C. (1997). *Through my own eyes: Single mothers and the cultures of poverty.* Cambridge, MA: Harvard University Press.

Kao, G. (1999). Psychological well-being and educational achievement among immigrant youth. In D.J. Hernandez (Ed.), *Children of immigrants: Health, adjustment, and public assistance* (pp. 410–477). Washington, DC: National Academies Press.

Liang, X., Fuller, B., & Singer J.D. (2000). Ethnic differences in child care selection: The influence of family structure, parental practices, and the home language. *Early Childhood Research Quarterly, 15*(3), 357–384.

Lynch, R.G. (2004). *Exceptional returns: Economic, fiscal and social benefits of investment in early childhood development.* Washington, DC: Economic Policy Institute.

Matthews, H., & Ewen, D. (2006). *Reaching all children? Understanding early care and education participation among immigrant families.* Washington, DC: Center for Law and Social Policy.

McLanahan, S., & Sandefur, G. (1994). *Growing up with a single parent: What hurts, what helps.* Cambridge, MA: Harvard University Press.

McLoyd, V. (1998). Socioeconomic disadvantage and child development. *American Psychologist, 53*(2), 185–204.

Mezey, J., Greenberg, M., & Schumacher, R. (2002). *The vast majority of federally-eligible children did not receive child care assistance in FY2000.* Washington, DC: Center for Law and Social Policy. Retrieved March 16, 2005, from http://www.clasp.org/publications/1in7ful.pdf

Millennial Housing Commission. (2002, May 20). *Meeting our nation's housing challenges: Report of the Bipartisan Millennial Housing Commission appointed by the Congress of the United States.* Washington, DC: U.S. Government Printing Office.

OECD Directorate for Education. (2006). *Early childhood education and care policy: Country note for Mexico.* Retrieved March 4, 2006, from www.oecd.org/dataoecd/11/39/34429196.pdf

Ruggles, S., Sobek, M., Alexander, T., Fitch, C.A., Goeken, R., Hall, P.K., et al. (2004). *Integrated Public Use Microdata Series: Version 3.0* [Machine-readable database]. Minneapolis, MN: Minnesota Population Center. Retrieved January 6, 2006, from http://www.ipums.org

Rumbaut, R.G. (1999). Passages to adulthood: The adaptation of children of immigrants in Southern California. In D.J. Hernandez (Ed.), *Children of immigrants: Health, adjustment, and public assistance* (pp. 478–545). Washington, DC: National Academies Press.

Saegert, S. (1982). Environment and children's mental health: Residential density and low income children. In A. Baum & J.E. Singer (Eds.), *Handbook of psychology and health, Vol. II. Issues in child health and adolescent health* (pp. 247–271). Hillsdale, NJ: Lawrence Erlbaum Associates.

Sewell, W.H., & Hauser, R.M. (1975). *Education, occupation and earnings.* New York: Academic Press.

Sewell, W.H., Hauser, R.M., & Wolf, W.C. (1980). Sex, schooling, and occupational status. *American Journal of Sociology, 83*(3), 551–583.

Shonkoff, J.P., & Phillips, D.A. (2000). *From neurons to neighborhoods: The science of early child development.* Washington, DC: National Academies Press.

Takanishi, R. (2004). Leveling the playing field: Supporting immigrant children from birth to eight. *The Future of Children, Special Issue on Children of Immigrants, 14*(2), 61–79.

UNICEF. (2005). *Child poverty in rich countries, 2005.* Innocenti Report Card No. 6. Florence, Italy: UNICEF Innocenti Research Centre.

U.S. Census Bureau. (1990). *Table QT-P1. Age and sex: 1990 universe: Hispanic origin population 1990 summary tape file 1 (STF 1) - 100-percent data geographic area: United States.* Retrieved July 5, 2000, from http://factfinder.census.gov/servlet/DatasetMainPageServlet?_program=DEC&_tabId=DEC1&_submenuId=datasets_1&_lang=en&_ts=179668739916

U.S. Census Bureau. (1994). *Housing of lower-income households* (Statistical Brief, SB/94/18). Retrieved January 9, 2006, from http://www.census.gov/aspd/www/statbrief/sb94_18.pdf

U.S. Census Bureau. (2000). *Final projections consistent with 1990 census (for 2000–2100) released by the Census Bureau on January 13, 2000.* Retrieved October 23, 2006, from http://www.census.gov/population/www/projections/popproj.html

U.S. Census Bureau. (2004). *Interim projections consistent with Census 2000 (for 2000–2050) released by the Census Bureau on March 18, 2004.* Retrieved October 23, 2006, from http://www.census.gov/population/www/projections/popproj.html

Uttal, L. (1999). Using kin for child care: Embedment in the socioeconomic networks of extended families. *Journal of Marriage and the Family, 61*(4), 845–857.

Zimmermann, W., & Tumlin, K. (1999). *Patchwork policies: State assistance for immigrants under welfare reform* (Occasional Paper No. 24). Washington, DC: The Urban Institute.

Chapter 11
Appendix

The data in this Appendix were compiled by Donald J. Hernandez, Nancy A. Denton, and Suzanne E. Macartney for the Center for Social and Demographic Analysis, University at Albany, State University of New York, with funding from The William and Flora Hewlitt Foundation.

Appendix Table 11.1. Percent officially poor or basic budget poor, and percent with father or mother limited English proficient, for children ages 0–8 by race–ethnicity

	Official poverty	Baseline basic budget poverty	Baseline basic budget poverty plus health care and child care/ ECE for all children	Father limited English proficient	Mother limited English proficient
Total	16.4	22.3	43.4	11.7	12.2
White	9.1	12.2	31.1	1.8	1.9
Black	33.0	40.7	64.2	3.1	2.7
Hispanic[a]	26.4	39.2	65.5	46.2	42.9
Asian	9.7	16.7	32.8	33.5	39.1
Hawaiian/Pacific Islander	18.8	26.0	50.9	3.3	3.4
American Indian	30.8	36.8	62.5	7.7	7.1

Source: U.S. Census Bureau, 2000.

Note: Race groups exclude Hispanics.

[a]Hispanic includes all Hispanic-origin children regardless of race.

Appendix Table 11.2.   Percent and number of children ages 0–8, by immigrant country or race-ethnic origin

Immigrant country or race/ethnic origin	Percent	Number
Total	100.0	33,681,915
Children in native-born families	79.4	26,732,109
White	57.0	19,181,106
Black	13.4	4,509,448
Puerto Rican, mainland origin	0.9	286,360
Puerto Rican, island origin	0.7	234,379
Mexican	3.8	1,271,262
Other Hispanic/Latino	1.7	576,684
Asian	0.6	200,233
Hawaiian/Pacific Islander	0.1	43,696
Native American	1.3	428,941
Children in immigrant families	20.7	6,949,806
Mexico	8.5	2,871,825
Central America	1.5	512,631
Cuba	0.3	112,960
Dominican Republic	0.5	171,863
Haiti	0.3	94,486
Jamaica	0.3	111,604
Caribbean, English speaking	0.3	107,876
South America	1.0	327,226
Japan	0.2	56,708
Korea	0.4	140,545
China	0.4	141,021
Hong Kong	0.1	43,516
Taiwan	0.2	50,415
Philippines	0.8	256,768
Hmong	0.1	31,301
Cambodia	0.1	36,410
Laos	0.1	43,028
Thailand	0.1	24,121
Vietnam[a]	0.6	192,936
India	0.6	184,426
Pakistan/Bangladesh	0.2	74,532
Afghanistan	0.0	9,358
Iran	0.1	47,205
Iraq	0.1	19,464
Israel/Palestine	0.1	37,257
Other West Asia	0.3	110,161
Former USSR	0.4	116,266
Other Europe, Canada[a]	1.8	604,911
Africa, Blacks	0.4	133,850
Africa, Whites[a]	0.2	67,693
Other	0.7	217,443

Source: U.S. Census Bureau, 2000.

[a] "Vietnam" includes Indochina not specified; "other Europe, Canada" includes Australia and New Zealand; "Africa, Whites" includes Asian Africans.

Appendix Table 11.3. Distribution across states of children ages 0–8 who are race–ethnic minorities or in immigrant families

	Percent of U.S. total living in each state	
State	Young children in minority families (%)	Young children in immigrant families (%)
United States, total	100.00	100.00
Alabama	1.37	0.29
Alaska	0.26	0.16
Arizona	2.56	2.65
Arkansas	0.66	0.29
California	21.61	30.71
Colorado	1.38	1.35
Connecticut	0.92	0.99
Delaware	0.25	0.14
District of Columbia	0.36	0.16
Florida	5.97	6.63
Georgia	3.38	1.84
Hawaii	0.80	0.56
Idaho	0.23	0.28
Illinois	4.75	4.97
Indiana	1.06	0.61
Iowa	0.29	0.33
Kansas	0.62	0.56
Kentucky	0.50	0.26
Louisiana	1.80	0.36
Maine	0.06	0.09
Maryland	2.02	1.47
Massachusetts	1.29	2.05
Michigan	2.46	1.59
Minnesota	0.71	0.90
Mississippi	1.25	0.13
Missouri	1.06	0.50
Montana	0.12	0.05
Nebraska	0.32	0.31
Nevada	0.93	1.17
New Hampshire	0.07	0.15
New Jersey	3.09	4.09
New Mexico	1.19	0.62
New York	7.23	9.69
North Carolina	2.51	1.45
North Dakota	0.07	0.04
Ohio	2.09	0.96
Oklahoma	1.12	0.44
Oregon	0.75	1.10
Pennsylvania	2.16	1.39
Rhode Island	0.22	0.36
South Carolina	1.36	0.36
South Dakota	0.13	0.06
Tennessee	1.30	0.52
Texas	12.47	11.95
Utah	0.49	0.68
Vermont	0.03	0.07
Virginia	2.15	1.71
Washington	1.55	2.12
West Virginia	0.11	0.07
Wisconsin	0.87	0.69
Wyoming	0.08	0.04

Source: U.S. Census Bureau, 2000.

Appendix Table 11.4. Percent of children ages 0–8 in the United States and in each state who are race–ethnic minorities or in immigrant families

	Percent who are	
State	Race-ethnic minorities	In immigrant families
United States	39.6	20.6
Alabama	34.9	3.9
Alaska	40.4	12.6
Arizona	51.9	28.1
Arkansas	28.3	6.5
California	66.8	49.0
Colorado	35.2	18.0
Connecticut	30.9	17.2
Delaware	35.2	10.3
District of Columbia	86.9	20.7
Florida	47.9	27.8
Georgia	44.1	12.5
Hawaii	83.6	28.8
Idaho	18.0	11.4
Illinois	41.1	22.5
Indiana	19.0	5.7
Iowa	11.5	6.8
Kansas	24.9	11.7
Kentucky	14.4	3.9
Louisiana	44.0	4.6
Maine	5.6	5.0
Maryland	43.3	16.4
Massachusetts	24.4	20.1
Michigan	27.1	9.1
Minnesota	16.3	10.6
Mississippi	46.9	2.6
Missouri	21.4	5.3

Appendix Table 11.4. *(continued)*

State	Percent who are	
	Race-ethnic minorities	In immigrant families
Montana	15.8	3.8
Nebraska	20.1	10.2
Nevada	49.2	32.3
New Hampshire	7.1	7.7
New Jersey	41.1	28.4
New Mexico	69.1	19.1
New York	44.3	30.9
North Carolina	36.2	10.9
North Dakota	12.7	4.3
Ohio	20.6	5.0
Oklahoma	36.2	7.5
Oregon	25.8	19.7
Pennsylvania	21.7	7.3
Rhode Island	26.4	22.1
South Carolina	39.6	5.5
South Dakota	19.1	4.3
Tennessee	26.6	5.5
Texas	59.6	29.9
Utah	18.8	13.5
Vermont	6.0	7.6
Virginia	35.3	14.6
Washington	29.4	20.9
West Virginia	7.5	2.6
Wisconsin	18.8	7.7
Wyoming	17.8	5.2

Source: U.S. Census Bureau, 2000.

Appendix Table 11.5. Percent who are first generation or second generation, for children ages 0–8 in immigrant families by country of origin

Country of origin	First generation (foreign born)	Second generation (U.S. born with foreign-born parents)
All immigrant origins	12.7	87.3
Mexico	12.0	88.0
Central America	7.7	92.3
Cuba	9.1	90.9
Dominican Republic	9.1	90.9
Haiti	10.2	89.8
Jamaica	6.2	93.8
Caribbean, English speaking	7.3	92.7
South America	15.3	84.7
Japan	24.5	75.5
Korea	22.2	77.8
China	23.2	76.8
Hong Kong	8.5	91.5
Taiwan	5.7	94.3
Philippines	7.4	92.6
Hmong	7.3	92.7
Cambodia	5.8	94.2
Laos	6.2	93.8
Thailand	27.3	72.7
Vietnam	9.9	90.1
India	17.4	82.6
Pakistan/Bangladesh	20.4	79.6
Afghanistan	7.2	92.8
Iran	5.0	95.0
Iraq	14.0	86.0
Israel/Palestine	12.6	87.4
Other West Asia	11.7	88.4
Former USSR	40.0	60.0
Other Europe, Canada	12.7	87.3
Africa, Blacks	15.6	84.4
Africa, Whites	13.3	86.8
Other	15.8	84.2

Source: U.S. Census Bureau, 2000.

Appendix Table 11.6. Family mobility and immigrant situation percentages, for children ages 0–8, by immigrant country or race/ethnic origin

	Parent in United States fewer than 10 years	Child moved in past 5 years[a]	One immigrant parent, one nonimmigrant parent	Mixed-status nuclear family[b]
Total	39.5	55.1	29.9	63.5
Children in native-born families	—	54.3	—	—
White	—	52.0	—	—
Black	—	60.9	—	—
Puerto Rican, mainland origin	—	60.2	—	—
Puerto Rican, island origin	33.0	63.8	—	—
Mexican	—	59.7	—	—
Other Hispanic/Latino	—	61.6	—	—
Asian	—	50.9	—	—
Hawaiian/Pacific Islander	—	62.3	—	—
Native American	—	56.1	—	—
Children in immigrant families	39.7	58.2	29.9	63.5
Mexico	41.2	59.2	23.2	75.2
Central America	34.6	57.8	23.5	75.6
Cuba	27.3	53.8	47.0	39.6
Dominican Republic	41.4	55.4	33.6	65.1
Haiti	39.5	55.6	15.2	61.0
Jamaica	28.1	54.3	43.7	56.1
Caribbean, English speaking	28.4	50.9	36.4	52.9
South America	40.1	62.4	39.1	57.2
Japan	54.3	67.9	51.7	57.3
Korea	34.6	64.8	25.5	47.0
China	44.4	56.0	8.0	56.0
Hong Kong	23.9	43.4	27.0	26.8
Taiwan	28.0	47.4	22.7	38.5
Philippines	36.5	55.4	41.5	43.8
Hmong	29.7	54.5	4.0	68.1
Cambodia	15.7	51.4	12.6	59.2
Laos	17.0	51.5	14.2	60.6
Thailand	33.6	55.6	39.4	51.5
Vietnam[c]	37.1	52.5	13.2	41.2
India	57.9	61.7	9.2	58.8
Pakistan/Bangladesh	62.6	67.0	8.4	56.5
Afghanistan	39.4	55.6	9.9	44.5
Iran	21.2	49.2	37.5	35.6
Iraq	52.6	59.5	19.2	44.5
Israel/Palestine	35.6	49.2	50.7	40.0
Other West Asia	43.1	54.3	29.9	41.7
Former USSR	58.5	71.6	12.0	48.0
Other Europe, Canada[d]	35.4	56.1	62.2	54.9
Africa, Blacks	55.9	64.2	18.4	60.7
Africa, Whites[e]	44.7	57.1	44.3	47.4
Other	37.2	58.3	62.5	57.4

Source: U.S. Census Bureau, 2000.

Note: Dashes indicate that sample size is too small to produce statistically reliable results or that category does not apply to the native group.

[a]For children ages 5–17 years.

[b]At least one sibling or parent is not a U.S. citizen, and at least one sibling or parent is a U.S. citizen.

[c]"Vietnam" includes Indochina not specified.

[d]"Other Europe, Canada" includes Australia and New Zealand.

[e]"Africa, Whites" includes Asian Africans.

Appendix Table 11.7. Family composition in the home percentages, children ages 0–8, by immigrant country or race/ethnic origin

	Two-parent family	Mother-only family	Father-only family	Four or more siblings ages 0–17	Two or more nuclear families in home[a]	Grandparent in home	"Responsible" grandparent[b]	Child 0–17 other than sibling in home	Other adult relative in home	Non-relative in home
Total	77.7	19.1	3.3	13.3	1.4	10.0	3.3	5.4	10.9	4.6
Children in native-born families	75.4	21.2	3.4	12.3	1.1	9.1	3.4	4.3	7.7	3.6
White	84.9	12.3	2.8	10.8	0.5	6.0	2.0	2.4	5.2	2.8
Black	42.8	52.3	5.0	17.1	2.3	16.7	7.4	8.9	14.0	5.1
Puerto Rican, mainland origin	52.1	43.2	4.8	13.4	2.4	16.5	6.6	8.5	13.4	5.6
Puerto Rican, island origin	64.4	32.2	3.4	17.2	2.1	12.7	4.2	8.2	16.2	5.2
Mexican	64.0	30.8	5.2	14.4	3.6	20.2	7.7	10.7	15.2	6.3
Other Hispanic/Latino	63.1	32.5	4.4	12.9	2.5	17.4	6.9	8.4	12.2	5.5
Asian	76.8	17.7	5.5	9.0	1.6	14.7	4.5	4.9	8.7	5.2
Hawaiian/Pacific Islander	70.4	24.1	5.5	20.0	3.3	22.5	8.7	10.6	17.9	6.5
Native American	68.6	25.5	5.9	18.0	2.4	14.8	6.9	8.7	14.4	5.5
Children in immigrant families	86.4	10.9	2.7	17.0	2.4	13.3	2.9	9.5	23.1	8.4
Mexico	86.2	10.6	3.1	23.1	4.0	13.0	3.1	15.5	32.9	12.1
Central America	81.5	14.6	3.8	14.8	2.7	14.4	3.7	12.2	29.0	14.5
Cuba	85.4	12.0	2.6	9.7	1.1	16.3	3.3	3.7	11.7	5.1
Dominican Republic	66.5	29.6	3.9	11.6	2.3	16.7	5.2	8.9	24.6	8.8
Haiti	73.7	23.3	3.0	20.7	1.5	15.3	3.3	8.1	26.6	6.9
Jamaica	66.6	28.8	4.6	12.3	1.9	15.9	4.7	8.4	20.0	5.6
Caribbean, English speaking	72.6	23.5	3.9	10.7	1.3	15.8	4.2	6.7	20.7	4.8
South America	85.6	11.9	2.5	8.5	1.7	13.5	2.7	6.5	19.1	9.1

Japan	94.2	5.1	0.7	7.1	0.2	3.4	0.8	0.6	3.6	2.0
Korea	92.8	5.9	1.4	3.5	0.1	11.8	1.9	1.5	7.7	2.3
China	90.7	7.5	1.8	4.1	1.1	23.5	5.0	3.3	12.0	4.0
Hong Kong	95.9	3.0	1.1	4.1	0.5	18.3	4.2	1.4	10.1	2.3
Taiwan	93.4	5.4	1.2	3.5	0.1	11.1	1.3	1.2	7.0	3.0
Philippines	87.8	10.1	2.1	9.3	1.9	23.8	4.3	6.1	18.6	6.6
Hmong	91.5	7.2	1.4	70.2	3.1	23.5	1.9	10.8	28.0	3.4
Cambodia	74.2	22.4	3.4	32.2	2.5	23.2	4.8	10.0	26.7	8.4
Laos	86.8	9.6	3.6	35.2	2.0	22.0	3.6	10.3	26.3	6.3
Thailand	87.5	10.2	2.3	27.8	3.7	19.5	3.5	9.8	20.4	4.8
Vietnam[c]	86.7	10.5	2.8	14.9	1.5	17.8	3.7	5.5	21.4	6.7
India	95.1	3.3	1.6	3.9	1.0	18.4	2.2	3.1	11.2	2.7
Pakistan/Bangladesh	94.0	3.8	2.1	18.5	1.4	14.6	2.6	5.0	19.1	4.0
Afghanistan	92.3	4.4	3.3	18.8	1.3	12.0	1.4	5.9	20.9	2.8
Iran	93.9	4.5	1.5	7.7	0.0	13.4	1.2	0.6	9.1	2.2
Iraq	93.0	5.0	1.9	24.0	0.6	13.1	2.3	3.7	14.6	0.8
Israel/Palestine	95.6	3.7	0.8	28.3	0.6	4.1	1.1	1.7	9.2	2.1
Other West Asia	94.3	3.7	2.0	18.3	0.8	10.2	1.6	2.6	10.8	2.9
Former USSR	90.7	7.4	1.9	17.0	0.3	12.3	2.2	1.6	9.1	2.4
Other Europe, Canada[d]	92.5	6.3	1.2	9.7	0.4	6.0	1.0	1.7	6.5	2.5
Africa, Blacks	80.8	15.3	4.0	21.9	0.6	8.5	1.4	5.6	21.1	5.2
Africa, Whites[e]	93.8	4.9	1.3	9.7	0.4	6.8	0.9	1.6	7.9	2.8
Other	90.6	7.9	1.6	15.1	0.7	6.1	1.4	3.2	9.1	3.1

Source: U.S. Census Bureau, 2000.

[a] A nuclear family consists of at least one child and the child's parent(s).

[b] Grandparents who have primary responsibility for the care of their grandchildren.

[c] "Vietnam" includes Indochina not specified.

[d] "Other Europe, Canada" includes Australia and New Zealand.

[e] "Africa, Whites" includes Asian Africans.

249

Appendix Table 11.8a. Parental employment percentages, for children ages 0–8, by immigrant country or race/ethnic origin

	Father works full time[a]	Father works part time[b]	Father does not work	Mother works full time	Mother works part time	Mother does not work	Other adult worker in home[c]
Total	78.7	16.5	4.8	32.8	36.2	31.1	11.6
Children in native-born families	81.0	14.7	4.2	34.1	38.1	27.8	9.5
White	84.1	13.0	2.9	32.7	38.6	28.7	7.7
Black	65.9	22.4	11.8	40.6	37.0	22.4	13.2
Puerto Rican, mainland origin	72.3	18.5	9.2	34.2	35.3	30.6	13.4
Puerto Rican, island origin	63.6	21.8	14.6	28.0	32.3	39.7	10.6
Mexican	72.9	20.6	6.4	34.7	36.2	29.1	17.7
Other Hispanic/Latino	74.5	19.6	5.9	34.7	37.0	28.3	14.8
Asian	80.4	15.6	4.0	37.1	35.5	27.4	14.0
Hawaiian/Pacific Islander	68.8	23.2	8.0	32.6	36.0	31.4	21.1
Native American	64.4	26.2	9.4	30.9	39.4	29.6	12.9
Children in immigrant families	70.8	22.6	6.6	27.5	28.9	43.5	19.8
Mexico	65.4	27.5	7.1	20.8	27.6	51.7	26.9
Central America	69.1	24.0	7.0	29.3	31.6	39.2	27.2
Cuba	77.7	16.7	5.6	40.6	28.4	30.9	14.2
Dominican Republic	62.0	25.5	12.5	29.8	31.0	39.2	19.3
Haiti	68.9	21.0	10.0	44.5	29.8	25.6	17.9
Jamaica	71.2	19.9	8.9	50.4	30.8	18.9	17.7
Caribbean, English speaking	73.6	18.8	7.5	42.5	27.1	30.3	17.0
South America	74.5	20.3	5.2	29.8	31.9	38.3	18.7
Japan	79.1	17.2	3.7	17.6	21.7	60.7	3.5
Korea	74.8	19.3	5.9	26.5	26.6	47.0	7.4

China	75.6	19.0	5.4	41.2	29.0	29.8	14.3
Hong Kong	80.8	15.7	3.4	42.8	26.1	31.0	10.7
Taiwan	82.4	13.5	4.1	35.4	23.7	40.9	6.4
Philippines	77.1	17.4	5.5	48.8	29.4	21.7	21.5
Hmong	62.6	20.4	17.0	32.0	27.9	40.1	16.7
Cambodia	64.3	18.7	17.0	38.2	22.4	39.4	18.3
Laos	66.6	19.6	13.7	40.4	27.4	32.2	20.8
Thailand	66.3	18.6	15.1	33.0	30.0	37.0	15.1
Vietnam[d]	74.6	18.6	6.9	36.8	28.1	35.1	20.1
India	80.9	15.1	4.0	31.8	25.4	42.8	12.3
Pakistan/Bangladesh	70.3	25.0	4.8	13.1	19.9	67.0	13.5
Afghanistan	68.0	24.9	7.0	17.9	27.7	54.4	12.6
Iran	82.4	14.0	3.6	25.1	30.8	44.0	7.1
Iraq	68.9	17.8	13.3	18.5	25.2	56.3	11.0
Israel/Palestine	74.3	18.3	7.3	17.9	27.1	55.0	5.3
Other West Asia	73.1	18.6	8.3	16.7	23.6	59.7	8.0
Former USSR	68.7	23.0	8.3	27.3	32.2	40.5	9.1
Other Europe, Canada[e]	80.0	16.2	3.9	27.8	33.2	39.0	7.0
Africa, Blacks	68.6	24.5	6.9	38.1	33.3	28.6	12.8
Africa, Whites[f]	76.2	19.6	4.3	24.9	29.6	45.5	6.1
Other	79.8	15.4	4.8	28.4	33.8	37.8	7.5

Source: U.S. Census Bureau, 2000.

[a]Full time indicates the parent works 35 hours per week or more, 48 weeks a year or more.

[b]Part time indicates the parent works less than full time.

[c]Adult workers are age 18 or more, earning $2,500 per year or more.

[d]"Vietnam" includes Indochina not specified.

[e]"Other Europe, Canada" includes Australia and New Zealand.

[f]"Africa, Whites" includes Asian Africans.

Appendix Table 11.8b. Parental employment percentages, for children ages 0–8, by immigrant country or race/ethnic origin

	Father full time, mother full time[a]	Father full time, mother part time[b]	Father full time, mother not working	Father part time, mother full time	Father part time, mother part time	Father part time, mother not working	Father not working, mother working	Neither parent working
Total	25.8	28.1	25.7	4.1	6.7	5.4	2.5	1.8
Children in native-born families	27.2	30.7	24.1	4.1	6.3	3.9	2.4	1.3
White	26.5	32.3	25.8	3.5	5.6	3.6	1.7	0.9
Black	34.3	22.1	12.2	7.6	9.8	4.2	6.5	3.2
Puerto Rican, mainland origin	28.3	24.9	21.2	5.3	7.1	5.4	4.8	3.0
Puerto Rican, island origin	23.3	20.2	21.2	4.9	8.9	7.8	5.7	8.0
Mexican	27.2	25.8	21.6	5.4	8.8	5.8	3.0	2.4
Other Hispanic/Latino	27.4	26.4	22.4	4.6	8.8	5.4	3.0	2.0
Asian	30.0	28.4	23.6	4.9	6.0	3.7	2.1	1.3
Hawaiian/Pacific Islander	24.8	23.2	22.8	5.0	9.0	7.9	4.1	3.2
Native American	22.3	25.0	18.8	6.2	11.6	7.7	4.5	3.9
Children in immigrant families	21.0	19.3	30.9	4.1	7.9	10.5	2.8	3.5
Mexico	15.1	16.5	34.2	3.4	9.2	14.8	2.6	4.1
Central America	21.7	20.1	27.7	4.6	9.3	9.9	3.2	3.4
Cuba	34.4	20.4	23.5	4.3	6.5	5.8	2.9	2.2
Dominican Republic	21.2	17.9	23.8	6.0	10.0	9.3	5.9	5.9
Haiti	33.6	18.1	17.5	7.3	9.4	4.4	5.4	4.3
Jamaica	38.9	20.2	12.8	8.5	7.5	3.6	5.7	2.8
Caribbean, English speaking	33.0	18.0	23.3	6.1	6.2	6.2	4.6	2.5
South America	23.3	22.4	29.1	4.1	8.1	8.0	2.2	2.9
Japan	13.4	16.8	49.0	2.2	3.5	11.5	1.6	2.1
Korea	21.9	19.7	33.2	3.2	5.3	10.8	2.0	3.9

China	33.2	19.9	22.8	5.2	7.4	6.1	3.1	2.3
Hong Kong	35.5	19.8	25.8	5.5	5.9	4.2	2.4	1.0
Taiwan	31.5	18.3	32.6	2.4	4.1	7.0	2.2	1.9
Philippines	38.9	20.7	17.9	7.1	6.9	3.1	3.9	1.5
Hmong	25.7	17.2	19.7	4.7	7.5	8.2	4.3	12.8
Cambodia	31.3	15.3	17.9	4.8	6.3	7.1	6.1	11.1
Laos	33.1	17.0	16.9	6.0	7.5	5.9	4.1	9.6
Thailand	26.4	19.5	20.5	3.3	6.7	8.7	5.7	9.2
Vietnam[c]	31.1	18.0	25.9	4.3	7.6	6.6	3.1	3.5
India	26.6	20.1	34.5	3.5	4.4	7.1	2.0	1.8
Pakistan/Bangladesh	10.3	14.0	46.4	1.6	5.1	17.9	1.3	3.5
Afghanistan	13.3	18.9	37.3	2.9	9.1	12.4	2.4	3.7
Iran	19.5	26.4	36.6	3.8	4.1	6.1	1.3	2.2
Iraq	14.2	17.7	36.7	1.5	7.0	9.5	3.2	10.2
Israel/Palestine	14.0	20.0	40.4	2.7	5.6	10.1	1.9	5.3
Other West Asia	13.1	17.5	42.8	1.9	4.4	12.2	2.3	5.9
Former USSR	20.9	21.7	26.5	3.8	8.3	10.5	3.2	5.1
Other Europe, Canada[d]	21.7	25.8	32.6	4.0	6.3	5.8	2.1	1.7
Africa, Blacks	28.0	22.2	18.8	6.8	10.0	7.6	3.6	3.0
Africa, Whites[e]	19.6	22.9	33.8	3.4	5.9	10.1	1.7	2.5
Other	21.5	26.8	31.6	3.9	5.5	5.9	2.9	1.8

Source: U.S. Census Bureau, 2000.

[a]Full time indicates the parent works 35 hours per week or more, 48 weeks a year or more.

[b]Part time indicates the parent works less than full time.

[c]"Vietnam" includes Indochina not specified.

[d]"Other Europe, Canada" includes Australia and New Zealand.

[e]"Africa, Whites" includes Asian Africans.

Appendix Table 11.8c. Parental employment percentages, for children ages 0–8, by immigrant country or race/ethnic origin

	Children in one-parent families				All children		
	Parent works more than full time[a]	Parent works full time or more[b]	Parent works part time[c]	Parent does not work	Father works more than full time	Mother works more than full time	Two parents work more than full time
Total	5.8	42.1	35.5	22.4	23.3	4.1	1.5
Children in native-born families	5.9	42.4	36.1	21.5	24.5	4.3	1.5
White	8.5	49.1	34.9	16.0	29.7	4.6	1.8
Black	3.5	37.2	37.7	25.1	8.3	3.5	0.7
Puerto Rican, mainland origin	3.4	33.9	35.1	31.0	12.0	3.1	0.7
Puerto Rican, island origin	2.0	25.0	31.1	43.9	10.7	2.3	0.6
Mexican	4.3	38.1	35.5	26.4	15.1	3.2	0.9
Other Hispanic/Latino	4.9	38.5	36.9	24.6	16.3	3.9	1.1
Asian	8.2	45.6	34.3	20.1	25.3	5.5	2.4
Hawaiian/Pacific Islander	3.0	36.2	40.7	23.1	13.0	3.7	0.8
Native American	4.8	34.8	38.9	26.3	15.1	3.1	1.0
Children in immigrant families	5.8	40.2	31.4	28.5	18.7	3.2	1.2
Mexico	4.5	34.8	31.1	34.1	13.3	1.8	0.5
Central America	5.2	40.9	33.5	25.6	14.4	2.8	0.8
Cuba	4.4	47.5	26.5	26.0	25.4	5.1	2.3
Dominican Republic	4.4	31.4	30.7	37.8	10.5	2.8	0.4
Haiti	4.3	46.6	30.6	22.9	10.1	3.3	0.8
Jamaica	5.3	50.4	31.7	17.9	12.9	4.8	1.0
Caribbean, English speaking	4.9	46.6	29.7	23.6	14.4	4.2	1.1
South America	7.4	45.0	31.5	23.6	23.7	3.8	1.5
Japan	4.8	46.4	28.1	25.5	34.2	3.1	1.5
Korea	10.3	40.0	32.0	28.0	31.1	5.2	3.0

China	12.6	53.0	34.0	13.0	21.6	6.4	3.2
Hong Kong	9.5	43.7	29.7	26.6	27.0	5.8	3.4
Taiwan	7.4	43.0	31.1	25.9	25.2	5.8	3.2
Philippines	5.5	52.3	32.9	14.7	15.6	5.0	1.2
Hmong	0.8	36.7	33.8	29.5	5.7	1.8	1.1
Cambodia	5.6	37.3	17.7	45.1	11.0	5.1	1.8
Laos	4.8	44.3	28.7	27.0	11.3	4.1	1.2
Thailand	5.6	42.7	32.4	24.9	15.9	4.2	1.7
Vietnam[d]	6.1	41.9	32.5	25.6	17.3	5.0	2.4
India	9.3	49.3	28.0	22.7	25.8	4.7	2.6
Pakistan/Bangladesh	10.3	37.8	30.1	32.1	26.1	2.0	1.1
Afghanistan	4.6	18.1	24.9	57.0	19.6	3.1	0.0
Iran	14.4	54.6	22.7	22.8	38.2	5.6	2.6
Iraq	10.3	46.6	10.8	42.6	22.6	3.1	1.4
Israel/Palestine	12.7	39.2	30.3	30.5	34.3	3.8	1.9
Other West Asia	12.3	42.1	35.0	22.9	30.0	3.0	1.4
Former USSR	9.8	45.7	35.5	18.7	22.4	4.3	1.7
Other Europe, Canada[e]	10.2	47.2	33.3	19.5	33.1	5.0	2.4
Africa, Blacks	8.7	47.6	30.6	21.8	14.4	4.1	1.2
Africa, Whites[f]	8.9	41.6	34.3	24.1	32.9	4.9	2.8
Other	9.0	47.0	33.8	19.2	30.6	4.3	1.4

Source: U.S. Census Bureau, 2000.

[a]More than full time indicates the parent works 50 hours per week or more, 48 weeks per year or more.

[b]Full time indicates the parent works 35 hours per week or more, 48 weeks per year or more.

[c]Part time indicates the parent works less than full time.

[d]"Vietnam" includes Indochina not specified.

[e]"Other Europe, Canada" includes Australia and New Zealand.

[f]"Africa, Whites" includes Asian Africans.

Appendix Table 11.8d. Parental employment percentages, for children ages 0–8, by immigrant country or race/ethnic origin

	Children with fathers employed full time[a]				Children with mothers employed full time			
	Father is a high school graduate	Father is not a high school graduate	Father is English fluent	Father is limited English proficient (LEP)	Mother is a high school graduate	Mother is not a high school graduate	Mother is English fluent	Mother is limited English proficient (LEP)
Total	82.7	60.8	80.7	64.0	35.7	19.4	34.2	21.8
Children in native-born families	83.9	59.9	81.3	63.9	36.2	19.7	34.3	27.1
White	86.2	65.4	84.2	73.5	34.0	19.7	32.7	27.8
Black	70.9	44.0	65.9	64.2	46.2	20.5	40.6	39.2
Puerto Rican, mainland origin	77.9	53.1	72.8	66.5	40.5	15.4	34.9	25.6
Puerto Rican, island origin	72.0	47.7	68.6	53.5	35.2	15.6	32.3	20.2
Mexican	77.9	57.8	73.9	62.0	40.0	20.0	35.4	27.4
Other Hispanic/Latino	79.4	56.0	75.2	65.8	39.3	19.2	35.3	27.4
Asian	82.4	50.9	80.9	—[b]	38.4	19.3	37.2	31.3
Hawaiian/Pacific Islander	70.6	56.5	69.6	—	34.8	20.0	32.6	—
Native American	69.2	46.6	65.5	40.8	34.6	16.8	31.1	26.8
Children in immigrant families	76.6	61.7	77.1	64.0	33.0	18.9	34.0	21.1
Mexico	72.4	62.0	70.5	63.1	28.4	16.7	28.5	17.0
Central America	75.3	63.7	74.1	65.6	34.8	24.2	34.9	25.7
Cuba	81.4	63.9	84.3	65.1	44.4	23.6	45.2	30.1
Dominican Republic	68.8	52.2	67.8	58.1	35.2	20.5	37.0	25.4
Haiti	72.1	61.7	72.4	64.9	48.7	36.0	47.7	41.1
Jamaica	73.8	60.5	71.2	—	52.9	38.5	50.5	—
Caribbean, English speaking	76.8	59.5	74.1	—	47.2	22.5	42.7	—
South America	77.1	63.2	80.0	66.8	31.5	22.2	34.2	25.0

Japan	79.5	—	82.3	71.9	17.0	—	25.9	8.4
Korea	75.3	60.7	82.9	63.5	26.4	26.8	32.9	20.5
China	78.9	60.6	83.6	68.0	44.0	29.2	49.5	34.9
Hong Kong	83.4	57.4	84.9	72.9	44.3	31.4	46.4	37.6
Taiwan	82.8	—	84.9	78.9	35.9	—	41.7	30.1
Philippines	78.3	59.1	79.0	69.5	50.0	31.4	50.9	42.0
Hmong	73.6	47.8	73.0	58.7	41.7	24.1	42.7	28.1
Cambodia	73.9	49.4	71.5	59.7	46.8	27.8	44.8	34.5
Laos	72.5	57.6	72.9	63.2	47.7	32.5	45.2	37.4
Thailand	75.3	38.6	79.0	51.8	40.4	19.9	38.5	28.0
Vietnam[c]	80.0	60.8	82.2	69.4	41.5	28.2	42.6	33.6
India	82.2	63.8	82.9	72.9	32.9	21.4	33.9	26.4
Pakistan/Bangladesh	72.1	58.0	74.6	61.3	15.0	5.1	18.1	8.0
Afghanistan	69.6	—	75.6	—	23.2	1.5	24.7	—
Iran	83.4	—	85.7	69.6	25.6	16.0	29.9	11.3
Iraq	74.0	60.4	75.1	60.7	23.1	9.2	29.0	8.8
Israel/Palestine	77.5	55.3	78.7	60.5	18.7	13.1	20.4	10.8
Other West Asia	75.5	57.0	76.3	63.6	18.8	6.5	19.8	10.9
Former USSR	70.3	54.0	80.4	55.7	28.9	11.3	37.6	16.5
Other Europe, Canada[d]	81.5	67.4	82.7	66.9	28.5	21.8	28.9	22.8
Africa, Blacks	70.0	54.1	71.4	57.4	41.5	20.2	44.2	22.0
Africa, Whites[e]	77.4	54.5	78.6	65.1	25.3	19.4	28.0	14.3
Other	81.7	61.7	81.8	62.9	28.9	23.3	28.7	25.5

Source: U.S. Census Bureau, 2000.

[a]Full time indicates the parent works 35 hours per week or more, 48 weeks a year or more.

[b]A dash indicates that the sample size is too small to produce statistically reliable results.

[c] "Vietnam" includes Indochina not specified.

[d]"Other Europe, Canada" includes Australia and New Zealand.

[e]"Africa, Whites" includes Asian Africans.

257

Appendix Table 11.9. Parental and other household member earnings percentages, for children ages 0–8, by immigrant country or race/ethnic origin

	Fathers earning below 100% of minimum wage[a]	Fathers earning from 100% to below 200% minimum wage[b]	Mothers earning below 100% of minimum wage	Mothers earning from 100% to below 200% minimum wage	One or two adult workers in the home[c]	Three adult workers in the home	Four or more adult workers in the home
Total	4.6	19.7	13.0	34.0	87.0	5.0	2.0
Children in native-born families	4.0	17.3	12.8	33.4	88.7	4.0	1.2
White	3.3	15.2	11.5	31.4	92.5	3.5	0.9
Black	7.5	27.3	16.6	38.8	78.0	4.9	1.3
Puerto Rican, mainland origin	5.9	23.5	13.5	34.9	77.8	4.8	1.7
Puerto Rican, island origin	6.6	29.8	15.6	39.8	73.1	5.0	1.5
Mexican	6.5	26.6	15.6	38.9	80.7	7.6	3.7
Other Hispanic/Latino	6.3	24.9	16.3	37.5	82.4	6.4	2.3
Asian	2.6	12.5	8.4	22.7	86.3	6.2	3.3
Hawaiian/Pacific Islander	5.2	22.2	12.9	36.6	81.0	7.3	5.2
Native American	8.3	28.8	19.2	40.3	82.1	5.4	2.0
Children in immigrant families	6.7	27.9	13.9	36.9	80.6	8.5	5.1
Mexico	9.2	39.7	20.7	48.8	75.2	10.8	7.6
Central America	6.8	33.9	16.6	44.7	74.9	11.5	7.7
Cuba	4.9	21.5	9.2	32.6	85.5	7.4	2.4
Dominican Republic	8.9	29.3	16.3	40.9	74.0	7.7	3.5
Haiti	4.9	31.8	10.7	40.2	80.1	8.6	2.8
Jamaica	4.9	19.9	8.3	29.3	81.6	8.6	2.9
Caribbean, English speaking	4.8	20.1	8.3	26.6	82.1	7.2	3.4
South America	4.9	21.8	11.8	35.0	82.2	8.7	4.4
Japan	2.9	11.2	9.6	29.1	93.8	1.6	0.6
Korea	5.0	15.5	8.7	26.1	90.3	3.0	1.1

China	9.5	16.7	10.6	20.9	86.9	6.7	3.7
Hong Kong	4.6	12.0	5.0	16.9	89.8	6.6	1.9
Taiwan	2.6	7.4	6.7	13.5	92.1	4.2	0.7
Philippines	2.6	15.7	5.8	24.5	79.7	10.4	7.6
Hmong	5.2	37.5	11.7	46.1	72.4	8.9	3.9
Cambodia	5.8	24.1	9.6	37.4	69.7	8.6	4.2
Laos	7.0	30.1	12.0	40.4	73.0	9.4	7.0
Thailand	3.2	25.4	9.8	39.4	77.2	8.1	4.5
Vietnam[d]	6.0	20.5	11.0	35.2	79.4	9.2	6.5
India	3.3	11.0	6.8	21.2	89.0	5.7	2.9
Pakistan/Bangladesh	7.3	22.6	14.4	31.4	88.5	4.7	2.0
Afghanistan	9.5	26.9	—[e]	—[e]	85.3	4.2	2.6
Iran	4.8	10.1	5.5	21.5	92.0	3.1	0.9
Iraq	7.0	27.7	18.1	32.7	79.3	5.1	2.2
Israel/Palestine	6.0	14.6	10.7	18.3	90.9	2.3	0.5
Other West Asia	5.9	17.7	9.4	27.2	88.6	3.4	0.9
Former USSR	5.8	18.4	9.4	24.3	86.6	4.3	1.4
Other Europe, Canada[f]	3.1	13.5	8.0	25.8	92.3	3.6	0.9
Africa, Blacks	4.3	21.9	8.9	29.5	85.3	6.6	1.3
Africa, Whites[g]	5.0	14.8	8.8	23.0	92.6	2.6	1.0
Other	3.1	12.4	9.1	24.9	91.9	3.7	1.1

Source: U.S. Census Bureau, 2000.

[a]"Below 100% of minimum wage" is earning less than $5.15 per hour.

[b]"From 100% to below 200% of minimum wage" is earning $5.15 to less than $10.30 per hour.

[c] Adult workers are age 18 or older, earning $2,500 or more per year.

[d]"Vietnam" includes Indochina not specified.

[e]A dash indicates that the sample size is too small to produce statistically reliable results.

[f]"Other Europe, Canada" includes Australia and New Zealand.

[g]"Africa, Whites" includes Asian Africans.

Appendix Table 11.10. Parental education percentages, for children ages 0–8, by immigrant country or race/ethnic origin

	Father has 0–4 years of school	Father has 0–8 years of school	Father is not a high school graduate	Father is a high school graduate or has some college	Father is a college graduate	Mother has 0–4 years of school	Mother has 0–8 years of school	Mother is not a high school graduate	Mother is a high school graduate or has some college	Mother is a college graduate
Total	1.8	6.1	18.1	54.1	27.8	1.6	5.5	18.2	58.0	23.8
Children in native-born families	0.3	1.6	11.9	59.1	29.0	0.2	1.6	12.8	62.5	24.7
White	0.1	1.4	9.8	57.7	32.6	0.1	1.2	8.9	61.4	29.7
Black	0.6	1.6	18.6	67.8	13.5	0.4	1.8	22.0	66.9	11.2
Puerto Rican, mainland origin	0.5	2.5	22.5	64.6	12.9	0.5	3.4	25.4	64.3	10.2
Puerto Rican, island origin	3.1	9.6	34.6	53.8	11.6	1.9	8.7	36.4	53.7	9.9
Mexican	1.0	3.8	24.7	62.1	13.2	0.8	4.6	26.2	63.4	10.4
Other Hispanic/Latino	0.7	2.7	20.8	63.2	16.0	0.5	3.5	22.8	64.5	12.6
Asian	0.2	0.7	6.2	48.0	45.8	0.4	1.2	7.0	52.1	40.9
Hawaiian/Pacific Islander	0.2	0.7	12.6	70.4	17.0	0.6	2.3	15.2	72.1	12.7
Native American	0.5	2.6	21.4	67.3	11.3	0.3	2.4	20.8	68.8	10.4
Children in immigrant families	7.2	21.4	39.2	37.0	23.9	6.6	20.1	38.9	41.1	20.1
Mexico	12.9	40.3	67.0	28.8	4.2	11.0	36.9	65.0	31.3	3.8
Central America	10.8	29.5	53.7	37.2	9.1	10.4	27.9	52.2	39.9	7.8
Cuba	1.2	4.5	21.6	50.9	27.5	0.7	2.6	18.2	55.8	26.1
Dominican Republic	4.0	15.2	40.9	46.7	12.4	2.9	12.6	36.9	52.2	10.8
Haiti	3.2	8.6	30.7	53.7	15.7	4.1	10.0	32.8	54.4	12.8
Jamaica	1.0	3.3	19.7	59.6	20.8	0.3	1.6	17.5	63.2	19.3
Caribbean, English speaking	1.3	5.1	18.4	60.2	21.4	1.4	4.1	18.7	63.1	18.2
South America	1.4	6.5	18.3	51.2	30.5	1.5	5.4	17.8	55.6	26.6

Japan	0.3	0.8	3.0	33.4	63.6	0.1	0.4	2.9	53.7	43.4
Korea	0.3	0.8	3.5	41.6	54.9	0.6	1.4	5.4	48.9	45.7
China	3.5	9.7	18.2	25.7	56.0	3.8	9.4	18.8	30.8	50.4
Hong Kong	1.0	2.8	9.9	29.6	60.6	1.4	4.0	11.5	34.7	53.8
Taiwan	0.6	0.8	2.3	16.0	81.6	0.4	0.8	2.4	26.7	70.9
Philippines	0.4	1.6	6.0	55.1	38.9	0.6	2.0	6.4	46.8	46.7
Hmong	28.5	31.4	42.6	49.2	8.2	36.1	39.1	54.9	40.5	4.6
Cambodia	15.2	19.7	39.3	45.9	14.8	21.3	26.3	45.2	46.5	8.3
Laos	18.9	23.7	39.4	51.5	9.1	23.8	29.1	47.9	45.9	6.2
Thailand	13.5	15.8	24.4	48.8	26.8	18.4	22.0	35.8	44.5	19.7
Vietnam[a]	5.7	10.8	28.4	43.4	28.2	7.4	15.1	35.4	45.3	19.3
India	0.8	1.5	7.3	17.9	74.8	0.6	1.8	9.2	24.2	66.6
Pakistan/Bangladesh	1.0	3.4	13.1	28.1	58.9	2.4	6.0	19.7	37.7	42.6
Afghanistan	2.4	3.0	14.2	61.6	24.2	5.6	10.7	24.5	56.9	18.7
Iran	0.2	0.9	3.4	28.7	67.9	0.3	0.8	5.4	44.7	49.9
Iraq	7.5	16.1	37.9	40.7	21.4	8.7	17.3	32.9	47.8	19.3
Israel/Palestine	0.9	3.5	14.2	42.0	43.9	1.0	3.2	12.8	47.6	39.5
Other West Asia	1.4	5.0	12.9	39.1	48.1	2.0	5.9	17.5	49.1	33.4
Former USSR	0.5	1.4	9.8	44.3	46.0	0.6	1.1	8.9	46.6	44.5
Other Europe, Canada[b]	0.8	2.8	10.6	48.6	40.8	0.6	2.6	9.5	55.1	35.5
Africa, Blacks	1.8	3.5	8.8	37.3	53.9	4.4	7.8	16.1	55.7	28.2
Africa, Whites[c]	0.6	1.5	5.3	32.9	61.8	0.7	2.1	7.6	40.8	51.6
Other	0.8	2.6	9.7	42.5	47.8	0.6	2.4	9.3	51.9	38.8

Source: U.S. Census Bureau, 2000.

[a] "Vietnam" includes Indochina not specified.

[b] "Other Europe, Canada" includes Australia and New Zealand.

[c] "Africa, Whites" includes Asian Africans.

Appendix Table 11.11. Limited English proficiency percentages, for children ages 0–8, by immigrant country or race/ethnic origin

	Bilingual	Limited English proficiency									
	Child is English fluent and speaks another language at home[a]	Child is limited English proficient (LEP)[a]	Child is LEP and father is LEP[a]	Child is LEP and mother is LEP[a]	Father is LEP	Mother is LEP	Father or mother is LEP	Both father and mother are LEP	Linguistically isolated household[b]	Parent(s) in U.S. fewer than 10 years and LEP[c]	Parents in U.S. 10 or more years and LEP[c]
Total	10.0	8.7	3.0	2.9	12.2	11.7	14.0	9.3	7.2	27.8	25.2
Children in native-born families	3.3	1.8	0.2	0.3	1.4	1.7	2.4	0.6	0.7	20.6	14.7
White	1.4	0.7	0.1	0.1	0.6	0.7	1.1	0.2	0.2	—[d]	—
Black	1.5	0.8	0.0	0.0	0.7	0.8	1.1	0.1	0.3	—	—
Puerto Rican, mainland origin	25.1	11.7	0.9	1.3	7.1	7.8	10.3	2.2	4.1	—	—
Puerto Rican, island origin	44.0	30.2	6.9	8.8	33.0	35.7	45.0	18.6	20.6	20.6	14.7
Mexican	18.6	10.2	1.2	1.5	8.3	8.6	11.4	3.9	4.0	—	—
Other Hispanic/Latino	19.2	9.3	1.0	1.2	7.2	7.8	10.4	3.1	4.2	—	—
Asian	5.1	2.6	0.4	0.3	2.4	2.8	3.8	1.1	1.3	—	—
Hawaiian/Pacific Islander	12.0	5.2	0.8	0.7	4.4	4.3	6.1	1.8	1.9	—	—
Native American	7.3	4.5	0.8	0.9	4.8	4.6	6.3	2.4	1.9	—	—
Children in immigrant families	36.4	35.7	12.5	13.0	48.7	50.0	58.6	38.6	31.8	28.0	25.6
Mexico	38.1	52.4	19.7	20.0	69.3	67.1	78.7	56.0	44.6	35.7	35.5
Central America	45.1	38.0	13.3	13.9	59.3	61.1	70.2	48.0	39.1	28.6	37.4
Cuba	50.0	24.1	6.3	6.4	34.6	30.3	41.4	21.7	19.6	22.4	14.0
Dominican Republic	50.3	39.1	12.3	14.7	59.5	62.5	72.8	43.8	40.3	34.6	33.1
Haiti	42.0	24.3	7.9	8.6	46.1	47.7	55.8	35.1	28.8	27.9	25.8
Jamaica	4.0	1.5	0.2	0.2	2.0	1.7	2.6	0.6	0.7	1.2	1.2
Caribbean, English speaking	5.6	2.3	0.5	0.5	3.2	2.8	4.4	1.1	1.3	1.7	1.9

Group										
South America	49.0	26.1	7.5	8.7	41.7	48.2	56.6	31.6	27.3	30.1	20.7
Japan	27.9	33.1	10.3	12.7	31.1	47.4	50.7	27.5	26.3	38.1	6.8
Korea	36.9	28.6	10.5	11.7	41.9	52.0	56.8	36.6	34.0	28.3	23.9
China	40.3	41.9	13.8	13.9	51.3	56.8	61.3	46.3	40.8	34.4	25.0
Hong Kong	38.4	29.8	9.5	11.0	33.8	40.4	45.8	28.1	25.4	16.3	27.2
Taiwan	52.0	27.0	8.8	10.2	41.6	53.7	59.2	35.5	33.7	21.4	34.5
Philippines	20.1	9.7	2.2	2.4	19.3	23.7	30.1	12.0	9.8	14.8	11.6
Hmong	24.1	69.8	32.7	32.9	72.9	73.5	79.7	66.1	48.8	28.1	50.9
Cambodia	33.0	45.3	17.5	17.8	61.3	63.9	69.8	53.2	37.1	11.8	56.6
Laos	37.8	45.7	18.3	17.9	64.4	61.1	70.7	53.5	34.7	14.7	52.5
Thailand	27.8	33.8	12.9	13.4	46.6	51.7	59.9	37.1	26.9	26.8	26.6
Vietnam[e]	37.5	45.4	15.9	17.0	60.0	64.9	71.0	52.8	44.4	31.6	37.2
India	49.0	19.8	3.6	4.7	19.7	27.6	31.4	15.7	13.7	21.5	9.2
Pakistan/ Bangladesh	53.7	30.3	6.7	10.0	32.4	49.6	54.1	27.3	23.0	39.4	13.6
Afghanistan	50.2	30.6	—	—	40.7	51.6	57.6	33.8	24.6	25.4	30.2
Iran	45.0	17.4	3.4	4.3	20.7	25.6	31.6	14.2	12.5	12.9	15.6
Iraq	48.7	27.9	7.8	9.7	43.4	51.9	59.0	35.5	28.0	43.1	13.3
Israel/Palestine	44.3	17.2	4.6	4.6	23.8	25.8	35.4	13.7	13.1	17.6	10.9
Other West Asia	46.1	20.1	4.0	5.6	25.0	35.0	41.8	17.5	15.7	26.2	11.9
Former USSR	41.2	34.8	12.5	12.5	47.4	49.0	56.0	39.6	32.8	44.7	9.6
Other Europe, Canada[f]	26.7	10.5	2.9	2.9	17.2	17.0	22.8	10.9	9.7	13.2	6.1
Africa, Blacks	21.8	16.4	3.1	4.6	19.5	27.4	30.9	14.9	15.1	22.7	6.9
Africa, Whites[g]	29.7	13.9	3.0	3.4	18.3	22.5	27.4	13.1	11.6	18.9	6.2
Other	17.1	8.5	2.1	2.4	10.6	11.5	15.2	6.5	5.6	7.4	5.4

Source: U.S. Census Bureau, 2000.

[a]For children ages 5–17 years.

[b]Households in which no one over the age of 13 speaks English exclusively or very well.

[c]These two columns together include all children with at least one LEP parent. The column labeled "Parent(s) LEP and in U.S. fewer than 10 years" includes all children with an LEP parent in the home and with at least one parent who has been in the U.S. fewer than 10 years. The column labeled "Parents LEP and in U.S. 10 or more years" includes all children with at least one LEP parent in the home, and the parent (in a single parent-home) or both parents (in a two-parent home) have lived in the U.S. for 10 or more years.

[d]A dash indicates that the sample size is too small to produce statistically reliable results or that category does not apply to the native group.

[e]"Vietnam" includes Indochina not specified.

[f]"Other Europe, Canada" includes Australia and New Zealand.

[g]"Africa, Whites" includes Asian Africans.

263

Appendix Table 11.12a. Poverty percentages, of children ages 0–8, by immigrant country or race/ethnic origin

	Near official poverty (below 200% of threshold)	Official poverty (below 100% of threshold)	Deep official poverty (below 50% of threshold)	Basic budget poverty (based on all costs)[a]	Basic budget poverty (based on food, housing, other necessities, transportation, and child care)	Basic budget poverty (based on food, housing, other necessities, and transportation)	Basic budget poverty (based on food, housing, and other necessities)	Basic budget poverty (based on food and housing)
Total	38.7	16.4	7.1	43.4	37.4	22.3	18.4	12.1
Children in native-born families	35.7	15.0	6.8	39.5	33.7	19.1	15.7	10.6
White	27.5	9.0	3.5	31.0	25.4	11.9	9.2	5.6
Black	60.8	34.5	18.4	65.0	58.7	41.6	36.1	26.6
Puerto Rican, mainland origin	53.5	29.5	15.1	62.8	57.1	40.0	35.2	26.0
Puerto Rican, island origin	63.0	35.9	19.4	70.3	64.6	46.9	42.2	31.5
Mexican	49.7	22.2	9.4	54.8	47.7	30.0	24.8	16.0
Other Hispanic/Latino	49.2	22.3	10.3	54.8	47.3	29.5	24.4	16.4
Asian	23.0	8.6	3.4	29.9	25.7	14.2	11.6	7.3
Hawaiian/Pacific Islander	44.5	18.3	6.6	54.1	47.4	30.2	26.4	16.0
Native American	56.4	26.7	12.0	58.3	50.4	32.4	26.5	18.1
Children in immigrant families	50.3	21.8	8.2	58.1	51.9	34.3	28.8	17.8
Mexico	70.0	31.3	10.7	76.4	69.3	47.3	39.5	23.8
Central America	57.9	23.4	8.3	67.9	60.6	41.0	34.1	20.4
Cuba	33.8	12.7	5.5	38.8	32.4	22.2	18.6	10.3
Dominican Republic	62.2	32.0	16.0	74.6	68.6	50.0	43.9	31.0
Haiti	55.6	23.3	10.4	68.6	61.5	40.9	34.4	21.7
Jamaica	39.2	15.2	7.2	52.4	46.1	27.8	23.4	14.6
Caribbean, English speaking	38.9	16.2	9.1	52.3	44.8	28.0	24.1	15.8
South America	38.2	14.7	5.8	49.0	42.7	27.1	22.5	13.5

Japan	23.6	7.7	4.5	29.2	25.1	12.3	10.5	7.1
Korea	29.6	11.6	6.6	37.3	32.4	19.3	16.5	10.8
China	29.8	12.1	3.3	37.2	32.7	22.4	18.8	11.1
Hong Kong	17.1	6.1	2.1	23.6	20.8	12.0	10.2	6.1
Taiwan	15.1	6.3	3.0	19.2	15.8	9.4	7.8	5.7
Philippines	20.9	5.4	2.2	29.3	23.6	11.3	8.6	4.7
Hmong	73.3	35.7	14.5	81.5	77.8	47.7	42.2	30.6
Cambodia	55.1	30.7	13.5	62.5	56.7	40.8	37.9	27.8
Laos	56.1	25.7	8.9	61.9	55.1	32.6	29.0	20.5
Thailand	47.1	22.3	9.8	52.7	47.3	30.9	26.5	19.4
Vietnamb	37.3	16.0	6.0	45.5	39.1	26.0	21.3	14.4
India	18.4	6.6	2.8	23.7	20.3	11.4	9.4	5.9
Pakistan/Bangladesh	48.6	23.0	7.6	56.2	51.5	36.6	31.9	21.8
Afghanistan	47.4	24.7	10.9	61.0	54.5	36.8	34.4	22.6
Iran	18.6	9.6	4.3	24.1	21.3	13.4	12.4	8.8
Iraq	52.0	28.2	10.7	57.0	49.8	35.3	33.0	21.2
Israel/Palestine	33.7	19.9	11.3	43.6	38.9	26.7	24.9	18.8
Other West Asia	40.1	19.2	8.7	47.9	43.4	28.2	25.0	16.2
Former USSR	38.1	19.1	7.7	45.5	40.5	26.9	24.0	16.2
Other Europe, Canadac	23.5	8.4	3.8	30.6	25.9	13.7	11.3	7.1
Africa, Blacks	43.3	19.4	9.4	55.0	49.2	30.4	26.0	17.6
Africa, Whitesd	27.6	12.0	6.1	36.1	31.4	18.8	16.2	10.6
Other	26.2	9.8	4.3	33.0	28.4	16.6	13.6	8.5

Source: U.S. Census Bureau, 2000.

a"Basic budget poverty" is based on all costs for a decent standard of living, including food, housing, other necessities, transportation for work, child care, and health insurance.

b "Vietnam" includes Indochina not specified.

c"Other Europe, Canada" includes Australia and New Zealand.

d"Africa, Whites" includes Asian Africans.

Appendix Table 11.12b. Poverty percentages, of children ages 0–8, by immigrant country or race/ethnic origin

	Children in official poverty			Children in basic budget poverty[a]		
	Father has 0–8 years of school	Father not a high school graduate	Father is a high school graduate or has more education	Father has 0–8 years of school	Father is not a high school graduate	Father is a high school graduate or has more education
Total	35.3	28.1	6.4	79.8	69.9	28.6
Children in native-born families	34.5	24.8	5.5	70.8	61.4	26.3
White	32.3	20.6	4.3	68.1	56.2	23.3
Black	39.9	35.0	12.0	73.6	70.0	40.5
Puerto Rican, mainland origin	—[b]	30.0	9.8	—	72.1	40.3
Puerto Rican, island origin	46.7	38.3	14.0	84.0	80.6	49.7
Mexican	35.8	28.2	8.5	76.2	70.8	37.1
Other Hispanic/Latino	34.9	27.6	8.9	77.4	70.7	37.1
Asian	—	17.7	4.0	—	56.2	21.5
Hawaiian/Pacific Islander	—	31.7	10.3	—	72.0	45.8
Native American	42.5	37.2	15.2	76.8	72.9	45.7
Children in immigrant families	35.4	31.6	10.7	82.1	78.8	40.3
Mexico	36.3	33.5	18.0	83.2	81.4	62.2
Central America	28.9	26.3	11.2	81.0	78.2	50.3
Cuba	—	20.8	7.2	—	62.8	27.2
Dominican Republic	33.8	31.9	14.1	84.6	81.4	58.1
Haiti	—	29.1	11.5	—	81.4	54.4
Jamaica	—	16.0	6.2	—	66.0	36.9
Caribbean, English speaking	—	19.8	8.2	—	64.1	39.9
South America	28.5	22.3	9.3	75.6	70.1	39.7
Japan	—	—	5.6	—	—	26.7

Korea	35.2	50.7	—	10.1	17.0	—
China	27.7	78.8	83.1	7.9	30.2	32.1
Hong Kong	17.9	60.6	—	3.1	24.3	—
Taiwan	16.4	—	—	4.9	—	—
Philippines	24.9	54.3	—	3.6	12.4	—
Hmong	71.9	94.3	—	18.8	54.1	—
Cambodia	41.5	76.4	—	10.5	38.5	—
Laos	52.9	72.8	—	16.6	35.2	—
Thailand	41.6	79.2	—	11.9	49.3	—
Vietnam[c]	33.1	65.8	70.2	8.9	24.2	30.9
Indochina total[d]	40.2	72.8	79.3	11.0	33.1	43.5
India	19.8	60.3	—	4.9	20.3	—
Pakistan/Bangladesh	51.5	82.9	—	18.6	46.9	—
Afghanistan	57.7	—	—	18.7	—	—
Iran	21.7	—	—	7.3	—	—
Iraq	44.7	75.1	—	17.9	42.4	—
Israel/Palestine	36.9	78.5	—	14.2	48.4	—
Other West Asia	42.3	78.5	—	15.9	34.7	—
Former USSR	40.7	75.7	—	15.7	40.3	—
Other Europe, Canada[e]	25.2	53.1	59.1	5.6	15.5	20.8
Africa, Blacks	47.1	83.8	—	12.0	45.6	—
Africa, Whites[f]	32.6	66.3	—	9.6	28.1	—
Other	26.1	64.9	74.3	5.9	23.1	35.3

Source: U.S. Census Bureau, 2000.

[a]Basic budget poverty is based on all costs for a decent standard of living, including food, housing, other necessities, transportation for work, child care, and health insurance.

[b]A dash indicates that the sample size is too small to produce statistically reliable results or category does not apply to the native group.

[c]"Vietnam" includes Indochina not specified.

[d]"Indochina, total" includes Hmong, Cambodia, Laos, Thailand, and Vietnam.

[e]"Other Europe, Canada" includes Australia and New Zealand.

[f]"Africa, Whites" includes Asian Africans.

Appendix Table 11.12c. Poverty percentages, of children ages 0–8, by immigrant country or race/ethnic origin

	Children in official poverty				Children in basic budget poverty[a]			
	Father working full time[b]	Both parents working full time	Parent(s) in United States fewer than 10 years[c]	Both parents in United States 10 years or more[d]	Father working full time	Both parents working full time	Parent(s) in United States fewer than 10 years	Both parents in United States 10 years or more
Total	4.6	0.6	26.5	24.0	28.8	12.9	65.0	63.4
Children in native-born families	3.1	0.5	—[e]	45.2	24.1	9.8	77.1	78.2
White	2.6	0.4	—	—	21.8	7.8	—	—
Black	5.1	0.8	—	—	33.7	17.6	—	—
Puerto Rican, mainland origin	5.6	0.4	—	—	38.1	16.7	—	—
Puerto Rican, island origin	6.9	1.5	41.8	45.2	47.8	23.7	77.1	78.2
Mexican	6.3	0.7	—	—	37.1	17.5	—	—
Other Hispanic/Latino	5.9	0.6	—	—	35.8	17.0	—	—
Asian	1.5	0.0	—	—	18.3	6.3	—	—
Hawaiian/Pacific Islander	4.7	1.8	—	—	39.2	19.2	—	—
Native American	7.1	0.7	—	—	39.6	19.6	—	—
Children in immigrant families	10.5	1.3	26.0	23.3	47.1	26.2	64.7	63.0
Mexico	18.9	2.5	35.2	31.0	69.9	45.8	80.7	78.2
Central America	11.1	1.8	27.3	24.5	59.3	39.1	75.3	71.0
Cuba	3.4	0.2	23.1	10.7	26.0	12.1	63.0	38.3
Dominican Republic	9.5	0.8	35.1	33.4	58.6	37.9	80.0	75.9
Haiti	8.0	2.0	30.1	20.5	54.6	39.7	77.0	65.9
Jamaica	1.9	0.5	18.2	17.1	32.5	19.5	59.7	55.0
Caribbean, English speaking	4.3	0.3	21.0	17.2	35.6	17.9	61.4	53.8
South America	5.5	0.5	18.5	16.7	38.1	19.6	59.4	54.4

Japan	1.8	0.3	8.3	11.1	21.5	10.4	31.4	35.2
Korea	3.1	0.9	20.6	9.4	26.6	15.1	53.6	37.1
China	6.2	1.9	16.4	11.3	27.9	15.8	47.1	39.0
Hong Kong	2.7	1.0	13.1	5.3	14.9	6.1	44.3	20.5
Taiwan	1.4	0.2	11.6	5.3	11.3	4.9	30.1	15.7
Philippines	1.6	0.0	6.4	5.4	21.8	10.0	33.9	29.6
Hmong	19.3	—	—	30.7	76.5	—	—	77.7
Cambodia	5.4	0.2	27.4	34.5	42.4	26.6	60.1	68.1
Laos	12.5	2.1	34.6	25.4	50.9	35.0	73.7	61.8
Thailand	6.1	0.8	30.8	25.4	36.9	26.1	58.7	62.2
Vietnam[f]	5.6	0.6	21.2	15.0	32.8	16.8	58.5	41.7
Indochina total[g]	7.7	0.9	25.8	21.8	40.1	25.0	62.6	53.9
India	2.6	0.4	7.5	5.2	17.1	10.0	25.0	23.0
Pakistan/Bangladesh	13.4	5.6	26.8	17.4	46.8	26.7	61.3	50.7
Afghanistan	12.3	—	—	—	52.0	—	—	—
Iran	2.7	0.3	22.1	8.2	16.6	4.6	44.4	21.2
Iraq	12.9	—	42.7	13.0	43.8	—	75.0	42.8
Israel/Palestine	8.9	0.0	19.0	22.2	34.2	11.4	44.3	53.3
Other West Asia	7.4	0.7	25.7	18.5	36.6	11.2	57.0	48.7
Former USSR	7.7	0.2	27.1	13.4	31.7	9.5	60.0	38.7
Other Europe, Canada[h]	2.6	0.3	10.6	13.1	22.3	8.0	35.6	40.3
Africa, Blacks	5.0	0.1	25.6	12.4	40.5	22.6	63.7	47.5
Africa, Whites[i]	4.5	1.0	16.7	11.4	26.7	10.1	46.5	35.2
Other	3.1	0.4	10.4	17.5	23.5	11.9	33.5	48.1

Source: U.S. Census Bureau, 2000.

[a]"Basic budget poverty" is based on all costs for a decent standard of living, including food, housing, other necessities, transportation for work, child care, and health insurance.

[b]Full time indicates the parent works 35 hours per week or more, 48 weeks a year or more.

[c]At least one parent in the United States fewer than 10 years.

[d] Both parents in a two-parent family or single parent in a one-parent family in the United States 10 years or more.

[e]A dash indicates that sample size is too small to produce statistically reliable results or category does not apply to the native group.

[f]"Vietnam" includes Indochina not specified.

[g]"Indochina, total" includes Hmong, Cambodia, Laos, Thailand, and Vietnam.

[h]"Other Europe, Canada" includes Australia and New Zealand.

[i]"Africa, Whites" includes Asian Africans.

Appendix Table 11.12d. Poverty percentages, of children ages 0–8, by immigrant country or race/ethnic origin

	Children in official poverty				Children in basic budget poverty[a]			
	Father is English fluent	Father is limited English proficient (LEP)	In linguistically isolated households[b]	Not in linguistically isolated households	Father is English fluent	Father is limited English proficient (LEP)	In linguistically isolated households	Not in linguistically isolated households
Total	8.0	26.9	34.2	14.9	31.3	71.0	77.5	40.7
Children in native-born families	7.5	24.4	46.2	14.7	30.0	58.3	78.7	39.3
White	5.8	20.5	34.7	8.9	26.4	46.7	67.4	30.9
Black	16.3	17.6	46.2	34.3	46.0	46.5	78.8	64.9
Puerto Rican, mainland origin	13.6	24.9	58.2	28.2	46.1	64.3	87.3	61.8
Puerto Rican, island origin	17.9	31.5	56.0	30.5	54.3	72.7	88.3	65.6
Mexican	12.4	23.5	42.4	21.3	43.8	62.5	77.0	53.9
Other Hispanic/Latino	12.0	22.6	48.4	21.1	42.8	60.7	79.6	53.7
Asian	4.7	—[c]	—	8.3	23.4	—	—	29.6
Hawaiian/Pacific Islander	12.7	—	—	17.7	48.7	—	—	53.8
Native American	18.7	43.3	51.8	26.1	50.3	75.7	83.0	57.8
Children in immigrant families	11.0	27.2	33.1	16.4	39.3	72.3	77.4	49.0
Mexico	21.7	31.4	37.1	26.2	64.3	79.8	84.2	70.0
Central America	13.6	23.2	30.7	18.5	51.7	74.6	80.1	60.1
Cuba	5.5	18.8	28.8	8.7	23.1	57.2	69.3	31.3
Dominican Republic	16.7	24.6	40.6	26.0	55.7	75.8	85.5	67.2
Haiti	11.1	23.7	31.1	20.0	54.2	72.6	79.9	64.1
Jamaica	8.1	—	—	14.9	42.3	—	—	52.1
Caribbean, English speaking	10.1	—	—	15.8	44.1	—	—	52.0
South America	6.8	18.5	25.6	10.5	32.7	62.8	71.4	40.5

Japan	5.1	8.2	9.8	7.0	28.7	24.2	30.9
Korea	5.9	16.7	20.4	7.1	23.8	52.2	27.0
China	4.3	19.3	20.6	6.2	15.4	57.4	21.0
Hong Kong	1.8	11.8	15.3	3.0	12.8	40.5	16.4
Taiwan	2.9	8.9	10.6	4.1	12.7	24.0	16.0
Philippines	3.8	5.3	9.4	5.0	24.1	37.1	27.7
Hmong	17.4	39.9	42.8	28.8	61.3	89.0	70.9
Cambodia	16.3	24.7	35.4	27.8	41.5	63.9	57.8
Laos	12.4	30.3	34.5	21.0	44.8	69.5	57.5
Thailand	7.5	36.6	37.1	16.7	31.7	72.6	45.4
Vietnam[d]	8.0	16.7	21.4	11.6	30.2	50.5	37.2
Indochina total[e]	10.0	23.3	27.4	16.8	35.5	60.3	46.3
India	4.8	10.8	11.5	5.8	18.5	39.8	20.5
Pakistan/Bangladesh	17.0	33.3	37.3	18.6	46.7	74.1	49.7
Afghanistan	14.2	—	—	20.5	53.4	—	56.3
Iran	5.4	20.1	28.6	6.9	18.1	42.6	20.4
Iraq	13.7	44.8	—	18.8	44.7	71.4	48.5
Israel/Palestine	14.3	34.3	—	17.6	36.6	62.7	41.4
Other West Asia	14.8	28.8	35.4	16.1	40.1	67.8	43.2
Former USSR	5.7	31.8	36.7	10.5	23.2	67.2	32.3
Other Europe, Canada[f]	4.8	15.4	19.9	7.2	23.6	49.9	27.9
Africa, Blacks	10.3	34.2	46.6	14.4	44.7	73.4	50.0
Africa, Whites[g]	7.3	25.3	34.6	9.0	27.7	63.9	31.0
Other	5.8	22.9	32.7	8.4	26.4	58.8	31.2

Source: U.S. Census Bureau, 2000.

[a]"Basic budget poverty" is based on all costs for a decent standard of living, including food, housing, other necessities, transportation for work, child care, and health insurance.

[b]Households in which no one older than the age of 13 speaks English exclusively or very well.

[c]A dash indicates that the sample size is too small to produce statistically reliable results or category does not apply to the native group.

[d]"Vietnam" includes Indochina not specified.

[e]"Indochina, total" includes Hmong, Cambodia, Laos, Thailand, and Vietnam.

[f]"Other Europe, Canada" includes Australia and New Zealand.

[g]"Africa, Whites" includes Asian Africans.

Appendix Table 11.12e. Poverty percentages, of children ages 0–8, by immigrant country or race/ethnic origin

	Children officially poor					Children not officially poor				
	Moved in past 5 years[a]	Working parent(s)	Moderate housing cost burden (30%–50% income)[b]	Severe housing cost burden (>50% income)[c]	Overcrowded housing[d]	Moved in past 5 years	Working parent(s)	Moderate housing cost burden (30%–50% income)	Severe housing cost burden (>50% income)	Overcrowded housing
Total	28.8	72.1	20.9	56.4	40.0	24.7	97.8	17.3	4.3	16.7
Children in native-born families	28.7	70.3	19.7	56.6	28.6	24.4	97.8	16.4	3.8	10.2
White	28.2	77.2	20.4	56.7	19.5	23.6	98.7	15.8	3.7	6.6
Black	29.8	65.0	18.7	56.9	31.9	28.4	94.4	18.6	4.2	19.5
Puerto Rican, mainland origin	26.3	56.7	16.3	66.8	35.4	26.4	94.8	22.4	5.6	20.2
Puerto Rican, island origin	32.3	51.3	18.2	65.1	43.3	30.8	94.9	21.5	5.1	30.3
Mexican	26.4	68.1	22.7	53.7	45.7	24.8	95.0	17.8	3.8	28.2
Other Hispanic/Latino	29.0	69.0	19.8	57.3	41.2	25.5	95.6	18.6	4.4	24.1
Asian	25.6	66.9	17.5	63.0	40.7	21.2	96.9	19.0	6.5	15.6
Hawaiian/Pacific Islander	28.3	71.0	19.0	58.9	60.3	28.2	95.3	23.4	6.1	38.0
Native American	26.3	70.7	20.6	42.0	43.6	26.7	95.7	13.2	2.9	23.9
Children in immigrant families	28.9	76.7	24.0	56.0	70.4	25.8	97.7	21.1	6.2	43.5
Mexico	28.5	80.6	28.1	46.8	77.4	26.3	96.9	20.0	4.4	64.5
Central America	26.7	77.1	24.2	60.7	74.8	25.7	97.2	23.9	6.1	57.2
Cuba	32.7	68.8	18.1	69.1	54.4	26.2	98.1	22.5	7.9	26.6
Dominican Republic	28.8	58.0	16.3	70.7	55.5	25.7	95.5	23.2	8.8	46.3
Haiti	30.9	69.7	15.8	74.6	60.9	26.0	97.3	27.1	8.6	42.5
Jamaica	25.6	62.2	11.1	81.1	37.5	24.8	97.5	25.7	8.4	26.4
Caribbean, English speaking	25.5	64.2	7.9	82.6	41.4	23.7	97.1	24.7	10.4	27.7
South America	32.3	73.2	15.1	76.2	57.2	27.8	97.8	25.2	8.7	32.1

Japan	35.5	68.0	12.2	81.8	31.1	30.5	99.0	22.5	7.9	14.9
Korea	38.0	63.9	7.7	89.6	56.8	30.0	98.4	24.1	9.8	32.8
China	21.0	81.9	20.0	63.4	64.8	22.0	98.9	18.5	6.7	31.9
Hong Kong	—[e]	—	—	—	—	19.2	99.7	18.8	7.9	21.7
Taiwan	—	—	—	—	—	22.0	98.0	21.0	8.0	15.4
Philippines	22.6	74.2	16.5	67.6	54.0	26.8	98.2	19.8	5.0	37.3
Hmong	—	—	—	—	—	29.2	96.5	15.4	0.2	72.1
Cambodia	34.8	46.5	28.3	54.9	81.0	21.0	95.2	18.2	3.4	52.7
Laos	28.9	64.7	26.2	50.5	77.9	24.1	96.3	14.1	5.2	53.7
Thailand	—	—	—	—	—	23.8	97.1	22.0	6.9	35.2
Vietnam[f]	29.7	72.1	21.8	63.0	65.6	21.8	97.7	20.0	6.3	40.8
Indochina total[g]	30.4	65.0	25.8	54.1	75.6	22.7	97.1	18.8	5.4	45.6
India	27.8	72.1	12.1	80.8	54.2	24.2	99.0	17.4	5.6	30.3
Pakistan/Bangladesh	31.1	82.7	17.1	76.7	68.8	28.5	98.5	22.8	8.1	48.2
Afghanistan	—	—	—	—	—	22.5	98.7	29.6	17.5	35.1
Iran	—	—	—	—	—	22.8	99.5	23.1	13.2	17.9
Iraq	—	—	—	—	—	23.4	98.1	25.0	13.3	28.7
Israel/Palestine	—	—	—	—	—	23.1	98.5	22.8	10.1	23.6
Other West Asia	27.1	71.1	10.4	83.8	52.7	22.5	98.3	24.0	10.3	26.1
Former USSR	40.4	74.2	21.4	63.0	67.7	28.9	98.3	20.8	5.8	29.6
Other Europe, Canada[h]	31.6	74.1	14.4	73.4	37.5	25.4	99.1	20.0	6.8	11.9
Africa, Blacks	31.5	70.6	22.1	64.1	65.1	26.6	98.9	20.5	6.1	42.7
Africa, Whites[i]	28.3	73.5	11.2	78.0	51.6	23.3	99.4	21.5	6.9	20.9
Other	30.7	75.3	12.7	71.1	47.7	27.5	98.8	20.4	6.2	15.1

Source: U.S. Census Bureau, 2000.

a For children ages 5–17 years.

b Moderate housing cost burden indicates the household pays at least 30% but less than 50% of its income for housing.

c Severe housing cost burden indicates the household pays 50% of its income or more for housing.

d More than one person per room.

e A dash indicates that the sample size is too small to produce statistically reliable results or that the category does not apply to the native group.

f "Vietnam" includes Indochina not specified.

g "Indochina, total" includes Hmong, Cambodia, Laos, Thailand, and Vietnam.

h "Other Europe, Canada" includes Australia and New Zealand.

i "Africa, Whites" includes Asian Africans.

Appendix Table 11.12f. Poverty percentages, of children ages 0–8, by immigrant country or race/ethnic origin

	Children basic budget poor					Children not basic budget poor				
	Moved in past 5 years[a]	Working parent(s)	Moderate housing cost burden (30%–50% income)[b]	Severe housing cost burden (>50% income)[c]	Overcrowded housing[d]	Moved in past 5 years	Working parent(s)	Moderate housing cost burden (30%–50% income)	Severe housing cost burden (>50% income)	Overcrowded housing
Total	27.5	87.0	27.2	27.7	34.8	24.0	98.6	10.8	1.4	9.6
Children in native-born families	27.4	86.1	26.9	27.7	23.4	23.8	98.6	10.4	1.2	6.2
White	26.3	91.6	28.6	24.4	15.9	23.3	99.1	10.7	1.3	4.3
Black	29.9	77.8	24.3	33.9	29.6	27.1	96.2	8.0	0.9	13.3
Puerto Rican, mainland origin	27.0	76.0	25.7	36.9	31.3	25.5	96.5	12.1	1.1	13.4
Puerto Rican, island origin	32.0	71.4	24.7	37.4	41.0	29.9	97.6	10.0	0.9	20.9
Mexican	25.8	82.8	26.6	26.3	42.3	24.7	96.5	9.5	1.0	19.7
Other Hispanic/Latino	27.9	83.3	25.7	28.6	37.7	24.6	97.4	10.6	1.1	16.2
Asian	25.1	85.9	26.2	31.2	33.6	20.3	98.0	15.8	2.9	11.0
Hawaiian/Pacific Islander	28.6	86.3	28.9	28.0	53.7	27.4	96.4	14.8	1.0	28.4
Native American	26.0	83.2	21.2	21.9	37.9	27.8	97.3	6.6	1.3	16.9
Children in immigrant families	27.5	89.1	27.9	27.7	64.7	25.2	98.5	13.1	2.2	28.4
Mexico	27.6	90.0	26.7	22.7	74.0	25.1	97.2	9.0	1.1	51.1
Central America	25.9	89.8	29.6	26.9	69.9	26.3	98.1	12.1	1.7	43.4
Cuba	29.9	87.2	32.0	36.6	48.1	25.5	98.8	15.6	2.4	19.1
Dominican Republic	26.4	78.6	24.1	37.4	54.3	27.9	97.6	11.7	2.4	34.6
Haiti	28.1	87.3	28.4	34.2	53.9	25.4	98.3	16.0	1.3	31.0
Jamaica	25.1	86.1	31.4	35.3	36.0	25.0	98.9	14.9	1.8	19.3
Caribbean, English speaking	24.9	85.4	25.8	39.6	40.2	23.3	98.6	17.7	2.8	18.7
South America	29.6	89.5	32.3	35.4	50.7	27.5	98.7	15.5	2.4	21.6

Japan	29.8	90.9	33.6	38.1	27.0	31.2	99.0	16.8	3.5	11.7
Korea	33.8	87.2	29.8	45.2	53.8	29.2	98.7	17.7	3.4	24.8
China	20.9	92.9	30.6	32.5	61.5	22.6	99.0	11.7	2.4	20.8
Hong Kong	21.3	92.2	26.9	39.7	51.6	19.2	99.8	17.0	2.6	15.9
Taiwan	29.8	88.3	24.4	46.6	39.3	21.1	98.5	19.4	4.4	12.2
Philippines	28.5	92.8	29.0	24.0	55.3	26.0	98.6	15.8	1.8	31.1
Hmong	29.3	83.0	24.7	15.7	87.2	27.6	—[e]	—	—	—
Cambodia	29.9	69.2	28.2	30.0	71.8	17.3	98.3	9.6	1.2	43.6
Laos	27.9	82.2	23.0	26.0	74.0	21.2	97.8	7.7	1.8	36.7
Thailand	30.3	79.7	30.7	26.7	68.7	20.7	99.1	15.1	4.1	19.5
Vietnam[f]	27.5	87.5	29.2	31.1	59.6	19.5	98.6	12.9	2.1	32.6
Indochina total[g]	28.3	83.1	27.5	27.6	68.0	19.8	98.5	12.0	2.1	33.6
India	26.3	90.7	33.3	36.4	51.9	23.9	99.2	12.0	2.5	25.6
Pakistan/Bangladesh	30.3	91.6	29.3	41.1	64.9	27.8	98.9	11.6	1.7	37.7
Afghanistan	—	—	—	—	—	22.5	—	—	—	—
Iran	27.7	87.4	20.9	63.4	41.7	22.2	99.5	21.8	6.7	15.4
Iraq	27.8	78.3	27.5	45.2	50.7	21.5	99.9	17.9	6.0	20.4
Israel/Palestine	23.9	86.8	24.1	50.6	47.9	22.0	98.8	16.9	4.4	17.7
Other West Asia	23.4	87.0	27.6	47.6	45.9	23.4	98.8	15.8	2.9	17.8
Former USSR	34.9	87.2	31.1	33.9	59.6	27.9	99.1	12.5	2.4	17.7
Other Europe, Canada[h]	27.7	91.6	30.7	34.5	28.1	25.3	99.4	14.5	2.7	7.8
Africa, Blacks	28.4	88.8	30.1	30.8	59.1	26.3	99.0	9.3	0.7	32.2
Africa, Whites[i]	22.6	90.2	32.0	37.5	42.7	24.8	99.6	13.6	3.0	14.5
Other	28.2	90.5	30.6	33.1	37.0	27.7	99.5	14.3	2.4	9.1

Source: U.S. Census Bureau, 2000.

[a]For children ages 5–17 years.

[b]Moderate housing cost burden indicates the household pays at least 30% but less than 50% of its income for housing.

[c]Severe housing cost burden indicates the household pays 50% or more of its income for housing.

[d]More than one person per room.

[e]A dash indicates that the sample size is too small to produce statistically reliable results or the category does not apply to the native group.

[f]"Vietnam" includes Indochina not specified.

[g]"Indochina, total" includes Hmong, Cambodia, Laos, Thailand, and Vietnam.

[h]"Other Europe, Canada" includes Australia and New Zealand.

[i]"Africa, Whites" includes Asian Africans.

Appendix Table 11.13. Housing situation percentages, of children ages 0–8, by immigrant country or race/ethnic origin

	In families with home owned by parents[a]	In families with moderate housing cost burden (30–50% income)[b]	In families with severe housing cost burden (50%+ income)[c]	Living in overcrowded housing[d]
Total	62.5	17.9	12.8	20.6
Children in native-born families	65.7	16.9	11.7	13.0
White	75.2	16.2	8.4	7.9
Black	36.7	18.6	22.3	23.8
Puerto Rican, mainland origin	35.1	20.6	23.6	24.7
Puerto Rican, island origin	29.9	20.3	26.6	35.0
Mexican	51.5	18.9	14.8	32.1
Other Hispanic/Latino	51.5	18.9	16.2	28.0
Asian	70.0	18.9	11.4	17.8
Hawaiian/Pacific Islander	45.4	22.4	15.6	42.1
Native American	54.5	15.1	13.3	29.1
Children in immigrant families	50.1	21.7	17.0	49.5
Mexico	42.9	22.5	17.6	68.6
Central America	37.1	24.0	18.8	61.4
Cuba	67.5	21.9	15.7	30.3
Dominican Republic	23.3	21.0	28.5	49.3
Haiti	43.1	24.5	23.9	46.7
Jamaica	51.9	23.5	19.4	28.1
Caribbean, English speaking	52.5	22.0	22.0	29.9
South America	50.9	23.7	18.6	35.9
Japan	50.2	21.7	13.6	16.2
Korea	55.5	22.2	19.0	35.6

China	67.0	18.7	13.6	36.0
Hong Kong	85.0	19.3	11.3	24.3
Taiwan	83.0	20.4	12.5	17.4
Philippines	66.0	19.7	8.3	38.2
Hmong	42.2	21.6	12.9	79.6
Cambodia	46.0	21.2	19.2	61.2
Laos	53.3	17.2	16.8	59.8
Thailand	55.9	23.3	16.0	45.4
Vietnam[e]	62.9	20.4	15.3	44.9
Indochina total[f]	57.2	20.3	15.7	52.0
India	58.0	17.0	10.5	31.9
Pakistan/Bangladesh	40.0	21.6	23.9	53.0
Afghanistan	51.4	26.6	30.7	42.1
Iran	74.1	21.6	20.4	21.7
Iraq	60.6	23.4	28.4	37.7
Israel/Palestine	58.5	20.0	24.5	30.9
Other West Asia	58.9	21.4	24.3	31.2
Former USSR	53.9	20.9	16.7	36.8
Other Europe, Canada[g]	67.6	19.5	12.4	14.0
Africa, Blacks	37.5	20.7	17.3	47.0
Africa, Whites[h]	57.0	20.2	15.4	24.7
Other	68.4	19.7	12.5	18.3

Source: U.S. Census Bureau, 2000.

[a]Parent or householder.

[b]Moderate housing cost burden indicates the household pays at least 30% but less than 50% of its income for housing.

[c]Severe housing cost burden indicates the household pays 50% or more of its income for housing.

[d]More than one person per room.

[e]"Vietnam" includes Indochina not specified.

[f]"Indochina, total" includes Hmong, Cambodia, Laos, Thailand, and Vietnam.

[g]"Other Europe, Canada" includes Australia and New Zealand.

[h]"Africa, Whites" includes Asian Africans.

Appendix Table 11.14. Percent of children enrolled in pre-K/nursery school, kindergarten, or grade school, by immigrant country or race–ethnic origin

	Pre-K/nursery school			Kindergarten		Grade school	Any school	
	Age 3	Age 4	Age 5	Age 4	Age 5	Age 5	Age 4	Age 5
Total	36.3	57.6	34.4	4.0	47.3	3.3	61.6	85.1
Children in native-born families	37.9	60.1	36.7	3.1	45.5	3.0	63.2	85.1
White	37.3	60.8	38.4	2.2	43.9	2.2	63.0	84.5
Black	44.8	62.1	32.9	6.6	50.0	5.5	68.7	88.4
Puerto Rican, mainland origin	39.3	56.9	28.6	5.4	55.4	3.8	62.2	87.7
Puerto Rican, island origin	31.0	48.8	28.0	6.7	51.6	5.7	55.4	85.3
Mexican	28.3	47.9	31.2	4.5	47.3	4.2	52.4	82.6
Other Hispanic/Latino	32.8	55.1	33.2	3.5	47.5	2.9	58.6	83.6
Asian	43.1	64.6	32.2	2.6	54.0	2.2	67.2	88.3
Hawaiian/Pacific Islander	30.2	58.9	22.4	1.9	57.6	5.1	60.8	85.1
Native American	31.9	54.7	32.9	2.7	45.5	3.7	57.4	82.1
Children in immigrant families	29.9	48.0	25.9	7.3	54.4	4.7	55.3	85.0
Mexico	17.9	35.3	23.0	8.2	54.0	5.4	43.5	82.4
Central America	25.2	42.7	23.9	9.2	55.6	4.1	51.9	83.7
Cuba	37.2	60.8	30.0	5.8	47.4	6.2	66.7	83.6
Dominican Republic	33.2	51.6	19.4	9.7	61.9	5.4	61.3	86.7
Haiti	48.1	59.5	25.9	12.7	54.0	8.6	72.3	88.5
Jamaica	48.4	65.6	25.8	10.0	59.5	5.2	75.6	90.5
Caribbean, English speaking	44.4	59.0	25.6	9.7	58.2	6.9	68.7	90.6
South America	37.9	57.2	28.2	7.0	55.3	4.5	64.2	87.9
Japan	48.3	67.5	37.2	3.1	53.2	1.4	70.6	91.8
Korea	45.0	64.9	34.0	5.1	53.9	1.7	70.1	89.5
China	46.9	66.3	30.9	7.6	56.9	3.3	73.9	91.1
Hong Kong	52.6	74.6	32.4	3.7	62.5	1.3	78.3	96.2

Taiwan	54.5	76.3	33.4	2.6	57.9	1.8	78.9	93.1
Philippines	27.1	48.3	22.1	2.5	57.2	3.9	50.9	83.2
Hmong	19.7	24.7	18.1	8.4	57.1	6.4	33.1	81.6
Cambodia	19.5	28.6	19.0	9.1	53.1	6.9	37.7	78.9
Laos	16.4	35.2	19.2	2.9	52.9	5.6	38.2	77.7
Thailand	36.1	49.5	28.1	2.5	52.4	3.5	51.9	84.0
Vietnam[a]	25.9	47.3	25.0	8.1	54.9	5.3	55.4	85.2
Indochina[b]	24.4	41.7	23.1	7.1	54.4	5.5	48.8	83.0
India	43.3	64.9	33.2	3.9	53.5	3.9	68.9	90.5
Pakistan/Bangladesh	27.7	47.4	24.8	8.4	54.7	6.3	55.8	85.8
Afghanistan	—[c]	—	—	—	—	—	—	—
Iran	53.8	72.1	36.9	4.5	48.4	2.6	76.7	87.9
Iraq	24.6	42.9	—	5.6	—	—	48.5	—
Israel/Palestine	60.5	67.5	28.5	11.4	58.6	7.8	78.9	94.8
Other West Asia	35.9	58.2	26.0	5.4	56.4	4.9	63.6	87.3
Former USSR	36.8	52.5	24.5	6.6	51.7	2.5	59.2	78.7
Other Europe, Canada[d]	45.0	64.7	32.8	4.1	52.7	2.7	68.8	88.2
Africa, Blacks	49.0	61.4	29.9	11.2	51.9	7.3	72.6	89.0
Africa, Whites[e]	43.8	67.3	28.7	5.2	56.6	6.0	72.5	91.3
Other	42.4	65.8	34.2	4.5	49.7	2.3	70.3	86.2

Source: U.S. Census Bureau, 2000.

[a]"Vietnam" includes Indochina not specified.

[b]"Indochina, total" includes Hmong, Cambodia, Laos, Thailand, and Vietnam.

[c]A dash indicates that the sample size is too small to produce statistically reliable results.

[d]"Other Europe, Canada" includes Australia and New Zealand.

[e]"Africa, Whites" includes Asian Africans.

Appendix Table 11.15. Number of children enrolled in pre-K/nursery school, kindergarten, or grade school, by immigrant country or race–ethnic origin

	Pre-K/nursery school			Kindergarten		Grade school	Any school	
	Age 3	Age 4	Age 5	Age 4	Age 5	Age 5	Age 4	Age 5
Total	1,314,312	2,149,368	1,309,318	148,144	1,799,003	126,014	2,297,512	3,234,335
Children in native-born families	1,087,388	1,781,094	1,105,491	92,461	1,370,796	89,076	1,873,555	2,565,363
White	769,569	1,299,661	831,633	46,098	950,417	47,869	1,345,759	1,829,919
Black	211,077	308,501	169,881	32,769	258,075	28,471	341,270	456,427
Puerto Rican, mainland origin	12,251	16,981	9,177	1,605	17,769	1,209	18,586	28,155
Puerto Rican, island origin	7,522	12,156	7,354	1,663	13,562	1,487	13,819	22,403
Mexican	40,329	65,981	42,444	6,152	64,394	5,717	72,133	112,555
Other Hispanic/Latino	21,156	35,219	21,179	2,248	30,360	1,846	37,467	53,385
Asian	9,602	15,019	6,974	616	11,705	473	15,635	19,152
Hawaiian/Pacific Islander	1,381	2,687	1,020	86	2,622	233	2,773	3,875
Native American	14,501	24,889	15,829	1,224	21,892	1,771	26,113	39,492
Children in immigrant families	226,924	368,274	203,827	55,683	428,207	36,938	423,957	668,972
Mexico	55,529	112,283	75,110	26,095	176,484	17,580	138,378	269,174
Central America	14,333	23,229	13,945	4,988	32,432	2,396	28,217	48,773
Cuba	4,230	7,260	3,931	693	6,210	812	7,953	10,953
Domincan Republic	5,358	10,323	3,782	1,949	12,053	1,057	12,272	16,892
Haiti	4,515	6,188	2,826	1,324	5,904	945	7,512	9,675
Jamaica	6,211	8,491	3,142	1,296	7,238	633	9,787	11,013
Caribbean, English speaking	5,291	6,864	3,107	1,123	7,059	837	7,987	11,003
South America	12,985	20,864	10,403	2,553	20,421	1,672	23,417	32,496
Japan	3,271	3,984	2,411	182	3,454	94	4,166	5,959
Korea	6,720	9,666	5,591	763	8,871	273	10,429	14,735
China	8,992	11,055	4,988	1,272	9,190	535	12,327	14,713
Hong Kong	2,351	4,085	1,540	202	2,975	61	4,287	4,576

Taiwan	2,884	4,253	1,849	143	3,201	97	4,396	5,147
Philippines	7,579	13,720	6,621	714	17,100	1,158	14,434	24,879
Hmong	627	893	752	304	2,371	265	1,197	3,388
Cambodia	692	1,226	780	388	2,185	282	1,614	3,247
Laos	697	1,736	877	145	2,413	254	1,881	3,544
Thailand	1,109	1,357	777	68	1,451	97	1,425	2,325
Vietnam[a]	5,566	10,085	5,301	1,730	11,623	1,124	11,815	18,048
Indochina[b]	8,691	15,297	8,487	2,635	20,043	2,022	17,932	30,552
India	9,840	12,604	6,100	765	9,831	711	13,369	16,642
Pakistan/Bangladesh	2,244	4,097	2,225	731	4,909	568	4,828	7,702
Afghanistan	240	401	245	121	595	—[c]	522	840
Iran	2,696	3,810	1,964	240	2,578	140	4,050	4,682
Iraq	558	1,036	445	135	1,191	148	1,171	1,784
Israel/Palestine	2,343	2,759	1,203	468	2,474	328	3,227	4,005
Other West Asia	4,322	7,545	3,237	694	7,036	611	8,239	10,884
Former USSR	5,248	6,771	3,096	857	6,541	315	7,628	9,952
Other Europe, Canada[d]	29,893	42,442	22,438	2,705	36,094	1,859	45,147	60,391
Africa, Blacks	7,364	8,657	4,329	1,578	7,508	1,052	10,235	12,889
Africa, Whites[e]	3,367	5,035	2,156	391	4,251	451	5,426	6,858
Other	9,869	15,555	8,656	1,066	12,564	583	16,621	21,803

Source: U.S. Census Bureau, 2000.

[a] "Vietnam" includes Indochina not specified.

[b] "Indochina, total" includes Hmong, Cambodia, Laos, Thailand, and Vietnam.

[c] A dash indicates that the sample size is too small to produce statistically reliable results.

[d] "Other Europe, Canada" includes Australia and New Zealand.

[e] "Africa, Whites" includes Asian Africans.

12

RACIAL AND ETHNIC GAPS IN SCHOOL READINESS

Jeanne Brooks-Gunn, Cecilia Elena Rouse, and Sara McLanahan

Are children ready to learn when they enter kindergarten? Teachers believe that more than two of five are not (based on a late 1990s survey of 3,500 kindergarten teachers; Rimm-Kaufman, Pianta, & Cox, 2000). Areas of concern include poor academic skills, difficulties working in a group, and problems following directions. Black and Hispanic children are more likely than White kindergartners to be rated as not being ready to learn upon school entry. This chapter explores what we know about racial and ethnic gaps in school readiness and what we can do about these gaps.

At the end of high school, Black and Hispanic youth are much less likely to do well in school than White students. For example, looking at the National Assessment of Education Progress data from 2002, 42% of White high school students, compared with 16% and 22% of Black and Hispanic students, earned a rating of "solid academic performance" on the reading test administered (Grigg, Daane, Jin, & Campbell, 2003). These ethnic and racial gaps are seen in other subject areas in high school. They are also seen in elementary and middle school (Jencks & Phillips, 1998).

Social scientists, educators, and policy makers all agree that closing these gaps is a national priority. In fact, the No Child Left Behind Act (NCLB) of 2002 (PL 107-110) has reducing these achievement differences as a major goal. This chapter focuses on ethnic and racial gaps as children enter school. Are such gaps seen in preschoolers and kindergartners? If so, what accounts for them? Finally, what policies might reduce these gaps? The goal of public policy should be to ensure that racial and ethnic minority children begin school on an equal footing to children from majority backgrounds (Rouse, Brooks-Gunn, & McLanahan, 2005).

A substantial portion—about one half—of the achievement test gap in high school exists at the time children enter kindergarten (Phillips, Crouse, & Ralph, 1998). Children who are doing poorly in preschool and kindergarten are likely to continue to do poorly through

The contents of this chapter are drawn from Rouse, C., Brooks-Gunn, J., & McLanahan, S. (2005). School readiness: Closing racial and ethnic gaps. *The Future of Children, 15*(1).

elementary and high school. This influences their prospects for high school graduation, postsecondary schooling, and employment (Baydar, Brooks-Gunn, & Furstenberg, 1993; Feinstein & Bynner, 2004). Children who have difficulty with their peers, who are disruptive in the classroom, and who are aggressive (compared with other kindergartners) are more likely to have school problems in elementary and middle school (Hamre & Pianta, 2001). Evidence also suggests that having high rates of behavior problems (or severe problems) early on is predictive of similar problems in adolescence, which, in turn, is associated with poor school performance, substance use, and juvenile delinquency (Nagin & Tremblay, 1999, 2001).

This chapter reviews racial and ethnic gaps in early childhood achievement, focusing on verbal ability tests, general cognitive tests, and early reading and mathematics tests, primarily as measured in large multisite or nationally representative studies. Much less is known about ethnic and racial gaps in behavior problems, such as aggression, inattention, and self-control; what evidence does exist is discussed in this chapter.

These early gaps are likely due to differences in family demographic characteristics, parenting behaviors, child care experiences, and individual characteristics (such as medical conditions). Some of the evidence for these varied influences is included in this chapter. In addition, as is reviewed here, it is possible to provide services and early education that may reduce these gaps. Indeed, intervention programs that target the preschooler seem to be more effective in enhancing school achievement and reducing problem behaviors in the adolescent years than programs initiated in elementary and high school (at least based on the programs that have been developed to date), as argued by James Heckman and Alan Krueger (2004) and other scholars (Shonkoff & Phillips, 2001). If preschool programs are cost-effective (as they seem to be), then much more effort might be made to intervene early in children's lives rather than wait until later.

This chapter is divided into four sections. The first section reviews what is known about racial and ethnic gaps in school readiness (Rock & Stenner, 2005). The focus is on behavioral and cognitive competencies. More is known about Black–White than about other racial and ethnic gaps (such as Hispanic–White gaps) because of the available data; this is reflected throughout the chapter. Also, research has tended to concentrate on academic aspects of school readiness rather than the behavioral or health aspects.

The second section examines the circumstances that are likely to contribute to these gaps and is based on a volume of *The Future of Children* that we edited and that includes six different papers (Rouse et al., 2005). These papers focus on the social and economic resources of the family (Duncan & Magnuson, 2005), on the health of the child (Currie, 2005), on birth weight (Reichman, 2005), on parenting behaviors and the home environment (Brooks-Gunn & Markman, 2005), and on child care (Magnuson & Waldfogel, 2005). William Dickens (2005) also wrote a paper on genetics. He finds no evidence for genetic contributions to cognitive and achievement gaps between race and ethnic groups, even though these competencies have a hereditable component. Each author conducted a literature review to estimate the size of racial and ethnic gaps in each factor as well as the strength of the links between each contributing factor and school readiness. From this information, each author then estimated what the decrease in the school readiness gaps would be if racial and ethnic differences in each contributing factor were eliminated.

Third, this chapter explores what programs and policies might be implemented to reduce the school readiness gaps. The possibilities range from tax credits to job training, to human capital investment, to health care, to parenting programs, to early childhood education. Each is briefly considered in this section.

Finally, we discuss the most promising programs and policies that, based on the evidence reviewed, are the best bets for reducing the racial and ethnic gaps in school readiness. These programs and policies have been chosen based on what is known about the effectiveness of various options, privileging the knowledge gleaned from experimental evaluations (random assignment) in making recommendations.

RACIAL AND ETHNIC GAPS IN SCHOOL READINESS MEASURES

Cognitive, language, and achievement measures of school readiness exist, as do measures of behaviors. The former are tapped using verbal ability, general cognition, and early achievement assessments, for the most part. Tests used to estimate test score gaps include the *Peabody Picture Vocabulary Test—Revised* (PPVT-R; Dunn & Dunn, 1981), the *Stanford-Binet Intelligence Scale, 4th Edition* (Thorndike, Hagen, & Sattler, 1986), the *Wechsler Preschool and Primary Scale of Intelligence–Revised* (WPSSI; Wechsler, 1989), the *Woodcock-Johnson Psychoeducational Battery—Revised* (Woodcock & Johnson, 1989), and the *Early Childhood Longitudinal Study–Kindergarten (ECLS-K) Battery* (National Center for Education Statistics, 2001). Behavior is most frequently assessed using the *Child Behavior Checklist* (CBCL; Achenbach & Rescorla, 2001), the *Behavioral Problems Index* (BPI; Peterson & Ziv, 1986), and the *Social Skills Rating Scales* (SSRS); constructs such as aggression, anxiety, inattention, self-control, and approaches to learning are tapped. Parents and teachers rate children on the frequency or severity of a list of behaviors (for a review, see Rock & Stenner, 2005).

Scores on most cognitively oriented tests in preschool and kindergarten are predictive of later achievement, estimated to be 25%–36% of the variance in later test scores. In the recent ECLS-K study, kindergarten test scores account for about 60% of the variance in third-grade test scores (Rock & Stenner, 2005). Therefore, racial and ethnic test score gaps seen in preschool and kindergarten are predictive of such gaps in later years.

Gaps have been reported for academic and behavioral school readiness (see Rock & Stenner, 2005, pp. 24–25). For example, on verbal ability and general cognition, Black preschoolers score more than one standard deviation (SD) below White preschoolers (when differences are not adjusted for social and economic family background differences; Brooks-Gunn, Klebanov, & Duncan, 1996; Brooks-Gunn, Klebanov, Smith, Duncan, & Lee, 2003; Phillips, Brooks-Gunn, Duncan, Klebanov, & Crane, 1998). These differences are reduced substantially when background differences are taken into account (40%–70%). No comparable data exist for Hispanics.

Using the ECLS-K battery, Blacks have math scores that are 64% of a standard deviation lower than Whites, and their reading scores are 40% lower. These differences are reduced by 70%–80% when social and family background differences are taken into account (Fryer & Levitt, 2004). The results are similar for Hispanic–White gaps. Therefore, the gaps are much smaller when using the ECLS-K than the PPVT-R or IQ tests (about one half of a standard deviation versus more than one standard deviation). Rock and Stenner (2005) discussed some of the reasons that the test score gaps are larger for verbal ability and general cognition than for achievement tests. Race or ethnic test bias does not seem to account for the differences (Nisbett, 1998).

Using the ECLS-K teacher ratings, White children have higher scores on approaches to learning (.36 of a SD) and self-control (.38 of a SD) and lower scores on externalizing problems (.31 of a SD) than Black children (these are raw scores). The gaps are smaller for Hispanics (.21 of a SD for approaches to learning and .13 of a SD for self-control, favoring White children).

What does it mean to say there is a one standard deviation difference between Whites and Blacks or between Whites and Hispanics on a school achievement test? Rock and Stenner (2005), using the Lexile Calculator (http://www.lexile.com/Calculator/LexileCalculator.asp), illustrated as follows:

> Randomly selecting one Black child and one White child and comparing their scores, the White child will exceed the Black child 76% of the time and the Black child will exceed the White child 24% of the time.
>
> Stated differently, if a class with equal numbers of White and Black children is divided by race into two equal-size groups based on ability, then Black students will compose roughly 70% and Whites will compose roughly 30% of the students in the lower performing group.
>
> If a school district chooses only the top-scoring 5% of students for entry into gifted classrooms, such classes will have 13 times more Whites than Blacks (pp. 26–27).

These examples show the vast disparity in Black and White students if they differ by one standard deviation on an academic achievement test. They also demonstrate that a difference of even one half of a standard deviation will result in many more Black than White children not doing well in school.

Even though adjusting for several social and economic background differences reduces these gaps, it does not eliminate them. These findings motivate a more detailed examination of the five conditions discussed in the next section. It is also important to remember that in the real world, adjustments are not made for family background; therefore, for an individual Black or Hispanic child, quite substantial racial and ethnic gaps exist and are relevant.

ACCOUNTING FOR RACE AND ETHNIC TEST SCORE GAPS

A variety of factors contribute to these school readiness gaps, including social and economic factors, birth weight, child health, parenting behaviors, and child care experiences. This section reviews the evidence for each. It is important to emphasize that the estimates of the amount of variance each factor contributes to the test score gaps are likely inflated, given that the factors themselves are related. For example, social and economic factors account for a large portion of the variance, and so do parenting behaviors. However, the two are related in that mothers with higher education and more family income also talk more to their children and provide more cognitively stimulating activities. When family background and parenting are considered at the same time, they both contribute to the test score gap, but not as much as the sum of the two.

In analyses in which measures of most of the five factors are considered, test score gaps in achievement scores, verbal ability scores, and IQ test scores are reduced by about 70%–80% (Brooks-Gunn et al., 1996, 2003; Fryer & Levitt, 2004; Phillips, Brooks-Gunn,

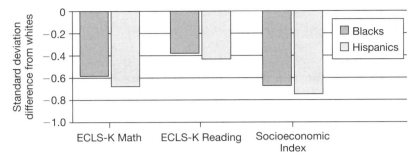

Figure 12.1. Racial and ethnic gaps in selected test scores and in family socioeconomic status for kindergartners. (*Source:* Duncan & Magnusson, 2005.)

et al., 1998). Neighborhood residence (i.e., in an affluent or poor neighborhood) and intergenerational factors (e.g., grandparents' education; immigration status) also contribute to the gap (Brooks-Gunn et al., 1996; Leventhal, Xue, & Brooks-Gunn, 2006; Phillips, Brooks-Gunn, et al., 1998), although their influence is not as great as family background and parenting. According to recent estimates from the ECLS-K, such analysis can account for around 90% of the test score gap with factors that are potentially modifiable; about four fifths to three quarters of the gap can be accounted for when other tests are used (such as IQ tests).

Family Social and Economic Background

The family social and economic conditions of White children are much better than those of Black and Hispanic children. Striking disparities are seen in maternal education, family structure (married, cohabiting, or single parents), family income, and neighborhood resources (Duncan, Brooks-Gunn, & Klebanov, 1994). Racial and ethnic differences, although less stark, are also seen for maternal age, parental employment, and instability of residence.

So, it comes as no surprise that when the family social and economic background variables of different ethnic and racial groups are compared using the same metric as has been used for test score gaps, Black children are residing in families that are 70% of a standard deviation below White children, and Hispanic children are 78% of a standard deviation below White children (see Figure 12.1 which uses data from the ECLS-K as an illustration). Test scores gaps, as presented earlier, are between 50% and 100% of a standard deviation (lower for the ECLS-K, from which Figure 12.1 is derived).

Social and economic background is often measured using a composite variable called socioeconomic status, which includes parental income, education, family structure, neighborhood income, maternal age, and work status (Brooks-Gunn & Duncan, 1997; Hauser & Warren, 1997; Mueller & Parcel, 1981). Family background is highly associated with school readiness, both academic and behavioral; links are seen in some studies as early as age 1 and almost always by age 2 (Klebanov, Brooks-Gunn, McCarton, & McCormick, 1998).

Studies sometimes measure these constructs separately to understand the relative importance of each condition for a particular aspect of child well-being (Duncan et al., 1994; Duncan, Yeung, Brooks-Gunn, & Smith, 1998; Smith, Brooks-Gunn, & Klebanov, 1997). At the risk of vast oversimplification, the order of importance of the three main background factors goes from parental education to family income (typically deep and persistent poverty) to family structure (Dearing, McCartney, & Taylor, 2001; Duncan & Brooks-Gunn, 1997; Mayer, 1997; Phillips, Brooks-Gunn, et al., 1998). Income may be more highly associated with cognitive and academic outcomes, and family structure may be more highly associated with behavioral outcomes (McLanahan, 1997).

The links between family background and child well-being may, in some cases, be due to the fact that children whose parents are poor, have little education, and are single might also have parents who have mental and physical health problems and who exhibit less competent parenting (e.g., are less sensitive, are more harsh, talk less, provide fewer stimulating activities). The children themselves are more likely to be low birth weight and have health problems. These factors are considered in the following sections.

Low Birth Weight

Low birth weight is defined as less than 2,500 grams; children born at very low birth weight (less than 1,500 grams) are often distinguished from those born low birth weight but above 1,500 grams. Between 7% and 8% of all births in the United States are less than 2,500 grams, with three quarters of these births being 1,500 grams or more (Martin et al., 2002; Reichman, 2005).

Children born at low birth weight are more likely to die in the first year of life (although rates of survival have increased dramatically in the last 40 years, especially for those who are very low birth weight; for example, for babies born between 1,000 and 1,499 grams, 1-year survival rates climbed from 45% in 1960 to 93% in 2000; Reichman, 2005). Children who survive are more likely to have cognitive and physical problems, such as cerebral palsy, mental retardation, deafness, and learning difficulties, making it likely that more of these children will be less ready for school than full birth weight children (Klebanov, Brooks-Gunn, & Duncan, 1994; McCormick, Brooks-Gunn, Workman-Daniels, Turner, & Peckham, 1992; Pinto-Martin et al., 2004).

Black babies are twice as likely as White babies to be born low birth weight (about 13% versus 6.5%). Although Hispanic mothers generally give birth to low birth weight babies at the same rate as White mothers, rates are much higher for mothers of Puerto Rican descent than for those of Mexican descent (more than 9% versus 6%; Martin et al., 2002). Such racial and ethnic differences are not totally explained by social and economic resources. Lifestyle differences are thought to be operating (Guendelman, 1994) an idea that is reinforced by the fact that immigrant mothers are less likely to have low birth weight births than native-born mothers, regardless of race or ethnicity. Survival rates of low birth weight babies are similar across racial and ethnic groups.

The effect of low birth weight on racial test score gaps has been estimated to be a little less than 2% (age 5–6 PPVT-R scores in the National Longitudinal Survey of Youth–Child Supplement [NLSY-CS]; Brooks-Gunn et al., 2003) to 3%–4% (imputed IQ test scores based on birth weight, using 2000 vital statistics data; Reichman, 2005). These estimates do not control or adjust for family social and economic differences between Black and White children.

Health of Children

Currie (2005) summarized the literature on racial and ethnic disparities in health, focusing on health problems with a relatively high prevalence (because if very few children are affected by a particular problem, reducing racial and ethnic disparities in them would not reduce the overall test score gap by much) and on health conditions with known links to school performance. Asthma, attention-deficit/hyperactivity disorder (ADHD), lead poisoning, anemia, and iron deficiency are examined in her article.

Asthma   Asthma, a common chronic health condition, accounts for the most trips to emergency rooms, the most absences from school, and the most hospitalizations of children. Children with asthma may be more likely to have low school readiness scores (Fowler, Davenport, & Garg, 1992; Halterman et al., 2001). It is not clear whether such effects are less for children whose asthma is well controlled.

About 13% of those under age 18 have been diagnosed with asthma; Blacks have higher rates than Whites or Hispanics (15.7%, 12.2%, and 11.2%, respectively; Currie, 2005). Asthma attacks reported in the last 6 months are also higher among Blacks (7.7%, 5.7%, and 4%, respectively; Akinbami, LaFleur, & Schoendorf, 2002). Asthmatic Black and Hispanic children may be less likely than asthmatic White children to have appropriate care and medication (Lieu et al., 2002). However, according to Currie's estimates, the racial disparities in asthma are likely to account for a small percentage of the variance in school readiness gaps (about 2%; Currie, 2005).

Lead Exposure   Children may be exposed to lead in paint, drinking water (lead was used to solder pipes), gasoline, canned food, and some ceramic dishes. The federal government now regulates lead in all of these situations, which has dramatically reduced the number of young children with high lead levels. For example, in the late 1970s, more than 88.2% of 1- to 5-year-olds had blood lead levels above 10 micrograms/deciliter compared with 2.2% in 1999–2000 (National Health and Nutrition Examination Survey [NHANES] data; Centers for Disease Control and Prevention [CDC]). High levels are more likely in 1- to 5-year-old Black children by a factor of 4 (NHANES data; Meyer et al., 2003).

Although estimates of the size of the links between high lead levels and IQ test scores differ, Currie used a conservative estimate of a 5-point IQ test score decrement due to high lead levels. Racial disparities in high lead levels account for up to 0.2% of a standard deviation in school readiness scores.

Iron Deficiency   Iron deficiency has negative effects on cognition, the immune system, and metabolic functioning. Iron deficiency in children is less widespread today than in the late 1970s, most likely thanks to iron-fortified cereals and the Women, Infants, and Children (WIC) program (Looker, Cogswell, & Gunter, 2002; Looker, Dallman, Carroll, Gunter, & Johnson, 1997). Rates of iron deficiency were between 15% and 30% in the late 1970s for preschool children but had decreased to 3%–9% in 1999–2000. At that time, Black preschoolers were twice as likely to be iron deficient as White preschoolers (16% versus 8%). However, it is not clear whether reducing the racial disparities would reduce racial gaps in school readiness, given the mixed results regarding cognition functioning of randomized interventions offering iron supplementation to children (Grantham-McGregor & Ani, 2001).

Attention-Deficit/Hyperactivity Disorder   ADHD, which is characterized by inattention and restlessness in at least two settings, is associated with not being ready for school. Symptoms of ADHD are present before age 7. National prevalence rates differ, although in the National Health Interview Survey (NHIS), a little more than 4% of boys and a little fewer than 2% of girls have "clinically significant" ADHD symptoms. Black boys have the highest rate, then Whites, and then Hispanics (5.7%, 4.3%, and 3.1%, respectively; Bloom et al., 2003). Blacks are less likely to be treated for ADHD (i.e., in the 1997 medical expenditure panel, 4.4% of Whites and 1.7% of Blacks were treated for ADHD; Olfson et al., 2003).

Currie estimates that up to 10% of the racial gap in school readiness might be explained by racial differences in ADHD. She notes that even though the prevalence estimates are relatively small, the effects of ADHD on school readiness are relatively large.

Summary　In brief, child health conditions, at least the ones reviewed by Currie, might explain up to 12%–14% of the racial gap in school readiness. She cautioned that this is an upper-bound estimate because these health conditions are also associated with family poverty and because Black families are much more likely than White families to be poor.

Parenting Behavior

In their article, Brooks-Gunn and Markman (2005) described parenting as the myriad activities that parents engage in either with or for their children. They divide these activities into seven categories of behaviors: nurturance, discipline, teaching, language, monitoring, management, and materials. After each category was defined, using measures that social scientists typically use, they examined whether ethnic and racial differences exist. Then, they examined how much of the gap in school readiness might be explained by the presence of racial and ethnic differences in parenting.

These researchers also consider the evidence for the premise that parenting behaviors influence child well-being. It is possible that the so-called effects of parenting are really due to other factors, including 1) family social, education, and economic conditions; 2) genetic similarities between parent and child; 3) child characteristics; and 4) other unmeasured characteristics. Although all four factors are important, the researchers noted that these other factors do not account completely for links between parenting and child outcomes, as is reviewed in their article (Caspi et al., 2004; Collins, Maccoby, Steinberg, Hetherington, & Bornstein, 2001; Duyme, Dumaret, & Tomkiewiez, 1999; Patterson, DeBaryshe, & Ramsey, 1989; Raikes et al., 2006; Singer et al., 2004; Trouton, Spinath, & Plomin, 2002).

Finally, Brooks-Gunn and Markman (2005) gave serious consideration to whether one can compare parenting measures across racial and ethnic groups. Three issues were raised: 1) whether parenting behaviors are universal or specific to time and place, 2) how representative the parenting behaviors typically measured and developed for middle-class White samples are of other groups, and 3) whether a particular society privileges certain parenting behaviors. In general, all societies exhibit these seven categories of parenting behaviors (Harkness & Super, 1995). However, they may differ in their emphasis of one over another (e.g., in some societies, parents talk more to their young children than parents in other societies; Greenfield, Keller, Fuligni, & Maynard, 2003). Although the measuring schemes developed for middle-class White samples have generally worked quite well for other groups (i.e., they have adequate reliability and validity), sometimes certain behaviors valued by a group are not measured (e.g., the importance of compliance in some societies); current measures are not effective in assessing the ways in which parents induce compliance in their children (Wasserman, Rauh, Brunelli, Garcia-Castro, & Necos, 1990). Sometimes, a coding system aggregates certain parenting behaviors in ways that often obscure parenting patterns in certain groups. An example is that Black mothers are more likely than White mothers to exhibit both authoritarian and authoritative behaviors in a pattern that is termed "tough love"; this construct is rarely measured (Brooks-Gunn & Chase-Lansdale, 1995). Finally, it is true that some parenting behavior habits, which may be more frequent in middle-class samples, are privileged in many studies. They are also the aspects of parenting that are most highly correlated with academic school readiness (language and teaching). Parenting behaviors less likely to be correlated with school readiness are less often measured. It is not that one class of parenting behaviors is better than another; it is just that one may be more highly correlated with school readiness and, ultimately, school achievement in our society. These are also the aspects of parenting that are targeted in intervention programs.

Nurturance   Nurturance involves ways of expressing love, affection, and care. Measures include being responsive to a child's needs; being sensitive to changes in a child's behaviors; and not being detached, intrusive, or negative. The Home Observation for Measurement of the Environment (HOME; Bradley & Caldwell, 1984) inventory is often used to assess warmth (via observation and a checklist), whereas other measures have involved videotaping parent–child interactions (e.g. the three-bag procedure, National Institute of Child Health and Development [NICHD] Early Child Care Research Network, 1999; the Early Head Start Study, Berlin, Brady-Smith, & Brooks-Gunn, 2002; Ispa et al., 2004) and coding them later as well as coding live interactions (e.g. Nursing Child Assessment Satellite Training [NCAST] Barnard, 1994).

Black mothers exhibit somewhat lower levels of sensitivity than White mothers, as measured by videotaped interactions, at about 20% of a standard deviation (Brooks-Gunn & Markman, 2005; Ryan, Brady-Smith, & Brooks-Gunn, 2004). The more negative behaviors listed previously are seen more frequently in Black than White mothers (Berlin, Brady-Smith, & Brooks-Gunn, 2002; Berlin, Brooks-Gunn, Spiker, & Zaslow, 1995).

Discipline   Discipline involves parents' responses to child behaviors that they consider appropriate or inappropriate, depending on a child's age and gender and on parental beliefs, upbringing, and culture. Sometimes harsh behaviors are coded from videotapes or observed during a home visit; sometimes mothers are asked about their discipline strategies and about the frequency of spanking (Bradley, 2002; Fuligni, Han, & Brooks-Gunn, 2004; Leventhal, Selner-O'Hagan, Brooks-Gunn, Bingenheimer, & Earls, 2004; Smith & Brooks-Gunn, 1997). Black mothers are somewhat more likely to spank their children than White mothers. These differences are 10%–20% of a standard deviation.

Teaching   Teaching includes strategies for providing skills or information to the child. Typically, a parent and child are given a problem-solving task and observers watch and code the interaction. Quality of assistance is measured (Chase-Lansdale, Brooks-Gunn, & Zamsky, 1994; Spiker, Ferguson, & Brooks-Gunn, 1993; Sroufe, Egeland, & Kreutzer, 1990). Also, the HOME inventory includes items related to teaching that are often summed for a learning stimulation scale (Linver, Brooks-Gunn, & Cabrera, 2004; Klebanov et al., 1994). These items are answered by mothers.

Although less is known about the teaching category, the available evidence suggests that Black mothers teach less than White mothers (it is difficult to place a standard deviation estimate on these parenting behaviors given the lack of information; Brooks-Gunn & Markman, 2005).

Language　Language use is often measured by observing parents and children at home—sometimes for hundreds of hours—and making transcripts from audiotapes of the conversations (Clark, 1993; Hart & Risley, 1995; Huttenlocher et al., 1991; Weizman & Snow, 2001). Observers also observe parental language use by having a parent read a book to the child; parents vary in how often they ask the child questions and expand on what is in the story (Britto & Brooks-Gunn, 2001; Ninio, 1983; Snow & Ninio, 1986). Some variants of the HOME inventory also have items about reading frequency (Bradley & Caldwell, 1984; Linver et al., 2004).

Language differs quite a bit across racial and ethnic groups. Black mothers talk less to their children, read books with them less, and have fewer books and reading materials in the home (Fuligni, Han, & Brooks-Gunn, 2004; Phillips et al., 1998; Raikes et al., 2006). Hispanic mothers also read less and have fewer reading materials in the home (data are not available regarding overall conversation). These differences are between 20% and 60% of a standard deviation.

Materials　The HOME inventory also includes items about materials in the home that are cognitively and linguistically stimulating. These include number of books in the home, number of magazine or newspaper subscriptions, toys for learning the alphabet, and so forth (Bradley, Corwyn, McAdoo, & Garcia-Coll, 2001; Raikes et al., 2006). The extensiveness of materials is associated with family income, which is not surprising (Mayer, 1997).

Learning materials are less frequent in Black and Hispanic children's homes than in White children's homes (Clark, 1993; Dickinson & Tabors, 2001; Hart & Risley, 1995, 1999; Huttenlocher et al., 1991). The two former groups have about 40%–60% of a standard deviation less learning materials than the latter group.

Monitoring　Monitoring is referred to as "keeping track." Even when parents are not directly interacting with their children, they are often paying attention to what their children are doing (e.g., what television shows are being watched, whether the television is on, whether a child in another room is awake or asleep, whether a very quiet toddler in another room is getting into mischief). For young children, measurement of this frequent activity is almost nonexistent (with the exception of time-use diaries, although some do not explicitly ask about monitoring; Fuligni & Brooks-Gunn, 2004). Information on racial or ethnic differences does not exist.

Management　This category includes scheduling events, completing events and everyday tasks, and the consistency and stability of the family routine. Typically, these aspects of parenting are not measured frequently or well. Perhaps the most common items tapping management involve whether children are getting the recommended number of well-baby and well-child visits, whether children are getting immunized on time, and whether preschoolers are taken to the dentist. The HOME inventory also includes items on taking children to the park, outside, and to visit relatives (Fuligni & Brooks-Gunn, 2004; Klebanov et al., 1998). Family routines are of interest theoretically but are not often measured. Items include regularity of bedtime and routines (singing, reading, praying), regularity of mealtime, and who eats together (Boyce, Jensen, James, & Peacock, 1983; Love et al., 2002). Little is known about whether racial or ethnic differences exist.

Summary   Ethnic and racial differences in parenting during early childhood are found for the five categories of parenting on which there are data. Where differences exist, Black mothers have lower scores than White mothers; the same seems to be true for Hispanic mothers, although the data base is thin. These effects are quite large—between one fifth and three fifths of a standard deviation (remember that the effects for family background were three fifths to four fifths of a standard deviation). If the disparity in parenting styles were reduced, racial school readiness gaps would decrease by 25%–60%. The previously mentioned estimates might suggest even larger effects; however, it must be remembered that the aforementioned parenting measures are related to one another, so each estimate given is not picking up unique variance.

Early Child Care and Education

In their article, Magnuson and Waldfogel (2005) explored whether Black, White, and Hispanic children have similar experiences of child care and education. Preschool education and center-based care (especially high-quality care) are associated with better school readiness (Barnett, 1995; Campbell & Ramey, 1995; Currie, 2001; Henry et al., 2003; Karoly et al., 1998; NICHD Early Child Care Research Network & Duncan, 2003; Ramey & Ramey, 1998; Reynolds, 1995; Schweinhart, Barnes, & Weikart, 1993). If Black and Hispanic preschoolers are less likely than White preschoolers to get preschool education or to be placed in center-based care, then part of the gap in school readiness could be offset by providing these children with such services.

Many preschools rely on family fees to operate; children from poorer families are less likely to attend such programs. Public funding pays for Head Start and pre-kindergarten (pre-K) programs; the former only serves poor children, and the latter are often targeted toward families or communities with low income (although a few states offer universal pre-K programs). Child care subsidies are available for working poor families; they vary as a function of locale and family income. Head Start serves 3- and 4-year-olds, and pre-K serves 4-year-olds. Tax credits also exist.

By age 4, about 60% of children are in some sort of preschool or care setting, compared with about 17% of 2-year-olds (Magnuson & Waldfogel, 2005). About 14% of 4-year-olds were in public school–based preschool programs in 2002 (Smith, Kleiner, Parsad, & Farris, 2003). Georgia, Oklahoma, and the District of Columbia offer these programs to all 4-year-olds, and a little more than one half of eligible children are enrolled in each state (Magnuson & Waldfogel, 2005). Head Start serves about 10% of 3- and 4-year-olds, or about 65% of those eligible (Currie & Neidell, 2003).

Based on the Current Population Survey (CPS), Black 3-year-olds are more likely than White children of the same age to be enrolled in any type of preschool (49% and 43% in 1998–2000); only 23% of Hispanic 3-year-olds were enrolled (Magnuson & Waldfogel,

2005). More 4-year-olds are in preschool (around 60%), although Hispanics still lag the other two groups in enrollment.

Using data from the Head Start Bureau and the 2000 Decennial Census, Magnuson and Waldfogel (2005) determined that Black and Hispanic preschoolers are more likely than White children to be enrolled in Head Start (20% and 15% compared with 4%), which is to be expected because Head Start serves primarily low-income families. Magnuson and Waldfogel's estimation of enrollment rates is a calculation based on the number of Head Start slots available, not the number of children served, which is larger because of turnover. Consequently, these estimates likely understate the number of children who have ever participated in Head Start (Magnuson and Waldfogel, 2005).

If Head Start did not exist (assuming that these low-income children would not be in private preschools), overall gaps in preschool enrollment might increase by 9% for Black children and 31% for Hispanics (both compared with White children). These estimates are derived by subtracting each group's rate of attendance in Head Start from its October CPS rates of preschool attendance. For example, because 19% of Black 4-year-olds are in Head Start and CPS data indicate that 72% of Black 4-year-olds are in preschool, without access to Head Start (and without enrollment in other programs), their enrollment rate would be 53%. By comparison, only 5% of White 4-year-olds are in Head Start, so without access to Head Start (and without enrollment in other programs), their enrollment rate would fall from 67% to 62%, resulting in a Black–White enrollment gap of 9% (compared with Black children's current enrollment advantage of 5%).

Assuming that Head Start enhances school readiness skills by 60% of a standard deviation (the authors base this estimate on data from the Chicago Child Parent Center evaluation; Reynolds, 1995), then the school readiness gap between Black and White children would be larger than it is (because more Black than White children attend Head Start). Even if the estimate of beneficial effects of Head Start were lower (say, 30% of a standard deviation), significant reductions in the gap would still accrue if Head Start were to cease to exist.

Preschool programs vary widely in terms of quality. Do racial or ethnic differences appear for overall quality of preschool programs? Few data exist to answer this question. However, in the Cost, Quality and Outcomes Study, conducted in four states, White children were in higher quality care than were Black children (Burchinal & Cryer, 2003). The difference was about 30% of a standard deviation. And, in a slightly different analysis looking at all types of care rather than just center-based and preschool, using the NICHD Study of Early Child Care, the quality of care experienced by White children was 70% of a standard deviation higher than that of Black children (Burchinal & Cryer, 2003).

The possible effects of increasing preschool enrollment of Black and Hispanic children in reducing the school readiness gap as well as the possible effects of increasing the quality of care are estimates. Estimates are provided for different levels of increased enrollment (five scenarios) using different estimates of the beneficial effects of such enrollment on preschool reading scores (15%, 25%, and 65% of a standard deviation increase; Magnuson & Waldfogel, 2005). If Hispanic children's enrollment rose from 40% to 60%, the Hispanic–White reading gap would be reduced by 3%–13% of a standard deviation. If 80% of Hispanic children were enrolled and the rate did not change for White children (60%), the gap would be reduced by 6%–26% of a standard deviation. The Black–White gap would not be reduced as much because the rates of Black and White preschool enrollment are so similar. Targeting children by income (enrolling all children who are poor or all children whose families' incomes are below 200% of the poverty line) would also reduce the gaps, but not by as much as estimated above using a standard deviation gap, which differs from the way the data are presented by Magnuson and Waldfogel (2005).

Increasing quality also would reduce the ethnic and racial gaps; however, these reductions would be smaller because effects of quality tend to be smaller overall. The authors estimate the effects at 10%, 20%, and 30% of a standard deviation (Magnuson & Waldfogel, 2005). If enrollment levels are not increased, even though quality is, the potential benefits to reducing the gap are quite small (about 2%–7% of a standard deviation). Increasing quality and enrollment for Black and Hispanic children or for all low-income children would reduce the gap by up to 12% of a standard deviation for Black and 18% for Hispanic preschoolers.

Intervention Strategies for Reducing Racial and Ethnic Gaps

Many programs and policies have the potential to reduce the racial and ethnic gaps in school readiness. Which ones are most promising, based on available evidence from well-designed experimental evaluations? In this section, program efficacy is reviewed for income supplementation and parent employment, parent education programs, programs to prevent low birth weight, health care to prevent or treat chronic health conditions, parenting programs, and preschool programs.

Income Supplementation   Increasing family income is one avenue to reducing the gaps in school readiness. However, the racial differences in family income are huge, estimated to be at least $30,000 (Duncan & Magnuson, 2005). Current policies and programs, and even large expansions of these programs, may narrow the income gap but will not even come close to eliminating it. At the same time, correlational studies suggest that reducing deep and persistent poverty, especially in the preschool years, has the potential to increase school achievement (Dearing, McCartney, & Taylor, 2001; Duncan & Brooks-Gunn, 1997; Duncan et al., 1998; Smith et al., 1997). Most programs and policies are oriented toward minimizing the number of families in poverty and maximizing the number of parents who are employed.

The welfare reform experiments of the last decade are informative. These programs, by and large, have resulted in more parents being employed, although some but not all have increased family income (and family income increases are themselves modest—the largest being $1,000–$2,000 a year; Krueger & Whitmore, 2001). Achievement of children in early elementary school only improved in those experiments where family income increased. Duncan and Magnuson (2005) estimated that for every $1,000 in additional family income, school achievement increased by 7% of a standard deviation. Krueger and Whitmore estimated that a 20% increase of a standard deviation increase in test scores from the Tennessee STAR class-size experiment could boost future earnings between $5,000 and $50,000, depending on assumed discount and future earnings growth rates. The 7% of a standard deviation found would increase earnings by one third of these amounts. Although modest, these gains are similar to those estimated by other authors for reductions in health disparities or for increases in quality of child care.

Another strategy involves the Earned Income Tax Credit, which is a refundable tax credit targeting working low-income parents. The maximum credit for a two-child family was $4,200 in 2002 (Council of Economic Advisors, 1998). Almost 19 million families got this tax credit that same year. It also supports parental employment and is, in part, associated with the dramatic rise in employment for poor parents, especially single parents. The impact of this program on school readiness is not known and would be difficult to estimate, given the lack of experimental data.

Parental Education   Another approach to enhancing family social and economic resources targets poorly educated parents. Enhancing work skills and increasing years of schooling might affect children, given the links between parental education and child school readiness. Similar to the findings on income, it is likely that impacts of education, or increased education, will matter the most for mothers who have not completed high school (Haveman & Wolfe, 1995).

Many of the welfare reform experiments have mandated education or work skill training. Such participation has been associated with better school readiness, in some cases by 25% of a standard deviation in some but not all experiments. It is likely that overall estimates would be more modest, in the range of 12%.

Other approaches include encouraging teenage mothers to stay in school or even to mandate that they stay in school, providing mentoring for at-risk adolescents (not parents), providing summer school for struggling high school students, increasing funding for community colleges, and increasing financial aid packages for postsecondary education. In general, such programs have had only very modest success (Duncan & Magnuson, 2005).

Marriage Promotion   Given that children whose parents are married do better in elementary school and that single parenthood is much more prevalent in Black and Hispanic than White families, marriage promotion is another avenue to reducing readiness gaps. Some, but not all, of the welfare reform experiments have increased marriage rates to a modest degree, even though that was not the central purpose of these programs (Duncan & Magnuson, 2005).

A promising development is the initiation of programs to promote marriage, with an emphasis on providing relational and emotional skills to low-income couples, both those who are married and those who are not (Dion, 2005). Data are not yet available regarding these programs (Knab & McLanahan, 2006).

Prevention of Low Birth Weight   A variety of strategies have been employed to prevent low birth weight. These include increasing access to prenatal care and getting women into such care early in their pregnancy, expanding Medicaid eligibility and services, providing social support and educational services (often through home visiting), doing medical interventions, reducing smoking, and enhancing nutrition. Some but by no means all of these programs have resulted in fewer low birth weight births (Reichman, 2005).

Although the efficacy of improving access to prenatal care is difficult to prove or disprove (because it would be unethical to withhold prenatal care for the sake of a randomized trial), increases in the proportion of pregnant women receiving such care over the past 30 years have not resulted in lower rates of low birth weight (Klerman et al., 2001; Martin et al., 2002), even though racial gaps in income have decreased over time. Also, more Whites receive prenatal care than do Blacks (Martin et al., 2002). Expanding Medicaid, in some cases, has reduced rates of low birth weights, with effects possibly being stronger for Blacks than Whites. An interesting study found that changes in Medicaid hospital payments in California lowered the rate of low birth weights for Black babies (Aizer, Lleras-Muney, & Stabile, 2004; Almond & Chay, 2003). Although many experiments have been conducted on programs that offer education or social support to pregnant women, they have not altered the low birth weight rate (Lu, Tache, Alexander, Kotelchuck, & Halfon, 2003). Participation in WIC, however, has been shown to reduce the proportion of low-weight births (Bitler & Currie, 2005; Kowaleski-Jones & Duncan, 2002; Reichman & Teitler, 2003).

Health Care   Solutions to the disparities in chronic health conditions include increasing access to health care, linking prevention and treatment of health conditions with family-based services, reaching more young children through WIC, and linking health and educational services. Again, some of these strategies, but not all of them, have shown some promise.

Currie (2005) argued that expanding health insurance coverage might not make much of a difference in reducing racial health disparities. This is because Medicaid and the State Children's Health Insurance Program (S-CHIP) have been greatly enhanced since the mid-1990s. Therefore, almost all poor and near-poor children are eligible for public health insurance (Lewitt, Bennet, & Behrman, 2003). However, some eligible children are not enrolled, and many who are get acute but not preventative care (Kuhlthau, Nyman, Ferris, Beal, & Perrin, 2004). One idea is to make all children eligible for Medicaid services and then charge premiums on a sliding scale (Lewitt et al., 2003), although this is unlikely to eliminate disparities in chronic health conditions altogether.

Family-based services are another way to deliver services. A widely replicated and successful program is the Nurse Home Visiting Program developed by David Olds (Olds et al., 1999). Incorporating health services into preschool is another tested strategy. Head Start has been offering health services since its inception. In a 20-year-old study by Abt Associates, children in Head Start were more likely to have seen a dentist, to be immunized, and to be screened for hearing and vision (Currie & Neidell, 2003). An interesting recent analysis of Head Start budgets reports that programs spending proportionately more of their budget on health and education than on other services have children who have higher achievement test scores later in childhood (Currie & Neidell, 2003).

Finally, the WIC program may be part of the reason that the rate of anemia (iron deficiency) declined between the mid-1970s and the mid-1980s (Yip, Binkin, Fleshood, & Trowbridge, 1987). Almost 60% of all infants are eligible for WIC (with about 45% receiving benefits; Bitler, Currie, & Scholz, 2003). The proportion of children in WIC drops steeply during the toddler period. WIC provides coupons to buy specific nutritional foods and also helps families get preventative health care. Therefore, keeping children in WIC after their first year might be a promising strategy for reducing disparities.

Parenting Programs   Programs focusing on altering parenting behaviors include those that are home based (often termed *home visiting*) programs, center-based early childhood education programs with a parenting component, family literacy programs, and programs targeting child behavior problems by changing parenting behaviors (Brooks-Gunn, Berlin, & Fuligni, 2000; Brooks-Gunn & Markman, 2005). Experimental evaluations have consistently reported beneficial effects on parenting behaviors. Some, but not all, studies also find that children's school readiness scores are also enhanced. A summary of each follows.

Home-visiting programs and center-plus-home-visiting programs mostly target families who are poor and who have little education. More evaluations have targeted Black and urban families than White, Hispanic, or rural families. The programs have targeted nurturance, discipline, stimulating activities, materials, and teaching. All of these parenting behaviors have been altered by programs with well-trained home visitors and center staff that see families relatively frequently. Home-visiting programs are more likely to influence nurturance than other parenting behaviors (Brooks-Gunn et al., 2000; van Ijzendoorn, Juffer, & Duyvesteyn, 1995). Some programs also target parental emotional health, typically measuring maternal depressive symptoms (Brooks-Gunn et al., 2000). Fewer of these home-visiting programs report effects on maternal mental health than on parenting behaviors; altering mental health might require more focused treatment of depressive symptoms. Differential effects of parenting interventions for mothers who are and are not depressed have been found in some studies (Love et al., 2005). The authors' premise here is that programs might want to target services to families with mental health issues because program effects might be largest for this group.

Few programs have actually tried to increase maternal language output (although all stress talking to and reading with the child). A few literacy programs have tried to change how parents read with their children; the goal is to use more and more varied language. Grover Whitehurst and colleagues (1994) have developed a successful program that trains mothers and teachers to read with an emphasis on asking children questions, providing feedback to their responses, initiating conversations, and delving into children's understanding of concepts (Dickinson & Neuman, 2006; Whitehurst et al., 1994).

Parent behavior training programs have also been successful in reducing children's behavior problems. A successful exemplar is the Incredible Years Curriculum, developed by Carolyn Webster-Stratton, which has been used in Head Start programs with mothers and teachers (Webster-Stratton, 1998; Webster-Stratton, Reid, & Hammond, 2001; Webster-Stratton & Taylor, 2001).

When it comes to children, few home-visiting programs have altered children's school readiness (Barnett, 1995; Gomby, Larner, Stevenson, Lewit, & Behrman, 1995; Olds et al., 2004). In contrast, the center-based early childhood education programs with a parenting component have improved vocabulary, reading and math achievement, and IQ test scores, with some effects continuing through adolescence in studies that have followed children that long (Barnett, 2002; Campbell, Ramey, Pungello, Sparling, & Miller-Johnson, 2002; Karoly et al., 1998). Although only a few programs have reported very modest reductions in behavior problems, those with long-term follow-ups have reported reductions in juvenile delinquency and teenage pregnancy. We do not know whether center-based programs with and without parenting components have similar effects (because almost every center program that has been evaluated has a parent component); however, part of the beneficial effects on school readiness seem to be through the effects on parents (Bradley et al., 1994; Love et al., 2002). At the same time, pre-K programs such as those in Oklahoma, which do not have a large parent component, have shown positive effects on school readiness (Gormley, Gayer, Phillips, & Dawson, 2005).

Although evidence is limited, the positive effects of such programs may be greater when mothers have a high school education or less, have low psychological resources, and are first-time parents; they also may be greater for Black than White mothers. These findings might indicate that parenting programs are likely to reduce racial disparities (Brooks-Gunn & Markman, 2005).

Preschool Programs   High-quality model early childhood education programs, which have enrolled poor children, have reported positive effects on school readiness, school success, and even adult well-being. At the beginning of school, effects were between 30% and 70% of a standard deviation. These programs provided developmentally appropriate education, with most also having health, nutrition, and parenting components. Teachers were highly educated and trained, and child-to-staff ratios were low. Children attended programs for full or half days, typically for two or more years, and efforts were made to ensure that children attended on a regular basis. Unfortunately, these characteristics are not seen in the majority of preschool programs nationwide.

Certain categories of programs seem to be of higher quality (such as the state-funded, school-based pre-k programs) than others; the first evaluations suggest that this model is effective (Gormley et al., 2005). Attendance in pre-k classes increased language skills by 39% of a standard deviation, with the largest effects for Black and Hispanic children attending the program full day (Gormley et al., 2005).

Evidence for Head Start is mixed; although Head Start programs vary in quality, in general the teachers have lower education and training than do teachers in pre-k programs. Effects of Head Start programs from 30 years ago were quite modest, although positive (Lee, Brooks-Gunn, Schnur, & Liaw, 1990). Sibling comparisons suggest that Head Start has modest beneficial effects, although findings vary by ethnicity and race (Currie & Thomas, 1995; Garces, Thomas, & Currie, 2002). None of these studies are based on randomized assignment. A Head Start Impact Study, using random assignment, is in the field at the present time; preliminary results suggest modest effects (more along the lines of 10%–20% of a standard deviation). Whether such modest effects will be sustained is not known. Early Head Start, which provides services to infants and toddlers, has also reported modest effects overall (although for programs that offered both home-visiting and center-based care, the effects are often more than 25% of a standard deviation; Love et al., 2005).

BEST BETS

The introduction to the special issue of *The Future of Children* (Rouse et al., 2005), on which this chapter is based, discusses which programs and policies might be best bets for closing racial and ethnic gaps in school readiness. Some programs are unlikely to make any differences—these include increasing public health insurance coverage (poor children are already covered, although efforts need to be made to enroll eligible children) and providing educational and support programs for reducing low birth weight. Small reductions might occur by implementing more educational and skill programs for low-education mothers, income supplementation for welfare-to-work program participants, and enhanced Earned Income Tax Credits. Nutrition programs, particularly WIC, have been somewhat effective in reducing low birth weight and anemia (and could provide screening for chronic health conditions).

The most promising approach might be to increase access to high-quality, center-based, early education programs. Such programs should be available to all low-income

3- and 4-year-olds (Rouse et al., 2005). These programs would have the characteristics of the model preschool programs that have proved so effective—low child-to-staff ratios, highly educated teachers, and well-designed, cognitively and linguistically stimulating curricula. Most current programs do not have these features. Ideally, these programs would identify children with moderate to severe behavior problems and offer training to their parents (and their teachers). Another parenting component could involve literacy and reading because programs emphasizing these skills have been effective. As Head Start does, all programs would offer health referrals and screening. And, finally, more planning should be done to coordinate pre-k and kindergarten programs, which often are very separate.

REFERENCES

Achenbach, T.M., & Rescorla, L.A. (2001). *Manual for ASEBA school-age forms & profiles.* Burlington: University of Vermont, Research Center for Children, Youth, & Families.

Aizer, A., Lleras-Muney, A., & Stabile, M. (2004, April). *Access to care, provider choice, and racial disparities in infant mortality* (NBER Working Paper No. W10445). Available from the Social Science Research Network (SSRN) at http://ssrn.com/abstract=533004

Akinbami, L.J., LaFleur, B.J., & Schoendorf, K.C. (2002). Racial and income discrepancies in childhood asthma in the United States. *Ambulatory Pediatrics, 2*(5), 382–387.

Almond, D., & Chay, K.Y. (2003). *The long-run and intergenerational impact of poor infant health: Evidence from cohorts born during the civil rights era.* Cambridge, MA: National Bureau of Economic Research. Available from the National Bureau of Economic Research at www.nber.org/~almond/cohorts.pdf

Barnard, K. (1994). *NCAST teaching scale.* Seattle: University of Washington, School of Nursing.

Barnett, W.S. (1995). Long-term effects of early childhood programs on cognitive and school outcomes. *The Future of Children, 5*(3), 25–50.

Barnett, W.S. (2002). Early childhood education. In A. Molner (Ed.), *School reform proposals: The research evidence* (p. 1). Greenwich, CT: Information Age Publishing.

Baydar, N., Brooks-Gunn, J., & Furstenberg, F.F. (1993). Early warning signs of functional illiteracy: Predictors in childhood and adolescence. *Child Development, 64,* 815–829.

Berlin, L.J., Brady-Smith, C., & Brooks-Gunn, J. (2002). Links between childbearing age and observed maternal behaviors with 14-month-olds in the Early Head Start Research and Evaluation Project. *Infant Mental Health Journal, 23,* 104–129.

Berlin, L.J., Brooks-Gunn, J., Spiker, D., & Zaslow, M.J. (1995). Examining observational measures of emotional support and cognitive stimulation in black and white mothers of preschoolers. *Journal of Family Issues, 16*(5), 664–686.

Bitler, M.P., & Currie, J. (2005). Does WIC work? The effects of WIC on pregnancy and birth outcomes. *Journal of Policy Analysis and Management, 24*(1), 73–91.

Bitler, M.P., Currie, J., & Scholz, J.K. (2003). WIC eligibility and participation. *Journal of Human Resources, 38,* 1139–1179.

Bloom, B., Cohen, R.A., Vickerie, J.L., & Wondimu, E.A. (2003). Summary health statistics for U.S. children: National Health Interview Survey, 2001. *Vital Health Statistics Series, 10*(216), 1–54.

Boyce, W.T., Jensen, E.W., James, S.A., & Peacock, J.L. (1983). The family routines inventory: Theoretical origins. *Social Science and Medicine, 17*(4), 193–200.

Bradley, R.H. (2002). Environment and parenting. In M. Bornstein (Ed.), *Handbook of parenting: Vol. 2. Biology and ecology of parenting* (p. 281). Hillsdale, NJ: Lawrence Erlbaum Associates.

Bradley, R.H., & Caldwell, B. (1984). *Home observation for measurement of the environment.* Little Rock, AR: University of Arkansas.

Bradley, R.H., Corwyn, R.F., McAdoo, H.P., & Garcia-Coll, C.G. (2001). The home environment of children in the United States, part 1: Variations by age, ethnicity, and poverty status. *Child Development, 72*(6), 1844–1867.

Bradley, R.H., Whiteside, L., Mundfrom, D.J., Casey, P.H., Caldwell, B.M., & Barrett, K. (1994). Impact of the Infant Health and Development Program (IHDP) on the home environments of infants born prematurely and with low birth weight. *Journal of Educational Psychology, 86*(4), 531–541.

Britto, P.R., & Brooks-Gunn, J. (Eds.). (2001). The role of family literacy environments in promoting young children's emerging literacy skills. *New Directions for Child and Adolescent Development, 92.*

Brooks-Gunn, J., Berlin, L.J., & Fuligni, A.S. (2000). Early childhood intervention programs: What about the family? In J.P. Shonkoff & S.J. Meisels (Eds.), *Handbook on early childhood intervention* (2nd ed., pp. 549–588). New York: Cambridge University Press.

Brooks-Gunn, J., & Chase-Lansdale, L. (1995). Adolescent parenthood. In M. Bornstein (Ed.), *Handbook of parenting: Vol.3. Status and social conditions of parenting* (p. 113). Mahwah, NJ: Lawrence Erlbaum Associates.

Brooks-Gunn, J., & Duncan, G.J. (1997, Summer/Fall). The effects of poverty on children. *The Future of Children, 7,* 55–71.

Brooks-Gunn, J., Klebanov, P.K., & Duncan, G.J. (1996). Ethnic differences in children's intelligence test scores: Role of economic deprivation, home environment, and maternal characteristics. *Child Development, 67,* 396–408.

Brooks-Gunn, J., Klebanov, P.K., Smith, J., Duncan, G.J., & Lee, K. (2003). The black–white test score gap in young children: Contributions of test and family characteristics. *Applied Developmental Science, 7,* 239–252.

Brooks-Gunn, J., & Markman, L.B. (2005). The contributions of parenting to ethnic and racial gaps in school readiness. *The Future of Children, 15*(1), 139–168.

Burchinal, M.R., & Cryer, D. (2003). Diversity, child care quality, and developmental outcomes. *Early Childhood Research Quarterly, 18,* 401–426.

Campbell, F.A., & Ramey, C.T. (1995). Cognitive and school outcomes for high-risk African American students at middle adolescence: Positive effects of early intervention. *American Educational Research Journal, 32,* 743–772.

Campbell, F., Ramey, C.T., Pungello, E., Sparling, J.J., & Miller-Johnson, S. (2002). Early childhood education: Young adult outcomes from the Abecedarian Project. *Applied Developmental Science, 6*(1), 42–57.

Caspi, A., Moffitt, T.E., Morgan, J., Rutter, M., Taylor, A., Arseneault, L., et al. (2004). Maternal expressed emotion predicts children's antisocial behavior problems: Using monozygotic-twin differences to identify environmental effects on behavioral development. *Developmental Psychology, 40*(2), 149–161.

Chase-Lansdale, L., Brooks-Gunn, J., & Zamsky, E. (1994). Young African-American multigenerational families in poverty: Quality of mothering and grandmothering. *Child Development, 65*(2), 373–393.

Clark, E. (1993). *The lexicon in acquisition.* New York: Cambridge University Press.

Collins, W.A., Maccoby, E.A., Steinberg, L., Hetherington, M.E., & Bornstein, M.H. (2001). Contemporary research on parenting: The case for nature and nurture. *American Psychologist, 55*(2), 218–232.

Council of Economic Advisers. (1998). *Good news for low income families: Expansions in the earned income tax credit and the minimum wage.* Washington, DC: Author.

Currie, J. (2001). Early childhood intervention programs: What do we know? *Journal of Economic Perspectives, 15,* 213–238.

Currie, J. (2005). Health disparities and gaps in school readiness. *The Future of Children, 15,* 117–138.

Currie, J., & Neidell, M. (2003, November). *Getting inside the 'black box' of Head Start quality: What matters and what doesn't* (Working Paper No. 10091). Cambridge, MA: National Bureau of Economic Research.

Currie, J., & Thomas, D. (1995). Does Head Start make a difference? *American Economic Review, 85,* 341–364.

Dearing, E., McCartney, K., & Taylor, B.A. (2001). Change in family income-to-needs matters more for children with less. *Child Development, 72*(6), 1779–1793.

Dickens, W.T. (2005). Genetic differences and school readiness. *The Future of Children, 15,* 55–69.

Dickinson, D., & Neuman, S. (Eds.). (2006). *Handbook of early literacy research* (Vol. 2). New York: Guilford.

Dickinson, D.K., & Tabors, P.O. (Eds.). (2001). *Beginning literacy with language: Young children learning at home and school.* Baltimore: Paul H. Brookes Publishing Co.

Dion, M.R. (2005). Healthy marriage programs: Learning what works. *The Future of Children, 15*(2), 139–156.

Duncan, G., & Brooks-Gunn, J. (1997). *Consequences of growing up poor.* New York: Russell Sage.

Duncan, G.J., Brooks-Gunn, J., & Klebanov, P.K. (1994). Economic deprivation and early-childhood development. *Child Development, 65,* 296–318.

Duncan, G.J., & Magnuson, K.A. (2005). Can family socioeconomic resources account for racial and ethnic test score gaps? *The Future of Children, 15,* 35–54.

Duncan, G., Yeung, W.J., Brooks-Gunn, J., & Smith, J.R. (1998). How much does childhood poverty affect the life chances of children? *American Sociological Review, 63,* 406–423.

Dunn, L.M., & Dunn, L.M. (1981). *Peabody Picture Vocabulary Test–Revised.* Circle Pines, MN: American Guidance Service.

Duyme, M., Dumaret, A.-C., & Tomkiewiez, S. (1999). How can we boost IQs of 'dull' children?: A late adoption study. *Proceedings of the National Academy of Sciences, 96*(15), 8790–8794.

Feinstein, L., & Bynner, J. (2004). The importance of cognitive development in middle childhood for adulthood socioeconomic status, mental health, and problem behavior. *Child Development, 75,* 1329–1339.

Fowler, M.G., Davenport, M.G., & Garg, R. (1992). School functioning of U.S. children with asthma. *Pediatrics, 90*(6), 939–944.

Fryer, R., & Levitt, S.D. (2004). Understanding the black–white test score gap in the first two years of school. *Review of Economics and Statistics, 86,* 447–464.

Fuligni, A.S., & Brooks-Gunn, J. (2004). Measuring mother and father shared caregiving: An analysis using the panel study of income dynamics-child development supplement. In R. Day & M. Lamb (Eds.), *Conceptualizing and measuring father involvement.* Mahwah, NJ: Lawrence Erlbaum Associates.

Fuligni, A.S., Han, W.J., & Brooks-Gunn, J. (2004). The infant–toddler HOME in the second and third years of life. *Parenting: Science and Practice, 4,* 139–159.

Garces, E., Thomas, D., & Currie, J. (2002). Longer-term effects of Head Start. *American Economic Review, 92,* 999–1012.

Gomby, D., Larner, M.B., Stevenson, C.S., Lewit, E.M., & Behrman, R.E. (1995). Long-term outcomes of early childhood programs: Analysis and recommendations. *The Future of Children, 5*(3), 6–24.

Gormley, W.T., Gayer, T., Phillips, D., & Dawson, B. (2005). The effects of universal pre-k on cognitive development. *Developmental Psychology, 41*(6), 872–884.

Grantham-McGregor, S., & Ani, C. (2001). A review of studies on the effect of iron deficiency on cognitive development on children. *Journal of Nutrition, 131,* 649–666.

Greenfield, P.M., Keller, H., Fuligni, A., & Maynard, A. (2003). Cultural pathways through universal development. *Annual Review of Psychology, 54,* 461–490.

Grigg, W.S., Daane, M.C., Jin, Y., & Campbell, J.R. (2003). *The nation's report card: Reading 2002* (NCES No. 2003-531). Washington, DC: U.S. Department of Education, Institute of Education Sciences, National Center for Education Statistics.

Guendelman, S. (1994). Mexican women in the United States. *The Lancet, 344*(8919), 352.

Halterman, J.S., Montes, G., Aligne, C.A., Kaczorowski, J.M., Hightower, A.D., & Szilagyi, P.G. (2001). School readiness among urban children with asthma. *Ambulatory Pediatrics, 1*(4), 201–205.

Hamre, B.R., & Pianta, R.C. (2001). Early teacher–child relationships and the trajectory of children's school outcomes through eighth grade. *Child Development, 72,* 625–688.

Harkness, S., & Super, C. (1995). Culture and parenting. In M. Bornstein (Ed.), *Handbook of parenting, Vol. 2. Biology and ecology of parenting* (p. 211). Mahwah, NJ: Lawrence Erlbaum Associates.

Hart, B., & Risley, T.R. (1995). *Meaningful differences in the everyday experience of young American children.* Baltimore: Paul H. Brookes Publishing Co.

Hart, B., & Risley, T.R. (1999). *The social world of children learning to talk.* Baltimore: Paul H. Brookes Publishing Co.

Hauser, R., & Warren, J.R. (1997). Socioeconomic indexes for occupations: A review, update, and critique. *Sociological Methodology, 27*(1), 177–298.

Haveman, R., & Wolfe, B. (1995). The determinants of children's attainments: A review of methods and findings. *Journal of Economic Literature, 23,* 1829–1878.

Heckman, J., & Krueger, A. (2004). *Inequality in America: What role for human capital policies?* (B.M. Friedman, Ed.). Cambridge, MA: MIT Press.

Henry, G.T., Henderson, L.W., Ponder, B.D., Gordon, C.S., Mashburn, A.J., & Rickman, D.K. (2003). *Report of the findings from the early childhood study.* Atlanta: Georgia State University, Andrew Young School of Policy Studies.

Huttenlocher, J., Haight, W., Bryk, A., Seltzer, M., & Lyons, T. (1991). Early vocabulary growth: Relation to language input and gender. *Developmental Psychology, 27,* 236–248.

Ispa, J.M., Fine, M.A., Halgunseth, L.C., Harper, S., Robinson, J., Boyce, L., et al. (2004). Maternal intrusiveness, maternal warmth, and mother–toddler relationship outcomes: Variations across low-income ethnic and acculturation groups. *Child Development, 75*(6), 1613–1631.

Jencks, C., & Phillips, M. (1998). The black–white test score gap: An introduction. In C. Jencks & M. Phillips (Eds.), *The black–white test score gap* (pp. 3–4). Washington, DC: Brookings.

Karoly, L.A., Greenwood, P.W., Everingham, S.S., Houbé, J., Kilburn, M.R., Rydell, C.P., et al. (1998). *Investing in our children: What we do and don't know about the costs and benefits of early childhood interventions.* Santa Monica, CA: RAND.

Klebanov, P.K., Brooks-Gunn, J., & Duncan, G.J. (1994). Does neighborhood and family poverty affect mother's parenting, mental health and social support? *Journal of Marriage and the Family, 56*(2), 441–455.

Klebanov, P.K., Brooks-Gunn, J., McCarton, C., & McCormick, M.C. (1998). The contribution of neighborhood and family income to developmental test scores over the first three years of life. *Child Development, 69*(5), 1420–1436.

Klerman, L.V., Ramey, S.L., Goldenberg, R.L., Marbury, S., Hou, J., & Cliver, S.P. (2001). A randomized trial of augmented prenatal care for multiple-risk, Medicaid-eligible African-American women. *American Journal of Public Health, 91*(1), 105–111.

Knab, J., & McLanahan, S. (2006). Measuring cohabitation: Does how, when, and who you ask matter? In S. Hofferth and L. Casper (Eds.), *Handbook of measurement issues in family research* (pp. 19–33). Mahwah, NJ: Lawrence Erlbaum Associates.

Kowaleski-Jones, L., & Duncan, G.J. (2002). Effects of participation in the WIC program on birth weight: Evidence from the national longitudinal survey of youth. *American Journal of Public Health, 92*(5), 799–803.

Krueger, A., & Whitmore, D. (2001). The effect of attending a small class in the early grades on college test taking and middle school test results: Evidence from project STAR. *Economic Journal, 11,* 1–28.

Kuhlthau, K., Nyman, R.M., Ferris, T.G., Beal, A.C., & Perrin, J.M. (2004). Correlates of use of specialty care. *Pediatrics, 113*(3), e249–e255.

Lee, V., Brooks-Gunn, J., Schnur, E., & Liaw, F.R. (1990). Are Head Start effects sustained? A longitudinal follow-up of disadvantaged children attending Head Start, no preschool, and other preschool programs. *Child Development, 61*(2), 495–507.

Leventhal, T., Martin, A., & Brooks-Gunn, J. (2004). The Home Observation for Measurement of the Environment (HOME) Inventory—Early Childhood: Across five national datasets in the third and fifth year of life. *Parenting: Science and Practice, 4,* 161–188.

Leventhal, T., Selner-O'Hagan, M.B., Brooks-Gunn, J., Bingenheimer, J.B., Earls, F. (2004). The homelife interview for the Project on Human Development in Chicago Neighborhoods: Assessment of parenting and home environment for 3–15 year olds. *Parenting: Science and Practice, 4,* 211–241.

Leventhal, T., Xue, Y., & Brooks-Gunn, J. (in press). Immigrant differences in school-age children's verbal trajectories: A look at four racial/ethnic groups. *Child Development.*

Lewitt, E., Bennet, C., & Behrman, R. (2003). Health insurance for children: Analysis and recommendations. *The Future of Children, 13*(1), 1–4.

Lieu, T.A., Lozano, P., Finkelstein, J.A., Chi, F.W., Jensvold, N.G., Capra, A.M., et al. (2002). Racial/ethnic variation in asthma status and management practices among children in managed medicaid. *Pediatrics, 109*(5), 857–865.

Linver, M., Brooks-Gunn, J., & Cabrera, N. (2004). The home observation for measurement of the environment (HOME) inventory: The derivation of conceptually designed subscales. *Parenting: Science and Practice, 4*(2, 3), 99–114.

Looker, A.C., Cogswell, M.E., & Gunter, E.W. (2002). Iron deficiency-United States, 1990-2000. *Morbidity and Mortality Weekly Report, 51*(40), 897–899.

Looker, A.C., Dallman, P.R., Carroll, M.D., Gunter, E.W., & Johnson, C.L. (1997). Prevalence of iron deficiency in the United States. *Journal of the American Medical Association, 277*(12), 973–976.

Love, J.M., Kisker, E.E., Ross, C.M., Brooks-Gunn, J., Schochet, P., Boller, K., et al. (2002). *Making a difference in the lives of infants and toddlers and their families: The impacts of Early Head Start* (Report prepared for the Administration for Children and Families, U.S. Department of Health and Human Services). Princeton, NJ: Mathematica Policy Research.

Love, J.M., Kisker, E., Ross, C., Raikes, H., Constantine, J., Boller, K., et al. (2005). The effectiveness of Early Head Start for 3-year-old children and their parents: Lesson for policy and programs. *Developmental Psychology, 41*(6), 885–901.

Lu, M.C., Tache, V., Alexander, G.R., Kotelchuck, M., & Halfon, N. (2003). Preventing low birth weight: Is prenatal care the answer? *Journal of Maternal-Fetal and Neonatal Medicine, 13*(6), 362–380.

Magnuson, K.A., & Waldfogel, J. (2005). Early childhood care and education: Effects on ethnic and racial gaps in school readiness. *The Future of Children, 15,* 169–196.

Martin, J.A., Hamilton, B.E., Sutton, P.D., Ventura, S.J., Menacker, F., & Munson, M.L. (2002, February). Births: Final data for 2000. *National Vital Statistics Report, 52*(10).

Mayer, S. (1997). *What money can't buy: Family income and children's life chances.* Cambridge, MA: Harvard University Press.

McCormick, M.C., Brooks-Gunn, J., Workman-Daniels, K., Turner, J., & Peckham, G.J. (1992). The health and developmental status of very low-birth-weight children at school age. *Journal of the American Medical Association, 267*(16), 2204–2208.

McLanahan, S.S. (1997). Parent absence or poverty: Which matters more? In G.J. Duncan & J. Brooks-Gunn (Eds.), *Consequences of growing up poor.* New York: Russell Sage.

Meyer, P.A., Pivetz, T., Dignam, T.A., Homa, D.M., Schoonover, J., Brody D., et al. (2003). Surveillance for elevated blood lead levels among children—United States, 1997–2001. *Morbidity and Mortality Weekly Reports Surveillance Summary, 52*(10), 1–21.

Mueller, C., & Parcel, T.L. (1981). Measures of socioeconomic status: Alternatives and recommendations. *Child Development, 52,* 13–30.

Nagin, D.S., & Tremblay, R.E. (1999). Trajectories of boys' physical aggression, opposition, and hyperactivity on the path to physically violent and non-violent juvenile delinquency. *Child Development, 70,* 1181–1196.

Nagin, D.S., & Tremblay, R.E. (2001). Parental and early predictors of persistent physical aggression in boys from kindergarten to high school. *Archives of General Psychiatry, 58,* 389–394.

National Center for Education Statistics, U.S. Department of Education. (2001). ECLS-K Base year data files and electronic codebook. Washington, DC: Author.

National Institute of Child Health and Development Early Child Care Research Network. (1999). Child care and mother–child interaction in the first three years of life. *Developmental Psychology 35,* 1399.

National Institute of Child Health and Development Early Child Care Research Network, & Duncan, G.J. (2003). Modeling the impacts of child care quality on children's preschool cognitive development. *Child Development, 74,* 1454–1475.

Ninio, A. (1983). Joint book reading as a multiple vocabulary acquisition device. *Developmental Psychology, 19,* 445.

Nisbett, R.E. (1998). Race, genetics and IQ. In C. Jenks & M. Phillips (Eds.), *The black–white test score gap* (pp. 86–102). Washington, DC: Brookings.

No Child Left Behind Act of 2001, PL 107-110, 115 Stat. 1425, 20 U.S.C. §§ 6301 *et seq.*

Olds, D.L., Henderson, C.R., Jr., Kitzman, H.J., Eckenrode, J.J., Cole, R.E., & Tatelbaum, R.C. (1999). Prenatal and infancy home visitation by nurses: Recent findings. *The Future of Children, 9*(1), 44–65.

Olds, D., Kitzman, H., Cole, R., Robinson, J., Sidora, K., & Luckey, D.W., et al. (2004). Effects of nurse home-visiting on maternal life course and child development: Age 6 follow-up of a randomized trial. *Pediatrics, 114*(6), 1550–1559.

Olfson, M., Gameroff, M.J., Marcus, S.C., & Jensen, P.S. (2003). National trends in the treatment of attention deficit hyperactivity disorder. *American Journal of Psychiatry, 160*(6), 1071–1077.

Patterson, G., DeBaryshe, B., & Ramsey, E. (1989). A developmental perspective on antisocial behavior. *American Psychologist, 44*(2), 329.

Peterson, J.L., & Zill, N. (1986). Marital disruption, parent–child relationships, and behavior problems in children. *Journal of Marriage and the Family, 48*(2), 295–307.

Phillips, M., Brooks-Gunn, J., Duncan, G., Klebanov, P., & Crane, J. (1998). Family background, parenting practices, and the Black–White test score gap. In C. Jencks & M. Phillips (Eds.), *The Black-White test score gap* (103–145). Washington, DC: Brookings.

Phillips, M., Crouse, J., & Ralph, J. (1998). Does the black–white test score gap widen after children enter school? In C. Jencks & M. Philips (Eds.), *The black–white test score gap* (229–272). Washington, DC: Brookings.

Pinto-Martin, J., Whitaker, A., Feldman, J., Cnaan, A., Zhao, H., & Bloch, J.R., et al. (2004). Special education services and school performance in a regional cohort of low birth weight infants at age nine. *Pediatric and Perinatal Epidemiology, 18*(2), 120–129.

Raikes, H., Pan, B.A., Luze, G., Tamis-Le Monda, C.S., Brooks-Gunn, J., Constantine, J., et al. (2006, July/August). Mother–child bookreading in low-income families: Correlates and outcomes during the first three years of life. *Child Development, 77,* 924–953.

Ramey, C.T., & Ramey S.L. (1998). Early intervention and early experience. *American Psychologist, 53*(2), 109–120.

Reichman, N.E. (2005). Low birth weight and school readiness. *The Future of Children, 15,* 91–116.

Reichman, N.E., & Teitler, J.O. (2003). Effects of psychosocial risk factors and prenatal interventions on birth weight: Evidence from New Jersey's Health Start program. *Perspectives on Sexual and Reproductive Health, 35*(3), 130–137.

Reynolds, A.J. (1995). One year of preschool or two: Does it matter? *Early Childhood Research Quarterly, 10,* 1–31.

Rimm-Kaufman, S.E., Pianta, R.C., & Cox, M.J. (2000). Teachers' judgments of problems in the transition to kindergarten. *Early Childhood Research Quarterly, 15,* 147–166.

Rock, D.A., & Stenner, A.J. (2005). Assessment issues in the testing of children at school entry. *The Future of Children, 15,* 15–34.

Rouse, C., Brooks-Gunn, J., & McLanahan, S. (2005). Introducing the issue; School readiness: Closing racial and ethnic gaps. *The Future of Children, 15,* 5–14.

Ryan, R.M., Brady-Smith, C., & Brooks-Gunn, J. (2004). Videotaped interactions in the Early Head Start Research and Evaluation Project. *The Evaluation Exchange, 10*(3), 24.

Schweinhart, L.J., Barnes, H.V., & Weikart, D.P. (1993). *Significant benefit of the High/Scope Perry Preschool Study through age 27.* Ypsilanti, MI: High/Scope Press.

Shonkoff, J., & Phillips, D. (2001). *From neurons to neighborhoods: The science of early childhood development.* Washington, DC: National Academies Press.

Singer, L., Minnes, S., Short, E., Arendt, R., Farkas, K., Lewis, B., et al. (2004). Cognitive outcomes of preschool children with prenatal cocaine exposure. *Journal of the American Medical Association, 291*(20), 2448–2456.

Smith, J., & Brooks-Gunn, J. (1997). Correlates and consequences of harsh discipline for young children. *Archives of Pediatric and Adolescent Medicine, 151*(8), 777–786.

Smith, J., Brooks-Gunn, J., & Klebanov, P. (1997). The consequences of living in poverty on young children's cognitive development. In G. Duncan & J. Brooks-Gunn (Eds.), *Consequences of growing up poor* (pp. 132–189). New York: Russell Sage.

Smith, T., Kleiner, A., Parsad, B., & Farris, E. (2003). *Prekindergarten in U.S. public schools.* Washington, DC: U.S. Department of Education, National Center for Education Statistics.

Snow, C., & Ninio, A. (1986). The contracts of literacy: What children learn from learning to read books. In W. Teale & E. Sulzby (Eds.), *Emergent literacy: Writing and reading* (pp. 116–117). Norwood, NJ: Ablex.

Spiker, D., Ferguson, J., & Brooks-Gunn, J. (1993). Enhancing maternal interactive behavior and social competence in low birth weight, premature infants. *Child Development, 64,* 754–768.

Sroufe, A., Egeland, B., & Kreutzer, T. (1990). The fate of early experience following developmental change: Longitudinal approaches to individual adaptation in childhood. *Child Development, 61*(5), 1363–1373.

Thorndike, R.L., Hagen, E.P., & Sattler, J.M. (1986). *Stanford-Binet Intelligence Scale* (4th ed.). Chicago: Riverside.

Trouton, A., Spinath, F.M., & Plomin, R. (2002). Twins early development study (TEDS): A multivariate, longitudinal genetic investigation of language, cognition and behavior problems in childhood. *Twin Research, 5,* 444–448.

U.S. Centers for Disease Control. (2003). *Children's blood lead levels in the United States.* Available from Centers for Disease Control and Prevention (CDC) at http://www.cdc.gov/nceh/lead/research/kidsBLL.htm#Tracking

van Ijzendoorn, M., Juffer, F., & Duyvesteyn, M. (1995). Breaking the intergenerational cycle of insecure attachment: A review of the effects of attachment based interventions on maternal sensitivity and infant security. *Journal of Child Psychology and Psychiatry and Allied Disciplines, 36*(2), 225–248.

Wasserman, G.A., Rauh, V.A., Brunelli, S.A., Garcia-Castro, M., & Necos, B. (1990). Psychosocial attributes and life experiences of disadvantaged minority mothers: Age and ethnic variations. *Child Development, 61*(2), 566–580.

Webster-Stratton, C. (1998). Preventing conduct problems in Head Start children: Strengthening parenting competencies. *Journal of Consulting and Clinical Psychology, 66*(5), 715–730.

Webster-Stratton, C., Reid, J., & Hammond, M. (2001). Preventing conduct problems, promoting social competence: A parent and child training partnership in Head Start. *Journal of Child Clinical Psychology, 30*(3), 283–302.

Webster-Stratton, C., & Taylor, T. (2001). Nipping early risk factors in the bud: Preventing substance abuse, delinquency, and violence in adolescence through interventions targeted at young children (0-8 years). Prevention Science, 2(3), 165–192.

Wechsler, D. (1989). *Wechsler Preschool and Primary Scale of Intelligence–Revised.* New York: Harcourt Assessment.

Weizman, Z.O., & Snow, C.E. (2001). Lexical input as related to children's vocabulary acquisition: Effects of sophisticated exposure and support for meaning. *Developmental Pyschology, 37*(2), 265–279.

Whitehurst, G., Epstein, J.N., Angell, A.L., Payne, A.C., Crone, D.A., & Fischel, J.E. (1994). Outcomes of an emergent literacy intervention in Head Start. *Journal of Educational Psychology, 86*(4), 542–555.

Woodcock, R.W., & Johnson, M.B. (1989). *Woodcock-Johnson Psychoeducational Battery–Revised.* Allen, TX: DLM.

Yip, R., Binkin, N.J., Fleshood, L., & Trowbridge, F.L. (1987). Declining prevalence of anemia among low-income children in the United States. *Journal of the American Medical Association, 258*(12), 1619–1623.

13

CO-CONSTRUCTING
THE TRANSITION TO SCHOOL

Reframing the Novice Versus Expert Roles of Children,
Parents, and Teachers from a Cultural Perspective

Fabienne Doucet and Jonathan Tudge

R esearchers have long recognized that the transition to school for young children is one of the most important steps in their development (Entwisle & Alexander, 1993; Mangione & Speth, 1998; Ramey & Ramey, 1994). Beyond the educational process, children also must learn to negotiate which attitudes and behavior habits are most adaptive to the school culture (Beery, 1984). School represents one of the first formal settings in which children are faced with new ideas and ways of doing things. Although this process may appear unilateral, sociocultural factors such as race/ethnicity,[1] region of origin, and social class play important roles in shaping how the transition to school is perceived, how children are prepared for it, and how easily the transition is made (Doucet, 2000; Swick, Brown, & Boutte, 1994). This chapter presents the argument that the transition to school is a cultural process, one that is experienced differently by different groups of people based on cultural characteristics, expectations, and goals. Specifically, there is a strong case for the importance of reframing current constructions of parents' and teachers' roles in fa-

We wish to thank all the participants (particularly the children) who so generously gave their time. We also gratefully acknowledge the financial support of the Spencer Foundation and the University of North Carolina at Greensboro (funding provided to the second author) and the Center for Developmental Science, Chapel Hill, for its support of the first author at the time of data collection. The views expressed are solely those of the authors.

[1]Our use of race/ethnicity (or racial/ethnic) denotes our perspective that race, used alone to distinguish among people based on perceived hereditary characteristics (most often skin color), is socially constructed and limiting in its ability to help us understand the complex nuances of identity and cultural variability. Ethnicity is a more helpful construct because it encompasses shared cultural traits, with national origin or ancestry as the point of reference (Betancourt & López, 1993). However to deny the powerful role that race (i.e., skin color) plays in everyday life in the United States would be misguided (Appiah & Gutmann, 1998). Thus, we use race/ethnicity to acknowledge that, as a social construction, race is a meaningful concept that has an impact on everyday life, but because we are interested here in cultural variation, ethnicity captures more accurately the way in which we frame shared values and beliefs based on ancestry.

cilitating the transition to school to account for the ways in which culture informs and shapes developmental processes.

Children of color[2] comprise close to half of the age 0–4 population in the United States today (U.S. Census Bureau, 2000). One in five children in the United States is a child of immigrant parents (Rong & Preissle, 1998). According to He and Hobbs (1999), by the year 2030, minority children ages 5 and younger will outnumber their nonminority counterparts by a half million.[3]

Whether the children of newly arrived immigrants or of groups with multiple generations of residence in the United States, children of color represent the future of the changing racial/ethnic landscape in this country, whereby groups once referred to as minorities slowly are becoming the majority (Doucet & Hamon, in press; He & Hobbs, 1999). These tremendous changes have brought tremendous challenges for the U.S. educational system, one of the most significant of which is the preparation of teachers (the majority of whom are White and middle class) to work effectively with children of color. Given the extraordinary numbers of very young children from diverse backgrounds entering formal schooling in the United States, it is clear that researchers and practitioners involved in teacher education must invest in the preparation of kindergarten teachers who are equipped to engage these young minds in ways that are meaningful and respectful of the diversity present in their classrooms (Broussard, 2000; Davidson Locke & Phelan, 1993; Fuller, 1992a, 1992b; Scrimsher & Tudge, 2003; Wiggins & Follo, 1999).

Ramey and Ramey (1994) described the transition to school as a developmental and transactional process—developmental in that children's concerns evolve and change as they move from preparing for and then entering school to being adjusted to the school environment, and transactional in that schools, families, children, and communities all are involved in creating a supportive educational experience for children. Much of the literature focusing on the transition to school examines the issue from one of these two perspectives. Thus, a number of studies examine the links among specific types of preschool experiences and the children's subsequent degree of success after they enter school (Field, 1991; Gullo & Burton, 1992, 1993; Haskins, 1989; Howes, 1988, 1990; National Institute of Child Health and Human Development [NICHD] Early Child Care Research Network, 2000). Much of the work on the quality of child care and the impact of Head Start and other similar programs falls into this category (Barnett, 1995; Lee, Brooks-Gunn, & Schnur, 1988; Lee, Brooks-Gunn, Schnur, & Liaw, 1991; Magnuson, Meyers, Ruhm, & Waldfogel, 2004; Ramey et al., 1999; Ramey, Lanzi, Phillips, & Ramey, 1998; Takanishi & DeLeon, 1994). An extensive portion of the literature deals more with home–school links, with the most attention paid to these links after the child has gone to school (Epstein, 1986; Gutman & McLoyd, 2000; Hoover-Dempsey & Sandler, 1995, 1997; Ramey et al., 1998).

---

[2]The authors use the term "of color" to refer to U.S. native and immigrant groups with ancestry in Africa, Asia, Latin America, and Oceania.

[3]He and Hobbs (1999) *define minority* as "The combined population of people who are Black, American Indian, Eskimo, Aleut, Pacific Islander, or of Hispanic origin (who may be of any race [sic]). Equivalently, the Minority population comprises all people other than non-Hispanic Whites (who are termed the 'non-Minority' population when compared with the combined Minority population group)" (p. 1).

Research on the impact of parental involvement with children's teachers and teachers' attempts to show parents how they can help their children make an easy and successful transition to school fall into this category (Berger, 1995; Comer, 1993; Gelfer, 1991; Honig, 1979; Leeper, Witherspoon, & Day, 1984; Mangione & Speth, 1998; Pianta, Cox, Taylor, & Early, 1999; Read, Gardner, & Mahler, 1993; Swick, 1992). An alternative approach to home–school links is one that focuses on aspects of the home environment that make the transition to school more or less easy (Bradley, 1995; Christian, Morrison, & Bryant, 1998; Clarke & Kurtz-Costes, 1997; Parker, Boak, Griffin, Ripple, & Peay, 1999). This is the approach adopted by Philip and Carolyn Cowan and their colleagues (Cowan, Cowan, Ablow, Johnson, & Measelle, 2005).

Cowan et al.'s study of 100 children and their two-parent families began in the year prior to kindergarten entry and followed the children through the first 2 years of school, using a five-domain model (individual psychological adjustment; family relationships, both with the child and as a couple; the ways in which the parents themselves had been raised; and stresses and supports outside the family) to explain the children's successful adaptation to school. The research also involved an intervention component that attempted to alleviate risk factors ("unresolved marital conflict [and] ineffective parenting"; Cowan et al., 2005, p. 14) that might make adaptation to school more difficult. As the authors point out, there is a glaring need for longitudinal studies that deal with the transition to school from the perspective of the home, rather than that of the school, and their research does a fine job in showing clear links connecting children's adaptation to school with such household dynamics as authoritative parenting, children's autonomy, the quality of the parents' relationships (both with one another and with their children), and the children's perceptions of those relationships. A major weakness of this research is that the sample is overwhelmingly White (84%) and relatively wealthy (79% above the median family income in the area from which the participants were drawn [the San Francisco Bay area]).

The goal of this chapter is to examine children's transition to school from a broader perspective than those listed above by framing this developmental transition as a cultural process. To understand the links between children's experiences in the years before they go to school and their transition to school, it makes most sense to take a cultural perspective. Culture is powerfully implicated in (among many other things) the types of settings that are made available to children, the experiences the children have in those settings, the types of interactions that are encouraged and discouraged, and beliefs about what count as competent behavior habits. This argument is one that is rooted in theory, particularly the contextualist theories of Lev Vygotsky and Urie Bronfenbrenner.

THEORIZING CO-CONSTRUCTION

As we have written elsewhere (Tudge, Doucet, & Hayes, 2001; Tudge & Hogan, 2005), contextualist theories take an interactionist and ecological view of human development, paying particular attention to everyday activities that are influenced both by characteristics of the individuals involved and the context (proximal and distal) in which those activities are taking place (see Goldhaber, 2000; Pepper, 1942). Bronfenbrenner's theory (Bronfenbrenner, 1989, 1993, 1995, 1999; Bronfenbrenner & Morris, 1998) illustrates this nicely; at the center of this theory are proximal processes, the regularly occurring activities and interactions with other people, objects, and symbols in the developing individual's environment. For Bronfenbrenner, these proximal processes are the "engines of development" (1993); it is by engaging in them that individuals learn what is expected of them, which activities are considered appropriate or inappropriate for them, how they are expected to engage in these activities, the ways other people will deal with them, and the ways in which they are expected to deal with others. People initiate activities themselves and try to draw others into those activities, and it is in the course of these activities that they try out different roles and observe the roles of others, both with regard to themselves and with others.

As Bronfenbrenner and Morris (1998) point out, however, these proximal processes are influenced both by characteristics of the individuals involved and by the environment. Age, gender, temperament, motivation, experience with the activity, experience with the other or others who are also engaged in the activity—all are implicated in the processes by which any activity is altered by the characteristics of the individuals involved. As for the environment, activities are only possible within contexts, and although the contexts can have an impact on the activities that go on within them, the contexts themselves are also transformed in the course of engagement in the activity. Context is partially represented by the settings in which individuals engage in activities, settings to which Bronfenbrenner referred as *microsystems*. Children always develop in more than a single microsystem, and Bronfenbrenner (1979) coined the term *mesosystem* to highlight the match or mismatch of children's everyday experiences across different microsystems such as home and school.

The nature of experiences in any microsystem—why children are encouraged to be in some settings and not others; why the settings are established in the ways they are; or why adults encourage some activities, discourage others, and never even consider the possibility of yet other activities—can be explained in part by the specific characteristics (values, beliefs, resources, and so forth) that individuals possess. However, such questions relate even more importantly to the social group (e.g., class, race/ethnicity, religion) of which the individuals are a part.

In this context, *culture* refers to any group that has a shared set of values, beliefs, practices, access to resources, social institutions, and a sense of identity, and that communicates those values, beliefs, and so forth to the next generation. According to this definition, different societies constitute different cultural groups, but it is clearly important to recognize that culture is far from a unitary construct. To the extent that Americans share values, beliefs, practices, access to resources, and a sense of identity as Americans, they may be thought of as members of a culture distinct from Angolans or Japanese. However, within the United States, it is clear that different racial/ethnic or social-class groups also qualify as different cultures to the extent that the definition also applies to them. Blacks and Whites in the United States may share the past 200 years of history, but they have experienced the same events in markedly different ways. Not surprisingly, although they may share a sense of identity as Americans (when contrasting themselves with people from other societies), they also may have distinct identities and differing values, beliefs, and practices.

Similarly, a good case can be made for different social classes within any society being considered different cultures on the grounds that, as Kohn and others have argued, members of different classes have different values and beliefs about child rearing that stem from their different life experiences and that are linked to different ways of raising their children (Kohn, 1979, 1995; Luster, Rhoades, & Haas, 1989; Tudge & Putnam, 1997). Although Whites and Blacks may be considered different cultural groups when focusing on racial/ethnic patterns, to the extent that middle-class Whites and working-class Whites have different access to resources; differing values, beliefs, and practices; and differing identities of themselves, they also constitute different cultures. The same argument, of course, applies to Blacks or members of any specific ethnic group from different social classes.

For Bronfenbrenner, then, research on any aspect of human development, including development across important ecological transitions such as the transition to school, requires focusing on the mutual interplay of individual activities and interactions on the one hand and cultural contextual features on the other. A similar claim can be made in terms of Vygotsky's theory. Vygotsky is probably best known, at least in educational circles, for his concept of the zone of proximal development, which is typically equated with scaffolding (Berk & Winsler, 1995; Bodrova & Leong, 1996; Brown & Ferrara, 1985). However, Vygotsky never meant for this concept to stand alone, nor did he view it as central to his theory. Rather, it is a theory in which the types of interpersonal interactions that occur within a zone of proximal development can only be explained through reference to aspects of the individual and to the broader context, specifically the cultural–historical context, that gives meaning to the interactions (Hogan & Tudge, 1999; Tudge & Scrimsher, 2003).

However, given that teachers often try to scaffold children's learning and, although the term is not typically used in this context, scaffold parents' understanding of what is expected of their children in the classroom, it is worth examining Vygotsky's view of the zone of proximal development in more detail. As has been pointed out elsewhere (Bodrova & Leong, 1996; Tudge & Scrimsher, 2003; Van der Veer & Valsiner, 1991), it is important to note that *obuchenie,* the key Russian word Vygotsky used to describe the concept, has been translated in very different ways by different translators. Some have translated this word, in the same sentence, to mean "instruction" (e.g., Vygotsky, 1934/1987) and others to mean "learning" (e.g., Vygotsky, 1935/1978) although these words have quite different meaning in English. The problem stems from the fact that, in Russian, *obuchenie* means "teaching/learning," treating this phenomenon as an integrated whole. Vygotsky (1934/1987) wrote that:

> [Teaching/learning] is only useful when it moves ahead of development. [When it does,] it impels or wakens a whole series of functions that are in a stage of maturation lying in the zone of proximal development. (p. 212)

Clearly, the meaning varies greatly if either "instruction" or "learning" is substituted for "teaching/learning." When translated as "instruction," the concept lends itself well to a more teacher-focused unidirectional flow, the sort of process that is often found in teacher-directed scaffolding. When translated as "learning," the concept appears to markedly reduce the role of the teacher. However, when translated more appropriately, the concept carries the idea of both teacher and child engaged in a joint activity that can create a zone of proximal activity:

> We propose that an essential feature of [teaching/learning] is that it creates the zone of proximal development; that is, [teaching/learning] awakens a variety of developmental processes that are able to operate only when the child is interacting with people in his environment and in collaboration with his peers. (Vygotsky, 1935/1978, p. 90)

In other words, what Vygotsky was calling for was neither a didactic approach to teaching, in which the teacher's job is to discover what the children's zones of proximal developments are and provide appropriate instruction, nor an approach that puts the onus on children, but, rather, a collaborative process between teachers and children.

From this perspective, teaching children also involves learning from them, to understand not only the more specific skills and concepts they need to advance their current level of thinking (something that interactions that create a zone of proximal development share with scaffolding) but also the way in which the children think about learning, their learning styles, their views about school, their lives at home, and their differing cultural backgrounds. This is not simply a matter of teachers gaining more information about their children as a way to teach them more effectively, although this may be one consequence. Just as many teachers realize that they learn new material best while teaching it, the children, while teaching their teachers about themselves and their ways of thinking, are likely to become more drawn into the process of learning.

There are two main ways in which these theories are relevant to the transition to school. The first and more obvious way is that the more teachers try to create zones of proximal development in those who are just entering school by encouraging the process of teaching and learning, the more likely children are going to feel comfortable and accepted in school. Children's high levels of comfort and acceptance may not be the ultimate goal, but they certainly make for a convenient start. The second way is more relevant to the aims of this chapter because precisely the same argument that has been made with regard to teacher–child relationships can be made regarding teacher–parent relationships.

FRAMING THE TRANSITION TO SCHOOL: CURRENT TRENDS

Taylor, Clayton, and Rowley (2004) reviewed the literature on parents' influences on their young children's academic development and concluded that much of what is known comes from one of two perspectives. The first is focused on "what parents do," that is, the behavior habits in which parents engage that help or hinder their children's school-related success. The second examines "who parents are," or the attitudinal, cultural, socioeconomic, and other personal characteristics that are believed to influence parents' academic socialization practices. Our own examination of the transition to school literature suggests that underlying reports of "what parents do" with respect to preparation for school are some important assumptions about "who parents are." Although not explicitly described as such, reports of transition practices among parents suggest one of two approaches: 1) parents [read White and/or middle-class parents], having taught their children their ABCs and 123s and having read to their children from infancy, talk to their children about the upcoming change, visit the school both to orient the children to the new classroom and to meet the teacher, and send their children on their way, confident that the children will adapt to the new environment with relative ease; or 2) parents [read Black/dark-skinned and/or poor parents] who do not own and/or do not read books to their children realize that the time has come for their children to begin kindergarten and, assuming they have learned enough in preschool, send them on their way with little thought to developing a relationship with the teacher and with no plans or time to be actively involved in the children's schooling. Although the summary above is overly simplistic, it does capture some of the underlying assumptions regarding who is prepared for school (and who is not) and why this is the case. Along these lines, some research on the lack of preparedness of working-class and poor, (mostly) minority children (Connell & Prinz, 2002; Stipek & Ryan, 1997; Wright, Diener, & Kay, 2000; Zill & Collins, 1995) fails to acknowledge the mainstream values dictating the behavior habits that are deemed appropriate for school preparation (Taylor et al., 2004). There is thus a lack of continuity between home and school values.

According to Mangione and Speth (1998), continuity is an important feature of successful transitions to formal schooling. This continuity includes links between home, school, and community services—which they term *horizontal continuity*—as well as service linkages across time (e.g., preschool to school, elementary school to middle school)—which they term *vertical continuity.* Although both are important, the literature on the transition to school is limited when it comes to evidence of horizontal continuity. Much more work exists at the theoretical and conceptual level (Brown, Amwake, Speth, & Scott-Little, 2002; Decker, 2001; Decker & Decker, 2002; Early Childhood Laboratory Network Program, 1995) than in real-life examples of successful models, particularly for early childhood education. One outstanding exception is the well-known School Development Program created by Comer in the 1970s (Comer, 1993; Comer, Haynes, Joyner, & Ben-Avie, 1996, 1999; Haynes & Comer, 1996; Haynes, Comer, & Hamilton-Lee, 1988). As Haynes and Comer (1996) explained,

> Education, in our view, is a holistic process in which significant adults—parents, school staff, and responsible members of the community—work together to help children develop well along multiple pathways. We have established mechanisms and procedures through which school staff, parents, and members of the wider community participate in a collaborative process of making critically important decisions that impact children's lives. (p. 501)

Another twist on the school–community partnership links schools with a local university that collaborates with schools to meet mutually constructed goals, such as Chicago's Erikson Institute School Project (Chen & Horsch, 2003). The project involved teaming up with nine public elementary schools, focusing on enacting change in the early years of schooling (prekindergarten through third grade).

With respect to vertical continuity (Mangione & Speth, 1998), the issue that has received by far the most attention is that of children's readiness for school. In 1989, United States President George H.W. Bush, along with the state governors at the time, instituted six goals for American education, the first of which declared that "by the year 2000, all children in America will start school ready to learn" (Action Team on School Readiness, 1992, cited in Shepard, Kagan, & Wurtz, 1998, p. 128). As Meisels (1999) pointed out, much has been made about the meaning of school readiness since that time. Numerous scholars have questioned the validity of the readiness concept because it has very definite political overtones and thus provokes questions about whose interests are met by such a concept. An obvious problem with the readiness concept is that it is not concrete or easily defined (Hitz & Richter, 1993; Lewit & Baker, 1995). This is problematic in general, but it becomes especially troublesome when considering the multiple variations in children's contexts. In a study of elementary schools in the Rocky Mountain region of the United States, Cooney (1995) found that "the teachers, parents, specialists and principals all tended to reinforce White middle-class values, interest, and concerns" (p. 164) despite the multiethnic composition of the area. Thus, the rhetoric of school readiness fails to acknowledge that schools and teachers, first and foremost, want children to be ready for school *culture* (Cooney, 1995). By not acknowledging this overarching goal, practitioners make invisible a process that clearly prioritizes the goals and values of one very specific cultural group (i.e., both White and middle class). As a consequence, the strengths that children from varying backgrounds bring to the educational table cannot be recognized.

Tharp and Gallimore (1988) argued that the lower achievement scores of many children of color could be related to the cultural dissonance between schools' structures and home cultures. As Swick, Brown, and Boutte (1994) asserted, because teachers are not educated about African American children's learning styles, and, more importantly, because variations in these children's learning styles often are framed as weaknesses, Black children are less likely than their White counterparts to be considered "ready" by teachers and other assessors. However, the problems do not rest only at the level of race/ethnicity. Social class is also powerfully implicated in one's life experiences, and research has shown that working-class and poor children experience cultural dissonance in mainstream classrooms (Boutte & DeFlorimonte, 1998; Heath, 1983; Lareau, 1987, 2000). In Bronfenbrenner's (1979) terms, this is a classic case of a mesosystem mismatch. Of course, White middle-class children's experiences do not precisely mirror those they have in school; the only time children at home engage in the particular instructional style so commonly found in school is when they are "playing school," and "show-and-tell" sessions rarely, if ever, feature at home. Instead, the cultural expectations of home and school are such that children from the same cultural group as the teacher are likely to have a far easier time making the adjustment to school than when those expectations are out of alignment (Scrimsher & Tudge, 2003). Moreover, intersections among race/ethnicity and class further complicate relationships between teachers and their students (Graue, 1999; Graue, Kroeger, & Prager, 2001; Heath, 1983; Lareau, 1989; Lareau & Horvat, 1999; Rimm-Kaufman & Pianta, 2000; Serpell, Baker, & Sonnenschein, 2005).

Hitz and Ritcher (1993) outlined the two major perspectives on school readiness: the educational and the legal. Theoretically, from the educational standpoint, readiness has to do with how prepared children are to perform tasks such as reciting the alphabet, counting, and writing their names. The legal aspect of readiness, on the other hand, has to do with every state's duty to provide all children with equal access to educational services regardless of their backgrounds or abilities. As the researchers pointed out, however, this compartmentalization is actually a false dichotomy. Legal requirements to have all children in school by a certain age are confused with educational readiness, and school systems, researchers, and policy makers work to create measures to assess exactly when children are intellectually ready to begin learning school material (Lewit & Baker, 1995). As the age for school entry, which varies by state, increases, kindergarten curricula become more demanding, and even when the age stays the same, middle-class and affluent mothers retain their children for an extra year in hopes of giving them a developmental advantage over their younger classmates who are judged to be less ready or less prepared (Graue, 1992, 1993a, 1993b; Shepard, 1997). As Morrison's work has shown, however, holding children back does not ensure they will learn better or be in less danger of academic risk (Morrison, Griffith, & Alberts, 1997).

For all of the attention that has been given to children's readiness for school, it is striking how little has been made of the necessity for schools and teachers to be ready for children (Carlton & Winsler, 1999; Graue, 1992; Hitz & Richter, 1993). Rather than putting the onus on children's readiness to learn, President George H.W. Bush's declaration might have read, "By the year 2000, all schools will be ready to learn about the children who populate their classrooms and the families that raise those children." In fact, few researchers have written about the National Education Goals Panel's (NEGP) recommendations for "ready schools" (for notable exceptions, see Murphey & Burns,

2002; Pianta, Rimm-Kaufman, & Cox, 1999). In 1998, the NEGP assembled a group of advisors to identify the characteristics of "ready schools" and to share useful strategies with school and community leaders (NEGP, 1998). According to the advisory group, there are 10 keys to ready schools:

1. Ready schools smooth the transition between home and school.

2. Ready schools strive for continuity between early care and education programs and elementary schools.

3. Ready schools help children learn and make sense of their complex and exciting world.

4. Ready schools are committed to the success of every child.

5. Ready schools are committed to the success of every teacher and every adult who interacts with children during the school day.

6. Ready schools introduce or expand approaches that have been shown to raise achievement.

7. Ready schools are learning organizations that alter practices and programs if they do not benefit children.

8. Ready schools serve children in communities.

9. Ready schools take responsibility for results.

10. Ready schools have strong leadership. (p. 5)

For the purposes of the current conversation, this section focuses on the first and the fifth items because they are the areas in which the role of culture has been neglected. Specifically, smooth transitions between home and school require that teachers understand and respect the home just as much as the parents understand and respect the school. For the teachers and school staff who interact with children to be successful, they must rethink their approach to children and parents (Doucet, 2002b). When it comes to teachers and parents, however, a clear gap in communication often emerges; in the same way that teachers tend to treat children in a top-down fashion, trying to scaffold children to fit the school rather than trying to learn from them and encouraging a mutual adaptation (thus creating zones of proximal development in which all children can learn), they tend to treat parents as novices to the educational "game." In this top-down model, teachers take on the role of experts who own the knowledge about schooling (Doucet, 2002a, in press).

One area in which the top-down approach to parental roles is particularly evident is in the literature surrounding parental involvement, which narrowly dictates why, when, and how parents should play a role in their children's education (Fine, 1993; Graue, 1993a, 1993b; Graue et al., 2001; Mapp, 2003; Pérez Carreón, Drake, & Calabrese Barton, 2005). Several dangers are associated with such a one-sided approach, or the "school-to-home transmission model" (Swap, 1993). One such danger is the ease with which teachers' biases can inform not only their constructions of what is needed for a successful transition to school but also their perceptions of whether children and their parents even are capable of preparing for a successful transition. As Rimm-Kaufman, Pianta, and Cox (2000) reported, nonminority teachers in schools with large minority populations reported higher rates of problems in the transition to kindergarten than did minority teachers in similar schools. Given the pervasive assumption that minority parents are not as involved in their children's educational endeavors (Phenice, Martinez, & Grant, 1986), teachers' preexisting biases could set them up to engage parents less as partners in facilitating the transition to school.

The problem is not only that teachers might perceive children of color as academically unprepared. As researchers have reported, kindergarten teachers are more interested in children's social skills and self-reliance than in the academic knowledge with which they enter the kindergarten classroom (Heaviside & Farris, 1993; Lin, Lawrence, & Gorrell, 2003; Rimm-Kaufman et al., 2000). Social competence has been identified as an important characteristic of readiness for school (Carlton & Winsler, 1999), a successful transition to school (Huffman, Mehlinger, & Kerivan, 2000), and school achievement (Foulks & Morrow, 1989). Yet, teachers' perceptions of children's social skills are far from objective (Entwisle, Alexander, Pallas, & Cadigan, 1988). Mendez, McDermott, and Fantuzzo (2002) noted that perceptions of social competence can be impacted by a range of factors, including temperament, gender, race/ethnicity, and class. For example, in a comparison of teacher ratings of children's social competence using ECLS-K data, Idzelis (2005) found that teachers were more likely to rate immigrant children from African countries (as well as African American children of nonimmigrant origin) as having poorer social skills compared with other children in the sample. Variations in assessments of competence also emerge when comparing teacher versus parental evaluations of children (Gray, Clancy, & King, 1981).

A related risk is that of miscommunication and misunderstanding with teachers who are not familiar with the social interaction styles of children of color and their parents (Lareau, 1987, 2002; Lareau & Horvat, 1999; Tharp & Gallimore, 1988; Willis, 1992; Wilson & Banks, 1994). A clear example of this is the different ways in which White and African American adults ask questions of children (Delpit, 1995; Heath, 1983). Specifically, White adults tend to give children directions by asking questions (e.g., "Brian, would you like to tell us about your project?") and to ask questions to which they already know the answer (e.g., "What color are my glasses?"), whereas African American adults tend to communicate requests to children directly ("James, it is your turn to tell us about your project.") and ask children questions to which they do not know the answer ("What color is your sofa at home?").

Similarly, Tharp (1989) reported on variations in communication style among Navajo, Hawaiian, and Anglo children and teachers. Among the Navajo people, a long period of silence after a person has asked a question is a sign that the listener is reflecting on the question and giving the speaker time to say all that needs to be said. White teachers, used to immediate responses from White children, could mistakenly assume that silence on the part of Navajo children is a sign of indifference or ignorance. For Hawaiian children, on the other hand, overlapping conversations are a common part of everyday communication, and White teachers unfamiliar with this "talk-story" style of conversation could mistake perfectly acceptable "interruptions" of other children as rudeness.

Gaps in communication also can arise when parents are not native speakers of English. Apprehension about navigating an unfamiliar educational system, insecurity that something may be "lost in translation" (Hoffman, 1989), and, for some, reliance on children to serve as translators can all engender a sense of powerlessness among parents (Doucet, 2005; Pérez Carreón et al., 2005; Trueba, 2004). Unfortunately, these parents' hesitation to contact or engage their children's teachers in conversations about the children's progress (or lack thereof) may be misinterpreted by teachers as lack of interest (Doucet, 2002a).

REFRAMING THE TRANSITION
TO SCHOOL: THE ROLE OF CULTURE

Parents and children should be allowed a place at the "experts" table so that teachers learn from them how to provide children with experiences that prepare them for the transition (Delpit, 1995; Doucet, 2002a, 2002b). Teachers' attempts to inform parents about what is going on in the classroom and what they are trying to accomplish with the children, as well as their efforts to involve parents in their children's education, all deserve recognition. These efforts are extremely important in helping children make successful transitions to school. However, applying the theoretical perspective laid out in this chapter would be far more beneficial. Rather than providing parents with scaffolding to teach them how to help their children, teachers would make more of a long-term beneficial impact on their children's development by applying the teaching/learning approach to their dealings with the children's parents described in this chapter. In both cases, zones of proximal development can be created. Delpit (1995) wrote about the frustration teachers of color feel trying to communicate with White teachers about how best to serve the concerns of children of color in their classrooms. Calling it a "silenced dialogue," Delpit described a process in which teachers of color shared their experiences with their colleagues, hoping to provide them with culturally nuanced insights, only to be met with responses about what *research* has shown are best practices or what progressive pedagogies suggest are better approaches for teaching. Teachers of color, unable to share their stories, experiences, and wisdom, felt silenced in conversations on how to teach children from their own cultural communities.

At this point, it might be helpful to return to the issue of culture, invoking both the fact that Vygotsky's theory is a cultural–historical theory (not a theory of zones of proximal development) and Bronfenbrenner's insistence that what goes on between individuals is profoundly influenced not only by the characteristics of the individuals concerned but also by the context in which those interactions occur, a context that is simultaneously proximal (the microsystem) and distal (the macrosystem, or culture). Cultures are distinguished by values, beliefs, practices, a sense of identity, and an attempt (explicit or implicit) to pass on those values, beliefs, and so forth to the following generation. Although cultures are transformed (and transform themselves) over historical time, the passing on of cultural ways of making sense of the world to the next generation also ensures a good degree of continuity over historical time.

In some cases, similarities between the teacher's culture and that of the children are clear. This occurs when both teacher and children share ethnic, regional, or socioeconomic backgrounds. Teachers and parents are then likely to have common values, beliefs, practices, and a sense of identity, although individual differences ensure that this commonality is likely rather than definite. Cultural compatibility is one of the central tenets of the Kamehameha Elementary Education Program (KEEP, Tharp & Gallimore, 1988). The KEEP model requires teachers to work collaboratively with students and to understand the communication styles of Hawaiian children, which include multiple overlapping conversations and communication, or "talk-story" (Tharp, 1989). KEEP Schools fund a teacher-training program called the Preservice Education for Teachers of Minorities (PETOM), which actively recruits students to teach in their home communities (PETOM, 1993), believing that these students are best equipped to serve the children in their own communities.

However, in many other cases there is no such concordance, either because the teacher has a different cultural background than the students or because the student body is culturally heterogeneous (Fuller, 1992b). In these latter cases, the children's transition to school and sub-sequent performance in school can only be enhanced if the teacher is both willing to teach and learn from the children and their parents. This is not to suggest that children should only be taught by teachers who share their cultural characteristics. Grant and Secada (1990) and Sleeter and Grant (1987) warned that, taken to the extreme, cultural compatibility models could be used to justify segregation of children and teachers of color and also to provide an "easy out" to White teachers who would not have to learn how to teach these children (Bloch & Swadener, 1992). Whether the teacher comes from the same community in which he or she is teaching, his or her first job should be to learn from the children and parents he or she serves.

One reason that this is important involves issues of social class. Although there is clearly a good deal of controversy about appropriate definitions of social class (Duncan & Magnuson, 2003; Ensminger & Fothergill, 2003; Holden & Edwards, 1989), Kohn (1977, 1979, 1995) argued convincingly that class differences in child rearing (among many other things) are related to parents' current conditions of life, particularly in the workplace, and their past experiences of education. Income also plays a role, but with the powerful exception of families living in or close to poverty, its role is less important than education and occupation.

Kohn (1979) argued that whereas all parents want their children to be successful, they differ in what strategies they believe will help their children attain success. If, based on a parent's educational experiences, success has required following the teachers' rules, regurgitating what the teacher has taught, and so forth, and if success in the workplace has required arriving on time and carefully carrying out the boss's instructions, it is not surprising that such a parent's approach to raising children might involve stressing doing what one is told, being neat and organized, and so forth. Whether this approach brings success or failing to take this approach inhibits success, parents with these types of experiences would most likely teach their children at home that these types of qualities will lead to success.

By contrast, parents who have gone to college are more likely to have progressed far enough in terms of education to have been encouraged to think for themselves rather than simply follow what the teacher has said (something they may not have experienced in an educational setting since preschool or kindergarten). If their occupational success depends less on following instructions than on thinking for themselves, they are more likely to encourage their children to be self-directing, not simply following rules, as a likely way to become successful.

If families are defined as middle class when the parents have a college degree and a professional occupation and as working class when the parents have not been to college and when their jobs do not require a great deal of self-direction, teachers, by definition, are middle class. If some or all of the children in a kindergarten class are from working-class backgrounds, one can see an immediate clash of values, beliefs, and practices if the teacher tries to set up the classroom in such a way that the children are encouraged to choose which "center" to go to, expected to work relatively independently, or encouraged to do group work without much teacher direction. If working-class children have more difficulty doing these things than do middle-class children, this is no more of a limitation than the fact that middle-class children might have more difficulty than working-class children fitting into a tightly structured classroom in which they are expected to do just as the teacher wants. In both cases, home experiences and those experiences of the classroom are mismatched. Rather than argue that one way is correct and the other not, it would be helpful for teachers to know the prevailing values, beliefs, and practices in the children's homes so they could find ways of bridging gaps between sets of expectations (the teacher's and the home's). This would require conversation between teachers and parents—not the teacher explaining what she or he wants and expects but an interchange in which both teacher and parents could learn from each other.

The idea that typical sets of experiences (whether the parents' experiences in their own schooling or in the workplace, or the child's experiences in the typical settings in which they are placed) should be counted as cultural practices can be taken further by examining the types of literacy experiences that middle-class and working-class children have in the home. As Heath (1983, 1986) demonstrated, White children from these two types of backgrounds engaged in many early literacy activities, but the manner of engagement was quite different in the two groups, with working-class children being encouraged to say the words in the books correctly and the middle-class children being drawn to make connections between what was in the books and what was in their own experiences. When these children enter school, their past experiences with books and literacy fit relatively well or relatively poorly with the teachers' expectations for reading. It is not a question of one or another group being deficient, but the likelihood of a mismatch of expectations will only make the transition to school that much more difficult. Only when the teacher has learned about the children's past experiences can she or he best help the children. The fact that the teacher has made the effort to discuss those experiences and learn from the parents can only help strengthen the connection between children and school.

For historical reasons, all of the issues that have been raised in this chapter regarding social class are likely to be magnified when talking about cultural differences that stem from ethnic or racial differences. This should not be confused with a cultural relativity approach—it is not reasonable to argue that some schools are right for working-class children but not middle-class children any more than it is reasonable to condone school segregation on the basis of race/ethnicity or national origin, particularly because this is a society in which middle-class White values link much more clearly to status, power, and wealth (Delpit, 1988, 1995; Ladson-Billings, 1994, 2001). Certainly, culturally sensitive pedagogical practices should be incorporated into the classroom (Ladson-Billings, 2001), but beyond that, as others have argued (Bloch & Swadener, 1992; Delpit, 1988; Fine, 1993; Grant & Secada, 1990; Graue et al., 2001), issues of power and access to educational capital must be addressed if diversity in U.S. classrooms is to become a source of strength rather than an excuse for failure.

NEW DIRECTIONS IN RESEARCH

Some research has considered the unique contributions of culture and the wealth of knowledge offered by parents; such research suggests that there is indeed cultural variation in expectations, beliefs, and practices with respect to children's schooling. For example, Okagaki and Sternberg (1993) found that immigrant parents from Cambodia, Mexico, the Philippines, and Vietnam placed a higher value on conforming behavior habits than did their Anglo American and Mexican American counterparts, among whom autonomous behavior habits were regarded more highly. In terms of their beliefs about markers of intelligent first graders, Asian parents in the sample rated motivation and self-management higher than social skills, whereas social skills were highly important to Hispanic parents' conceptualizations of intelligent first graders. Ruth Chao (1994) explored the parenting styles of Chinese immigrant and European

American mothers of preschoolers to illuminate why Chinese children seemed to perform so well in school considering that, according to research, "authoritarian" parenting leads to negative outcomes, including poor academic achievement, and that traditionally Chinese parents have been identified as authoritarian. Challenging the description of Chinese parenting as "controlling," Chao argued that the Chinese concept for what researchers have described as "authoritarian" parenting includes the notion of "training"—an important distinction.

In terms of practices related to schooling, Gallimore and Goldenberg (2001) found that immigrant parents of Hispanic origin rarely engaged their children in reading before the age of 5 because it was not believed that children had reached the "age of reason" before that time. Instead, parents focused on their children's moral development and the development of good social skills (such as politeness), which, from these parents' frame of reference, were important even for the youngest of children. Along similar lines, Doucet (2000) found that African American parents framed preparation for the transition to school more broadly as preparation for the real world and thus highlighted skills that would serve children in this comprehensive endeavor. For these parents, children's ability to take care of themselves (from physical self-care to knowledge of basic safety), to demonstrate curiosity and intelligence, to display social competence (good manners, kindness), and to negotiate race relations were just as important for being prepared to go to school as were basic skills in literacy and numeracy.

Tudge and colleagues (Tudge & Doucet, 2004; Tudge, Odero, Hogan, & Etz, 2003; Tudge, Tammeveski, Meltsas, Kulakova, & Snezhkova, 2001) have approached the issue of the links, if any, between the preschool years and what happens after children enter formal schooling from the perspective of the regularly occurring activities and interactions in which young children from a variety of different cultural contexts are involved. Working from a theoretical framework that views the intersection of culture and everyday practices as key to development, Tudge et al. conducted ethnographic observations of how and with whom young children spent their time. Tudge et al. also interviewed the children's parents to understand, among other things, their values and beliefs. The children were observed and the parents were interviewed when the children were between 3 and 4 years of age, and more data (interviews and questionnaires) were gathered during the first few years the children were in school. Data using the same methodology have been gathered from a single city in each of Russia, Estonia, Finland, Korea, Kenya, and Brazil, as well as in the United States with equal numbers of European American and African American families (Tudge, 2005). In each city, equal numbers of middle-class and working-class families were recruited, with class membership being determined by education and occupation criteria.

This study reveals that children in different cultural communities engage in different types of activities. For example, in the U.S. sample, and just focusing on those activities that Tudge and colleagues felt might be relevant to school, middle-class White children were far more likely than their working-class peers to be involved in activities involving verbal interaction with adults. This was true of conversation (defined as the more cognitively sophisticated talk about the past or future) or the exchange of information (i.e., lessons) about literacy, numeracy, or about the world in general (whether specific skills or about nature). In Black communities, the differences between the social-class groups were not as marked, although middle-class children were more likely than their working-class counterparts to be involved in more discussions about literacy, numeracy, and the world. However, children from both groups were less likely to be involved with conversation with adults than either group from the White community. Middle-class children in both the White and the Black communities were more likely to be involved in pretend play and to engage with objects that might help with literacy (such as looking at books or being read to) and numeracy than their working-class peers (Tudge & Doucet, 2004). It is interesting to note, however, that those working-class Black children who attended formal child care centers were far more likely to participate in school-related lessons than those who did not (Tudge, Doucet, Odero, Sperb, Piccinini, et al., 2006).

There is thus good evidence that young children's school-relevant experiences differ by virtue of the specific cultural community of which they are a part. What, if any, are the implications after they enter school? In three of the four communities, children who had engaged as preschoolers in more school-relevant lessons (about literacy, numeracy, and so forth) were much more likely to be perceived as academically competent by their teachers when they were in second or third grade (correlations ranging from .49 to .55). The exception was White working-class children, who had participated in almost no such lessons. Similarly, children in three of the four communities (middle-class Black children were the exception) who had had more lessons about the world (skills, nature, and safety) were more likely to be viewed as more competent (correlations from .3 to .5). Middle-class children who had had more interpersonal lessons (about politeness, getting along with others, and so forth) were also more likely to be viewed as more competent (.58 for the White children, .21 for the Black children). The remaining activity that involved verbal interaction with others, namely, conversation with adults, was also clearly linked to teachers' perceptions of competence 4 years later in three of the four groups, strikingly so in the case of the working-class White children (.87), less so for the middle-class children (.4 in the White community, .23 in the Black community). Interestingly, those activities that did not necessarily involve interaction with an adult (pretend play and playing with school-relevant objects) were only positively related to later competence for working-class White children (pretend play, .39) and middle-class Black children (play with school-relevant objects, .43); working-class Black children who had been involved in more pretend play were actually viewed as less competent by their teachers (−.37).

These data reveal that middle-class children are more likely than their working-class peers, during the years before they go to school, to engage in the types of activities that are linked to school success, and these differences are magnified in the case of White children. These results are in agreement with the literature on children's early language and literacy experiences (Dickinson & Tabors, 2001; Hart & Risley, 1995, 1999), showing how those early experiences are related to both class and race/ethnicity and having clear implications for the transition to school.

There are two ways of looking at this issue. The traditional way is to simply view members of groups that are not White and middle class as having an impairment that needs to be made up if success is to occur. An alternative position is that schools have privileged the goals and practices of one particular group without considering ways of building on the more typically occurring experiences of other groups. For example, as Serpell et al. (2005) found in their research on early literacy experiences, the Black children in their study were more likely to play word games and to draw and write than Whites, and middle-class Blacks were far more likely than children from the other communities to engage in oral storytelling. A similar point can be made regarding parents' beliefs about educationally relevant activities. For example, although 70% of the parents in Serpell et al.'s Early Childhood

Project focused on decoding skills as one of the major signs of their children starting to read, middle-class parents, both Black (82%) and White (42%), were far more likely to mention motivational factors as being important than were working-class parents (fewer than 20%). These different views reflect different strengths on which teachers could build. But without talking to children and parents about the parents' beliefs and the children's prior experiences, teachers are unlikely to know what they can build on.

CONCLUSION

The transition to school is a cultural process, although the complex roles that culture plays in this critical developmental juncture often are not recognized. The theoretical bases for these claims come from two contextual theories. First, Bronfenbrenner's ecological perspective encourages a viewing of culture from the broadest level (i.e., the macrosystem) to the most proximate (i.e., the microsystem). Thus, schools operate within a specific cultural framework, but this framework does not always reflect the values and beliefs of the families the schools serve. Furthermore, Vygotsky's cultural–historical model, with its focus on education and relationships among teachers and students, demands that teaching and learning be seen as a transactional process—that is, teaching/learning.

Recognizing the transition to school as a cultural process means moving away from models that try to generalize a universal (or even national) model for how children experience the transition to school as well as for how parents conceptualize this transition. Projections suggest that the U.S. population will continue to increase in racial/ethnic diversity (see He & Hobbs, 1999) and that economic changes related to globalization, outsourcing, and wage stagnation will further the gap between asset owners and wage earners (Collins, Leondar-Wright, & Sklar, 1999). It is crucial that teachers be prepared to appropriately address diversity in their classrooms (Fuller, 1992b) and, by extension, to address diversity among these children's parents. For children to make the transition to school successfully, current conceptions of the roles children and their parents play in informing the schooling process also will need to be expanded to make room for diverse approaches (Graue, 1993a). This "transition as cultural process" perspective also means that teachers will need to suspend their expectations that children will experience the transition in the same way, just as they must suspend expectations that all children learn to read the same way (Delpit, 1988), communicate the same way (Tharp, 1989), or behave the same way (Wilson & Banks, 1994). Finally, schools themselves must be made more appropriate for adapting to the concerns of an ever-changing child population. To do so, all of the relevant players must actively construct schooling experiences together.

REFERENCES

Appiah, K.A., & Gutmann, A. (1998). *Color conscious: The political morality of race.* Princeton, NJ: Princeton University Press.

Barnett, S. (1995). Long-term effects of early childhood programs on cognitive and school outcomes. *The Future of Children, 5*(3), 25–35.

Beery, M.E. (1984). *Kindergarten entry: A study of transition.* Unpublished doctoral dissertation, Ohio State University, Columbus.

Berger, E.H. (1995). *Parents as partners in education: The school and home working together* (4th ed.). New York: Merrill/Macmillan.

Berk, L.E., & Winsler, A. (1995). *Scaffolding children's learning: Vygotsky and early childhood education.* Washington, DC: National Association for the Education of Young Children.

Betancourt, H., & López, S.R. (1993). The study of culture, ethnicity, and race in American psychology. *American Psychologist, 48*(6), 629–637.

Bloch, M., & Swadener, B.B. (1992). Relationships between home, community and school: Multicultural considerations and research issues in early childhood. In C.A. Grant (Ed.), *Research and multicultural education: From the margins to the mainstream* (pp. 165–183). Washington, DC: The Falmer Press.

Bodrova, E., & Leong, D.J. (1996). *Tools of the mind: The Vygotskian approach to early childhood education.* Englewood Cliffs, NJ: Prentice Hall.

Boutte, G.S., & DeFlorimonte, D. (1998). The complexities of valuing cultural differences without overemphasizing them: Taking it to the next level. *Equity & Excellence in Education, 31*(3), 54–62.

Bradley, R.H. (1995). Environment and parenting. In M.H. Bornstein (Ed.), *Handbook of parenting: Vol. 2. Biology and ecology of parenting* (pp. 235–261). Mahwah, NJ: Lawrence Erlbaum Associates.

Bronfenbrenner, U. (1979). *The ecology of human development.* Cambridge, MA: Harvard University Press.

Bronfenbrenner, U. (1989). *Ecological systems theory.* Greenwich, CT: JAI Press.

Bronfenbrenner, U. (1993). The ecology of cognitive development: Research models and fugitive findings. In R.H. Wozniak & K.W. Fischer (Eds.), *Development in context: Acting and thinking in specific environments. The Jean Piaget symposium series* (pp. 3–44). Hillsdale, NJ: Lawrence Erlbaum Associates.

Bronfenbrenner, U. (1995). Developmental ecology through space and time: A future perspective. In P. Moen, G.H. Elder, Jr., & K. Luscher (Eds.), *Examining lives in context: Perspectives on the ecology of human development* (pp. 619–647). Washington, DC: American Psychological Association.

Bronfenbrenner, U. (1999). Environments in developmental perspective: Theoretical and operational models. In S.L. Friedman & T.D. Wachs (Eds.), *Measuring environment across the life span: Emerging methods and concepts* (pp. 3–28). Washington, DC: American Psychological Association.

Bronfenbrenner, U., & Morris, P.M. (1998). The ecology of developmental processes. In W. Damon & R.M. Lerner (Eds.), *Handbook of child psychology, Vol. 1: Theories of human development* (pp. 993–1028). New York: John Wiley & Sons.

Broussard, C.A. (2000). Preparing teachers to work with families: A national survey of teacher education programs. *Equity & Excellence in Education, 33*(2), 41–49.

Brown, A.L., & Ferrara, R.A. (1985). Diagnosing zones of proximal development. In J.V. Wertsch (Ed.), *Culture, communication, and cognition: Vygotskian perspectives* (pp. 273–305). New York: Cambridge University Press.

Brown, E.G., Amwake, C., Speth, T., & Scott-Little, C. (2002, Fall). The Continuity Framework: A tool for building home, school, and community partnerships. *Early Childhood Research & Practice, 4*(2). Retrieved October 28, 2005, from http://ecrp.uiuc.edu/v4n2/brown.html

Carlton, M.P., & Winsler, A. (1999). School readiness: The need for a paradigm shift. *The School Psychology Review, 28*(3), 338–352.

Chao, R.K. (1994). Beyond parental control and authoritarian parenting style: Understanding Chinese parenting through the notion of cultural training. *Child Development, 65,* 1111–1119.

Chen, J.-Q., & Horsch, P. (2003). *Effective partnering for school change: Improving early childhood education in urban classrooms.* New York: Teachers College Press.

Christian, K., Morrison, F.J., & Bryant, F.B. (1998). Predicting kindergarten academic skills: Interactions among child care, maternal education, and family literacy environments. *Early Childhood Research Quarterly, 13,* 501–521.

Clarke, A.T., & Kurtz-Costes, B. (1997). Television viewing, educational quality of the home environment, and school readiness. *Journal of Educational Research, 90*(5), 279–285.

Collins, C., Leondar-Wright, B., & Sklar, H. (1999). *Shifting fortunes: The perils of the growing American wealth gap.* Boston: United for a Fair Economy.

Comer, J.P. (1993). *School power: Implications of an intervention project* (2nd ed.). New York: The Free Press.

Comer, J.P., Haynes, N.M., Joyner, E.T., & Ben-Avie, M. (Eds.). (1996). *Rallying the whole village: The Comer process for reforming education.* New York: Teachers College Press.

Comer, J.P., Haynes, N.M., Joyner, E.T., & Ben-Avie, M. (Eds.). (1999). *Child by child: The Comer process for change in education.* New York: Teachers College Press.

Connell, C.M., & Prinz, R.J. (2002). The impact of childcare and parent–child interactions on school-readiness and social skills development for low-income African American children. *Journal of School Psychology, 40*(2), 177–193.

Cooney, M.H. (1995). Readiness for school or for school culture? *Childhood Education, 71*(3), 164–167.

Cowan, P.A., Cowan, C.P., Ablow, J.C., Johnson, V.K., & Measelle, J.R. (Eds.). (2005). *Family context of parenting in children's adaptation to elementary school.* Mahwah, NJ: Lawrence Erlbaum Associates.

Davidson Locke, A., & Phelan, P. (1993). Cultural diversity and its implications for schooling: A continuing American dialogue. In P. Phelan & A.L. Davidson (Eds.), *Renegotiating cultural diversity in American schools* (pp. 1–26). New York: Teachers College Press.

Decker, L.E. (2001). Allies in education. *Principal Leadership, 2*(1), 42–46.

Decker, L.E., & Decker, V. (2002). *Home, school, and community partnerships.* Lanham, MD: Scarecrow Press.

Delpit, L. (1988). The silenced dialogue: Power and pedagogy in educating other people's children. *Harvard Educational Review, 58*(3), 280–298.

Delpit, L. (1995). *Other people's children: Cultural conflict in the classroom.* New York: The New Press.

Dickinson, D.K., & Tabors, P.O. (Eds.). (2001). *Beginning literacy with language: Young children learning at home and in school.* Baltimore: Paul H. Brookes Publishing Co.

Doucet, F. (2000). *The transition to school in middle class and working class African American families: A study of beliefs, values, and practices.* Unpublished doctoral dissertation, University of North Carolina at Greensboro.

Doucet, F. (2002a, April). *L'éducation: The missing link for Haitian parents.* Paper presented at the National Coalition for Haitian Rights conference on Developing a National Haitian-American Agenda: Moving Forward Together, Miami, FL.

Doucet, F. (2002b, March). *Understanding those we serve: Toward an agenda for culturally-sensitive childcare services.* Keynote address presented at the New York YWCA-sponsored conference on Child Care: Bridging the Cultural Gap, New York.

Doucet, F. (2005). Divergent realities: The home and school lives of Haitian immigrant youth. *Journal of Youth Ministry, 3*(2), 37–65.

Doucet, F. (in press). "They just have more of a lesson plan": How African American parents construct their roles and the roles of teachers in preparing children for the transition to school. *Early Childhood Research Quarterly.*

Doucet, F., & Hamon, R.R. (under review). A nation of diversity: Demographics of the United States of America and their implications for families. In B. Sherif-Trask & R.R. Hamon (Eds.), *Cultural diversity and families: Expanding perspectives.* Thousand Oaks, CA: Sage Publications.

Duncan, G.J., & Magnuson, K.A. (2003). Off with Hollingshead: Socioeconomic resources, parenting, and child development. In M.H. Bornstein & R.H. Bradley (Eds.), *Socioeconomic status, parenting, and child development. Monographs in parenting series* (pp. 83–106). Mahwah, NJ: Lawrence Erlbaum Associates.

Early Childhood Laboratory Network Program. (1995). *Continuity in early childhood: A framework for home, school, and community linkages.* Washington, DC: U.S. Department of Education.

Ensminger, M.E., & Fothergill, K. (2003). A decade of measuring SES: What it tells us and where to go from here. In M.H. Bornstein & R.H. Bradley (Eds.), *Socioeconomic status, parenting, and child development* (pp. 13–27). Mahwah, NJ: Lawrence Erlbaum Associates.

Entwisle, D.R., & Alexander, K.L. (1993). Entry into school: The beginning school transition and educational stratification in the United States. Annual Review of Sociology, *19,* 401–423.

Entwisle, D.R., Alexander, K.L., Pallas, A.M., & Cadigan, D. (1988). A social psychological model of the schooling process over first grade. *Social Psychology Quarterly, 51*(3), 173–189.

Epstein, J.L. (1986). Parents' reactions to teacher practices of parent involvement. *Elementary School Journal, 86,* 277–294.

Field, T.M. (1991). Quality infant day-care and grade school behavior and performance. *Child Development, 62,* 863–870.

Fine, M. (1993). [Ap]parent involvement: Reflections on parents, power, and urban public schools. *Teachers College Record, 94*(4), 682–709.

Foulks, B., & Morrow, R.D. (1989). Academic survival skills for the youngest child at risk for school failure. *Journal of Educational Research, 82,* 158–165.

Fuller, M.L. (1992a). Monocultural teachers and multicultural students: A demographic clash. *Teaching Education, 4*(2), 87–93.

Fuller, M.L. (1992b). Teacher education programs and increasing minority school populations: An educational mismatch? In C.A. Grant (Ed.), *Research and multicultural education: From the margins to the mainstream* (pp. 184–200). Washington, DC: Falmer Press.

Gallimore, R., & Goldenberg, C. (2001). Analyzing cultural models and settings to connect minority achievement and school improvement research. *Educational Psychologist, 36,* 45–56.

Gelfer, J.I. (1991). Teacher–parent partnerships: Enhancing communications. *Childhood Education, 67*(3), 164–167.

Goldhaber, D.E. (2000). *Theories of human development: Integrative perspectives.* Mountain View, CA: Mayfield Publishing.

Grant, C.A., & Secada, W.G. (1990). Preparing teachers for diversity. In W.R. Houston (Ed.), *Handbook of research on teacher education* (pp. 403–422). New York: Macmillan.

Graue, E. (1999). Integrating diverse perspectives on kindergarten contexts and practices. In R.C. Pianta & M.J. Cox (Eds.), *The transition to kindergarten* (pp. 109–142). Baltimore: Paul H. Brookes Publishing Co.

Graue, M.E. (1992). Social interpretations of readiness for kindergarten. *Early Childhood Research Quarterly, 7,* 225–243.

Graue, M.E. (1993a). Expectations and ideas coming to school. *Early Childhood Research Quarterly, 8,* 53–75.

Graue, M.E. (1993b). Social networks and home–school relations. *Educational Policy, 7*(4), 466–490.

Graue, M.E., Kroeger, J., & Prager, D. (2001). A Bakhtinian analysis of particular home–school relations. *American Educational Research Journal, 38*(3), 467–498.

Gray, C.A., Clancy, S., & King, L. (1981). Teacher versus parent reports of preschoolers' social competence. *Journal of Personality Assessment, 45*(5), 488–493.

Gullo, D.F., & Burton, C.B. (1992). Age of entry, preschool experience, and sex as antecedents of academic readiness in kindergarten. *Early Childhood Research Quarterly, 7,* 175–186.

Gullo, D.F., & Burton, C.B. (1993). The effects of social class, class size and prekindergarten experience on early school adjustment. *Early Child Development and Care, 88,* 43–51.

Gutman, L.M., & McLoyd, V.C. (2000). Parents' management of their children's education within the home, at school, and in the community: An examination of African-American families living in poverty. *The Urban Review, 32*(1), 1–24.

Hart, B., & Risley, T.R. (1995). *Meaningful differences in the everyday experience of young American children.* Baltimore: Paul H. Brookes Publishing Co.

Hart, B., & Risley, T.R. (1999). *The social world of children: Learning to talk.* Baltimore: Paul H. Brookes Publishing Co.

Haskins, R. (1989). Beyond metaphor: The efficacy of early childhood education. *American Psychologist, 44,* 274–282.

Haynes, N.M., & Comer, J.P. (1996). Integrating schools, families and communities through successful school reform. *School Psychology Review, 25*(4), 501–506.

Haynes, N.M., Comer, J.P., & Hamilton-Lee, M. (1988). The School Development Program: A model for school improvement. *Journal of Negro Education, 57*(1), 11–21.

He, W., & Hobbs, F. (1999). *The emerging minority marketplace: Minority population growth: 1995 to 2050.* Washington, DC: U.S. Department of Commerce, Minority Business Development Agency. Retrieved June 1, 2005, from http://www.mbda.gov/documents/mbdacolor.pdf

Heath, S.B. (1983). *Ways with words: Language, life, and work in communities and classrooms.* Cambridge, England: Cambridge University Press.

Heath, S.B. (1986). What no bedtime story means: Narrative skills at home and school. In B.B. Schieffelin & E. Ochs (Eds.), *Language socialization across culture* (pp. 97–124). Cambridge, England: Cambridge University Press.

Heaviside, S., & Farris, E. (1993). *Public school kindergarten teachers' views on children's readiness for school* (NCES No. 93-410). Washington, DC: U.S. Department of Education, Office of Educational Research and Improvement.

Hitz, R., & Richter, S. (1993). School readiness: A flawed concept. *Principal, 72*(5), 10–13.

Hoffman, E. (1989). *Lost in translation: A life in a new language.* New York: Penguin.

Hogan, D.M., & Tudge, J.R.H. (1999). Implications of Vygotsky's theory for peer learning. In A.M. O'Donnell & A. King (Eds.), *Cognitive perspectives on peer learning* (pp. 39–65). Mahwah, NJ: Lawrence Erlbaum Associates.

Holden, G.W., & Edwards, L.A. (1989). Parental attitudes toward child rearing: Instruments, issues, and implications. *Psychological Bulletin, 106,* 29–58.

Honig, A. (1979). *Parent involvement in early childhood education.* Washington, DC: National Association for the Education of Young Children.

Hoover-Dempsey, K.V., & Sandler, H.M. (1995). Parental involvement in children's education: Why does it make a difference? *Teachers College Record, 97*(2), 310–332.

Hoover-Dempsey, K.V., & Sandler, H.M. (1997). Why do parents become involved in their children's education? *Review of Educational Research, 67*(1), 3–42.

Howes, C. (1988). Relations between early child care and schooling. *Developmental Psychology, 24,* 53–57.

Howes, C. (1990). Can the age of entry and the quality of infant child care predict behaviors in kindergarten? *Developmental Psychology, 26,* 292–303.

Huffman, L.C., Mehlinger, S.L., & Kerivan, A.S. (2000). Risk factors for academic and behavioral problems at the beginning of school. In *Off to a good start: Research on the risk factors for early school problems and selected federal policies affecting children's social and emotional development and their readiness for school.* Chapel Hill, NC: University of North Carolina, FPG Child Development Center.

Idzelis, M.L. (2005). *A study of the protective factors in the social adjustment of immigrant children in the classroom.* Unpublished doctoral dissertation, The University of Connecticut, Storrs.

Kohn, M.L. (1977). *Class and conformity: A study in values* (2nd ed.). Chicago: University of Chicago Press.

Kohn, M.L. (1979). The effects of social class on parental values and practices. In D. Reiss & H. Hoffman (Eds.), *The American family: Dying or developing* (pp. 45–68). New York: Plenum Press.

Kohn, M.L. (1995). Social structure and personality through time and space. In P. Moen, G.H. Elder, Jr., & K. Luscher (Eds.), *Examining lives in context: Perspectives on the ecology of human development* (pp. 141–168). Washington, DC: American Psychological Association.

Ladson-Billings, G. (1994). *The dreamkeepers: Successful teachers of African American children* (2nd ed.). Chicago: University of Chicago Press.

Ladson-Billings, G. (2001). *Crossing over to Canaan: The journey of new teachers in diverse classrooms.* San Francisco: Jossey-Bass.

Lareau, A. (1987). Social class differences in family–school relationships: The importance of cultural capital. *Sociology of Education, 60,* 73–85.

Lareau, A. (1989). *Home advantage: Social class and parental intervention in elementary education.* Philadelphia: Falmer Press.

Lareau, A. (2000). Social class and the daily lives of children. *Childhood, 7*(2), 155–171.

Lareau, A. (2002). Invisible inequality: Social class and childrearing in black families and white families. *American Sociological Review, 67*(5), 747–776.

Lareau, A., & Horvat, E.M. (1999). Moments of social inclusion and exclusion: Race, class, and cultural capital in family–school relationships. *Sociology of Education, 72,* 37–53.

Lee, V., Brooks-Gunn, J., & Schnur, E. (1988). Does Head Start work? A 1-year follow-up comparison of disadvantaged children attending Head Start, no preschool, and other preschool programs. *Developmental Psychology, 5,* 719–734.

Lee, V., Brooks-Gunn, J., Schnur, E., & Liaw, F.R. (1991). Are Head Start effects sustained? A longitudinal follow-up comparison of disadvantaged children attending Head Start, no preschool, and other preschool programs. *Child Development, 61,* 495–507.

Leeper, S.H., Witherspoon, R.L., & Day, B. (1984). *Good schools for young children* (5th ed.). New York: Macmillan.

Lewit, E.M., & Baker, L.S. (1995). School readiness. *The Future of Children, 5*(2), 128–139.

Lin, H., Lawrence, F.R., & Gorrell, J. (2003). Kindergarten teachers' views of children's readiness for school. *Early Childhood Research Quarterly, 18,* 225–237.

Luster, T., Rhoades, K., & Haas, B. (1989). The relation between parental values and parenting behavior: A test of the Kohn hypothesis. *Journal of Marriage and the Family, 51,* 139–147.

Magnuson, K.A., Meyers, M.K., Ruhm, C.J., & Waldfogel, J. (2004). Inequality in preschool education and school readiness. *American Educational Research Journal, 41*(1), 115–157.

Mangione, P.L., & Speth, T. (1998). The transition to elementary school: A framework for creating early childhood continuity through home, school, and community partnerships. *The Elementary School Journal, 98*(4), 381–398.

Mapp, K.L. (2003). Having their say: Parents describe why and how they are engaged in their children's learning. *School Community Journal, 13*(1), 35–64.

Meisels, S.J. (1999). Assessing readiness. In R.C. Pianta & M.J. Cox (Eds.), *The transition to kindergarten* (pp. 39–66). Baltimore: Paul H. Brookes Publishing Co.

Mendez, J.L., McDermott, P., & Fantuzzo, J. (2002). Identifying and promoting social competence with African American preschool children: Developmental and contextual considerations. *Psychology in the Schools, 39*(1), 111–123.

Morrison, F.J., Griffith, E.M., & Alberts, D.M. (1997). Nature–nurture in the classroom: Entrance age, school readiness, and learning in children. *Developmental Psychology, 33*(2), 254–262.

Murphey, D.A., & Burns, C.E. (2002). Development of a comprehensive community assessment of school readiness. *Early Childhood Research and Practice, 4*(2). Retrieved October 20, 2005, from http://ecrp.uiuc.edu/v4n2/murphey.html

National Education Goals Panel. (1998, February). *Ready schools: A report of the Goal 1 Ready Schools Resource Group.* Washington, DC: Author.

National Institute of Child Health and Human Development Early Child Care Research Network. (2000). The relation of child care to cognitive and language development. *Child Development, 71,* 960–980.

Okagaki, L., & Sternberg, R.J. (1993). Parental beliefs and children's school performance. *Child Development, 64*(1), 36–56.

Parker, F.L., Boak, A.Y., Griffin, K.W., Ripple, C., & Peay, L. (1999). Parent–child relationship, home learning environment, and school readiness. *School Psychology Review, 28,* 413–425.

Pepper, S.C. (1942). *World hypotheses: A study in evidence.* Berkeley: University of California Press.

Pérez Carreón, G., Drake, C., & Calabrese Barton, A. (2005). The importance of presence: Immigrant parents' school engagement experiences. *American Educational Research Journal, 42*(3), 465–498.

Phenice, L., Martinez, E., & Grant, G. (1986). Minority family agendas: The home–school interface and alternative schooling model. In R.J. Griffore & R.P. Boger (Eds.), *Child rearing in the home and school* (pp. 121–156). New York: Plenum Press.

Pianta, R.C., Cox, M.J., Taylor, L.C., & Early, D.M. (1999). Kindergarten teachers' practices related to the transition into school: Results of a national survey. *Elementary School Journal, 100,* 71–86.

Pianta, R.C., Rimm-Kaufman, S.E., & Cox, M.J. (1999). Introduction: An ecological approach to kindergarten transition. In R.C. Pianta & M.J. Cox (Eds.), *The transition to kindergarten* (pp. 3–12). Baltimore: Paul H. Brookes Publishing Co.

Preservice Education for Teachers of Minorities. (1993). *Kamehameha Journal of Education, 4,* 1–9.

Ramey, C.T., Campbell, F.A., Burchinal, M.R., Bryant, D.M., Wasik, B.H., Skinner, M.L., et al. (1999). *Early learning, later success: The Abecedarian study.* Chapel Hill, NC: FPG Child Development Institute.

Ramey, S.L., Lanzi, R.G., Phillips, M.M., & Ramey, C.T. (1998). Perspectives of former Head Start children and their parents on school and the transition to school. *The Elementary School Journal, 98*(4), 311–328.

Ramey, S.L., & Ramey, C.T. (1994). The transition to school: Why the first few years matter for a lifetime. *Phi Delta Kappan, 76*(3), 194–199.

Read, K., Gardner, P., & Mahler, B.C. (1993). *Early childhood programs: Human relationships and learning* (2nd ed.). New York: Harcourt Brace.

Rimm-Kaufman, S.E., & Pianta, R.C. (2000). An ecological perspective on the transition to kindergarten: A theoretical framework to guide empirical research. *Journal of Applied Developmental Psychology, 21*(5), 491–511.

Rimm-Kaufman, S.E., Pianta, R.C., & Cox, M.J. (2000). Teachers' judgments of problems in the transition to Kindergarten. *Early Childhood Research Quarterly, 15*(2), 147–166.

Rong, X.L., & Preissle, J. (1998). *Educating immigrant students: What we need to know to meet the challenges.* Thousand Oaks, CA: Corwin Press.

Scrimsher, S., & Tudge, J. (2003). The teaching/learning relationship in the first years of school: Some revolutionary implications of Vygotsky's theory. *Early Education and Development, 14*(3), 293–312.

Serpell, R., Baker, L., & Sonnenschein, S. (2005). *Becoming literate in the city: The Baltimore Early Childhood Project.* New York: Cambridge University Press.

Shepard, L.A. (1997). Children not ready to learn? The invalidity of school readiness testing. *Psychology in the Schools, 34*(2), 85–97.

Shepard, L.A., Kagan, S.L., & Wurtz, E. (1998). Goal 1 early childhood assessments resource group recommendations. *Young Children, 43*(3), 52–54.

Sleeter, C., & Grant, C.A. (1987). An analysis of multicultural education in the United States. *Harvard Educational Review, 57*(4), 421–444.

Stipek, D.J., & Ryan, R.H. (1997). Economically disadvantaged preschoolers: Ready to learn but further to go. *Developmental Psychology, 33,* 711–723.

Swap, S. (1993). *Developing home–school partnerships.* New York: Teachers College Press.

Swick, K.J. (1992). *An early childhood school–home learning design: Strategies and resources.* Champaign, IL: Stipes.

Swick, K.J., Brown, M., & Boutte, G.S. (1994). African American children and school readiness: An analysis of the issues. *Journal of Instructional Psychology, 21*(2), 183–192.

Takanishi, R., & DeLeon, P.H. (1994). A head start for the 21st century. *American Psychologist, 49,* 120–122.

Taylor, L.C., Clayton, J.D., & Rowley, S.J. (2004). Academic socialization: Understanding parental influences on children's school-related development in the early years. *Review of General Psychology, 8*(3), 163–178.

Tharp, R.G. (1989). Psychocultural variables and constants: Effects on teaching and learning in schools. *American Psychologist, 44,* 349–359.

Tharp, R.G., & Gallimore, R. (1988). *Rousing minds to life: Teaching, learning, and schooling in social context.* New York: Cambridge University Press.

Trueba, E.H.T. (2004). *The new Americans: Immigrants and transnationals at work.* Lanham, MD: Rowman & Littlefield.

Tudge, J. (2005). *The everyday lives of young children: Culture, class, and child-rearing in diverse societies.* Manuscript in preparation.

Tudge, J., & Doucet, F. (2004). Early mathematical experiences: Observing young Black and White children's everyday experiences. *Early Childhood Research Quarterly, 19,* 21–39.

Tudge, J., Doucet, F., & Hayes, S. (2001). Theory, method and analysis: Necessary interconnections in the study of children and families. *Contrapontos: Revista de Educao [Counterpoints: The Journal of Education], 1*(3), 11–22.

Tudge, J., Doucet, F., Odero, D., Sperb, T., Piccinini, C., & Lopes, R. (2006). A window into different cultural worlds: Young children's everyday activities in the United States, Kenya, and Brazil. *Child Development (Special Issue on Race, Ethnicity, and Culture in Child Development), 77*(5), 1446–1469.

Tudge, J., & Hogan, D.M. (2005). An ecological approach to observations of children's everyday lives. In S. Greene & D.M. Hogan (Eds.), *Researching children's experience* (pp. 102–121). Thousands Oaks, CA: Sage Publications.

Tudge, J., Odero, D., Hogan, D.M., & Etz, K.E. (2003). Relations between the everyday activities of preschoolers and their teachers' perceptions of their competence in the first years of school. *Early Childhood Research Quarterly, 18,* 42–64.

Tudge, J., & Putnam, S. (1997). The everyday experiences of North American preschoolers in two cultural communities: A cross-disciplinary and cross-level analysis. In J. Tudge, M. Shanahan, & J. Valsiner (Eds.), *Comparisons in human development: Understanding time and context* (pp. 252–281). New York: Cambridge University Press.

Tudge, J., & Scrimsher, S. (2003). Lev S. Vygotsky on education: A cultural-historical, interpersonal, and individual approach to development. In B.J. Zimmerman & D.H. Schunk (Eds.), *Educational psychology: A century of contributions* (pp. 207–228). Mahwah, NJ: Lawrence Erlbaum Associates.

Tudge, J., Tammeveski, P., Meltsas, M., Kulakova, N., & Snezhkova, I.A. (2001, April). *The effects of young children's everyday activities: A longitudinal study in the United States, Russia, and Estonia.* Paper presented at the biennial meetings of the Society for Research in Child Development, Minneapolis, MN.

U.S. Census Bureau. (2000). *Census 2000 Summary File 4.* Washington, DC: Author.

Van der Veer, R., & Valsiner, J. (1991). *Understanding Vygotsky: A quest for synthesis.* Oxford, England: Blackwell.

Vygotsky, L.S. (1978). Interaction between learning and development. In M. Cole, V. John-Steiner, S. Scribner, & E. Souberman (Eds.), *Mind in society: The development of higher psychological processes* (pp. 79–91). Cambridge, MA: Harvard University Press. (Originally published 1935)

Vygotsky, L.S. (1987). *The collected works of L.S. Vygotsky, Vol. 1. Problems of general psychology* (N. Minick, Trans.). New York: Plenum. (Original work published 1934)

Wiggins, R.A., & Follo, E.J. (1999). Development of knowledge, attitudes and commitment to teach diverse student populations. *Journal of Teacher Education, 50,* 94–105.

Willis, M.G. (1992). Learning styles of African American children: A review of the literature and interventions. In A.K.H. Burlew, W.C. Banks, H.P. McAdoo, & D.A.Y. Azibo (Eds.), *African American psychology: Theory, research, and practice* (pp. 260–278). Newbury Park, CA: Sage Publications.

Wilson, T.L.Y., & Banks, B. (1994). A perspective on the education of African American males. *Journal of Instructional Psychology, 21*(1), 97–101.

Wright, C., Diener, M., & Kay, S.C. (2000). School readiness of low-income children at risk for school failure. *Journal of Children & Poverty, 6*(2), 99–117.

Zill, N., & Collins, M. (1995). *Approaching kindergarten: A look at preschoolers in the United States* (Statistical Analysis Report NCES 95-280). Washington, DC: U.S. Department of Education.

14

FATHER INVOLVEMENT DURING EARLY CHILDHOOD

Jason Downer, Ph.D.

Sensitive, supportive parenting is one of the most consistent and robust predictors of academic and social performance during the critical early school years and beyond (e.g., Barth & Parke, 1993; Burchinal, Peisner-Feinberg, Pianta, & Howes, 2002; Estrada, Arsenio, Hess, & Holloway, 1987; Morrison & Cooney, 2002; Pianta, Smith, & Reeve, 1991). Although the term *parent* implies the inclusion of both mothers and fathers, the vast majority of these investigations into supportive parenting are in fact studies of mothering, with a sole focus on maternal behaviors and mother–child relationships and a notable lack of attention to fathers and their roles during children's early schooling. Until recently, efforts to research fatherhood have been plagued by oversimplified definitions of fathers' involvement in the lives of their children. However, in the past 2 decades, investigators from multiple disciplines have developed increasingly complex conceptualizations of fathering within the context of diverse family life, suggesting multiple ways in which men can be involved and make unique contributions to children's development during the early school years.

There are several compelling reasons for studying father involvement during early childhood (ages 3–8) and the transition to school. First, fathers are known to make direct and indirect contributions to children's development of cognitive and socioemotional competencies above and beyond maternal contributions (Amato & Rivera, 1999; Cabrera, Tamis-LeMonda, Bradley, Hofferth, & Lamb, 2000). Second, children at risk for school adjustment problems—often overrepresented in low-income, minority families—are likely to be faced with a diverse, dynamic array of father-involvement experiences that provide a source of contextual variation about which little is known. Third, fathers tend to be more involved with their children during infancy and early childhood than during middle childhood and adolescence (Yeung, Sandberg, Davis-Kean, & Hofferth, 2001), and fathers who are most involved early on are also the most involved during later childhood (Aldous, Mulligan, & Bjarnason, 1998; National Institute of Child Health and Human Development [NICHD], Early Child Care Research Network [ECCRN], 2000). Finally, early childhood is a time when children are repeatedly confronted with the challenge of adapting to new environments outside the home, a process that fathers' style of play and use of language may be especially suited to support (Grossmann et al., 2002; Lamb & Tamis-LeMonda, 2004; Paquette, 2004; Roggman, 2004).

The intent of this chapter is to discuss father involvement during early childhood and bring attention to the potential significance of fathering during the transition to school. To achieve a thorough appreciation of the role that fathers can play in children's early learning, it is first necessary to establish who should be considered "fathers." Men who do and do not have biological ties to children and who do or do not have co-residence with children may have a significant impact on children's lives. The initial section of this chapter therefore addresses the question—what is the contemporary definition of a father? The chapter then draws from recent conceptual and empirical work to define father involvement and describe the amounts and types of father involvement (e.g., quantity, quality) that occur during early childhood. Next, the chapter moves to a review of literature about the mechanisms through which father involvement may influence children's cognitive and socioemotional development throughout the school transition period. The chapter concludes with identification of specific research and practice issues that need to be addressed to advance understanding of father involvement in early childhood (ages 3–8) and its potential role in facilitating the transition into the school environment.

WHO ARE FATHERS?

Hernandez and Brandon (2002) aptly asked, "Who are the fathers of today?" in a recent chapter that underscores the challenges of defining the term *father* in today's age of diverse family structures. The list of ways in which men can take on the role of a father is lengthy; father status is often determined by a combination of or distinction between shared genetics and diverse sociocultural expectations and norms about fatherhood and families. In a rudimentary sense, men's father status can be distinguished along the following dimensions: relationship to a child, residential status, and relationship to a child's mother (Hofferth & Anderson, 2003). The most common scenario remains the two-parent, intact family in which a biological father lives with and is married to his child's biological mother. In 2002, 74% of children younger than 5 years old were living in this type of family context (U.S. Department of Health and Human Services [DHHS], 2004). Because a large proportion of young children live with their biological fathers, there is a real need for continued emphasis on conducting studies in two-parent family contexts that explicitly examine the potential value of father involvement. However, there is a clear trend toward more children living in nonnuclear household arrangements, particularly those in low-income and minority families. In fact, young children at risk for early school problems are likely to experience a range of diverse fathering experiences, particularly cohabiting, nonresidential, and social fathers, about which relatively little has been known until recent years (Coley, 2001).

Cohabiting Fathers

From 1990 to 1997, the number of cohabiting couples (i.e., living together but not married) in the United States increased by 50%, and a quarter of these couples gave birth to a new child (Casper & Cohen, 2000). Rapidly rising numbers of cohabiting couples parallel a trend toward single mothers of young children living with at least one other adult rather than alone with her children (Acs & Nelson, 2001; Smock, 2000). More than 1.5 million children under the age of 15 were living in a cohabiting family in 1998 compared with fewer than 200,000 just 18 years earlier (U.S. Census Bureau, 1999). In the Fragile Families project, it was noted that more than 50% of young, unmarried parents were living together at the time of their newborn's birth (Garfinkel & McLanahan, 2000). Under cohabiting arrangements, children may live with their biological father or a romantic partner of their mother. Regardless, cohabitation seems to occur more often in African American and Hispanic American families than European American ones and is highly associated with a dynamic family structure that changes within 5 years in 90% of cases (Graefe & Lichter, 1999). Although providing children with a potential father figure, a cohabiting arrangement is also liable to result in the disruption of such relationships. There is clearly a need to better understand the role of fathers in cohabiting contexts to discern benefits or detriments to young children's preparation for entry into school.

Nonresidential Biological Fathers

Much has been written about the aftermath of divorce and the role that nonresidential biological fathers play in the lives of their children, such as responsibilities for visitation and child support (Amato & Sobolewski, 2004; Lamb, 2002). Far less is known about never-married, nonresidential biological fathers and their relationships with children, a scenario that occurs at a high rate in disadvantaged minority families (Coley, 2001). The emphasis of media coverage and research often rests on financial obligations and high numbers of never-married, nonresidential fathers who fall short of meeting their financial responsibilities toward their biological children (Miller, Garfinkel, & McLanahan, 1997). However, there is some evidence that more of these men are providing financial support through informal routes than was previously thought (Coley & Chase-Lansdale, 1999; Edin & Lein 1997) and that fatherhood is a meaningful experience in their lives (Nelson, Clampet-Lundquist, & Edin, 2002). There is much to be learned about the role that never-married, nonresidential fathers play in their young children's lives and, in particular, why seemingly strong, early commitments to newborn children do not translate into more consistent, active involvement during early childhood and the transition to school.

Social Fathers

A seemingly endless number of fatherhood scenarios exist for biological fathers, but the complexity of defining fatherhood does not end there. As rates of divorce and nonmarital childbearing have increased in past decades, so has discussion of men who have come to be known as "social fathers" or "father figures." These men typically fall into one of two categories—biological mother's romantic partner or a child's male relative—and they may or may not live in the child's residence. It appears that in roughly one third to one half of cases in which preschool-age children experience little to no contact with their biological fathers, mothers report an involved/available father figure (Black, Dubowitz, & Starr, 1999; Jayakody & Kalil, 2002), whereas for school-age children, social father involvement is estimated at about 25% (Coley, 1998). Some have proposed that African American families have particularly strong kinship networks in which helping to parent and care for all children is a cultural norm, leading to greater acceptance and occurrence of social fathering in these communities (Dunifon & Kowalewski-Jones, 2002; Hill, 1972). Although less frequently discussed in the literature, another group of social fathers may surface during the transition to school as children become old enough to participate in community events and are more connected with a school context, opening up the pool to male youth group leaders, school teachers, coaches, and so forth.

Given the sheer number of family structures in contemporary society, children are experiencing contact and relationships with multiple male caregivers now more than ever, sometimes simultaneously and other times scattered chronologically. This diversity in children's experiences with fathers, both biological and nonbiological, provides a challenge for understanding and clarifying the role of fathers in family life during early childhood and the transition to school. For instance, ambiguity about the role of fathers and father figures in a child's life may lead to discontinuity and instability, precluding the development of close, supportive fathering relationships. On the other hand, multiple men in the life of a child could complement one another in a way that would provide the child with an adaptive set of interpersonal and financial resources. In recognition of the growing number of fatherhood types and the need to expand a weak knowledge base about father involvement in both typical and atypical family contexts, it is necessary to study men under the conditions of cohabitation, nonresidential parenting, and social fathering to identify distinct and common patterns of involvement with young children during early schooling.

CONCEPTUALIZING INVOLVEMENT

The role of fathers in child development, often coined "involvement," is a continually evolving concept that has resulted in different definitions of the ideal father and has made the assessment of father involvement challenging (Pleck & Pleck, 1997). Coltrane and Parke (1998) argued that the cultural norm of fatherhood has never truly been uniform, despite popular opinions to the contrary, and that contemporary thought on the conceptualization of fatherhood often relies on precedents from past eras. The current consensus is that father involvement is a multifaceted concept, incorporating elements of both quantity and quality of time spent in diverse fathering activities (Lamb & Tamis-LeMonda, 2004; Tamis-LeMonda & Cabrera, 2002).

Brief History of Research on Father Involvement

At the beginning of the 20th century, the father's traditional role as breadwinner and disciplinarian was supplanted by a novel perspective on fatherhood referred to as masculine domesticity (Marsh, 1988). Because of increased job security and suburbanization, fathers began to spend more family-focused leisure time at home, leading to a shift in father–child relations toward more companionship and affection (Griswold, 1997). Attitudes toward fatherhood have shifted several times since the turn of the 20th century, alternating between the traditionally patriarchal, breadwinner role and a push toward greater child care responsibility and more affectionate father–child bonds (Coltrane & Parke, 1998; Griswold, 1997; LaRossa, Gordon, Wilson, Bauran, & Jaret, 1991). Particularly since World War II, there has been an increased emphasis on men expanding their nurturant, companion role with children (Griswold, 1997). This shift in image for fathers coincided directly with the increasing percentage of mothers of young children entering the work force (Lamb, 2000).

In the 1970s and 1980s, father involvement was most frequently measured by the number of hours that fathers spent with their children (e.g., child care duties, play) or through calculating fathers' financial contributions to their families (Lamb, 2000). A deficit-based, father-absence paradigm was also popularized (Blankenhorn, 1995; Popenoe, 1996) in which father involvement was thought of as a dichotomous variable and comparisons of child outcomes were based on residential versus nonresidential father status. Opponents of this father-absence approach note that it fails to address the processes by which fathers' actual involvement might be linked to their children's development (Silverstein & Auerbach, 1999).

Contemporary, Multifaceted Involvement

In recent years, the definition and assessment of father involvement has become more complex, expanding to focus on quantity of diverse involvement activities as well as the quality of this involvement. The tripartite model of father involvement, pioneered by Lamb (1986, 1987), extended the notion of involvement beyond child care duties into the three domains of responsibility, availability, and engagement. Although engagement encompasses all direct father–child contact and interactions, the responsibility and availability domains involve child-related planning activities (e.g., calling a recreation center for basketball registration) and general accessibility (e.g., picking up the child at school in an emergency), respectively. Epstein's (1996) typology, commonly adopted as a generic framework for thinking about parent involvement in education, also reflects this wide range of parental contributions to early schooling in that it includes direct contact with schools, provision of learning opportunities at home, and even basic child care activities.

Numerous extensions of Lamb's multidimensional approach have surfaced in the past 2 decades, either expounding on a particular aspect of the model or adding yet another domain to a rapidly expanding list. Theorists have broken down responsibility into direct and indirect components (Pleck & Masciadrelli, 2004; Pleck & Stueve, 2001); for example, direct, process-oriented responsibility refers to taking initiative for and monitoring a child's care, whereas indirect responsibility may involve making child care arrangements (Peterson & Gerson, 1992) or facilitating peer-play opportunities (Parke, 2002). Others have described multiple aspects of *responsible fathering,* which includes financial support, direct child care, emotional support, and efforts to establish legal paternity (Doherty, Kouneski, & Erickson, 1998).

Also using the tripartite model as a foundation, Palkovitz (1997) emphasized three distinct domains of fathering: cognitive, affective, and behavioral involvement. The behavioral component is akin to engagement in Lamb's model and has been the primary focus of research (Pleck, 1997); however, the inclusion of cognitive and affective aspects of involvement constitutes a shift toward considering how fathers psychologically experience the time spent with children and the personal meaning attributed to father–child relationships (Hawkins & Palkovitz, 1999). For example, children's presence regularly has an impact on fathers' cognitive processes, such as planning and evaluating daily experiences, as well as the expression or restraint of emotions. In turn, these cognitive and affective experiences of fatherhood may be linked to behavioral involvement, and vice versa, in a way that affects the quality of father–child interactions and relationships.

Integrating Quantity and Quality of Involvement

In addition to identifying diverse facets of involvement, the *quality* of interactions between fathers and children has become a centerpiece of what is called *positive father involvement* (Pleck, 1997). Typically, this framework for involvement integrates the amount of time that fathers spend in diverse activities with children and the quality of parenting and/or the relationship between the father and child. Ways of describing the quality of fathering mirror longstanding mothering frameworks, pointing to warmth, nurturance, sensitivity, responsiveness, cognitive stimulation, and support of autonomy as ideal for child development (Lamb & Tamis-LeMonda, 2004; Paquette, 2004). However, there continues to be room for improvement in operationalizing high-quality cognitive and affective involvement, as well as discerning how these various elements of father involvement relate to one another in optimal form.

An integration of historical and contemporary thought about defining involvement suggests that multidimensionality best reflects the complexity of fathering roles in the lives of young children. This multidimensionality is manifested in what a father does with or for his child (behavioral, financial responsibility); how a father thinks about his child (cognitive); and how a father feels toward his child (affective) during the transition to school. Additional layers of quantity and quality are then applied to each of these involvement constructs to ascertain a fathering "dose" and its influence on a child's preparation for school. As an example, consider the case of Joe, the never-married father of 4-year-old Lisa, who lives across town with her mother.

Joe is responsible for picking up Lisa from preschool every Tuesday and often excitedly talks with her in the car about what happened that day in the classroom. He drops her off at home, at which point he encourages Lisa to read her favorite book before bedtime, indicates that he looks forward to seeing her in a few days, and tells her that he loves her. As Joe drives home, he experiences intense feelings of pride as he recalls the new words that Lisa was using in their conversation. Later that evening at his second job, Joe becomes frustrated with a customer, but quickly calms down as he thinks about how much he wants to impress his boss, receive a promotion, and secure the more flexible schedule that will allow him to spend more time with Lisa on the weekends.

Note in this example that Joe takes his role as father seriously and is often *involved* cognitively and affectively, even though his time spent with Lisa is minimal. This translates into behaviors at work that may increase the amount of time that he can spend with her and, even during brief contacts, help create a smoother transition into high-quality interactions that convey support, caring, and enthusiasm for learning. In contrast, what if Joe considered responsibility for his daughter's needs to be a burden and constant source of frustration? This affective tenor could reduce both the amount and quality of his direct involvement with Lisa, thus reducing his effectiveness as a supportive resource. More work is needed to explain how these multiple components of involvement interact with one another and how they may do so differently under different circumstances (e.g., if Lisa's mother decides that Joe is not providing enough child support and restricts his contact). This integration will help create a model of father involvement that strikes a balance between comprehensiveness and clarity (Cabrera et al., 2000) and recognizes the direct and indirect roles that fathers play in young children's lives.

WHAT ARE FATHERS DOING?

The role of fathers in contemporary society is far less straightforward than it was even a few decades ago (Coltrane, 1996), resulting in a wide range of involvement activities during early childhood and elementary school. Before moving to the question of whether fathering plays a key role in determining children's readiness for school, it is important to understand what fathers are doing with children prior to and during the transition to school. When possible, the following section reports findings specifically for children during the transition to school (ages 3–8), but samples often include a larger age range.

Time Spent with Children

To what extent and in what ways do fathers spend time with their young children? There are two consistently striking patterns in "time spent" data cutting across multiple sources of information: father engagement and accessibility in two-parent households has increased in the past 30 years, and this involvement slowly but steadily decreases as children grow older (Aldous et al., 1998; Bianchi, 2000; Bond, Galinsky, & Swanberg, 1998; Pleck & Masciadrelli, 2004; Sandberg & Hofferth, 2001). Using time diary methodology in the 1997 Child Development Supplement to the Panel Study of Income Dynamics (PSID), fathers in two-parent households are noted to average 68 minutes in direct interaction with children ages 3–8 during weekdays and are accessible to their children for approximately the same amount of time (resulting in a total of 2 hours and 16 minutes each weekday; Yeung et al., 2001). On the weekends, these numbers increase, with fathers actively engaged in activities with their children for an average of 3.4 hours and accessible for about another 3 hours, totaling more than 6 hours of involvement for a weekend day. These daily hours are somewhat higher than those reported in other studies (Bianchi, 2000; Zuzanek, 2000), but this is not a function of self-serving bias (most data were reported by mothers) and may in part be related to the inclusion of older children in comparable studies with whom fathers are less engaged (Pleck & Masciadrelli, 2004).

So, what types of activities are fathers engaged in with their young children? Play and interactive companionship activities are the most frequently cited contexts for father–child interactions, regardless of a study's methodology or sample (Hofferth, Pleck, Stueve, Bianchi, & Sayer, 2002; McBride & Mills, 1993; Robinson & Godbey, 1997; Yeung et al., 2001). These activities are also the most regular activities for mothers to engage in with young children, but play takes up a larger proportion of fathers' total time spent with children than it does for mothers (Lamb, 1997; Pleck & Masciadrelli, 2004).

Perhaps most interesting are the relative amounts of time that fathers spend with children compared with mothers in two-parent households. In the 1980s and early 1990s, estimates of fathers' relative engagement with and accessibility to children were about 44% and 66% the estimates for mothers, respectively (Pleck, 1997); although low, these numbers suggest a significant increase compared with data spanning the mid-1960s and 1970s (Lamb, Pleck, Charnov, & Levine, 1985). Mothers continue to dominate time spent with children relative to fathers, but recent data indicate that fathers in two-parent households continue to increase their relative engagement and accessibility. In particular, on the weekends for children ages 3–8, fathers may be approaching equal partnership with mothers, averaging about 87% time engaged or accessible across all types of activities and as high as

91% and 95% for caregiving and social activities (Yeung et al., 2001). Similarly, in terms of responsibility for young children in two-parent households, 17% of fathers in 1977 were listed as primary caregivers for preschoolers when mothers worked (O'Connell, 1993), whereas by 1996, this proportion had risen to 23% (Child Trends, 2002).

Evidence is mixed regarding the influence of racial/ethnic differences on the amount and type of time fathers spend with children within two-parent households. When controlling for factors that typically reduce the amount of time children are engaged with fathers, such as family size and nonbiological father status, weekly father engagement and accessibility do not appear to systematically differ based on race/ethnicity (Hofferth, 2003; Yeung et al., 2001). However, on the weekends, African American fathers may spend less time and Hispanic American fathers may spend more time with children than European American fathers (Yeung et al., 2001). Fathers from both minority groups also may demonstrate more responsibility for parenting than European American fathers (Hofferth, 2003), perhaps related in African American families to adoption of more egalitarian beliefs and roles in the home (Billingsley, 1992).

Far less is known about the time that fathers spend with children in less traditional household arrangements. Stepfathers and cohabiting nonbiological fathers seem to spend less time with residential children than biological fathers (Hofferth & Anderson, 2003; Hofferth et al., 2002). Their responsibility for supporting other nonresidential children may play a role in this reduced time (Hofferth & Anderson, 2003); however, some theorists have proposed an evolutionary explanation, suggesting that biological fathers are more engaged than nonbiological fathers because of the potential genetic benefits of this investment (Anderson, Kaplan, & Lancaster, 1999). Nonresidential father involvement, either biological or social, is perhaps the most challenging to quantify given that these men are often less accessible to researchers than those that live with young children. Mainly reviewing literature about children with divorced parents, Amato & Sobolewski (2004) suggested that many children rarely see or spend time with their nonresidential biological fathers; however, fathers who remain highly involved after a divorce are actually growing in number. And, father–child contacts for never-married, often nonresidential fathers actually appear to be quite frequent during a child's first few years of life (Coley & Chase-Lansdale, 1999; McLanahan & Sandefur, 1994; McLanahan, Garfinkel, Brooks-Gunn, & Zhao, 1997), although likely diminishing over time (Carlson & McLanahan, 2002). Again, there is a real need to gather objective data about the frequency and types of involvement by fathers and social fathers outside of two-parent intact families, including information about barriers to and supports of this involvement.

Nature and Quality of Interactions with Children

Given the trend toward greater involvement by fathers, the nature and quality of their relationships and interactions with preschool- and early elementary school–age children become of great interest. This is especially true because proximal influences are expected to provide the most substantial contribution to children's developmental outcomes (Bronfenbrenner & Morris, 1998). However, a major point of contention when considering father–child interactions is that measurement systems mostly have been developed using mothers as a template (Hawkins & Palkovitz, 1999; Marsiglio, Day, & Lamb, 2000; Roggman, Fitzgerald, Bradley,

& Raikes, 2002), focusing on behaviors such as warmth, sensitivity, and support. When applying this template to fathers, they actually tend to be as consistently warm and responsive toward their young children as mothers, both when observed and when asked to report about the relationship (Clarke-Stewart, 1978; Lamb & Lewis, 2004; Notaro & Volling, 1999; Tamis-LeMonda, Shannon, Cabrera, & Lamb, 2004). This picture differs somewhat depending on the type of father, however, with stepfathers and nonbiological fathers demonstrating a less nurturing relationship with children than biological fathers (Coleman, Ganong, & Fine, 2000; Hofferth & Anderson, 2003; MacDonald & DeMaris, 1996).

Applying a maternal template to father–child relationships allows for easy comparisons with mothering. Yet, worthy of more attention is the possibility that fathers are interacting with young children in distinct ways from mothers, which may serve the function of "opening children to the outside world" (Paquette, 2004, p. 198) and empowering them to successfully handle the transition from home to schooling contexts. For example, attachment theorists and others have suggested that the playful companion role that many fathers tend to enter into with their young children includes more persistent, intense support for autonomy than mothers typically provide (Grossmann et al., 2002; Harkness & Super, 1992; Murphy, 1997). Paquette (2004) described it as follows:

> Men seem to have a tendency to surprise children, to destabilize them momentarily, and to encourage them to take "risks," thus enabling children to learn to be brave in unfamiliar situations and to stand up for themselves. (p. 212)

In other words, fathers may challenge young children to be more independent, self-reliant, and self-regulated. Consider, for example, a father who consistently provides opportunities for active, physical, and rowdy play within a safe context. Such experiences offer the child a chance to develop assertiveness and confidence, as well as learn how to regulate during physical and affective stimulation. These are personal qualities that will serve children well during adjustment to early schooling.

Fathers also interact with and speak to young children in distinct ways from mothers, which could be conducive to assisting with the transition to new environments, such as schools and classrooms during the kindergarten transition. Specifically, fathers tend to have more linguistically challenging communicative interactions with children than do mothers (Lamb & Tamis-LeMonda, 2004). For example, fathers of young children use more wh- (e.g., what, why) questions, imperatives, directives, requests for clarification, and other more complex forms of speech (Bellinger & Gleason, 1982; Kavanaugh & Jirkovsky, 1982; Leaper, Anderson, & Sanders, 1998; Marcos, 1995; McLaughlin, White, McDevitt, & Raskin, 1983; Ratner, 1988; Tomasello, Conti-Ramsden, & Ewert, 1990). These unexpected and perhaps unconventional uses of language with young children may facilitate cognitive flexibility and ease of adaptation.

School Involvement

Given the centrality of parents to children's early learning, school-based parent-involvement practices have been incorporated into Head Start national performance standards since 1975 and, more recently, into No Child Left Behind Act (PL 107-110) legislation that funds Title I prekindergarten and elementary school programs (Henrich & Blackman-Jones,

2006). School-based involvement, defined here as parents' direct engagement with children in schools or contact with school personnel, is not to be confused with educational involvement, which might also include home-based educational and teaching activities between fathers and children (Epstein, 1996; Fantuzzo, Tighe, & Childs, 2000). There is very limited information about the involvement of fathers in children's school experiences during prekindergarten and early elementary education, as summarized next.

The prevailing perspective is that men are much less likely than mothers to be found at school-related functions (Fagan & Palm, 2004). In perhaps the most comprehensive study of father involvement in schools, as part of the 1996 National Household Education Survey, parents were asked about their participation in four types of school-related activities during the kindergarten through 12th-grade period: attendance at a school meeting, attendance at a scheduled parent–teacher conference, attendance at a school/class event, and serving as a volunteer at the school (Nord, Brimhall, & West, 1997). Within two-parent households, mothers were much more likely to report a high level of involvement in these school activities (56% involved in 3–4 activities) than fathers (27%). In fact, 48% of fathers in these families reported involvement in only one or fewer school activities. This is in stark contrast to single-parent, father-led families in which fathers reported a level of school involvement that was more similar to mothers than fathers in two-parent households.

Interestingly, mothers in single-parent households (34% of the sample) also reported on nonresidential father involvement in schools (Nord et al., 1997). A quarter of these nonresidential fathers had absolutely no contact with the study children in the past year. Those nonresidential fathers who had some contact in the past year were reportedly much less involved in their children's school than residential fathers—69% had participated in no school activities in the past year, 31% had attended at least one school activity, and 9% had been involved in three or four activities. Nonresidential fathers were more involved in school when they were paying child support and when the child's mother was more stable financially, but nonresidential fathers were less involved in school if their children were older.

In addition to this large-scale, national study, a host of smaller studies provided information about fathers' involvement in early education and child care settings, again suggesting limited school involvement (Downer & Mendez, 2005; Fagan, 1999; Fagan & Press, 2000; Gary, Beatty, & Weaver, 1987). In the late 1990s, Fagan and colleagues reported a set of findings from research with fathers and father figures who had preschool-age children. Seventy-one percent of these fathers rarely or never volunteered in their children's preschools, 73% rarely or never attended parent meetings or conferences, and 49% rarely or never communicated with the preschool teacher (Fagan, 1999). McBride and colleagues have also reported relatively low levels of preschool center involvement for fathers within Caucasian, middle-class families (Garinger & McBride, 1995; McBride & Rane, 1997). With another sample of preschoolers who lived in two-parent households, even when fathers did report coming into the preschool setting, they were much less likely to communicate with teachers than were mothers (Fagan, 1997; Fagan & Press, 2000), suggesting a discomfort or uncertainty about interacting with teachers. Another recent study of low-income, African American fathers of Head Start children indicated that they were more likely to report involvement with their children at home than at school (Downer & Mendez, 2005). Such a finding suggests that a sole focus on center- and classroom-based involvement may underestimate fathers' involvement in home-based learning activities and the value that they place on education for their children.

Although limited in scope, consistent findings indicate that, by and large, fathers, whether living with their children or not, rarely visit the school and classroom environments of their young children. Low school-involvement rates, however, do not necessarily mean that fathers lack investment in their children's education. Rather, fathers may be more likely to engage in home-based educational involvement, such as reading a book, helping with a school project, or asking a child about his or her school day, than school-based activities (Downer & Mendez, 2005). In contrast to a deficit approach that focuses on what fathers are *not* doing (e.g., volunteering in classrooms), it may be more effective to invest a school's parent-involvement resources in creative efforts to encourage, support, and expand fathers' home-based educational involvement. Furthermore, low school involvement could be a function of how this involvement is measured, thus underestimating fathers' involvement; for instance, the NHES does not cover other school-related involvement activities such as dropping off and picking up children from school, which may be a more likely role for working fathers. Finally, it is worth noting that early childhood settings are often a female-dominated culture that may unconsciously be more welcoming to mothers than fathers, thus leading to a less comfortable environment for men.

HOW AND WHY FATHERS MAKE A DIFFERENCE

Children's positive adjustment to school settings and their development of foundational academic and socioemotional competencies during the school transition is essential, given the relative stability of academic trajectories after third grade (Entwisle, Alexander, & Olson, 1997). Although much is known about the importance of family experience and mother–child interactions in support of development during early childhood (e.g., Bornstein & Tamis-LeMonda, 1989; Pianta & Harbers, 1996), only recently has the unique contribution of father involvement during this period been more consistently considered. Despite the lack of a "grand unifying theory" of fatherhood (Roggman et al., 2002, p. 6), evidence suggests that fathers can have both direct and indirect influences on development during early childhood (Lamb & Tamis-LeMonda, 2004). In fact, the application of a developmental ecological model, as described by Rimm-Kaufman & Pianta (2000), is well suited to describing the ways that father involvement can have an impact on children's readiness for and adjustment to school. Within such a model, proximal processes, or the direct interactions that children have within dyads and settings, are conceptualized as the primary means by which early learning is promoted (Bronfenbrenner & Morris, 1998).

Although father–child interactions serve as proximal processes, fathers may also indirectly have an influence on child development through provision of financial and social capital within a child's immediate family system. An understanding of these pathways of influence is essential for thinking about how father involvement can be supported in a way that has the greatest impact on children at risk for school adjustment problems. The following sections provide an overview of the trends in empirical findings about fathers' influence on young children's development, including father absence in single-parent households, direct effects, indirect effects, and an integrated developmental ecological model.

Father Absence in Single-Parent Households

Early father-involvement studies simply compared the outcomes of children with residential fathers versus children with fathers who lived outside the home, either due to divorce or remaining unmarried (Lamb & Tamis-LeMonda, 2004). Results of this work sparked the "responsible fathering" movement, which reached the consensus that father absence in the case of single-parent households had consistently negative effects on children's concurrent development and developmental trajectories (Blankenhorn, 1995; Lerman, 1993; Seltzer & Bianchi, 1988). However, despite the significant findings, this all-or-none distinction overlooked the more intricate aspects of how a father's thoughts, affect, and behaviors may be related to his children's well-being, regardless of residential status or relationship with a child's mother. In fact, a recent meta-analysis indicated that bivariate correlations between children's outcomes and father absence from the home were actually somewhat lower than expected, given recently publicized attention to fatherlessness (Amato & Gilbreth, 1999). The claim of an essential link between father absence and child outcomes is now recognized as an oversimplification of the issue (Hawkins & Dollahite, 1997; Silverstein & Auerbach, 1999); specifically, distinguishing the effects of father absence from those of economic disadvantage can be difficult in poor, single-mother households (Lamb, 2002; McLanahan, 1999; McLoyd, 1998).

Direct Father Involvement

As the field moves beyond the limited perspective of fathers missing from single-parent households, studies are incorporating more sophisticated measures of direct father involvement and consistently demonstrating that fathers' involvement is positively associated with young children's development (Cabrera et al., 2000; Lamb & Tamis-LeMonda, 2004). One review article (Marsiglio, Amato, Day, & Lamb, 2000) reported 55 studies in the 1990s that investigated the father–child relationship within intact families and its impact on child outcomes (for young children and adolescents). Medium-size effects were generally found between fathers' authoritative parenting and children's lower internalizing and externalizing behavior problems. Although Amato and Rivera's meta-analysis (1999) noted only nine studies in which father–child relationships and children's outcomes were independently observed and maternal involvement was controlled, the majority of these studies also indicated that father involvement was uniquely and positively associated with children's development. This positive impact of fathers' involvement appears to be consistent for families from different racial backgrounds (Amato & Rivera, 1999), whereas some studies have even indicated a larger positive effect of father involvement in low-income, African American families than in Caucasian families (Yogman, Kindlon, & Earls, 1995).

Specifically in early childhood, research has identified positive links between fathers' warmth/nurturance, sensitivity/responsivity, and authoritative parenting style and children's cognitive development, academic achievement, and socioemotional competence (Cowan, Cowan, Ablow, et al., 2005; NICHD ECCRN, 2004; Yeung, Duncan, & Hill, 2000). For example, fathers who sensitively support children's independent exploration during preschool make positive contributions to those children's emotional security at the age of 16; these contributions have been found to be even more effective than mothers' support (Grossmann, Kindler, & Strasser, 2003). Positive father engagement with 6-year-old children has also been associated at age 7 with higher cognitive abilities, academic achievement, and social maturity (Gottfried, Gottfried, & Bathurst, 1988). Importantly, these associations appear to be lasting, as suggested by a study that found fathers' warmth with children at age 5 to be a significant predictor of children's well-being as adults in their early 40s (Franz, McClelland, & Weinberger, 1991).

Studies of the relationship between father involvement and children's developmental outcomes are much less abundant for low-income, minority, and nontraditional families, the very contexts in which children are most at risk for school adjustment problems. For nonresidential fathers, frequency of contact and child-reported quality of the father–child relationship have not been significantly related to positive adjustment, whereas authoritative fathering does appear to be a significant predictor of children's well-being (Amato & Gilbreth, 1999; Marsiglio, Amato, et al., 2000). In a recent critical review of fathering studies within African American families, Coley (2001) reported that father presence is often associated with positive cognitive development and school functioning for young children, whereas social and emotional development may be influenced more by the emotional quality of the father–child relationship than by mere presence or availability. For example, in low-income, urban African American families, fathers' and father figures' parenting satisfaction and nurturance in interactions with 3-year-old children were predictive of greater cognitive and language competence (Black et al., 1999). Across time from ages 2 to 3, even after controlling for demographic factors such as level of education and employment status, supportive parenting by low-income fathers (i.e., observed sensitivity, positive regard, cognitive stimulation) was predictive of children's cognitive and receptive language abilities (Tamis-LeMonda, et al., 2004). Evidently, children benefit from interactions with a warm, responsive, supportive, and cognitively stimulating father or father figure, regardless of the family and cultural context in which that relationship is embedded (Amato & Fowler, 2002).

Integrating the above empirical findings, father–child interactions and relationships appear to be significantly and uniquely associated with children's cognitive and socioemotional development, above and beyond mothers' influence. Such proximal influence is not merely a function of "being there"; rather, it involves sensitive, warm, responsive, nurturing, and supportive parenting behaviors that parallel effective mother–child interactions. This pattern of influence, which appears to hold true whether or not fathers live with their children (Amato & Gilbreth, 1999), raises the question of whether fathers actually play a distinct role from mothers or other supportive adults available to children. Although the answer is far from definitive, fathers and mothers appear to interact differently with their children in some instances (Paquette, 2004), and these discrepancies in behavioral style may hold unique benefits for children (Grossmann et al., 2002; Paquette, 2004) that require further empirical inquiry.

Indirect Father Involvement

The contribution of fathers to children's development cannot be completely accounted for by assessing direct engagement in father–child interactions. Instead, a father's role needs to be considered from an ecological perspective to examine the ways that fathers affect and are affected by myriad processes that occur within two-parent intact and nontraditional family systems (Pleck & Masciadrelli, 2004). Clear evidence shows that fathers can make contributions to children's development through less direct means, mostly by making more financial or social capital available to their children. Identification of these indirect pathways could offer promising new targets for intervention, focusing on systemic changes to facilitate children's school readiness.

In terms of financial capital, child support payments (particularly voluntary ones) have consistently been associated with children's well-being (Argys, Peters, Brooks-Gunn, & Smith, 1998; McLanahan, Seltzer, Hanson, & Thomas, 1994). For example, a recent meta-analysis indicated that child support payments to mothers were associated with more educational success and fewer externalizing problems (Amato & Gilbreth, 1999). This provision of economic resources is a way for fathers to be involved in a supportive fashion, even without one-to-one interactions, suggesting the importance of continued emphasis on job creation for low-income men and stringent enforcement of child support payments for nonpoor fathers (Greene & Moore, 2000).

Marital relationships, and particularly marital conflict, are also consistently linked with the quality of parents' relationships with their children and children's social, emotional, and academic development (Cowan, Cowan, Ablow, et al., 2005; Cox, Paley, & Harter, 2001; Cummings, Goeke-Morey, & Raymond, 2004; Emery, 1999). Findings uphold the hypothesis that marital distress and conflict result in compromised parenting skills and/or parent–child relationships (Cummings & Davies, 1994, 2002), with father–child relationships actually being more susceptible to marital problems than mother–child interactions (Coiro & Emery, 1998; Frosch, Mangelsdorf, & McHale, 2000; Owen & Cox, 1997). However, one recent study provided evidence that children's perceptions of marital conflict contribute to the influence of the conflict on their emotional functioning (Ablow, 2005), suggesting that the field's understanding of mechanisms by which marital distress influences children would benefit from further inquiry focused on multimethod, multirater assessments.

Other contextual factors, including psychological functioning of parents (Cummings, Keller & Davies, 2005; Simons, Lorenz, Wu, & Conger, 1993) and work experiences (Cowan & Cowan, 2000; McHale & Crouter, 1992), may also play a role in how fathers indirectly influence young children's development (Clements, Lim, & Chaplin, 2002). As Cummings and O'Reilly (1997) discussed, there remains a lack of investigation into how fathers' psychological functioning is tied to both maternal mental health and marital quality, considering that they all relate to parenting and children's outcomes. For instance, anger in the context of depressive symptomatology may be especially relevant to fathers' influence within the family context (Du Rocher Schudlich & Cummings, 2003). In addition, a father may have an indirect protective influence on his children's development through his support of the mother, particularly in circumstances such as maternal depression (Tannenbaum & Forehand, 1994). Fathers' work life may also contribute indirectly to children's school adaptation, and not merely through hours spent away from the home that reduce the amount of father–child interactions. Schulz (2005) reported that work experiences in a sample of dual-earner, intact families were related in a number of ways with children's academic and social adjustment to kindergarten. When controlling for the number of hours worked, fathers' investment in their jobs was positively related to teacher ratings of their children's early social and academic functioning. Children were also more adaptive in kindergarten when mothers reported feeling satisfied with the amount of support that their husbands provided regarding work decisions. Perhaps this positive investment in work and support for work decisions leads to more harmonious family interactions, which, in turn, create a nurturing, supportive environment that contributes to children's early school adaptation. However, there remains an absence of explicit tests of mediation that could speak to the mechanisms through which a father's anger or psychological investment in work has an impact on his child.

Multidimensional Father Involvement: A Developmental Ecological Model

The most promising and relevant longitudinal studies of the transition to school, although few in numbers and inclusive mostly of Caucasian, middle-class, intact families, are those that follow children across the preschool through early elementary school period, include assessments of father and mother involvement, and take other contextual inputs into careful consideration. Two of these efforts, the National Institute of Child Health and Development Study of Early Child Care and Youth Development (NICHD SECCYD) and the Schoolchildren and their Families Study (SFS), are illustrations of using a developmental ecological model to learn more about fathers' direct and indirect involvement and its potential contributions to children's school readiness and adjustment to elementary school.

Data from the comprehensive, prospective NICHD SECCYD offer a unique opportunity to identify direct and indirect pathways of fathers' influence on children's early reading and math achievement and socioemotional competence and also to consider how fathering is affected by maternal and paternal psychological functioning and marital support. The NICHD SECCYD data set is ideally suited for this purpose because of the availability of a large two-parent household sample, complete data on family structure and process over time prior to and after school entry, and parallel assessments of mothers and fathers. As of now, the NICHD Early Child Care Research Network (ECCRN) has produced two manuscripts that exemplify a process-oriented approach to examining direct and indirect fathering effects as applied to the transition to school. In the first study of 648 families in which fathers were married to and living with their children's mother, children's adjustment to school from 54 months through second grade was significantly predicted by fathering sensitivity and support for autonomy beyond mother–child interactions (NICHD ECCRN, 2004). Indirect fathering influences in the form of emotionally supportive marriages were also evident. Teachers reported fewer internalizing problems for children whose mothers reported higher marital intimacy, whereas teacher ratings suggested positive social adjustment with teachers and peers when fathers reported higher marital support.

Other analyses with the NICHD SECCYD data set were reported in a second paper about academic development from 54 months to third grade (NICHD ECCRN, 2006). With a sample of more than 600 two-parent intact families, a multigroup longitudinal mediation analysis was conducted to examine observed mothers' and fathers' sensitive support of children's autonomy from 54 months to third grade, children's observed self-reliance in the classroom from first through third grade, teacher ratings of teacher–child relationships from first through third grade, and children's reading and math achievement from 54 months to third grade. Controlling for achievement scores at 54 months and mothers' sensitivity, results indicated that fathers' sensitivity in interactions with their children at 54 months was uniquely predictive of third-grade achievement, which was attributable to contributions to growth in self-reliance from first to third grade, although only for boys (NICHD ECCRN, 2006). In fact, boys appeared to benefit from the sensitive behaviors of both parents, whereas girls' achievement during this time was only associated with mothers' support. The NICHD SECCYD clearly includes rich multiinformant, multimethod, and longitudinal information about family processes in two-parent households that allows for concurrent consideration of father– and mother–child relationships and indirect pathways such as marital support or parental psychological functioning in predicting children's academic and socioemotional adjustment to school.

The SFS offers another exemplar for designing and conducting studies about father involvement to address direct and indirect pathways of influence on young children's school readiness. Cowan, Cowan, Ablow, and colleagues (2005) followed a sample of 100 intact families with preschool-age children through first grade, explicitly focusing on family processes during the transition to school. Researchers gathered data about children's academic and social competence from multiple informants (parents, teachers, children); parents' self-perceptions (e.g., self-concept, mental health); self-reported and observed parenting and marital functioning; parents' family of origin; work and social support; and observed whole-family interactions. The breadth of measurement with a multisystemic focus allowed for multiple analyses of fathers' direct and indirect contributions to children's cognitive and socioemotional development, thus revealing both the significance and complexity of these influences. For example, controlling for mothers' parenting, fathers' authoritative parenting during preschool was predictive of fewer behavior problems and greater academic and social competence in kindergarten and was associated with better math and reading achievement during first grade (Mattanah, 2005). Interestingly, when fathers' encouragement of autonomy declined from preschool to kindergarten, teachers rated children as having more externalizing and internalizing behavior problems in first grade. Indirect fathering influences were also identified, as reported previously, and further demonstrate the importance of considering father roles from an ecological, systems perspective (Cowan, Cowan, Ablow, et al., 2005).

The NICHD SECCYD and SFS address many shortcomings of other research about fathers' roles during early childhood. These studies are longitudinal in design and include both mothers and fathers so that the dynamic nature of fathering can be examined as a unique factor in children's lives. Use of observational and multiinformant methodology provides thorough measurement of multifaceted father involvement and avoids the common pitfalls and biases of mothers reporting about fathers' behaviors or fathers only rating themselves. In addition, both studies made concerted efforts to measure family and other contextual factors in recognition of the fact that a father's role is best understood in an ecological context. Although generalizable to many families in the United States, the samples of these studies are limited to intact families and provide little data about children at greatest risk for school adjustment problems. These comprehensive longitudinal studies demonstrate the utility of using a developmental ecological model to examine father involvement's direct and indirect influences; however, this model now needs to be applied to other fathering contexts, such as minority families and cohabiting households.

FUTURE TRENDS FOR RESEARCH AND PRACTICE

Since the mid-1990s, developmental science has experienced a notable upswing in empirical interest and activity regarding fatherhood. The most frequently downloaded article from *Child Development* in the first half of 2005 focused on the relative contribution of fathers to the language and cognitive development of 2- and 3-year-olds in an Early Head Start sample (Tamis-LeMonda et al., 2004), and in 2003, a new, multidisciplinary, peer-reviewed *Fathering* journal was created to further knowledge about men as parents. In addition to this increased scientific scrutiny of father involvement, fathers and marriage have been central to several federal policy initiatives, including President Clinton's Fatherhood and President Bush's Healthy Marriage Initiatives. Much of this attention has been spurred by the changing demography of families in the United States, wherein the proportion of children growing up in traditional two-parent households has decreased (DHHS, 2004); in fact, children from African American families live with both parents in fewer than 40% of cases. However, it is equally important to note that the majority of children still grow up in two-parent, intact families, and there is still much for the field to learn about how fathers contribute to young children's school readiness within this family context.

As a means of moving fatherhood inquiry forward, this chapter recognizes a need for the early childhood field to tackle the dual challenge of applying a developmental ecological model to the study of fathers within two-parent households and empirical inquiry of father involvement within underresearched, but increasingly common, family contexts. In addition, there is a need to apply advances in knowledge about father involvement to the development of practical interventions, which can be used in the context of experimental designs to assess causal mechanisms through which fathers influence children's early development and adaptation to early school contexts.

Researching Fathers of Young Children

Nowhere is increased empirical attention to the role of fathers in young children's development more evident than in systematic alterations and supplements to the methodology of large-scale, longitudinal studies of early childhood and related family processes. In 1996, as part of the Early Head Start (EHS) Research and Evaluation Project, a fatherhood workgroup expanded data collection to include father interviews and videotaped father–child interactions (Brooks-Gunn, Berlin, Leventhal, & Fuligni, 2000). In addition, the Fragile Families and Child Wellbeing Study (1998–1999) followed a group of predominantly unwed parents and their newborn children from birth into early childhood and explicitly included the children's fathers in data collection from the beginning (Brooks-Gunn et al., 2000). Although parenting literature has become more inclusive of fathers in the last 20 years (Cabrera et al., 2000; Lamb & Tamis-LeMonda, 2004), it is important to consider that empirical articles in clinical and developmental psychology journals have demonstrated no change over time in the number of fathers included in published research on child development and developmental psychopathology, and the inclusion of fathers in such research remains a rarity (Phares, Fields, Kamboukos, & Lopez, 2005). In fact, much remains unknown about fathers during early childhood and the transition to school that can be addressed by further attention to research design and methodological improvements. Clearly, there remains an enormous need for investigation of fathering influences on young children's development under both traditional (i.e., two-parent, intact family) and nontraditional circumstances (e.g., nonresidential father involvement, cohabitation, social father presence) as well as with racial/ethnic minority families.

In particular, Cowan and colleagues noted a shortage of longitudinal prospective studies that comprehensively assess family context, including fathers, and its association with children's achievement and socioemotional competence both before and after children enter elementary school (Cowan, Cowan, Ablow, et al., 2005). Regardless of family structure and residential status of biological or social fathers, truly understanding children's experiences requires that researchers conduct more process-oriented inquiries that consider both father– and mother–child interactions, as well as other factors within the family system (e.g., parent mental health) that affect developing competencies (Cox & Paley, 2003; Cummings, Goeke-Morey, & Raymond, 2004). There is a real need for research that targets *how* and *why* father involvement assists children during adaptation to school settings, focusing on mediation, moderation, and causal mechanisms.

Future inquiries must also improve measurement of fathering behaviors in a way that is distinct from mothering behaviors (Paquette, 2004) and that also features cognitive and affective aspects of involvement (Hawkins & Palkovitz, 1999). Such innovation in assessment can help to construct a definition of fathering quality that captures both its commonalities with mothering quality and the nature of father–child interactions that may get missed by traditional maternal measures. Finally, increased efforts are needed to understand father involvement in its ethnic, cultural, and nontraditional family contexts.

Developing Interventions to Support Father Involvement

As fathers continue to play so many different roles in the lives of young children, and expectations for mothers shift according to new cultural norms and economic realities, no "one size fits all" intervention can foster supportive father involvement during early schooling. Supporting positive father involvement requires attention and sensitivity to the type of father(s), particular dimension(s) of involvement, and family and cultural contexts that are targeted. In the past decade, practical attempts to alter father involvement have taken many forms including family-based group interventions, school-based efforts, fathering support groups, strict child support policies, and initiatives to strengthen marriages. Although promising, the majority of these interventions have not incorporated an evaluative component to provide information about their effectiveness (Fagan & Hawkins, 2001). To generate ideas for further development and rigorous empirical testing, a few father-involvement intervention efforts are described next.

Fagan and colleagues in Philadelphia have implemented a variety of father-involvement interventions, particularly targeting low-income, minority men with children enrolled in Head Start (Fagan & Iglesias, 1999; Fagan & Palm, 2004; Fagan & Stevenson, 1995). One effort, Men as Teachers, used a self-help format in which African American fathers were empowered to take the lead of a small group focused on improving parenting skills and increasing fathering efficacy. The curriculum, codeveloped with fathers from the Head Start center, addressed issues related to being an African American male and father (e.g., effect of racism on fathering) as well as specific child-rearing strategies (e.g., positive discipline strategies). A small experimental study of the group's benefits indicated that participation over the course of 6 weeks was positively associated with fathers' beliefs about their ability to help children learn, regardless of residential status (Fagan & Stevenson, 2002); however, other outcomes were less positive for nonresidential fathers than residential ones, such as self-esteem and satisfaction with parenting. In fact, Greif (2005) suggested that noncustodial parents may have deeper and more expansive therapeutic needs than can be addressed in such a short, peer-guided group. Regardless, this type of support group for men as parents, particularly minority fathers, is a popular and growing trend that is being replicated throughout the country (Franklin & Davis, 2001).

Another father-involvement initiative in Philadelphia incorporates several strategies for improving men's involvement in young children's lives. This initiative, based in the School District of Philadelphia's prekindergarten Head Start program, integrates several components:

encouragement of volunteering in classrooms, weekly programs in Head Start sites called Father's Day, staff training concerning work with fathers, support groups for fathers, and provision of father–child activity opportunities. Over the course of 2 years in the late 1990s, 91 fathers participated in the project, the majority of whom were single and never married (55.2%), biological (68.4%), and residential fathers (71.9%). A quasiexperimental outcome evaluation indicated that fathers who were highly involved in the project increased their time of direct interaction, accessibility, and support for children's learning (Fagan & Iglesias, 1999). Participating fathers also had children who scored higher on a math readiness assessment from pre- to posttest. In contrast, fathers participating in the intervention did not significantly change their child-rearing behaviors, nor did children improve in the area of prosocial skills. Interestingly, residential status of the father did not alter the effects of the intervention, possibly because nonresidential fathers in this project were more motivated than those who chose not to participate or because the study lacked power to detect effects due to small sample size.

Family-based interventions are another mechanism through which to stimulate change in father involvement. In a recent monograph, Cowan and colleagues provided detailed findings from the SFS, a family-focused intervention with predominantly Caucasian, two-parent intact families with children about to enter kindergarten (Cowan, Cowan, Ablow, et al., 2005). This project explicitly targeted the transition of a child into the school system as a time when the family system experiences stress and instability, thus providing an opportunity to offer alternative strategies to handling family challenges. The intervention consisted of participation in group sessions that focused either on marital or parenting issues. Findings indicated that fathers in the parenting intervention group became less authoritarian during the preschool–kindergarten period, whereas marital conflict was reduced in the marital-focused intervention group (Cowan, Cowan, & Heming, 2005). Changes in fathers' direct parenting and the marital relationship mediated children's adaptation during the kindergarten to first-grade period, but in different ways. Improvements in fathers' parenting were related to significant declines in child withdrawal and depression, whereas improvements in marital functioning were linked to increases in child academic competence and reductions in externalizing behaviors. These findings highlight a possible two-pronged approach to intervention in which both marital and parenting factors are addressed during the transition to school.

A recently published book, *Clinical and Educational Interventions with Fathers,* illustrates the diverse range of practical applications based on the fatherhood literature reviewed in this chapter (Fagan & Hawkins, 2001). Chapter topics include anger management groups, therapeutic support groups for African American men, training early education staff to work with fathers, faith-based approaches to fatherhood interventions, legal support for fathers during custody trials, and parent education courses for incarcerated men. As empirical inquiry provides a clearer picture of the direct and indirect influences of fathering on children's early development in different family contexts, there will be more opportunities to evaluate the effects of existing and innovative interventions that attempt to change aspects of fathering to test the mechanisms through which father involvement has an impact on children's academic and socioemotional competence during the transition to school.

CONCLUSION

Children's transition to school requires adaptation to novel settings and greater connection to contexts outside of the family. The increase in available data about fathers and fathering has contributed to a growing appreciation of the role that fathers can play in the care and education of young children during this transition to school (Lamb, 1997, 2004). In particular, fathers may challenge young children's language and self-reliance in ways that make the adjustment to new settings during the transition to school more manageable. And yet, with increased diversification of family life in the past decade, there is still much to be learned about children's experiences with cohabiting fathers, nonresidential fathers, and social fathers that may enhance or detract from their adjustment to early schooling. It is critical that the momentum behind increased scrutiny of fathers be sustained, perhaps through a dual focus on gathering epidemiological and ethnographic data about understudied groups and discerning what cognitive, affective, and behavioral qualities of fathering best support young children during the dynamic shift into early schooling environments.

REFERENCES

Ablow, J.C. (2005). When parents conflict or disengage: Children's perceptions of parents' marital distress predict school adaptation. In P.A. Cowan, C.P. Cowan, J.C. Ablow, V.K. Johnson, & J.R. Measelle (Eds.), *The family context of parenting in children's adaptation to elementary school* (pp. 189–208). Mahwah, NJ: Lawrence Erlbaum Associates.

Acs, G., & Nelson, S. (2001). Honey I'm home. Changes in living arrangements in the late 1990s. *Assessing the New Federalism* (Policy Brief, Series B, No. B-38). Washington, DC: The Urban Institute.

Aldous, J., Mulligan, G.M., & Bjarnason, T. (1998). Fathering over time: What makes the difference? *Journal of Marriage and the Family, 60*(4), 809–820.

Amato, P.R., & Fowler, F. (2002). Parenting practices, child adjustment, and family diversity. *Journal of Marriage and Family, 64,* 703–716.

Amato, P.R., & Gilbreth, J.G. (1999). Nonresident fathers and children's well-being: A meta-analysis. *Journal of Marriage and the Family, 61,* 557–573.

Amato, P.R., & Rivera, F. (1999). Paternal involvement and children's behavior. *Journal of Marriage and the Family, 61,* 375–384.

Amato, P.R., & Sobolewski, J.M. (2004). The effects of divorce on fathers and children: Nonresidential fathers and stepfathers. In M.E. Lamb (Ed.), *The role of the father in child development* (pp. 341–367). Hoboken, NJ: John Wiley & Sons.

Anderson, K.G., Kaplan, H., & Lancaster, J. (1999). Paternal care by genetic fathers and stepfathers: I. Reports from Albuquerque men. *Evolution and Human Behavior, 20,* 405–431.

Argys, L.M., Peters, H.E., Brooks-Gunn, J., & Smith, J.R. (1998). The impact of child support dollars on cognitive outcomes. *Demography, 35*(2), 159–173.

Barth, J.M., & Parke, R.D. (1993). Parent–child relationship influences on children's transition to school. *Merrill-Palmer Quarterly, 39*(2), 173–195.

Bellinger, D.C., & Gleason, J.B. (1982). Sex differences in parental directives to young children. *Sex Roles, 8,* 1123–1139.

Bianchi, S.M. (2000). Maternal employment and time with children: Dramatic change or surprising continuity? *Demography, 37,* 402–414.

Billingsley, A. (1992). *Climbing Jacob's ladder: The enduring legacy of African-American families.* New York: Simon & Schuster.

Black, M.M., Dubowitz, H., & Starr, R.H. (1999). African American fathers in low income, urban families: Development, behavior, and home environment of their three-year-old children. *Child Development, 70,* 967–978.

Blankenhorn, D. (1995). *Fatherless America: Confronting our most urgent social problem.* New York: Basic Books.

Bond, J.T., Galinsky, E., & Swanberg, J.E. (1998). *The 1997 national survey of the changing workforce.* New York: Families and Work Institute.

Bornstein, M.H., & Tamis-LeMonda, C.S. (1989). Maternal responsiveness and cognitive development in children. *New Directions for Child Development, 43,* 49–61.

Bronfenbrenner, U., & Morris, P.A. (1998). The ecology of developmental processes. In W. Damon & R.M. Lerner (Eds.), *Handbook of child psychology, Vol. 1. Theoretical models of human development* (pp. 993–1028). Hoboken, NJ: John Wiley & Sons.

Brooks-Gunn, J., Berlin, L.J., Leventhal, T., & Fuligni, A. (2000). Depending on the kindness of strangers: Current national data initiatives and developmental research. *Child Development, 71,* 257–267.

Burchinal, M.R., Peisner-Feinberg, E., Pianta, R.C., & Howes, C. (2002). Development of academic skills from preschool through second grade: Family and classroom predictors of developmental trajectories. *Journal of School Psychology, 40,* 415–436.

Cabrera, N.J., Tamis-LeMonda, C.S., Bradley, R.H., Hofferth, S., & Lamb, M.E. (2000). Fatherhood in the twenty-first century. *Child Development, 71,* 127–136.

Carlson, M.J., & McLanahan, S.S. (2002). Fragile families, father involvement, and public policy. In C.S. Tamis-LeMonda & N. Cabrera (Eds.), *Handbook of father involvement: Multidisciplinary perspectives* (pp. 461–488). Mahwah, NJ: Lawrence Erlbaum Associates.

Casper, L., & Cohen, P. (2000). How does the POSSLQ measure up? *Demography, 37,* 237–245.

Child Trends. (2002). *Charting parenthood: A statistical portrait of fathers and mothers in America.* Washington, DC: Author.

Clarke-Stewart, K.A. (1978). And Daddy makes three: The father's impact on mother and young child. *Child Development, 49*(2), 466–478.

Clements, M.L., Lim, K.G., & Chaplin, T.M. (2002, November). Marriage, parenting, and coparenting: Effects of context, parent gender, and child gender on interactions. In F.M. Hughes (Chair), *Bridging the marital dyad and the family triad: A process-oriented approach.* Symposium conducted at the 36th annual convention of the Association for the Advancement of Behavior Therapy, Reno, NV.

Coiro, M.J., & Emery, R.E. (1998). Do marriage problems affect fathering more than mothering? A quantitative and qualitative review. *Clinical Child & Family Psychology Review, 1,* 23–40.

Coleman, M., Ganong, L., & Fine, M. (2000). Reinvestigating remarriage: Another decade of progress. *Journal of Marriage and the Family, 62,* 1288–1307.

Coley, R.L. (1998). Children's socialization experiences and functioning in single-mother households: The importance of fathers and other men. *Child Development, 69*(1), 219–230.

Coley, R.L. (2001). (In)visible men: Emerging research on low-income, unmarried, and minority fathers. *American Psychologist, 56,* 743–753.

Coley, R.L., & Chase-Lansdale, P.L. (1999). Stability and change in paternal involvement among urban African American fathers. *Journal of Family Psychology, 13,* 416–435.

Coltrane, S. (1996). *Family man: Fatherhood, housework, and gender equity.* New York: Oxford University Press.

Coltrane, S., & Parke, R.D. (1998). *Reinventing fatherhood: Toward an historical understanding of continuity and change in men's family lives.* Philadelphia: National Center on Fathers and Families.

Cowan, C.P., & Cowan, P.A. (2000). *When partners become parents: The big life change for couples.* Mahwah, NJ: Lawrence Erlbaum Associates.

Cowan, C.P., Cowan, P.A., & Heming, G. (2005). Two variations of a preventive intervention for couples: Effects on parents and children during the transition to school. In P.A. Cowan, C.P. Cowan, J.C. Ablow, V.K. Johnson, & J.R. Measelle (Eds.), *The family context of parenting in children's adaptation to elementary school* (pp. 277–314). Mahwah, NJ: Lawrence Erlbaum Associates.

Cowan, P.A., Cowan, C.P., Ablow, J.C., Johnson, V.K., & Measelle, J.R. (2005). *The family context of parenting in children's adaptation to elementary school.* Mahwah, NJ: Lawrence Erlbaum Associates.

Cox, M.J., & Paley, B. (2003). Understanding families as systems. *Current Directions in Psychological Science, 12*(5), 193–196.

Cox, M.J., Paley, B., & Harter, K. (2001). Interparental conflict and parent–child relationships. In J.H. Grych & F.D. Fincham (Eds.), *Interparental conflict and child development* (pp. 249–272). Cambridge, England: Cambridge University Press.

Cummings, E.M., & Davies, P.T. (1994). *Children and marital conflict: The impact of family dispute and resolution.* New York: Guilford Press.

Cummings, E.M., & Davies, P.T. (2002). Effects of marital conflict on children: Recent advances and emerging themes in process-oriented research. *Journal of Child Psychology and Psychiatry, 43,* 31–63.

Cummings, E.M., Goeke-Morey, M.C., & Raymond, J. (2004). Fathers in family context: Effects of marital quality and marital conflict. In M.E. Lamb (Ed.), *The role of the father in child development* (4th ed., pp. 196–221). Hoboken, NJ: John Wiley & Sons.

Cummings, E.M., Keller, P.S., & Davies, P.T. (2005). Towards a family process model of maternal and paternal depressive symptoms: Exploring multiple relations with child and family functioning. *Journal of Child Psychology and Psychiatry, 46*(5), 479–489.

Cummings, E.M., & O'Reilly, A.W. (1997). Fathers in family context: Effects of marital quality on child adjustment. In M.E. Lamb (Ed.), *The role of the father in child development* (3rd ed., pp. 49–65). Hoboken, NJ: John Wiley & Sons.

Doherty, W.J., Kouneski, E.F., & Erickson, M.F. (1998). Responsible fathering: An overview and conceptual framework. *Journal of Marriage and the Family, 60,* 277–292.

Downer, J.T., & Mendez, J. (2005). African American father involvement and preschool children's school readiness. *Early Education and Development, 16,* 317–340.

Dunifon, R., & Kowalewski-Jones, L. (2002). Who's in the house? Race differences in cohabitation, single parenthood, and child development. *Child Development, 73*(4), 1249–1264.

Du Rocher Schudlich, T.D., & Cummings, E.M. (2003). Parental dysphoria and children's internalizing symptoms: Marital conflict styles as mediators of risk. *Child Development, 74*(6), 1663–1681.

Edin, K., & Lein, L. (1997). *Making ends meet: How single mothers survive welfare and low-wage work.* New York: Russell Sage Foundation.

Emery, R.E. (1999). *Marriage, divorce, and children's adjustment* (2nd ed.). Thousand Oaks, CA: Sage.

Entwisle, D.R., Alexander, K.L., & Olson, L.S. (1997). *Children, schools, and inequality.* Boulder, CO: Westview Press.

Epstein, J.L. (1996). Perspectives and previews on research and policy for school, family, and community partnerships. In A. Booth & J.F. Dunn (Eds.), *Family–school links: How do they affect educational outcomes?* (pp. 209–246). Mahwah, NJ: Lawrence Erlbaum Associates.

Estrada, P., Arsenio, W.F., Hess, R.D., & Holloway, S.D. (1987). Affective quality of the mother–child relationship: Longitudinal consequences for children's school-relevant cognitive functioning. *Developmental Psychology, 23,* 210–215.

Fagan, J. (1997). Patterns of mother and father involvement in child care. *Child and Youth Care Forum, 26,* 113–126.

Fagan, J. (1999). *Predictors of father and father figure involvement in pre-kindergarten Head Start.* Philadelphia: National Center on Fathers and Families.

Fagan, J., & Hawkins, A.J. (2001). *Clinical and educational interventions with fathers.* New York: The Haworth Clinical Practice Press.

Fagan, J., & Iglesias, A. (1999). Father involvement program effects on fathers, father figures, and their Head Start children: A quasi-experimental study. *Early Childhood Research Quarterly, 14*(2), 243–269.

Fagan, J., & Palm, G. (2004). *Fathers and early childhood programs.* Clifton Park, NY: Thomson Delmar Learning.

Fagan, J., & Press, J. (2000, November). *Determinants of parental drop off and pick up from day care.* Paper presented at the National Council on Family Relations annual conference, Minneapolis, MN.

Fagan, J., & Stevenson, H. (1995). Men as teachers: A self-help program on parenting for African American men. *Social Work with Groups, 17*(4), 29–43.

Fagan, J., & Stevenson, H.C. (2002). An experimental study of an empowerment-based intervention for African American Head Start fathers. *Family Relations, 51,* 191–198.

Fantuzzo, J., Tighe, E., & Childs, S. (2000). Family Involvement Questionnaire: A multivariate assessment of family participation in early childhood education. *Journal of Educational Psychology, 92,* 367–376.

Franklin, A.J., & Davis, T. (2001). Therapeutic support groups for primary intervention for issues of fatherhood with African American men. In J. Fagan & A.J. Hawkins (Eds.), *Clinical and educational interventions with fathers* (pp. 45–66). New York: The Haworth Clinical Practice Press.

Franz, H.A., McClelland, D.C., & Weinberger, J. (1991). Childhood antecedents of conventional social accomplishment in midlife adults: A 36-year prospective study. *Journal of Personality and Social Psychology, 60,* 586–595.

Frosch, C.A., Mangelsdorf, S.C., & McHale, J.L. (2000). Marital behavior and the security of preschooler–parent attachment relationships. *Journal of Family Psychology, 14,* 144–161.

Garfinkel, I., & McLanahan, S. (2000). Fragile families and child well-being: A survey of new parents. *Focus, 21,* 9–11.

Garinger, J.G., & McBride, B.A. (1995). Successful parent involvement strategies in prekindergarten at-risk programs. *School Community Journal, 5,* 59–78.

Gary, L., Beatty, L., & Weaver, G. (1987). *Involvement of black fathers in Head Start.* Final report submitted to the Department of Health and Human Services, ACF, Grant No. 90-CD-0509. Institute for Urban Affairs and Research, Howard University, Washington, DC.

Gottfried, A.E., Gottfried, A.W., & Bathurst, K. (1988). Maternal employment, family environment, and children's development: Infancy through the school years. In A.E. Gottfried & A.W. Gottfried (Eds.), *Maternal employment and children's development: Longitudinal research* (pp. 11–58). New York: Plenum.

Graefe, D., & Lichter, D. (1999). Life course transitions of American children: Parental cohabitation, marriage and single motherhood. *Demography, 36,* 205–217.

Greene, A.D., & Moore, K.A. (2000). Nonresident father involvement and child well-being among young children in families on welfare. *Marriage and Family Review, 29,* 159–180.

Greif, G.L. (2005). Group work with noncustodial parents. In G.L. Greif & P.H. Ephross (Eds.), *Group work with populations at risk* (pp. 126–134). New York: Oxford University Press.

Griswold, R.L. (1997). Generative fathering: A historical perspective. In A.J. Hawkins & D.C. Dollahite (Eds.), *Generative fathering: Beyond deficit perspectives* (pp.71–88). Thousand Oaks, CA: Sage.

Grossmann, K., Grossmann, K.E., Fremmer-Bombik, E., Kindler, H., Scheuerer-Englisch, H., & Zimmerman, P. (2002). The uniqueness of the child–father attachment relationship: Fathers' sensitive and challenging play as a pivotal variable in a 16-year longitudinal study. *Social Development, 11*(3), 307–331.

Grossmann, K., Kindler, H., & Strasser, K. (2003). *Father support during early childhood: Effects on adolescents' representations of attachment and partnership.* Paper presented at the meetings of the Society for Research in Child Development, Tampa, FL.

Harkness, S., & Super, C. (1992). The cultural foundations of fathers' roles: Evidence from Kenya and the United States. In B. Hewlett (Ed.), *Father–child relations: Cultural and biosocial contexts* (pp. 191–211). New York: Aldine de Gruyter.

Hawkins, A.J., & Dollahite, D.C. (1997). Beyond the role-inadequacy perspective of fathering. In A.J. Hawkins & D.C. Dollahite (Eds.), *Generative fathering: Beyond deficit perspectives* (pp. 3–16). Thousand Oaks, CA: Sage.

Hawkins, A.J., & Palkovitz, R. (1999). Beyond ticks and clicks: The need for more diverse and broader conceptualizations and measures of father involvement. *Journal of Men's Studies, 8,* 11–32.

Henrich, C.C., & Blackman-Jones, R. (2006). Parent involvement in preschool. In E. Zigler, W. Gilliam, & S. Jones (Eds.), *A vision for universal preschool education.* Oxford: Cambridge University Press.

Hernandez, D.J., & Brandon, P.D. (2002). Who are the fathers of today? In C.S. Tamis-LeMonda & N. Cabrera (Eds.), *Handbook of father involvement: Multidisciplinary perspectives* (pp. 33–62). Mahwah, NJ: Lawrence Erlbaum Associates.

Hill, R.B. (1972). *The strengths of Black families.* New York: Emerson Hall.

Hofferth, S.L. (2003). Race/ethnic differences in father involvement in two-parent families. *Journal of Family Issues, 24,* 185–216.

Hofferth, S.L., & Anderson, K.G. (2003). Are all dads equal? Biology versus marriage as a basis for paternal investment. *Journal of Marriage and Family, 65,* 213–232.

Hofferth, S.L., Pleck, J., Stueve, J.L., Bianchi, S., & Sayer, L. (2002). The demography of fathers: What fathers do. In C.S. Tamis-LeMonda & N. Cabrera (Eds.), *Handbook of father involvement: Multidisciplinary perspectives* (pp. 63–90). Mahwah, NJ: Lawrence Erlbaum Associates.

Jayakody, R., & Kalil, A. (2002). Social fathering in low-income, African American families with preschool children. *Journal of Marriage and Family, 64,* 504–516.

Kavanaugh, R.D., & Jirkovsky, A.M. (1982). Parental speech to young children: A longitudinal analysis. *Merrill-Palmer Quarterly, 28,* 297–311.

Lamb, M.E. (1986). *The father's role: Applied perspectives.* Hoboken, NJ: John Wiley & Sons.

Lamb, M.E. (1987). *The father's role: Cross-cultural perspectives.* Mahwah, NJ: Lawrence Erlbaum Associates.

Lamb, M.E. (1997). *The role of the father in child development* (3rd ed.). Hoboken, NJ: John Wiley & Sons.

Lamb, M.E. (2000). The history of research on father involvement: An overview. *Marriage and Family Review, 29,* 23–42.

Lamb, M.E. (2002). Nonresidential fathers and their children. In C.S. Tamis-LeMonda & N. Cabrera (Eds.), *Handbook of father involvement: Multidisciplinary perspectives* (pp. 169–184). Mahwah, NJ: Lawrence Erlbaum Associates.

Lamb, M.E. (2004). *The role of the father in child development* (4th ed.). Hoboken, NJ: John Wiley & Sons.

Lamb, M.E., & Lewis, C. (2004). The development and significance of father–child relationships in two-parent families. In M.E. Lamb (Ed.), *The role of the father in child development* (4th ed., pp. 272–306). Hoboken, NJ: John Wiley & Sons.

Lamb, M.E., Pleck, J.H., Charnov, E., & Levine, J.A. (1985). Paternal behavior in humans. *American Psychologist, 25,* 883–894.

Lamb, M.E., & Tamis-LeMonda, C.S. (2004). The role of the father: An introduction. In M.E. Lamb (Ed.), *The role of the father in child development* (4th ed., pp. 1–31). Hoboken, NJ: John Wiley & Sons.

LaRossa, R., Gordon, R.J., Wilson, A., Bauran, A., & Jaret, C. (1991). The fluctuating image of the 20th century American father. *Journal of Marriage and the Family, 53*(4), 987–997.

Leaper, C., Anderson, K.J., & Sanders, P. (1998). Moderators of gender effects on parents' talk to their children: A meta-analysis. *Developmental Psychology, 34,* 3–27.

Lerman, R.I. (1993). A national profile of young unwed fathers. In R.I. Lerman & T.J. Ooms (Eds.), *Young unwed fathers: Changing roles and emerging policies* (pp. 27–51). Philadelphia: Temple University Press.

MacDonald, W.L., & DeMaris, A. (1996). Parenting stepchildren and biological children: The effects of stepparents' gender and new biological children. *Journal of Family Issues, 17,* 5–25.

Mattanah, J.F. (2005). Authoritative parenting and the encouragement of children's autonomy. In P.A. Cowan, C.P. Cowan, J.C. Ablow, V.K. Johnson, & J.R. Measelle (Eds.), *The family context of parenting in children's adaptation to elementary school* (pp. 119–138). Mahwah, NJ: Lawrence Erlbaum Associates.

Marcos, H. (1995). Mother–child and father–child communication in the second year: A functional approach. *Early Development and Parenting, 2,* 49–61.

Marsh, M. (1988). Suburban men and masculine domesticity, 1870–1915. *American Quarterly, 40,* 165–188.

Marsiglio, W., Amato, P., Day, R., & Lamb, M.E. (2000). Scholarship on fatherhood in the 1990s and beyond. *Journal of Marriage and the Family, 62,* 1173–1191.

Marsiglio, W., Day, R., & Lamb, M.E. (2000). Exploring fatherhood diversity: Implications for conceptualizing father involvement. *Marriage and the Family Review, 29,* 269–293.

McBride, B.A., & Mills, G. (1993). A comparison of mother and father involvement with their preschool age children. *Early Childhood Research Quarterly, 8,* 457–477.

McBride, B.A., & Rane, T.R. (1997). Father/male involvement in early childhood programs: Issues and challenges. *Early Childhood Education Journal, 25*(1), 11–15.

McHale, S.M., & Crouter, A.C. (1992). You can't always get what you want: Incongruence between sex-role attitudes and family work roles and its implications for marriage. *Journal of Marriage & the Family, 54,* 537–547.

McLanahan, S.S. (1999). Father absence and the welfare of children. In E.M. Hetherington (Ed.), *Coping with divorce, single parenting, and remarriage: A risk and resiliency perspective* (pp. 117–145). Mahwah, NJ: Lawrence Erlbaum Associates.

McLanahan, S.S., Garfinkel, I., Brooks-Gunn, J., & Zhao, H. (1997). *Fragile families.* Unpublished manuscript.

McLanahan, S.S., & Sandefur, G. (1994). *Growing up with a single parent: What hurts, what helps?* Cambridge, MA: Harvard University Press.

McLanahan, S.S., Seltzer, J.A., Hanson, T.L., & Thomas, E. (1994). Child support enforcement and child well-being: Greater security or greater conflicts. In I. Garfinkel, S.S. McLanahan, & P.K. Robins (Eds.), *Child support and child well-being* (pp. 239–254). Washington, DC: Urban Institute Press.

McLaughlin, B., White, D., McDevitt, T., & Raskin, R. (1983). Mothers' and fathers' speech to their young children: Similar or different? *Journal of Child Language, 10,* 245–252.

McLoyd, V.C. (1998). Socioeconomic disadvantage and child development. *American Psychologist, 53,* 185–204.

Miller, C., Garfinkel, I., & McLanahan, S. (1997). Child support in the U.S.: Can fathers afford to pay more? *Review of Income and Wealth, 43,* 261–281.

Morrison, F., & Cooney, R. (2002). Parenting and academic achievement: Multiple paths to early literacy. In J. Borkowski, S. Ramey Landesman, & M. Bristol-Power (Eds.), *Parenting and the children's world: Influences on academic, intellectual, and social-emotional development* (pp. 141–160). Mahwah, NJ: Lawrence Erlbaum Associates.

Murphy, L.B. (1997). Fathers. *Zero to Three, 18*(1), 9.

National Institute of Child Health and Human Development, Early Child Care Research Network. (2000). Factors associated with fathers' caregiving activities and sensitivity with young children. *Journal of Family Psychology, 14*(2), 200–219.

National Institute of Child Health and Human Development, Early Child Care Research Network. (2004). Father's and mother's parenting behavior and beliefs as predictors of child social adjustment in the transition to school. *Journal of Family Psychology, 18*(4), 628–638.

National Institute of Child Health and Human Development, Early Child Care Research Network. (2006, March). *Longitudinal mediation of the impact of fathers' sensitive support for autonomy on early achievement in grade school: The role of social adjustment.* Presentation at the biennial meeting of the Society for Research in Adolescence, San Francisco, CA.

Nelson, T., Clampet-Lundquist, S., & Edin, K. (2002). Sustaining fragile fatherhood: Father involvement among low-income, noncustodial African American fathers in Philadelphia. In C.S. Tamis-LeMonda & N. Cabrera (Eds.), *Handbook of father involvement: Multidisciplinary perspectives* (pp. 525–553). Mahwah, NJ: Lawrence Erlbaum Associates.

Nord, C.W., Brimhall, D., & West, J. (1997). *Fathers' involvement in their children's schools.* U.S. Department of Education, Office of Educational Research and Improvement, Washington, DC.

Notaro, P.C., & Volling, B.L. (1999). Parental responsiveness and infant–parent attachment: A replication study with fathers and mothers. *Infant Behavior & Development, 22*(3), 345–352.

O'Connell, M. (1993). *Where's papa? Fathers' role in child care.* Washington, DC: Population Reference Bureau.

Owen, M.T., & Cox, M.J. (1997). Marital conflict and the development of infant–parent attachment relationships. *Journal of Family Psychology, 11,* 152–164.

Palkovitz, R. (1997). Reconstructing "involvement": Expanding conceptualizations of men's caring in contemporary families. In A.J. Hawkins & D.C. Dollahite (Eds.), *Generative fathering: Beyond deficit perspectives* (pp. 200–216). Thousand Oaks, CA: Sage.

Paquette, D. (2004). Theorizing the father–child relationships: Mechanisms and developmental outcomes. *Human Development, 47,* 193–219.

Parke, R.D. (2002). Fathers and families. In M.H. Bornstein (Ed.), *Handbook of parenting* (2nd ed., Vol. 3, pp. 27–73). Mahwah, NJ: Lawrence Erlbaum Associates.

Peterson, R.R., & Gerson, K. (1992). Determinants of responsibility for child care arrangements among dual-earner couples. *Journal of Marriage and the Family, 54,* 527–536.

Phares, V., Fields, S., Kamboukos, D., & Lopez, E. (2005). Still looking for poppa. *American Psychologist, 60*(7), 735–736.

Pianta, R.C., & Harbers, K.L. (1996). Observing mother and child behavior in a problem-solving situation at school entry: Relations with academic achievement. *Journal of School Psychology, 34,* 307–322.

Pianta, R.C., Smith, N., & Reeve, R.E. (1991). Observing mother and child behavior in a problem-solving situation at school entry: Relations with classroom adjustment. *School Psychology Quarterly, 6,* 1–15.

Pleck, E.H., & Pleck, J.H. (1997). Fatherhood ideals in the United States: Historical dimensions. In M.E. Lamb (Ed.), *The role of the father in child development* (3rd ed., pp. 33–48). Hoboken, NJ: John Wiley & Sons.

Pleck, J.H. (1997). Paternal involvement: Levels, sources, and consequences. In M.E. Lamb (Ed.), *The role of the father in child development* (3rd ed., pp. 66–103). Hoboken, NJ: John Wiley & Sons.

Pleck, J.H., & Masciadrelli, B.P. (2004). Paternal involvement by U.S. residential fathers: Levels, sources, and consequences. In M.E. Lamb (Ed.), *The role of the father in child development* (4th ed., pp. 222–271). Hoboken, NJ: John Wiley & Sons.

Pleck, J.H., & Stueve, J.L. (2001). Time and paternal involvement. In K. Daly (Ed.), *Minding the time in family experience: Emerging perspectives and issues* (pp. 205–226). Oxford, England: Elsevier.

Popenoe, D. (1996). *Life without father.* New York: Free Press.

Ratner, N.B. (1988). Patterns of parental vocabulary selection in speech to very young children. *Journal of Child Language, 15*(3), 481–492.

Rimm-Kaufman, S.E., & Pianta, R.C. (2000). An ecological perspective on the transition to kindergarten: A theoretical framework to guide empirical research. *Journal of Applied Developmental Psychology, 21*(5), 491–511.

Robinson, J.P., & Godbey, G. (1997). *True for life: The surprising ways Americans use their time.* University Park, PA: Pennsylvania State University.

Roggman, L.A. (2004). Do fathers just want to have fun? Commentary on theorizing the father–child relationship. *Human Development, 47,* 228–236.

Roggman, L.A., Fitzgerald, H.E., Bradley, R.H., & Raikes, H. (2002). Methodological, measurement, and design issues in studying fathers: An interdisciplinary perspective. In C.S. Tamis-LeMonda & N. Cabrera (Eds.), *Handbook of father involvement: Multidisciplinary perspectives* (pp. 1–30). Mahwah, NJ: Lawrence Erlbaum Associates.

Sandberg, J.F., & Hofferth, S.L. (2001). Changes in parental time with children. *Demography, 38,* 423–436.

Schulz, M.S. (2005). Parents' work experiences and children's adaptation to school. In P.A. Cowan, C.P. Cowan, J.C. Ablow, V.K. Johnson, & J.R. Measelle (Eds.), *The family context of parenting in children's adaptation to elementary school* (pp. 237–254). Mahwah, NJ: Lawrence Erlbaum Associates.

Seltzer, J.A., & Bianchi, S.M. (1988). Children's contact with absent parents. *Journal of Marriage and the Family, 50,* 663–677.

Silverstein, L.B., & Auerbach, C.F. (1999). Deconstructing the essential father. *American Psychologist, 54,* 397–407.

Simons, R.L., Lorenz, F.O., Wu, C., & Conger, R.D. (1993). Social network and marital support as mediators and moderators of the impact of stress and depression on parental behavior. *Developmental Psychology, 29*(2), 368–381.

Smock, P. (2000). Cohabitation in the United States: An appraisal of research themes, findings, and implications. *Annual Review of Sociology,* 1–20. Washington, DC: American Sociological Association.

Tamis-LeMonda, C.S., & Cabrera, N. (Eds.). (2002). *Handbook of father involvement: Multidisciplinary perspectives.* Mahwah, NJ: Lawrence Erlbaum Associates.

Tamis-LeMonda, C.S., Shannon, J.D., Cabrera, N.J., & Lamb, M.E. (2004). Fathers and mothers at play with their 2- and 3-year-olds: Contributions to language and cognitive development. *Child Development, 75*(6), 1806–1820.

Tannenbaum, L., & Forehand, R. (1994). Maternal depressive mood: The role of the father in preventing adolescent problem behaviors. *Behavior Research and Therapy, 32,* 321–325.

Tomasello, M., Conti-Ramsden, G., & Ewert, B. (1990). Young children's conversations with their mothers and fathers: Differences in breakdown and repair. *Journal of Child Language, 17*(1), 115–130.

U.S. Census Bureau. (1999). *Unmarried-couple households by presence of children.* Retrieved November 21, 2005, from http://www.census.gov/population/socdemo/ms-la/tabad-2.txt

U.S. Department of Health and Human Services. (2004, July). *Trends in the well-being of America's children and youth.* Retrieved November 21, 2005, from http://aspe.hhs.gov/hsp/03trends

Yeung, W.J., Duncan, G.J., & Hill, M.S. (2000). Putting fathers back in the picture: Parental activities and children's adult outcomes. *Marriage and Family Review, 29,* 97–113.

Yeung, W.J., Sandberg, J.F., Davis-Kean, P.E., & Hofferth, S.L. (2001). Children's time with fathers in intact families. *Journal of Marriage and Family, 63,* 136–154.

Yogman, M.W., Kindlon, D., & Earls, F. (1995). Father involvement and cognitive/behavioral outcomes of preterm infants. *Journal of the American Academy of Child and Adolescent Psychiatry, 34*(1), 58–66.

Zuzanek, J. (2000). *The effects of time use and time pressure on child–parent relationships.* Waterloo, Ontario: Otium.

INDEX

Page numbers followed by *f* indicate figures; those followed by *t* indicate tables.